# TRANSNATIONAL CORPORATIONS AND HUMAN RIGHTS

This volume offers a systematic overview of the different tools through which the human rights accountability of transnational corporations may be improved. It first examines the responsibility of States in controlling transnational corporations, emphasising both the limits imposed by the protection of the rights of investors under investment treaties and the potential of the US Alien Tort Claims Act and other similar extraterritorial legislations. It then turns to self-regulation by transnational corporations, through the use of codes of conduct or international framework agreements. It then discusses recent attempts at the global level to improve the human rights accountability of corporations by the direct imposition on corporations of obligations under international law. Finally, it considers the use of public procurement policies or of conditionalities in the lending policies of multilateral lending institutions in order to incentivize TNCs to behave ethically. Altogether, the book offers a rigorous legal analysis of these different developments and critically appraises their potential.

**Volume 12: Studies in International Law**

# Transnational Corporations and Human Rights

*Edited by*

Olivier De Schutter

·HART·
PUBLISHING

OXFORD AND PORTLAND, OREGON
2006

Published in North America (US and Canada) by
Hart Publishing
c/o International Specialized Book Services
920 NE 58th Avenue, Suite 300
Portland, OR 97213-3786
USA
Tel: +1 503 287 3093 or toll-free: (1) 800 944 6190
Fax: +1 503 280 8832
E-mail: orders@isbs.com
Web Site: www.isbs.com

Hart Publishing, 16c Worcester Place, Oxford, OX1 2JW
Telephone: +44 (0)1865 517530 Fax: +44 (0) 1865 510710
E-mail: mail@hartpub.co.uk
Website: http://www.hartpub.co.uk


British Library Cataloguing in Publication Data
Data Available


ISBN-13: 978-1-84113-653-0 (paperback)
ISBN-10: 1-84113-653-0 (paperback)

Typeset by Compuscript Ltd, Shannon
Printed and bound in Great Britain by
TJ International Ltd, Padstow, Cornwall

# Contents

# List of Contributors

*The Editor*

**Olivier De Schutter** is professor of human rights law at the University of Louvain (Belgium) and at the College of Europe (Natolin), Member of the Global Law School Faculty at New York University, and the Coordinator of the EU Network of Independent Experts on Fundamental Rights.

*The Contributors*

**Cristina Chiomenti** is member of the Italian Bar; LL.M in International Legal Studies of New York University (Grotius Scholar); Lawyer in the Corporate Department of Studio Legale Chiomenti, Rome, Italy; Graduate cum laude of the Law Faculty of the University of Rome La Sapienza.

**Jacob Gelfand** received his J.D. from New York University School of Law in 2005.

**Terra Lawson-Remer** (Juris Doctor, NYU School of Law, 2006) is currently completing a Doctorate of Philosophy in Law & Society at the NYU Graduate School of Arts and Science. Her work focuses primarily on property rights, economic development, and trade law.

**Fiona McLeay** is General Counsel at World Vision Australia, a large private international aid and development NGO. Prior to commencing at World Vision, she was Special Counsel at law firm Clayton Utz. Her areas of interest include the intersection of human rights and corporate social responsibility and the role of law in development.

**Chu Yun Juliana Nam**, B.Com/LL.B(Hons)(Syd), LL.M. in International Legal Studies (NYU), is currently an officer at the WTO Trade Law Branch of the Department of Foreign Affairs and Trade in Canberra, Australia. She has previously practised law at a private law firm in Sydney and assisted a member of the UN International Law Commission, Geneva as an NYU International Law & Human Rights Student Fellow.

**Ana Piquer** holds an LL.M. in International Legal Studies from NYU.

**Lisa R Price** received her J.D. from New York University School of Law in 2005. She is currently an associate in the Financial Services Group of Dechert LLP in New York.

**Ryan Suda** holds a BA (1998, *summa cum laude*) and JD (2005, *magna cum laude*) from New York University. He is an associate at a law firm in New York city.

**Inés Tófalo** is currently an associate at Simpson Thacher & Bartlett LLP's New York office. She is working on Capital Markets and Credit deals, mainly for transnational clients. She is also undertaking pro bono representation of three asylum seekers from Togo, Guinea and Tchad, and collaborating with an Argentina NGO on a human rights project.

**Andrew J. Wilson**, LL.B (Hons) (Edinburgh), LL.M (NYU), is currently CPE candidate, City Law School, London.

**Katherine Zeisel** is a graduate of the New York University School of Law, where she was a founding member of Law Students for Human Rights. She is currently employed at the Center for Battered Women's Legal Services at Sanctuary for Families as an advocate for victims of domestic violence.

# 1

# The Challenge of Imposing Human Rights Norms on Corporate Actors

## OLIVIER DE SCHUTTER

THIS COLLECTION OF essays offers a broad overview of the questions raised by the imposition of human rights obligations on transnational corporations (TNCs). Section II of this chapter offers an outline of the rest of the chapters contained in the book. First, however, Section I of this chapter, which is conceived as an introduction to the general themes of the volume, presents the general context in which the question of the human rights responsibilities of TNCs has developed. It reviews the push towards improving the accountability of these actors in the United Nations (UN), in the Organization for Economic Cooperation and Development (OECD), and in the International Labour Organization (ILO), as part of the movement in favor of the New International Economic Order during the 1970s or in response to that movement. This introduction then describes the initiatives which are the outcome of the second wave of corporate social responsibility. These more recent initiatives resulted from the critique, especially by civil society organisations, of the form taken by economic globalization since the early 1990s. Despite certain superficial similarities, especially with regard to its outcomes, this second wave of initiatives is markedly different from the first. Developing countries, which were at the forefront of the project of the New International Economic Order, now appear suspicious of, if not hostile to, the imposition of human rights obligations on TNCs. The pressure on companies is also significantly stronger now than previously, both because of the mobilization of non-governmental organizations (NGOs) and the communication tools they now have at their disposal, and because of the threat of legal suits against companies for human rights violations, especially before the United States federal courts. It is in this context that the Secretary-General of the UN proposed a Global Compact in 1999, and that the UN Sub-Commission on the Promotion and Protection of Human Rights adopted, in 2003, a set of Norms on the Human Rights Responsibilities of Transnational Corporations and Other

Business Enterprises. It is also under this pressure to improve the human rights accountability of corporations that voluntary initiatives by business have developed exponentially during recent years. The question today is how to ensure consistency between these different initiatives, and whether the time is ripe for a more ambitious development.

## I. THE GENERAL CONTEXT

### 1. The 1970s: Codifying the Conduct of Transnational Corporations under the New International Economic Order

The debate on the question of the human rights responsibilities of companies is hardly new. The insistence on an improved control of the activities of TNCs has accompanied the vindication of a 'New International Economic Order' in the early 1970s,[1] which the recently decolonized States pushed forward during that period. A draft Code of Conduct on Transnational Corporations[2] was even being prepared up to 1992 within the UN Commission on Transnational Corporations, established as a follow-up to a report prepared by a group of experts upon the request of the Economic and Social Council.[3] The UN Draft Code of Conduct provided, inter alia, that 'Transnational corporations shall respect human rights and fundamental freedoms in the countries in which they operate. In their social and industrial relations, transnational corporations shall not discriminate on the basis of race, colour, sex, religion, language, social, national and ethnic origin or political or other opinion. Transnational corporations shall conform to government policies designed to extend equality of opportunity and treatment.' The Draft Code failed to be adopted, however, because of major disagreements between industrialized and developing countries, in particular on the reference to international law and on the inclusion in the Code of standards of treatment for TNCs:[4]

---

[1] See the resolution adopted by the General Assembly of the United Nations on 1 May 1974, calling for a New International Economic Order (UN doc A/Res/3201 (S-VI)). This resolution was followed upon, in particular, by GA Res 3281(XXIX) of 15 January 1975, UN GAOR Supp (No 31), UN doc A/9631 (1975), The Charter of Economic Rights and Duties of States, reproduced in (1975) 14 ILM 251–65.

[2] UN doc E/1990/94, 12 June 1990.

[3] Ecosoc Res 1974/1721 of 24 May 1974; 'The Impact of Multinational Corporations on the Development Process and on International Relations, Report of the Group of Eminent Persons to Study the Role of Multinational Corporations in Development and in International Relations', UN doc E/5500/Rev.1/Add 1 (1974).

[4] See the Report by the Secretary General, *The impact of the activities and working methods of transnational corporations on the full enjoyment of all human rights, in particular economic, social and cultural rights and the right to development, bearing in mind existing international guidelines,*

while the industrialized countries were in favor of a Code protecting TNCs from discriminatory treatment or other behavior of host States which would be in violation of certain minimum standards, the developing States primarily sought to ensure that TNCs would be better regulated, and in particular would be prohibited from interfering either with political independence of the investment-receiving States or with their nationally defined economic objectives. Although a compromise solution was found on these differing expectations in 1980, when it was agreed that the Draft Code would comprise two parts, one regulating the activities of TNCs, and the other relating to the treatment of TNCs,[5] the conflicting views about what each of those parts should contain ultimately proved insuperable.

It is also in the context created in the 1970s, where the developed States feared that certain abuses by TNCs, or their interference with local political processes, might lead to hostile reactions from developing States, and possibly to the imposition of restrictions on the rights of foreign investors, and where the 'Group of 77' non-aligned (developing) countries insisted on their permanent sovereignty over natural resources and on the need to improve the supervision of the activities of transnational corporations, that the OECD adopted, on 21 June 1976, the Guidelines for Multinational Enterprises. These Guidelines have been revised on a number of occasions since their initial adoption, and most recently in 2000, when the supervisory mechanism was revitalized and when a general obligation on multinational enterprises to 'respect the human rights of those affected by their activities consistent with the host government's international obligations and commitments' was stipulated.[6] Although they are addressed

---

*rules and standards relating to the subject-matter*, UN Sub-Commission on Prevention of Discrimination and Protection of Minorities, UN doc E/CN.4/Sub.2/1996/12, 2 July 1996, paras 61–62. See also on this attempt, SKB Assante, 'United Nations: International Regulation of Transnational Corporations' (1979) 13 *Journal of World Trade Law* 55; W Spröte, 'Negotiations on a United Nations Code of Conduct on Transnational Corporations' (1990) 33 *German Yearbook of International Law* 331; P Muchlinski, 'Attempts to Extend the Accountability of Transnational Corporations: The Role of UNCTAD', in Menno T Kamminga and Saman Zia-Zarifi (eds), *Liability of Multinational Corporations under International Law* (The Hague, Kluwer Law International, 2000), pp 97–117; N Jägers, *Corporate Human Rights Obligations: in Search of Accountability* (Antwerpen, Oxford and New York, Intersentia, 2002), pp 119–24.

[5] P Muchlinski, 'Attempts to Extend the Accountability of Transnational Corporations: The Role of UNCTAD', above n 4, at p 100 (referring to Ecosoc Res 1980/60 of 24 July 1980).

[6] See para 2 of the Chapter on 'General Policies'. On the context in which the OECD launched the revitalization of the Guidelines for Multinational Enterprises, see J. Murray, 'A new phase in the regulation of multinational enterprises: the role of the OECD', 30 *Industrial Law Journal* 255 (2001); Jan Huner, 'The Multilateral Agreement on Investment and the Review of the OECD Guidelines for Multinational Enterprises', in Menno T. Kamminga and Saman Zia-Zarifi (eds), *Liability of Multinational Corporations under International Law*, above n 4, at 197–205.

only to the 30 member States of the OECD and the handful of non-member countries who have chosen to adhere to them, the Guidelines still constitute the most widely used instrument defining the obligations of multinational enterprises.[7] As illustrated by the fact that they were adopted as part of the Declaration on International Investment and Multinational Enterprises, which in its other parts sought to facilitate trade among OECD countries in particular by requiring the parties to adopt the principle of national treatment and by seeking to minimize the risk of conflicting requirements being imposed on multinational enterprises, the Guidelines were seen as a means to encourage the opening up of foreign economies to foreign direct investment. They sought to ensure that all States parties would contribute, by the setting of national contact points and their cooperation with the OECD Investment Committee,[8] to ensuring a certain level of control on the activities of multinational enterprises incorporated under their jurisdiction, even if this supervision remains purely voluntary and may not lead to the imposition of sanctions.

Almost simultaneously, the ILO adopted the Tripartite Declaration of Principles concerning Multinational Enterprises and Social Policy.[9] As stated in its Preamble, the Tripartite Declaration is based on the finding that 'the advances made by multinational enterprises in organizing their operations beyond the national framework may lead to abuse of concentrations of economic power and to conflicts with national policy objectives and with the interest of the workers. In addition, the complexity of multinational enterprises and the difficulty of clearly perceiving their diverse structures, operations and policies sometimes give rise to concern either in the home or in the host countries, or in both.' The aim of the Tripartite Declaration of Principles, then, is to 'encourage the positive contribution which multinational enterprises can make to economic and social progress and to minimize and resolve the difficulties to which their various operations may give rise, taking into account the United Nations resolutions advocating the Establishment of a New International Economic

---

[7] The Guidelines are addressed to the governments of the 30 States parties of the Organisation, but have also been adopted by the governments of Argentina, Brazil, Chile, Estonia, Israel, Latvia, Lithuania and Slovenia. These governments 'recommend to multinational enterprises operating in or from their territories the observance of the Guidelines' (Declaration on International Investment and Multinational Enterprises, 27 June 2000, I). There is therefore no territorial limitation to the application of the Guidelines. As most multinational enterprises are domiciled in industrialized countries that are members of the OECD, the Guidelines are practically of almost universal applicability to transnational business enterprises.

[8] Previously called the Committee on International Investment and Multinational Enterprises (CIME).

[9] Tripartite Declaration of Principles concerning Multinational Enterprises and Social Policy, adopted by the Governing Body of the ILO at its 204th Session (November 1977), and revised at the 279th Session (November 2000).

Order.'[10] Apart from specific references to fundamental workers' rights as guaranteed under conventions and recommendations adopted within the ILO—including the ILO Declaration on Fundamental Principles and Rights at Work, adopted in June 1998 by the International Labor Conference[11]—such as references to the principles of freedom of association[12] and the right to collective bargaining,[13] the prohibition of arbitrary dismissals,[14] or the protection of health and safety at work,[15] the Tripartite Declaration contains a general provision relating to the obligation to respect human rights. Paragraph 8 of the chapter on General Policies states that:

> All the parties concerned by this Declaration should respect the sovereign rights of States, obey the national laws and regulations, give due consideration to local practices and respect relevant international standards.[[16]] They should respect the Universal Declaration of Human Rights and the corresponding International Covenants adopted by the General Assembly of the United Nations as well as the Constitution of the International Labour Organization and its principles according to which freedom of expression and association are essential to sustained progress. They should contribute to the realization of the ILO Declaration on Fundamental Principles and Rights at Work and its Follow-up, adopted in 1998.[[17]] They should also honour commitments which they have freely entered into, in conformity with the national law and accepted international obligations.

It is also noteworthy that, although the Tripartite Declaration insists on the requirement that all parties to the Declaration—including, thus, the employers—'respect the sovereign rights of States', and states that multinational enterprises 'take fully into account established general policy objectives of the countries in which they operate' and that their activities should be 'in harmony with the development priorities and social aims and structure of the country in which they operate',[18] the standards on

---

[10] Para 2.
[11] Para 8.
[12] Paras 42–48.
[13] Paras 49–56.
[14] Para 27.
[15] Paras 37–40.
[16] This has led to the following interpretation by the ILO, under the procedure for the interpretation of the Tripartite Declaration set out below: 'There is no reasonable basis for interpreting the Declaration to permit the exemption of any party from complying with substantive safeguards under either domestic laws or international standards. This would be inconsistent with the Declaration's ultimate goal, laid out in paragraph 5, of furthering social progress. (GB.272/MNE/1 confidential, para 21)' (*Belgian Case no 2* (1997–1998)).
[17] This sentence was added in para 8 when the Tripartite Declaration was revised, in November 2000.
[18] Para 10.

social policy developed under ILO conventions and recommendations are to be complied with, even where the host country either would not be bound by certain of those instruments, or where, even though bound, the host government would be acting in violation of those international obligations.[19] In this respect, the ILO Tripartite Declaration goes even beyond the provision of the OECD Guidelines for Multinational Enterprises: by referring to the obligation of multinational enterprises to 'respect the human rights of those affected by their activities *consistent with the host government's international obligations and commitments*', the OECD Guidelines suggest that the foreign investor should comply with any international instruments ratified by the host country, even if local regulations or local practice are not themselves in conformity with those instruments ; the ILO Tripartite Declaration states that, even where certain core ILO instruments have not been ratified by the host State, they nevertheless should be 'referred to' by these investors 'for guidance in their social policy'.

Although of high moral significance because of its adoption by consensus by the ILO Governing Body at which governments, employers and workers are represented, the Tripartite Declaration remains, as such, a non-binding instrument: the Declaration, we are told in its introductory chapter, 'sets out principles in the fields of employment, training, conditions of work and life and industrial relations which governments, employers' and workers' organizations and multinational enterprises are recommended to observe on a voluntary basis; its provisions shall not limit or otherwise affect obligations arising out of ratification of any ILO Convention.'[20] Governments, however, are to report on a quadriennial

---

[19] See, in particular, para 9 of the Tripartite Declaration : 'Governments which have not yet ratified Conventions Nos 87 [concerning Freedom of Association and Protection of the Right to Organise], 98 [concerning the Application of the Principles of the Right to Organise and to Bargain Collectively], 111 [concerning Discrimination in Respect of Employment and Occupation], 122 [concerning Employment Policy], 138 [concerning Minimum Age for Admission to Employment] and 182 [concerning the Prohibition and Immediate Action for the Elimination of the Worst Forms of Child Labour] are urged to do so and in any event to apply, to the greatest extent possible, through their national policies, the principles embodied therein and in Recommendations Nos. 111 [concerning Discrimination in Respect of Employment and Occupation], 119 [concerning Termination of Employment at the Initiative of the Employer], 122 [concerning Employment Policy], 146 [concerning Minimum Age for Admission to Employment] and 190 [concerning the Prohibition and Immediate Action for the Elimination of the Worst Forms of Child Labour]. Without prejudice to the obligation of governments to ensure compliance with Conventions they have ratified, in countries in which the Conventions and Recommendations cited in this paragraph are not complied with, all parties should refer to them for guidance in their social policy'.

[20] Para 7. The Addendum to the Tripartite Declaration of Principles concerning Multinational Enterprises and Social Policy adopted by the Governing Body of the International Labour Office at its 238th Session (Geneva, November 1987) and 264th Session (November 1995) states that '[i]n keeping with the voluntary nature of the Declaration all of its provisions, whether derived from ILO Conventions and Recommendations or other sources, are recommendatory, except of course for provisions in Conventions which are binding on the member States which have ratified them.'

basis to the Governing Body on the implementation of the Declaration, and the Governing Body may make recommendations on the basis of the examination of these reports by the the Subcommittee on Multinational Enterprises of the Committee on Legal Issues and International Labour Standards.[21] Moreover, under the *Procedure for the Examination of Disputes concerning the Application of the Tripartite Declaration of Principles Concerning Multinational Enterprises and Social Policy by Means of Interpretation of Its Provisions*,[22] governments may request an interpretation of the Tripartite Declaration, either on their own initiative or upon a request made by workers' or employers' international or representative national organizations.[23] This request is transmitted to the Subcommittee on Multinational Enterprises, a subcommittee of the ILO Governing Body's Committee on Legal Issues and International Labour Standards, the three officers of which (representing respectively the governments, the workers and the employers) may decide that the request is admissible (or 'receivable', in the jargon of the Declaration),[24] leading it to ask the ILO for the interpretation requested. Once the draft reply of the ILO is received, the proposed interpretation of the Tripartite Declaration is voted upon within the Subcommittee on Multinational Enterprises, and if approved by the Governing Body of the ILO, will be forwarded to the parties

---

[21] This Subcommittee is composed of 18 members (six from each of the three groups – governments, workers and employers – which reflect the tripartite structure of the ILO).

[22] Adopted by the Governing Body of the ILO, at its 232nd Session (Geneva, March 1986). Para 1 of this *Procedure* states that its purpose is 'to interpret the provisions of the Declaration when needed to resolve a disagreement on their meaning, arising from an actual situation, between parties to whom the Declaration is commended.' In interpreting this paragraph, the ILO has considered that '[t]here must be an actual dispute, arising out of a factual situation, between the parties for an interpretation to be necessary. Therefore, requests for interpretation must be supported by factual evidence to show that there is a dispute. (GB.229/13/13, Appendix, para 13)' (*BIFU Case*, 1984–1985). In April 1992, the International Union of Food and Allied Workers' Associations (IUF) submitted, on behalf of one of its members, a formal request for an interpretation of the Tripartite Declaration, complaining about the decision of a multinational enterprise to expand its investment in a country where, according to the IUF, there was a total disregard for all workers' and human rights, so that in the view of the IUF such an investment could not be said to contribute to 'economic and social progress' (paras 2 and 8 of the Tripartite Declaration). The Subcommittee on Multinational Enterprises considered, however, that the request was not receivable, insofar as 'a situation that did not relate to an actual dispute between workers and management or between the enterprise and the government was not an "actual situation" requiring an interpretation. There was no evidence of an actual dispute between workers and management or government leading to a disagreement over the interpretation of the Declaration (...). (GB.255/10/12)'.

[23] These organisations may make such a request themselves if the government refuses to do so or has failed to react within three months of having received such a request. See para 6 of the *Procedure for the Examination of Disputes concerning the Application of the Tripartite Declaration of Principles Concerning Multinational Enterprises and Social Policy by Means of Interpretation of Its Provisions*, above n 22.

[24] If the three officers cannot reach an agreement unanimously, the question shall be referred to the full Committee for decision (see para 4).

concerned and made public in the *Official Bulletin* of the ILO, although the names of any specific corporations concerned are withheld.

Neither the 1976 OECD Guidelines for Multinational Enterprises nor the 1977 ILO Tripartite Declaration of Principles concerning Multinational Enterprises and Social Policy may be described as effective instruments imposing human rights obligations on transnational enterprises.[25] These instruments impose on States certain obligations of a procedural nature: in particular, States must set up national contact points (NCPs) under the OECD Guidelines in order to promote the Guidelines and to receive 'specific instances', or complaints by interested parties in cases of non-compliance by companies; they must report on a quadriennal basis under the ILO Tripartite Declaration on the implementation of the principles listed therein. However, both these instruments are explicitly presented as non-binding instruments, with respect to the multinational enterprises whose practices they ultimately seek to address. The statements adopted by the NCPs at the close of procedures initiated under the revised OECD Guidelines for Multinational Enterprises are generally weak, and the procedure itself before the NCPs is mostly considered as unsatisfactory by the NGOs which, across some 45 'specific instances' they have presented to the NCPs since 2000, have relied on this mechanism: the NCPs have no investigative powers;[26] the procedures followed lack transparency and are seen as biased towards the interests of business; and, as they belong to the governmental apparatus, the NCPs are neither independent[27] nor even, in most cases, impartial in the consideration of the complaints they

---

[25] For a comparison of these tools, see Bob Hepple, *Labour Laws and Global Trade* (Oxford and Portland, Oregon, Hart Publishing, 2005), at pp 78–85.

[26] Although para 20 of the 'Commentary on the Implementation Procedures of the OECD Guidelines on Multinational Enterprises' (in *The OECD Guidelines on Multinational Enterprises*, revision 2000, at p 57) refers to the fact that the NCP may 'pursue enquiries and engage in other fact finding activities', this statement must be replaced in its context: it is made in order to encourage NCPs to receive 'specific instances' even where Guidelines-related questions arise in non-adhering countries. It is in order to emphasize that the NCPs may nevertheless contribute to compliance with the Guidelines in such a situation that the Commentary mentions that it remains possible in such an instance for the NCP to 'take steps to develop an understanding of the issues involved.'

[27] The States adhering to the OECD Guidelines on Multinational Enterprises are recognized a broad margin of appreciation in how to set up their national contact point. However, in conformity with the principle of 'functional equivalence', a set of core criteria has been laid down which they should take into account in organising the NCPs: 'Since governments are accorded flexibility in the way they organise NCPs, NCPs should function in a visible, accessible, transparent, and accountable manner. These criteria will guide NCPs in carrying out their activities and will also assist the CIME in discussing the conduct of NCPs' (para 8 of the 'Commentary on the Implementation Procedures of the OECD Guidelines on Multinational Enterprises' (above, n 26)). Neither the principles of independence nor that of impartiality are mentioned among those core criteria.

receive.[28] Moreover, no sanctions may be imposed on multinational enterprises which either refuse to cooperate with the NCP, or are found to be in violation of the Guidelines. Under the OECD Guidelines, the only incentive for companies to comply resides in the adverse publicity they will be subjected to if they refuse to cooperate in identifying a solution to the 'specific instance' presented to an NCP.[29] Such an incentive is even absent from the procedures for the supervision and interpretation of the ILO Tripartite Declaration.

## 2. The 1990s: the Second Wave of Corporate Responsibility

The question of the human rights responsibilities of TNCs has been spectacularly revived, however, since the mid 1990s, and the improvements brought to the OECD Guidelines on Multinational Enterprises in 2000, especially with respect to the treatment of complaints by the NCPs established by each adhering government, may be seen as illustrative of a much broader development. This revival in turn is part of a more general critique of the path taken by economic globalization. It also has more immediate causes. Certain highly visible legal suits have been filed before United States and European courts against parent companies whose subsidiaries or affiliates were accused of directly committing human rights violations, or—more frequently—of being complicit in human rights violations committed by the States in which they operated. In the United States in particular, such suits have been based on an inventive use by litigants, relying often on the class action mechanism,[30] of the

---

[28] These critiques are developed in the report released in September 2005 by OECD Watch, an international network of NGOs promoting corporate accountability: see OECD Watch, *Five Years On. A Review of the OECD Guidelines and the National Contact Points*, available at www.oecdwatch.org.

[29] Under the terms of the 'Procedural Guidance' given to the NCPs by the Decision of the OECD Council of 27 June 2000 (OECD doc DAFFE/IME/WPG (2000)9), '[i]f the parties involved do not reach agreement on the issues raised, [the NCP may] issue a statement, and make recommendations as appropriate, on the implementation of the Guidelines.' Moreover, 'after consultation with the parties involved, [the NCP may] make publicly available the results of these procedures unless preserving confidentiality would be in the best interests of effective implementation of the Guidelines.' Finally, 'At the conclusion of the procedures, if the parties involved have not agreed on a resolution of the issues raised, they are free to communicate about and discuss these issues,' although 'information and views provided during the proceedings by another party involved will remain confidential, unless that other party agrees to their disclosure.'

[30] See more generally, on the specific procedural advantages which potential plaintiffs in such cases are recognized under the Federal Rules of Civil Procedure, which imply that the usefulness of the Alien Tort Claims Act may be limited as a model to be followed by other jurisdictions, Beth Stephens, 'Translitigating *Filartiga*: A Comparative and International Law Analysis of Domestic Remedies For International Human Rights Violations' (2002) 27 *Yale Journal of International Law* 1.

Alien Tort Claims Act 1789 (ATCA). That statute, a part of the First Judiciary Act 1789, provides that '[t]he district courts shall have original jurisdiction of any civil action by an alien for a tort only, committed in violation of the law of nations or a treaty of the United States.'[31] The United States federal courts have agreed to read this provision as implying that they have jurisdiction over enterprises either incorporated in the United States or having a continuous business relationship with the United States, where foreigners, victims of violations of international law[32] wherever such violations have taken place, seek damages from enterprises which have committed those violations or are complicit in such violations as they may have been committed by State agents.[33] Although its practical consequences remain to be seen, and although the procedural hurdles in using the ATCA should not be underestimated, the litigation following its revival has served to shed light on the risks involved in the activities of TNCs operating in States where human rights may be violated on a routine basis.[34]

The debate on how to improve the human rights accountability of TNCs has gained further momentum at the international level since two developments have occured. First, at the 1999 Davos World Economic Forum, the UN Secretary General Kofi Annan proposed to the world of business a Global Compact based on shared values in the areas of human rights, labour, and the environment, to which anti-corruption was added in 2004. The ten principles to which participants in the Global Compact adhere are derived from the Universal Declaration of Human Rights, the ILO's Declaration on Fundamental Principles and Rights at Work, the Rio Declaration on Environment and Development, and the UN Convention Against Corruption. The process is voluntary. It is based on the idea that good practices should be rewarded by being publicized, and that they

---

[31] 28 USC §1350.

[32] The United States Supreme Court considers that, when confronted with such suits, the US federal courts should 'require any claim based on the present-day law of nations to rest on a norm of international character accepted by the civilized world and defined with a specificity comparable to the features of the 18th-century paradigms (violation of safe conducts, infringement of the rights of ambassadors, and piracy) which Congress had in mind when adopting the First Judiciary Act 1789 (*Sosa v Alvarez-Machain*, No 03-339, slip op at 30–31 (US Sup Ct, 2004)).

[33] See in particular *John Doe I v Unocal Corp*, 395 F.3d 932, 945–46 (9th Cir, 2002) (complicity of Unocal with human rights abuses committed by the Burmese military); and *Wiwa v Royal Dutch Petroleum Co*, 2002 WL 319887, *2 (SDNY, 2002) (complicity of Shell Nigeria and its parent companies Shell UK and Royal Dutch in the human rights abuses committed by the Nigerian police).

[34] For a synthesis of the litigation against companies based on the ATCA, see chs 2, 3 and 4 of Sarah Joseph, *Corporations and Transnational Human Rights Litigation* (Oxford and Portland, Oregon, Hart Publishing, 2004). In the other chapters of the book, the author also seeks to provide an overview of the litigation against companies for human rights abuses under other jurisdictions.

should be shared in order to promote a mutual learning among businesses.[35] The companies acceding to the Global Compact are to 'embrace, support and enact, within their sphere of influence,' the ten (initially nine) principles on which it is based, and they are to report annually on the initiatives they have taken to make those principles part of their operations. The two first principles relate to human rights: under Principle 1, 'Businesses should support and respect the protection of internationally proclaimed human rights'; under Principle 2, they should 'make sure that they are not complicit in human rights abuses.'

Second, after a wide consultation of all relevant stakeholders including in particular the business community, the UN Sub-Commission for the Promotion and Protection of Human Rights approved in Resolution 2003/16 of 14 August 2003, the set of 'Norms on the Responsibilities of Transnational Corporations and Other Business Enterprises with regard to Human Rights'.[36] The draft Norms essentially present themselves as a restatement of the human rights obligations imposed on companies under international law. It is based on the idea that 'even though States have the primary responsibility to promote, secure the fulfillment of, respect, ensure respect of and protect human rights, transnational corporations and other business enterprises, as organs of society, are also responsible for promoting and securing the human rights set forth in the Universal Declaration of Human Rights,' and therefore 'transnational corporations and other business enterprises, their officers and persons working for them are also obligated to respect generally recognized responsibilities and norms contained in United Nations treaties and other international instruments.'[37] Principle 1 of the draft Norms reflects their overall approach on the scope of the human rights obligations of companies:

> States have the primary responsibility to promote, secure the fulfillment of, respect, ensure respect of and protect human rights recognized in international as well as national law, including ensuring that transnational corporations and

---

[35] As stated on the website of the Global Compact (www.unglobalcompact.org): 'The Global Compact is a purely voluntary initiative. It does not police or enforce the behavior or actions of companies. Rather, it is designed to stimulate change and to promote good corporate citizenship and encourage innovative solutions and partnerships.'

[36] UN doc E/CN.4/Sub.2/2003/12/Rev.2 (2003); and for the Commentary, which the Preamble of the draft Norms states is 'a useful interpretation and elaboration of the standards contained in the Norms,' UN doc E/CN.4/Sub.2/2003/38/Rev.2 (2003). On the drafting process of these draft Norms and a comparison with previous attempts of a similar nature, see David Weissbrodt and Muria Kruger, 'Current Developments: Norms on the Responsibilities of Transnational Corporations and Other Business Enterprises with Regard to Human Rights' (2003) 97 *American Journal of International Law* 901; David Weissbrodt and Muria Kruger, 'Human Rights Responsibilities of Businesses as Non-State Actors', in Ph Alston (ed), *Non-State Actors and Human Rights* (Oxford, Oxford University Press, 2005), pp 315–50.

[37] Preamble, 3d and 4th Recital.

other business enterprises respect human rights. Within their respective spheres of activity and influence, transnational corporations and other business enterprises have the obligation to promote, secure the fulfillment of, respect, ensure respect of and protect human rights recognized in international as well as national law, including the rights and interests of indigenous peoples and other vulnerable groups.

The notion of 'sphere of influence', which the Global Compact also relies upon, is therefore crucial to understanding the extent of the obligations which the draft Norms seek to impose on companies. It is, however, a relatively vague notion, and is best understood as a compromise between two ideas: on the one hand, companies are not to be equated to the States in which they operate, which are primarily responsible for the provision of public services such as health or education, and for the maintenance of law and order; on the other hand, the more companies are powerful, the more it will be justified to impose on them to exercise leverage on their business partners or on the host government to ensure that they, too, comply with the set of internationally recognized human rights. How then can the notion be made operational? The explanation provided by the Global Compact website is not particularly helpful. It states that the concept, although 'not defined in detail by international human rights standards,'

> will tend to include individuals to whom the company has a certain political, contractual, economic or geographic proximity. Every company, both large and small, has a sphere of influence, though obviously the larger and more strategically significant the company, the larger the company's sphere of influence is likely to be.[38]

As to the Commentary to the draft Norms – adopted by the UN Sub-Commission on Human Rights along with the draft Norms themselves, and providing an authoritative explanation of their content – this states:

> Transnational corporations and other business enterprises shall have the responsibility to use due diligence in ensuring that their activities do not contribute directly or indirectly to human abuses, and that they do not directly or indirectly benefit from abuses of which they were aware or ought to have been aware. Transnational corporations and other business enterprises shall further refrain from activities that would undermine the rule of law as well as governmental and other efforts to promote and ensure respect for human rights, and shall use their influence in order to help promote and ensure respect for human rights. Transnational corporations and other business enterprises shall inform

---

[38] www.unglobalcompact.org

themselves of the human rights impact of their principal activities and major proposed activities so that they can further avoid complicity in human rights abuses.

This latter statement clearly links the question of the 'sphere of influence' of companies with the requirement that they are not complicit in human rights abuses, a requirement also formulated in the UN Global Compact (Principle 2). Just like the notion of 'sphere of influence', the notion of complicity—which also has been criticized for its vagueness[39]— may be examined both in the relationships between the concerned company and its business partners, and in the relationships between that company and the country in which it operates. Although these two situations may be fused in practice, when a company has a partnership or joint venture with the host government, they nevertheless are analytically distinct, and should thus be considered separately. Offering a typology of the situations where a corporation may be said to be complicit in human rights violations committed by its business partners or by the host government in the country where it operates certainly is the most urgent task facing legal doctrine today in this field. Neither the draft Norms nor, indeed, any other mechanism for improving the accountability of multinational corporations for human rights obligations, will be workable unless these notions are adequately clarified.[40]

Although the notion of 'sphere of influence' therefore presents close affinities with the concept of complicity, the two notions nevertheless have distinct functions to fulfill. The notion of complicity serves to identify the responsibility of companies where another entity, their business partners (their suppliers or subcontractors) or the host government, commits human rights abuses, which are considered as criminal offences under either international or internal law. In order to identify whether the company is directly complicit in such abuses, we will have to ask, first, whether it aided and abetted the commission of the violation. Under the case-law of the international criminal tribunals, for instance, which in turn inspired the United States federal jurisdictions for the application of the ATCA, such assistance will be considered to lead to a finding of complicity where it has a substantial effect on the commission of the

---

[39] See, eg, Gregory Wallace, 'Fallout from Slave-Labor Case is Troubling' (1997) 150 *New Jersey LawJournal* 896.

[40] Useful attempts are, eg, Andrew Clapham, 'State responsibility, corporate responsibility, and complicity in human rights violations', in Lene Bomann-Larsen and Oddny Wiggen (eds), *Responsibility in World Business. Managing Harmful Side-effects of Corporate Activity* (Tokyo, New York and Paris, United Nations University Press, 2004), pp 50–81; Andrew Clapham and Scott Jerbi, *Categories of Corporate Complicity in Human Rights Abuses* (2001), available at http://www.business-humanrights.org/Clapham-Jerbi-paper.htm.

abuse,[41] and where it is given with the knowledge that it would have such an effect, whether or not the accomplice shares the *mens rea* of the direct perpetrator.[42] Other forms of complicity have been put forward, however.[43] Where a company is in a joint venture with the host government or with another private actor and has knowledge of, or should have known of, human rights violations committed by that partner in the fulfilment of the agreement, the company should be considered complicit in the violation for not having put an end to the business relationship. We may also ask, for instance, whether the company benefited from the abuse, for example in instances where the state security forces repress peaceful

---

[41] Under the ATCA, it has been authoritatively held that the standard for aiding and abetting is 'knowing practical assistance or encouragement that has a substantial effect on the perpetration of the crime': *John Doe I v Unocal Corp*, 395 F.3d 932, 945–46 (9th Cir, 2002) (judgment filed 18 September 2002). This standard is borrowed from the approach of international criminal tribunals. See, eg, *Prosecutor v Furundzija*, IT-95-17/1-T (10 December 1998), reprinted in 38 ILM 317 (1999), where the International Tribunal for the former Yugoslavia (ICTY) held that 'the *actus reus* of aiding and abetting in international criminal law requires practical assistance, encouragement, or moral support which has a substantial effect on the perpetration of the crime' (at § 235). As emphasized by the *Unocal* judgment delivered on 18 September 2002 by the United States Court of Appeals for the 9th Circuit, the ICTY considered that, in order to qualify, 'assistance need not constitute an indispensable element, that is, a *conditio sine qua non* for the acts of the principal' (*Furundzija* at § 209; see also *Prosecutor v Kunarac*, IT-96-23-T and IT-96-23/1-T, § 391 (22 February 2001), available at http://www.un.org/icty/foca/trialc2/judgement/index.htm ('The act of assistance need not have caused the act of the principal'): it suffices that the acts of the accomplice 'make a significant difference to the commission of the criminal act by the principal' (*Furundzija* at § 233)). Under the criterion used by the ICTY, which borrows from the precedents set by the United States and British military courts and tribunals dealing with the Nazi war crimes in the aftermath of the Second World War, the acts of the accomplice will have the required '[substantial] effect on the commission of the crime' where 'the criminal act most probably would not have occurred in the same way [without] someone act[ing] in the role that the [accomplice] in fact assumed.' *Prosecutor v Tadic*, ICTY-94-1, § 688 (7 May 1997), available at http://www.un.org/icty/tadic/trials2/judgement/index.htm. The International Criminal Tribunal for Rwanda also considers that the *actus reus* for aiding and abetting consists in any act of assistance, whether physical or moral, which substantially contributes to the commission of the crime: *Prosecutor v Musema*, ICTR-96-13-T (27 January 2000), available at http://www.ictr.org/.

[42] Again, this is the understanding of the *mens rea* required for the existence of direct complicity under the ATCA. Quoting from § 245 of the *Furundzija* case of the ICTY and from § 180 of the *Musema* case of the ICTR, the United States Court of Appeals for the 9th Circuit noted that 'it is not necessary for the accomplice to share the *mens rea* of the perpetrator, in the sense of positive intention to commit the crime' and that, 'in fact, it is not even necessary that the aider and abettor knows the precise crime that the principal intends to commit'; '[r]ather, if the accused "is aware that one of a number of crimes will probably be committed, and one of those crimes is in fact committed, he has intended to facilitate the commission of that crime, and is guilty as an aider and abettor"'.

[43] See the *Report of the United Nations High Commissioner for Human Rights to the 56th session of the General Assembly*, UN doc A/56/36 (2001) (distinguishing direct, beneficial and silent complicity); or the OHCHR briefing paper, 'The Global Compact and Human Rights : Understanding Sphere of Influence and Complicity', available from the website of the UN Global Compact (http://www.unglobalcompact.com/Issues/human_rights/index.html), at p 18.

protest against business activities. Finally, when in the face of systematic or continuous human rights violations in the host country, the company remains silent, refusing to denounce these abuses which the company was aware of or should have been aware of, we may ask whether it should not be considered the 'silent accomplice' of those violations: apart from the fact that, in such situations, direct complicity may be alleged—insofar as by remaining silent in the face of violations the company lends its moral support to those crimes, thus contributing to the instigation of such crimes[44]—there exists a 'growing acceptance within companies that there is something culpable about failing to exercise influence in such circumstances.'[45] It is this four-tiered approach to complicity which the website of the Global Compact advocates. Similarly, in its 2005 report to which I return hereunder, the Office of the High Commissioner for Human Rights states that:

> Four situations illustrate where an allegation of complicity might arise against a company. First, when the company actively assists, directly or indirectly, in human rights violations committed by others; second, when the company is in a partnership with a Government and could reasonably foresee, or subsequently

---

[44] For instance, in the Trial Chamber judgment delivered in the case of *Prosecutor v Akayesu*, the International Criminal Tribunal for Rwanda convicted a village mayor as an accomplice as it considered that his presence 'sent a clear signal of official tolerance for sexual violence', thus in effect encouraging the offence (*Prosecutor v Akayesu*, Case No ICTR-96-4-T (Trial Chamber), 2 September 1998). According to the charges of the indictment, 'Jean Paul Akayesu knew that the acts of sexual violence, beatings and murders were being committed and was at times present during their commission. Jean Paul Akayesu facilitated the commission of the sexual violence, beatings and murders by allowing the sexual violence and beatings and murders to occur on or near the bureau communal premises. By virtue of his presence during the commission of the sexual violence, beatings and murders and by failing to prevent the sexual violence, beatings and murders, Jean Paul Akayesu encouraged these activities.' The judgment of 2 September 1998 follows this argument: 'The Tribunal finds, under Article 6(1) of its Statute [according to which 'A person who planned, *instigated*, ordered, committed or otherwise aided and abetted in the planning, preparation or execution of a crime referred to in Articles 2 to 4 of the present Statute (genocide, crime against humanity, war crimes defined as serious violations of Article 3 common to the Geneva Conventions of 12 August 1949 for the Protection of War Victims, and of Additional Protocol II thereto of 8 June 1977), shall be individually responsible for the crime'], that the Accused aided and abetted the following acts of sexual violence, by allowing them to take place on or near the premises of the bureau communal, while he was present on the premises in respect of [multiple acts of rape] and in his presence in respect of [an act of rape and other sexual offences] and by facilitating the commission of these acts through his words of encouragement in other acts of sexual violence, which, by virtue of his authority, sent a clear signal of official tolerance for sexual violence, without which these acts would not have taken place' (§§ 693 and 694). In the subsequent judgment of 1 June 2001 filed by the Appeals Chamber in the same case (§§ 474 to 483), it was clarified that Art 6(1) of the Statute did not require that the incitement to commit a crime be 'direct and public', despite the fact that, with respect to the crime of genocide, Art 2 § 3, c) of the Statute of the ICTR provides that 'direct and public incitement' to commit this crime is punishable.

[45] *Report of the United Nations High Commissioner for Human Rights to the 56th session of the General Assembly*, above n 43, para 111.

obtains knowledge, that the Government is likely to commit abuses in carrying out the agreement[46]; third, when the company benefits from human rights violations even if it does not positively assist or cause them; and fourth, when the company is silent or inactive in the face of violations.[47]

The notion of complicity is a legal notion which originates in the criminal law. It has been relied upon in the context of litigation based on the ATCA, however, although this statute provides for the possibility to invoke the civil liability of certain actors for violations of the law of nations. In the words of the United States Court of Appeals for the Ninth Circuit, this is justified insofar as 'what is a crime in one jurisdiction is often a tort in another jurisdiction, and this distinction is therefore of little help in ascertaining the standards of international human rights law': the Court therefore considered in that case that 'the standard for aiding and abetting in international criminal law is similar to the standard for aiding and abetting in domestic tort law, making the distinction between criminal and tort law less crucial in this context.' But insofar as it appears in the Global Compact and in the draft Norms, the notion of complicity is used in a broader sense, which should not necessarily be limited to the significance it takes in the criminal law context. It is here that the complementary notion of 'sphere of influence' has a role to play. By stating that companies have human rights responsibilities within their sphere of activity and influence, the UN draft Norms seek to clarify that the extent of these responsibilities depends both on the scope of the impact of their activities and on the capacity of the companies to influence the other actors with whom they may interact. These two dimensions correspond, respectively, to the negative and the positive obligations companies may have to respect, protect and promote human rights. Indeed, under the draft Norms, companies are not only imposed with an obligation to respect the human rights set forth in the draft Norms by abstaining from adopting certain measures which would violate those rights; they also are under a positive duty to ensure respect of those rights, to protect and promote them.

---

[46] Although, in the description of this category of complicity, reference is made only to the business partner of a company which is a government, the same reasoning should hold for the situation where the business partner is a private understanding. This is confirmed by the OHCHR briefing paper, 'The Global Compact and Human Rights: Understanding Sphere of Influence and Complicity' (referred to above n 43), which describes as 'complicity in case of joint venture' the situation where 'the company has a common design or purpose with its contractual partner to fulfil the joint venture. It knew or should have known of the abuses committed by the partner'.

[47] *Report of the United Nations High Commissioner on Human Rights on the responsibilities of transnational corporations and related business enterprises with regard to human rights*, 15 February 2005, UN doc. E/CN.4/2005/91, para 34 (citing International Council on Human Rights Policy, *Beyond Voluntarism: Human rights and the developing international legal obligations of companies* (Geneva, February 2002), pp 125–36).

In principle, the notion of 'sphere of influence' should answer the question of how far such positive obligations reach. It should encourage us to identify different 'circles of influence', ie categories of situations and persons or communities affected (directly or more remotely) by the activities of the corporation and towards whom, therefore, the corporation has more or less wide-ranging obligations. However, it may be more fruitful to focus, rather than on these circles of influence, on a set of procedural obligations imposed on corporations which would ensure that they take into account their human rights obligations in planning and executing their activities, including in the selection of their business partners. In that sense, while useful in the hands of the rule-maker, or for the company which seeks to understand the expectations which the community has developed about its responsibility towards human rights, the notion of 'sphere of influence' may be too vague if left completely in the hands of the adjudicator: it may serve as a guideline in order to develop the legal obligations of corporations under both international and national law or in order to define the content of codes of conduct or of other standards adopted on a voluntary basis, but it may require further implementation before it can be fully applicable, for example in the context of civil litigation alleging the liability of the corporation for certain violations committed.

## 3. The Next Steps

It is too early to predict what will result from the movement launched by the adoption by the UN Sub-Commission on Human Rights of the draft Norms, which are currently being 'road-tested' within the Business Leaders Initiative on Human Rights.[48] The presentation of the draft Norms to the UN Commission on Human Rights led it to recommend that the Economic and Social Council request a further report from the Office of the High Commissioner for Human Rights (OHCHR). That study was prepared between May 2004 and early 2005. According to the terms of the UN Commission on Human Rights decision 2004/116, its purpose was to set out:

> the scope and legal status of existing initiatives and standards relating to the responsibility of transnational corporations and related business enterprises with regard to human rights, inter alia, the [draft Norms on the Human Rights Responsibilities of Transnational Corporations and Other Business Enterprises] and, identifying outstanding issues, to consult with all relevant stakeholders in compiling the report, ... and to submit the report to the Commission at its

---

[48] www.blihr.org

sixty-first session [March–April 2005] in order for it to identify options for strengthening standards on the responsibilities of transnational corporations and related business enterprises with regard to human rights and possible means of implementation.

On the basis of the consultations of the OHCHR, the report[49] identified a number of arguments put forward either by employers or by States against the draft Norms.[50] In particular, stakeholders critical of the Norms asserted, these Norms would represent 'a major shift away from voluntary adherence by business to international human rights standards and the need for this shift has not been demonstrated';[51] indeed, they added, 'the binding approach adopted in the draft Norms could also be counter-productive, drawing away from voluntary efforts and focusing on the implementation of only bare minimum standards.' Moreover, the imposition of legal responsibilities on business could 'shift the obligations to protect human rights from Governments to the private sector and provide a diversion for States to avoid their own responsibilities.' Finally, by seeking to impose on businesses to 'promote, secure the fulfilment of, respect, ensure respect of and protect human rights,' they would be misstating international law, as 'only States have legal obligations under the international human rights law.'

This first set of critiques challenges the very approach of the Sub-Commission on Human Rights in adopting the draft Norms, and which is reflected in Principle 1, cited above. In the next section of this chapter, I offer certain arguments in response to these critiques.[52] The argument according to which international human rights law imposes obligations only on States fails to recognize the precedents in international criminal law of international law imposing obligations directly on private individuals: thus, even if the draft Norms may be seen as innovating, they are not moving into entirely unchartered territory, and from the point of view at least of the principles of international law, there is nothing in their approach which may be denounced as unorthodox. There are two more important points to make in response, however. First, although the

---

[49] *Report of the United Nations High Commissioner on Human Rights on the responsibilities of transnational corporations and related business enterprises with regard to human rights*, 15 February 2005, UN doc E/CN.4/2005/91.

[50] See para 20 of the *Report*.

[51] This argument of the adversaries of the draft Norms is of course in contradiction with another argument put forward by some critics, which is that 'The draft Norms duplicate other initiatives and standards, particularly the OECD Guidelines for Multinational Enterprises and the ILO Tripartite Declaration' (para. 20, (i), of the *Report*). The stakeholders critical of the draft Norms obviously do not form a coherent group, nor do they have one single coherent set of arguments to present.

[52] See Section II.3 below, pp. 29–34.

imposition of direct obligations on companies under international law is one possible outcome of the draft Norms, this is neither a necessary outcome, nor the only outcome which can be imagined. The Norms themselves mention that the Norms could encourage UN human rights treaty bodies to better monitor the obligations of the States parties to the treaties they apply, which—as part of their general obligation to protect human rights under their jurisdiction—already are legally obliged to control private actors whose behavior could lead to human rights violations.[53] Thus, rather than imposing direct obligations under international law on companies, the Norms could, if adopted, instead impose stricter obligations on States parties to international human rights instruments, by clarifying the extent of their obligation to protect: far from 'shift[ing] the obligations to protect human rights from Governments to the private sector and provid[ing] a diversion for States to avoid their own responsibilities', the Norms in fact could thus reinforce the existing international obligations of States. Second—and this argument follows directly from the first—where the critics of the draft Norms assert that these Norms misstate international law, as 'only States have legal obligations under the international human rights law', they entertain a confusion between the content of international law and its tools. Although traditionally international law addresses itself to the State, it is common for the State to be imposed with an obligation to control private actors under its jurisdiction; in such a situation, although the law of international State responsibility constitutes the mechanism on which international law relies for its enforcement, the material object of the international norms is to impose obligations on private actors. Indeed, the direct application of international law before national jurisdictions illustrates how even rules of international law, in particular those contained in international treaties, may easily apply to private parties, provided they are sufficiently precise and may therefore be considered self-executing.

A second set of critiques addressed to the draft Norms adopted by the Sub-Commission on Human Rights is directed instead to the content of the human rights obligations they list. It is said, for instance, that the content of human rights the document is based on is inaccurate, as it refers to instruments whose status and levels of ratification vary widely. This argument is closely related to another argument according to which 'the legal

---

[53] Although Principle 16 of the Norms states, perhaps imprudently, that '[t]ransnational corporations and other business enterprises shall be subject to periodic monitoring and verification by United Nations, other international and national mechanisms already in existence or yet to be created, regarding application of the Norms', the corresponding Commentary refers (in (b)) to the mechanisms which, at UN level, already exist in order to monitor compliance by States with their human rights obligations, and which could seek inspiration from the Norms.

responsibilities on business identified in the draft Norms go beyond the standards applying to States. In particular, the wording of the draft Norms imposes duties on business to meet standards under treaties that a State in which a company was operating might not have ratified.' What these critics are thus indicating implicitly is the usefulness of defining at the universal level a set of standards applicable to corporations, in a context where the human rights obligations of States may vary widely, and where there are even more strikingly varying levels of implementation. As recalled above, both the OECD Guidelines on Multinational Enterprises and the ILO Tripartite Declaration refer, in defining the content of the human rights obligations of companies, not to the local rules or practices in the host State, but to the international commitments of the host State (in the case of the OECD Guidelines) or to the relevant international standards, whatever the precise set of international instruments ratified by that State (in the case of the Tripartite Declaration). It is precisely because the commitments of States under international human rights law are variable that there is a need to define a set of standards applicable to the business community, both in order to ensure that companies will not invoke the bad human rights record of the host government in order to escape their liability for complicity in certain abuses, and in order to prevent any temptation by a government to seek out potential foreign investors at the expense of human rights under their jurisdiction.

A third set of critiques concern the implementation measures which the Norms envisage. The Norms, it is said, may be unworkable: 'The vagueness of some of the provisions in the draft Norms would make it difficult for a tribunal to adjudicate any communication that came before it and the reporting requirements in the draft Norms are burdensome.' This vagueness also results from the fact that, in the concrete implementation of the general principles contained in the draft Norms, balancing decisions would be required, which should more appropriately be made by governments: 'Some human rights require Governments to decide on the most appropriate form of implementation, balancing often competing interests. The democratic State is in a more appropriate position to make such decisions than companies.' In fact, it is at this level that the discussion should now take place. As argued above, even though the content of the various rights listed in the draft Norms is well defined in the international law of human rights, and even though the notion of complicity is relatively well circumscribed as it is well known in the context of criminal law, it may be necessary in other respects to develop the draft Norms before they may become fully operational. This is not a reason for not using the draft Norms as the departure point for further initiatives, in particular for the adoption of an international instrument imposing on States an obligation to control the TNCs incorporated under their jurisdiction: on the contrary, it demonstrates the need for further action in order for the draft Norms to have an impact. In sum, the critiques addressed to the draft Norms on the Responsibilities of Transnational Corporations and Other Business Enterprises with Regard to Human Rights adopted in 2003 by the UN Sub-Commission on Human Rights merely demonstrate that, in their present form, these Norms may not be sufficiently clear and detailed to impose legal obligations directly on the companies to which they are addressed. But this does not invalidate current attempts to build on the Norms in order to clarify those obligations and set up monitoring mechanisms which would ensure that they are effectively complied with. On the contrary, such attempts should be encouraged, precisely because the Norms may not be treated as self-sufficient, even apart from their current lack of legal status.

In April 2005, the UN Commission on Human Rights requested that the UN Secretary General appoint a Special Representative to identify ways through which the accountability of TNCs for human rights violations may be improved.[54] On 28 July 2005, Professor John Ruggie, a professor at the John F Kennedy School of Government of Harvard University and hitherto closely involved with the process of the UN Global Compact, was appointed Special Representative of the UN Secretary General. As defined by Resolution 2005/69 of the UN Human Rights Commission, his task is:

(a) To identify and clarify standards of corporate responsibility and accountability for transnational corporations and other business enterprises with regard to human rights;

(b) To elaborate on the role of States in effectively regulating and adjudicating the role of transnational corporations and other business enterprises with regard to human rights, including through international cooperation;

(c) To research and clarify the implications for transnational corporations and other business enterprises of concepts such as 'complicity' and 'sphere of influence';

(d) To develop materials and methodologies for undertaking human rights impact assessments of the activities of transnational corporations and other business enterprises;

(e) To compile a compendium of best practices of States and transnational corporations and other business enterprises.

The description of the mandate of the Special Representative was the result of a compromise within the UN Commission on Human Rights, in

---

[54] UN Commission on Human Rights Res 2005/69, 'Human rights and transnational corporations and other business enterprises', adopted on 20 April 2005 by a recorded vote of 49 votes to three, with one abstention (chap XVII, E/CN.4/2005/L.10/Add.17).

which the creation of the mandate itself was obtained only against the absence of any explicit reference to the draft Norms of the UN Sub-Commission for the Promotion and Protection of Human Rights. Thus, while further developments may be expected to take place in this field after 2007—when the Special Representative should deliver his final report—the regulatory approach clearly favored by the UN Sub-Commission on Human Rights when it adopted the draft Norms may or may not be retained. The essays collected in this volume arrive therefore at the most crucial time, as they deal with the most important issues which the Special Representative will be facing, and on which he is to report back to the UN Human Rights Council. The next section presents these chapters in the logical order in which they are arranged.

## II. OUTLINE OF THE BOOK

This volume seeks to offer a systematic overview of the different tools through which the human rights accountability of TNCs may be improved. Part I of the book first examines the responsibility of States in controlling TNCs, emphasizing both the limits imposed by the protection of the rights of investors under investment treaties and the constraints States face in the competition for scarce investment, and, yet, the potential of the United States ATCA and other similar extra-territorial legislation, through which States ensure that corporate actors are effectively controlled. Part II of the book then turns to self-regulation by TNCs, through the use of codes of conduct or international framework agreements. Part III discusses further the recent attempts at global level to improve the human rights accountability of corporations by the direct imposition on corporations of obligations under international law. Finally, Part IV reviews the role of incentive-based mechanisms to achieve the same result: it considers the use of public procurement policies or of conditionalities in the lending policies of multilateral lending institutions in order to incentivize TNCs to behave ethically. Each Part of the book thus corresponds to one approach to the question of the human rights obligations of corporations.

### 1. The Responsibility of States in Controlling Transnational Corporations

Improving the accountability of TNCs for human rights violations may be done through four avenues, which are complementary in theory, but are often presented as alternative routes in political and legal discourse. It may be envisaged, first, to impose on States a responsibility to control corporate actors. The State in which the corporation is domiciled may control the activities of that corporation even when these are pursued abroad, either directly or through the setting up of a subsidiary corporation with a distinct legal personality (home State responsibility). The 'receiving' State where the corporation has its activities also may be said to be under an obligation to protect the human rights of its population (host State responsibility). The four chapters of Part I explore different facets of these State responsibilities. Chapter two addresses the imposition of human rights obligations on TNCs by their home States, using the specific example of the United States ATCA. The other chapters focus by contrast on the host State. The ability of the receiving State to control foreign investors operating on its territory may be severely constrained by the restrictions imposed by investment or free trade treaties to which it is a party, as such treaties may contain certain protections in favor of those foreign investors. Moreover, as States are competing for scarce foreign investment to fuel their economic growth, and as the shift to services in global trade implies that competition between States becomes increasingly global and increasingly depends on the regulatory framework and the level of wages rather than on the natural endowment of States, they may be reluctant to impose too stringent standards on the foreign corporations wishing to invest under their jurisdiction, as they have even more reasons than previously to fear the relocalization of those investments. Chapters three and four examine these issues, concentrating on bilateral investment treaties and export-processing zones specifically. These chapters both illustrate the risks of regulatory competition and of granting extensive protections to economic actors without imposing on them corresponding obligations, in order to attract investment. This concern was also one important aspect of the negotiations on the North American Free Trade Agreement (NAFTA). Chapter five examines the adequacy of the solution which the Clinton administration favored when it sought to reassure those who feared that this agreement would lead to social and environmental dumping, ie to the lowering by a State of social and environmental standards in order to improve the competitiveness of undertakings operating in that State, or to limit the risk of outsourcing or relocation.

Under the current regime of international State responsibility, a State may not be held responsible for the activities of a private person, unless that person is in fact acting on the instructions of, or under the direction or control of, that State in carrying out the conduct.[55] However, it is equally clear that States may adopt extra-territorial legislation based on the 'active personality principle', ie on the competence of each State to control its nationals wherever they operate, provided at least that

---

[55] See further text corresponding to nn 83–85 below.

they do not interfere with the sovereign rights of the territorial State.[56] Chapter two, by Andrew Wilson, examines the exemplary function that the United States ATCA has fulfilled in ensuring that corporations based in the United States or having a continuous business relationship with the United States may be sued for damages by the victims of human rights violations attributable to the activities of those corporations wherever they occur. The litigation which, since the mid 1990s, relies on the ATCA in order to file civil claims before United States federal courts for the violations allegedly committed by corporations or in which they are complicit, is studied here as a typical example of the 'home State' ensuring that 'its' corporations are being controlled even with respect to their activities abroad, through a legislative instrument which—although this was certainly not its initial purpose[57]—in fact provides for an extra-territorial jurisdiction of the United States federal courts. This chapter shows in detail which difficulties are raised by the application, through concepts of internal law, of rules of international law. Which standards should be applied when a corporation is allegedly complicit in human rights abuses committed by the host government; under which conditions a private actor may be said to directly violate norms of international law; and, indeed, how exactly the 'law of nations' whose violation may give rise to civil liability under the ATCA should be circumscribed: all these are issues on which much uncertainty remains. This uncertainty may be attributed in large part to the fact that the United States federal jurisdictions are in disagreement about the division of tasks, in providing answers to these questions, between internal and international law. The differences between judicial circuits on these questions may not be settled decisively soon, because of the strong incentives corporate defendants have to settle the claim before the litigation ends: whether or not they fear an unfavorable final outcome, companies may prefer even a relatively costly settlement to the stain on their reputation which may result from a long judicial procedure. The specific contribution of Andrew Wilson is to expose the remaining uncertainties of the ATCA, and to compare the respective merits of the different solutions which appear in the case-law. But as to the fact of uncertainty itself, no clear solution—except perhaps legislative action—emerges.

---

[56] On the question of the extra-territorial competence of States, see Olivier De Schutter, 'L'incrimination universelle de la violation des droits sociaux fondamentaux', in *La compétence universelle, Revue de droit de l'Université libre de Bruxelles* (vol 30, 2004-2), and *Annales de droit de Louvain* (vol 64, 2004, n°1–2), 209–45.

[57] The question of the original intent of the so-called 'Alien Tort Claims Act' is still debated. See, eg, Anne-Marie Burley, 'The Alien Tort Statute and the Judiciary Act of 1789: A Badge of Honor', (1989) 83(3) *American Journal of International Law* 461.

Chapter three, by Ryan Suda, demonstrates the difficulties the host States who receive international investors may encounter when they are bound by a bilateral investment treaty (BIT). Such treaties, which have been greatly expanding in numbers since the early 1990s,[58] provide extensive protections to foreign investors. They typically contain clauses providing for admission and establishment of the foreign investor and for the national treatment in the post-establishment phase (ie prohibiting discrimination between local companies and foreign investors). They often include a 'most-favored nation' clause. They guarantee to the foreign investor a 'fair and equitable treatment', which includes in particular a protection against expropriation, whether de jure or de facto, which may be invoked in the face of what may be termed 'regulatory takings' under United States constitutional law.[59] Many BITs also include guarantees of free transfers of funds and repatriation of capitals and profits. Finally, they usually contain dispute settlement provisions, both State–State and State–investor, thus ensuring that any dispute between the foreign investor and the host State will be subjected to arbitration, often through arbitral panels set up under the International Centre for the Settlement of Investment Disputes, which the Convention on the Settlement of Investment Disputes between States and Nationals of other States has set up as part of the World Bank Group.[60] Suda shows how the obligations imposed by such bilateral investment treaties on States hosting foreign direct investment may in practice constitute an obstacle to those States fully complying with their international human rights obligations, especially because of the chilling effect they may have on the adoption of new, more demanding local regulations which could affect the profitability of the investment.

[58] See United Nations Conference on Trade and Development (UNCTAD), *World Investment Report 2004, The Shift Towards Services* (New York and Geneva, UNCTAD, 2004), fig 1.6. (at p 8) (table exhibiting the growing numbers of bilateral investment treaties and double taxation treaties concluded during the period 1990–2003, with a peak growth during 1994–99).

[59] For a comparison between the protection of the rights of investors under Chapter 11 of the North American Free Trade Agreement (NAFTA) (17 December 1992, (1993) 32 ILM 289 (chs 1–9), (1993) 32 ILM 605 (chs 10–22)) and the prohibition of takings under US constitutional law, see David Schneiderman, 'NAFTA's Takings Rule: American Constitutionalism Comes to Canada', (1996) 46 *University of Toronto Law Journal* 499; and Vicki Been and Joel C Beauvais, 'The Global Fifth Amendment? NAFTA's Investment Protections and the Misguided Quest for an International "Regulatory Takings" Doctrine', (2003) 78 *New York University Law Review* 30. Been and Beauvais convincingly demonstrate that certain interpretations of NAFTA provide a considerably wider protection to foreign investors than would be provided under the Fifth Amendment to the United States Constitution.

[60] 575 UNTS 159, reprinted in (1965) 4 ILM 532.

Chapter four, by Chu Yun Juliana Nam, considers another vulnerability of the 'receiving' States—and thus, of the difficulties they may encounter in seeking to impose human rights obligations on the companies that operate under their jurisdiction—which results from the fact that these States are competing for scarce foreign direct investment, and therefore may fear the flight of investors if they impose too far-reaching requirements on investors, who may be tempted to relocate into more welcoming countries. The phenomenon of export-processing zones which this chapter describes is a typical illustration of the consequences of such a competition for investment in which many developing States are caught: as a result of such competition—which, it will be noted, also explains why States agree to the conclusion of bilateral investment treaties despite the limitations this entails on their regulatory autonomy[61]—States may be tempted to lower their environmental and labor standards, or the tax requirements they impose, in order to attract foreign investors, often to the detriment of the long-term interests of the local community. The paradox is that, although in many cases the working conditions in export-processing zones are not worse and often are better even than in other sectors of the local economy—indeed, the wages are typically significantly higher—,the high visibility of these zones, because of the number of TNCs which operate under the specific conditions they provide, ensures that the violations of labor rights which occur under those 'zones' are regularly denounced, especially by global unions. This, however, may be less paradoxical than it may seem. Both the low regulatory standards in export-processing zones and the weak enforcement of whichever standards do exist, and also the absence of positive returns to the local economy of the host State, are clearly attributable to the pressure of the global economy, and to the extreme ease with which, often, foreign investors will be able to leave a zone in order to relocate elsewhere. In that sense, export-processing zones are a natural target for human rights activists and unions, in the views of whom they epitomize certain of the worse aspects of globalization.

Chapter five, by Ana A Piquer, examines whether harmonization of labor standards is the only possible answer to the dilemmas of such regulatory competition, or whether a mechanism such as that of the North American Agreement on Labor Cooperation (NAALC), a side agreement to the NAFTA 1992, could constitute an alternative. One way

---

[61] See Andrew T Guzman, 'Why LDCs Sign Treaties That Hurt Them: Explaining the Popularity of Bilateral Investment Treaties' (1997–98) 38 *Virginia Journal of International Law* 640 (demonstrating that the interests of developing countries as a group should be distinguished from the interests of individual least developed countries (LDCs) when they compete with one another for scarce foreign investment).

to see the NAALC is as a compromise solution between a form of regulatory competition potentially destructive of labor standards and the harmonization of labor standards, which may be seen by certain developing States as depriving them of their comparative advantage on the global markets.[62] It therefore justified a detailed examination not only of the reasons which were put forward by the Clinton administration when it advocated in favor of that solution, but also of the results of the side agreement more than 10 years after it entered into force. The conclusions which Ana Piquer reaches, on the basis of the available studies on the impact of the NAFTA, are not particularly encouraging. They deserve to be paid careful attention, especially if the project of the Free Trade of the Americas is to move forward and borrow from the NAFTA its solution to the risk of social dumping.

## 2. Self-regulation of Transnational Corporations

A second tool for the improvement of the human rights accountability of corporations is through self-regulation. In principle, self-regulation should not be an alternative to the imposition of regulatory standards. In fact, however, the initiatives adopted voluntarily by companies are often presented as having a number of advantages which rules-based approaches do not offer: voluntary initiatives, it is said, do not fall into the trap of the 'one-size-fits-all' approach; they are flexible; and they ensure the commitment of corporations where regulatory approaches lead to avoidance strategies. Such voluntary approaches are therefore proposed as an alternative, and a more desirable one, to regulatory initiatives.

How credible is this alternative? The 2005 report by the OHCHR adopted a cautious position on the issue, noting simply that 'company and market initiatives have their limits and are not necessarily comprehensive in their coverage nor a substitute for legislative action. Importantly, while voluntary business action in relation to human rights works for the well-intentioned and could effectively raise the standard of other

---

[62] For other discussions on this subject, see in particular Jack I Garvey, 'Current Development: Trade Law and Quality of Life – Dispute Resolution under the NAFTA Side Accords on Labor and the Environment' (1995) 89 *American Journal of International Law* 439; Laura O Pomeroy, 'The Labor Side Agreement under the NAFTA: Analysis of Its Failure to Include Strong Enforcement Provisions and Recommendations for Future Labor Agreements Negotiated with Developing Countries' (1996) 29 *George Washington Journal of International Law and Economy* 769. For a report critical of the insufficiencies of the NAALC, see Human Rights Watch, *Trading Away Rights. The Unfulfilled Promise of NAFTA's Labor Side Agreement*, April 2001, vol 13, No 2(B), available on www.hrw.org. The report contains in particular an extensive analysis of the cases presented under the NAALC to the National Administrative Offices established under the agreement by the United States, Mexico, and Canada.

companies, there remains scepticism amongst sectors of civil society as to their overall effectiveness.'[63] The two chapters comprising Part II of the book show what may feed such scepticism, while at the same time illustrating the potential of voluntary initiatives.

Chapter six, by Fiona McLeay, offers an in-depth discussion of the efficacy of codes of conduct, which are the clearest manifestation of such voluntary initiatives adopted by companies in order to improve their reputation and to answer to the calls for corporate social responsibility. Codes of conduct, however, appear in many different forms: they differ by their content, by the monitoring mechanisms they may or may not include, and by the level (the individual company, the sector, the country or group of countries) at which they are drafted and proposed for adoption.[64] While acknowledging the limitations of codes, the chapter by Fiona McLeay recognizes the small but important role that codes of conduct may have in promoting and realizing human rights in the operation of business. It identifies ways in which their implementation can have a direct positive impact on the human rights of workers. It also discusses indirect benefits which are possible as the culture of companies is improved and awareness of human rights is raised among both workers and governments in the developing world. The chapter concludes that codes should be encouraged with a view to maximizing these benefits and for their value as practical examples of the way in which human rights norms can be integrated into business activity. However, McLeay insists that codes should not be seen as a panacea for the complex problem of human rights abuses which are connected with the activities of TNCs in the developing world. The use of codes should not be encouraged at the expense of other mechanisms for remedying these problems, including taking account of the inequities inherent in the process of globalization itself.

International framework agreements (IFAs) are concluded between a TNC and a global union in order to protect the fundamental social rights of the employees of the company concerned in all its operations. Such agreements go beyond most codes of conduct by the active implication of unions in the monitoring of the undertakings of the company which has

---

[63] *Report of the United Nations High Commissioner on Human Rights on the responsibilities of transnational corporations and related business enterprises with regard to human rights*, 15 February 2005, above n 47, at para 45.

[64] A working party of the Trade Committee of the OECD has produced an extensive inventory of codes of corporate conduct: see 'Codes of corporate conduct: an inventory' (TD/TC/WP(98)74/FINAL, 99 pages). This overview of codes of corporate conduct is based on information submitted by OECD member governments and non-governmental sources. It reviews 233 codes, issued by individual companies, by business groups, or by intergovernmental organisations. A revised and extended comparative study was presented in 2001 (OECD doc TD/TC/WP(2001)10/FINAL).

signed the agreement. Chapter seven, by Lisa R Price, offers an interesting discussion of this new development—most of the IFAs have been concluded since 2000, and there were only a handful in 1995—putting a particular emphasis on the role of the unions in the implemention of such agreements. In what has been described of a new paradigm emerging in the management of economic globalization, adequate regulation is seen to depend on involving a variety of actors in voluntary initiatives, both at the local and the global level, and it is this that IFAs would most clearly exhibit. The chapter by Price describes the new collaborative paradigm for labor relations which IFAs exhibit. It explores the theoretical underpinnings behind the agreements, placing them further within the context of the collaborative paradigm. It also considers in detail several IFAs that have been tested, evaluating the degree to which they have operated successfully in practice. Finally, the chapter closes by identifying the problems that continue to plague these agreements.

## 3. Direct Liability of Transnational Corporations under International Law

A third tool for improving the human rights accountability of corporations is by the direct imposition on corporations of obligations under international law. This, indeed, is how most commentators have interpreted the initiative of the UN Sub-Commission for the Promotion and Protection of Human Rights when it adopted its Draft set of Norms on the Human Rights Responsibilities of Transnational Corporations and Other Business Enterprises in August 2003.[65] But the idea of international law imposing obligations directly on private actors is not a new one. It is this idea which lies at the heart of international criminal law since the Nuremberg trials: individuals, not States as 'abstract entities',[66] may commit international crimes, defined as such directly under international law. The chapters in Part III examine the issues raised under this approach to improving the human rights accountability of corporations. Chapter eight, by Asimina-Manto Papaioannou, offers a detailed case study on how the reference to the OECD Guidelines on Multinational Enterprises may serve to define the human rights responsibilities of

---

[65] On this development, see the text corresponding to nn 36–47 above.

[66] In the words of the International Military Tribunal at Nuremberg: '... individuals can be punished for violations of international law. Crimes against international law are committed by men, not by abstract entities, and only by punishing individuals who commit such crimes can the provisions of international law be enforced' (*Trial of German major war criminals (Goering et al)*, International Military Tribunal (Nuremberg) sentence of 30 September and 1 October 1946, reproduced in 41 *American Journal of International Law* (1947) 172–333).

companies in the context of the fuelling of the civil war in the Congo, as documented by the Panel of Experts on the Illegal Exploitation of Natural Resources and Other Forms of Wealth of the Democratic Republic of Congo set up in the UN Security Council to investigate this matter. In her contribution to the book, Asimina-Manto Papioannou examines the pronouncements of the Panel of Experts with regard to the involvement of corporations in the area, but she also offers an evaluation of the Panel's working methods and results. Finally, she makes reference to the way the governments of the countries in which the corporations involved are registered followed up on the Panel's findings.

In Chapter nine, Cristina Chiomenti looks at the potentiality that the International Criminal Court (ICC) could extend its jurisdiction to corporate actors, when its statute is revised in 2009, seven years after entering into force. Under the present Statute of the International Criminal Court legal persons are not included in its jurisdiction.[67] However, national and international legislation increasingly contemplate the criminal liability of corporations; and as recalled by a number of authors who have recently returned to the British and American war crimes tribunal set up after the Second World War,[68] the involvement of corporations in the international crimes over which the ICC has jurisdiction can be generally imagined in the form of complicity. Chiomenti therefore explores whether the jurisdiction of the ICC should not be extended to legal persons, in order to include such most serious forms of corporate criminal conduct. This leads her to examine the most delicate issues raised by the criminal liability of corporations, especially concerning *mens rea*—the 'intent' of corporations—and complicity—specifically in respect of the conduct of TNCs operating in foreign countries. Her conclusion is that, should the jurisdiction of ICC extend to legal persons, specific rules and criteria would be required in those two areas.

Chapter ten, by Jacob Gelfand, offers an evaluation of the UN Norms on the Human Rights Responsibilities of Transnational Corporations and Other Business Enterprises, focusing especially on the question of which mechanisms could ensure that these norms are effectively enforced. In the draft Norms, the UN Sub-Commission on the Promotion and

---

[67] See, for a detailed examination of the negotiations of the Statute of the International Criminal Court on this issue, Andrew Clapham, 'The Question of Jurisdiction Under International Criminal Law Over Legal Persons : Lessons from the Rome Conference on an International Criminal Court', in Menno T. Kamminga and Saman Zia-Zarifi (eds.), *Liability of Multinational Corporations under International Law*, Kluwer Law International, The Hague, 2000, pp. 139–195.

[68] See in particular Anita Ramasastry, 'Corporate Complicity: From Nuremberg to Rangoon. An Examination of Forced Labor Cases and their Impact on the Liability of Multinational Corporations' (2002) 20 *Berkeley Journal of International Law* 91.

Protection of Human Rights listed a number of possible avenues. It clearly expressed a preference for the direct monitoring of TNCs and other enterprises by the UN, through procedures both transparent and independent, and including the possibility for NGOs to file complaints of violations of the Norms.[69] But it also listed the other impacts an endorsement of the Norms could have, for instance on the interpretation of existing instruments in the field of corporate social responsibility containing only vague or general references to human rights, on the clarification of the obligations of States to protect human rights by controlling corporate actors, on the negotiation by trade unions of agreements with TNCs, or on the evaluation by corporations of their own practices or the conduct of human rights impact assessments before the implementation of certain projects which may adversely affect human rights.[70] As to the development of the draft Norms into a legally binding instruments imposing direct obligations on TNCs and other business enterprises, the conclusion of Jacob Gelfand is sceptical: 'While attaining binding status is a legitimate goal, it is not realistic in the short term. Instead, the Norms should be used as an explicitly non-binding, and therefore flexible, document that restates human rights obligations, suggests new means of enforcement and monitoring, and ultimately encourages corporate, political, and social actors to work together to ensure human rights protection by TNCs becomes less aspirational and more real.' It will be noted, however, that most of the uses the UN Sub-Commission on the Promotion and Protection of Human Rights envisages for the Norms on the Human Rights Responsibilities of Transnational Corporations and Other Business Enterprises do not require that they are formally attributed a legally binding character: for the document to serve as a reference point for further initiatives, it is sufficient that it is recognized as having moral authority in the view of the stakeholders concerned. It is uncertain that it has yet achieved this status. In its decision 2004/116, the UN Commission on Human Rights specifically affirmed that 'document E/CN.4/Sub.2/2003/12/Rev.2 [containing the draft norms on the responsibilities of TNCs and other business enterprises with regard to human rights] has not been requested by the Commission and, as a draft proposal, has no legal standing, and that the Sub-Commission should not perform any monitoring function in this regard.' This statement was welcomed by the International Chamber of Commerce, which stated in the course of the consultations conducted by the OHCHR on 'Responsibilities of transnational corporations and related business enterprises with

---

[69] See Principle 16 of the draft Norms. On the UN Norms generally, see the text corresponding to nn 36–47 above.
[70] See the Commentary to Principle 16 of the draft Norms.

regard to human rights'[71] that it 'cannot accept the approach taken by the draft developed by the Sub-Commission. It is simply not feasible to transfer the responsibilities of the State with regards to human rights onto business because of governments' unwillingness and/or lack of capacity to meet their responsibilities effectively. No initiative or standard with regard to business and human rights can replace the primary role of the State and national laws in this area.'[72] Within the UN Commission on Human Rights, the United States opposed the proposed resolution concerning human rights and TNCs and other business enterprises which requested the appointment of a Special Representative of the Secretary General on this question, arguing that the text adopted 'a negative tone towards international and national business, treating them as potential problems rather than the overwhelmingly positive forces for economic development and human rights that they are.'[73] These public statements by major actors are indicative of the enormous resistance any attempt to impose legally binding standards on corporations at the universal level would be facing.

As mentioned above, the notion of 'complicity' is one of the most heavily contested notions used by the draft Norms, and one whose vague contours are seen to constitute a major obstacle to these Norms being attributed one day a legally binding character. In Chapter eleven, Inés Tófalo proposes a detailed study of the notion, and proposes a typology of the situations in which complicity may be invoked where a corporation is present in a country where systematic human rights violations are committed. She proposes a structure and a consistent vocabulary as tools to argue distinctions across different types of complicity. The working typology of complicity ranges from direct complicity, where TNCs are committing human rights abuses jointly with State agents or are otherwise participating in those abuses, to indirect complicity, in situations where a TNC finances or provides tools facilitating violations of human rights, to incidental complicity, including the situation where complicity would result from the mere presence of the TNC in an area where human rights abuses are pandemic.

Taken together, the chapters in Part III show that, while it may be possible to model an understanding of an international responsibility of corporations in the same way as it has been possible to develop an understanding of the responsibility of the individual under international criminal

---

[71]   On the context of the consultation, see the text corresponding to nn 48–50 above.

[72] Letter from Maria Livanos Cattaui, Secretary General of the International Chamber of Commerce, to Mr D Kedzia, Chief of the Research and Right to Development Branch at the OHCHR, 20 September 2004, available from the website of the ICC: http://www.iccwbo.org/display7/doctype1/index.html

[73] According to the explanations made public by the United States on 20 April 2005. These explanations are available on the Business and Human Rights site of Amnesty International: http://www.amnestyusa.org/business/un_norms.html

law, the conceptual difficulties in doing so should not be underestimated. At the same time, we should not be held hostage to an understanding of international law—outdated in fact, and unworkable in practice—that sees it as being exclusively the law of inter-State relations. Writing in 1912, perhaps at the height of the postivist doctrine in international law, L Oppenheim could write: 'Since the law of nations is based on the common consent of individual States, and not of individual human beings, States solely and exclusively are subjects of international law.'[74] This classical approach resulted in creating an artificial obstacle to the recognition of 'non-State' entities as subjects of international law.[75] It has now been acknowledged, however, that international legal personality results from the capacity of the subject to hold rights or to be imposed with duties under international law, and to exercise those rights or be held accountable to such duties in the international legal process.[76] Thus, the recognition of an international legal personality of TNCs should not be seen as a prerequisite to the imposition of obligations on such entities, just as it has not been considered a prerequisite for the recognition of rights of these actors, for instance, under free trade agreements or investment liberalization agreements guaranteeing the rights of investors and ensuring that they have access to a procedure for a determination of their claims under such instruments.[77] The attribution of rights and duties, and of an international legal capacity, do not follow from legal personality, as if to give a certain substantive content to that legal personality once it is recognized;

[74] Lassa Oppenheim, *International Law. A Treatise*, 2nd edn (London, 1912), vol I, p 19.

[75] See Philip Alston, 'The 'Not-a-Cat' Syndrome: Can the International Human Rights Regime Accommodate Non-State Actors?', in Philip Alston (ed), *Non-State Actors and Human Rights*, Series of the Collected Courses of the Academy of European Law (Oxford, Oxford University Press, 2005), p 3.

[76] The International Court of Justice ruled in the *Reparations for Injuries Suffered in the Service of the United Nations* case that the UN is a 'subject of international law and capable of possessing international rights and duties, and that it has the capacity to maintain its rights by bringing international claims'. It based its conclusion that the UN has an international legal personality on the finding that 'the Organisation was intended to exercise and enjoy, and is in fact exercising and enjoying, functions and rights which can only be explained on the basis of the possession of a large measure of international personality and the capacity to operate upon an international plane' (1949 ICJ Rep 179).

[77] On this question, see in particular D Kokkini-Iatridou and P de Waart, 'Foreign Investments in Developing Countries – Legal Personality of Multinationals in International Law' (1983) 14 *Netherlands Yearbook of International Law* 87; P Malanczuk, 'Multinational Enterprises and Treaty-Making – A Contribution to the Discussion on Non-State Actors and the "Subjects" of International Law' in Vera Gowlland-Debaas (ed), *Multilateral Treaty-Making. The Current Status of Challenges to and Reforms Needed in the International Legislative Process*, Proceedings of the American Society of International Law/Graduate Institute of International Studies, Forum Geneva, 16 May 1998, (Martinus Nijhoff Publications, 2000), p 35; Jonathan Charney, 'Transnational Corporations and Developing Public International Law' (1983) *Duke Law Journal* 748, especially at 774–76; and the excellent discussion in Nicola Jägers, *Corporate Human Rights Obligations: In Search of Accountability*, above n 4, at pp 19–35.

rather, international legal personality follows from the attribution of rights and duties, and from the recognition in fact of an international legal capacity of certain actors in the international legal process. Should a code of conduct be adopted tomorrow, for instance, under a resolution of the UN Human Rights Council creating a new thematic procedure making it possible to monitor the activities of TNCs under the code,[78] we would then have to conclude that TNCs had acquired an international legal personality to that extent, just as we may conclude that they are exercising their rights, as international legal subjects, when they seek to vindicate rights attributed to them under an investment treaty. This is not to say, of course, that the rights or duties of TNCs should be seen as identical to those of the States: the International Court of Justice, we are well aware, has observed that '[t]he subjects of law in any legal system are not necessarily identical in their nature or in the extent of their rights, and their nature depends upon the needs of the community.'[79] But to restrict a definition of international legal personality to the capacity to act in the international legal order just as States may act—for example, by the conclusion of treaties or by sending and receiving diplomatic missions—would be purely tautological: it would be denying the international legal personality of entities other than States on the basis that only States have the capacity to act as States.[80]

## 4. Incentivizing Socially Responsible Corporate Conduct

Whether or not they are under a legal obligation to observe human rights and whether or not there exist mechanisms to ensure that they comply with such an obligation, corporations may be incentivized to do so. Part IV considers two such tools, through which either States or international organisations may use their economic muscle to encourage corporations to take into account their responsibilities towards human rights in the planning and conduct of their activities. Chapter twelve, authored by Kathy Zeisel, examines the use of selective public procurement schemes by States for that purpose, discussing in particular whether this would be acceptable under the Agreements of the World Trade Organization

---

[78] Indeed, this is one of the possible outcomes of the current discussion on the follow-up to the draft Norms on the Human Rights Responsibilities of Transnational Corporations and Other Business Enterprises adopted in 2003 by the UN Sub-Commission on Human Rights: see David Weissbrodt and Muria Kruger, 'Human Rights Responsibilities of Businesses as Non-State Actors', above n 36, at 345.

[79] *Reparations for Injuries Suffered in the Service of the United Nations* case, 1949 ICJ Rep 178.

[80] See Philip Alston, 'The "Not-a-Cat" Syndrome: Can the International Human Rights Regime Accommodate Non-State Actors?', above n 75, at 20, and his critique of B Cheng, 'Introduction to Subjects of International Law', in M Bedjaoui (ed), *International Law. Achievements and Prospects* (Paris, Unesco, 1991), p 23.

(WTO). Selective public procurement seeks to ensure fulfillment of international human rights obligations by requiring companies that wish to bid on public contracts to make a specific level of commitment to protecting human rights, thereby creating an incentive for companies and their host States to improve human rights conditions. The chapter by Zeisel argues that selective public procurement policies by States are permissible under international law, including under international trade law generally and the GATT/WTO agreements specifically. After providing a background on selective public procurement, including a typology of the types of selective public procurement, it examines selective public procurement in practice in the United States and the European Union as well as the perspective of developing States and international institutions. It then examines the legitimacy of selective public procurement through discussion of theoretical and pragmatic justifications for and against selective public procurement. It finally proceeds to analyze the legality of selective public procurement under the law of the WTO.

Chapter thirteen, by Terra Eve Lawson-Remer, considers how the International Finance Corporation (IFC), the private sector lending arm of the World Bank Group, could contribute to improving respect for human rights in the projects to which it lends its support. The purpose of this chapter is to argue that the IFC can and should require inclusion of commitments regarding sustainable development and human rights in the legal covenants that often govern large private-sector investments. The Baku-Tiblisi-Ceyhan (BTC) Pipeline Project, which the chapter examines in depth, illustrates both the risk of States being pressured by foreign investors wishing to obtain government guarantees that insulate their investment from risk, and the potential role multilateral lending institutions might play in limiting the detrimental effects of such imbalance in bargaining power. Lawson-Remer explores the relationship (or lack thereof) between the legal framework underlying the Baku-Tbilisi-Ceyhan oil pipeline project and the IFC, and she argues that the IFC would more effectively further its purported mission of promoting environmentally and socially sustainable development by requiring this legal framework to be compatible with the effective enforcement of evolving international environmental and human rights norms.

Both of these chapters are particularly timely, as the WTO is largely denounced for imposing the requirements of free trade above other values and for closing the possibilities for States to promote human rights where this may lead to discriminatory behaviour, ie where this could be seen as a pretext to perpetuate protectionist practices, and as the IFC is presently revising its operational protocols in order to better take into consideration the requirements of international human rights law.

### III. BEYOND THE STATE?

A final consideration may be in order. It is a note of caution. As the essays collected in this volume show, a number of mechanisms—private codes of conduct, of course, but also intergovernmental codes of conduct such as the OECD Guidelines on Multinational Enterprises, codes of conduct proposed by NGOs which may contain a reliable and independent supervisory mechanism, or international framework agreements—already exist which seek to address directly the behavior of TNCs. Such mechanisms could be further developed in the future. The draft Norms on the Responsibilities of Transnational Corporations and Other Business Enterprises with Regard to Human Rights insist, however, in the opening sentence in Principle 1, that 'States have the primary responsibility to promote, secure the fulfilment of, respect, ensure respect of and protect human rights recognized in international as well as national law, including ensuring that transnational corporations and other business enterprises respect human rights'; the savings clause contained in the final principle of the Norms restates that 'Nothing in these Norms shall be construed as diminishing, restricting, or adversely affecting the human rights obligations of States under national and international law ...'. Indeed, whatever progress is made on the question of the accountability of TNCs with regard to human rights, this should not restrict the scope of the obligation imposed on States under international law to protect the human rights of all persons under their jurisdictions. And it should not constitute an obstacle to improving State responsibility where a need to do so may appear.

States have the primary responsibility to protect and promote human rights. This not only means that, wherever they operate, TNCs should be effectively controlled by the territorially competent State on whose national territory they pursue their activities, as the UN human rights treaty bodies have repeatedly stated.[81] Neither should this be seen as simply imposing an obligation on all States to facilitate the protection of human rights by the territorial State, in particular, by not concluding agreements, such as bilateral or multilateral investment treaties or free trade agreements, which, by providing extensive guarantees to the investors, may result in depriving the territorial State from its capacity to effectively protect human rights of all persons under its jurisdiction.[82]

---

[81] Indeed, as recalled earlier (above, n 53 and corresponding text), whatever progress is made in the direction of a clarification of the human rights responsibilities of TNCs may encourage these monitoring bodies to require that States provide more extensive and more precise evidence about the measures they are taking to ensure that TNCs operating under their jurisdiction do not by their activities violate the human rights of others.

[82] For a more detailed examination, see Olivier De Schutter, 'Transnational Corporations as Instruments of Human Development', in Philip Alston and Mary Robinson (eds), *Human Rights and Development: Towards Mutual Reinforcement* (Oxford, Oxford University Press, 2005), pp 403–44.

These obligations are important and should not be neglected. But the international responsibility of States in the context of economic globalization, where TNCs have gained an almost unprecedented influence and bargaining power vis-à-vis the States in which they operate, may have to be expanded even further.

The obligations of States towards internationally recognized human rights may imply that States should, insofar as legally and practically possible, control the activities abroad of the corporations which are incorporated under their jurisdiction, and over which, therefore, they may exercise control by the adoption of extra-territorial legislation, although as a matter of course this obligation should be understood without prejudice of the sovereign rights of the territorial State. Although, under the current rules of State responsibility for internationally wrongful acts, a State may not be held responsible for acts of private parties unless such parties have in fact acted on the instructions of, or under the direction and control of, that State in carrying out those acts,[83] strong arguments exist in favor of imposing such a responsibility in specific fields, such as with respect to certain acts committed by corporations abroad. Indeed, precedents exist. Article 4(2) of the 1997 OECD Convention on Combating

---

[83] See Article 8 of the Articles on the Responsibility of States for Internationally Wrongful Acts (UN doc A/56/10 (2001)), as taken note of by the UN General Assembly (Res 56/83 (2001)). Of course, this clause seeks to incorporate the position taken by the International Court of Justice in the case of *Military and Paramilitary Activities in and against Nicaragua (Nicaragua v United States of America) (merits)* 1986 ICJ Rep, p 14, at pp 64–65, para 115 ('[f]or this conduct [of the *contras*] to give rise to legal responsibility of the United States, it would in principle have to be proved that that State had effective control of the military or paramilitary operations in the course of which the alleged violations were committed'). This is not the place to enter into a discussion of this rule and whether it should allow for certain exceptions in particular circumstances. But we should note here that certain authors have considered that, notwithstanding this rule, the home States of corporations should be held responsible in certain circumstances for the conduct of those corporations on the territory of a foreign State – ie either where they have actual or constructive knowledge that these corporations will cause harm, or where they give active assistance to that conduct –: see Muthucumaraswamy Sornarajah, 'Linking State Responsibility for Certain Harms Caused by Corporate Nationals Abroad to Civil Recourse in the Legal Systems of Home States', in Craig Scott (ed), *Torture as Tort. Comparative Perspectives on the Development of Transnational Human Rights Litigation* (Oxford and Portland Oregon, Hart Publishing, 2001), pp 491–512; Muthucumaraswamy Sornarajah, *The International Law on Foreign Investment*, 2nd edn (Cambridge, Cambridge University Press, 2004), pp 182–202. The author argues that, as there exists 'a general duty in international law not to cause harm to other states', where 'a state knows that its nationals' activities will cause, or are causing, harm to other states or their people's, it is consistent with this duty that it should prevent such harm' (at p 197). Moreover, M Sornarajah derives a duty to control one State's nationals operating abroad from the right of that State to exercise its diplomatic protection: 'As a matter of general principle, if the state has the right to have its nationals protected abroad, a concomitant duty to ensure that the nationals act in a manner consistent with international norms should be recognised' (*ibid*). The wording is identical in the chapter 'Linking State Responsibility for Certain Harms Caused by Corporate Nationals Abroad to Civil Recourse in the Legal Systems of Home States', at p 507.

Bribery of Foreign Public Officials in International Business Transactions provides that: 'Each Party which has jurisdiction to prosecute its nationals for offences committed abroad shall take such measures as may be necessary to establish its jurisdiction to do so in respect of the bribery of a foreign public official.'[84] Under the 1982 UN Convention on the Law of the Sea, flag States are under a duty to 'effectively exercise [their] jurisdiction and control in administrative, technical and social matters over ships flying [their] flag' (Article 94). There is no reason not to consider whether there exist sufficiently weighty reasons to impose similar obligations relating to the control of a State's nationals where the conduct of corporations in violation of internationally recognized human rights norms is concerned, especially where the territorial State hosting the activities of the corporation is either unwilling or unable effectively to protect the human rights of populations under its jurisdiction.

If the conclusion of an international treaty for that purpose is required, imposing a duty on the States parties effectively to control the TNCs over which they may exercise jurisdiction, this avenue should be explored.[85] Indeed, this would preempt any fear that the formulation of the human rights obligations of corporations will lead to a diminishing of the responsibilities of States to uphold human rights; and it would ensure that corporations will not be imposed with responsibilities which should be assumed by the States in which they operate. It is crucial that, in the course of identifying the human rights responsibilities of corporations, the primary responsibility of States under the current international law of human rights be recalled and emphasized. An improved regulation of TNCs by initiatives adopted at a global level should not be seen as a substitute for the obligations of States towards human rights: such initiatives should be seen, rather, as complementing such obligations, and as facilitating the fulfilment by all States of their human rights obligations. An international

---

[84] The OECD Bribery Convention was adopted on 21 November 1997 and entered into force on 15 February 1999. On the contribution of this instrument, see PM Nichols, 'Regulating Transnational Bribery in Times of Globalisation and Fragmentation' (1999) 24 *Yale Journal of International Law* 257. The UN Convention against Corruption also provides that a State party may establish its jurisdiction over an offence as established under the Convention where it is committed by a national of that State party (Art 42(2), b)). The Convention was adopted by the General Assembly by resolution 58/4 of 31 October 2003 and entered into force in December 2005, after the number of 30 ratifications was reached.

[85] In favor of such a development, see Emeka A Duruigbo, *Multinational Corporations and International Law. Accountability and Compliance Issues in the Petroleum Industry* (Ardsley, NY, Transnational Publications, 2003), at pp 204–8; and International Council on Human Rights Policy, *Beyond Voluntarism: Human Rights and the Developing International Legal Obligations of Companies* (Geneva, 2002), at p 157 (available at http://www.ichrp.org/public/publications.php?id_projet=13&lang=AN).

convention codifying the obligations of States with respect to the imposition of human rights obligations on the companies over which they have jurisdiction—because the company operates or is domiciled under the jurisdiction of the State concerned—would serve that purpose. By clarifying the human rights obligations of companies both for the territorial (host) State and for the 'sending' (home) State, moreover, such a treaty would avoid approaches to the human rights obligations of companies which lead to conflicting requirements.

***

Before being revised for publication in this book, these chapters were prepared and discussed as working papers in the context of the seminar on 'Transnational Corporations and Human Rights' which I had the pleasure of teaching during the 2004–05 Fall Term, at New York University School of Law, as a Visiting Global Law Professor. I am immensely grateful to all the students who took part in that seminar, with enthusiasm and talent. The students whose papers could not be presented in this series should be considered co-authors of what has been a truly collective enterprise.

# Part I

# The Responsibilities of States in Controlling Transnational Corporations

# 2

# Beyond Unocal: Conceptual Problems In Using International Norms To Hold Transnational Corporations Liable Under The Alien Tort Claims Act

ANDREW J WILSON

## I. INTRODUCTION

PERHAPS IT DOES not take much to excite the legal imagination; but section 9 of the Federal Judiciary Act of 1789 has done so with distinction. The text of what has come to be known as the 'Alien Tort Claims Act'[1] is well known:

> The district courts shall have original jurisdiction of any civil action by an alien for a tort only, committed in violation of the law of nations or a treaty of the United States.[2]

With its archaic inscrutability and almost homeopathic brevity, the ATCA creates conceptual headaches at every turn. The question of *corporate* liability under the statute is the latest of these to arise. Claims under the ATCA might be analyzed in four layers, namely:

(1)    jurisdiction *ratione personae*;
(2)    attachment of liability to the defendant;

---

[1] The heading of the section as it appears in the United States Code is 'Alien's action for tort': 28 USC § 1350. Authors use different nomenclature in referring to the statute. The most usual renditions are 'Alien Tort Statute' and 'Alien Tort Claims Act', but alternative forms of words are common. 'Alien Tort Claims Act' (or more often abbreviated to 'ATCA') will be the preferred appellation in the present chapter.

[2] 28 USC § 1350 (1948). In this chapter I am considering claims based on 'the law of nations' — understood to mean customary international law – in contradistinction to those brought under 'a treaty of the United States'. The latter have thus far been few; as and when they do arise they are likely to present problems of their own. For a brief anticipatory exegesis of these potential difficulties as they pertain to the environmental law sphere, see Stephen L Kass and Jean M McCarroll, 'After Sosa: Claims Under the Alien Tort Claims Act – Part I', *The New York Law Journal*, 27 August 2004.

(3)   enforcement of the judgment;

(4)   judicial propriety.

In this chapter I intend to concentrate on the issues raised at the level of attachment of liability, as that is where the most distinctive and problematic conceptual issues arise in this context. True it is, for example, that establishing jurisdiction *ratione personae* over a corporation will involve the application of troublesome legal fictions regarding its 'presence' within the forum's territorial jurisdiction; this, indeed, precipitated Total's exit from the *Unocal* litigation.[3] But such difficulties, as is well known, are not specific to the ATCA.[4] With enforcement, too, we have seen great obstacles. Radovan Karadzic, 'tagged' whilst attending the United Nations (UN), had returned to the Balkans by the time the judgment against him was handed down; the torturer Peña-Irala in the *Filártiga* case[5] had actually been deported. But in the case of a corporation, as distinct from an individual, where there is jurisdiction there are likely to be assets; and where there are assets damages are likely to be paid. Under the fourth heading we might place, for example, the act of state, international comity and political question doctrines. Perhaps surprisingly, these have until now posed very little problem to ATCA claims, something which may be changing.[6] This too, however, is not specific to the corporate context.

Hence the focus of this chapter is on the second 'level' identified. I use the non-technical nomenclature of 'attachment' here instead of 'imputation' or 'attribution', which have term-of-art connotations under public international law. I take 'attachment of liability' to include three basic

---

[3] *Doe v Unocal Corp*, 248 F.3d 915.

[4] Indeed, it is worth noting here that much of the criticism of the Act's 'overreaching' would be more properly directed at the forms of personal jurisdiction that are used in conjunction with it, notably 'tag' (based on the - often ephemeral - presence of the defendant in the United States) and 'doing business' jurisdiction, especially in its 'general' form. Each is highly controversial in its own right: consider the proposal for an International Convention on Jurisdiction and Foreign Judgments in Civil and Commercial Matters, which is now frozen as a result of polarisation in the Hague Conference on Private International Law. See Linda J Silberman, 'Comparative Jurisdiction in the International Context: Will the Proposed Hague Judgments Convention Be Stalled?' (2002) 52 *De Paul Law Review* 319; and the rather ragged current Interim Text (not substantively updated since June 2001), at http://www.hcch.net/index_en.php?act=progress.listing&cat=4. The recognition of judgments aspect of the project has been severed and proceeded on separately in the interests of progress (ibid).

[5] *Filártiga v Pena-Irala*, 630 F.2d 876 (2nd Cir, 1980).

[6] Footnote 21 in the *Sosa* judgment, which I discuss below, refers to the 'possible limitation' of 'a policy of case-specific deference to the political branches' in the conduct of foreign affairs: *Sosa v Alvarez-Machain*, No 03-339, slip op at 39 (US Sup Ct, 2004). Mention is then made of *In Re South African Apartheid Litigation*, with respect to which the Mbeki administration's sovereignty-based objections have been backed up by the US State Department; the note all but approves the State Department's position. Sure enough, in November 2004, Sprizzo J threw out *In Re South African Apartheid Litigation* on a motion to dismiss: 346 F.Supp.2d 538 (SDNY, 2004).

issues: whether corporations acting alone can violate international law; whether they can do so through participation in the actions of a State; and how and in what circumstances responsibility might percolate up the corporate structure to the ultimate parent. I shall deal with those three issues in turn, then examine some of the policy objections to the statute. First of all, however, it is necessary to provide some comment on the Supreme Court's view of ATCA.

## II. NOTE: *SOSA* AT THE SUPREME COURT

Only one ATCA case has yet reached the Supreme Court. On 29 June 2004, the court decided *Sosa v Alvarez-Machain* in favour of the defendants. The judgment, inevitably, has been claimed as a victory by both the defenders of the ATCA and its critics. Much the most important aspect of it, however, is that the court did not do as the Bush administration suggested and take the opportunity to obliterate the Act. First, the notion that ATCA was 'stillborn'—because it provided jurisdiction without a cause of action, and the latter was not anywhere else furnished—was expressly dismissed. Congress would not have enacted a statute as a mere 'jurisdictional convenience to be placed on the shelf for use by a future Congress or state legislature that might, some day, authorise the creation of causes of action or itself decide to make some element of the law of nations actionable for the benefit of foreigners.'[7] Second, the court adhered to the—hardly controversial—view that 'the law of nations' means international law not as it was when the statute was first enacted, but as it stands today. Thus the ATCA is freed from a possible eighteenth-century time-warp in which, for example, slavery would not be counted as illegal.

On the other hand, the court appeared to set a fairly steep threshold for an international norm to cross in order to be considered a 'violation of the law of nations' for ATCA purposes. The central passage is as follows:

> We assume ... that no development in the two centuries from the enactment of §1350 to the birth of the modern line of cases beginning with *Filartiga* ... has categorically precluded federal courts from recognising a claim under the law of nations as an element of common law ... Still, there are good reasons for a restrained conception of the discretion a federal court should exercise in considering a new cause of action of this kind. Accordingly we think courts should require any claim based on the present-day law of nations to rest on a norm of international character accepted by the civilised world and defined with a specificity comparable to the features of the 18th-century paradigms we have recognised.[8]

---

[7] *Sosa v Alvarez-Machain*, No 03-339, slip op at 24 (US Sup Ct, 2004).
[8] *Ibid*, slip op at 30-31.

The perennial *Paquete Habana* test, with its emphasis on the custom 'of civilised nations' and respected legal scholarship, is once again in evidence.[9] Indeed, with regard to the writings of jurists, the 'paradigms' mentioned, primarily 'violation of safe conducts, infringement of the rights of ambassadors, and piracy',[10] are drawn from the words of Blackstone and Vattel. The early case of *US v Smith*, which exemplifies a similar approach, is cited with approval for its definition of piracy. There, the court relied exclusively on the writings of jurists such as Grotius and Bynkershoek; Story J notes of the former that, in writing of piracy, 'though he nowhere defines the crime, in precise terms, yet there seems to be no doubt as to what he understood to be comprehended in that crime.'[11] The standard announced, then, is sensitive to the process of discovering a norm of customary international law. In addition, whilst *Sosa* itself is a clear 'state action'[12] case—Jose Sosa and other defendants were acting on behalf of the Drug Enforcement Administration—the 'paradigms' identified relate also to purely individual conduct; indeed, piracy is perhaps the prototype international crime. In this sense, the judgment is encouraging from the point of view of holding private parties such as corporations liable under ATCA. Considering how the court could have decided—and indeed was urged to decide—the case, the judgment is encouraging for proponents of the Act in general. Taken at its most favourable, what the court decides is simply that courts must apply the law, not make it. At any rate, it is certainly no more onerous than the familiar requirement that international norms relied on under ATCA be 'definable, obligatory (rather than hortatory) and universally condemned'.[13]

Ultimately, however, the court's conclusion upon the merits is not especially helpful as a signpost for the future, simply because of the narrowness of the holding. The majority found it sufficient 'to hold that a single illegal detention of less than a day, followed by the transfer of custody to lawful authorities and a prompt arraignment, violates no norm of customary international law so well defined as to support the creation of a federal remedy.'[14] Its holding is consistent with its observation that 'many nations recognise a norm against arbitrary detention, but that consensus is at a high level of generality' and its rejection of Alvarez's reliance on the International Court of Justice's (ICJ's) judgment in the *Tehran Hostages* case on the basis that the detention there was 'far longer and harsher than

---

[9] *Ibid*, slip op at 40.
[10] *Ibid*, slip op at 20.
[11] *United States v Smith*, 18 US 153, at 163 note *h*.
[12] See the discussion of the 'State action' requirement in Section IV below.
[13] *Forti v Suarez-Mason*, 672 F.Supp 1531, at 1539-40 (ND Cal, 1987). Similar requirements are posited in other ATCA cases.
[14] *Sosa v Alvarez-Machain*, No 03-339, slip op at 44-45 (US Sup Ct, 2004).

Alvarez's.[15] The implication is that a more egregious case of arbitrary detention may have met the test announced. Moreover, the case did not involve on its facts, nor did the judgment explicitly discuss *obiter dictum*, either of the two elements which will occupy the greater part of the rest of this chapter, namely *corporate* and *third-party* liability.

The three sections following are directed at each of three important questions which present themselves under the banner of 'attachment of liability' described above. Section III deals with the threshold issue whether a corporation is capable of violating international law at all. Section IV concerns the imputation to corporations of responsibility for the acts of others. Section V includes a discussion of the liability of a parent corporation for the wrongful acts of its subsidiary, invariably a further issue on the facts of ATCA cases against corporations.

### III. THE THRESHOLD QUESTION: CAN CORPORATIONS VIOLATE INTERNATIONAL LAW?

Conceptualising the way in which ATCA should operate evokes one of the key frustrations with international law: whilst there is no shortage of norms, mechanisms for enforcement of those standards are critically lacking. However, with ATCA the problem is, in a sense, the reverse. The existence of the *remedy*, as the Supreme Court acknowledged in *Sosa*, is there in black and white, whilst the obligations covered, being creatures of customary international law, are often far less clear. However, the Act represents a tantalizing opportunity for the meaningful enforcement of rights conferred and duties owed under international law itself. Liability under the Act is triggered where '(1) an alien sues (2) for a tort (3) committed in violation of ... international law.'[16] The word 'tort' here is apt to mislead, because international law, as discussed below, lacks a rigid separation between torts and crimes, whereas domestic law clearly does possess a distinct category of violations called 'torts'. Most likely its use in the statute refers either to *domestic* torts—the ambiguity accounted for by archaic phraseology—or in a more generic sense, simply to 'wrongs'[17] that contravene the law of nations—what we would now call violations of international law. As was noted in *Sosa*, international law and domestic common law in the late eighteenth century were not seen as formally separate in the way they are today. It is submitted that the statute is best

---

[15] *Ibid* at 42, fn 27.
[16] *Kadic v Karad ic*, 70 F.3d 232, at 238 (2nd Cir, 1995).
[17] Although now obsolete, the use of the word 'tort' to refer to an wrong or injury in the general (that is, not specifically juristic) sense was still current in the eighteenth century. *See Oxford English Dictionary*, 2nd edn (Oxford, Oxford University Press, 1989).

viewed as a point of nexus or interface between international and domestic law that allows *violations* (in the general sense) of the former to be treated as *torts* under the latter. The Supreme Court therefore took the correct approach in looking to international law to provide the substantive law for these purposes.[18] By making violations of *international law* actionable, Congress has mandated a choice of law which courts are bound to follow.[19] Additionally, from a policy point of view, the Act targets not 'garden-variety municipal torts' but violations of the law of nations. To look to domestic law for causes of action, therefore, would obviate this aspect of the statute.[20]

Clearly, then, a threshold question here is whether a corporation is capable of violating international law at all. It is worth noting at this stage that most courts considering ATCA claims against corporations have simply assumed that they can be held liable under the statute on the same basis as individuals; the one court that did engage in a fully reasoned review of the issue came to the same conclusion.[21] However, it is useful to examine this question in its own right. I shall first consider whether corporations are bound by international criminal law, then discuss their obligations under international human rights law more generally.

## 1. Obligations under International Criminal Law

It has never been the case that only States were capable of bearing duties under international law. The prohibitions on high seas piracy and the slave trade are the classic examples of international obligations binding directly on individuals.[22] Nuremberg and its progeny inspired a huge expansion in the range and specificity of obligations in this category, culminating in the definitions contained in the Rome Statute of the International Criminal Court. The international legal duties of *natural*

---

[18] For a brief survey of alternative approaches taken by Circuit and District courts, see *Wiwa v Royal Dutch Petroleum Co*, 226 F.3d 88, at 105, fn 12 (2nd Cir, 2000).

[19] Federal courts generally look to the American Law Institute's *Restatement (Second) of Conflict of Laws* (1971) in deciding conflict of laws questions. The basic substantive provision is §6, which requires that, subject to the Constitution, a court follow legislative directives on choice of law: para 1.

[20] *Xuncax v Gramajo*, 886 F.Supp 162, at 183 (D Mass, 1995).

[21] *Presbyterian Church of Sudan v Talisman Energy*, Inc, 244 F.Supp 2d 289 (SDNY, 2003).

[22] It bears mention that the slave trade is quintessentially a commercial crime, which at its height was usually committed by corporations as well as the natural persons working for them. Ratner notes in this connection that 'the first true example of international human rights law was a response to commercially-oriented violations of rights': 'Corporations and Human Rights: A Theory of Legal Responsibility' (2001) 111 *Yale Law Journal* 443, at 465.

persons extend at a very minimum to those derived from the narrow class of human rights norms that comprise international criminal law. That much is now clear to the point of triteness. A more vexed question is whether *companies*, as well as natural persons, are bound by these norms. Although the International Military Tribunal (IMT) had been cautious in examining the question of criminal organizations, presumably influenced by the fact that a declaration of criminality under its Charter could lead to the death penalty for those shown to have been members of the criminalised group,[23] the US Military Tribunal at Nuremberg seemed receptive to the concept of corporate responsibility for the crimes it tried. Despite its lack of jurisdiction over the corporations as such, in the *IG Farben* and *Krupp* cases[24] the Tribunal consistently spoke in terms of their having committed and participated in international crimes, for example in the following passage:

> [T]he proof establishes beyond a reasonable doubt that offences against property as defined in Control Council Law No 10 were committed *by Farben*, and that these offences were connected with, and an inextricable part of the German policy for occupied countries ... The *action of Farben* and its representatives, under these circumstances, cannot be differentiated from acts of plunder or pillage committed by officers, soldiers, or public officials of the German Reich ... Such action *on the part of Farben* constituted a violation of the Hague Regulations.[25]

As counsel for the defendant in *Presbyterian Church of Sudan v Talisman* noted, however,[26] criminal liability of legal persons failed to make it into the final draft of the Rome Statute. Article 23 of the Preparatory Committee's draft specifically recognized the court's jurisdiction over legal persons in respect of all crimes within its competence.[27] However,

---

[23] See Andrew Clapham, 'The Question of Jurisdiction Under International Criminal Law Over Legal Persons', in Menno T Kamminga and Saman Zia-Zarifi (eds), *Liability of Multinational Corporations under International Law* (The Hague, Kluwer, 2000) 139, at pp 160—65.

[24] *United States v Carl Krauch et al*, Trials of War Criminals before the Neurenberg Military Tribunals under Control Council Law No 10, vols VII—VIII; *United States v Alfried Krupp et al, ibid*, vol IX

[25] Quoted by Schwartz J in *Presbyterian Church of Sudan v Talisman Energy, Inc*, 244 F.Supp 2d 289, at 315–16 (SDNY, 2003) (emphasis added). See further the excerpts from *United States v Krauch* and *United States v Krupp* quoted in Andrew Clapham, 'The Question of Jurisdiction Under International Criminal Law Over Legal Persons', above n 23.

[26] See Memorandum of Law in Support of Defendant Talisman Energy Inc's Motion to Dismiss, 13 May 2001, 2002 WL 32495947, text corresponding to fn 5.

[27] *Report of the Preparatory Committee on the Establishment of an International Criminal Court. Part I: Draft Statute for the International Criminal Court*, A/CONF.183/2/Add.1, 14 April 1998. Article 23 provided in relevant part as follows:

> 5. *The Court shall also have jurisdiction over legal persons, with the exception of States, when the crimes committed were committed on behalf of such legal persons or by their agencies or representatives.*

discussion of Article 23 as it stood in that draft was constrained somewhat by the introduction of a French proposal which instead provided for an organization to be declared criminal *as such* if a crime were found to have been committed *on its behalf*.[28] This was 'Nuremberg in reverse': just as under Control Council Law No 10 criminal responsibility of an individual could attach by association with a criminal organization, so under the French proposal the criminal responsibility of a legal person could attach by association with a natural person who committed a crime within the jurisdiction of the court. Thus, rather than provide for corporate liability under international criminal law *per se*, the French proposal envisaged in effect an *ancillary* offence of 'being a criminal organisation'. The debate in the Committee of the Whole centred around the French modifications, which raised political hackles because of their (superficial) resemblance to Articles 9 and 10 of the Nuremberg Charter.[29] Other objections focused on the practical problems of implementing the other part of France's proposal, which bound States parties themselves to enforce judgments made against organizations,[30] something which, of course, would be very difficult for those States that did not recognise corporate criminal responsibility. The dominant view seems to have been that criminal responsibility for legal persons was in principle desirable, but that the practical issues were simply too complex to be agreed upon in the short time available.[31] The opinion that corporations were *incapable* of breaching international criminal law (which, needless to say, would have been a relevant view to have expressed at that juncture) was notably absent from the discussion. In the end, although 'all delegations' to the Working Group on General Principles of Criminal Law 'had recognised the great merits of the relevant proposal ... some had felt that it would perhaps be premature to introduce that notion.'[32] It is therefore difficult to draw from these discussions any firm conclusions about corporate responsibility under international criminal law. However, the absence of challenges to the idea in principle, together with the focus on overcoming the practical barriers to imposing liability,

---

6. *The criminal responsibility of legal persons shall not exclude the criminal responsibility of natural persons who were perpetrators or accomplices in the same crimes.*

[28] France: Proposal regarding Article 2, A/CONF.183/C.1/L.3, 16 June 1998. The proposal provided that '[w]hen the crime was committed by a natural person on behalf or with the assent of a group or organization of every [sic] kind, the Court may declare that this group or organisation is a criminal organization,' and provided for penalties. Interestingly, the possibility, provided for in the Preparatory Committee's draft at Art 23, para 5, that crimes could be committed by an 'agency' of a legal person, was not included in the French proposal.

[29] See eg the comments of the Chinese delegate: Summary records of the meetings of the Committee of the Whole: First Meeting, 16 June 1998, A/CONF.183/C.1/SR.1 at para 36.

[30] *Ibid* at para 6, cl 2.

[31] *Ibid* at paras 32–66, especially the Chairman's comments at paras 50 and 66.

[32] Summary records of the meetings of the Committee of the Whole: Twenty-Sixth Meeting, 8 July 1998, A/CONF.183/C.1/SR.26 at para 10.

must be regarded as strongly encouraging. Andrew Clapham, who served as legal adviser to one of the delegations at the Rome Conference, points out that no delegation even posed 'the question *whether* legal persons are bound by international criminal law,' and puts the delegates' caution down, rather, to a fear of granting the court jurisdiction over *States themselves* 'by the back door', by way of activities carried out by State-owned businesses.[33] In the ATCA context, that policy objection has little force given the application of the Foreign Sovereign Immunities Act, which represents the sole means of suing a foreign government or an 'agency or instrumentality' thereof in the United States.[34]

The conceptual difficulties involved in using criminal norms as the basis for tort liability are more metaphysical than real. International law, as a perpetually emergent system, does not lend itself to the use of such analytical compartments as 'civil' and 'criminal'. Its mechanisms of compliance are scarcely so well developed as to warrant the assertion that certain obligations fall into the exclusive province of one or another category. The obligations that comprise international criminal law are fundamentally human rights norms, binding on individuals by way of Nuremberg's overarching rule of reason that responsibility can be imposed on individuals (and presumably, *mutatis mutandis*, powerful corporations) where that is *necessary to uphold the law*. Moreover, as Harold Koh points out, 'even if for some reason international law did not impose civil liability directly, there is nothing to prevent domestic law (eg the ATS) from supplementing international criminal law remedies with civil remedies arising out of domestic law.'[35] 'To read §1350's reference to "the law of nations" as requiring international agreement on the *type* of action available ... would be to effectively nullify that portion of the statute.'[36] And as the Supreme Court recognised in *Sosa*, Congress cannot have intended to enact a nullity.


## 2. General International Obligations

Corporations bear certain duties explicitly under international law. Several conventions and other international legal instruments identify obligations for companies operating in the international sphere, particularly in the

---

[33] Andrew Clapham, 'The Question of Jurisdiction Under International Criminal Law Over Legal Persons', above n 23 (italics in original).

[34] 28 USC 1330, 1602–11; see *Argentine Republic v Amerada Hess Shipping Corporation*, 488 US 428, at 434–35 per Rehnquist CJ (1989) (FSIA is 'sole basis for obtaining jurisdiction over a foreign state in our courts').

[35] Koh, 'Separating Myth from Reality About Corporate Responsibility Litigation' (2004) 7 *J Int'l Econ L* 263, at 267.

[36] *Xuncax v Gramajo*, 886 F.Supp 162, at 180–81 (D Mass, 1995), quoting Edwards J in *Tel-Oren v Libyan Arab Republic*, 726 F.2d 774 (internal quotation marks and parentheses omitted).

fields of environmental damage and corrupt business practices.[37] Some of these even assert the criminal liability of corporations.[38] Against this background Koh asks, 'how can it be that corporations can be held responsible under international law for their complicity in oil spills, but not for their complicity in genocide? How can corporations be held liable under European law for anti-competitive behaviour, but not for slavery?'[39] The orthodox answer, presumably, would be that 'the number of entities with international legal personality *for particular purposes* is considerable,' but that 'the *context* of problems remains paramount.'[40] In other words, that no matter how many corporate obligations international law eventually recognizes, each will remain *sui generis* and the sum of them will never add up to general corporate international legal personality. Whilst, contrary to this notion, there is no particular reason why at some point the build-up of specific obligations might not amount to sufficient State practice and *opinio juris* to establish corporations as international legal actors in some more general sense, it is not possible to state with confidence that that point has yet been reached. Moreover, many of the conventions cited in this context do not themselves embody duties of corporations, but rather are specifically addressed only to States parties, requiring *them* to proscribe and punish certain behavior under domestic law.[41] It is thus not possible to infer corporate international legal personality from the accumulation of regulatory regimes mentioned by Koh.

However, I submit that human rights norms can be seen as binding corporations directly at customary international law. Certain corporations now possess power that approaches or even surpasses that of many States,[42] with a capacity to effect human rights depredations to match. In this setting, then, a simple rule of reason dictates that they should also bear similar human rights obligations. The Universal Declaration, it should be

[37] See, for examples, Radu Mares (ed), *Business and Human Rights: A Compilation of Documents* 2–137 (Leiden, Martinus Nijhoff Publishers, 2004); Ratner, 'Corporations and Human Rights: A Theory of Legal Responsibility' (2001) 111 *Yale Law Journal* 443, at 475–88; Koh, 'Separating Myth from Reality About Corporate Responsibility Litigation' (2004) 7 *J Int'l Econ L* 263, at 264–66.

[38] See, for examples, Andrew Clapham, *The Question of Jurisdiction Under International Criminal Law Over Legal Persons*, above n 23.

[39] Koh, 'Separating Myth from Reality About Corporate Responsibility Litigation', above n 37.

[40] Ian Brownlie, *Principles of Public International Law*, 6th edn (Oxford, Oxford University Press, 2003), at p 67. Italics in the original.

[41] For four examples, see 'Corporate Liability for Violations of International Human Rights Law' (2001) 114 *Harvard Law Review* 2025, at 2032–33 and fn 49.

[42] In 1997, taking gross domestic product (GDP) for States and revenue for companies, of the top 100 most powerful economic actors in the world, 49 were nations and 51were companies: Worth Loomis, 'The Responsibility of Parent Corporations for the Human Rights Violations of Their Subsidiaries', in Michael K Addo (ed), *Human Rights Standards and the Responsibility of Transnational Corporations* (The Hague, Kluwer, 1999), 145, at p 155.

remembered, was enacted 'to the end that every individual *and every organ of society* ... shall strive ... to promote respect for these rights and freedoms and ... to secure their universal and effective recognition and observance.'[43] More recently, there have been efforts to catalogue definitively the human rights obligations of corporations. Kofi Annan's Global Compact, whilst voluntary in itself, comprises principles expressly drawn from existing standards;[44] the commentary acknowledges that '[t]he responsibility for human rights does not rest with governments or nation-states alone.'[45] The newly-drawn UN Norms on the Responsibilities of Transnational Corporations and Other Business Enterprises, too, have been characterised by their Reporter as a restatement and clarification of the *existing* human rights duties of corporations.[46] The orthodox position, that 'international law is virtually silent with respect to corporate liability for violations of human rights,'[47] has never really been true, and is quickly becoming less and less tenable. Additionally, corporate legal personality is so universally accepted as to constitute a 'general principle of law recognized by civilized nations.'[48] In *Barcelona Traction*, the ICJ had the corporate entity in mind when it stated that 'international law is called upon to recognise institutions of municipal law that have an important and extensive role in the international field.'[49]

Viewed in light of the foregoing, the appropriate question is not whether there is any positive doctrinal reason to hold corporations liable under international law, but whether there is any reason that they should be *excluded* from liability. I have already mentioned the rule of reason articulated by the Nuremberg IMT: that the enforcement of international law sometimes requires that entities other than States be held liable.

[43] UN doc A/811, Preamble (emphasis added). This principle was developed in the 1999 Declaration on the Right and Responsibility of Inidviduals, Groups and Organs of Society to Promote and Protect Universally Recognised Human Rights and Fundamental Freedoms, which affirms the responsibility of 'individuals, groups, institutions and non-governmental organisations' in promoting human rights: GA Res 53/144, UN doc A/RES/53/144, Art 18. The connection is explicitly drawn in the UN Norms: 'transnational corporations and other business enterprises, as organs of society, are also responsible for promoting and securing the human rights set forth in the Universal Declaration of Human Rights': Norms on the Responsibilities of Transnational Corporations and Other Business Enterprises with Regard to Human Rights, UN doc E/CN.4/Sub.2/2003/12/Rev.2 (2003), Preamble, third paragraph.

[44] United Nations Global Compact, available at: http://www.unglobalcompact.org/content/AboutTheGC/TheNinePrinciples/thenine.htm

[45] *Ibid*, Commentary to Principle One, available at: http://www.unglobalcompact.org/content/AboutTheGC/TheNinePrinciples/prin1.htm

[46] David Weissbrodt and Muria Kruger, 'Current Developments: Norms on the Responsibilities of Transnational Corporations and Other Business Enterprises with Regard to Human Rights' (2003) 97 *American Journal of International Law* 901, at 913–15, 921.

[47] 'Corporate Liability for Violations of International Human Rights Law', above n 41.

[48] Statute of the International Court of Justice, Art 38(1)(c).

[49] *Case concerning the Barcelona Traction, Light and Power Company*, 1970 ICJ Rep 3, at paras 37–38.

International law is fundamentally a 'natural law' system, animated by concern for humankind; it is only now recovering from the formalism with which it became infected in the nineteenth century. This, indeed, may be one of the reasons why the ATCA seems so strange to the eyes of twenty-first century international lawyers: it is a product of 'the law of nations' as it used to be, free from more 'modern' doctrinal shackles that have seemed to confine its reach to States alone. If a firm is capable of depredations of internationally-recognized human rights, it should be liable for those depredations. Thus Judge Schwartz in *Talisman*, in the face of sceptical affidavits from some very prestigious international lawyers,[50] rightly concluded that '[a] corporation is a juridical person and possesses no *per se* immunity under US domestic or international law.'[51] Even apart from their often huge power, corporations may warrant closer scrutiny than individuals. The philosopher Larry May has suggested that the corporate setting engenders 'personal value transformation' in individuals acting within the organization, which may cause them to make decisions they would not have made acting alone.[52] This kind of 'group-think' can be dangerous, especially in combination with knowledge of corporate impunity.

## IV. IMPUTATION OF RESPONSIBILITY TO CORPORATIONS

### 1. The 'State Action' Requirement

Thus there is a large corpus of human rights norms that corporations might violate acting alone; federal courts, however, have not seen it this way. One notorious feature of ATCA cases has been the 'State action' requirement. Courts handling ATCA claims have usually asserted that only a State may *directly* violate an international law norm, with the exception of a small category of offences of 'universal concern', apparently coterminous with those cited in the American Law Institute's Restatement (Third) of Foreign Relations Law as attracting universal jurisdiction.[53] For the Ninth Circuit in *Unocal*, this translated to 'crimes like slave trading, genocide or war crimes,' together with other crimes under international law when committed in furtherance of crimes in the smaller category.[54]

---

[50] Professors James Crawford and Christopher Greenwood gave expert statements to the defence: see Memorandum of Law in Support of Defendant Talisman Energy Inc's Motion to Dismiss, 13 May 2001, 2002 WL 32495947.

[51] *Presbyterian Church of Sudan v Talisman Energy, Inc*, 244 F.Supp 2d 289, 319 (SDNY, 2003).

[52] May, *Sharing Responsibility* (Chicago, University of Chicago Press, 1992), ch 4.

[53] *Kadic v Karad ic*, 70 F.3d 232, 239 (2nd Cir, 1995). See the discussion of universal jurisdiction in this section.

[54] *John Doe I v Unocal Corp*, 395 F.3d 932, at 945–46 (9th Cir, 2002).

The courts may have been led into error here by the fact that the original modern case—*Filártiga*—concerned torture. Under the 1984 Torture Convention,[55] and its predecessor the 1975 Torture Declaration[56]—which the judgment quotes in full[57]—one of the conditions of liability is that the offender be acting under State authority. Thus official capacity is built into the definition of the *offence itself*, which might for that reason more appropriately be termed '*official* torture'. Indeed, in the Rome Statute of the International Criminal Court, the 'public official' requirement is deleted.[58] Additionally, the misconception that most human rights violations require State action seems to have been erroneously reinforced by the Torture Victim Protection Act (TVPA), which includes a specific 'actual or apparent authority, or color of law, of any foreign nation' requirement.[59] But the TVPA is a different statute.[60] In contradistinction to the ATCA, it applies only to action related to foreign governments, and it does not require that suit be brought by 'an alien'. Moreover, it covers only 'official torture' and extrajudicial killing, each of which can by definition only be committed by a State.[61] Finally, an interpretation of ATCA that requires that the defendant in most cases be a State actor also sits uneasily in the wider federal statutory scheme. It necessitates steering a precarious path between the ATCA on the one hand and the Foreign Sovereign Immunities Act (FSIA) on the other. An individual (or corporation) must be enough of a 'State actor' to qualify for ATCA liability; but not too much, or else the FSIA will render it immune.

However, corporations for the most part do not violate human rights acting alone; much more common is the situation where a corporation *assists* government or other actors (local warlords, for example) in violating human rights norms, or provides the *opportunity* for the violation. *Unocal* is an instance of this latter type of situation. It was alleged that the defendant corporation had hired the 'Myanmar Military' to provide

---

[55] Convention Against Torture and Other Cruel, Inhuman or Degrading Treatment or Punishment 1984, Art 1(1): '... when such pain or suffering is inflicted by or at the instigation of or with the consent or acquiescence of a public official or other person acting in an official capacity.' Note also Art 1(2): 'This article is without prejudice to any international instrument or domestic legislation which does or may contain provisions of wider application.'

[56] Declaration on the protection of all persons from being subjected to torture and other cruel, inhuman or degrading treatment or punishment, GA Res., 3452 (XXX), 9 December 1975, UN doc A/1034.

[57] *Filártiga v Peña-Irala*, 630 F.2d 876, at 883.

[58] UN doc A/CONF.183/9, 17 July 1998, Art 7(2)(e).

[59] 28 USC § 1350, *note*.

[60] Indeed, whilst the courts have generally been receptive to the idea of suing corporations under the ATCA, it has been held that the use of the word 'individual' in the TVPA excludes this possibility: *Beanal v Freeport McMoRan, Inc*, 969 F.Supp 362, at 381–82 (EDLa, 1997), aff'd 197 F.3d 161 (5th Cir, 1999).

[61] The latter in the sense that the qualifier 'extrajudicial' cannot sensibly be applied to the actions of individuals, who are incapable, acting alone, of performing a 'judicial' killing.

security for its pipeline project, knowing of its history of brutality, then failed to act when it became aware that the army was using forced labor and perpetrating ethnic cleansing along the pipeline route.[62] My contention, advanced below, is that in situations where a corporation is alleged to have participated in some way in the violation of another, whether the primary violator is a State actor or not, liability should be imputed to the corporation if it is found, under international law principles, to have been *complicit* in the violation.[63] Contrast this with a 'State action' requirement, which, first, denies that a corporation could ordinarily violate international law in conjunction with any actor *other* than a State; and, second, even where there has been State action, requires that the corporation effectively *be* the State in order for a violation to exist.

## 2. Choice of Law for Principles of Third-party Liability

This brings us to a second cluster of errors commonly made in applying the ATCA. Having looked to international law for standards of conduct associated with liability as a principal violator, it makes little sense to turn to domestic law for the rules governing *complicity* in such conduct. What is required is a *violation of international law*, and such a violation has simply not taken place unless the actor has failed to live up to duties imposed on it by that particular body of law. There is no principled basis for proceeding as Reinhardt J did in *Unocal*, and treating third-party liability rules as 'ancillary legal questions', separate from other parts of the definition of the wrong to such an extent that a different choice of law is warranted.[64] Nevertheless, most courts dealing with third-party liability under ATCA have applied notions of complicity derived from federal law.

This use of domestic law may stem from the view of the ATCA as an exercise of 'universal jurisdiction'.[65] That analysis was most recently expounded by Breyer J in *Sosa*, whose approach involved a search for

---

[62] 395 F.3d 932, at 932–45.

[63] Of course, where some form of participation by the State is part of the definition of the specific offence itself — as with official torture — such participation will have to be proved as an element of the violation, in addition to any complicity theory that might be brought to bear. See the discussion in the preceding and following subsections.

[64] 395 F.3d 932, at 963: 'I do not agree that the question of Unocal's tort liability should be decided by applying any international law test at all. Rather, in my view, the *ancillary legal question* of Unocal's third-party tort liability should be resolved by applying general federal common law tort principles, such as agency, joint venture, or reckless disregard' (emphasis added).

[65] This is a view with which some commentators have, usually just in passing, agreed: see eg Rabkin, 'Universal Justice: The Role of Federal Courts in International Civil Litigation', (1995) 95 *Columbia Law Review* 2120, at 2139–41; 'Corporate Liability for Violations of International Human Rights Law', above n 41, at 2044.

international 'procedural consensus' that the offence in question would attract universal jurisdiction.[66] Universal jurisdiction is a species of jurisdiction to proscribe. Conceptually speaking, therefore, the fact that an offence is one of 'universal jurisdiction' simply means that States may (or perhaps in some cases must) exercise their own lawmaking capacity to make the relevant offence punishable *under domestic law* no matter where in the world it takes place, or who commits it. The 1949 Geneva Conventions are a case in point:

> The High Contracting Parties undertake to enact any legislation necessary to provide effective penal sanctions for persons committing, or ordering to be committed, any of the grave breaches of the present Convention
> Each High Contracting Party shall be under the obligation to search for persons alleged to have committed, or to have ordered to be committed, such grave breaches, and shall bring such persons, regardless of their nationality, before its own courts. It may also, if it prefers, and in accordance with the provisions of its own legislation, hand such persons over for trial to another High Contracting Party concerned, provided such High Contracting Party has made out a prima facie case.[67]

The fact that a crime attracts universal jurisdiction does not of itself mean that it also violates international law. However, it is true that crimes which attract universal jurisdiction at customary law tend to be the most serious offences; and for that reason the same acts which constitute crimes attracting universal jurisdiction also tend in fact to be violations of international law. Non-State actors hailed into domestic courts using universal jurisdiction are thus punished under *domestic law*. Thus if we see ATCA as an exercise of universal jurisdiction, it might be reasonable to use domestic standards of third-party liability. It is submitted, however, that ATCA cannot be seen as an exercise of universal jurisdiction. The latter is fundamentally *criminal* in nature: jurisdiction to punish is taken on the basis of *custody of the defendant*, generally following an unaccepted offer to turn him over to the authorities of a State with a stronger connection to the crime.[68] It is thus an exceptional ground of jurisdiction, designed for situations where the defendant would otherwise escape punishment; the paradigm case being high seas piracy. By contrast, with ATCA cases, courts use ordinary bases of civil jurisdiction which would be employed in respect of any civil suit coming before them. Indeed, ATCA itself makes *no provision at all* with regard to jurisdiction. Rather, what is significant

---

[66] *Sosa v Alvarez-Machain*, No 03-339, Op of Breyer J (US Sup Ct, 2004).
[67] Geneva Red Cross Conventions 1949, Convention I, Art 49; Convention II, Art 50; Convention III, Art 129; Convention IV, Art 146, 75 UNTS 31, 85, 135 and 287.
[68] See 'Harvard Research Draft Convention on Jurisdiction with Respect to Crime' (1935) 29 *Am J Int'l L Supp* 443, Art 10(a).

about it is the type of *substantive* norms it embraces. As observed above, it acts as a nexus for the enforcement of duties imposed by norms of international law. Indeed, the statute's substantive reach is a further indication that it cannot be viewed as an exercise of universal jurisdiction. The list of offences in respect of which universal jurisdiction is authorised as a matter of customary international law is extremely short, in all probability not extending beyond 'crimes against peace', crimes against humanity and war crimes.[69] On the *Sosa* test, discussed above, ATCA would clearly embrace customary norms far beyond this range. Thus the theory of ATCA as an exercise of 'universal jurisdiction' conflates two issues which should be kept separate: first, the available heads of jurisdiction *ratione personae*; and second, the substantive norms with which the statute interfaces. We should therefore not be tempted to bring in domestic principles of third-party liability on the theory that ATCA simply permits courts to exercise universal jurisdiction.

A final argument for the application of municipal rather than international law here is that international law simply fails to provide any guidance on third-party liability, and federal law must fill the gaps.[70] However, I shall endeavour to demonstrate in the next subsection that this 'interstitial' use of federal law is unnecessary, because international law is well capable of furnishing appropriate standards of complicity.

Whilst the Ninth Circuit in *Unocal* appeared to look to international law to provide standards of complicity, its approach was somewhat unstable. First, the court left open the possibility that domestic law might be the proper law in other cases.[71] This suggestion is incompatible with the view, advanced above, of ATCA as laying down a specific choice of law rule. Second, it purported to justify its reliance on the ICTY's *Furundzija* test[72] by reference to that test's resemblance to domestic law standards.[73] Indeed, the court claimed to be applying a 'slightly modified' version of that test, although the exact nature of the 'modification' is not made clear.[74] This approach is fundamentally wrong-headed—for the

---

[69] See eg Malcolm Shaw, *International Law*, 5th edn (Cambridge, Cambridge University Press, 2005), at p 597.

[70] A species of this argument is made by Reinhardt J in *Unocal*: 395 F.3d 932, at 965–66 (9th Cir, 2002).

[71] 'We however agree with the District Court that *in the present case*, we should apply international law.' This was apparently because the violations alleged all concerned *jus cogens* norms: *ibid*, at 948.

[72] Discussed in the next subsection.

[73] This is how the majority confronted Reinhardt J's contention that federal law should have been used: *John Doe I v Unocal Corp*, 395 F.3d 932, at 950ff (9th Cir, 2002) (quoting, inter alia, the American Law Institute's *Restatement of Torts*).

[74] *Ibid*, at 951: 'Especially given the similarities between the *Furundzija* international criminal standard and the Restatement domestic tort standard, we find that application of a slightly modified *Furundzija* standard is appropriate in the present case.'

reasons stated above, if anything the relationship is the reverse: domestic law should follow international law in this context. Thus the Ninth Circuit drew back from a decisive choice of international law. As a result, '[c]ourts that attempt to follow *Unocal* may find themselves caught between the approach *Unocal* explicitly announces and the approach *Unocal* implicitly employs.'[75] Needless to say, this state of affairs is problematic; moreover, as I shall discuss below, it provides grist to the mill of the anti-ATCA lobby.

### 3. Complicity in the Acts of a Foreign State

Under the conception I am advancing, a corporation could violate international law in connection with the conduct of a foreign government in three ways. First, it could itself engage in 'State' action within the meaning of the principles of State responsibility. This would be the case where, for example, a corporation carries out certain government functions, such as customs checks, which are sometimes performed by airlines. In a situation like that, the corporation would not merely be responsible for the conduct of the State: it would *be* the State. 'States', it should be remembered, are in themselves only abstract entities, which, as the Permanent Court of International Justice (PCIJ) had it in the *German Settlers in Poland* case, 'can act only by and through their agents and representatives.'[76] The extent of liability of State 'agents and representatives', then, is defined and circumscribed by the rules of State immunity. It is accordingly not possible to sue a State instrumentality under ATCA;[77] hence that question lies beyond the scope of this chapter.

Second, there are those violations, such as 'official torture', that require a particular connection to State action as one element of the definition of the offence. Of course, it goes without saying that each element of a violation must be proved. If one of those elements is State action, then the plaintiff clearly will have to show that there has been State action according to the definition built into the particular norm in question. Only if that is established would it be appropriate to examine questions of *complicity* in that primary violation.

---

[75] 'Ninth Circuit uses international law to decide applicable substantive law under Alien Tort Claims Act', 116 Harvard Law Review 1525, at 1532 (arguing for the application of federal common law in ATCA cases).

[76] Advisory Opinion of 10 September 1923, PCIJ Rep, Ser B No 6, p 22.

[77] The FSIA is the sole basis for such claims: see *Argentine Republic v Amerada Hess Shipping Corporation*, 488 US 428, at 434–35 per Rehnquist CJ (1989).

Finally, and most significantly for present purposes, a corporation might be *complicit* in the wrongful actions of State actors. So long as we are no longer constrained by strict formalism regarding the subjects of international law, it is easy to conclude that such liability, in principle, must exist. Ryskamp J wrote in *Eastman Kodak v Kavlin*: 'it would be a strange tort system that imposed liability on state actors but not on those who conspired with them to perpetrate illegal acts through the coercive use of state power.'[78] The logic of that statement applies with equal force to international law. If a State can violate a particular norm, so can those who assist that State in doing so; that much is obvious. Problems arise, once more, when we proceed to the next stage, that of discerning concrete standards. Under *Sosa* these will have to be widely accepted and well defined.

Ratner's approach suggests that the principles of *State* responsibility be used 'in reverse', to impute responsibility from States to corporations.[79] However, it is submitted that those principles are inapposite in this context. They are designed for the situation in which an entity can be counted as an organ or 'emanation' of the State, standing in the relationship of subordinate. Here, by contrast, we are concerned with State and private entities acting *together*, on a formally equal footing: the private entity, in other words, is not assimilated to the State.[80] Indeed, as Ratner recognizes, the corporation may in fact be the 'commander' in the relationship.[81] This would be a fair characterization of the situation described in *Wiwa*: Shell/Royal Dutch reportedly recruited the Nigerian police and military to suppress Ogoni dissent, providing those forces with transport, logistical support, and weapons.[82] It is possible, however, to discern customary standards of complicity appropriate for this type of State—private entity relationship.

*Unocal*, too, was not a 'State action' case. The court found that the acts of the military were perpetrated in furtherance of *slavery*, which is one of the offences perceived as not requiring State action under the ATCA.[83] The court was therefore concerned with the *general* principles of third-party liability, rather than any test specific to discovering whether the defendant was a 'State actor'. It applied the test for 'aiding and abetting' from the Yugoslavia Tribunal case of *Furundzija*:

> [T]he Trial Chamber holds the legal ingredients of aiding and abetting in international criminal law to be the following: the *actus reus* consists of practical assistance, encouragement, or moral support which has a substantial effect on

---

[78] 978 F.Supp 1078, at 1091 (SD Fl, 1997).

[79] Steven R Ratner, 'Corporations and Human Rights: A Theory of Legal Responsibility' (2001) 111 *Yale Law Journal* 443, at 497–98.

[80] If it were, it would be FSIA-immune. See above.

[81] Ratner, above n 79, at 504–6.

[82] *Wiwa v Royal Dutch Petroleum Co* 2002 WL 319887, at *2 (SDNY, 2002).

[83] See discussion above.

the perpetration of the crime. The *mens rea* required is the knowledge that these acts assist the commission of the offence.[84]

That test was developed from an examination of a range of sources, including jurisprudence from the post-War Allied tribunals in Germany, the Rome Statute of the International Criminal Court, and the ICTY's own prior case-law.[85] Whilst it is true that the Chamber must work within the context of its own statute, in so far as it was informed by the foregoing sources, its judgment is a valuable statement of the customary law of aiding and abetting. And precisely because the standard does emerge from such widely accepted sources, it can comfortably be said to meet the *Sosa* pedigree requirements discussed above. Of course, it is applied in *Furundzija* as a criminal standard; but, as argued above, rigid separations between civil and criminal norms at international law are unhelpful. Besides, if anything, the 'criminal' threshold for aiding and abetting will be higher (that is, more protective of the defendant) than the 'civil' one; so there can be little room for objection by defendants to the choice of the former. Controversy has surrounded the inclusion of 'moral support' in the *Furundzija* definition.[86] This concern, however, is once again overstated. It is clear from the judgment that the crucial element of the *'actus reus'* is that it had 'a substantial effect on the commission of the crime'; moreover, the *mens rea* is furnished by knowledge of the assistance thus supplied. If the conduct of the defendant had such an effect, and the defendant knew it, it is entirely reasonable that there should be liability, whatever the precise nature of the conduct. 'Moral support', thus defined, is also arguably cognate with the emerging international norm of 'silent complicity' which I discuss in the following paragraph.

### 4. Complicity and Developing International Law

In parallel with the process of cataloguing—and thereby underscoring—the human rights responsibilities of companies, norms on the types of complicity of which they may be guilty are also in the process of crystallizing. These developing rules would, it is submitted, place corporations in the position of defenders of human rights in countries in which they invest, in recognition of their often immense relative power vis-à-vis host

---

[84] *Prosecutor v Anto Furundzija*, ICTY Trial Chamber II, 10 December 1998, para 234, available at: http://www.un.org/icty/furundzija/trialc2/judgement/index.htm.

[85] *Ibid*, paras 192–249.

[86] The Ninth Circuit left consideration of moral support 'to another day', but noted that an analogous principle of liability is envisaged in the American Law Institute, *Restatement (Second) of Torts*. Given that the majority justified its use of the *Furundzija* test precisely on its resemblance to domestic law (see discussion in subsection 1 of this section), this must be regarded as a strong indication of the court's approval – albeit *obiter* – of 'moral support': *John Doe I v Unocal Corp*, 395 F.3d 932, at 951 and fn 28 (9th Cir, 2002).

State governments. The Sullivan Principles, the *locus classicus* of 'corporate social responsibility', were designed as an 'incentive for companies to shake the pillars of apartheid.'[87] When accountability finally came, South Africa's Truth and Reconciliation Commission held a special hearing on the role of business in supporting the apartheid State. In assessing this, the Commission posed itself the question whether business *could have done more* to prevent the outrages of the past.[88] It criticized the inaction of those business groupings with sufficient 'bargaining power' to have had a positive influence on the State, whose 'power could have been used more aggressively to promote reform.'[89]

The Global Compact, too, insists on a proactive role for corporations: 'Companies interact with all levels of government in the countries in which they operate. They therefore have the *right and responsibility* to express their views on matters that affect their operations, employees, customers *and the communities of which they are a part*.'[90] Under Principle Two, businesses should 'make sure that they are not complicit in human rights abuses.'[91] The commentary to this Principle employs a tripartite analysis, comprising 'direct', 'beneficial', and 'silent' complicity.[92] The last takes place where a corporation fails to 'raise the question' of human rights abuse with the competent authorities.[93] Clapham and Jerbi, developing the themes of the Compact, have identified 'growing expectations that corporations should do everything in their power to promote universal human rights' and 'growing acceptance within companies that there is something culpable in failing to exercise influence' on host State governments to end rights depredations.[94]

Under the draft Norms, TNCs would be obliged to 'promote, secure the fulfilment of, respect, ensure respect of and protect' human rights '[w]ithin their respective *spheres of activity and influence*.'.[95] The Commentary explains that TNCs would be required by the Norms to 'use due diligence in ensuring ... that they do not directly or indirectly benefit

---

[87] See Frey, 'The Legal and Ethical Responsibilities of Transnational Corporations in the Protection of International Human Rights' (1997) 6 *Minnesota Journal of Global Trade* 153, at 174–75.

[88] Truth and Reconciliation Commission of South Africa, *Report*, vol 4, ch 2, paras 124–48.

[89] *Ibid*, para 49.

[90] United Nations Global Compact, Principle One, available at: http://www.unglobalcompact.org/ (emphasis added).

[91] *Ibid*, Principle Two.

[92] *Ibid*, Commentary to Principle Two, available at: http://www.unglobalcompact.org/

[93] *Ibid*.

[94] Andrew Clapham and Scott Jerbi, *Categories of Corporate Complicity in Human Rights Abuses*, available at: http://209.238.219.111/Clapham-Jerbi-paper.htm

[95] Norms on the Responsibilities of Transnational Corporations and Other Business Enterprises with Regard to Human Rights, UN doc E/CN.4/Sub.2/2003/12/Rev.2 (2003), Art 1 (emphasis added).

from abuses of which they were aware or ought to have been aware' and to *'use their influence* in order to help promote and ensure respect for human rights.'[96] The concept of 'sphere of influence' is a useful one in that it incorporates into the analysis an appreciation of the extent of the corporation's practical power; since not all firms are equally powerful, it is only sensible that their responsibilities should be keyed to their capacities. As Mary Robinson has stated, '[i]t is not a question of asking business to fulfil the role of government, but of asking business to promote human rights *in its own sphere of competence.*'[97]

Whilst the stricter standards of complicity evidenced by the foregoing are perhaps not yet firmly established in international law, as international acceptance of it grows it is likely to be cited with increasing frequency in ATCA cases. International law is only now—belatedly—formally recognizing the power possessed by many TNCs, and the obstacles to regulation they present. Naturally, business sees these developments as overreaching and burdensome.[98] But increased human rights obligations for such entities are essential. 'Globalization', broadly speaking, involves two worldwide social processes: *internationalization* and *privatization*. What this means is that power is increasingly concentrated in the hands of international business. In this climate—from which, after all, they are able to extract substantial benefit—corporations must expect their protective duties to develop accordingly. Tougher standards of complicity, wedded to the notion of 'sphere of influence', constitute a suitable formula for firm but fair evolution.

## V. PIERCING THE CORPORATE VEIL

Perhaps more than anything else, it is their complex organizational structures that make TNCs slippery subjects for any legal regime. Western firms, compelled to do so by law or self-interest, invariably operate abroad through subsidiaries incorporated under host State law. Traditional company law would treat these subsidiaries as entirely distinct juridical persons. This conception produces, for example, a legal schematic of the business entity 'British Petroleum', which most would see as an integrated whole with its head office in the United Kingdom, as

---

[96] Commentary on the Norms on the Responsibilities of Transnational Corporations and Other Business Enterprises with Regard to Human Rights, UN doc E/CN.4/Sub.2/2003/38/Rev.2 (2003) (emphasis added).

[97] Mary Robinson, 'The Business Case for Human Rights', in *Visions of Ethical Business* (London, Financial Times Management, 1998).

[98] Not surprisingly, this was the general flavour of business comments submitted to the Commission regarding the UN Norms. See http://www.ohchr.org/english/issues/globalization/business/contributions.htm.

around 1,200 completely separate corporations.[99] Jurisdiction in a federal court over foreign subsidiaries is unlikely to be obtained.[100] Additionally, subsidiaries—especially when they have been created for individual projects—are seldom the 'deep pockets' their parent companies are; nor does their being hauled into court carry the same public relations clout as a summons served on a brand-name firm. The 'corporate veil', then, is the final obstacle to be overcome if we wish to hold corporations, or rather, the corporations we want, liable under the ATCA. As a preliminary matter, it is submitted that here we are in the realm of *domestic* rather than international law. The corporate veil is a protection offered by States to their own corporations. The law under which the defendant is incorporated, or failing that the law of its primary place of business, should therefore be used.[101] In cases against United States corporations, this will point to the law of their State of incorporation, and with foreign corporations to the law of their home country. However, on these matters there is likely to be a significant degree of identity between the laws of home States.[102] In any event, it is possible to frame some general comments about when piercing might be appropriate in this context.

The justification for erecting legal boundaries between a corporation and its investors is, of course, that by limiting the financial risk to investors investment is encouraged. In a contract paradigm, this makes

[99] Philip I Blumberg, 'Accountability of Multinational Corporations: The Barriers Presented by Concepts of the Corporate Juridical Entity' (2000–2001) *Hastings International and Company Law Review* 297, at 303.

[100] At an early stage of the *Unocal* litigation, the French oil company Total – which held a 62% stake in the Yadana pipeline project, to Unocal's 28% – was removed from the suit on the basis that its California subsidiaries were not its alter egos, and were therefore insufficient to ground personal jurisdiction: *Doe v Unocal Corp*, 248 F.3d 915.

[101] This result is indicated by American Law Institute, *Restatement (Second) of Conflict of Laws* §302 (1971), which entails application of the law of the place of incorporation, save where another State has a 'more significant relationship'. This may be the case where the corporation is incorporated under the law of one State (the exemplar is Delaware) but has only a nominal presence there and does business primarily elsewhere. This conclusion is also supported by an 'interest analysis': the policy of protection is presumably designed to boost the local economy, and the 'social and economic consequences' of holding a parent liable for the acts of its subsidiary will be felt where the corporation primarily does business. See eg Robert Sedler, 'The Territorial Imperative: Automobile Accidents and the Significance of a State Line' (1971) 9 *Duquesne Law Review* 394.

[102] For the English law perspective, see Richard Meeran, 'The Unveiling of Transnational Corporations: A Direct Approach', in Michael K Addo (ed), *Human Rights Standards and the Responsibility of Transnational Corporations* (The Hague, Kluwer, 1999). Whilst there are moves, especially in Europe, to reverse the traditional approach in cases of parent liability for the acts of subsidiaries (creating a presumption *in favour* of liability), the laws of the 'big five' TNC home States (France, Germany, Japan, the United Kingdom and the United States) all basically follow the 'entity law' approach, discussed below, when it comes to corporations that are not formally related to one another. See Larry C Backer (ed), *Comparative Corporate Law: United States, European Union, China and Japan: Cases and Materials* 1077–97 and 1114–16 (Durham, NC, Carolina Academic Press, 2002).

sense: those contracting with a corporation either can be assumed to have taken into account the associated financial risk, or *ex hypothesi* enjoy the protection of other mechanisms such as consumer protection legislation. The principle begins to break down, however, where two factors are present. The first is the use of corporate groups, that is to say, the phenomenon of corporations owned entirely by other corporations. This gives rise to the spectre of many overlapping and compounding layers of limited liability, and the possibility of using the corporate form not to encourage investment but to avoid liability. Philip Blumberg argues that 'entity law' is 'a legal conception that is manifestly anachronistic' because it fails to recognize the modern reality of the economically integrated corporate group.[103] The second is the commission of *torts*, rather than contract violations, by the corporation at the bottom of the chain: these are not transactions in respect of which it can be said that the plaintiff had accepted the financial risk involved in dealing with an entity that is legally fenced off from those that finance it.[104] However, in his survey of around 4,000 'piercing' cases, Thompson found that courts were *less* likely to lift the veil on corporate groups than on individual shareholders, and that within the category of corporate group cases, piercing took place in tort cases less than half as frequently than it did in contract cases.[105] Thompson suggests that this may be a product, inter alia, of the requirement, often laid down in piercing judgments, of a 'strong showing of misuse of the corporate form, not just economic integration of the corporate group.'[106] Prima facie, then, entity law appears to represent to ATCA suits a significant road-block.

Piercing law, as both Thompson and Blumberg note, is beset by a woeful lack of consistency. The flip-side of this, however, is that it is extremely malleable: the underlying concept probably cannot be stated any more specifically than 'fairness' or 'justice'. This gives rise to the possibility of a *sui generis* rule for human rights cases. Coye-Huhn has argued for a 'per se piercing' rule where a subsidiary commits a violation sufficient for an ATCA claim.[107] Parent companies would be positively required under such a rule to make sure that they inform themselves of the activities of their subsidiaries, and to steer those activities away from human rights violations. This is an attractive proposition, at least as regards 'subsidiaries' properly so-called; but consideration needs to be given to the definition of that term.

---

[103] Philip I Blumberg, 'Accountability of Multinational Corporations: The Barriers Presented by Concepts of the Corporate Juridical Entity', above n 99, at 303.

[104] See Robert B Thompson, 'Piercing the veil within corporate groups: Corporate shareholders as mere investors' (1998) 13 *Connecticut Journal of International Law* 379, at 384–5, fn 33.

[105] *Ibid*, at 385–86.

[106] *Ibid*, at 380.

[107] Scott Coye-Huhn, 'No more hiding behind forms, factors and flying hats: A proposal for a per se piercing rule for corporations that violate the Law of Nations under the Alien Tort Claims Statute' (2004) 72 *University of Cincinnati Law Review* 743.

Worth Loomis, himself a former Chief Executive Officer, gives the example of a Japanese business in which his company acquired a 50 per cent interest, but over which it could exercise little control because of the closed nature of Japanese corporate culture.[108] By contrast, Unocal owned only a 28 per cent interest in the Myanmar joint venture, but apparently enjoyed a greater degree of influence over its running. Piercing, as traditionally understood, is appropriate where the two corporations each in fact form part of the same business enterprise, such that the 'veil' between them is recognised as artificial. This will depend, basically, upon the level of control exercised by the parent over the subsidiary.

In both *Wiwa* and *Unocal*, however, corporate veil arguments are relegated to footnotes, wherein they are rather perfunctorily cast aside. In each, the involvement of the parent corporations in the activities complained of was sufficient to hold them *directly* liable under principles of third-party liability, without the need to equate the parent with the subsidiary for legal purposes.[109] Nevertheless, in each case the court would have been willing to pierce, on the basis that Royal Dutch/Shell and Unocal were the 'alter egos' of their subsidiaries.[110] It is not possible to draw any firm conclusions from the decided cases. It is submitted, however, that the seriousness of the acts complained of in ATCA cases would justify the emergence of a stricter set of legal requirements for corporate groups vis-à-vis such violations, if not quite a per se piercing rule. In parallel with the developing norm against 'silent complicity', the test for whether responsibility should flow up the chain of investment should involve a comparison between what the corporation did to avert the wrongful conduct of the firm in which it is invested and what it *could have* done. If more could have been done by the former, there should be liability. There is no sense in blaming a corporation where it would have been powerless to act otherwise; equally, corporations must inform themselves, to the greatest degree feasible, of the activities of their subsidiaries and joint ventures, and failure to do so should be considered culpable. Where they find wrongdoing, they should endeavour to stop it. Again, default in this obligation should mean liability. This is not a per se rule, but rather one based on what could reasonably have been expected of the 'parent' in the circumstances.[111] Thus, any positive obligations imposed on the

---

[108] Worth Loomis, 'The Responsibility of Parent Corporations for the Human Rights Violations of Their Subsidiaries', in Michael K Addo (ed), *Human Rights Standards and the Responsibility of Transnational Corporations* (The Hague, Kluwer, 1999), 145, at p 151.

[109] *Wiwa v Royal Dutch Petroleum Co*, 2002 WL 319887, at *13–*14 (SDNY, 2002); *John Doe I v Unocal Corp*, 395 F.3d 932, at 952–53 (9th Cr, 2002).

[110] *Wiwa v Royal Dutch Petroleum Co*, above n 109, at fn 14; *John Doe I v Unocal Corp*, above n 109, at 953, fn 30.

[111] An important caveat is that what is 'reasonable' cannot depend on what is 'usual corporate practice', which has been the standard in some past piercing cases.

'parent' will not go beyond action the parent would have or should have been capable of taking with regard to its subsidiary in the circumstances. Fundamentally, *vigilance* on the part of parent corporations is required.

## VI. HAVE WE AWOKEN A MONSTER? THE POLICY ARGUMENT

Whilst we should not automatically assume that to encourage litigation against corporations under ATCA would be to the good, grim warnings of the consequences of the statute are exaggerated. Basically the argument is that the risk of litigation under the ATCA will significantly chill investment abroad. This argument is specious: the United States is perhaps the world's most litigious society, and the scale of *purely domestic* damages awards bids fair to horrify foreign businesspeople. Yet one could hardly assert that the United States repels investment. In the midst of this, the number of ATCA suits against corporations is vanishingly small.[112] The *Sosa* test, discussed above, will keep such cases confined to the realm of the most firmly established norms of international law. Additionally, a remedy under the ATCA is unlikely where one would be available in the country in which the violation occurred, an 'exhaustion of local remedies' requirement having been more or less confirmed in *Sosa*.[113] This is not a case of litigants flocking to the United States simply to get massive payouts, especially when we consider that ATCA cases themselves rarely succeed. Moreover, those groups likely to bring ATCA claims simply do not possess the resources necessary to litigate on a truly grand scale.

There is, in short, no precedent for an 'avalanche' of litigation, and no likelihood of such developing. If, as I have argued, corporations have duties under international law, *why not* hold a firm accountable when it breaches one of those duties? Once more the burden of proof is on the opponents of the statute: they must produce convincing reasons why such a corporation should be permitted to *escape* liability. Whilst the ATCA may be just rising from its slumber, impunity for corporate misconduct is awake and rampant; and that is scarcely a situation that provides much incentive for good behaviour.

The value of ATCA suits, as several NGOs have recognized, lies not in massive damages payouts but in embarrassing corporations into changing their conduct. This rests on the notion that their reputation can be

---

[112] 'Only 25 suits have ever been filed against companies under the ATCA. This compares to 250,000 civil proceedings commencing annually in US federal courts, and 15 million civil suits filed in state courts': Human Rights Watch, *Myths and Facts About the Alien Tort Claims Act* (14 May 2003), available at: http://hrw.org/campaigns/atca/myths.htm

[113] *Sosa v Alvarez-Machain*, No 03-339, slip op at 39, fn 21 (US Sup Ct, 2004). The doctrine of *forum non conveniens* can operate to the same effect. For the factors that are applied in assessing *forum non conveniens*, see *Wiwa v Royal Dutch Petroleum Co*, above n 109, at *28–*31.

publicly tarnished in a court of law. Not only ethical consumerism, but also ethical *investing*, represent increasingly lucrative slices of the economy; in various sectors, companies' bottom lines depend as much on image as anything else.[114] Meanwhile, information on corporate human rights records is finding its way onto the internet and into the public conscience. Firms, it should be noted, are much more susceptible to *deterrence* than emotionally and ideologically driven individuals, for the springs of corporate action are fairly transparent. The profit-motive dominates, and business exercises caution where profits are under threat. Which is not to lend support to Hufbauer's and Mitrokostas' doom-laden prediction that 'the chill to trade and investment could entirely offset whatever liberalisation agreements are negotiated in the Doha Development Round.'[115] The fact is that corporations can and do turn profits *without* getting involved in wrongful conduct. Moreover, a climate of respect for human rights is good for business; corporations which bemoan the expense involved in promoting human rights would do well to reflect on the amount that social instability and its attendant sluggish economic conditions cost them in the long run. Worth Loomis points out that '[b]usiness thrives under the rule of law, private property rights, separated powers and free speech.'[116] Stable infrastructure and a solid skills-base, rather than mere cheap, unskilled labor, is increasingly the preoccupation of companies seeking to invest abroad.[117] Thus the 'business case for human rights,' in Mary Robinson's language, is clear.[118]

Even if ATCA suits put United States companies at a competitive disadvantage, the 'advantage' of which they are thereby divested is nothing other than the ability to participate in violations of the most fundamental human rights without fear of consequence. Complaining about this is rather like worrying about the impact on the arms industry of declaring world peace. Far from being 'beside the point' in the face of persisting impunity (and hence, we might suppose, persisting 'competitive advantage') abroad,[119] the fact that some corporations and not others may be held

---

[114] See New Economics Foundation, *Ethical Consumerism Report 2003* (on ethical consumerism in the UK) (publication details?); Social Investment Forum, 2003 *Report on Socially Responsible Investing Trends in the United States* (Washington DC, Social Investment Forum, 2003).

[115] Gary Clyde Hufbauer and Nicholas K Mitrokostas, *Awakening Monster: The Alien Tort Statute of 1789* (Washington DC, Institute for International Economics, 2003), at pp 2–3.

[116] Worth Loomis, above n 108, at pp 153–54.

[117] UN Conference on Trade and Development, *World Investment Report 1999: Foreign Direct Investment and the Challenge of Development* (New York, United Nations Publications, 1999), at pp 313–15.

[118] See Mary Robinson, 'The Business Case for Human Rights' in *Visions of Ethical Business* (London Financial Times Management, 1998).

[119] Emeka Duruigbo, 'The economic cost of Alien Tort litigation: A response to "Awakening Monster: The Alien Tort Statute of 1789"' (2004) 14 *Minnesota Journal of Global Trade* 1, at 29.

accountable can only increase public pressure on other TNC home States to enact their own 'ATCAs', or better yet, to take direct responsibility for policing the acts of their corporations beyond their borders. Uniformity is scarcely sufficient justification for maintaining impunity worldwide. The 'competitive advantage' argument is, in point of fact, less powerful than it might at first seem, since many foreign TNCs could be subject to ATCA anyway, on the basis of the business they do in the United States.[120] This, moreover, means that *host* States which purport to offer business advantages in the shape of the ability to violate human rights will be less likely to succeed vis-à-vis corporations which could be subject to suit in the United States; which in turn reinforces the attractiveness to investors of those jurisdictions that *do* effectively protect human rights.

Finally, there are the foreign policy arguments. The current White House and State Department have displayed more hostility towards the statute than in previous administrations. One of their most striking claims was that a suit involving abuses by the Indonesian army could threaten diplomatic efforts in the war on terrorism.[121] This is a perverse argument. The campaign against global terrorism is meant to be directed towards *safeguarding* human freedom and dignity, not masking widespread violations of human rights in order to sweeten abusive regimes. Dismayingly, however, the Executive's position fits with its general effort to erode the power of the other branches of government when it comes to foreign policy.[122] This is not to deny that there may be cases in which friendly relations between the United States and other nations would indeed be threatened by allowing a suit to go forward; but that should be decided case-by-case, as the Supreme Court suggested in *Sosa*. Pointedly, potential interference with the war on terror was not listed as an example of a situation in respect of which a federal court should recuse itself.[123] Such an assessment is required under the 'act of State' doctrine, which has generally received short shrift in ATCA cases.[124] The latter trend is all to the good. It must be remembered that norms actionable under ATCA must be

---

[120] In *Wiwa* the defendant's 'investor relations office' in New York City was sufficient contact for an assertion of jurisdiction *ratione personae* by the Second Circuit: *Wiwa v Royal Dutch Petroleum Company*, 226 F.3d 88 (2nd Cir, 2000), at 94–98.

[121] See Emeka Duruigbo, above n 119, at 22–25.

[122] See David Golove and Stephen Holmes, 'Terrorism and Accountability: Why Checks and Balances Apply Even in "The War on Terrorism"' (2004) 2 *New York University Review and Law and Security* 2.

[123] *Sosa v Alvarez-Machain*, No 03-339, slip op at 39, fn 21 (US Sup Ct, 2004).

[124] For an overview, see *Wiwa v Royal Dutch Petroleum Co*, 2002 WL 319887, at *27–*28 (SDNY, 2002). 'Act of State' is an odd doctrine at any rate. It is supposedly based on the separation of powers (see *Banco Naçional de Cuba v Sabbatino* 376 US 398, at 425 (1964)), but it operates against the checks and balances which are the object of that doctrine by limiting the power of the judicial branch vis-à-vis foreign relations.

universally accepted; this means, *ex hypothesi*, that the 'target' State has also accepted them. This point is all the stronger in the field of fundamental human rights, which are now established as matters of *international* concern, not falling exclusively within the domestic jurisdiction of States.

## VIII. CONCLUSION

Hard cases, of course, make bad law; but the same may be true of easy ones. What the *Unocal* case confirms is that companies sued under ATCA will be held to at least the same standard as private individuals. But beyond that, what can we take from it? The conduct of the corporation in question[125] was so egregious that, morally speaking, we find no difficulty in condemning it, and the judges could not help feeling the same. For example, the Ninth Circuit had before it 'evidence that Unocal could influence the army not to commit human rights violations, that the army might otherwise commit such violations, and that Unocal knew this.'[126] Consider the memo from a company representative which read, '[o]ur assertions that the Myanmar Military has not expanded and amplified its usual methods around the pipeline on our behalf may not withstand much scrutiny.'[127] Any reasonable legal standard would have condemned Unocal for its conduct. Yet this diminishes somewhat the value of such cases as precedents, or at least as predictors of future developments. The true test of ATCA's scope will come soon, however, in the shape of several ongoing claims with less, so to speak, obvious legal bases. *In Re South African Apartheid Litigation* was dismissed—once again on a motion to dismiss—by a judge of the Southern District of New York in November 2004.[128] That case actually represents a 'mixed bag' of different claims against corporations for their role in supporting apartheid. They are accused, inter alia, of providing the regime with its basic, day-to-day material means of support such as transportation and computer technology—two of the defendants are General Motors and IBM.[129] At least one of the cases, that brought by the Khulumani support group, will be appealed to the Second Circuit.[130]

---

[125]    Assuming that it can eventually be proved: the procedural posture of the various cases is such that ATCA has yet to be tested against a corporation on the merits.

[126]    *John Doe I v Unocal Corp*, 395 F.3d 932, at 939 (9th Cir, 2002).

[127]    *Ibid*, at *5.

[128]    346 F.Supp.2d 538 (SDNY, 2004).

[129]    See Complaint and Jury Trial Demand, *Khulumani et al v Barclays National Bank Ltd et al* ('*Khulumani Complaint*'), paras 536–62; 587–602, available at http://www.apartheid-reparations.ch/en/reparationen.php

[130]    See Khulumani Support Group, *Khulumani International lawsuit appeal lodged*, at http://khulumani.net/content/view/538/61/

The inconsistencies regarding choice of law in decisions under the ATCA are unhelpful, and need to be cleared up. Apart from the simple unfairness caused by a lack of legal certainty, corporations need to know precisely what the law is before they can change their behavior to conform to it. Otherwise, either *Awakening Monster*'s prophecy of a reduction in investment in the developing world might just come to pass, or alternatively corporations may decide simply to take the risk and ignore their obligations. Moreover, ambiguities in the law are only so much grist to the mill of the counter-ATCA movement. Hufbauer and Mitrokostas themselves decry '[e]lastic definitions of the "law of nations", flexible choices as to substantive law, and "aiding and abetting" and "color of law" liability.'[131] Their first worry will be largely assuaged should the standard announced by the Supreme Court in *Sosa* endure. I have argued in this chapter that the solution to their second (although presumably not one of which they would approve) is to opt decisively for international law: dilettantism is indeed impermissible where legal certainty is the goal. The third is the most problematic. International law, however, is by no means without standards for complicity liability; and *some* degree of corporate complicity in human rights depredations *must* be forbidden. In fact the *Furundzija* standard chosen by the *Unocal* court may be regarded as one of the more favourable definitions available as far as defendants are concerned.

It is not possible to pretend that ATCA is a perfect, or even a particularly helpful or efficient, means for holding TNCs to account. It is scarcely possible to tackle directly the wider social malaise of corporate involvement in human rights abuse merely by bringing individual lawsuits, although it may facilitate insertion of the issue into the public imagination. Similarly, however, the goal of publicizing a problem can be thwarted by the limitations of litigation as a form. Unocal—which has recently been acquired by ChevronTexaco, one of the defendants named in Khulumani's case—has settled the case against it, reportedly for a sum of at least $15 million.[132] This has naturally been hailed as a 'big win for human rights.'[133] However, if the defendant offers a generous settlement, plaintiff's counsel is bound, ethically and professionally, to advise his client to take it, together with the attendant gagging orders, and this may be less costly to the company involved than the negative publicity a trial would generate. The upshot is that we may never see an ATCA case against a corporation go to trial, with the result that no allegations will ever be fully judicially investigated or officially proved. In

---

[131] Gary Clyde Hufbauer and Nicholas K Mitrokostas, above n 115, at 55.
[132] See Daphne Eviatar, 'A Big Win for Human Rights', *The Nation*, 9 May 2005.
[133] *Ibid*.

this sense the ATCA, should it prove useful against firms' motions to dismiss, is liable to become a victim of its own success. Multiple lawsuits, moreover, are an inefficient use of resources. However, accountability for some is better than accountability for none, and even if ATCA proves to be a paper tiger in itself, it has sown the seeds of enhanced awareness of corporate malfeasance in association with tyrannical regimes.[134]

---

[134] A number of NGOs now have specific ATCA-related campaigns: see eg Amnesty International: http://www.amnestyusa.org/business/atca.html; EarthRights: http://www.earthrights.org/atca/index.shtml; Human Rights Watch: http://www.hrw.org/campaigns/atca/; Khulumani: http://khulumani.net/

# 3

# The Effect of Bilateral Investment Treaties on Human Rights Enforcement and Realization

RYAN SUDA

## I. INTRODUCTION

I N 2003, AN arbitral tribunal constituted under the Spain–Mexico bilateral investment treaty (BIT) ordered Mexico to pay $5.5 million in com-
pensation to a Spanish corporation that had operated a landfill in
Mexico prior to the denial, by a Mexican federal agency, of the renewal
application for the landfill's operating permit. The tribunal held that the
non-renewal, which was predicated on environmental- and health-related
violations of the permit conditions and on community opposition to the
landfill, violated two of the investment protection provisions in the BIT.[1]

The scenario in that arbitration, *Técnicas Medioambientales Tecmed SA v
United Mexican States*,[2] is one that threatens to play out countless times
around the world. By virtue of their pervasiveness, BITs have the potential to have a significant global impact on human rights enforcement.
Although this chapter will address the negative implications of BITs for
human rights, BITs may have positive consequences for human rights as
well, inasmuch as the foreign direct investment protected by BITs may
promote economic growth, development and employment.[3] However,
there is little evidence that BITs have stimulated foreign direct investment

---

[1] *Técnicas Medioambientales Tecmed SA. v United Mexican States* (ICSID Case No
ARB(AF)/00/2) (2003) [hereinafter *Tecmed*], at http://www.worldbank.org/icsid/cases/
laudo051903FINAL.pdf (Spanish original version), http://www.worldbank.org/icsid/
cases/laudo-051903%20-English.pdf (unofficial English translation). All quotations will be
from the unofficial English translation.

[2] *Ibid.*

[3] See, eg, UN Economic and Social Council, *Human Rights, Trade and Investment, Report of
the High Commissioner for Human Rights*, UN doc E/CN.4/Sub.2/2003/9 (2 July 2003)
[hereinafter 'UNESC Report'], para 6, available at http://www.unhchr.ch/Huridoca.nsf/
(Symbol)/E.CN.4.Sub.2.2003.9.En?Opendocument

(FDI), leading commentators to question the utility of granting strong rights to investors in BITs.[4]

## 1. Bilateral Investment Treaties: A Low-profile, but Significant, Legal Regime

Bilateral investment treaties comprise a legal regime that is widespread and growing, but that, due to its decentralized structure and lack of transparency, has not yet attracted the notice (or notoriety) aroused by, for example, the investment chapter of the North American Free Trade Agreement (NAFTA).[5] There are more than 2,300 BITs worldwide;[6] 176 countries are party to at least one BIT.[7] BITs have the potential to

[4] See, eg, Mary Hallward-Driemeier, *Do Bilateral Investment Treaties Attract FDI?* (World Bank, 2003), at 22–23, available at http://econ.worldbank.org/files/29143_wps3121.pdf; Luke Eric Peterson, *International Human Rights in Bilateral Investment Treaties and in Investment Treaty Arbitration* (International Institute for Sustainable Development, 2003) [hereinafter 'IISD 2003'], at 35-36, available at http://www.iisd.org/pdf/2003/ investment_int_human_rights_bits.pdf; below n 35.

[5] This is true despite strong similarities between NAFTA's Chapter 11 and the provisions of many BITs. See below n 76.

[6] Press Release, United Nations Conference on Trade and Development, 'South–South Investment Agreements Proliferating', UN doc UNCTAD/PRESS/PR/2004/036 (23 November 2004), available at http://www.unctad.org/Templates/webflyer.asp?docid= 5637&intItemID=1634&lang=1 (half that number have been ratified). In addition, an increasing number of bilateral free trade agreements cover investment in terms similar to those of BITs. See United Nations Conference on Trade and Development, *World Investment Report 2003*, 89 [hereinafter 'UNCTAD 2003'], http://www.unctad.org/Templates/webflyer.asp? docid=3785&intItemID= 2527&lang=1&mode=downloads. It has been pointed out that '18,145 BITs would be needed to ensure full coverage of the world's 191 economies': *ibid* at 96, n 10.

[7] United Nations Conference on Trade and Development, *Quantitative Data on Bilateral Investment Treaties and Double Taxation Treaties* (data as of 2003), available at http://www.unctad.org/Templates/WebFlyer.asp?intItemID=3150&lang=1 (last visited 2 December 2004); UNCTAD 2003, above n 6, at 89. By the end of 2003, developed countries were party to 1,211 BITs. United Nations Conference on Trade and Development, *World Investment Report 2004* (2004), at 85 and 87, fig II.33 [hereinafter 'UNCTAD 2004'], available at http://www.unctad.org/Templates/webflyer.asp?docid=5209&intItemID=2983&lang =1& mode=downloads. Central and Eastern European countries were party to more than 700 BITs, having signed 26 in 2003: *ibid*, at 75 and fig II.26. Among developing countries, African countries were party to 567 BITs, having signed 35 in 2003: *ibid* at 42 and 45, fig II.5. Asian and Pacific countries were party to more than 1,000 BITs, having concluded 36 in 2003: *ibid* at 52 and 54, fig II.11. Latin American and Caribbean countries were party to 421 BITs, having concluded eight in 2003: *ibid* at 64 and fig.II.18. For corresponding data from 2002, see UNCTAD 2003, above n 6, at 74 and fig II.31 (developed countries); 64–65 and 66, fig II.24 (Central and Eastern European countries); 36–37 and 37, fig II.4 (African countries); 48 and 49, fig II.10 (Asian and Pacific countries); and 55–56 and 56, fig II.17 (Latin American and Caribbean countries). See also United Nations Conference on Trade and Development, *Bilateral Investment Treaties 1959–1999*, UN doc UNCTAD/ITE/IIA/2 (2000) [hereinafter 'UNCTAD 2000'], at 5, fig 2 ('Number of BITs concluded by developing countries, by decade, 1960–1999'), 6, fig 3 ('BITs between developing countries, by region and decade, 1960–1999'); 17, fig 5 ('Number of BITs concluded by Central and Eastern European Countries, by decade, 1960–1999'), available at http://www.unctad.org/en/docs/poiteiiad2.en.pdf.

govern immense flows of capital: the inflow of FDI to developing countries in 2002 was \$162.1 billion,[8] more than triple the inflows of official development assistance.[9]

Although BITs have attracted little public notoriety,[10] investors are becoming increasingly aware of them, with the result that more and more arbitration cases are being brought under investment treaties:[11] at the International Centre for the Settlement of Investment Disputes (ICSID), the only arbitral body to keep public records, the number of BIT arbitrations initiated in 2003 was 30, double the number initiated in 2002.[12] The potential for arbitration under BITs is further enhanced by the fact that many BITs define nationality based on situs of incorporation,

---

[8] UNCTAD, 2003, at 7, tbl 1.2. BITs currently do not govern the entirety of those capital flows, but rather 'an estimated 7% of the stock of world FDI and 22% of the FDI stock in developing and [Central and Eastern European] countries': UNCTAD 2003, above n 6, at xvi.

[9] Inflows of official development assistance totaled \$53.7 billion in 2002. See Rémi Bachand and Stéphanie Rousseau, 'Droits et Démocratie', (2003) *International Investment and Human Rights: Political and Legal Issues* 2 (citing J Randel *et al*, *The Reality of Aid* 145 (Ibon Foundation, 2002), available at http://www.eldis.or/static/DOC14477.htm).

[10] One NGO, the Europe Centre, characterizes the situation in this way: 'Bilateral treaties ... are not very visible to public opinion, many of them have been reached on the sly and [they] are even more harmful to rights of peoples than international or regional treaties in force or in process.' See Europe Centre, Written statement submitted by Europe Centre [to the UN Commission on Human Rights], UN doc E/CN.4/Sub.2/2004/NGO/10 (12 July 2004), at 3, available at http://www.choike.org/documentos/tlc_un.pdf. See also *ibid* at 3 ('Our planet is wrapped in a thick weft of international, regional and bilateral economic and financial agreements and treaties that have subordinated or taken the place of the basic tools of international and national human rights law (including the right to a safe environment), national Constitutions, economic legislation directed to national development and labour and social laws that tend to alleviate inequalities and exclusion').

[11] See Aaron Cosbey *et al*, *Investment and Sustainable Development: A Guide to the Use and Potential of International Investment Agreements* (International Institute for Sustainable Development, 2004) [hereinafter 'IISD 2004'], at 15 ('[a]ll evidence points to a significant increase in the use of BITs and other investment agreements since the late 1990s'), available at http://www.iisd.org/pdf/2004/investment_invest_and_sd.pdf. A number of factors help explain the increase:

> Among [the factors] is surely a growing realization on the part of investors and their legal counsel that the tool is available and, as shown by recent rulings, useful. As well, ... there is a proliferation of classes of possible investor litigants (investments, major investors, minority investors), and of types of measures covered. There is also the possibility of multiple proceedings, and the potential for 'forum shopping'—searching for a home state that offers the protection of a BIT.

*Ibid* at 16.

[12] See *ibid* at 16, fig 1 (citation omitted); see also IISD 2003, above n 4, at 14–15 (performing similar analysis through 2002). When other investment-based investor–State arbitrations are included, such as those under non-BIT treaties such as FTAs and IIAs generally, the same trend is noticeable:

> [t]he cumulative total of all known cases brought under bilateral, regional (eg NAFTA) or plurilateral (eg Energy Charter Treaty) agreements that contain investment clauses, or international investment agreements (IIAs), is now 160 ... [w]ell over half (92) of the 160 known claims were filed within the past three years. Virtually none of them was initiated by governments.

which effectively allows investors to adopt a 'home State of conven-ience' and 'treaty-shop' for favorable investment treaty provisions.[13] Few BITs require that investors be resident for a period of time to qual-ify as nationals of a contracting State, and some in fact dispense with nationality altogether, requiring only permanent residence in a contract-ing State as a predicate for coverage under the treaty.[14] The flexibility of the provisions even allows investors to 'swap' their nationality, incorpo-rating in a foreign nation and subsequently availing themselves of the foreign investment protections in their former home country, as occurred in a case under the Ukraine–Lithuania BIT.[15] The increase in the number of investment treaty arbitrations is ominous from a human rights perspective because, as will be discussed below, investor–State

United Nations Conference on Trade and Development, *Occasional Note: International Investment Disputes on the Rise* (29 November 2004), at 1, available at http://www.unctad.org/sections/dite/iia/docs/webiteiit20042_en.pdf (also noting that '[i]nternational investment disputes arising from investment agreements are on the increase, at times involving tens of millions of dollars'). Discussing the UNCTAD data, Luke Eric Peterson notes that:

> While a lack of transparency hinders a full accounting of this form of legal activity, the study did find significant annual growth in the number of known claims, particularly over the last 5 years...even when [34 recent claims against Argentina] are controlled for, invest-ment treaty arbitration is on an upward trajectory, with 14 non-Argentine claims mounted in 2001, 17 in 2002, 24 in 2003, and 20 as of November 2004. In every instance, the actual number of investment treaty arbitrations is likely higher, as claims under some rules (UNCITRAL, ICC, SCC, etc) may proceed without any publicity.

Luke Eric Peterson, 'UNCTAD Releases Data on Incidence of Investment Treaty Arbitration', *INVEST-SD: Investment Law and Policy Weekly News Bulletin* (IISD, Winnipeg, Canada), 29 November 2004, available at http://www.iisd.org/pdf/2004/investment_investsd_nov29_2004.pdf.

[13] See IISD 2003, above n 4, at 20–21.

[14] See Luke Eric Peterson, 'Tribunal dismisses BIT suit against United Arab Emirates on grounds of nationality', *INVEST-SD: Investment Law and Policy Weekly News Bulletin* (IISD, Winnipeg, Canada), 23 August 2004, available at http://www.iisd.org/pdf/2004/invest-ment_investsd_aug23_2004.pdf ('few investment treaties are known to impose more restric-tive requirements – such as an express requirement that the investor have been resident for some period of time in the putative home state—in order to qualify as a covered investor under the treaty. Indeed, on occasion, treaties will move in the opposite direction and extend their protections beyond nationals, to include permanent residents—as is the case in some Canadian bilateral investment treaties').

[15] See Luke Eric Peterson, 'ICSID Tribunal splits sharply over question of corporate nation-ality', *INVEST-SD: Investment Law and Policy Weekly News Bulletin* (IISD, Winnipeg, Canada), 11 June 2004, available at http://www.iisd.org/pdf/2004/investment_investsd_june11_2004.pdf ('many investment treaties may be drafted so liberally as to permit investors of one country to incorporate in another country, and for the newly-created entity to adopt the nationality of that new state. The nominally "foreign" investor may then re-invest in their country of origin at some later date, and lay claim to the treaty rights that are offered by their country of origin to foreign nationals'); Luke Eric Peterson, 'Chairman of Tribunal Resigns After Dissenting in Investment Arbitration', *INVEST-SD: Investment Law and Policy Weekly News Bulletin* (IISD, Winnipeg, Canada) 18 July 2004, available at http://www.iisd.org/pdf/2004/investment_investsd_july16_2004.pdf.

arbitrations under BITs present a danger of creating a legal regime lacking safeguards of transparency, legitimacy or accountability: a regime skewed towards investors, but one that nevertheless passes judgment on important public interest issues.[16]

As a general rule, BITs are not concluded between two developed countries.[17] Although, as one might expect, a plurality of BITs consists of treaties concluded between one developed and one developing country ('North–South' treaties),[18] perhaps more surprising is the fact that developing countries have been concluding BITs with other developing countries in increasing numbers ('South–South' treaties).[19] This chapter attempts to demonstrate that BITs have the potential to restrict State capacity to regulate in the public interest in the sphere of human rights. If

---

[16] See below, at sections II.3.C and V.1.D.

[17] See UNCTAD 2003, above n 6, at xvi ('[BITs] are not concluded between developed countries'), 96, n 9 ('BITs are not concluded between developed countries, as their legal systems reflect investor protection standards evolved over many years of experience with such issues'); Andrew T Guzman, 'Why LDCs Sign Treaties that Hurt Them: Explaining the Popularity of Bilateral Investment Treaties' (1998) 38 *Virginia Journal of International Law* 639, at 680 ('no two developed countries have entered into a BIT with one another'). But see UNCTAD 2000, above n 7, at 4 ('There are only a few (11) BITs between developed countries, the reason being that investment relations among developed countries are dealt with in a number of instruments adopted under the auspices of the OECD, to which all developed countries belong').

[18] As of July 2004, the following were the proportions of BITs worldwide based on the status of the contracting parties as developed ('North'), developing ('South'), or Central and Eastern European ('CEE'): North–South: 39%; South–South: 28%; CEE–South: 13%; others: 20%. See Press Release, United Nations Conference on Trade and Development, above n 6. Cf Guzman, above n 17, at 641–42 (BITs 'typically signed between developed and developing nations').

[19] See Press Release, United Nations Conference on Trade and Development, above n 6 ('[a]greements on investments between developing countries have increased substantially in both number and geographical coverage over the past decade, according to UNCTAD data released today. This wave of South–South international investment agreements (IIAs) includes 653 bilateral investment agreements (BITs), 312 double taxation treaties (DTTs) and 49 preferential trade and investment agreements (PTIAs) between developing countries'); UNCTAD 2003, above n 6, at 89 ('more BITs are being concluded between developing countries as well as between them and economies in transition ... [t]oday, more than 45% of the BIT universe does not include developed countries'); bilaterals.org, *South–South BITs* ('Bilateral investment treaties signed between the governments of two "developing" countries represent the largest portion of BITs signed in recent years'), available at http://www.bilaterals.org/rubrique.php3?id_rubrique=58 (last visited 14 January 2005); UNCTAD 2000, above n 7, at 1–2 ('[i]nitially, BITs were concluded between a developed and a developing country, usually at the initiative of the developed country ... [t]his pattern has changed since the late 1980s and especially in the 1990s, as developing countries and economies in transition began to sign BITs between themselves in great numbers'); Antonio R Parra, International Centre for the Settlement of Investment Disputes, 'ICSID and Bilateral Investment Treaties' (2000) 17 *ICSID News* 7 (in the 1980s, '[c]ountries that had previously refrained from signing BITs, such as China and the United States, launched BIT programs. With more of them being made among developing and socialist countries, it became increasingly inappropriate to regard BITs as simply North-South instruments'), available at http://www.worldbank.org/icsid/news/n-17-1-7.htm.

that assertion is accurate, one might ask why States continue to negotiate and conclude BITs. Why do States choose to tie their hands, to restrict their sovereignty in this fashion? There are several relevant factors, which also help explain both the historical North–South orientation of BITs and the increasing South–South orientation.

Traditionally, developed countries would request BITs from developing countries as a means of protecting the developed country's investors.[20] Developing countries would sign the treaties in order to attract FDI, which can help build national capacities.[21] In addition to guaranteeing substantive investor protections by signing BITs, developing countries also signal their embrace of the dominant neoliberalist economic ideology, making them more appealing to foreign investors.[22]

---

[20] See UNCTAD 2000, above n 7, at 1 ('[i]nitially, BITs were concluded between a developed and a developing country, usually at the initiative of the developed country. The developed country—typically a capital exporting country—entered into a BIT with a developing country—typically a capital importing country—in order to secure additional and higher standards of legal protection and guarantees for the investments of its firms than those offered under national laws').

[21] See *ibid* ('[t]he developing country, on the other hand, would sign a BIT as one of the elements of a favourable climate to attract foreign investors'). See also UNCTAD 2003, above n 6, at 85 ('[c]ountries seek FDI to promote their growth and development. With its package of tangible and intangible assets, FDI can contribute directly and indirectly to building national capabilities'). There are several reasons for the increasing popularity of FDI:

> The growing appreciation of the benefits of FDI reflects several factors. Concessional aid is declining, and various financial crises have created a preference for long-term and more stable capital inflows. Access to innovative technologies is more important. And some of the earlier fears about FDI may have been exaggerated, given the economic benefits that many developing countries have drawn from FDI. Many governments are now more confident in dealing with TNCs. And TNCs have learned to be more responsive to the concerns and priorities of host countries.

*Ibid* (internal citation omitted). See also UNESC Report, above n 3, at para 20 ('States originally adopted bilateral investment agreements (BITs) to protect investment in response to the uncertainty of the cold war and the decolonization period where unilateral government actions such as asset stripping or nationalization of industries exposed foreign investors to risks, often without compensation. Since the cold war, States have increasingly viewed BITs as vehicles for liberalizing investment by reducing constraints on investment opportunities as a means of attracting investment'). For a brief history of BITs, see Nicolaas Jan Schrijver, *Sovereignty Over Natural Resources: Balancing Rights and Duties in an Interdependent World* (1995), 182–83, available at http://www.ub.rug.nl/eldoc/dis/jur/n.j.schrijver.

[22] See Pierre Sauvé, 'Scaling Back Ambitions on Investment Rule-Making at the WTO', (2001) 2 *Journal of World Investment* 529, at 3 ('in a context of worldwide unilateral investment regime liberalization, many host countries in the developing world have come to appreciate the 'signaling' benefits afforded by bilateral investment protection agreements. The latter send clear signals to international investors that recently enacted policy reforms are unlikely to be reversed, thereby reducing risk premia for investors'), available at http://www.cid.harvard.edu/cidtrade/Papers/Sauve/sauveinvest.pdf; Press Release, United Nations Conference on Trade and Development, '29 Bilateral Investment Treaties Signed by Least Developed Countries in Brussels', UN doc LDCIII/PRESS/08/Rev.1 (18 May 2001) ('[b]y signing [BITs], developing countries in particular are sending a strong signal to the business community worldwide, as well as to their own investors, of their

Although developing countries may desire to attract FDI by signing BITs, the strength of the investment protections contained in the treaties may have developed out of circumstances of disparate bargaining power between developed and developing countries.[23] However, since

commitment to providing a predictable and stable legal investment framework'), available at http://www.unctad.org/Templates/Webflyer.asp?docID=2914&intItemID=2068&lang=1; UNCTAD 2003, above n 6, at 89–91 (BITs 'could signal that a host country's attitude towards FDI has changed and its investment climate is improving—and [thereby improve a country's ability] to obtain access to investment insurance schemes. Indeed, investors appear to regard BITs as part of a good investment framework'). Thomas Wälde makes a similar point:

> Why would countries accept such disciplines [investor protection provisions]? They have to accept it, because becoming members of these international conventions is a sign that you are part of the club. You are joining the global economy. If you want the benefits, you have to accept the disciplines. If you don't, you are an 'out' State, a pariah; your reputation suffers, and everybody will do less business with you and then only with much higher security margins.

Thomas Wälde, 'Current Issues in Investment Disputes: Comments' (2001) *The CEPMLP Internet Journal*, available at http://www.dundee.ac.uk/cepmlp/journal/html/forum_8.html.

[23] See below n 404 and associated text; Guzman, above n 17, at 680 ('[o]ne explanation for the North–South nature of BITs is the bargaining power of the two sides. Without a BIT, a particular developing country will have a much lower level of investment than otherwise. Investment in a developed country, on the other hand, is much less likely to be sensitive to the presence of such treaties. Developing countries, therefore, are much more eager to reach an agreement on investment with a major capital-exporting country and the capital-exporting countries can, in turn, demand strong protections for their foreign investors'); Choike.org/Third World Institute, *Bilateral trade agreements: case studies* ('[i]t is generally recognized that bilateral agreements, especially between a developing and a developed country, are not the best option and that multilateral negotiations and agreements are preferable as they are less discriminatory and allow a better bargaining position for the developing countries'), available at http://www.choike.org/nuevo_eng/informes/2269.html (last visited 14 January 2005).

There is some evidence of bargaining power disparity in the fact that some North–South treaties are broader in scope than most South–South treaties, going beyond investor protection to include investment liberalization provisions:

> the overwhelming number of BITs cover only the post-establishment stage of investment, leaving admission and establishment—which have the greatest development implications—to be determined autonomously by host countries. On the other hand, asymmetries in bargaining power put weaker economies at a disadvantage in the negotiations of bilateral agreements. Although this applies in all negotiating situations, it is particularly relevant in agreements between large developed countries and small and poor developing ones—and when bilateral agreements go beyond a narrow coverage. In some recent cases, the principal objective of investor protection has been complemented with liberalization clauses related to the right of establishment and an expanded list of restricted performance requirements. So, ... developing countries may be entering IIAs of broader scope.

UNCTAD 2003, above n 6, at 93. See also Press Release, United Nations Conference on Trade and Development, above n 6 ('[a]s a rule, South–South BITs deal mainly, and exclusively, with investment protection and promotion (ie they do not grant free access and establishment, unlike the western hemisphere BITs); they refrain from explicitly prohibiting performance requirements; and they limit transparency requirements to the stage after the adoption of laws and regulations'); bilaterals.org, *South–South BITs*

the late 1980s, the line between capital-exporting and capital-importing countries has blurred as developing countries have been increasingly acting not only as host States of FDI, but also as home States of outward-flowing capital.[24] The desire to protect their own investors gives

('[o]ften, [South–South BITs] do not go as far as North–South BITs in terms of setting new policy standards and privileges for transnational corporations'), available at http://www.bilaterals.org/rubrique.php3?id_rubrique=58 (last visited 14 January 2005); UNCTAD 2003, above n 6, at xvi ('BITs are primarily instruments to protect investors, although recent agreements by a few countries also have more of a liberalizing effect'), 89 ('[t]he early focus [in BITs] on protection, treatment and dispute settlement—the reason for these treaties—remains at their centre. But a few countries extend them with provisions for the right to establishment, performance requirements and employment of key foreign personnel. These changes—mainly in recent BITs, including those being renegotiated—are giving rise to a new generation of BITs with greater obligations, with more far-reaching implications'); below n 184 and associated text (discussing liberalization provisions of US and Canadian BITs).

 The existence of a bargaining power disparity also appears corroborated by the fact that developing countries retreat from such strong provisions in situations where they are hosting FDI:

 investment protection had until the advent of the NAFTA and the MAI been conducted almost exclusively on a bilateral, North–South, basis ... [the MAI negotiations and NAFTA] have shown how the juxtaposition of (i) a broad definition of investment; (ii) far-reaching protection against expropriation, including compensation for investors in the advent of 'indirect' forms of expropriation (so-called 'regulatory takings'); and (iii) private party recourse to dispute settlement, ie investor–state arbitration, can give rise to complex, politically sensitive, and often unanticipated policy challenges when pursued among countries with a long history of regulatory activism.

 The lesson has been sobering, suggesting that what works well and is fairly uncontroversial within highly asymmetrical power relations and when investment flows are unidirectional in nature, looks considerably less attractive, and indeed more problem-prone, when applied to countries with significant two-way investment ties and where internationally-active firms have an equal ability to defend their property rights in each other's (or before international) courts.

 Viewed in this light, it is not altogether surprising that many countries have shown growing hesitancy on the issues of how broad to define investment; whether a political market exists in support of multilateral investment protection disciplines (and if so, how broad such disciplines should be on expropriation grounds); and whether, all things considered, private investors should be allowed to challenge state conduct and afforded direct standing in dispute resolution proceedings. Paradoxically, such questioning is taking place at a time when bilateral investment treaties that feature many of the provisions that undermined the MAI negotiations and are proving controversial in a NAFTA and WTO setting, are being signed in record numbers.

Sauvé, above n 22, at 3. See also below nn 401–4 and associated text (developed countries beginning to limit the breadth of BIT provisions, spurred by contexts such as NAFTA where they are importers, and not just exporters, of FDI).

[24] See UNCTAD 2000, above n 7, at 2 ('[the North–South] pattern has changed since the late 1980s and especially in the 1990s, as developing countries and economies in transition began to sign BITs between themselves in great numbers. As a result, the dividing line for BIT partners between capital exporting and capital importing countries no longer holds true and, in many instances, countries approach BITs with the dual purpose of protecting their outward investments to, while attracting inward investment from, the other BIT partner'); UNCTAD 2003, above n 6, at 89 ('more BITs are being concluded between developing countries as well as between them and economies in transition, reflecting the emergence of firms from these countries as foreign investors'); United Nations Conference on Trade and

developing countries an additional incentive to sign BITs, not just with developed countries but also with other developing countries.[25]

These factors may not completely explain the popularity of BITs among developing countries, given a paradox that commentators have identified. In the decolonization period, developing countries waged a successful campaign to negate the assertion that the Hull Rule, which mandates 'prompt, adequate and effective' compensation for State expropriations, represents customary international law.[26] It seems paradoxical that, after establishing that the Hull Rule did not constitute international law, developing countries would turn around in droves and sign BITs, which contain an expropriation standard even more stringent than the Hull Rule.[27]

Development, Trade and Development Board, Commission on Investment, Technology and Related Financial Issues, *Home Country Measures*, UN doc TD/B/COM.2/EM.8/L.1 (14 November 2000) (experts at the Expert Meeting on Home Country Measures, held from 8–10 November 2000 in Geneva, 'noted that 90 per cent of all FDI originates in developed countries, but that developing countries are increasingly becoming home countries [of firms that choose to invest abroad] as well'), available at http://www.unctad.org/en/docs/ c2em8l1.en.pdf; United Nations Conference on Trade and Development, *Expert Meetings* ('The discussion [at the expert meeting on home country measures] confirmed that the issue of outward investment and technology transfer promotion has grown beyond the North–South divide, with a number of developing home countries also actively promoting outward investment'), available at http://www.unctad.org/Templates/ Page.asp?intItemID=2369&lang=1&print=1 (last visited 14 January 2005).

[25] See UNCTAD 2000, above n 7, at 2 ('the dividing line for BIT partners between capital exporting and capital importing countries no longer holds true and, in many instances, countries approach BITs with the dual purpose of protecting their outward investments to, while attracting inward investment from, the other BIT partner'). UNCTAD itself has facilitated the signing of South–South BITs in greater numbers through its 'initiative aimed at strengthening investment cooperation between developing countries by providing them an opportunity to negotiate bilateral investment treaties (BITs) and bilateral treaties for the avoidance of double taxation of income and capital (DTTs)': UNCTAD 2000, above n 7, at 2–4 (box); see also Press Release, United Nations Conference on Trade and Development, '29 Bilateral Investment Treaties Signed by Least Developed Countries in Brussels', UN doc LDCIII/PRESS/08/Rev.1 (18 May 2001) ('Nine of the world's poorest countries, mostly from francophone Africa, signed 29 bilateral investment treaties (BITs) here today with developed and other developing countries, paving the way for increased FDI flows and economic cooperation. ... The treaties, signed at ministerial level during the Third UN Conference on the Least Developed Countries [LDCs] ... were concluded during a round of intensive negotiations for francophone LDCs organized and facilitated earlier this year by the secretariat of [UNCTAD] ... Countries are increasingly concluding BITs in order to promote and protect foreign direct investments and to foster international economic cooperation'), available at http://www.unctad.org/Templates/Webflyer.asp?docID=2914&intItemID=2068&lang=1.

[26] See Guzman, above n 17, at 644–51.

[27] This paradox has been noted and analyzed by several commentators. See *ibid* at fn 14 and associated text. As Guzman explains, the expropriation standard in BITs is more stringent than the Hull standard for several reasons. First, inasmuch as covered investments are often defined to include licenses and contractual obligations, BITs reach investor–State relationships that would not be subject to the Hull Rule. See *ibid* at 642, 655–58; cf Luke Eric Peterson, 'Tribunal rules in Jordan dispute; rejects extension of MFN to cover procedural issues', *INVEST-SD: Investment Law and Policy Weekly News Bulletin* (IISD, Winnipeg, Canada), 21 January 2005, available at http://www.iisd.org/pdf/2005/ investment_investsd_jan21_2005.pdf (citing an arbitral award in which an ICSID tribunal 'rejected the view that the Italy–Jordan BIT could be interpreted so as to elevate contractual

Several explanations of this paradox have been adduced.[28] Under what one commentator calls the 'LDC enlightenment theory',[29] developing countries have concluded that they will be able to attract more investment if they are able to bind themselves contractually not to expropriate without compensation.[30] A second theory posits that BITs are an attempt to clarify the status of investment protections under international law,[31] while a third supposes that developing countries obtain particularized benefits under BITs.[32] Finding none of these theories satisfactory, Guzman proposes that developing countries sign BITs because they 'face a prisoner's dilemma in which it is optimal for them, as a group, to reject the Hull Rule, but in which each individual LDC is better off "defecting" from the group by signing a BIT that gives it an advantage over other LDC in the competition to attract foreign investors.'[33]

undertakings to the plane of international law'). Second, most BITs apply to both direct and indirect expropriation, whereas the Hull rule covers only direct expropriation: see Guzman, above n 17, at 658. Finally, investor–State arbitration under BITs provides investors with a more effective enforcement mechanism, by virtue of its compulsory, neutral and binding nature, than does the Hull Rule: see *ibid* at 642, 657–58. Also relevant is the fact that, while the Hull Rule pertains only to expropriation, BITs contain further substantive protections of investment: see *ibid* at 658.

[28] See Guzman, above n 17, at 667–79 (surveying existing explanations of the behavior of developing countries).

[29] The acronym LDC refers to 'least developed countries'. See UNCTAD 2003, above n 6, at 33 (defining least developed countries as 'a special group of 49 economies').

[30] See Guzman, above n 17, at 667–68 (noting that this theory is unsatisfactory because 'the period in which BITs have been signed has overlapped considerably with the period in which [developing countries] sought to discredit the Hull Rule' and 'had developing countries decided, as a group, that providing greater protections for foreign investors served their interest, one would expect them to express that view at the [United Nations] General Assembly [as they had expressed opposition to the Hull Rule] ... [o]ne would also expect developing countries to have signed multilateral investment treaties rather than bilateral treaties').

[31] See *ibid* at 668 (noting that this theory is unsatisfactory because '[i]f the goal of BITs were to clarify existing rules, ... there is no reason for them to provide so much protection to investors' and 'it is difficult to understand why [developing countries] would undermine the Hull Rule ... only to adopt BITs to avoid the legal ambiguity generated by the demise of the Hull Rule').

[32] See *ibid* at 668–69 (noting that this theory is unsatisfactory because it 'is difficult to reconcile with the content of most bilateral treaties. There is little in such treaties that inures to the benefit of the host countries apart from the benefits that those countries enjoy from a regime of investor protection,' and the latter type of benefits were to be found also under the Hull Rule, which developing countries actively undermined).

[33] *Ibid* at 666–67. See also *ibid* at 669–80 (developing and expounding this hypothesis). An alternative to Guzman's explanation of the paradox is the possibility that developing countries opposed the Hull Rule when it was applied in the post-colonial context to investments that had been established under coercive conditions, but that the requirement of compensation for expropriation is more palatable to developing countries when applied to FDI that has been voluntarily sought by developing countries and established under less lopsided terms. One account of the circumstances leading to the passage in 1962 of UN General Assembly Resolution 1803, the Resolution on Permanent Sovereignty over Natural Resources, provides some support for the foregoing possibility, noting that Third World countries in the post-colonial era were subject to

In connection with the other factors mentioned above, Guzman's hypothesis goes some way to explaining the popularity of BITs among developing countries. Additionally, it should be noted that there is some indication that States are becoming more wary of the capacity of BITs to restrict sovereignty and are beginning to attempt to circumscribe some provisions.[34] This is a welcome trend that needs to go further. There is little evidence that BITs actually are effective in increasing FDI, suggesting that States are needlessly bearing the costs (in terms of diminished regulatory capacity) of such provisions while reaping little, if any, benefit.[35]

## 2. Relationship of Bilateral Investment Treaties to Public International Law

The relationship of BITs to public international law is unclear. For the purposes of this chapter, two unresolved questions have particular importance. The first is whether BITs merely codify public international law doctrines, or whether they provide stronger protections to investors than those found in international law. This may be referred to as the 'substantive' relationship of BITs to international law. The second question is, given a conflict between a provision in a BIT and a doctrine of customary law, which source takes precedence over the other. This might be called the question of 'priority'. The following addresses each of these questions in turn.

---

long-term concessions providing for the extraction of natural resources on terms extremely favorable to Western based transnational corporations. Although these agreements should have been highly suspect based on the circumstances under which they typically were negotiated, Third World governments were having little success with individual challenges—a series of which were made in arbitrations after World War II.

Therefore, Third World countries sought, through [Resolution 1803], to establish the right to expropriate foreign enterprises if they deemed it necessary to do so.... Rejecting the unspoken premise that foreign ownership was presumptively legitimate, and realizing that such a standard would preclude nationalizations in many poor nations, Third World leaders contended that the national tribunals of the host country, in accordance with national law, should determine compensation.

Ruth Gordon and Jon Sylvester, 'Deconstructing Development' (2004) 22 *Wisconsin International Law Journal* 1, 54–55.

[34] The 2004 US Model BIT, for example, implements changes to increase the transparency of arbitral proceedings, circumscribe the breadth of the expropriation standard, and eliminate the use of dual nationality by investors: see Luke Eric Peterson, 'US releases final draft of model investment treaty', *INVEST-SD: Investment Law and Policy Weekly News Bulletin* (IISD, Winnipeg, Canada)), 17 December 2004, available at http://www.iisd.org/pdf/2004/investment_investsd_dec17_2004.pdf. See also below nn 72, 392, 401, 402.

[35] See above n 4; UNCTAD 2003, above n 6, at 89–91 ('[w]hat has been the impact of BITs on FDI flows? An aggregate statistical analysis does not reveal a significant independent impact of BITs in determining FDI flows. At best, BITs play a minor role in influencing global FDI flows and explaining differences in their size among countries. Aggregate results do not

## A. The Substantive Relationship

As will be seen below in the discussions of particular provisions of BITs, the treaties in some respects appear to codify public international law. However, one view holds that there are so many BITs precisely because they derogate from otherwise prevailing standards of customary international law.[36] There is room for debate on the issue of whether BIT provisions

mean, however, that BITs cannot play a role in specific circumstances and for specific countries'). BITs, in and of themselves, cannot create a favorable investment climate:

> Why [the finding that BITs do not significantly impact FDI]? The policy framework is at best enabling, having by itself little or no effect on FDI flows. It has to be complemented by economic determinants that attract FDI, especially market size and growth, skills, abundant competitive resources and good infrastructure. As a rule, IIAs tend to make the regulatory framework more transparent, stable, predictable and secure—that is, they allow the economic determinants to assert themselves. And when IIAs reduce obstacles to FDI and the economic determinants are right, they can lead to more FDI. But it is difficult to identify the specific impact of the policy framework on FDI flows, given the interaction and relative importance of individual determinants.

*Ibid* at 91. See also *ibid* at 96–97, fn 13 ('[a] more recent test similar to UNCTAD's also found that "there was little independent role for BITs in accounting for the increase in FDI" by the end of the 1990s and that "countries that had concluded a BIT were no more likely to receive additional FDI than were countries without such a pact." But a study of determinants of FDI in CEE found that "bilateral investment treaties, the degree of enterprise reform and repatriation rules tended to stimulate FDI"') (internal citations omitted). Guzman's distributional assessment is another potential explanation of why BITs may not increase developing country welfare:

> BITs sharpen the competition for investment among potential hosts. This forces LDCs to offer greater and greater concessions to potential investors, bidding away the gains the host would otherwise enjoy. In effect, BITs make the market for foreign investment much more competitive by allowing competition in the "price" of investment, that is, the terms under which investment takes place.
>
> From the point of view of the welfare of developing countries as a group, the best of the three possible regimes is [the Charter of Economic Rights and Duties of States], followed by the Hull Rule (which only covers direct expropriation), followed by the BIT regime. The BIT regime is the least beneficial to LDCs because it includes the most expansive definition of investment and thereby allows greater competition among developing countries.
>
> ... without a mechanism to redistribute wealth between countries, the distributional consequences of a particular policy should be considered. The rise of BITs has reduced the market power held by developing countries, which, in turn, has reduced the benefit these countries can capture from any particular investment. For this reason, the BIT regime may actually reduce the overall welfare of developing countries

Guzman, above n 17, at 682–83. Guzman does argue, however, that 'from a global efficiency perspective, a regime that allows for contracting between host governments and investors is more efficient than a regime in which potential hosts cannot effectively commit to any particular behavior or agreement': *ibid* at 684. See also below n 391.

[36] See Paul Peters, 'Investment Risk and Trust: The Role of International Law', in Paul de Waart *et al*, *International Law and Development* (Dordrecht and Boston, Martinus Nijhoff, 1994), 131, at p 153. For other discussions of whether BITs constitute customary international law or *lex specialis*, see M Sornarajah, *The International Law on Foreign Investment* (Cambridge and New York, NY, Cambridge University Press, Grotius Publications, 1994), at pp 226–27, 253–54 and fn 69 (in particular, the expropriation clauses of BITs represent customary law

strengthen customary law standards or merely codify them. What is clear is that even those BIT provisions that facially reiterate customary international law have a greater impact, in practice, on State capacity to enforce human rights than do customary law doctrines, for several reasons.

First, the investor–State dispute resolution mechanism contained in most BITs makes the treaties more inhibiting of State regulatory action than is public international law because of the threat of large damages awards and consistent enforcement by private parties deeply invested in particular claims.[37] In the absence of a BIT, disputes would be resolved between the relevant States, either through a State-to-State procedure or through diplomatic channels. The political resolution of such disputes has less impact on State regulatory action than an investor–State procedure because rules are often bent in the interest of diplomatic expediency.[38]

In addition, investor–State arbitrations are skewed in favor of investors. Arbitrators often do not have the expertise necessary to give appropriate consideration to complex issues of public interest implicated by the regulations at issue.[39] The interpretation of BITs is likely to favor investors as well: '[s]ince most of the substantive provisions of the BIT

with regard to the conditions of public purpose and non-discrimination, but not with regard to the issue of compensation, which varies from treaty to treaty); Schrijver, above n 21, at 183–85; Paul E Comeaux and N Stephan Kinsella, *Protecting Foreign Investment Under International Law: Legal Aspects of Political Risk* (Dobbs Ferry, NY, Oceana Publications, 1996), at pp 74–76.

[37] Thomas Wälde points out some of arbitration's advantages for investors:

it provides an independent setting outside host state control for settling disputes ... In particular, it allows an investor to negotiate a particular contractual regime before the 'hostage effect' of fully committed investment with its reversal of bargaining power has taken place; it then protects such regime against legislative and administrative intervention. International investment arbitration has some benefit for the investor once a conflict has arisen and the investor/state relationship has broken down: It facilitates liquidation of the investment under the terms of an agreement and before an impartial tribunal. But much more importantly, it discourages host state agencies from interfering in the investment's contractual regime; the prospect of a drawn-out and costly arbitral procedure and of a negative arbitral award with its often considerable visibility and loss of face and reputation is one of the main reasons why government bureaucracies will often adhere to a previously negotiated contractual regime.

Thomas W Wälde, *Investment Arbitration Under the Energy Charter Treaty* (October 1998), at 6 (internal citations omitted), available at http://www.dundee.ac.uk/cepmlp/journal/html/Vol1/article1-10.pdf. See also Guzman, above n 17, at 642, 657–58 (investor–State arbitration under BITs provides investors with a more effective enforcement mechanism, by virtue of its compulsory, neutral and binding nature, than does customary international law); below n 54.

[38] Cf IISD 2004, above n 11, at 34 ('history shows that state-to-state mechanisms are more easily distorted [than investor-state mechanisms] by politics and influence, according better treatment to large players than to small and medium-sized enterprises, and ever subject to the political dynamics of the moment').

[39] See below n 203 and associated text.

concern the promotion and protection of foreign investment, it could be argued that any ambiguity should be interpreted in a way that would favor the rights granted to a foreign investor.'[40]

There is a danger that this slant in favor of investors could be transferred into general international law. Even if BITs exceed mere codification of customary international law, they may in turn function as a source of customary law by virtue of their prevalence and their repetition of standard clauses.[41]

## B. The Question of Priority

One way to conceive of the question of priority is to ask whether a customary law obligation would constitute an excuse for the violation of a BIT provision if a State were subject to conflicting obligations deriving from the two sources. While there is no hierarchy of sources of international law, 'if there is a clear conflict, treaties prevail over custom and custom prevails

---

[40] Rudolf Dolzer and Margrete Stevens, *Bilateral Investment Treaties* (The Hague and Boston, Martinus Nijhoff, 1995), at p 17.

[41] See Peters, above n 36, at p 153 (citing JHW Verzijl, 'General Subjects' (1969) 1 *International Law in Historical Perspective*)); Sornarajah, above n 36, at p 226 ('[i]t is possible that an accumulation of bilateral treaties which subscribe to the same standard of conduct could make that standard of conduct a principle of customary international law'). Even if some standards are divergent across BITs, it is 'possible that if there is concordance of standards in [BITs], such standards on which there is consistent agreement evidenced by such treaties could become international law': *ibid* at 226–27. But see Guzman, above n 17, at 685–86 ('"the repetition of common clauses in bilateral treaties does not create or support an inference that those clauses express customary law ... To sustain such a claim of custom one would have to show that apart from the treaty itself, the rules in the clauses are considered obligatory"') (citing Oscar Schachter, 'Compensation for Expropriation' (1984) 78 *American Journal of International Law* 121, at 126). Guzman argues that BITs are not representative of the *opinio juris* necessary to constitute international law because countries sign BITs out of economic motives, not a sense of legal obligation:

> If BITs are signed out of a sense of obligation or to clarify a legal obligation, they must be considered evidence of customary international law. On the other hand, if BITs are signed for reasons unrelated, or even contrary, to a country's sense of legal obligation, BITs are not evidence of customary international law...It is equally plausible that BITs represent a permissible derogation from the existing rules of customary law and that countries have pursued the treaties because it is in their economic interest to do so. This means that BITs offer no evidence concerning the rules of customary international law that govern compensation for appropriations.
>
> The absence of a sense of legal obligation is further demonstrated by the vigorous opposition of developing countries to the Hull Rule ... It is simply not possible to explain the paradoxical behavior of LDCs toward foreign investment based on a view that BITs reflect opinio juris.
>
> ... Developing countries have demonstrated that they do not feel an international legal obligation to provide full compensation for expropriation or to honor their contractual commitments to investors. On the other hand, they have, in pursuit of their economic self-interest, committed themselves to such behavior through BITs. BITs, therefore, do not reflect a sense of legal obligation but are rather the result of countries using the international tools at their disposal to pursue their economic interests.

Guzman, above n 17, at 686–87.

over general principles and the subsidiary sources.'[42] Treaties concluded later in time between the same parties will normally prevail over treaties granted later in time.[43] If BITs constitute *lex specialis*, they would be likely to prevail over human rights obligations derived from customary international law, but the resolution of a conflict between a BIT and human rights treaty might depend on which was concluded earlier and whether one or both were viewed as *lex specialis*.[44]

Even if BITs represent *lex specialis*, there are some potential justifications for asserting that human rights obligations could constitute an excuse for a State's violation of BIT provisions. First, human rights treaties concluded by the same parties subsequently to the conclusion of a BIT could potentially be viewed as altering the intent of the parties with respect to the BIT.[45] A second potential justification might be based on two conceptions of human rights treaties that Matthew Craven has identified as 'purposive' and 'cognitivist'.[46] These approaches are attempts to explain a characteristic of human rights treaties that has been identified by some international courts: namely that the obligations secured by human rights treaties are independent, to a certain

---

[42] Peter Malanczuk, *Akehurst's Modern Introduction to International Law*, 7th edn (London and New York, NY, Routledge, 1997), at p 57.

[43] Convention on the Law of Treaties (Vienna), Art 30, 23 May 1969, (1969) 8 ILM 679 (in force 27 January 1980).

[44] The relevant principles relating to the hierarchy of international legal sources have complicated interrelationships:

> Clearly a treaty, when it first comes into force, overrides customary law as between the parties to the treaty … But treaties can come to an end through desuetude … [which] often takes the form of the emergence of a new rule of customary law, conflicting with the treaty
>
> Thus, treaties and custom are of equal authority; the later in time prevails. This conforms to the general maxim of *lex posterior derogat priori* (a later law repeals an earlier law). However, in deciding possible conflicts between treaties and custom, two other principles must be observed, namely *lex posterior generalis non derogat priori speciali* (a later law, general in nature, does not repeal an earlier law which is more special in nature) and *lex specialis derogat legi generali* (a special law prevails over a general law).
>
> Since the main function of general principles of law is to fill gaps in treaty law and customary law, it would appear that general principles of law are subordinate to treaties and custom (that is, treaties and custom prevail over general principles of law in the event of conflict)…if there is a clear conflict, treaties prevail over custom and custom prevails over general principles.

Malanczuk, above n 42, at pp 56–57.

[45] Cf Bachand and Rousseau, above n 9, at 28 (discussing whether treaties external to the World Trade Organization (WTO) can be taken into account by the WTO's Dispute Settlement Body) (citing J Pauwelyn, 'The Role of Public International Law in the WTO: How Far Can We Go?' (2001) 95 *American Journal of International Law* 490).

[46] See Matthew Craven, 'Legal Differentiation and the Concept of the Human Rights Treaty in International Law' (2000) 11 *European Journal of International Law* 489, at 513–17 (identifying three possible approaches, 'formalist,' 'purposive' and 'cognitivist', to explain certain features of human rights treaties which differentiate them from treaties in other subject areas).

extent, of the bilateral reciprocal undertakings of States.[47] Under the 'purposive' conception,

> human rights treaties are properly understood to be concerned with the protec-
> tion of the legal interests of individuals or groups rather than those of states
> themselves. They embody (depending upon one's view) either a series of uni-
> lateral commitments on the part of participating states as regards individuals
> or groups falling within their jurisdiction, or a series of 'internationalized con-
> stitutional agreements' that seek to establish enforceable legal relations as
> between public authorities and the individuals in question. In either case, par-
> ticipating states may be seen to have certain procedural rights in order to effec-
> tuate, or protect, the object of that regime, but those rights are not directed
> towards the pursuit or protection of their own specific legal interests which are
> neither present nor relevant.[48]

The 'cognitivist' conception posits that 'human rights treaties [embody] certain "collective values" ... which both define and transcend individual states' legal interests.'[49] Either of these approaches could be used to support an argument that human rights obligations can justify the breach of a BIT provision because of the special character of human rights treaties. Under this view, human rights obligations, which exist independently of State interests, would supersede obligations contained in treaties that, based on a contractual model of reciprocal undertakings, instantiate only State interests.[50]

To the extent that the relationship of BITs to international law in general, and human rights norms in particular, is unclear, it would be of benefit to human rights enforcement and realization if the relationship were clarified through the inclusion in BITs of provisions requiring adherence by both parties to human rights obligations. This is discussed more fully in the conclusion to this chapter.

---

[47] See, eg, *ibid* at 510–13 (discussing *Austria v Italy* (1961) 4 *European Yearbook of Human Rights* (European Commission on Human Rights) 116).

[48] Craven, above n 46, at 514–15 (internal citations omitted).

[49] *Ibid* at 515.

[50] This argument might also find support in the statement by the International Court of Justice (ICJ) in the *Barcelona Traction* case that 'basic rights of the human person' are *erga omnes* obligations, perhaps suggesting that they also constitute *jus cogens* norms which cannot be abrogated by treaty. See Malanczuk, above n 42, at p 58 (noting that the ICJ considered some 'basic rights of the human person' as *erga omnes* obligations, 'without, however, expressly recognizing the concept of *ius cogens*') (emphasis in original) (citing *Barcelona Traction* case (*Belgium v Spain*), 1970 ICJ Rep 3, at paras 33–34). However, despite the dictum of the ICJ in the *Barcelona Traction* case, most human rights would likely not be considered *jus cogens* obligations. See Malanczuk, above n 42, at p 58 ('apart from the "basic rights of the human person" mentioned in the *Barcelona Traction* case, the only one which at present receives anything approaching general acceptance is the rule against aggression').

## 3. Intersection of Bilateral Investment Treaties with Human Rights

BITs may intersect with human rights enforcement and realization in several ways.[51] First, investors may use BIT provisions to challenge human rights-inspired regulations that affect their investment interest. This can impair the ability of States that host transnational corporations (TNCs) to impose human rights obligations on TNCs operating on their territory, a phenomenon which is the subject of Section II of this chapter. Second, investors may use BIT provisions to challenge host State policies aimed at progressive realization of human rights (such as affirmative action programs or policies designed to establish the social and economic conditions necessary to fulfill human rights obligations). Section III of this chapter will examine the ways in which BIT provisions can interfere with the progressive realization of human rights by host States. Finally, the host State and the foreign investor may be complicit in human rights violations related to a BIT dispute.[52]

In some situations in the third category, citizens will be entitled to seek relief either in local courts or, in some instances, ultimately through international or regional human rights mechanisms.[53] However, in each of these situations there is potential for a case to be tried consecutively in a human rights forum and an investment tribunal (or vice versa), or to be active in both forums simultaneously, putting the State in a situation of having conflicting obligations under international law: its human rights obligations on the one hand, whether derived from treaties or customary international law, and its BIT obligations on the other hand.[54] Section IV of this chapter, using the *Tecmed* arbitration as a case study, will examine the possibility that a State might aver to a human rights obligation as a defense to an investor claim in a BIT arbitration. The

[51] Cf IISD 2003, above n 4, at 16, 22–23; UNESC Report, above n 3, at para 31(a)–(d) (noting that investment treaties can impact on States' right and duty to regulate in four areas: the need to regulate some forms of investment, the flexibility to use some performance requirements and other measures, the flexibility to withdraw investment liberalization commitments in light of experience, and the flexibility to introduce new regulations to promote and protect human rights).

[52] See IISD 2003, above n 4, at 16–21.

[53] See *ibid* at 16–17; Craven, above n 46, at 511.

[54] Although the same conflict could arise between human rights obligations and property-related doctrines of customary international law, such as the expropriation doctrine, BITs have the potential to make the conflict much more acute by virtue of their investor–State arbitration provisions: see Steven R Ratner, *Corporations and Human Rights: A Theory of Legal Responsibility* (2001) 111 *Yale Law Journal* 443, at 459 ('Bilateral investment treaties are heavily skewed in favor of foreign investors. Beyond the substantive rights noted above, the BITs and NAFTA also provided investors a critical procedural right—to institute international arbitration without the consent of the host state to the individual arbitration and thereby bypass domestic courts entirely'); IISD 2004, above n 11, at 8 (the 'opaque ad hoc' dispute settlement mechanism is troubling because 'the disputes heard in such fora are dealing increasingly with matters of public policy—such as environmental regulation, protection of public health and safety, the provision of public services—in which the public at large clearly has a legitimate interest'); above n 37.

human rights implicated in the *Tecmed* dispute, as will be the case in most BIT arbitrations, were human rights which States are to realize progressively. It is clear that States must take steps to realize such rights; it is less clear at what speed these steps must be taken.[55] Due to their nature, it is unlikely that a defense based on such rights would prevail in any discrete investment arbitration. The analysis demonstrates, however, how such a defense might be constructed, and brings home the need for the investment treaty regime to be reformed to take better account of the human rights regime, which would ameliorate situations in which States face conflicting international legal obligations under the two regimes.

## II. LIMITATIONS ON HOST STATE CAPACITY TO IMPOSE HUMAN RIGHTS OBLIGATIONS ON TRANSNATIONAL CORPORATIONS

The provisions of bilateral investment treaties usually cover four substantive areas: admission, treatment, expropriation, and dispute settlement.[56] The admission provisions govern the conditions of entry of FDI into the host country.[57] In the areas of treatment and expropriation, modern BITs generally grant to investors a portfolio of 'rights' under the rubrics of 'national treatment' (stipulating that investors enjoy similar treatment to nationals of the host State), 'most-favored-nation treatment' (investors enjoy treatment similar to the best treatment accorded any third nation), 'absolute standards of treatment' (eg fair and equitable treatment; protection and security), 'capital transfer provisions guaranteeing transfer and repatriation of profits', and 'guarantees against expropriation or nationalization without compensation and due process.'[58] The dispute settlement clauses enable investors to challenge measures implemented by the host State in violation of the investor rights provisions.[59] BITs typically do not refer to international human rights obligations of the contracting parties, contain substantive clauses

---

[55] For example, Art 2(1) of the International Covenant on Economic and Social Rights (ICESCR) requires States 'to take steps, individually and through international assistance and co-operation, especially economic and technical, to the maximum of its available resources, with a view to achieving progressively the full realization of the rights recognized in the [ICESCR] by all appropriate means, including particularly the adoption of legislative measures': UN doc A/6316 (1966), 992 RTNU 2 (in effect 3 January 1976).

[56] See Dolzer and Stevens, above n 40, at p xii. For catalogues and analysis of standard BIT provisions, see generally *ibid*; Sornarajah, above n 36; United Nations Conference on Trade and Development, *Bilateral Investment Treaties in the Mid-1990s* (New York, NY, United Nations 1998) [hereinafter 'UNCTAD 1998']; UNCTAD 2003, above n 6; IISD 2004, above n 11. Cf US Department of State, Bureau of Economic and Business Affairs, *US Bilateral Investment Treaty Program* (15 September 2004), available at http://www.state.gov/e/eb/rls/fs/22422.htm (six core principles of US BITs).

[57] See, eg, Dolzer and Stevens, above n 40, at p 49.

[58] See IISD 2003, above n 4, at 8.

[59] See, eg, *ibid* at 9.

on human rights, nor condition investor rights upon investor duties to respect human rights.[60] Both parties to the agreement are, of course, bound by the investor rights provisions, but the effect of BITs is to 'impose restraints and obligations on the host State without including similar undertakings by the home State.'[61]

The following sections examine, on the basis of the decisions of arbitral tribunals, the effects on human rights enforcement of the provisions typically present in BITs. Before examining how tribunals have interpreted BIT provisions, it is necessary to point out that there are obstacles to determining whether fears of impingement on the capacity of host States to adopt regulations to protect and fulfill human rights have been, or are likely to be, borne out by arbitrations under BITs. First, the arbitration rules of several of the tribunals commonly incorporated in BITs do not require that arbitrations be made public.[62] Any disputes registered at the ICSID, a body incorporated in many BITs, are notified to the public on the ICSID docket,[63] but ICSID must keep the text of the awards private without the consent of both parties to publish.[64] Second, although arbitral tribunals 'will often take account of earlier awards, such that awards may be said to have some persuasive authority as precedents,' arbitral awards are technically binding only upon the parties to the arbitration.[65] Both of these circumstances hinder an attempt at comprehensive assessment of the status of legal doctrines under BITs and give rise to the potential for divergent rulings on similar facts.[66]

## 1. Expropriation and Stabilization Clauses

BITs generally reiterate the customary international law proposition that host States may expropriate foreign investments only if the taking is done for a public purpose and in accordance with the law (eg in a non-discriminatory fashion),[67] and only if the investor is compensated for the

---

[60] See *ibid* at 8–9 (noting, however, that '[s]ome South African BITs do contain *exceptions* which shelter certain forms of human rights-inspired legislation which might affect foreign investors. However, these provisions are very limited in scope—providing an exception only to one of more than a dozen investment treaty provisions').

[61] See Dolzer and Stevens, above n 40, at p 18.

[62] IISD 2003, above n 4, at 9–10.

[63] *Ibid.*

[64] See Luke Eric Peterson, *All the Roads Lead Out of Rome: Divergent Paths of Dispute Settlement in Bilateral Investment Treaties* (International Sustainable and Ethical Investment Rules Project, 2002), at pp 11–12; see also below n 194 and associated text.

[65] IISD 2003, above n 4, at 11. For more analysis of the dispute settlement provisions in BITs, see the discussion below, at section II.3.C.

[66] See below, at section II.3.C.3.

[67] See Sornarajah, above n 36, at p 253 ('[t]here is broad agreement that [under international law] the exercise of the right [of expropriation] should not be discriminatory and should have a basis in public purpose ... It is such customary law that is reiterated in [bilateral investment treaties]"). See also Dolzer and Stevens, above n 40, at p 97 ('[i]t is generally

expropriation.[68] Two classes of expropriation can be distinguished: 'direct' takings, which include expropriation, nationalization, confiscation, requisition or sequestration; and 'indirect' takings,[69] which comprise 'creeping' expropriations[70] and 'regulatory' takings.[71] Most BITs proscribe indirect as

accepted in international law that host States may expropriate foreign investments provided certain conditions are met, namely that the taking of the investments is done for a public purpose, in accordance with the law and against compensation').

[68] See Dolzer and Stevens, above n 40, at p 97 ('[i]t is generally accepted in international law that host States may expropriate foreign investments provided certain conditions are met, namely that the taking of the investments is done for a public purpose, in accordance with the law and against compensation'); Restatement (Third) of the Foreign Relations Law of the United States § 712 (1986) (a 'state is responsible under international law for injury resulting from: (1) a taking by the state of the property of a national of another state that (a) is not for a public purpose, or (b) is discriminatory, or (c) is not accompanied by provision for just compensation'). Cf Sornarajah, above n 36, at p 254 and fn 69 (due to variations in language among BITs, BITs do not create or reflect customary law on the issue of the compensation requirement for expropriation).

The expropriation clauses of BITs generally use terminology referring to 'expropriation' and 'nationalization', although additional terms used almost interchangeably to include both expropriation and nationalization (which itself includes 'indigenization', the transfer of property to nationals of the host state) are 'dispossession,' 'taking,' 'deprivation' or 'privation'. See Dolzer and Stevens, above n 40, at p 98. Dolzer and Stevens note that 'BITs generally do not define the term expropriation or any of the other terms denoting similar measures of forced dispossession. Furthermore, BIT practice shows that although the above terms may be used either alone or in combination, most often no distinctions have been attempted between the general concept of dispossession and the specific forms thereof. In fact most treaties do not even differentiate between expropriation and nationalization although it is generally recognized in legal doctrine that there are substantial differences between these two concepts': *ibid* at pp 97–98 (internal citations omitted); see also UNCTAD 1998, above n 56, at 65–73 (BIT expropriation clauses and doctrine); Sornarajah, above n 36, at pp 315–21 (illegal takings under international law); IISD 2004, above n 11, at 12–15 (expropriation under IIAs); UNCTAD 2003, above n 6, at 110–14 (nationalization and expropriation under IIAs).

[69] See Dolzer and Stevens, above n 40, at p 99, fn 268 (defining indirect takings).

[70] Creeping expropriations have been defined as 'an incremental but cumulative encroachment on one or more of the range of recognized ownership rights until the measures involved lead to the effective negation of the owner's interest in the property': UNCTAD 2003, above n 6, at 110–11.

[71] Regulatory takings have been defined as acts 'in which the exercise of governmental regulatory power ... diminishes the economic value of the owners' property without depriving them of formal ownership': *ibid* at 110–11. According to the Restatement (Third) of the Foreign Relations Law of the United States, 'a state is responsible for an expropriation of property "when it subjects alien property to taxation, regulation, or other action that is confiscatory, or that prevents, unreasonably interferes with, or unduly delays, effective enjoyment of an alien's property or its removal from the state's territory"': Allen S Weiner, 'Indirect Expropriations: The Need for a Taxonomy of "Legitimate" Regulatory Purposes' (2003) 5 *International Law Forum du Droit International* 166, at 167 (citing Restatement (Third) of the Foreign Relations Law of the United States § 712 cmt.g (1986)). The Iran–US Claims Tribunal stated that 'it is recognized in international law that measures taken by a State can interfere with property rights to such an extent that these rights are rendered so useless that they must be deemed to have been expropriated, even though the State does not purport to have expropriated them and the legal title to the property remains with the original owner': see Veijo Heiskanen, 'The Contribution of the Iran-United States Claims Tribunal to the Development of the Doctrine of Indirect Expropriation' (2003) *International Law Forum du Droit International* 176, at 181 (citing *Starrett Housing Corp v Government of the Islamic Republic of Iran* (1983) 4 Iran–US CTR 122, at 154).

well as direct uncompensated expropriations,[72] although some BITs qualify the indirect taking with 'a carve-out for normal regulatory powers.'[73]

These provisions can prevent host States from enforcing human rights norms against TNCs operating on their territory by making it too expensive, as a result of the compensation requirement, to regulate TNCs in the areas of environment, land use, public health and safety, and workers' rights.[74] The potential for expropriation clauses to impinge on State regulatory capacity became widely recognized as a result of arbitrations under

[72] BITs describe indirect takings variously as 'indirect', 'creeping', or 'de facto' expropriations: see Dolzer and Stevens, above n 40, at p 99, or prohibit measures 'tantamount to' or 'having an effect equivalent to' expropriation: see IISD 2003, above n 4, at 12.

The most recent US model BIT clarifies that the character of the government action, not simply its economic impact, is to be taken into account in determining whether the action constitutes an indirect expropriation: see Treaty between the Government of the United States of America and the Government of [Country] Concerning the Encouragement and Reciprocal Protection of Investment, at Annex B, para 4(a) (2004), available at http://www.state.gov/document/organization/38710.pdf. The US model BIT also provides that '[e]xcept in rare circumstances, nondiscriminatory regulatory actions by a Party that are designed and applied to protect legitimate public welfare objectives, such as public health, safety, and the environment, do not constitute indirect expropriations': *ibid* at Annex B, para 4(b). See also IISD 2004, above n 11, at 224, box VI.3 (describing three main approaches to BIT structure, including the 'Western Hemisphere approach' followed by the United States and Canada); below n 96 (according to one tribunal, public purpose does not mitigate compensation owed for direct expropriation); below nn 401–4 and associated text.

[73] UNCTAD 2003, above n 6, at 112. Some BITs also expressly require observance of due process: see *ibid*.

[74] See *ibid* at 112 (using environment as an example, noting that '[i]f regulatory takings give rise to compensation, ... a duty to compensate might inhibit a host country from enforcing its laws or from complying with international environmental agreements'); UNESC Report, above n 3, at para 31(c) ('[a] human rights approach would seek to avoid the situation where a requirement to pay compensations might discourage States from taking action to protect human rights—such a situation could reinforce the status quo or exacerbate human rights problems').

NGOs have pointed out that expropriation provisions have the potential to preclude '[b]ans on the production or sale of dangerous products[,] [l]aws designed to conserve valuable resources or land; and [r]equirements that recycled content be used, when possible, in the production process': Michelle Sforza *et al*, Center for Economic and Policy Research, *Writing the Constitution of a Single Global Economy: A Concise Guide to the Multilateral Agreement on Investment—Supporters' and Opponents' Views*, available at http://www.cepr.net/globalization/MAI/maioverv.html (last visited 15 September 2004) (commenting on the expropriation provision in the proposed and abandoned Multilateral Agreement on Investment (MAI)). Similarly, expropriation provisions might preclude 'health and safety regulations designed to protect workers': Robert Naiman and Neil Watkins, Center for Economic and Policy Research, *The Proposed MAI: Harmful to Workers*, available at http://www.cepr.net/globalization/MAI/mlabor3.html (last visited 9 September 2004) (commenting on the expropriation provision in the proposed and abandoned Multilateral Agreement on Investment (MAI)). Developing countries would be most affected by the compensation requirement, as Philippe Sands has noted in the environmental context: 'onerous levels of compensation awarded to investors could preclude poorer states from "taking effective measures to give effect to their international obligations ... since they will often not be in a position to finance an interference"': IISD 2003, above n 4, at 31 (citing Philippe Sands, '"Arbitrating Environmental Disputes", Draft Remarks on the occasion of the annual ICSID/ICC/AAA Colloquium' (10 November 2000, Washington, DC)).

the investor protection provisions of NAFTA,[75] which are substantially similar to the provisions in BITs.[76] In one notorious dispute, Ethyl Corp sued the government of Canada in 1996 for expropriation, claiming $250 million in damages, after Canada banned, for public health reasons, a gasoline additive produced by Ethyl. Canada settled the case, agreeing to pay $13 million in compensation to Ethyl and to repeal the ban.[77]

The unresolved issue of which State actions constitute indirect expropriation has particularly threatening implications for the human rights regulatory capacity of host States.[78] The UN High Commissioner for Human Rights has noted that '[t]o the extent that broad interpretations of expropriation provisions could affect States' willingness or capacity to introduce new measures to promote and protect human rights, then the use and interpretation of expropriation provisions is a cause of concern.'[79]

Many of the known arbitrations under BITs, MITs, and free trade agreements such as NAFTA concern environmental and land use regulations. The environment is relevant to consideration of a host State's capacity to impose human rights obligations on TNCs in two ways. First, there is a relationship between environment and human rights, inasmuch as impairment of environment can impair the human right to health: see below, at section IV.2.D.1, for a discussion of the human right to health; see also UNESC Report, above n 3, at para 35 ('government action in relation to chemicals and toxic wastes has flow-on effects in relation to the enjoyment of human rights such as the right to health or the right to water'). Second, environment-related arbitrations are relevant as an illustration of the limitations BITs may impose on host State capacity to regulate in the public interest, whether in any given case the particular interest be environment or human rights.

[75] See IISD 2003, above n 4, at 12. With regard to regulatory takings in the international context in general and the NAFTA context in particular, one commentator has rejected three traditional justifications for requiring compensation for expropriations by government: see Vicki Been, 'Does an International "Regulatory Takings" Doctrine Make Sense?' (2002) 11 *New York Environmental Law Journal* 49.

[76] See, eg, Dolzer and Stevens, above n 40, at p xiii ('the NAFTA Investment Chapter provisions cover much the same ground as BITs').

[77] See IISD 2003, above n 4, at 12–13. The case 'seemed to herald the possibility that a key tenet of the environmental movement, the "polluter pays principle", would be subverted into a "pay the polluter principle"': *ibid* (citing Howard Mann and Konrad von Moltke, International Institute for Sustainable Development, *NAFTA's Chapter 11 and the Environment: Addressing the Impacts of the Investor-State Process on the Environment* (1999), available at http://www.iisd.org/trade). The legal documents pertaining to the dispute are available at http://www.naftaclaims.com/disputes_canada/disputes_canada_ethyl.htm.

For summaries of other NAFTA arbitrations involving claims of regulatory expropriation, see 'Introduction to Regulatory Expropriations in International Law and Case Summaries' (2002) 11 *New York Environmental Law Journal* 1 (excerpting Vicki Been, 'NAFTA's Investment Protections and the Division of Authority for Land Use and Environmental Controls' (September 2002) 32 *Environmental Law Reporter (Environmental Law Institute)* 11001).

[78] See IISD 2003, above n 4, at 12–13; see also UNCTAD 2003, above n 6, at 111 ('[t]he major difficulty ... is how to identify the point at which a process of governmental action changes to an incremental deprivation of an owner's rights, such that the deprivation becomes the subject of a duty to compensate. If that definition is drawn too widely it will catch entirely legitimate regulatory and administrative action').

[79] UNESC Report, above n 3, at para 35.

## A. The Question of Indirect Expropriation

Although customary international law recognizes indirect expropriation,[80] it also exempts from the compensation requirement State acts that are 'commonly accepted as within the police power of states,' at least as expressed in the Restatement (Third) of the Foreign Relations Law of the United States.[81] Thus, customary international law purports not to require States to compensate foreign investors for that great portion 'of the activity of the modern state [which] entails regulating social and economic activity in ways that interfere substantially with the enjoyment of property rights.'[82]

The indirect expropriation jurisprudence of international tribunals has produced two doctrines of indirect expropriation, which have been called the 'sole effect' doctrine and the 'police powers' doctrine,[83] and the former departs from the doctrine as expressed in the Restatement.[84] Under the 'sole effect' doctrine, favorable to foreign investors, 'the crucial factor in determining whether an indirect expropriation has occurred is solely the effect of the governmental measure on the property owner; the purpose of the governmental measure is irrelevant in making that

---

[80] See Weiner, above n 71, at 167 (citing Restatement (Third) of the Foreign Relations Law of the United States § 712 cmt.g (1986)); Heiskanen, above n 71, at 181 (citing *Starrett Housing Corp v Government of the Islamic Republic of Iran* (1983) 4 Iran–US CTR 122, at 154).

[81] See Weiner, above n 71, at 168 ('as a corollary to the rules prohibiting "unreasonable interference" with an owner's enjoyment of her property, international law also recognizes that a state need not compensate foreign property owners for interference with property interests that results from "bona fide general taxation, regulation, forfeiture for crime, or other action of the kind that is commonly accepted as within the police power of states"') (citing Restatement (Third) of the Foreign Relations Law of the United States § 712 cmt.g (1986)).

[82] Weiner, above n 71, at 167–68. Examples of such regulation include: land use regulations; building, fire and housing codes; income taxes; occupational health and safety standards; minimum wage requirements; and environmental regulations, to name a few examples: see *ibid* at 168 (listing examples of types of regulation grounded in the police power); see also IISD 2003, above n 4, at p 12 ('[i]nternational law has long recognized that a certain category of regulations—what some have categorized as exercises of "police powers"—related to environment, public safety or correcting market imperfections, for example, would not need to be compensable').

[83] Maurizio Brunetti, 'Introduction' (2003) 5 *International Law Forum du Droit International* 150, at 151.

[84] Informing these doctrines is a policy debate about who should bear the costs of government regulation, the foreign investor or the public: see *ibid* at 150–51:

> Some argue that the state—and, ultimately, the taxpayer—should not be required to act as the insurer of last resort of the value of foreign investments affected by governmental regulations pursuing a legitimate public purpose; the effects of regulations on the value of foreign property represent the materialization of a political risk, the consequences of which the foreign investor must bear. Others argue, in contrast, that it is not for the foreign investor to bear, in each and every case, the financial brunt of governmental regulation aimed at some public welfare purpose; if the effect of a regulation on an investment is that of an expropriation, the state must compensate the foreign property owner.

determination.'[85] On the other hand, the 'police powers' doctrine does not restrict the analysis to the effects on the investor, but 'consider[s] the wider context ... taking into account the governmental interest involved.'[86] Currently, 'it does not seem possible to characterize either of the two approaches as dominant or as representing the mainstream of international thinking.'[87]

Some recent awards under BITs, however, indicate that the governmental purpose of regulation may not be accorded much weight in expropriation analysis by BIT tribunals. As mentioned above, in *Tecmed*, an ICSID arbitral tribunal found that the failure of a Mexican agency to renew an operating permit for a landfill constituted an expropriation in violation of the BIT between Spain and Mexico.[88] The tribunal ordered Mexico to pay US $5.5 million in compensation for the lost value of the investment.[89] The Mexican government argued that the failure to renew the permit was based in part on its police powers with respect to environmental and health concerns.[90] The tribunal, aligning itself with the 'sole effect' doctrine, held that the action was expropriatory because '[t]he government's intention is less important than the effects of the measures on the owner

---

[85] Rudolf Dolzer and Felix Bloch, 'Indirect Expropriation: Conceptual Realignments?' (2003) 5 *International Law Forum du Droit International* 155, at 158; see also Brunetti, above n 83, at 151; Weiner, above n 71, at 169–70. To this line of jurisprudence, Dolzer and Bloch assign the following cases: *Tippetts, Abett, McCarthy, Stratton v TAMS-AFFA et al* (1984) 6 Iran–US CTR 219; *Biloune v Ghana Investment Centre* (1989) 95 ILR 183; and *Metalclad Corp v United Mexican States* (2000) 119 ILR 615, at 638: see Dolzer and Bloch, above, at pp 161–63.

[86] Dolzer and Bloch, above n 85, at p 158. See also Brunetti, above n 83, at 151; Weiner, above n 71, at 170–71. To this line of jurisprudence, Dolzer and Bloch assign the following cases: *Oscar Chinn Case* (1934) PCIJ Series A/B., No 63, at 65; *Sea-Land Service, Inc v Iran* (1984) 6 Iran–US CTR 149; and *SD Myers Inc v Canada, Partial Award* (2000) 121 ILR 72. See Dolzer and Bloch, above n 85, at pp 159–61.

[87] Dolzer and Bloch, above n 85, at p 163. Nevertheless, there are varying assessments as to which of the doctrines currently has primacy in international law, with some commentators reading recent jurisprudence as favoring an effects doctrine and others of the opinion that the law will continue to give weight to public purposes when evaluating the compensability of indirect expropriations. Compare *ibid* ('it is perhaps fair to say that the more recent jurisprudence of arbitral tribunals seems to reveal a tendency of shifting the focus of the analysis away from the context and the purpose to the effects on the owner') with Weiner, above n 71, at 170 (the line of jurisprudence that 'appears to be gaining predominance today ... emphasizes the sovereign regulatory power of states').

This uncertainty is itself bad news for human rights enforcement: '[c]onfusion as to the boundaries of acceptable government regulation in this realm prevails at a worrying time, as there is clear evidence that investors have awakened to the existence of the full constellation of international investment treaties and are challenging host state laws in record numbers': IISD 2003, above n 4, at 13.

[88] See *Técnicas Medioambientales Tecmed SA v United Mexican States* (ICSID Case No ARB(AF)/00/2) (2003), at para 151, available at http://www.worldbank.org/icsid/cases/laudo051903FINAL.pdf (Spanish original version); http://www.worldbank.org/icsid/cases/laudo-051903%20-English.pdf (unofficial English translation).

[89] See *ibid* at para 197.

[90] See *ibid* at para 125.

of the assets or on the benefits arising from such assets affected by the measures.'[91] Likewise, in *Goetz v Republic of Burundi*,[92] decided in 1999 under the Belgium–Burundi BIT,

> the tribunal found that the revocation of a free trade zone (FTZ) license, which granted certain incentives and exceptions to a mineral mining enterprise, constituted an indirect expropriation. Essential to this holding was the fact that 'the revocation of their FTZ license forced [the complainants] to stop all activity ... thereby making their investment completely useless and depriving them of the benefits they could expect therefrom.' Thus, the measure, in the tribunal's opinion, had a 'similar effect' to expropriation.[93]

The tribunal found an expropriation despite the fact that the change in regulation had been undertaken in response to 'imperatives of public need ... or of national interest.'[94] The general development of expropriation doctrine in international law in the decisions of tribunals arbitrating both BIT disputes and non-BIT disputes (including NAFTA and Iran-United States Claims Tribunal awards)[95] reinforces the view that State capacity to impose

[91] See *ibid* at para 116. After examining the impact of the measure, the tribunal did assess whether the impact was proportional to the measure's stated aims: see below, section IV.2.B.2; IISD 2004, above n 11, at 15.

[92] *Antoine Goetz and others v Republic of Burundi* (ICSID Case No ARB/95/3) (1999), (2000) 15 ICSID Rev—FILJ 457 (award embodying the parties' settlement agreement of 10 February 1999) (French original), available at http://www.worldbank.org/icsid/cases/goetz.pdf; (2004) 6 ICSID Rep 5 (English version).

[93] Stuart G Gross, Note, 'Inordinate Chill: BITs, Non-NAFTA MITs, and Host-State Regulatory Freedom—An Indonesian Case Study', 24 *Michigan Journal Internationl Law* 893, at 948 (internal citations omitted).

However, in one recent case the tribunal held that 'an investor does not have a right [under the expropriation doctrine] to a modification of the laws of the host country': *MTD Equity Sdn Bhd and MTD Chile SA v Republic of Chile* (ICSID Case No ARB/01/7) (2004), at para 124, available at http://ita.law.uvic.ca/documents/MTD-Award.pdf. Chile authorized MTD to proceed with a development project, the authorization apparently contradicting Chile's own development policy; subsequently MTD was unable to secure a necessary permit: see *ibid* at paras 53, 57, 72, 80. The investor prevailed on its fair and equitable treatment claim, see *ibid* at para 166, but not its expropriation claim, see *ibid* at para 214. The court held that since the permit could not be issued under the relevant regulation, the investor had requested not just a permit, 'but a change in a regulation. It was the policy of the Respondent and its right not to change it. For the same reason, it was unfair to admit the investment in the country in the first place': *ibid* at para 214.

A similar result was reached in *Maffezini v Spain*: 'the investor's right to proceed with the development in question was always subject to the requirement of an [environmental impact assessment] and ... no rights of his were infringed when the government required him to conduct one': Gross, above, at 943–44 (discussing *Emilio Agustín Maffezini v Kingdom of Spain* (ICSID Case No ARB/97/7) (2000), (2002) 27 YB Com Arb 13, available at http://www.worldbank.org/icsid/cases/emilio_AwardoftheTribunal.pdf).

[94] See *Goetz* (ICSID Case No ARB/95/3) (1999), at para 126.

[95] See Heiskanen, above n 71, at 184–85 (although it has recognized the validity of the 'police powers' doctrine, the Iran–US Claims Tribunal has emphasized an effects-based analysis and effectively adopted the 'sole effects' doctrine in claims arising out of the Islamic Revolution).

human rights obligations on TNCs is undermined by expropriation clauses in BITs.[96]

## B. Stabilization and Economic Equilibrium Clauses

Stabilization clauses, also known as economic equilibrium clauses, are found in some BITs.[97] They 'generally aim at protecting the private parties to a contract from application of legislation or administrative measures subsequent to the conclusion of the contract.'[98] Stabilization clauses may have an effect similar to expropriation clauses. While

> [e]arlier models [of the clause] sought to incorporate and freeze the host coun-try's municipal law into the contract, ... current practice prefers to transfer the increased financial burden associated [with] more stringent standards [result-ing from a change in law] from the investor to the government, ie right to com-pensation. Economic stabilization clauses ... thus stand in direct confrontation with the sovereignty of the government to regulate for the public interest.[99]

In several international arbitrations (although not under BITs), the exis-tence of stabilization clauses contributed to the tribunal's decision that the expropriations at issue were illegal and deserving of compensation.[100] Stabilization clauses may protect investors, and thus hinder States from imposing human rights obligations, where a regulatory act would not otherwise constitute an illegal expropriation triggering compensation.[101]

---

[96] Further, one arbitral tribunal rejected the contention that, in the case of a direct expropri-ation motivated by a public purpose, public purpose should mitigate the amount of compen-sation owed: see IISD 2003, above n 4, at 30–31 (noting Philippe Sands's criticism of one ICSID case (not decided under a BIT) in which tribunal refused to take the environmental purpose of an expropriation into account in calculating damages) (citing *Compañia del Desarrollo de Santa Elena SA v Republic of Costa Rica* (2000) 39 ILM 317); see also UNCTAD 2003, above n 6, at 114. The requirement of compensation for direct expropriation may impact the ability of States progressively to realize their human rights obligations. See below, at section III.3.

[97] See United Nations Centre on Transnational Corporations, *Bilateral Investment Treaties* (New York, NY, United Nations, 1988), para 171. For more on stabilization clauses, see Sornarajah, above n 36, at pp 327–28; UNCTAD 1998, above n 56, at 87 and fn 130.

[98] Center for International Environmental Law, 'Comments to the IFC [International Financial Corporation]: Baku-Tblisi-Ceyhan Pipeline Project', [hereinafter 'CIEL Comments'] at 6, available at http://www.ciel.org/Publications/BTC_Comments_10Oct03.pdf (last visited 20 September 2004). See also Sornarajah, above n 36, at pp 328–32.

[99] CIEL Comments, above n 98, at 6. CIEL notes also that '[t]he focus of earlier stabiliza-tion clauses was to prevent nationalization or expropriatory effects of changing tax regimes': *ibid* at 6, fn 7.

[100] See Paul E Comeaux and N Stephan Kinsella, 'Reducing Political Risk in Developing Countries: Bilateral Investment Treaties, Stabilization Clauses, and MIGA and OPIC Investment Insurance' (1994) 15 *New York Law School Journal of International and Comparative Law* 1, at 26–27.

[101] See *ibid* at 30–31; see also UNESC Report, above n 3, at para 31(c) ('[a] human rights approach would seek to avoid the situation where a requirement to pay compensations might discourage States from taking action to protect human rights—such a situation could reinforce the status quo or exacerbate human rights problems').

## C. Regulatory Chill

The phenomenon in which States 'forego needed environmental and social legislation that might negatively affect the value of foreign investment, rather than risk potential liability,' is known as 'regulatory chill'.[102] Given the uncertainty about the status of indirect expropriation claims under BITs,[103] as well as uncertainty in the legal doctrines concerning the other BIT provisions examined below, alone the threat that a regulation could be challenged by a foreign investor may discourage States from attempting to enforce human rights obligations against TNCs operating on their territory.[104] The threat of a suit can be

---

[102] Gross, above n 93, at 899 and fn 36. See also UNCTAD 2003, above n 6, at 111 ('an expansive interpretation of "regulatory takings" can limit the national policy space by hindering a government's right to regulate, creating the risk of "regulatory chill", with governments unwilling to undertake legitimate regulation for fear of lawsuits from investors').

[103] See Dolzer and Bloch, above n 85, at p 155, fn 2 ('[i]t is widely assumed, both in the business and legal community, that the international takings doctrine is in disarray, that the jurisprudence is inconsistent and that results are rarely predictable').

[104] As expressed by two commentators, referring to the NAFTA Chapter 11 jurisprudence, '[t]he fear of being sued by a foreign investor may well have a chilling effect on states when they consider enacting legislation to respect, protect, promote or fulfill obligations relating to human rights': Bachand and Rousseau, above n 9, at 21. Another commentator notes that developing countries are most vulnerable to regulatory chill because investor claims of indirect expropriation and unfair treatment are based on violated investor expectations, and investor expectations of regulatory freedom are often high and thus easily violated in cases involving developing countries with weak regulatory regimes—precisely the countries that need to improve regulatory enforcement of human rights: see Gross, above n 93, at 899, fn 36. Thomas Wälde, from a somewhat different vantage point, expounds on the ways in which the threat of being subjected to international arbitration can impede State regulatory action:

the prospect of international arbitration can often quite effectively discourage host states against using sovereign powers for abrogating legal and contractual rights granted to an investor. In particular, it allows an investor to negotiate a particular contractual regime before the 'hostage effect' of fully committed investment with its reversal of bargaining power has taken place; it then protects such regime against legislative and administrative intervention. International investment arbitration has some benefit for the investor once a conflict has arisen and the investor/state relationship has broken down: It facilitates liquidation of the investment under the terms of an agreement and before an impartial tribunal. But much more importantly, it discourages host state agencies from interfering in the investment's contractual regime; the prospect of a drawn-out and costly arbitral procedure and of a negative arbitral award with its often considerable visibility and loss of face and reputation is one of the main reasons why government bureaucracies will often adhere to a previously negotiated contractual regime, a regime which they might otherwise easily repudiate relying on the government's sovereign and administrative prerogatives. This is even more acute in transition societies where in the continuing tradition of socialism and command economy culture state powers tend to prevail over contractual and proprietary rights. Bargaining with a government agency is much more comfortable for a foreign investor if it is 'in the shadow' of prospective international arbitration. It is hard to see what other leverage (except perhaps international financial institution pressure) is available to defend investors' rights against the predominant attitude of bureaucratic supremacy.

Wälde, above n 37, at 6–7 (internal citations omitted).

an 'effective pressure tactic for investors when a state's actions put their interests in jeopardy.'[105]

An example of regulatory chill in a BIT context played out recently in Indonesia.[106] After the Indonesian government banned open-pit mining in protected forests in 1999, a measure that would affect about 150 mining companies with operations and/or undeveloped mining exploration contracts in protected forests, a group of 'mainly foreign-owned mining companies ... threatened [in 2002] to launch international arbitration against the government of Indonesia,'[107] implying that they would allege indirect expropriation and a violation of fair and equitable treatment guarantees.[108] Two BITs and one multilateral investment treaty (MIT) would probably have been applicable.[109] Apparently in response to this threat, the Indonesian government retreated from the ban, first exempting several of the companies from the ban and promising to assess the situation of other affected companies, and then finally repealing the ban several months later.[110] Prior to the repeal, the Indonesian Environmental Minister stated, '[t]here were investment activities before the Forestry Act was effective. If shut down, investors demand compensation and Indonesia cannot pay [sic].'[111]

Similarly, the rejection by Canada's province of New Brunswick in June 2004 of a public scheme of automobile insurance also exhibits the characteristics of regulatory chill.[112] During consideration of the plan by the New Brunswick government, insurance industry officials threatened to sue under investment agreements signed by Canada, which include NAFTA's Chapter 11 and BITs with Eastern European countries, if a public insurance

---

[105] Bachand and Rousseau, above n 9, at 21. See also UNESC Report, above n 3, at para 35 (in ensuring human rights protection in the context of investment liberalization, 'it will be important to avoid a situation where the threat of litigation on the basis of broadly interpreted expropriation provisions has a "chilling effect" on government regulatory capacity, conditioning State action to promote human rights and a healthy environment by the commercial concerns of foreign investors'); IISD 2003, above n 4, at 23–24 and fn 72 ('BITs may be useful levers for foreign investors to invoke in the context of informal discussion with governments ...[in the NAFTA context], threats of investment treaty arbitration are known to have "chilled" government plans for public health inspired regulations').

[106] See generally Gross, above n 93.

[107] See *ibid* at 894.

[108] See *ibid* at 897.

[109] See *ibid* at 897–98 (reaching this conclusion on the basis of the 'nationalities' of the investors who were affected by the ban).

[110] See *ibid* at 894–95.

[111] See *ibid* at 895.

[112] See generally Luke Eric Peterson, 'Canadian Province Rejects Public Auto Insurance; Think-Tank Sees Treaty Chill', *INVEST-SD: Investment Law and Policy Weekly News Bulletin* (International Institute for Sustainable Development, Winnipeg, Canada), 2 July 2004, available at http://www.iisd.org/pdf/2004/investment_investsd_july2_2004.pdf; Luke Eric Peterson, 'International Treaty Implications Color Canadian Province's Debate over Public Auto Insurance', *INVEST-SD: Investment Law and Policy Weekly News Bulletin* (International Institute for Sustainable Development, Winnipeg, Canada), 11 May 2004, at http://www.iisd.org/pdf/2004/investment_investsd_may11_2004.pdf.

system were introduced.[113] Although it cannot be proven that the government failed to approve the plan as a result of the threats, it was reported that the government was advised that the implementation of the public scheme could constitute 'an expropriation of the market share of existing (foreign-owned) private players in the [New Brunswick] market.'[114]

## 2. Treatment

In the context of BITs, treatment 'refers to the legal regime that applies to investments once they have been admitted by the host State.'[115] While international law requires only 'a minimum of fairness in the treatment of foreigners and foreign investment,'[116] most BITs expressly incorporate the following standards, all of which are relevant to a State's human rights regulatory capacity: fair and equitable treatment; full protection and security; non-discrimination; and national and most-favored-nation treatment.

### A. Fair and Equitable Treatment

Most BITs guarantee that, for example, 'Each Contracting Party shall in its territory accord to investments made by investors of the other Contracting Party fair and equitable treatment.'[117] Because of the vagueness of the guarantee of 'fair and equitable treatment', and the fact that it may reach State action not rising to the level of indirect expropriation, it provides an attractive catch-all cause of action for investors.[118] Although it is a subject of debate whether the standard calls for something more than international law's minimum standard,[119] which is only violated by 'egregious' State conduct,[120] one commentator has concluded that the BIT standard does no more than 'guarantee investors basic rights of due

---

[113] See Luke Eric Peterson, 'Canadian Province Rejects Public Auto Insurance; Think-Tank Sees Treaty Chill', above n 112; Luke Eric Peterson, 'International Treaty Implications Color Canadian Province's Debate over Public Auto Insurance', above n 112.

[114] See Luke Eric Peterson, 'Canadian Province Rejects Public Auto Insurance; Think-Tank Sees Treaty Chill', above n 112.

[115] Dolzer and Stevens, above n 40, at p 58.

[116] *Ibid* at p 58.

[117] Agreement between the Government of the Republic of Cuba and the Government of the Kingdom of Denmark concerning the Promotion and Reciprocal Protection of Investments, 19 February 2001 [hereinafter Denmark–Cuba BIT], Art 4, available at http://www.unctad.org/sections/dite/iia/docs/bits/cuba_denmark.pdf. See generally Dolzer and Stevens, above n 40, at pp 58–60; UNCTAD 1998, above n 56, at 53–55; IISD 2004, above n 11, at 11–12; Sornarajah, above n 36, at pp 250–52.

[118] See Gross, above n 93, at 934.

[119] Ie whether it is intended to extend or merely to codify customary international law: see *ibid* at 935–36.

[120] See *ibid* at 936–37 (citing *Neer Claim* (1926) 4 RIAA 60 (US–Mex Gen Claims Comm'n, 1926)).

process, both administratively and judicially, which are rarely implicated when a State acts within its statutory authority.'[121]

The standard applied in some BIT cases does tend toward the international minimum standard,[122] finding a violation only where there is evidence 'showing bad faith, discriminatory intent, and/or ultra vires actions on the part of host-State government officials.'[123] In *Tecmed*,[124] however, the arbitral tribunal expressly rejected the position that the 'fair and equitable' clause in the Spain–Mexico BIT did nothing more than incorporate the customary international law minimum standard. The tribunal held that the scope of the provision was that resulting from an 'autonomous interpretation',[125] that is, different from the international law standard, because otherwise it 'would be deprived of any semantic content or practical utility of its own.'[126] In particular, the tribunal rejected the notion that bad faith or egregious behavior on the part of a State is necessary to sustain a violation of the clause.[127] While the tribunal seemed motivated by a perceived denial of due process,[128] it applied a standard that seems unattainable, as no democratic society can provide knowledge beforehand of 'any and all rules and regulations.' The decision appears to weaken a State's ability to impose human rights obligations on TNCs operating on its territory.[129]

---

[121] See Gross, above n 93, at 935.

[122] See *ibid* at 937 (referring to BIT and NAFTA cases).

[123] *Ibid* at 937 (referring to BIT and NAFTA cases) (continuing, '[i]n all other instances, including instances where host-State actions were not the model of clarity or fairness but were legally justified and non-discriminatory, no violation was found').

Expressly applying the minimum international standard, the tribunal in *Genin v Estonia* found that the Estonian government's decision to revoke the investor's banking license for seemingly technical reasons and without prior notice was not a violation of the US–Estonia BIT, because the decision was within the State's statutory authority, followed the applicable procedure, and was within reason: see *ibid* at 937–38 (discussing *Alex Genin, Eastern Credit Limited, Inc and AS Baltoil v The Republic of Estonia* (ICSID Case No ARB/99/2) (2001), (2002) 27 YB Com Arb 61, available at http://www.worldbank.org/icsid/cases/genin.pdf). Although the tribunal in *Maffezini v Spain*, decided under the Argentina–Spain BIT, did not explicitly adopt the minimum international standard, it nonetheless showed deference to decisions by State officials made pursuant to statutory authority, rejecting the investor's claim that the State should pay for a statutorily mandated Environmental Impact Assessment. See Gross, above n 93, at 938 (discussing *Emilio Agustín Maffezini v Kingdom of Spain* (ICSID Case No ARB/97/7) (2000), (2002) 27 YB Com Arb 13, available at http://www.worldbank.org/icsid/cases/emilio_AwardoftheTribunal.pdf).

[124] *Técnicas Medioambientales Tecmed SA v United Mexican States* (ICSID Case No ARB(AF)/00/2) (2003), available at http://www.worldbank.org/icsid/cases/laudo051903FINAL.pdf (Spanish original version); http://www.worldbank.org/icsid/cases/laudo-051903%20-English.pdf (unofficial English translation).

[125] *Ibid* at para 155.

[126] *Ibid* at para 156.

[127] See *ibid* at para 153 (citing the NAFTA arbitration *Mondev International Ltd v United States* (ICSID Case No ARB(AF)/99/2) (2002), at 40).

[128] See, eg, *Tecmed*, at para 173.

[129] See also the summary of this part of the award below, at section IV.2.B.3.

In *MTD Equity v Republic of Chile*,[130] decided 25 May 2004 under the Malaysia–Chile BIT,[131] suit was brought when an investment, the construction of a planned community in an area zoned for agricultural use, was approved by Chile's Foreign Investment Commission (FIC) but was later denied the necessary permits by the Ministry of Housing and Urban Development because it was inconsistent with the agency's urban development policy.[132] The tribunal explicitly applied the *Tecmed* standard,[133] holding that approval by the FIC of an investment project 'that is against the urban policy of the Government is a breach of the obligation to treat an investor fairly and equitably.'[134] In *Occidental Exploration and Production Co v Republic of Ecuador*,[135] decided 1 July 2004 under the US–Ecuador BIT,[136] the *Tecmed* standard was likewise applied by the tribunal,[137] although the tribunal somewhat inconsistently held that the BIT standard was *not* more demanding than the international minimum standard.[138] The tribunal held that a change in tax law to the detriment of the claimant was evidence of a legal and business framework that did not meet 'the requirements of stability and predictability under international law.'[139]

---

[130] *MTD Equity Sdn Bhd and MTD Chile SA v Republic of Chile* (ICSID Case No ARB/01/7) (2004), available at http://ita.law.uvic.ca/documents/MTD-Award.pdf. For an overview of the award, see Luke Eric Peterson, 'Malaysian firm wins BIT case against Chile; "wide scope" of MFN clause looms large', *INVEST-SD: Investment Law and Policy Weekly News Bulletin* (International Institute for Sustainable Development, Winnipeg, Canada), 23 August 2004, available at http://www.iisd.org/pdf/2004/investment_investsd_aug23_2004.pdf.

[131] See *MTD Equity* at para 1.

[132] See *ibid* at paras 42, 72.

[133] See *ibid* at paras 114–15.

[134] *Ibid* at para 166. However, the tribunal did not award the entire amount of compensation requested by the claimant (see *ibid* at para 242), because Chile was not 'responsible for the consequences of unwise business decisions or for the lack of diligence of the investor': *ibid* at para 167. The tribunal noted that 'BITs are not an insurance against business risk ... [the claimants'] choice of partner, the acceptance of a land valuation based on future assumptions without protecting themselves contractually in case the assumptions would not materialize, including the issuance of the required development permits, are risks that the Claimants took irrespective of Chile's actions': *ibid* at para 178 (citing *Emilio Agustín Maffezini v Kingdom of Spain* (ICSID Case No ARB/97/7) (2000), (2002) 27 YB Com Arb 13, available at http://www.worldbank.org/icsid/cases/emilio_AwardoftheTribunal.pdf).

[135] LCIA Case No UN 3467 (2004), available at http://ita.law.uvic.ca/documents/Oxy-EcuadorFinalAward_001.pdf. For an overview of the award, see Luke Eric Peterson, 'Occidental Wins Investment Arbitration Against Ecuador; Ecuador Vows "Appeal"' *INVEST-SD: Investment Law and Policy Weekly News Bulletin* (International Institute for Sustainable Development, Winnipeg, Canada), 16 July 2004, available at http://www.iisd.org/pdf/2004/investment_investsd_july16_2004.pdf

[136] See *Occidental* at para 5.

[137] See *ibid* at paras 185–86.

[138] See *ibid* at paras 188–191.

[139] See *ibid* at para 191. The tribunal found fault with the fact that 'the tax law was changed without providing any clarity about its meaning and extent and the practice and regulations were also inconsistent with such changes': *ibid* at para 184.

## B. Full Protection and Security

This clause, which requires that each party accord full protection and security to the investments made by the other party's investors,[140] is generally interpreted as imposing an obligation on the State to exercise due diligence in protecting foreign investment from injurious activities by the government or by private parties.[141] It is not interpreted as instantiating a strict liability standard such as to 'render a host State liable for any destruction of the investment even if caused by persons whose acts could not be attributed to the state'.[142]

In *Tecmed*,[143] the tribunal adopted the prevailing standard, holding that 'the guarantee of full protection and security is not absolute and does not impose strict liability upon the State that grants it'.[144] The tribunal rejected the claim for lack of evidence sufficient to conclude either that the authorities provided support to the community movement in opposition to the landfill or that the activity of the demonstrators could be attributed to the authorities pursuant to international law.[145] The tribunal did not foreclose the possibility that if such support had been proven, it would have constituted a violation of the clause. In *Occidental*,[146]

---

[140] See, eg, Agreement between Mauritius and the Federal Republic of Germany concerning the Encouragement and Reciprocal Protection of Investments, 25 May 1971, Art 3(1) ('Investments by nationals or companies of either Contracting Party shall enjoy full protection as well as security in the territory of the other Contracting Party') [hereinafter 'Germany–Mauritius BIT'], available at http://www.unctad.org/sections/dite/iia/docs/bits/germany_mauritius_gr_eng.pdf; Denmark–Cuba BIT, above n 117, at Art 2(1) ('[i]nvestments of investors of each Contracting Party shall at all times enjoy full protection and security in the territory of the other Contracting Party'). See generally Dolzer and Stevens, above n 40, at pp 60–61; UNCTAD 1998, above n 56, at 55; IISD 2004, above n 11, at 11–12; Sornarajah, above n 36, at pp 260–64.

[141] See Dolzer and Stevens, above n 40, at p 61. See also Chen Huiping, *OECD's Multilateral Agreement on Investment: A Chinese Perspective* (The Hague and New York, NY, Kluwer Law International, 2002), at p 113.

[142] Dolzer and Stevens, above n 40, at p 61 (noting, however, that 'given that the issue of physical protection (and compensation) is normally dealt with elsewhere in the modern treaties, it may be assumed that this provision in some measure serves to amplify the obligations that the parties have otherwise taken upon themselves'). See also Huiping, above n 141, at p 113.

[143] *Técnicas Medioambientales Tecmed SA v United Mexican States* (ICSID Case No ARB(AF)/00/2) (2003), available at http://www.worldbank.org/icsid/cases/laudo051903FINAL.pdf (Spanish original version); http://www.worldbank.org/icsid/cases/laudo-051903%20-English.pdf (unofficial English translation).

[144] *Ibid* at para 177.

[145] *Ibid* at paras 166–67. The claimant alleged that Mexican authorities violated the full protection and security clause by encouraging, fostering and supporting a community movement in opposition to the landfill and by failing to act 'as quickly, efficiently and thoroughly as they should have to avoid, prevent or put an end to the adverse social demonstrations expressed through disturbances in the operation of the Landfill or access thereto, or the personal security or freedom to move about of the members of [claimant's subsidiary]'s staff related to the Landfill': *ibid* at paras 175–76.

[146] LCIA Case No UN 3467 (2004), available at http://ita.law.uvic.ca/documents/Oxy-EcuadorFinalAward_001.pdf.

the tribunal held that a violation of the guarantee of fair and equitable treatment automatically constitutes a violation of the guarantee of full protection and security.[147] As an independent standard, this clause might in some circumstances interfere with a State's ability progressively to realize human rights, but it seems less likely to interfere with capacity to impose human rights obligations on TNCs.

## C. Non-discrimination and Reasonableness

What is generally known as the non-discrimination clause typically provides that neither party shall impair by unreasonable or discriminatory measures the management, maintenance, development, use, enjoyment, expansion, sale or disposition of investments in its territory of nationals or companies of the other party.[148] The clause thus has two components: the State is prohibited from impairing the investment through 'discriminatory' measures and through 'unreasonable' measures.[149]

One could imagine scenarios in which such clauses would impair a host State's ability to enforce human rights against TNCs.[150] The

---

[147] *Ibid* at para 187.

[148] See, eg, Dolzer and Stevens, above n 40, at p 62 (citing Agreement between the Government of the United Kingdom of Great Britain and Northern Ireland and the Government of Malaysia for the Promotion and Protection of Investments, 21 May 1981, Art 2(2) [hereinafter 'UK–Malaysia BIT']); *Tecmed*, at para 175 (citing Acuerdo para la promoción y protección recíproca de inversiones entre los Estados Unidos Mexicanos y el reino de España, 1996, Art 3(1) [hereinafter 'Spain–Mexico BIT']). Some BITs substitute 'arbitrary' for 'unreasonable'. See UNCTAD 1998, above n 56, at 55. See generally Dolzer and Stevens, above n 40, at pp 61–63; UNCTAD 1998, above n 56, at 55–56; IISD 2004, above n 11.

Under the international law prohibition of discriminatory treatment of aliens, discrimination is only actionable if two conditions are met: intent to injure the alien, combined with injury in fact: see Dolzer and Stevens, above n 40, at pp 61–62. Under the non-discrimination clause of a BIT, while an impairment of activities relating to a foreign investment could constitute the requisite injury component, intent would probably need to be proven for a violation of the non-discrimination clause to exist: see *ibid* at p 62 ('the stipulations on non-discrimination contained in many BITs ... would not be violated simply because more favorable treatment were accorded to nationals of another State').

[149] For an analysis of the effect of the choice of the conjunction ('and' versus 'or') used to join the words 'unreasonable' and 'discriminatory' in this BIT provision, see UNCTAD 1998, above n 56, at 55–56 (arguing that '[w]hen the provision uses the conjunction "and" instead of "or"', as in "unreasonable and discriminatory measures", it may be that the host country would have greater latitude for action; it would be free to discriminate as long as the discrimination was not unreasonable (or arbitrary)').

[150] The investment protection provisions in BITs could affect a State's regulatory capacity both by chilling or preventing the introduction of new laws and regulations and also by chilling or preventing enforcement actions taken under existing laws and regulations. Thus, although BITs do not contain 'rollback' provisions that require States to repeal existing laws, it would seem that BITs might effectively repeal existing laws by preventing their enforcement. Moreover, in some nations, international treaties are self-executing and take precedence over national law, again suggesting that, in such nations, existing law in conflict with BIT provisions might effectively be repealed by the entry into force of a BIT. Cf Free Trade Area of the Americas Working Group on Investment (Organization of American States,

non-discrimination clause could undermine 'living wage laws covering a certain class of investors, laws mandating union neutrality in specific industries, requirements to remain in a state or municipality for a minimum period of time, laws requiring severance payments to dislocated workers and communities, and other existing or proposed policies to stem capital flight and create high quality jobs for local citizens.'[151] The 'unreasonableness' provision could give excessive discretion to arbitral panels in validating investor challenges to host State environmental, land use, public health and worker safety regulation.[152]

Recent cases have found that State action does not violate the reasonableness standard so long as it is permitted by the applicable legal framework. In *Tecmed*,[153] the tribunal rejected the claim that the Mexican authorities' actions were 'legally groundless actions' (the formulation of the reasonableness standard in the Spain–Mexico BIT) or discriminatory.[154] The tribunal found the failure to renew the landfill permit not to have violated Mexican law nor to have taken place outside the Mexican

Inter-American Development Bank and United Nations Economic Commission for Latin America and the Caribbean), *Foreign Investment Regimes in the Americas: A Comparative Study*, § 5.5 ('[m]ost countries [surveyed] replied that, in compliance with their respective constitutional provisions, international treaties take legal precedence over national laws (with the exception of the constitution) and that they have direct effect'), http://alca-ftaa.iadb.org/eng/invest/PREFACE.HTM (last visited 16 January 2004). For a country-specific example, see Free Trade Area of the Americas Working Group on Investment (Organization of American States, Inter-American Development Bank and United Nations Economic Commission for Latin America and the Caribbean), *Legislation for Foreign Investment Statutes in Countries in Americas Comparative Study: Venezuela*, § 5.4 ('Article 8 of the Civil Procedure Code establishes: "In cases where Private International Law is applied, judges shall first consider public treaties of Venezuela with the respective State, on the point in question; where there are no such treaties, the provisions of laws of the Republic on the matter or what can be inferred from the spirit of national legislation shall apply; and finally, the generally accepted principles of such Law shall apply"'), http://alca-ftaa.iadb.org/eng/invest/VEN~1.HTM (last visited Jan.16, 2004). The homepage of the Working Group on Investment is http://www.ftaa-alca.org/ngroups/nginve_e.asp (last visited 16 January 2004).

[151] Michelle Sforza, 'MAI Provisions and Proposals: An Analysis of the April 1998 Text', *Public Citizen's Global Trade Watch* (Washington, DC, Public Citizen, July 1998), at Part I, section 1.B.2, available at http://www.citizen.org/trade/issues/mai/articles.fm?ID=7415.
[152] *Ibid.*
[153] *Técnicas Medioambientales Tecmed SA v United Mexican States* (ICSID Case No ARB(AF)/00/2) (2003), available at http://www.worldbank.org/icsid/cases/laudo051903FINAL.pdf (Spanish original version); http://www.worldbank.org/icsid/cases/laudo-051903%20-English.pdf (unofficial English translation).
[154] *Ibid* at paras 175 (citing the Spain–Mexico BIT, above n 148), para 179 (rejecting the claim). The tribunal's analysis of reasonableness and discrimination overlapped with its analysis of full protection and security (see *ibid* at paras 175–82), since all three standards are included in the same Article of the BIT: see *ibid* at para 175. It appears that the unreasonableness and discrimination challenges were rejected because there was insufficient evidence to conclude that the authorities did not act 'reasonably, in accordance with the parameters inherent in a democratic state': see *ibid* at para 177.

legal framework.[155] In *MTD Equity*,[156] while the tribunal held that the approval of an investment by Chile's Foreign Investment Commission contrary to the government's urban policy (with the result that the requisite permits for the project could not be issued) was unreasonable and thus a violation of the prohibition on unreasonable and discriminatory measures,[157] it did not accept the contention that the rejection by a government agency of an environmental impact statement for the project was unreasonable, since the agency had followed the prescribed procedure.[158]

### D. National and Most-favored-nation Treatment

Most BITs contain clauses that require the host State to accord foreign investors treatment no less favorable than (1) the treatment it accords its own nationals (national treatment) and (2) the treatment it accords nationals of any third country (most-favored-nation treatment, or MFN).[159]

A recent arbitration suggests that national treatment could be used to challenge State imposition of human rights obligations on TNCs if domestic corporations, even in other economic sectors, are not subject to the same obligations. This could conceivably arise in the context of decision-making by agencies responsible for regulating particular industries. In *Occidental*,[160] the tribunal accepted the position of the claimant, an oil company, that the discontinuation of its value-added tax (VAT) refunds violated the national treatment provision, since other exporters in Ecuador continued to enjoy VAT refunds.[161] Although the BIT provision restricted its application to foreign investors 'in like situations' as domestic companies, and the companies averred to by the claimant were purveyors of products dissimilar to oil (such as flowers, seafood products, and bananas), the tribunal held that the 'in like situations' condition was satisfied because the claimant and the domestic companies receiving VAT refunds were all exporters, and the purpose of protecting investors as

---

[155] *Ibid* at para 179.
[156] *MTD Equity Sdn Bhd and MTD Chile SA v Republic of Chile* (ICSID Case No ARB/01/7) (2004), available at http://ita.law.uvic.ca/documents/MTD-Award.pdf.
[157] See *ibid* at para 196.
[158] See *ibid* at paras 195–96.
[159] See Dolzer and Stevens, above n 40, at pp 63 (noting that many treaties limit the national treatment obligation to cases where the foreign and the domestic investor are similarly situated), 65; see also Huiping, above n 141, at pp 50–51 (noting that national treatment has less acceptance among developing countries, and where adopted it is usually accompanied by exceptions and restrictions). See generally Dolzer and Stevens, above n 40, at pp 63–66; UNCTAD 1998, above n 56, at 57–65; UNCTAD 2003, above n 6, at 102–10; IISD 2004, above n 11, at 10–11; Sornarajah, above n 36, at pp 250–52.
[160] LCIA Case No UN 3467 (2004), available at http://ita.law.uvic.ca/documents/Oxy-EcuadorFinalAward_001.pdf.
[161] See *ibid* at paras 168–79.

compared to local producers 'cannot be done by addressing exclusively the sector in which that particular activity is undertaken.'[162] No discriminatory intent is necessary, according to the tribunal, for a violation of the provision to exist.[163]

In addition to hindering State efforts to impose human rights obligations directly on TNCs, it has been suggested by NGOs that MFN clauses can 'end policies that pressure governments to reform by restricting investment' from TNCs whose home governments have poor records on human rights.[164] Conceivably this could also prevent restrictions on investment from TNCs who do business with such governments. Discussing the most-favored-nation clause in the proposed (and abandoned) MAI, one NGO argued that:

> [h]ad the MAI been in effect during the 1980s, successful divestment strategies to pressure the South African government to abolish apartheid would have been forbidden. In the US, cities and state governments divested from South African-owned banks, municipalities set up Shell-free zones banning investment by Royal Dutch Shell and its subsidiaries, and state and local governments dropped South African-owned firms as suppliers.[165]

Recent examples of divestment strategies that would be prohibited by most-favored-nation clauses might include:

> the proposed divestiture by the states of New York and California from Swiss-owned banks in retaliation for their collusion with the Nazi regime and for their reluctance to return funds to descendants of Holocaust victims who held Swiss bank accounts.[166]

These examples illustrate how MFN clauses may limit host State capacity to promote human rights extraterritorially by exerting control over domestic investment conditions.

Most-favored-nation treatment can be used to obtain two benefits for investors additional to the protections in the governing BIT: substantive protections and procedural advantages. In *MTD Equity*,[167] the tribunal

---

[162] See *ibid* at para 173.
[163] See *ibid* at para 177.
[164] Sforza, above n 151, at Part I, section 1.A.2. See also Robert Naiman and Neil Watkins, Center for Economic and Policy Research, *The Proposed MAI: Harmful to Workers*, http://www.cepr.net/globalization/MAI/mlabor3.htm (last visited 5 November 2004) (MFN means that investors and corporations cannot 'be held accountable for the conduct, laws or policies of their home governments').
[165] Sforza, above n 151, at Part I, section 1.A.2.
[166] *Ibid* at n 11.
[167] *MTD Equity Sdn Bhd and MTD Chile SA v Republic of Chile* (ICSID Case No ARB/01/7) (2004), available at http://ita.law.uvic.ca/documents/MTD-Award.pdf.

held that the claimant could have recourse to substantive investment protection provisions under the Denmark–Chile and Croatia–Chile BITs due to the MFN clause in the governing Malaysia–Chile BIT.[168] In the decision on jurisdiction in *Siemens v Argentine Republic*,[169] the tribunal permitted the claimant to evade the exhaustion of local remedies requirement in the Germany–Argentina BIT by invoking that treaty's MFN clause to access the dispute settlement provisions under the Chile–Argentina BIT, which has no requirement of exhaustion of local remedies.[170]

Finally, the suggestion that a State's administrative discretion to distinguish among investors based on human rights-related considerations potentially could be limited by both national treatment and MFN clauses finds some confirmation in *Tecmed*,[171] where the Spanish investor argued that the fact that its permit had not been renewed, while unlimited-term operating permits had been granted to another foreign-owned company and to government entities of the Mexican state of Sonora, constituted violations of MFN treatment and of national treatment.[172] While the tribunal rejected these arguments, it did so on the basis that the complained-of actions occurred prior to the BIT's entry into force.[173] The tribunal did not preclude the possibility that the actions otherwise would have constituted breaches of the BIT.

---

[168] See *ibid* at paras 100–4. For an overview of the award, see Peterson, above n 130. There is a debate about whether a provision sought to be incorporated via the MFN clause must relate to the subject matter in the governing BIT in order to be capable of incorporation: see generally UNCTAD 2003, above n 6, at 152–53, box V.4.

[169] ICSID Case No ARB/02/8 (2004), available at http://ita.law.uvic.ca/documents/SiemensJurisdiction-English-3August2004.pdf. For an overview of the decision, see Luke Eric Peterson, 'Tribunal upholds jurisdiction in *Siemens v Argentina*; MFN plays procedural role', *INVEST-SD: Investment Law and Policy Weekly News Bulletin* (International Institute for Sustainable Development, Winnipeg, Canada), 23 August 2004, available at http://www.iisd.org/pdf/2004/investment_investsd_aug23_2004.pdf.

[170] See *Siemens* at paras 107–9. Cf Luke Eric Peterson, 'Tribunal rules in Jordan dispute; rejects extension of MFN to cover procedural issues', *INVEST-SD: Investment Law and Policy Weekly News Bulletin* (International Institute for Sustainable Development, Winnipeg, Canada), 21 January 2005, available at http://www.iisd.org/pdf/2005/investment_investsd_jan21_2005.pdf (summarizing recent award under Italy–Jordan BIT, which held that MFN clause does not extend to dispute settlement procedures unless expressly so provided).

[171] *Técnicas Medioambientales Tecmed SA v United Mexican States* (ICSID Case No ARB(AF)/00/2) (2003), available at http://www.worldbank.org/icsid/cases/laudo051903FINAL.pdf (Spanish original version); http://www.worldbank.org/icsid/cases/laudo-051903%20-English.pdf (unofficial English translation).

[172] See *ibid* at paras 179–82.

[173] See *ibid* at para 181 (addressing claimant's allegations that Mexico's treatment of (1) Residuos Industriales Multiquim SA de CV, owned by a foreign investor, and (2) the prior operators and owners of the landfill, which were government entities of the Sonoran state, was more favorable than Mexico's treatment of claimant).

## 3. Other Provisions

In addition to the primary substantive provisions on expropriation and treatment examined above, several other features of BITs can have an impact on host State capacity to enforce human rights against TNCs.

### A. Definition of 'Investment'

The scope of the definition of covered investment in a BIT has implications for the capacity of host States to regulate TNCs on their territory, because the broader the scope of the definition, the greater the range of assets that are protected by the other provisions of the treaty. Recent BITs often define investment 'by a list of five groups of specific rights which usually include traditional property rights, rights in companies, monetary claims and titles to performance, copyrights and industrial property rights as well as concessions and similar rights.'[174] Generally BITs will apply both to investments made subsequently to the entry into force of the BIT as well as to investments that existed before the entry into force of the BIT, so long as the relevant dispute arose subsequently to the entry into force.[175]

---

[174] Dolzer and Stevens, above n 40, at p 26 (noting also that '[i]t is frequently stated that these illustrations are not exhaustive'); see also George M von Mehren *et al*, 'Navigating Through Investor-State Arbitrations—An Overview of Bilateral Investment Treaty Claims' (2004) 59 *Dispute Resolution Journal* 69, at 71. See generally Dolzer and Stevens, above n 40, at pp 25–31; UNCTAD 1998, above n 56, at 32–37; UNCTAD 2003, above n 6, at 99–102; IISD 2004, above n 11, at 9; Sornarajah, above n 36, at pp 239–45.

[175] See, eg, Agreement Between the Lebanese Republic and the Kingdom of Sweden on the Promotion and Reciprocal Protection of Investments, 15 June 2001 [hereinafter 'Sweden–Lebanon BIT'], Art 10 ('The present Agreement shall also apply to investments in the territory of a Contracting Party made in accordance with its laws and regulations by investors of the other Contracting Party prior to the entry into force of this Agreement. However, the Agreement shall not apply to disputes that have arisen before its entry into force'), available at http://www.unctad.org/sections/dite/iia/docs/bits/ sweden_lebanon.pdf; Agreement Between the Government of the Republic of Chile and the Government of the Republic of Croatia on the Reciprocal Promotion and Protection of Investments, 28 November 1994 [hereinafter 'Croatia–Chile BIT'], Art 2 ('[t]his Agreement shall apply to investments in the territory of one Contracting Party made in accordance with its legislation, prior to or after the entry into force of the Agreement, by investors of the other Contracting Party. It shall however not be applicable to disputes which arose prior to its entry into force or to disputes directly related to events which occurred prior to its entry into force'), available at http://www.unctad.org/sections/dite/iia/docs/bits/chile_croatia.pdf; Agreement Between the Hellenic Republic and the Arab Republic of Egypt on the Promotion and Reciprocal Protection of Investments, 16 July 1993, [hereinafter 'Greece–Egypt BIT'], Art 8 ('[t]his Agreement shall apply to investments made both prior to and after its entry into force by investors of one Contracting Party in the territory of the other Contracting Party in accordance with the latter's legislation'), available at http://www.unctad.org/sections/ dite/iia/docs/bits/egypt_greece.pdf.

The US model BIT, revised in 2004, provides that a '"covered investment" means, with respect to a Party, an investment in its territory of an investor of the other Party in existence as of the date of entry into force of this Treaty or established, acquired, or expanded thereafter': Treaty Between the Government of the United States of America and the Government of

While the restriction of host government capability to sanction TNCs that violate human rights, or to use licensing procedures to condition corporate behavior, threatens the ability of States to impose human rights obligations on TNCs, recent decisions in a BIT context have at least established some of the outer bounds of the scope of the term 'investment'. In the decision on jurisdiction in *Mihaly International Corp v Republic of Sri Lanka*,[176]

[Country] Concerning the Encouragement and Reciprocal Protection of Investment (2004 Model BIT), available at http://www.state.gov/documents/organization/38710.pdf (last visited 23 January 2005). See also *ibid*, Art 2(3) ('[f]or greater certainty, this Treaty does not bind either Party in relation to any act or fact that took place or any situation that ceased to exist before the date of entry into force of this Treaty'). Most existing US BITs will reflect the prior version of the US model BIT, from 1994, which took a similar approach. See, eg, Treaty Between the Government of the United States of America and the Government of El Salvador Concerning the Encouragement and Reciprocal Protection of Investment, 10 March 1999 [hereinafter 'US–El Salvador BIT'], Art. I(e) ('"covered investment" means an investment of a national or company of a Party in the territory of the other Party'), Art XVI(1) ('[this treaty] shall apply to covered investments existing at the time of entry into force as well as to those established or acquired thereafter'), Protocol, para 2 ('[t]he Parties confirm their mutual understanding that the provisions of this Treaty do not bind either Party in relation to any act or fact which took place or any situation which ceased to exist before entry into force of this Treaty'), available at http://www.unctad.org/sections/dite/iia/docs/bits/us_elsalvador.pdf. As Luke Eric Peterson indicates, the drafters of the most recent model BIT may have rejected a restriction on the applicability of US BITs to pre-existing investment contracts:

> The model BIT ... exhibits several noticeable changes from an earlier draft version of the model BIT circulated earlier this year by US authorities. In particular, authorities appear to have resolved a long-running inter-departmental debate over those investment agreements (for eg natural resources contracts) which may be arbitrable using the international disputes mechanism contained in the treaty. Whereas an earlier draft of the model treaty had covered only agreements that came into effect on or after the date of entry into force of the treaty, the November 2004 version of the US model BIT no longer imposes such a bar on the inclusion of pre-existing investment contracts.

Luke Eric Peterson, 'US releases final draft of model investment treaty', *INVEST-SD: Investment Law and Policy Weekly News Bulletin* (International Institute for Sustainable Development, Winnipeg, Canada), 17 December 2004, available at http://www.iisd.org/pdf/2004/investment_investsd_dec17_2004.pdf.

In the *Tecmed* dispute, the tribunal considered conduct of the respondent Mexican government which occurred subsequently to the signing of the Spain–Mexico BIT, but before the treaty entered into force, to be covered by the treaty. See *Técnicas Medioambientales Tecmed SA v United Mexican States* (ICSID Case No ARB(AF)/00/2) (2003), at para 172 ('the conduct of the Respondent between the date of execution of the Agreement (in view of the Respondent's determination to ratify it subsequently) and the effective date thereof, is incompatible with the imperative rules deriving from Article 4(1) of the Agreement as to fair and equitable treatment. This is particularly so since, according to Article 2(2) of the Agreement, it is applicable to investments made before its entry into force, a circumstance to be certainly considered when analyzing the conduct attributable to the Respondent that took place before that time but after the Respondent having executed the Agreement'), available at http://www.worldbank.org/icsid/cases/laudo051903FINAL.pdf (Spanish original version); http://www.worldbank.org/icsid/cases/laudo-051903%20-English.pdf (unofficial English translation).

[176] *Mihaly International Corp v Democratic Socialist Republic of Sri Lanka* (ICSID Case No ARB/00/2), (2002) 17 *ICSID Review–Foreign Investment Law Journal* 142, available at http://www.worldbank.org/icsid/cases/mihaly-award.pdf.

decided under the US–Sri Lanka BIT, the tribunal held that expenditures made prior to a contractual commitment by the State to admit the investment project did not constitute an investment.[177] In the jurisdictional decision in *Joy Mining v Egypt*,[178] decided under the UK–Egypt BIT, the tribunal distinguished between commercial contracts and investments in holding that a contract for the provision of mining equipment to Egypt was not an investment such as to confer jurisdiction under the BIT or the ICSID Convention.[179]

## B. Admission

The admission provision governs the circumstances under which investment will be admitted to a host country.[180] If the admission provision grants a 'right of establishment' or 'national treatment in the pre-establishment phase,'[181] it might require a State to admit investment even if, for example, the State objects to the investor's record of lack of respect for human rights. Once admitted, of course, the investment is then protected by the substantive provisions of the BIT.

Although most BITs 'preserve full host-government control over admission and establishment, while granting national treatment in the post-establishment phase of an investment,'[182] some BITs require that applications for licenses and entry of employees be given favorable consideration.[183] Going further, United States and Canadian BITs extend the national treatment and MFN standards to the pre-establishment phase as well.[184]

---

[177] See *ibid* at paras 48–61; see also Alejandro A Escobar, 'Introductory Note' (2002) 17 *ICSID Review–Foreign Investment Law Journal* 140, at 141, available at http://www.world-bank.org/icsid/cases/mihaly-intro.pdf.

[178] *Joy Mining Machinery Limited v Arab Republic of Egypt* (ICSID Case No ARB/03/11) (2004), available at http://www.asil.org/ilib/JoyMining_Egypt.pdf.

[179] See *ibid* at paras 43–61. For an overview of the decision, see Luke Eric Peterson, 'UK mining firm loses investment treaty claim against Egypt', *INVEST-SD: Investment Law and Policy Weekly News Bulletin* (International Institute for Sustainable Development, Winnipeg, Canada), 24 September 2004 (noting that 'While the tribunal noted that recent ICSID tribunals have "progressively given a broader meaning to the concept of investment," it stressed that a distinction needed to be preserved between ordinary sales contracts and investments (the latter being characterized by such features as: "a certain duration, a regularity of profit and return, an element of risk, a substantial commitment and that it should constitute a significant contribution to the host State's development")'), available at http://www.iisd.org/pdf/2004/investment_investsd_sept24_2004.pdf.

[180] See generally Dolzer and Stevens, above n 40, at pp 50–58, 76–78; UNCTAD 1998, above n 56, at 46–50.

[181] See UNCTAD 2003, above n 6, at 102.

[182] *Ibid* at 107.

[183] See Dolzer and Stevens, above n 40, at p 76 (citing Germany–China BIT).

[184] UNCTAD 2003, above n 6, at 108; see also UNCTAD 2004, above n 7, at 224, box VI.3 (terming this the 'Western Hemisphere approach'); Dolzer and Stevens, above n 40, at p 76 ('[w]ith the exception of US treaties, national and MFN standards are generally not extended to the admission procedure, but only begin to be operative after the investment has been approved or otherwise admitted by the host country'); Luke Peterson, 'Changing

## C. Investor–State Dispute Settlement

Since the 1980s, an investor–State dispute settlement mechanism has been a 'virtually standard' feature of BITs.[185] Usually these clauses do not require that local remedies be exhausted before international arbitration is invoked.[186] BITs may provide for arbitration under both institutional and ad-hoc arbitration processes. Under an institutional process, an institution supervises the conduct of the arbitration by the arbitral tribunal, a feature lacking in an ad hoc arbitration.[187] Institutions that supervise arbitrations include ICSID, the International Chamber of Commerce, and the Stockholm Chamber of Commerce.[188] An ad hoc arbitration may be governed by rules prescribed by the treaty which gave rise to the claim or by the rules drafted by the UN Commission on International Trade Law (UNCITRAL).[189] Each of these options is lacking in transparency, legitimacy and accountability[190] in ways that hinder the capacity of host States to impose human rights obligations on TNCs operating in their territory, because the result is an increase in legal uncertainty and costs, and a legal regime that favors the interests of investors. Developing countries, the usual targets for investor claims under BITs, often do not have the necessary human or monetary resources at their disposal to be able effectively to contest the claims.[191]

Investment Litigation, Bit by BIT' (2001) ('[m]ost BITs cover only investments which are already "sunk" or "established", but the BITs concluded by the United States—and many of those concluded by Canada—go further and extend national treatment and most-favored nation treatment to cover the entry and establishment of investments'), available at http://www.iisd.org/pdf/2001/trade_inv_litigation.pdf.

[185] See Peterson, above n 64, at 7; see also UNCTAD 2003, above n 6, at 115 (although investor–State mechanisms were 'virtually unknown before the introduction of the ICSID system in 1965[, m]ost bilateral and many regional agreements now include provisions on investor–State dispute settlement'); Dolzer and Stevens, above n 40, at p 130 ('[w]ith the entry into force in 1966 of the ICSID Convention, matters changed significantly in view of the fact that the Convention provided a complete, self-contained system for the settlement by arbitration of disputes between investors and their host States'). See generally *ibid* at 119–64; UNCTAD 1998, above n 56, at 87–104; UNCTAD 2003, above n 6, at 114–18; IISD 2004, above n 11, at 3–8, 34–35; Sornarajah, above n 36, at pp 265–73.

[186] See Peterson, above n 64, at 7–8.

[187] See *ibid* at 8.

[188] See *ibid* at 9.

[189] See *ibid* at 8.

[190] The following exposition draws heavily from Peterson, above n 64.

[191] See, eg, UNCTAD 2003, above n 6, at 117 ('[i]nternational arbitration itself can demand much in resources and expertise, possibly putting developing country parties at a disadvantage'); Peterson, above n 64, at 18 ('substantial costs make contestation of an arbitral claim an unattractive option for poorer developing countries'); Inaamul Haque and Ruxandra Burdescu, 'Monterrey Consensus on Financing for Development: Response Sought from International Economic Law' (2004) 27 *British Columbia International and Comparative Law Review* 219, at 253 ('costs of an international dispute resolution mechanism may be too great for a poor country to afford'). As Haque and Burdescu note, the costs of international arbitration are especially burdensome for the host State 'in cases where policies were formulated by a previous regime for corrupt motives': *ibid* at 253. This drain on resources can decrease a State's capacity to progressively realize human rights for its citizens.

**1. Transparency: Registration and Publication**   Of the possible arbitral processes listed above, only ICSID has a requirement that disputes be publicly registered, identifying the parties, the date of registration and an indication of the subject matter of the dispute.[192] However, those meager facts are often all that is available even under the ICSID rules: none of the mechanisms, including ICSID, require that the text of the awards be made public.[193] ICSID itself may publish an award only with the consent of both parties, although either party may unilaterally allow the award to be published elsewhere.[194] However, under the UNCITRAL rules, an award may be publicized only with the consent of both parties.[195] Although '[s]ometimes, awards will circulate in the international legal community, stripped of any identifying information,'[196] often, distribution is even more circumscribed: 'the major law firms will have access [to awards] through their representation of clients (investors and governments) in some cases and also through the activities of some partners as arbitrators.'[197] The secrecy enshrouding arbitral awards under BITs 'contributes to a skewed playing field,'[198] creating a body of law unavailable to governments and reinforcing regulatory chill by making it difficult for States to know how to regulate without running afoul of their international legal commitments.[199]

**2. Legitimacy: Selection of Arbitrators and Third-Party Access**   In BIT disputes, parties typically choose their own arbitrators (one is chosen by each party, with the third chosen jointly).[200] The dynamic among the arbitrators can have a significant impact on the tribunal's decision, and the 'close-knit nature' of the arbitration community,[201] as well as the fact that the same individuals often function variously as arbitrators and as counsel in different matters,[202] can lead to conflicts of interest. Specific credentials

---

[192] Peterson, above n 64, at 10, 11.
[193] *Ibid* at 11–12.
[194] See *ibid* at 12.
[195] See *ibid* at 12 (citing ICSID Convention, Art 32(5)).
[196] *Ibid* at 11.
[197] *Ibid* at 12.
[198] *Ibid* at 12.
[199] See *ibid* at 12.
[200] See *ibid* at 13.
[201] See *ibid* at 13–14; see also IISD 2004, above n 11, at 6 (citing M Sornarajah's critique that '[arbitrators'] concern for the values of the international community is weaker than their concern for contractual sanctity and the securing of their next appointment to a tribunal on the basis of their display of commercial probity and their loyalty to the values of multinational business').
[202] See Luke Eric Peterson, 'Dutch Court finds arbitrator in conflict due to role of counsel to another investor', *INVEST-SD: Investment Law and Policy Weekly News Bulletin* (International Institute for Sustainable Development, Winnipeg, Canada), 17 December 2004 ('[i]t is commonplace ... for international lawyers to serve as advocates in one or more investment treaty claims, at the same time as they may be sitting as arbitrators in other such cases—with the potential for facing the same types of legal issues in both contexts'), available at http://www.iisd.org/pdf/2004/investment_investsd_dec17_2004.pdf. In one recent

or expertise are not required of the arbitrators, even for disputes involving sensitive and complex public welfare and regulatory issues.[203] Further detracting from the legitimacy of BIT arbitrations is the fact that they are generally not accessible to third parties without the consent of both

situation where the same person was serving concurrently as an arbitrator in one case and as counsel in another, a Dutch court required the person, Prof Emmanuel Gaillard, to choose between the two roles. Professor Gaillard resigned as arbitrator:

> in an investment treaty arbitration between Telekom Malaysia and Ghana [after] a Dutch court ... effectively required [him] to choose between his arbitral work in the Telekom Malaysia case and his work as counsel in a separate ICSID proceeding involving an Italian construction consortium, *Consortium RFCC v Morocco* ... Gaillard had been instructing the Italian firm as it sought to annul an earlier ICSID award which rejected all of the Italian firm's claims against Morocco under the Italy–Morocco bilateral investment treaty ... It was these twin roles of counsel and arbitrator—so often undertaken by a growing number of international lawyers—which the Dutch Court objected to in this particular instance.
>
> In a decision of the District Court of The Hague dated October 18, 2004 ... the Court reasoned that Prof Gaillard, in his role as counsel to Consortium RFCC, would need to put forward all possible arguments against the award in the annulment proceeding taking place at ICSID. The Court held that such a duty was incompatible with Prof Gaillard's duty as arbitrator in the Telekom Malaysia arbitration, to be unbiased and open towards the validity of the award which had been rendered in the earlier RFCC case (and upon which lawyers for the Government of Ghana relied in part in their defence of Telekom Malaysia's claim).

See *ibid*. However, other tribunals have permitted attorneys to concurrently function variously as arbitrators and counsel: see *ibid* ('the Telekom Malaysia tribunal (consisting of [a panel of three arbitrators, including Prof Gaillard]) had earlier rejected Ghana's efforts to challenge ... Prof Gaillard. Likewise, the Secretariat of the Permanent Court of Arbitration, which is supervising the administration of the arbitration, also rejected a subsequent challenge by Ghana. Only upon turning to the Dutch Courts was Ghana successful in challenging Prof. Gaillard's appointment by Telekom Malaysia').

A recent proposal by ICSID suggests instituting disclosure requirements for arbitrators. See International Centre for Settlement of Investment Disputes, *Possible Improvements of the Framework for ICSID Arbitration*, at paras 16–17 (22 October 2004), http://www.worldbank.org/icsid/improve-arb.pdf. IISD responds that disclosure requirements, while welcome, will not do enough to eliminate conflicts of interest on the part of arbitrators:

> Conflict of interest includes both actual bias and the avoidance of any appearance of bias. Lawyers or their partners cannot sit as a judge one day and as an advocate on a similar issue another day. Judges cannot create decisions that might in some way aid their partners in another case or a firm client in a future potential situation. Yet, this is precisely what happens today in the international arbitration bar. This is not, and can never be, the hallmark of a mature legal system. Indeed, it is the antithesis of one. It must be ended.
>
> ...
>
> ... The legitimacy of the process today depends not just on disclosure documents, but an actual separation between the advocacy and judicial functions, especially when the balance between public and private interests is in dispute. We can no longer apply a lesser standard to international dispute settlement in this regard than we do to domestic dispute settlement. Indeed, the very fact that arbitrators can rule on domestic legal issues, and often do, shows the need to move to a system that reflects the same judicial distance from the practice of law required of domestic judges making rulings on these matters.

Aaron Cosbey *et al*, International Institute for Sustainable Development, *Comments on ICSID Discussion Paper, 'Possible Improvements of the Framework for ICSID Arbitration'* (December 2004), at 11 (proposing the use of 'rosters of arbitrators who do not have either an actual or perceived conflict of interest'), available at http://www.iisd.org/pdf/2004/investment_icsid_response.pdf.

[203] Peterson, above n 64, at 14. See also Cosbey *et al*, above n 202, at 11 ('[a]rbitrations today raise a wide range of issues of public versus private welfare').

parties to the dispute,[204] in contrast to domestic proceedings.[205] By making it more difficult for host States to prevail against investor claims, this lack of third-party access thus impacts on their capacity to impose human rights obligations on TNCs.

**3. Accountability: Precedent and Review**   Further contributing to the legal uncertainty of investor–State arbitrations under BITs are the lack of a consistent and binding body of precedent and the variances of review possibilities among the arbitral mechanisms. Several aspects of the 'one-off nature' of arbitrations make the process susceptible to inconsistent decisions on the same or similar facts.[206] Most BITs do not require that related cases be consolidated into a single proceeding, and in consecutive claims, common issues 'may have to be re-litigated in each new proceeding, which can lead to increased costs, inconsistent results, or both.'[207] The impact on human rights enforcement may be felt when:

> the prospect of multiple arbitrations—running in parallel or consecutively—sets up the very real situation where sensitive government regulations or measures will be scrutinized by a number of tribunals (under one or many different bilateral investment treaties with the host state) which could reach different, and even contradictory, conclusions.[208]

Finally, opportunity for review of arbitral awards is limited. Arbitrations under ICSID rules can be reviewed within the ICSID system, again out of the public eye, on limited grounds.[209] Under other arbitration rules, there

---

[204] See Peterson, above n 64, at 14–16; UNCTAD 2003, above n 6, at 118 ('interested third parties may have no standing before [an arbitral tribunal] and will be denied the possibility of a hearing').

[205] In a domestic forum, for example, if 'an investor and a host country are in dispute over the application of environmental regulations to the investment, [and] local communities affected by the environmental performance of that investment ... wish to participate as interested third parties[, t]his can be accommodated through rights of audience': UNCTAD 2003, above n 6, at 118.

[206] See Peterson, above n 64, at 16.

[207] See *ibid* at 16. This situation materialized in two recent cases, involving the Czech Republic, which produced contrary results on 'essentially the same facts and claims': IISD 2004, above n 11, at 7. Likewise, a multiplicity of related claims filed recently against Argentina have the potential to produce inconsistent results: see *ibid*; Michael D Goldhaber, 'Wanted: A World Investment Court', *The American Lawyer: Focus Europe* (Summer 2004) ('cases arising out of Argentina's peso crisis threaten to yield conflicting results on a scale much larger than the Lauder or SGS matters [the Czech cases and cases involving a Swiss engineering firm, respectively] ... Thirty-plus arbitrations, easily worth $10 billion, have been filed against Argentina, most by foreign investors who in the early nineties bought up newly privatized water and power utilities'), available at http://www.americanlawyer.com/focuseurope/investmentcourt04.html.

[208] Peterson, above n 64, at 16.

[209] See *ibid* at 18. Due to its status as part of the World Bank, ICSID is itself subject to conflicts of interest in investment disputes, as the IISD points out when considering the possibility of ICSID hosting an appellate mechanism for investment arbitrations:

> [ICSID] is financially and structurally dependant upon the Bank. The President of the World Bank chairs its Administrative Council. The Legal Vice President of the Bank is also

are limited possibilities for an award to be reviewed in domestic courts—and thus publicly—under the law of the place of the arbitration or the law of the place of enforcement.[210] However, this avenue is shrinking, 'as an increasing number of jurisdictions are adopting model laws which severely restrict the level of control which may be exercised over arbitral awards by domestic courts.'[211]

In addition to the concerns detailed above, the UN High Commissioner for Human Rights has pointed out the potential danger to human rights enforcement 'of allowing recourse to strong dispute settlement provisions under investment agreements in the absence of similarly strong accountability mechanisms for human rights issues arising in the context of investment.'[212] Section IV, below, addresses this issue in more detail.

### III. INTERFERENCE WITH PROGRESSIVE REALIZATION OF HUMAN RIGHTS

Just as BITs can limit the capacity of States to impose human rights obligations on TNCs, they can also hinder States from progressively providing for second- and third-generation human rights.[213] Such rights may include the second-generation rights to employment, medical care, housing, education, retirement insurance, cultural life, and food, and the third-generation rights to peace, development, a healthy environment, humanitarian aid, and the world's common cultural heritage.[214] While this section of the

Secretary General of ICSID. At the same time, the Bank routinely expresses specific positions regarding the values of investment agreements, and the interpretation of specific provisions and obligations and goals, and the role of the investor-state process. All of this means that the independence of ICSID as currently constituted is, from a conflict of interest perspective, undeniably compromised.

In addition, it is entirely possible that other parts of the World Bank Group may have a financial stake in a project brought to arbitration or in another project in similar circumstances facing related challenges as the circumstances generating a dispute. Again, this presents the potential for an actual or reasonably apprehended conflict of interest.

Cosbey *et al*, above n 202, at 13.

[210] See Peterson, above n 64, at 19–21.

[211] *Ibid* at 19 (citing Horacio Gregera-Naon, 'The Settlement of Investment Disputes Between States and Private Parties: An Overview from the Perspective of the ICC' (2000) 1 *Journal of World Investment*).

[212] UNESC Report, above n 3, at para 55.

[213] Each State that has ratified the International Covenant on Economic and Social Rights (ICESCR) has committed 'to take steps, individually and through international assistance and co-operation, especially economic and technical, to the maximum of its available resources, with a view to achieving progressively the full realization of the rights recognized in the [ICESCR] by all appropriate means, including particularly the adoption of legislative measures': ICESCR, above n 55, Art 2(1).

[214] See William H Meyer, *Human Rights and International Political Economy in Third World Nations: Multinational Corporations, Foreign Aid, and Repression* (Westport, CT, Praeger, 1998), at p 11. See also UNESC Report, above n 3, at para 29 ('[t]he Universal Declaration on

chapter will discuss ways in which specific BIT provisions may hinder the realization of human rights, as a general matter it is important to note that by locking States into protecting investment, BITs prevent States from responding as situations arise that are threatening to human rights, despite the consideration that 'at times, modification of commitments to liberalize investment might be necessary to protect against unforeseen consequences of liberalization which disproportionately affect the poor, disadvantaged or vulnerable.'[215] Even the potential positive benefits of privatization[216] may never be realized if States' inability to modify their investment commitments makes experimentation too costly.

The following sections will demonstrate that BIT provisions can prevent States from implementing policies that promote human rights by gradually laying the social and economic groundwork necessary for an increase in enjoyment of particular rights. Section III.1 will discuss prohibitions on performance requirements; section III.2 will discuss the national treatment standard; section III.3 will examine the compensation requirement associated with direct expropriation and nationalization; section III.4 will look at indirect expropriation through the lens of several arbitrations in the water privatization context; section III.5 will assess prohibitions on capital transfer restrictions and the definition of 'investment'; and section III.6 will briefly examine provisions governing the admission of investment into host countries.

---

Human Rights, the International Covenant on Economic, Social and Cultural Rights (ICESCR) and the International Covenant on Civil and Political Rights (ICCPR), amongst other treaties, recognize a series of civil, cultural, economic, political and social human rights carrying corresponding obligations on States—most of which can be affected, one way or another, by investment').

[215] UNESC Report, above n 3, at para 31(c). The report goes on to note:

> a human rights approach to investment liberalization raises the question of what degree of flexibility is appropriate with respect to withdrawing commitments to investment liberalization where human rights impact assessments indicate that this would be necessary to promote and protect human rights ... Importantly, a human rights approach would seek to avoid the situation where a requirement to pay compensations might discourage States from taking action to protect human rights—such a situation could reinforce the status quo or exacerbate human rights problems. Establishing a direct link between withdrawing commitments and promoting human rights obligations might be an important consideration to bear in mind in allowing flexibility to modify commitments and in determining the appropriateness of compensation case by case.

*Ibid*.

[216] See *ibid* at para 44 (acknowledging negative consequences of privatization, but noting also that 'privatization can promote investment into failing essential services in need of new technology, infrastructure and management and can play an important role in modernizing sectors such as telecommunications ... Given the need to attract investment into all sectors, including essential services related to the enjoyment of human rights, the question from a human rights perspective is how to optimize the benefits of investment while minimizing the challenges of privatization to individuals and communities, particularly those who are poor, disadvantaged or vulnerable') (internal citation omitted).

## 1. Prohibition of Performance Requirements

Performance requirements are conditions placed on foreign investors 'to act in ways considered beneficial to the host economy.'[217] Common performance requirements relate to local content, export performance, domestic equity, joint ventures, technology transfer, and employment of nationals.[218] Host States seek to use performance requirements because they are 'an important policy tool to enhance the benefits of inward FDI.'[219] Although BITs traditionally did not address performance requirements,[220] some BITs, including those concluded by the United States and Canada, now prohibit a range of performance requirements.[221] Even those agreements that do not explicitly prohibit performance requirements can operate, by virtue of the provisions on national treatment and most-favored-nation treatment, to restrict their use.[222] As set out in the following, the prohibition of performance requirements can interfere with a host State's ability progressively to realize human rights.[223]

### A. Domestic content, ownership and employment requirements

States may use performance requirements to promote a right to culture or a policy of non-discrimination:

> Maintaining flexibility in the use of certain performance requirements such as employment or local content requirements could be appropriate at times to promote the right to culture of particular cultural or linguistic minorities, or to respect the principle of non-discrimination through the introduction of affirmative action schemes to promote employment opportunities for disadvantaged or under-represented people.[224]

---

[217] UNCTAD 2003, above n 6, at 119. See generally Dolzer and Stevens, above n 40, at pp 79–81; UNCTAD 1998, above n 56, at 81–83; UNCTAD 2003, above n 6, at 119–23.

[218] See UNCTAD 2003, above n 6, at 119.

[219] *Ibid* at 119.

[220] See *ibid* at 121; Dolzer and Stevens, above n 40, at pp 79–80.

[221] See UNCTAD 2003, above n 6, at 121, 122, tbl.IV.1; see also Dolzer and Stevens, above n 40, at p 80 (discussing US BITs).

[222] See UNCTAD 2003, above n 6, at 152, box V.4; see also Dolzer and Stevens, above n 40, at p 79 (performance requirements can effectively discriminate against foreign investors).

[223] See Bachand and Rousseau, above n 9, at 18 (noting that NAFTA's prohibition of performance requirements is a 'prohibition on states' subordination of economic activity to certain social objectives [that] must be analyzed from the standpoint of human rights'); see also UNCTAD 2003, above n 6, at 121 (noting that some scholars caution against regulation or prohibition of performance requirements because 'host countries may deliberately choose to use performance requirements and take the risk of reducing FDI for the sake of specific development objectives') (citing VN Balasubramanyam, 'Brief comments on the note on development dimensions of FDI', Paper presented at the UNCTAD Expert Meeting on the development dimension of FDI: policies to enhance the role of FDI in the national and international context, Geneva, Switzerland (6–8 November 2002)).

[224] UNESC Report, above n 3, at para 31(b).

Prohibitions on domestic content and employment requirements can hinder the efforts of States progressively to achieve human rights objectives[225] because, as NGOs have pointed out, prohibitions of performance requirements can prevent States from implementing human rights-inspired development policies such as 'laws requiring foreign investors to form partnerships with local firms so as to foster local capital accumulation; laws that promote the development of local intellectual capital by requiring the employment of local managers; and ... the fledgling programs some Third World countries are developing to address the almost total absence of women in senior management positions.'[226] In addition, the prohibition of limitations on foreign ownership can threaten 'many developing countries' land redistribution policies.'[227] As one NGO notes, '[a] state that abrogates such [performance] requirements could be in breach of its human rights obligations.'[228]

## B. Technology transfers

As UNCTAD states, 'The transfer and dissemination of technology and the promotion of innovation are among the most important benefits that host countries seek from FDI. TNCs are the dominant source of innovation.'[229] Article 15(b) of the International Covenant on Economic, Social and Cultural Rights (ICESCR)[230] recognizes the right of every person to 'enjoy the benefits of scientific progress'; accordingly, BITs that prohibit States from conditioning admission of investment on the transfer of technology by TNCs conceivably can prevent a State from realizing its human rights obligations under the ICESCR.[231]

---

[225] See Bachand and Rousseau, above n 9, at 18 (discussing NAFTA's prohibitions on performance conditions, noting that '[w]hen states are prevented from requiring investors to attain certain levels of domestic content or purchase domestic products and services, they are deprived of an important means of ensuring that private economic activity has an impact on social development and, a fortiori, on the progressive realization of human rights').

[226] Michelle Sforza, Center for Economic and Policy Research, *Globalization, the Multilateral Agreement on Investment, and the Increasing Economic Marginalization of Women*, available at http://www.cepr.net/globalization/womfin.html (last visited 4 November 2004). See also The People's Movement for Human Rights Education, *International NGO Committee on Human Rights in Trade and Investment: Policy Statement*, at para 19, available at http://www.pdhre.org/involved/policy_statement.html (last visited 4 November 2004) (proposed (and now abandoned) MAI could prohibit performance requirements 'established with a human rights purpose, such as requiring a foreign investor to employ local workers, to provide training or to contribute in other ways to the local economy').

[227] Sforza, above n 226.

[228] The People's Movement for Human Rights Education, above n 226, at para 19.

[229] UNCTAD 2003, above n 6, at 129. See generally *ibid* at 129–33.

[230] ICESCR, above n 55, Art 15(b).

[231] See Bachand and Rousseau, above n 9, at 18–19 (discussing NAFTA's performance requirements).

## 2. National Treatment

The progressive realization of human rights principles such as non-discrimination is threatened by BIT prohibitions of national treatment (as well as by prohibitions of performance requirements). As stated in the Report of the UN High Commissioner for Human Rights:

> In the context of post-apartheid South Africa, the [National Water Act of the Republic of South Africa (Act No 36 of 1998)] envisages favourable treatment to racial minorities to redress the results of past racial and gender discrimination in the issuance of water licences. While such a measure could favour certain nationals over foreigners—including foreign investors that might seek access to water as a means of providing water and sanitation services—this might be necessary as a means of dealing with de facto discrimination. [The measure could violate national treatment provisions] despite the fact that the measure is intended to promote equality and diminish racial discrimination rather than act as a barrier to investment.... Similarly, it might be argued that such measures are performance requirements (local content).[232]

As one NGO notes, provisions such as national and most-favored-nation treatment that require States to repeal or refrain from implementing positive measures to protect vulnerable groups 'could cause the state to violate its international human rights obligations.'[233]

## 3. Direct Expropriation and Nationalization

The compensation requirement in BITs can prevent States from implementing large-scale reforms[234] aimed at realizing the right to self-determination

---

[232] UNESC Report, above n 3, at para 31(b). See also Sforza, above n 226 (discussing proposed and abandoned MAI) (asserting that national treatment could permit challenge of '[e]conomic development strategies in place to encourage capital accumulation among the poor and disenfranchised,' '[a]ny subsidies, aid, or grants set aside for local, women-owned business or agricultural development,' and specific programs such as 'India's programs to improve women's access to scarce land resources,' 'Pakistan's programs that provide low-income groups, including large numbers of women in microenterprises, access to financial services,' and 'Armenia's program to create employment opportunities for low-income groups, in which women are actively involved in choosing and evaluating projects').

[233] The People's Movement for Human Rights Education, above n 226, at paras 18–19 (discussion of proposed and abandoned MAI) (referring to 'numerous provisions of the ICESCR, CRC, CERD and CEDAW and other international human rights treaties,' including 'ICESCR articles 2 (non-discrimination), 7 (work and equal opportunity) and 11 (adequate standard of living)').

[234] Although the compensation requirement for expropriations would obtain under customary international law as well, the investor–State dispute resolution mechanism provided by BITs makes the provision more inhibiting of State regulatory action than is the public international law doctrine: see above, nn 37–40 and associated text.

through, for example, indigenization processes[235] or the transfer of rights to natural resources from private entities to the government.[236] The potential of BITs to disrupt human rights-driven reform efforts is illustrated by developments in South Africa, where the Minerals and Petroleum Resources Act (MRDA) of 2002 requires the transfer of all privately owned mineral rights to the South African State, which will then distribute licenses to businesses for exploitation of the rights.[237] The MRDA is part of the BEE program, a race-based affirmative action effort.[238] Under the MRDA, licenses to exploit the rights will be 'predicated upon corporate compliance with a range of policy objectives, including employment equity, human resources development, rural development, and housing and living

---

[235] Indigenization is the transfer of property to nationals of the host State. Dolzer and Stevens, above n 40, at p 98 and fn 265 (citing discussion of Nigeria's indigenization in Osunbor, 'Nigeria's Investment Laws and the State's Control of Multinationals' (1988) 3 *ICSID Review–Foreign Investment Law Journal* 38). Zimbabwe is facing investment treaty claims as a result of a land indigenization program:

> In 2001, the Pan African News Agency wire reported that the Zimbabwean government backed away from plans to acquire a number of foreign-owned farms, as part of its controversial land reform programme, following representations from Switzerland, Austria, Germany, Belgium, the Netherlands and Italy—often invoking the provisions of bilateral investment protection treaties concluded between those governments and Zimbabwe.
>
> And, in 2002, the High Court of Zimbabwe ordered the Zimbabwean government to refrain from the compulsory acquisition of a German-owned estate, 'unless such acquisition is done strictly in accordance' with the 1995 Germany–Zimbabwe bilateral investment treaty.
>
> However, in more recent times, the Zimbabwean government has accelerated its land reform efforts, and moved ahead with compulsory acquisitions of properties held by foreign nationals of states, including nationals who might enjoy protection under a bilateral investment treaty.
>
> ...
>
> INVEST-SD can confirm that a small number of Dutch nationals are now fighting the compulsory acquisition of their properties through the launch of investor-state arbitration under the terms of investment protection treaties.

Luke Eric Peterson, 'Zimbabwe facing treaty claims arising out of land reform programme', *INVEST-SD: Investment Law and Policy Weekly News Bulletin* (International Institute for Sustainable Development, Winnipeg, Canada), 21 January 2005, available at http://www.iisd.org/pdf/2005/investment_investsd_jan21_2005.pdf.

[236] In one such scenario, foreign investors who sought to sue the Democratic Republic of the Congo (DRC) after revocation of mining concessions by the State 'have been singled out for criticism in a special UN report on the illegal exploitation of natural resources in the DRC': Luke Eric Peterson, International Institute for Sustainable Development, *Research Note: Emerging Bilateral Investment Treaty Arbitration and Sustainable Development* (2003), at part 3(c) and fn 31 (citing United Nations, *Report of the Panel of Experts on the Illegal Exploitation of Natural Resources and Other Forms of Wealth of the Democratic Republic of the Congo* (2002), http://www.un.org/News/dh/latest/drcongo.htm).

[237] Luke Eric Peterson, 'US–Southern Africa Negotiations Stall; Race-based Affirmative Action an Obstacle?', *INVEST-SD: Investment Law and Policy Weekly News Bulletin* (International Institute for Sustainable Development, Winnipeg, Canada), 22 July 2004, available at http://www.iisd.org/pdf/2004/investment_investsd_july22_2004.pdf.

[238] *Ibid*; see also IISD 2003, above n 4, at 23.

conditions.'[239] Prior to the MRDA's passage, commentators warned[240] that it might violate expropriation provisions in BITs with the United Kingdom and Belgium and Luxembourg.[241] Although industry apparently decided for political reasons not to contest the law, the government, after talks with industry, dropped plans for more ambitious reforms.[242] The issue continues to play out, as plans to include exceptions to investor protections for the BEE program in a new United States–South Africa Free Trade and Investment Agreement may encounter objections from United States investors claiming to be disadvantaged relative to European investors, based on the lack of such exemptions in earlier BITs between South Africa and European countries.[243]

### 4. Indirect Expropriation: The Water Cases

Three pending cases in the context of water privatization illustrate the effect of BITs on host country efforts to realize the right to water for all citizens.[244] In *Compañía de Aguas del Aconquija SA. and Vivendi Universal v Argentine Republic*, Vivendi initiated an arbitration against Argentina under the France–Argentina BIT for violations of provisions including

---

[239] Luke Eric Peterson, 'South Africa's Plans for Black Economic Empowerment Confronting Foreign Investor Rights', *INVEST-SD: Investment Law and Policy Weekly News Bulletin* (International Institute for Sustainable Development, Winnipeg, Canada), 9 May 2003, available at http://www.iisd.org/pdf/2003/investment_investsd_may9_2003.pdf.

[240] These warnings were made in articles published in the *The Economist*, see Peterson, above n 237, and in South African news publications, see Peterson, above n 239. See also IISD 2003, above n 4, at 23 and fn 70 ('[f]oreign investors, including those in the mining sector, have reacted warily to [BEE proposals]; at times, threatening use of bilateral investment treaties in an effort to discourage some of the more far-reaching proposals being considered').

[241] Peterson, above n 239.

[242] *Ibid.* Had South Africa been compelled to withdraw the MRDA, it may have been in violation of its human rights obligations. See The People's Movement for Human Rights Education, above n 226, at para 21 ('[u]nder international human rights law, states have the obligation of non-retrogression, according to which states are not permitted to remove, weaken or withdraw from legislation and programs, which implement their human rights obligations').

[243] Peterson, above n 237.

[244] Additionally, three subsidiaries of Suez have initiated water privatization-related claims against Argentina at ICSID. See Peterson, above n 64, at 22 (citing *Aguas Provinciales de Santa Fe, SA, Suez, Sociedad General de Aguas de Barcelona, SA and Interagua Servicios Integrales de Agua, SA v Argentine Republic* (Case No ARB/03/17), *Aguas Cordobesas, SA., Suez, and Sociedad General de Aguas de Barcelona, SA v Argentine Republic* (Case No ARB/03/18), *Aguas Argentinas, SA., Suez, Sociedad General de Aguas de Barcelona, SA and Vivendi Universal, SA v Argentine Republic* (Case No ARB/03/19)).

The right to water is a component of the right to health. See below, at section IV.2.D.1. Although these cases involve the States' attempts, through privatization, progressively to realize the right to water by arranging for the provision of services that might otherwise be out of reach, in at least some of the cases the States may have, in a sense, been complicit in

those on expropriation and fair and equitable treatment, alleging that the government incited customers not to pay their water bills.[245] The tribunal initially ruled against the claims, taking jurisdiction but limiting itself to considering evidence outside the context of the relevant concession agreement, since the agreement specified that it could be interpreted exclusively by the provincial courts.[246] However, the award has since been annulled under ICSID's annulment process[247] and the proceeding reinstituted.[248]

In another case, Azurix Corporation, an Enron spin-off, filed a claim against Argentina, for $550 million in compensation, alleging violations of the expropriation, fair and equitable treatment, and security and protection provisions of the United States–Argentina BIT after the government warned customers 'to avoid drinking the local water and to minimize exposure to showers and baths, due to an outbreak of toxic bacteria in the local water supply,' and after the government allegedly failed to deliver

the eventual violation of the right, due to their failure (1) to effectively negotiate the concession agreements, see Bachand and Rousseau, above n 9, at 32, and (2) to permit public participation in negotiations, see Maria McFarland Sánchez-Moreno and Tracy Higgins, 'No Recourse: Transnational Corporations and the Protection of Economic, Social, and Cultural Rights in Bolivia' (2004) 27 *Fordham International Law Journal* 1663, at 1747 ('there is no doubt that the processes by which Cochabamba's water system was privatized and the new water law passed lacked transparency and public participation. With regard to the privatization negotiation, few opportunities for public input were available and the government made no effort to communicate to the public the nature of the deal with Aguas del Tunari. Finally, in order to ratify its deal with Aguas del Tunari, the government succeeded in passing a new water law in a hurried and deceptive manner, again undermining public participation...we approach the water war primarily as an illustration of how a State's failure to respect rights of public participation may contribute to the violation of substantive rights, particularly social, economic, and cultural rights'), 1665 ('the core problem involves Bolivia's failure to guarantee the procedural rights that are necessary for the effective protection of substantive ESC rights').

The following summaries draw primarily from IISD 2003, above n 4; for other accounts of these disputes, see Bachand and Rousseau, above n 9, at 31–32; Peterson, above n 64, at 22–24; UNESC Report, above n 3, at paras 51–54; Sánchez-Moreno and Higgins, above, at 1747–88; Erik J Woodhouse, 'The "Guerra del Agua" and the Cochabamba Concession: Social Risk and Foreign Direct Investment in Public Infrastructure' (2003) 39 *Stanford Journal of International Law* 295.

[245] IISD 2003, above n 4, at 26.

[246] See *Compañía de Aguas del Aconquija, SA & Compagnie Générale des Eaux v Argentine Republic States* (ICSID Case No ARB/97/3) (2000), at 2–3, available at http://www.worldbank.org/icsid/cases/ada_AwardoftheTribunal.pdf.

[247] See *Decision on Annulment, Compañía de Aguas del Aconquija, SA. & Vivendi Universal (formerly Compagnie Générale des Eaux) v Argentine Republic States* (ICSID Case No ARB/97/3) (2002), available at http://www.worldbank.org/icsid/cases/vivendi_annul.pdf; Luke Eric Peterson, 'New Tribunal Constituted in Long-Running Vivendi–Argentina Water Dispute', *INVEST-SD: Investment Law and Policy Weekly News Bulletin* (International Institute for Sustainable Development, Winnipeg, Canada), 11 May 2004, available at http://www.iisd.org/pdf/2004/investment_investsd_may11_2004.pdf.

[248] See IISD 2003, above n 4, at 27; Peterson, above n 247.

promised infrastructure.[249] In a third case, *Bechtel Corporation v Bolivia*, Bechtel filed a claim against Bolivia under the Netherlands–Bolivia BIT seeking $25 million in damages from Bolivia for expropriation.[250] Bolivia had granted exclusive rights to all water in Cochabamba, the country's third-largest city, including wells formerly possessed by communities.[251] There was a popular uprising after some water bills almost doubled, and a state of emergency was declared. As two commentators summarize, '[w]hen [Bolivia] reversed its decision on privatization in response to the pressure exerted by the population of Cochabamba, the corrective measures it implemented ran counter to its commitments under international investment law.'[252]

### 5. Prohibitions on Capital Transfer Restrictions; Definition of 'Investment'

Most BITs contain clauses guaranteeing the 'free transfer of all payments related to, or in connection with, an investment.'[253] Unfettered cross-border capital transfers can create financial and social instability,[254] inhibiting the ability of States to meet human rights obligations through development policies and other national initiatives.[255]

---

[249] IISD 2003, above n 4, at 27–28 (citing *Azurix Corp v the Argentine Republic* (ICSID Case No ARB/01/12) (2003)).

[250] Bachand and Rousseau, above n 9, at 31–32.

[251] IISD 2003, above n 4, at 28.

[252] Bachand and Rousseau, above n 9, at 32. See the discussion in the introduction to Part III on the potential of BITs to stifle State experimentation with privatization by making it too costly.

[253] UNCTAD 1998, above n 56, at 76. See generally Dolzer and Stevens, above n 40, at pp 85–96; UNCTAD 1998, above n 56, at 75–81; Sornarajah, above n 36, at pp 252–53.

[254] See UNESC Report, above n 3, at para 31(a) (capital transfer may contribute to financial crises with attendant social and political problems) (citing Center for International Environmental Law/El Instituto del Tercer Mundo/Preamble Center, *Investment Agreement of the Americas: Environmental, Economic and Social Perspectives* (1999), at 6, 12, available at http://ciel.org/Publications/miamiinvestmentpaper.pdf (last visited 12 September 2004)); see also UNESC Report, above n 3, at para 8 ('[i]n the 1990s several developing countries experienced surges and reversals of foreign capital flows that destabilized the local economy, particularly where the reversals were sudden and large') (discussing the effects of portfolio investment but noting that 'the distinction between FDI and more volatile investments is becoming blurred and investors are increasingly able to convert bricks and mortar investments into liquid assets which they can rapidly take out of the country. As such, some forms of FDI might have similar effects to short-term capital flows in times of crisis'); see also Bachand and Rousseau, above n 9, at 19.

[255] See UNESC Report, above n 3, at para 31 ('"States have the right and the duty to formulate appropriate national development policies that aim at the constant improvement of the well-being of the entire population and of all individuals, on the basis of their active, free and meaningful participation in development and in the fair distribution of the benefits resulting therefrom"') (citing Art 2(3) of the Declaration on the Right to Development). According to the UNESC Report, economic instability:

The broader the definition of 'investment', the greater the range of financial activities protected by the prohibitions on transfer restrictions. As UNCTAD states, '[t]he main question is not whether FDI should be defined as investment—it is. The question is what other investment should be granted the same status: portfolio investment (both equity and debt components), other capital flows (bank loans, non-bank loans and other flows) and various investment assets (both tangible and intangible, including intellectual property rights),'[256] since:

> [if such assets qualify as investments, o]bligations to meet financial transfer requirements could for many developing countries at times be difficult to fulfill. Possible complications could arise for macroeconomic management of capital flows of a type and magnitude that may be beyond the control of national governments. And volatile capital flows have implications for domestic financial stability.[257]

The scope of the definition of 'investment' thus impacts on the ability of host States to maintain a stable economic environment that is conducive to the progressive realization of human rights.

## 6. Admission

As noted above in section II.3.B, the admission clause may grant a 'right of establishment' or provide for 'national treatment in the pre-establishment phase,'[258] requiring a State to admit foreign investment in a situation in which it would otherwise deny entry. The admission clause thus amplifies the effects of the other investment protection provisions of BITs which erode a State's capacity progressively to realize human rights through reform policies that may include performance requirements, favor local over foreign investors, require the nationalization or indigenization of private property or restrict cross-border capital transfers.

---

can have negative effects on the enjoyment of human rights, straining available resources in national budgets needed for the progressive realization of economic, social and cultural rights and the right to development. The independent expert on the right to development noted that this was the general experience of the East Asian financial crisis in the second half of the 1990s, although it should be noted that the volatility of short-term capital flows was only one of many factors that led to the crisis.

*Ibid* at para 8 (discussing the effects of portfolio investment, but noting that 'the distinction between FDI and more volatile investments is becoming blurred and investors are increasingly able to convert bricks and mortar investments into liquid assets which they can rapidly take out of the country. As such, some forms of FDI might have similar effects to short-term capital flows in times of crisis').

[256] UNCTAD 2003, above n 6, at 100.
[257] *Ibid* at 99.
[258] *Ibid* at 102.

## IV. INTERSECTION WITH HUMAN RIGHTS OBLIGATIONS

### 1. Significance of a Human Rights Defense in Investment Arbitrations

The fact that States are subject to binding human rights obligations under treaties and customary international law, [259] as well as under domestic law, poses a question about the relationship between those obligations and the obligations imposed by BITs.[260] By using a human rights obligtion as a defense when a regulation is challenged under a BIT, could a State keep in place the regulation or reduce the amount of compensation due to the investor? Although 'there have been no known investment treaty arbitrations where host states have adverted to ... human rights obligations,'[261] there appears to be a possibility that in certain circumstances, arbitral tribunals constituted under BITs would be required to take a State's human rights obligations into account.

The importance of States raising human rights obligations before arbitral tribunals was emphasized in a report by the UN High Commissioner for Human Rights. The report notes that in the absence of an international mechanism for adjudicating claims against States by individuals alleging violations of economic and social rights, States should inject human rights

---

[259] A State's human rights obligations at international law might derive from treaties to which it is a party or from customary international law. See, eg, Bachand and Rousseau, above n 9, at 26, fn 80.

States' duties with regard to their human rights obligations can be broken down into three components: the obligation to respect (refrain from interfering with) the right; the obligation to protect (prevent violations by third parties of) the right; and the obligation to fulfill (take measures towards the full realization of) the right: see, eg, UNESC Report, above n 3, at para 29.

[260] In a situation currently playing out in Ecuador, the indigenous Kichwa people of Sarayacu are pursuing a remedy at the Inter-American Court of Human Rights in response to conflicts with an Argentine oil company partly owned by US investors: see generally Luke Eric Peterson, 'Human Rights Body Intercedes to Protect Indigenous Group Opposed to Oil Exploration', *INVEST-SD: Investment Law and Policy Weekly News Bulletin* (International Institute for Sustainable Development, Winnipeg, Canada), 23 May 2003, available at http://www.iisd.org/pdf/2003/investment_investsd_may23_2003.pdf; Marisa Handler, 'Indigenous tribe takes on big oil: Ecuadoran village refuses money, blocks attempts at drilling on ancestral land', *San Francisco Chronicle*, 13 August 2004, available at http://sfgate.com/cgi-bin/article.cgi?f=/c/a/2004/08/13/MNGHB86B4V1.DTL. Since Ecuador has signed BITs with Argentina and the United States, it is conceivable that the oil company would bring a claim against Ecuador to an arbitral tribunal if the concession contract is broken by the government as a result of the human rights proceeding, in which case 'the Ecuadorian Government could find itself caught between competing international legal obligations to indigenous groups on the one hand, and foreign investors on the other.' See Peterson, above.

[261] IISD 2003, above n 4, at 23; see also *ibid* at 31 (although petitioners couched argument about effect of damages on State's ability to provide water to its citizens in 'rights' language, they 'did not advert to any national or international human rights norms which might have reinforced their arguments').

considerations into investment treaty arbitrations, lest the development of international law fail sufficiently to take account of such rights:[262]

> [T]here is currently no international mechanism to consider complaints on all aspects of economic, social and cultural rights. On the other hand, under investment agreements, investors have recourse to international redress against States and States have redress against other States. This risks skewing the balance of protection in favour of investors, which in turn could lead to investment decisions favouring the interests of investors over the human rights of individuals and communities who could remain voiceless in the event of a conflict of interests and rights.[263]

The UN report encourages States to raise human rights obligations in investment treaty disputes 'in an attempt to secure interpretations of investment agreements and tribunal decisions that take into account the wider legal and social context.'[264]

---

[262] See UNESC Report, above n 3, at paras 41, 54–55.

[263] *Ibid* at para 41. The report notes the unevenness of international mechanisms to deal with human rights complaints by individuals:

> The Human Rights Committee has the authority to hear individual complaints in relation to civil and political rights while the Committee on the Elimination of Discrimination against Women (CEDAW) has the authority to consider individual complaints of women in relation to discrimination in the exercise of their human rights, including economic, social and cultural rights. The ILO has a series of mechanisms such as the Committee on Freedom of Association and its Fact-Finding and Conciliation Committee to consider complaints in relation to certain labour rights; however, these do not allow individual complaints nor do they address the interdependence of human rights owing to their focusing solely on labour standards.

*Ibid*. While there are also regional mechanisms to hear human rights complaints by individuals, the report identifies the limitations of one such mechanism in the inter-American context:

> While the Inter-American system includes a mechanism for individual complaints concerning economic, social and cultural rights, the tribunal has jurisdiction to hear complaints only in relation to workers' human rights and the right to education (the San Salvador Protocol). Internationally, there is still no comprehensive individual complaint mechanism for violations of economic, social and cultural rights.

*Ibid* at para 54. See also Bachand and Rousseau, above n 9, at 14 ('[e]ven more than most civil and political rights, the justiciability of most economic, social and cultural rights is deplorably limited at present'), 33 ('the difference between the mechanisms established in human rights law and investment law is a major problem with the relationship between those two bodies of law. While the investment agreements enable investors to sue states that impede the full enjoyment of an investor's property, international human rights treaties provide weak or non-existent remedies to citizens, however grave the violations').

[264] UNESC Report, above n 3, at para 55. An elaboration of this point immediately precedes the cited statement:

> the lack of mechanisms to resolve [non-commercial] issues risks weighing the balance in favour of resolving problems according to the terms of investment agreements which might not necessarily take into account the many other non-commercial dimensions of the issue at hand. To the extent that this prioritizes commercial considerations over other issues, it raises concerns for the promotion and protection of human rights which considers development not only in commercial terms but as 'economic, social, cultural and political development in which all human rights and fundamental freedoms can be fully realized.'

*Ibid* (citing Declaration on the Right to Development, Art 1).

## 2. Hypothetical Application: The Tecmed Case

Using the *Tecmed* arbitration as a case study, this section will consider how a State might go about raising a human rights defense.[265] First, the relationship of international law to investment arbitrations will be examined. The *Tecmed* award will then be summarized. Finally, there will be an analysis of how Mexico may have structured human rights-based defenses to Tecmed's claims.

### A. The Relationship of International Law to Investment Arbitrations

The law applicable to an investment dispute will be the law specified in the treaty, or if none is specified, the law agreed by the parties leading up to arbitration, or if none is agreed, the law determined as per the arbitration rules.[266] Some BITs stipulate that applicable law, in addition to comprising the provisions of the treaty itself, will include international law.[267] According to the Deputy Secretary-General of ICSID, 'because the treaties are instruments of international law, it should be implicit that arbitrators "should have recourse to the rules of general international law to supplement those of the treaty."'[268] Under the ICSID Convention, one set of arbitral rules, '"where the parties cannot agree on the applicable law, the Tribunal will apply the law of the host state and such rules of international

---

[265] This analysis was inspired in part by a research paper written by Luke Peterson for the International Institute for Sustainable Development:

> Further work needs to be undertaken in order to assess emerging investment treaty disputes through a human rights lens, so as to ascertain their possible implications for human rights issues. An essential part of this task will be to further analyse the prospect for human rights norms to be injected in to investment arbitrations, and weighed by Tribunals tasked with interpreting investment treaty obligations, in a manner which will be consonant with consideration of a host state's broader international commitments, including human rights.

IISD 2003, above n 4, at 31–32.

[266] See *ibid* at 10.

[267] See *ibid* at 10; Dolzer and Stevens, above n 40, at pp 128–29 (noting that '[g]enerally speaking, European treaties appear not to include references to the law that tribunals arbitrating disputes between Contracting Parties are to apply,' with the exception of treaties concluded by Germany, Switzerland and the United Kingdom, while 'US treaties normally provide that disputes between the Parties that are submitted to an arbitral tribunal shall be decided "in accordance with applicable rules of international law",' and '[r]ecent Chinese treaties have ... emphasized that such principles of international law that are to apply shall be recognized by both States').

[268] See IISD 2003, above n 4, at 10 (citing Antonio Parra, 'Applicable Substantive Law in ICSID Arbitrations Initiated Under Investment Treaties' (2001)16 *ICSID Review* 21); see also Dolzer and Stevens, above n 40, at p 129 ('normally it is presumed that international agreements are governed by international law').

law as may be applicable.'[269] In many cases, then, international law will be applicable to investment disputes to some extent, and in disputes where that is the case, arbitral tribunals may have the opportunity to consider international human rights obligations of States.[270] The Spain–Mexico BIT, which governed the *Tecmed* arbitration, provides that disputes thereunder will be decided in accordance with the provisions of the treaty and the applicable rules of international law.[271] Mexico's human rights obligations therefore could have been considered by the tribunal in *Tecmed*.

The consideration of human rights obligations by a BIT arbitral tribunal could conceivably occur in two situations: where the obligations are raised by one of the parties, and where the court considers the obligations *moto proprio*. The latter would likely only occur where, unlike in *Tecmed*, the investor and the state were complicit in human rights violations.[272] The former could have occured in *Tecmed*, and in the context of BITs, a State party's assertion of a human rights defense could potentially have two legal effects: first, in the case of an expropriation claim, liability could perhaps be avoided by arguing that the challenged measure was within the State's police powers and thus not an expropriation. Second, as a defense to other types of investor claims, or if the foregoing argument is rejected with regard to an expropriation claim, damages could potentially be reduced by arguing that the State's human rights obligations should mitigate the amount of compensation owed.[273] With regard to the first possibility, 'by referring to long-standing and broadly endorsed international human rights obligations,' a host State could argue that the challenged measure fulfilled a police power function.[274] If the tribunal adopted the indirect expropriations standard under which a public purpose does not preclude a measure from having expropriatory status, however, this argument would be unsuccessful *ab initio* in pre-

---

[269] IISD 2003, above n 4, at 10 (citing Washington Convention on the Settlement of Disputes Between States and Nationals of other States, 1965, 575 UNTS 159, 4 ILM 524 (1966)). This reference to rules of international law is meant to denote the sources enumerated in Art 38 of the Statute of the International Court of Justice: treaties, customary international law, and generally principles of law recognized by civilised nations, and subsidiary sources which include the opinions of jurists and judicial decisions. IISD 2003, above n 4, at 10 (citing Report of the World Bank Executive Directors on the Convention, para 40, Doc ICSID/2, 1 ICSID Rep 31).

[270] See IISD 2003, above n 4, at 10.

[271] See Spain–Mexico BIT, above n 148, Apéndice, Título Sexto, Derecho Aplicable ('Cualquier tribunal establecido conforme a este Apéndice decidirá las controversias que se sometan a su consideración de conformidad con las disposiciones de este Acuerdo y las reglas aplicables del Derecho Internacional'). See also *Técnicas Medioambientales Tecmed SA v United Mexican States* (ICSID Case No ARB(AF)/00/2) (2003), at para 116, available at http://www.worldbank.org/icsid/cases/laudo051903FINAL.pdf (Spanish original version), http://www.worldbank.org/icsid/cases/laudo-051903%20-English.pdf (unofficial English translation).

[272] See below n 334 and associated text.

[273] See IISD 2003, above n 4, at 30–31.

[274] *Ibid* at 30.

venting the measure from being deemed an expropriation. The second possibility, reduction of damages, would then come into play, at least where the BIT gives some discretion to the tribunal to determine the level of compensation.[275] For example, where expropriatory measures could be shown to be 'undertaken in the furtherance of competing human rights commitments,' the State's motive in pursuing the measures could be argued to reduce the level of compensation owed to the complaining investor.[276]

To establish the argument in either of these cases, the State would first have to establish that 'the measure had been taken to conform to an existing obligation' under customary or treaty law.[277] The State would then have to demonstrate that the BIT and the human rights obligation are incompatible, and, presumably, that 'no other measure could enable it to fulfill its [human rights] obligations.'[278] If the tribunal then decided, based on the traditional rules of interpretation of international law sources, to give precedence to the human rights obligation over the investment treaty obligation,[279] it is conceivable that the tribunal would find that a State was not liable under the BIT or owed reduced compensation.[280] In at least one

---

[275] *Ibid.*

[276] But see *ibid* at 30–31 (noting Philippe Sands' criticism of one ICSID case (not decided under a BIT) in which the tribunal refused to take the environmental purpose of an expropriation into account in calculating damages) (citing *Compañía del Desarrollo de Santa Elena SA v Republic of Costa Rica* (2000) 39 ILM 317). The suggested approach, adjusting compensation based on the State's motive for regulating, may have utility with regard to rights that must be promoted though progressive realization by the State:

> Similar concerns will certainly attend the arbitration of disputes implicating economic or social rights, such as the right to water. Because these rights are contingent upon the best-efforts of a state to utilize 'the maximum of its available resources, with a view to achieving progressively the full realization of the rights recognized in the covenant,' arbitrators ought to be awake to the human rights implications of any methodology used for evaluating compensation in such cases [because the level of compensation] will necessarily have a direct and measureable effect upon the level of "available resources" which may be harnessed to the effort to progressively realize the right in question.

IISD 2003, above n 4, at 31 (internal citation omitted).

[277] See Bachand and Rousseau, above n 9, at 26. The discussion in Bachand and Rousseau concerns the NAFTA context. Under NAFTA, the State would not have recourse to a human rights obligation in a treaty, because NAFTA has precedence over other treaties, with limited exceptions, see *ibid* at 25, although sometimes an obligation can exist independently and concurrently in both a treaty and customary international law: see *ibid* at 26, fn 80. In the BIT context, a State is likely to have more success adverting to a treaty-based norm than a customary norm (unless the norm is a *jus cogens* norm), because a BIT might be viewed as a *lex specialis* prevailing over a customary norm. See Sornarajah, above n 36, at pp 226–27; see also above n 41 (citing several discussions of whether BITs constitute customary international law or *lex specialis*).

[278] Bachand and Rousseau, above n 9, at 26.

[279] See *ibid* at 26; above, section I.2 (relationship of BITs to public international law).

[280] Tribunals might also have occasion to take human rights into account *moto proprio* in situations where peremptory norms of international law have been violated and the State was complicit in or enabled or ignored such violations. See IISD 2003, above n 4, at 18–20; below n 334.

known ICSID arbitration, a State raised a treaty obligation (although not a human rights obligation) as a defense of its treatment of an investor.[281] The tribunal rejected the defense because the treaty did not in fact mandate the State's action, but the tribunal did not appear to foreclose the possibility that a State's international obligations could justify the breach of a BIT.[282]

### B. Synopsis of the Tecmed Arbitration

As mentioned above, in the *Tecmed*[283] award, an ICSID arbitral tribunal found that the failure of a Mexican agency to renew an operating permit for a landfill constituted a violation of two clauses of the BIT between Spain and Mexico: the prohibition on expropriation without compensation, and the guarantee of fair and equitable treatment.[284] The tribunal ordered Mexico to pay US$5.5 million in compensation for the lost value of the investment.[285]

***1. The Facts***   In 1996 the claimant, Tecmed, purchased in a municipal auction a landfill near the town of Las Víboras in the municipality of Hermosillo, in the State of Sonora, Mexico.[286] Tecmed formed a corporation

---

If a State raised a BIT obligation as a defense to a human rights claim before a human rights tribunal, it seems that a similar analysis would govern, except that BITs concluded after the conclusion of the human rights treaty would be likely to be interpreted in light of the human rights obligations contained in the human rights treaty. Cf below, section IV.2.C.1.

[281] See *Southern Pacific Properties (Middle East) Limited v Arab Republic of Egypt* (1993) 32 ILM 933 at paras 150–54 .

[282] See *ibid* at para 154. One commentator characterizes the relevant part of the award as holding that 'obligations imposed by other international conventions entered into by a host state may be adverted to in that state's defence of its treatment of the investor': IISD 2003, above n 4, at 29 (continuing, 'the Tribunal took seriously the argument that a host state's failure to interfere with an investment, might have been contrary to its international law commitments under a UNESCO convention on the protection of cultural antiquities ... [a]lthough the argument was not persuasive on the facts of the case, nevertheless it signaled that ICSID Tribunals may take account of a state's broader international law commitments, in the course of assessing that state's compliance with its investment treaty commitments to foreign investors').

[283] *Técnicas Medioambientales Tecmed SA v United Mexican States* (ICSID Case No ARB(AF)/00/2) (2003) at para 116, available at http://www.worldbank.org/icsid/cases/laudo051903FINAL.pdf (Spanish original version), http://www.worldbank.org/icsid/cases/audo-051903%20-English.pdf (unofficial English translation). All quoted text is from the unofficial English version of the opinion.

[284] See *ibid* at paras 151 (expropriation), 174 (fair and equitable treatment). Tecmed also claimed violations of the full protection and security, nondiscrimination, most-favoured-nation treatment, national treatment and admission clauses, all of which claims the tribunal rejected. See *ibid* at paras 175–82.

[285] See *ibid* at para 197.

[286] See *ibid* at para 35. While it was disputed whether Tecmed had purchased the right to continue operating the plant under the existing permits in addition to having purchased the physical assets comprising the landfill, see *ibid* at paras 75–92, this issue was resolved in favor of Tecmed, see *ibid* at paras 90–91.

called Cytrar to operate the landfill.[287] Mexican regulations promulgated subsequently to the purchase[288] prohibited the siting of hazardous waste landfills within a particular distance from an urban center, a distance which exceeded the distance of the Cytrar landfill from Hermosillo;[289] the regulations did not apply to the landfill, however, since they did not have retroactive effect.[290] Community pressure to close the landfill resulted in Cytrar agreeing to relocate the operation to another site to be identified by the Mexican authorities.[291] Cytrar's request to continue operating the landfill under the existing permit of unlimited duration was denied, and Cytrar was issued a permit renewable annually.[292] In November 1998, the National Ecology Institute of Mexico (INE),[293] a federal agency within the Ministry of the Environment, Natural Resources and Fisheries (SEMARNAP),[294] issued a resolution[295] which denied the renewal of the permit, citing four violations of the permit with environmental and health implications.[296] At the time Tecmed filed its claim at

---

[287] See *ibid* at para 35 ('the holder of Tecmed's rights and obligations under the tender came to be Cytrar, a company organized by Tecmed for such purpose and to run the landfill operations').

[288] See *ibid* at para 109.

[289] See *ibid* at para 117.

[290] See *ibid* at para 141.

[291] See *ibid* at para 142.

[292] See *ibid* at para 38.

[293] See *ibid* at para 36. INE 'is in charge of Mexico's national policy on ecology and environmental protection, and is also the regulatory body on environmental issues': *ibid*.

[294] See *ibid* at para 36.

[295] See *ibid* at para 95.

[296] See *ibid* at para 99. The grounds for the non-renewal were:

(i) the Landfill was only authorized to receive waste from agrochemicals or pesticides or containers and materials contaminated with such elements; (ii) PROFEPA's delegates in Sonora had informed, in the official communication dated November 11, 1998, that the waste confined far exceeded the landfill limits established for one of the Landfill's active cells, cell No 2; (iii) the Landfill temporarily stored hazardous waste destined for a place outside the Landfill, acting as a 'transfer center,' an activity for which the Landfill did not have the required authorization; Cytrar was requested on October 16, 1997 to file reports in connection with this activity, but to date the relevant authorization had not been issued; and (iv) liquid and biological-infectious waste was received at the Landfill, an activity that was prohibited and that amounted to a breach of the obligation to notify in advance any change or modification in the scope of the Permit [and that constituted] unauthorized storage at the Landfill of liquid and biological-infectious waste.

*Ibid.*

Tecmed disputed the factual bases of the justifications for the non-renewal of the permit, claiming among other things that PROFEPA had investigated the landfill levels of cell no 2 and issued a small fine in connection with it, stating that the infringement 'did not have a "significant effect on public health or generate an ecological imbalance",' and that another fine addressing the temporary storage of hazardous waste and operation as a transfer center was accompanied by a statement that the infringements were not serious enough to justify revocation of the permit nor did they impact public health or generate an ecological

ICSID in July 2000,[297] negotiations on a relocation site for the landfill had been abandoned,[298] partly due to community opposition to one of the alternative sites.[299]

*2. The Expropriation Analysis*   The tribunal's analysis of the expropriation claim relied on a distinction between regulatory measures that merely decrease the value of an investor's assets, and therefore are not necessarily expropriatory, and those that completely deprive an investor's assets of value, which do constitute expropriation.[300] The standard the tribunal applied was that State actions, 'whether regulatory are not, are an indirect de facto expropriation if they are irreversible and permanent and if the assets or rights subject to such measure have been affected in such a way that "... any form of exploitation thereof ..." has disappeared; ie the economic value of the use, enjoyment or disposition of the assets or rights affected by the administrative action or decision have been neutralized or destroyed.'[301] As mentioned above,[302] the tribunal aligned itself with the

---

imbalance: see *ibid* at paras 100–2. At the arbitration, Mexico argued that the resolution had been motivated by public interest concerns in relation to (1) the protection of the environment and public health, and (2) the need to provide a response to community pressure regarding the landfill's location 'and Cytrar's violations during the operation, which some groups interpreted as harmful to the environment or the public health': see *ibid* at para 125. The tribunal appeared to view the asserted basis of the protection of the environment and public health as a post hoc rationalization: see *ibid* at para 124 ('the Arbitral Tribunal points out that [the resolution] does not suggest that the violations [of the permit] compromise public health, impair ecological balance or protection of the environment, or that they may be the reason for a genuine social crisis'); see also *ibid* at para 130.

    Several citations had been issued for environmental violations in the operation of the landfill and in the shipping of waste to the landfill: see *ibid* at paras 107, 123. The operation of the landfill and the shipping of waste were governed by different permits; at issue in the arbitration was only the operating permit: see *ibid* at paras 123, 134. To the extent that the community opposition was a response to the shipping of waste, the tribunal did not give it any weight in the analysis of the justifiability of the expropriation, since (1) it could not have formed a basis for the non-renewal of the operating permit, see *ibid* at para 134, (2) the authorities' decision to confine the waste in the landfill, rather than Cytrar's management of the shipping process, was what motivated that part of the community opposition, see *ibid* at para 136, and (3) the violations during the shipping activity did not provoke any serious response from the Mexican agencies, which meant they should not be given much weight in the proportionality analysis, see *ibid* at paras 137–38.

[297] See *ibid* at para 4.

[298] See *ibid* at para 112.

[299] See *ibid* at para 142, n 170.

[300] *Ibid* at para 115. Total loss of value, the court said, is 'one of the main elements to distinguish, from the point of view of an international tribunal, between a regulatory measure, which is an ordinary expression of the exercise of the state's police power that entails a decrease in assets or rights, and a de facto expropriation that deprives those assets and rights of any real substance': *ibid*.

[301] *Ibid* at para 116 (citing *In re Matos e Silva, Lda, and Others v Portugal* [1996] ECHR 37 (16 September 1996), http://hudoc.echr.coe.int).

[302] See above, section II.1.A.

'sole effect' doctrine,[303] holding that the INE resolution was expropriatory inasmuch as it deprived the landfill of all economic value by shutting it down permanently; even if the landfill were ever allowed by INE to reopen, the siting regulations would become applicable.[304] Additionally, the accumulation of toxic waste at the site would prevent it from being sold in the real estate market.[305]

In what can be considered dicta, the tribunal went on to perform an analysis[306] in which it did not limit itself to consideration only of the effects of the resolution,[307] but instead considered also the regulatory purpose of the resolution and the proportionality of the financial impact to the public interest served by the resolution. The tribunal first concluded that State action with a public regulatory purpose is not per se excluded from the prohibition on expropriations under the Spain–Mexico BIT.[308] The tribunal then moved to a proportionality analysis, stating that '[t]here must be a reasonable relationship of proportionality between the charge or weight imposed [on] the foreign investor and the aim sought to be realized by any expropriatory measure.'[309] Noting that the 'Resolution does not suggest that the violations [of the landfill's operating permit mentioned in the resolution as grounds for shutting down the operation] compromise public health, impair ecological balance or protection of the environment, or that they may be the reason for a genuine social crisis,'[310] and that aside from the violations,

---

[303] See *Tecmed* at para 116 ('[t]he government's intention is less important than the effects of the measures on the owner of the assets or on the benefits arising from such assets affected by the measures; and the form of the deprivation measure is less important than its actual effects').

[304] *Ibid* at para 117.

[305] *Ibid*.

[306] *Ibid* at paras 118–50.

[307] *Ibid* at para 118.

[308] See *ibid* at paras 119–22. While acknowledging that '[t]he principle that the State's exercise of its sovereign powers within the framework of its police power may cause economic damage to those subject to its powers as administrator without entitling them to any compensation whatsoever is undisputable,' *ibid* at para 119, the tribunal held that '[the fact that] the actions of [Mexico] are legitimate or lawful or in compliance with the law from the standpoint of [Mexico]'s domestic laws does not mean that they conform to the Agreement or to international law: "An Act of State must be characterized as internationally wrongful if it constitutes a breach of an international obligation, even if the act does not contravene the State's internal law—even if, under that law, the State was actually bound to act that way"': *ibid* at para 120 (citing J Crawford, *The International Law Commission's Articles on State Responsibility: Introduction, Text and Commentaries* (Cambridge, UK, and New York, NY, Cambridge University Press, 2002), at p 84). The tribunal concluded that, in its interpretation of the expropriation provision of the BIT, it found 'no principle stating that regulatory administrative actions are *per se* excluded from the scope of the Agreement, even if they are beneficial to society as a whole': *Tecmed* at para 121.

[309] *Tecmed* at para 122 (citing *In re Mellacher and Others v Austria* (1989) EHRR at 24, http://hudoc.echr.coe.int; *In re Pressos Compañia Naviera and Others v Belgium* (1995) EHRR at 19, http://hudoc.echr.coe.int).

[310] *Tecmed*, at para 124.

'the Resolution does not specify any reasons of public interest, public use or public emergency that may justify it,'[311] the tribunal held the resolution had in fact been motivated by "socio-political circumstances",[312] and that the economic impact of the resolution was disproportional to such considerations,[313] such that the resolution

---

[311] *Ibid* at para 125. In the arbitration Mexico claimed that such reasons were (1) the protection of the environment and public health, and (2) the need to provide a response to community opposition to the landfill. See *ibid*.

[312] See *ibid* at paras 129, 132. In arriving at this determination, the tribunal accorded weight to its perception that:

> INE, instead of deciding by itself—as it was empowered [to do] by law—as to the Permit's renewal on the basis of considerations exclusively related to INE's specific function linked to the protection of the environment, ecological balance and public health, consulted with the mayor of the Municipality of Hermosillo and the Governor of the State of Sonora as to Cytrar's requests related to the expansion of cell No 2 and the construction of cell No 3 in the Landfill. The only conclusion possible is that such consultation or inquiries were driven by INE's socio-political concerns, since it is not in dispute that INE and PROFEPA were the only entities legally authorized and technically competent to have a role in issues in which public health and protection of the environment in connection with the Landfill were involved.

*Ibid* at para 129. The tribunal was also influenced by 'the absence of any statement in the Resolution and in the opinions rendered by the municipal and state officers consulted by INE prior to issuing the Resolution about ... infringements committed by Cytrar and mentioned in the Resolution being infringements seriously or imminently affecting public health, ecological balance or the environment, together with the confirmation by PROFEPA that such infringements did not pose such dangers': *ibid* at para 130. The tribunal views response to community pressure as an improper basis for agency decision-making:

> Even the significance awarded by INE to the technical infringements [on which the Resolution is based] committed during the operation of the Landfill ... were actually strongly influenced by the community pressure and the political consequences faced by INE ... [the Director General of Hazardous Materials, Waste and Activities considered that the] expansion of cell [N]o 2 did not create current or future hazards for the protection of the environment or public health; she considered that such expansion increased INE's difficulties to manage community pressure and the related political consequences adverse to the landfill: '... as I had issued no written resolution authorizing the expansion of the cell, the fact that [Cytrar] commenced to expand the cell was a concern to me...the circumstance that the company had not helped me create trust among local authorities as it expanded the cells without any authorization, whether issued by me or local authorities, was included among [the elements favoring non-renewal of the permit].'

*Ibid* at para 130.

[313] See *ibid* at paras 139, 149. The tribunal relied on several considerations in arriving at this determination: the community opposition to the landfill was based primarily 'on the site's proximity to Hermosillo's urban center and on the circumstance, not attributable to Cytrar, that the site's location violated the applicable Mexican regulations': *ibid* at para 140; the fact that Cytrar had agreed to relocate the landfill as a result of community pressure, and did not breach or have the intention to breach that commitment: *ibid* at paras 142–43; Mexico presented no 'evidence that community opposition to the Landfill—however intense, aggressive and sustained—was in any way massive or went any further than the positions assumed by some individuals or the members of some groups that were opposed to the Landfill': *ibid* at para 144; and 'Cytrar's operation of the Landfill never compromised the ecological balance, the protection of the environment or the health of the people, and all

constituted an uncompensated expropriation in violation of the BIT and of international law.[314]

### 3. The Fair and Equitable Treatment Analysis

As noted above in section II.3.A, the tribunal rejected the notion that bad faith or egregious behavior on the part of a State is necessary to sustain a violation of the guarantee of fair and equitable treatment,[315] holding that the clause:

> requires the Contracting Parties to provide to international investments treatment that does not affect the basic expectations that were taken into account by the foreign investor to make the investment ... to act in a consistent manner, free from ambiguity and totally transparently in its relations with the foreign investor, so that it may know beforehand any and all rules and regulations that will govern its investments, as well as the goals of the relevant policies and administrative practices or directives, to be able to plan its investment and comply with such regulations. [316]

Tecmed's expectations upon the making of the investment, the tribunal found, 'were that the Mexican laws applicable to such investment, as well as the supervision, control, prevention and punitive powers granted to the authorities in charge of managing such system, would be used for the

the infringements committed were either remediable or remediated or subject to minor penalties': *ibid* at para 148. Ultimately, the tribunal's decision rested on its position that:

> [t]he actions undertaken by the authorities to face ... socio-political difficulties, where these difficulties do not have serious emergency or public hardship connotations, or wide-ranging and serious consequences, may not be considered from the standpoint of the Agreement or international law to be sufficient justification to deprive the foreign investor of its investment with no compensation, particularly if it has not been proved that Cytrar or Tecmed's behavior has been the determinant of the political pressure or the demonstrations that led to such deprivation, which underlie the Resolution and conclusively conditioned it ... [the resolution's closing of the landfill site] shows that INE concluded that the Permit granted to Cytrar should not be renewed and also that from then on nobody should be authorized to operate a hazardous waste landfill at the Las Víboras site, even if it was an operator whose behavior was so flawless that it could not give rise even to minor faults. Such conclusion was consistent with the requests of the Municipality of Hermosillo and the authorities of the state of Sonora with whom INE consulted ... While the Resolution is based on some [violations], apparently through a literal and strict interpretation of the conditions under which the Permit was granted, it would be excessively formalistic, in light of the above considerations, the Agreement and international law, to understand that the Resolution is proportional to such violations when such infringements do not pose a present or imminent risk to the ecological balance or to people's health, and the Resolution, without providing for the payment of compensation as required by Article 5 of the Agreement, leads to the neutralization of the investment's economic and business value and the Claimant's return on investment and profitability expectations upon making the investment.

*Ibid* at paras 147–49.

[314] See *ibid* at paras 139, 149.
[315] See *ibid* at para 153 (citing *Mondev International Ltd. v United States* (ICSID Case No ARB(AF)/99/2) (2002), at 40, 116 (NAFTA arbitration)).
[316] *Tecmed*, at para 154.

purpose of assuring compliance with environmental protection, human health and ecological balance goals underlying such laws.'[317]

The tribunal based its finding of a violation of the clause on two aspects of INE's conduct, one of which relates to the resolution,[318] and one of which relates to the replacement of the landfill's original permit of unlimited duration with a permit renewable annually, an administrative action which occurred prior to the BIT's entry into force but after its signing.[319] With regard to the resolution, the tribunal identified inconsistencies, contradictions and lack of transparency in INE's behavior inasmuch as it failed to provide (1) notice to Cytrar of the violations or irregularities which necessitated the issuance of the regulation, and (2) opportunity to correct any such violations.[320] These inconsistencies led the tribunal to deduce that INE's true aim was not to secure the correction of any such violations, but rather that it must have been either to coerce Cytrar to relocate the landfill,[321] which coercion would violate the guarantee of fair and equitable treatment,[322] or simply to close the landfill whether or not a relocation occurred,[323] in which case INE's concealment of this purpose was a violation of the guarantee, since it fell short of the required transparency.[324]

---

[317] *Ibid* at para 157.

[318] See *ibid* at paras 158–64.

[319] See *ibid* at paras 166–71, 172 ('[t]he contradiction and uncertainty inherent in INE's actions as to Cytrar and Tecmed is evidenced ... both in the initial stage of the processing of the necessary permits to operate the Landfill and when INE decided to put an end to such operation by means of the Resolution'). The BIT entered into force on 18 December 1996: *ibid* at para 53. The new permit was issued on 11 November 1996, *ibid* at para 170, and the resolution denying the permit renewal was issued on 25 November 1998, *ibid* at para 39. The tribunal considered Mexico's conduct prior to the effective date of the BIT not in isolation but in conjunction with its later conduct, (a) 'in light of the good faith principle (Arts 18 and 26 of the Vienna Convention [of 1969]),' which principle provides that after signing a treaty but before ratifying it, or after consenting to be bound by a treaty but before the treaty enters into force, a State shall refrain from acts which would defeat the object and purpose of the treaty; and (b) in light of Art 2(2) of the BIT, which provides that the BIT 'is applicable to investments made before its entry into force': *ibid* at para 172. Even without considering Mexico's conduct prior to the effective date of the BIT, according to the tribunal, Mexico's conduct subsequent to the entry into force of the BIT constituted a breach of the guarantee of fair and equitable treatment. See *ibid* at para 174 ('[Mexico]'s behavior [in the stages described in paras 153–64] amounts, in itself, to a violation of the duty').

[320] See *ibid* at paras 161–64, 173.

[321] See *ibid* at para 163.

[322] See *ibid* at para 163.

[323] See *ibid* at para 164.

[324] See *ibid* ('[t]he lack of transparency in INE's behavior and intention throughout the process that led to the Resolution, which does not reflect in full the reasons that led to the non-renewal of the Permit, cover up the final and real consequence of such actions and of the Resolution: the definitive closing of the activities at the Las Víboras landfill without any compensation whatsoever, whether Cytrar agreed or not, in spite of the expectations created, and without considering ways enabling it to neutralize or mitigate the negative economic effect of such closing by continuing with its economic and business activities at a different place ... [t]he refusal to renew the Permit in this case was actually used to permanently close

With regard to the permit, rather than allowing Cytrar to operate the landfill under the existing unlimited-duration permit after it had acquired the landfill in the auction, INE issued a new permit renewable annually, taking the position that 'the nature of the operation ... and the consequent expansion' required a new permit.[325] The tribunal viewed INE's action as a means of giving itself the discretion to terminate the permit without needing to meet the burden of proving violations before the Federal Environmental Protection Attorney's Office (PROFEPA).[326] This action violated the guarantee of fair and equitable treatment because INE failed to communicate to Cytrar that Cytrar needed to request a new permit, thus failing to disabuse Cytrar of its expectation that it would be able to continue to operate under the existing permit.[327] In summary, the tribunal held that 'INE's described behavior frustrated

---

down a site whose operation had become a nuisance due to political reasons relating to the community's opposition expressed in a variety of forms, regardless of the company in charge of the operation and regardless of whether or not it was being properly applied').

What the tribunal would have required of INE seems to have been, if the agency's purpose was to force a relocation, 'a clear and unequivocal expression of the will of the Mexican authorities to change their position [which had promised] the extension of the Permit [until the relocation could be accomplished],' or if the purpose was to close the landfill without a relocation, 'an explicit, transparent and clear warning addressed to Cytrar from the Mexican authorities that rejected conditioning the revocation of the Permit [on] the relocation of Cytrar's operations...to another place,' see *ibid* at para 160, and the payment of compensation:

> the decisive factor—for which Cytrar was not responsible—was the Landfill's location at the Las Víboras site and its proximity to Hermosillo's urban center, which was in violation of Mexican regulations and a source of community opposition and political unrest, but which was not—as confirmed by Mexican authorities—against the legitimacy of the Landfill's operation under Mexican law [because the regulations did not have retroactive effect]. If the inevitable consequence of this situation, evaluated by the Mexican authorities, was the refusal to renew the Permit and the closing of the site, such determination, from the [BIT]'s standpoint, should have been accompanied, as has already been decided, by the payment of the appropriate compensation.

*Ibid* at para 164.

[325] *Ibid* at para 168.

[326] See *ibid* at paras 43, 170 ('the purpose behind the annual renewal of permits was to facilitate INE's actions to put an end to the operations carried out by companies that, in INE's understanding, did not adjust their actions to the applicable legal provisions; ... this allowed INE to dispense with the more cumbersome procedure—of uncertain success—of obtaining the revocation of the permit by PROFEPA, which required that a case be opened and that the party subject to sanctions be given the opportunity to express its argumentations and defenses'), 171 ('[i]f the indefinite-duration permit dated May 4, 1994 had been transferred to Cytrar ... INE would not have been able to put an end to Cytrar's operation of the Landfill by means of the Resolution and the only remedy available for that purpose would have been the revocation on the basis of the infringements of the Permit used to justify the Resolution, which were not even considered by PROFEPA as deserving any sanction other than a fine').

[327] See *ibid* at paras 168 ('[t]here is no evidence that INE [stated] that Cytrar had actually to request a new permit which may differ from the existing one, instead of requesting the replacement of the [former permit-holder's name] with a new one; and no convincing evidence has been offered to support [Mexico]'s allegations as to the fact that, from the beginning, INE's officers instructed Cytrar to obtain a new "operating license" because, for example, as stated by [Mexico], the nature of the operation undertaken by Cytrar and the

Cytrar's fair expectations upon which Cytrar's actions were based and upon the basis of which [Tecmed]'s investment was made, or negatively affected the generation of clear guidelines that would allow [Tecmed] or Cytrar to direct its actions or behavior to prevent the non-renewal of the Permit, or weakened its position to enforce rights or explore ways to maintain the Permit.'[328]

## C. Legal Premises for Mexico's Assertion of Human Rights-based Defenses

Mexico is party to at least three treaties under which it is bound to honor human rights obligations that are relevant to the *Tecmed* case. The ICESCR[329] and the Additional Protocol to the American Convention on Human Rights in the Area of Economic, Social and Cultural Rights (the 'Protocol of San Salvador')[330] both require States parties to honor the human right to health; in the case of the ICESCR, the right to health has been interpreted to include the right to water. The International Covenant on Civil and Political Rights (ICCPR)[331] requires States parties to honor the human right to participate in the conduct of public affairs. Spain is also a party to both the ICESCR and the ICCPR.[332]

---

consequent expansion of the Landfill's installed capacity would so require it'), 171 ('INE unilaterally transformed a previous administrative act, which, as such, was presumed to be legitimate, had immediate effects and could only be interpreted in good faith as having accepted Cytrar's petition to be the transferee of the existing permits for the operation of the Landfill. The objective consequence of such transformation was to grant Cytrar a permit to operate the Landfill, which reduced Cytrar's entitlement to question actions that deprived it of the Permit or that had such effect').

[328] *Ibid* at para 173. See also *ibid* at para 172 (INE's behavior prior to and following the entry into force of the BIT constituted 'one and the same course of conduct characterized by its ambiguity and uncertainty which are prejudicial to the investor in terms of its advance assessment of the legal situation surrounding its investment and the planning of its business activity and its adjustment to preserve its rights').

[329] Above n 55. Mexico ratified the ICESCR on 23 June 1981: Office of the High Commissioner for Human Rights, United Nations, *Status of Ratifications of the Principal International Human Rights Treaties*, 9 June 2004, available at http://www.unhchr.ch/pdf/report.pdf (last viewed 14 October 2004).

[330] Organization of American States, Inter-American Commission on Human Rights, Additional Protocol to the American Convention on Human Rights in the Area of Economic, Social and Cultural Rights, 17 November 1988, available at http://www.cidh.oas.org/Basicos/basic5.htm. Mexico ratified the Additional Protocol on 16 April 1996; it entered into force 16 November 1999. See status of ratifications to Protocol of San Salvador, available at http://www.cidh.oas.org/Basicos/basic6.htm.

[331] UN GA res 2200A (1966) (entered into force on 23 March 1976), available at http://www.unhchr.ch/html/menu3/b/a_ccpr.htm. Mexico ratified the ICCPR on 23 June 1981: Office of the High Commissioner for Human Rights, United Nations, *Status of Ratifications of the Principal International Human Rights Treaties*, 9 June 2004, available at http://www.unhchr.ch/pdf/report.pdf (last viewed 14 October 2004).

[332] Spain is a party to the ICESCR and ICCPR, having ratified both on 27 July 1977: Office of the High Commissioner for Human Rights, United Nations, *Status of Ratifications of the Principal International Human Rights Treaties*, 9 June 2004, available at http://www.unhchr.ch/pdf/report.pdf (last viewed 14 October 2004).

These treaties guarantee two sets of human rights obligations that Mexico might have invoked as a defense to Tecmed's claims. First, Mexico might have argued that its commitments to the right to health and water required it to close the landfill.[333] Second, Mexico might have argued that, even in the absence of infringements by the landfill of the right to health, Mexico's commitment to two human rights, the rights to participation in the conduct of public affairs and to self-determination (which includes the right to sovereignty over wealth and natural resources), required it to give effect to the community opposition to the landfill, since those rights require that a community be able to change its mind about allowing investment activities even in the absence of proven violations (that is, simply to decide that the community does not want to permit certain activities after all).

Each of these human rights obligations will be examined below. First, however, two potential legal premises will be considered which might allow consideration of the obligations in an arbitration under the BIT: namely, the propositions (a) that the Spain–Mexico BIT should be read not to permit interference with Mexico's human rights obligations, and (b) that Spain is bound (as are Spanish corporations) by human rights commitments not to hinder Mexico's efforts to comply with its human rights obligations.[334]

*1. Principles of Treaty Interpretation*   Mexico's assertion of substantive human rights obligations as defenses to its alleged breach of the BIT could be premised on a claim that the Spain–Mexico BIT should be read not to permit interference with Mexico's human rights obligations. The obligations of States with regard to the right to health and the right to water extend to the negotiation and conclusion of treaties. The ICESCR requires

---

[333] Although it is not clear from the facts of the arbitration that the right to water was threatened by the activities of the landfill, it may be assumed that the storage and processing of toxic waste has the potential to negatively impact on water quality. As the UN High Commissioner for Human Rights has noted, 'government action in relation to chemicals and toxic wastes has flow-on effects in relation to the enjoyment of human rights such as the right to health or the right to water': see UNESC Report, above n 3, at para 35.

[334] A third position would be available where a *jus cogens* human rights norm had been violated, which is not the case in the *Tecmed* arbitration. In such a case the State could argue that the *jus cogens* norm supersedes the provisions of the BIT. This could also arise in the context of a concession contract which involves the violation of a *jus cogens* norm. If the State decides, for whatever reason, that it does not want to go through with the contract, and the investor sues under the applicable BIT, the host State might raise the peremptory norm as a defense to the validity of the contract.

If, on the other hand, the State wants the investor to complete its contractual performance but the State has allegedly inadequately fulfilled its contractual performance (such as the provision of infrastructure, etc) and the investor sues, the State will not raise the violation of the *jus cogens* norm because it wants the contract to remain valid. In that situation, the tribunal would perhaps be compelled to take notice of the norm *moto proprio*, either to refuse jurisdiction or to invalidate the contract. See IISD 2003, above n 4, at 18–20.

that '[i]n relation to the conclusion of other international agreements, States parties should take steps to ensure that these instruments do not adversely impact upon the right to health'[335] or the right to water.[336] A State violates its obligation to respect the right to health when it fails 'to take into account its legal obligations regarding the right to health when entering into bilateral or multilateral agreements with other States, international organizations and other entities, such as multinational corporations.'[337]

A State thus may be in violation of its human rights commitments if it concludes a treaty, such as a BIT, that will prevent it from honoring those commitments. Although Mexico would not have much success in arguing that its own breach, in the form of its entry into the BIT, of its human rights commitments excuses its violation of that BIT, it might more convincingly argue that the BIT and the human rights treaty should be construed in such a way as to minimize conflict between them: as far as possible, the BIT should be read to be consistent with Mexico's pre-existing human rights obligations. Taking this approach, Mexico could have argued that, due to the fact that Mexico and Spain were both bound under the ICESCR by the obligation not to conclude treaties that adversely impact on the right to health, the BIT should be construed, in light of those obligations, not to constrain a State's ability to prevent violations of the right to health. If the BIT is interpreted this way in the light of the ICESCR, the State's commitment to the right to health under the ICESCR would obviate any compensation requirement for an expropriation intended to prevent an infringement of the right to health: when read in light of the ICESCR, the BIT simply would not reach those situations. (Alternatively, with reference to the proportionality analysis performed by the *Tecmed* tribunal,[338] Mexico could have argued that if the BIT is read in the light of the ICESCR, a State is not required to provide compensation for the regulatory expropriation of an investment which threatens adversely to impact on the right to health, because the public interest in safeguarding the right to health, as expressed

---

[335] *General Comment No 14: Substantive Issues Arising in the Implementation of the International Covenant on Economic, Social and Cultural Rights: The right to the highest attainable standard of health (article 12 of the International Covenant on Economic, Social and Cultural Rights)*, Committee on Economic, Social and Cultural Rights, UN ESCOR, 22nd Sess, UN doc E/C.12/2000/4, (2000) [hereinafter 'CESCR General Comment 14'], at para 39, available at http://www.ohchr.org/english/bodies/cescr/comments.htm.

[336] *General Comment No 15: Substantive Issues Arising in the Implementation of the International Covenant on Economic, Social and Cultural Rights: The right to water (Articles 11 and 12 of the International Covenant on Economic, Social and Cultural Rights)*, Committee on Economic, Social and Cultural Rights, UN ESCOR, 29th Sess., UN doc E/C.12/2002/11 (2002) [hereinafter 'CESCR General Comment 15'], at para 35 ('[w]ith regard to the conclusion and implementation of other international and regional agreements, States parties should take steps to ensure that these instruments do not adversely impact upon the right to water') , available at http://www.ohchr.org/english/bodies/cescr/comments.htm.

[337] CESCR General Comment 14, above n 335, at para 50.

[338] See above nn 306–14 and associated text.

in the ICESCR, outweighs any economic impact on investors.) Likewise, the non-renewal of the permit should not constitute a violation of the guarantee of fair and equitable treatment, Mexico would argue, because it is unreasonable, in light of Mexico's human rights commitments, for an investor to have an expectation of being able to avail itself of the BIT's protections for an investment that will adversely impact on the right to health.

*2. Spain's Human Rights Obligations*  An alternative basis for Mexico's human rights-based defenses for the alleged breach of the BIT would be that, under the ICESCR, States parties must refrain from actions that interfere, directly or indirectly, with the enjoyment of the rights to health and water in other countries.[339] States must also prevent violations of the rights by third parties, such as their own citizens and companies, in other countries.[340] Spain is thus bound by the ICESCR to prevent violations in Mexico of the right to health and water by Spanish corporations. In addition, under Article 1(3) of the ICCPR, 'States must refrain from interfering in the internal affairs of other States and thereby adversely affecting the exercise of the right to self-determination';[341] Spain is therefore bound under the ICCPR not to impede the exercise of the right to self-determination in Mexico.

To assert this basis for its human rights defenses, Mexico should have argued in *Tecmed* that the BIT should be interpreted in the light not only of Mexico's human rights obligations, but also of Spain's human rights obligations. To minimize conflict between the BIT and the ICESCR and ICCPR, the BIT should not be read to permit Tecmed to invoke the BIT, an international treaty concluded by Spain, to force an interpretation of that treaty that, inasmuch as it effectively licenses the violation of human rights in Mexico by a Spanish corporation, is in conflict with Spain's human rights obligations.[342]

---

[339] CESCR General Comment 14, above n 335, at para 39; CESCR General Comment 15, above n 336, at para 31.

[340] See CESCR General Comment 14, above n 335, at para 39; CESCR General Comment 15, above n 336, at para 33; Sánchez-Moreno and Higgins, above n 244, at 1675 and fn 27 ('States' obligation to protect [economic, social and cultural] rights from violations by a third party implies that States have an obligation under international law to protect [economic, social and cultural] rights from violations by TNCs') (noting practical restrictions on enforcement of this obligation identified in Scott F Leckie, 'Violations of Economic, Social and Cultural Rights', in Theo C Van Boven *et al* (eds), *The Maastricht Guidelines on Violations of Economic, Social and Cultural Rights* (Netherlands Institute of Human Rights, 1998), at p 114 ('[w]hile it is legally possible to reach TNCs indirectly through a State's obligation to "protect" human rights, the immense influence that these mammoth entities exert often makes such options futile')).

[341] *General Comment No 12: The right to self-determination of peoples (Article 1)*, Human Rights Committee, UN HRCOR, 21st Sess (1984), reprinted in UN doc HRI/GEN/1/Rev.7 (2004) at 134, para 6 [hereinafter 'CCPR General Comment 12'], available at http://www.unhchr.ch/tbs/doc.nsf/(Symbol)/f3c99406d528f37fc12563ed004960b4?Opendocument.

[342] A related argument would be that Tecmed is itself bound by the human rights treaties to which Spain is a party. Whether Tecmed is bound by the ICESCR or the ICCPR depends in the first instance on whether corporations can be subjects of international law. The UN

## D. The Applicable Human Rights Obligations

In the context of the preceding two legal approaches, Mexico could have invoked two sets of human rights obligations: the right to health, with the concomitant right to water; and the rights to participation in the conduct of public affairs and to self-determination. The following examines in each case (i) the content of the obligations and (ii) potential defenses based on them.

### 1. *Rights to Health and to Water*

i. The Content of the Obligations

Article 12 of the ICESCR provides for the right to 'the highest attainable standard of physical and mental health.'[343] The UN Committee on Economic, Social and Cultural Rights ('the Committee') elucidated the

---

Committee on Economic, Social and Cultural Rights has suggested that the applicability of the obligations in the ICESCR extends beyond States to private actors, including those in the business sector, see CESCR General Comment 14, above n 335, at para 42 ('[w]hile only States are parties to the Covenant and thus ultimately accountable for compliance with it, all members of society—[including] the private business sector—have responsibilities regarding the realization of the right to health'), although commentators are divided on the issue. See, eg, Karl Josef Partsch, 'Individuals in International Law', in (1995) 2 *Encyclopedia of Public International Law* 957, at 961–62 (ICESCR 'is of a "promotional" character. It does not confer subjective rights upon individuals'; although ICCPR is not 'promotional' inasmuch as it contains obligations to be implemented immediately, it mentions only States parties, so that 'it appears doubtful that individuals may also be regarded as its addressees and that their position as subjects of international law is enforced'); David Kinley and Junko Tadaki, 'From Talk to Walk: The Emergence of Human Rights Responsibilities for Corporations at International Law' (2004 ) 44 *Virginia Journal of International Law* 931, at 947–48 ('the extent to which TNCs already possess an international legal status may be ascertained by enquiring whether TNCs have any existing rights or duties under international law. There is, in fact, ample evidence that TNCs do possess international rights and duties, and, with respect to their rights, the capacity to enforce them ... The legal (or quasi-legal) duties imposed on corporations have some potential authority, but as yet they remain ill-defined and ineffective. In short, the rudiments of an international legal framework may be discernable, but the legal content of the law is almost wholly absent'); Todd Weiler, 'Human Rights and Investor Protection: A New Approach for a Different Legal Order' (2004) 27 *British Columbia International and Comparative Law Review* 429, at 441 ('[i]nternational law purists might argue that international human rights conventions impose little or no obligations on the activities of non-state actors, and to the extent that they do impose obligations, their breach is a matter of dispute between the states that are party to the applicable treaty. As discussed above, this is far too narrow a reading of the state of the international legal order today'), 444 ('to the extent that international obligations appear to specifically contemplate regulating the conduct of individuals or transnational corporations as part of their object or operation, it would appear likely that a remedy should be provided that also contemplates action on an individual scale') (analysis drawing from Steven R Ratner, 'Corporations and Human Rights: A Theory of Legal Responsibility' (2001) 111 *Yale Law Journal* 443).

For a brief survey of potential approaches to imposing human rights liability directly on transnational corporations under international law, see Paul Redmond, 'Transnational Enterprise and Human Rights: Options for Standard Setting and Compliance' (2003) 37 *International Law* 69, 99–102.

[343] ICESCR, above n 55, at Art 12.

content of the obligation in its General Comment No 14.[344] There are four aspects to the normative content of the right to health: availability, accessibility, acceptability and quality.[345] The right is an inclusive one which includes, inter alia, 'underlying determinants of health' such as healthy environmental conditions and 'the participation of the population in all health-related decision-making at the community, national and international levels.'[346] The right to healthy natural and workplace environments, a component of the right to health:

> comprises, *inter alia*, ... the requirement to ensure an adequate supply of safe and potable water and basic sanitation [and] the prevention and reduction of the population's exposure to harmful substances such as radiation and harmful chemicals or other detrimental environmental conditions that directly or indirectly impact upon human health.[347]

The Committee has more fully addressed the right to water, a particular right included in the right to health, in its General Comment No 15.[348] Normatively, the right to water dictates that adequate water must satisfy certain standards with regard to availability, quality and accessibility.[349]

While the ICESCR enumerates broad positive obligations which States must work progressively to realize,[350] the ICESCR also contains some obligations with which States must immediately comply; such immediate obligations include the responsibility to guarantee that the rights will be exercised without discrimination and to take concrete steps towards the full realization of the rights.[351] The rights to health and water, like all human rights, impose three obligations on States parties: to respect, to protect, and to fulfill the rights.[352] The obligation to protect requires States

---

[344] See CESCR General Comment 14, above n 335. Other international documents also recognize the human right to health: see *ibid* at para 2; Center for Economic and Social Rights, *International Instruments on the Right to a Healthy Environment*, avalable at http://cesr.org/healthyenvironment/instruments (last visited 5 November 2004).

[345] See CESCR General Comment 14, above n 335, at para 12.

[346] *Ibid* at para 11.

[347] *Ibid* at para 15.

[348] See CESCR General Comment 15, above n 336. The Committee identified that the right to water is implicitly contained in Arts 11 and 12 of the ICESCR and explicitly safeguarded in Art 14(2) of the Convention on the Elimination of All Forms of Discrimination Against Women (1979) and Art 24(2) of the Convention on the Rights of the Child (1989). See CESCR General Comment 15, above n 336, at paras 3–4; see also IISD 2003, above n 4, at 24–26; UNESC Report, above n 3, at paras 47, 49(a), 52; Bachand and Rousseau, above n 9, at 32; see generally Center for Economic and Social Rights, *Right to Water Fact Sheet #3: Water in International & Constitutional Law*, available at http://cesr.org/healthyenvironment/cesr (last visited 14 October 2004).

[349] See CESCR General Comment 15, above n 336, at para 12.

[350] See ICESCR, above n 55, at Art 2(1).

[351] See CESCR General Comment 14, above n 335, at para 30; CESCR General Comment 15, above n 336, at para 17.

[352] See CESCR General Comment 14, above n 335, at para 33; CESCR General Comment 15, above n 336, at para 20.

parties to prevent third parties from interfering with the enjoyment of the respective right.[353] In particular, with regard to the right to water, the obligation to protect 'requires State parties to prevent third parties from ... polluting and inequitably extracting from water resources, including natural sources, wells and other water distribution systems.'[354] The right to fulfill includes the obligation to facilitate, that is 'to take positive measures that enable and assist individuals and communities to enjoy' each right, and the obligation to provide, that is to provide a right contained in the ICESCR 'when individuals or a group are unable, for reasons beyond their control, to realize that right themselves by the means at their disposal.'[355]

States may violate the ICESCR by omitting to 'take necessary measures arising from legal obligations'[356] or by failing 'to enforce relevant laws.'[357] In particular, States may violate the obligation to protect the right to health by failing 'to regulate the activities of individuals, groups or corporations so as to prevent them from violating the right to health of others' or by failing 'to enact or enforce laws to prevent the pollution of water, air and soil by extractive and manufacturing [and presumably other] industries.'[358] States may violate the obligation to protect the right to water by failing 'to enact or enforce laws to prevent the contamination and inequitable extraction of water.'[359]

## ii. A Defense Based on the Obligations[360]

The difficulty with raising a human rights obligation contained in the ICESCR is that those rights are broad ones which are to be realized progressively.[361] It would be difficult for Mexico to argue that due to its

---

[353] See CESCR General Comment 14, above n 335, at paras 33, 51; CESCR General Comment 15, above n 336, at paras 23, 44(b).

[354] CESCR General Comment 15, above n 336, at para 23.

[355] CESCR General Comment 14, above n 335, at para 37; CESCR General Comment 15, above n 336, at para 25.

[356] CESCR General Comment 14, above n 335, at para 49.

[357] CESCR General Comment 15, above n 336, at para 43.

[358] CESCR General Comment 14, above n 335, at para 51.

[359] CESCR General Comment 15, above n 336, at para 44(b).

[360] An initial obstacle which Mexico would have faced in raising a defense based on an obligation to protect the right to health and water is that the resolution denying the renewal of the landfill's operating permit was not based on an assertion by the State that the regulatory violations committed by the landfill 'compromise[d] public health, [or] impair[ed] ecological balance or protection of the environment,' see above n 310 and associated text, although the State later asserted public health as a reason for the denial of the renewal, see above n 311. The following analysis of potential human rights-based defenses will assume that public health concerns had been cited in the resolution.

[361] In general, the difficulty may be summarized as follows: because progressively realizable obligations require States to improve broad social and economic conditions, it is difficult to demonstrate that (a) a State is violating that obligation, and (b) if the State is violating it, the violation is due to any particular investment. It is easier to establish a violation of first-generation rights that impose negative obligations on States to refrain from taking certain

commitment to the right to health, it had no option but to violate the BIT by denying the renewal of the landfill's operating permit, since it seems unlikely that the existence of any single landfill could prevent Mexico from progressively realizing the right to health. Although Mexico has the obligation to protect the right to health from violations by third parties, it is likewise difficult to argue that any particular regulatory violations at the landfill violated a human right that requires progressive realization. And although Mexico's obligation to *take steps* to realize the right is immediate, not progressive,[362] it would again be difficult for Mexico to argue that it needed to take the particular step of denying the renewal of the landfill's permit in order for Mexico to avoid being in violation of its human rights commitments.

Nevertheless, supposing that Mexico established that its human rights commitment to the right to health or water required it to deny the renewal of the landfill's permit, the next question is how a tribunal would reconcile the State's competing investment treaty and human rights obligations. With regard to the expropriation claim, since the *Tecmed* tribunal applied the sole effects doctrine, it would likely have found that although the State's action was motivated by a legally binding human rights obligation, it was nevertheless an expropriatory action requiring compensation. However, in dicta, the court also performed a proportionality analysis comparing the State's motivations for the act to the economic impact on the investor. If the State's motivation had been more urgent, the proportionality analysis might have favored that motivation and influenced accordingly the tribunal's determination of whether an expropriation had occurred or whether compensation was required. The tribunal states that the community opposition to the landfill did not 'give rise ... to a serious urgent situation, crisis, need or social emergency that, weighed against the deprivation or neutralization of the economic or commercial value of [Tecmed]'s investment, permits reaching the conclusion that the Resolution did not amount to an expropriation under the Agreement and international law.'[363] This formulation does not rule out the possibility, however slight, that a State's enforcement of its human rights obligations may constitute a 'serious need' that could outweigh the neutralization of an investor's investment.

With regard to the fair and equitable treatment claim, if serious environmental violations with health implications occurred at the landfill, INE notified Cytrar of the violations, and the violations were not cor-

---

actions. If a BIT required a State to engage in such a violation, the human rights-based argument excusing a State's breach of the BIT would be stronger than it might be in the case of a human right that is to be progressively realized.

[362] See above n 351 and associated text.

[363] *Tecmed* at para 139.

rected, it seems likely that a tribunal would not consider the denial of the renewal of the permit to be a violation of the guarantee of fair and equitable treatment, since the *Tecmed* tribunal's concern centered around the lack of (1) transparency in INE's actions, (2) notice to Cytrar, and (3) opportunity to correct the violations, as well as around Cytrar's expectations that the Mexican legal apparatus 'would be used for the purpose of assuring compliance with environmental protection, human health and ecological balance goals underlying such laws.'[364] However, in the absence of any serious environmental violations, that is, if INE's position were simply that the presence of the landfill or its proximity to Las Víboras constituted a violation of Mexico's commitment to honor the right to health, it is likely that a tribunal would find that the permit non-renewal constituted a violation of the fair and equitable treatment guarantee. The *Tecmed* tribunal held that bad faith on the part of the State is not necessary to violate the standard,[365] and such a decision by Mexico, even if frankly communicated at the time of the decision, would contravene 'the basic expectations that were taken into account by the foreign investor [in making] the investment'[366] and the principle that the investor must 'know beforehand any and all rules and regulations that will govern its investments.'[367] According to this reasoning, if the site of the landfill constituted a violation of the right to health, it would be considered unfair and inequitable to have allowed Tecmed to purchase the landfill only to deny the renewal of the landfill's operating permit on that basis shortly thereafter.

## 2. Rights to Participation in the Conduct of Public Affairs and to Self-determination

i. The Content of the Obligations

Article 25(a) of the ICCPR provides that every citizen shall have the right and the opportunity to 'take part in the conduct of public affairs, directly or through freely chosen representatives.'[368] In General Comment

---

[364] *Ibid* at para 157.

[365] See *ibid* at para 153.

[366] *Ibid* at para 154.

[367] *Ibid*.

[368] For other potential sources of this right in international law, see Bachand and Rousseau, above n 9, at 29 (citing Universal Declaration on Human Rights, Art 21(3); Vienna Declaration and Programme of Action, § 8). The Aarhus Convention provides for a right to public participation in environmental decision-making: Convention on Access to Information, Public Participation in Decision-Making and Access to Justice in Environmental Matters, 25 June 1998, Art 6, UN doc ECE/CEP/43 (entered into force on 30 October 2001), http://www.unece.org/env/pp/treatytext.htm. Mexico is not a party to the Aarhus Convention. See United Nations Economic Commission for Europe, *Convention on Access to Information, Public Participation in Decision-Making and Access to Justice in Environmental Matters* (parties and signatories to the Convention), available at http://www.unece.org/env/pp/ctreaty.htm.

25[369] on the implementation of Article 25, the Office of the High Commissioner for Human Rights states that the conduct of public affairs 'is a broad concept which relates to the exercise of political power, in particular the exercise of legislative, executive and administrative powers. It covers all aspects of public administration, and the formulation and implementation of policy at international, national, regional and local levels.'[370] Ways in which citizens can take part in the conduct of public affairs, and which are protected by Article 25, are directly,[371] through elected representatives,[372] or 'by exerting influence through public debate and dialogue with their representatives or through their capacity to organize themselves.'[373] Furthermore, the right to health under the ICESCR encompasses a right of the community to participate in decision-making.[374] As the UN High Commissioner for Human Rights has stated, the right to participate in the conduct of public affairs requires 'institutions and mechanisms that are close to the people themselves so that people are empowered to change their own lives, improve their own communities, influence their destinies and hold accountable the decision makers and actors whose actions affect their rights.'[375]

The right to self-determination includes the right to community authority over decisions about natural wealth and resources, specifically guaranteed in Article 1(2) of the ICCPR and the ICESCR, which each provide that '[a]ll peoples may, for their own ends, freely dispose of their natural wealth and resources without prejudice to any obligations arising out of international economic co-operation, based upon the principle of mutual benefit, and international law.'[376] Article 1(1) of each of these conventions guarantees the broader principle that "[a]ll peoples have the right of self-determination. By virtue of that right they freely determine their political status and freely pursue their economic, social and cultural development.'[377] In General Comment 12[378] on the ICCPR, the Office of the High Commissioner on Human Rights emphasizes the importance of

---

[369] *General Comment No 25: The right to participate in public affairs, voting rights and the right of equal access to public service (Article 25)*, Human Rights Committee, UN HRCOR, 57th Sess, UN doc CCPR/C/21/Rev.1/Add.7 (1996) [hereinafter 'CCPR General Comment 25'], available at http://www.unhchr.ch/tbs/doc.nsf/0/d0b7f023e8d6d9898025651e004bc0eb?Opendocument.

[370] *Ibid* at para 5.

[371] See *ibid* at para 6.

[372] See *ibid* at para 7.

[373] *Ibid* at para 8.

[374] CESCR General Comment 14, above n 335, at para 11.

[375] UNESC Report, above n 3, at para 52.

[376] International Convention on Civil and Political Rights, above n 331, at Art 1(2); International Covenant on Economic and Social Rights, above n 55, at Art 1(2).

[377] International Convention on Civil and Political Rights, above n 331, at Art 1(1); International Covenant on Economic and Social Rights, above n 55, at Art 1(1).

[378] See CCPR General Comment 12, above n 341.

the right to self-determination.[379] In particular, the right to sovereignty over natural wealth and resources 'entails corresponding duties for all States and the international community.'[380]

## ii. A Defense Based on the Obligations

In the form of its component rights to exert influence and to organize, the right to participate in the conduct of public affairs is protected primarily by protecting freedom of expression, assembly, and association,[381] which were not impinged upon in the *Tecmed* case. However, Mexico might have argued that if an administrative agency is prevented from responding to citizens who exercise their rights to expression, assembly, and association,[382] those rights would be indirectly deprived of their effectiveness. Therefore, the argument would go, under the ICESCR and ICCPR, INE had to have the capability to take community expressions into account in order to avoid violating the right of citizens to exercise influence over the conduct of public affairs and to exercise their rights to self-determination and sovereignty over natural wealth and resources. The right of the community to participate in decision-making, a component of the right to health,[383] offers further support for the argument. This is not to say that INE had to make the decision it did, but that if community concerns are relevant to its decision-making[384] and it chooses to give weight to them, it may not be prevented from doing so.[385]

---

[379] 'The right of self-determination is of particular importance because its realization is an essential condition for the effective guarantee and observance of individual human rights and for the promotion and strengthening of those rights. It is for that reason that States set forth the right of self-determination in a provision of positive law in both Covenants and placed this provision as article 1 apart from and before all of the other rights in the two Covenants': *ibid* at para 1.

[380] *Ibid* at para 5.

[381] See CCPR General Comment 25, above n 369, at paras 8, 12, 25–26.

[382] The tribunal noted that '[t]he community's opposition to the Landfill, in its public manifestations, was widespread and aggressive': *Tecmed*, at para 108. In the tribunal's view, such opposition nevertheless did not justify the expropriation, since Mexico did not present 'any evidence that community opposition to the Landfill—however intense, aggressive and sustained—was in any way massive or went any further than the positions assumed by some individuals or the members of some groups that were opposed to the Landfill': *ibid* at para 144.

[383] CESCR General Comment 14, above n 335, at para 11.

[384] Community influence on the decision-making process extended beyond the holding of public demonstrations: the Sonora Human Rights Academy filed: (1) two complaints, one 'against SEMARNAP, PROFEPA, the State Legislature and the State Governor, [alleging] that the authorities had violated the State's sovereignty by authorizing the deposit of toxic waste from Baja California without the relevant permit by the competent local authorities' and the other 'before the National Commission of Human Rights', *Tecmed* at para 135; (2) a criminal complaint against Cytrar for environmental crimes; and (3) a challenge to the municipality's granting of the landfill's operating permit: see *ibid* at para 108; an NGO association filed a human rights claim with the State Commission of Human Rights against State and municipal authorities; and 'community organizations submitted a petition to the local office of SEMARNAP so that expressions of such associations and individual citizens [could] be considered upon [the evaluation] of the renewal [application] of the Permit': *ibid*.

[385] Mexico argued that INE's powers of permit renewal are discretionary and that the non-renewal of the landfill's permit was not an arbitrary exercise of the agency's powers: see *ibid*

With regard specifically to the expropriation claim, Mexico could have argued that applying a compensation requirement in such situations restricts the agency's ability to give effect to citizen participation in public affairs and to public sovereignty over natural wealth and resources, and therefore that no compensation should have been required in this instance. A corollary argument might be that the BIT should be construed away from an interpretation in which it would put the State in a situation of having to violate its pre-existing human rights obligations by virtue of being deterred from giving effect to community concerns that were deemed legitimate by an agency in the exercise of its discretion. With regard to the guarantee of fair and equitable treatment, Mexico might have argued that no fundamental expectations of Tecmed were disturbed by the non-renewal of the permit, since it would not have been reasonable for Tecmed to expect that a community does not have the right to influence decisions concerning its own welfare,[386] and that there is nothing unfair or inequitable about the legitimate operation, in good faith, of the democratic machinery of the polity.

## V. CONCLUSION

Of course, there are limitations to what can be accomplished by raising human rights obligations as defenses in investment treaty arbitrations, even if the defenses prove successful. Arbitral tribunals are not a forum for adjudicating FDI-related human rights claims against investors, and

---

at para 46. Prior to the issuance of the resolution denying the renewal of the landfill's permit, some indication of the bases on which the discretionary non-renewal would rest was given by 'a joint declaration issued by the federal, state and municipal authorities stating that although the inspections conducted did not provide "... evidence of any risk to health and the ecosystems ..." arising out of the Landfill, the relocation [of the landfill] was necessary to secure environmental safety in view of the rapid urban growth of Hermosillo, provide a response to the concerns that had been expressed and guarantee, in the long term, the environmental infrastructure to handle and dispose of industrial waste': *ibid* at para 110. The tribunal's interpretation of the situation, however, was that 'since [the groups opposed to the landfill] could not obtain the Permit's revocation due to the lack of [evidence of environment or public health violations]—as explained to them by INE and the municipal authorities—their ultimate goal was to close down the Landfill and make Cytrar relocate its operations': *ibid* at para 140; see also *ibid* at para 109. The issue might turn on two questions, then: whether it was beyond the discretion of INE to accord such weight to the environmental violations in the operation of the landfill that those violations necessitated the denial of the renewal of the permit; and if in fact it was beyond INE's discretion, whether community desire for a relocation of the landfill was itself a sufficient basis for the denial of the renewal of the permit. The tribunal acknowledged at least that 'there is no evidence proving the fact that INE's denial of the Permit [was] contrary to Mexican laws': *ibid* at para 182.

[386] One of Tecmed's allegations was that public disapproval of the landfill grew as a result of the election of a new mayor of Hermosillo: see *ibid* at para 42. The tribunal rejected the allegation that the mayor encouraged a citizens' movement against the landfill, however: see above, section II.2.B.

human rights adjudication mechanisms should be strongly supported.[387] Serious consideration should be given to modifying the structure and substance of any BITs concluded in the future, since to continue with the same paradigm of strong investor protection and dispute resolution provisions in BITs will be to pave a very dangerous path leading to the weakening of State capacity to enforce and progressively realize human rights. Some consideration of human rights in the investment regime would especially be helpful to address those situations where States are subject to competing international obligations.[388] The UN High Commissioner for Human Rights recommends implementing a 'human rights approach to investment liberalization,'[389] and several commentators suggest a

---

[387] See IISD 2003, above n 4, at 33–34. The IISD proposes including human rights obligations in BITs to facilitate the consideration of human rights norms in investment treaty arbitrations, but notes that:

> the inclusion of investor responsibilities in investment treaties would necessarily require that investment tribunals grapple more frequently and at an ever-greater level of sophistication with human rights norms. This presupposes ever-greater human rights expertise on the part of arbitrators, and invests these Tribunals with greater authority as fora where human rights concerns will be elaborated and interpreted. It must be stressed that investment tribunals would not become an adjudicative forum for human rights norms. Rather, they would only adjudicate investor rights, but in a manner which conditioned these investor rights on compliance of the investors with minimum human rights responsibilities. Naturally, it should be asked whether these ad-hoc Tribunals can be expected to have the legitimacy to be entrusted with such a critical task.

*Ibid* at 36.

[388]See, eg, UNESC Report, above n 3, at para 29 ('to the extent that investment affects [human] rights, the obligations on States in relation to individuals and groups should also be considered within the context of rights and obligations between States and toward investors'); Bachand and Rousseau, above n 9, at 34 ('designing innovative means to ensure that international investment law does not compromise respect for human rights obligations [is] an urgent task'); IISD 2003, above n 4, at 33 ('matters would be much clearer if investment treaties were to impose countervailing duties and responsibilities upon investors'), 34 ('procedural and substantive changes to strengthen the ability of investment arbitration might be needed in order to take into account competing human rights obligations of host states and investors').

For other human-rights motivated proposals for reform to investment treaties, see IISD 2003, above n 4, at 37–38.

[389] UNESC Report, above n 3, at para 56 (such an approach 'examines what complementary measures are needed to ensure an appropriate balance of rights and obligations between States and towards investors, bearing in mind States' responsibilities under human rights law'). The human rights approach would involve several courses of action: including the promotion and protection of human rights among the objectives of investment agreements; ensuring States' right and duty to regulate; promoting investors' obligations alongside investors' rights; promoting international cooperation as part of investment liberalization; promoting human rights in the context of privatization; increasing dialogue on human rights and trade; and undertaking human rights assessments of investment liberalization. See *ibid* at paras 57–63.

To strengthen human rights enforcement in the face of investment liberalization, the UN Commission on Human Rights has established 'a working group to consider options for the elaboration of an individual complaints mechanism under the ICESCR': *ibid* at para 41.

recalibration of the investment regime to reflect the goal of sustainable development,[390] especially since BITs have not been particularly effective at promoting investment.[391]

## 1. The Way Forward: Proposed Reforms

In concrete terms, there are several ways in which BITs should be recalibrated to reflect human rights obligations and goals. Ideally, the investment regime might consist of a single multilateral agreement rather than thousands of bilateral treaties. Regardless, however, of whether future investment treaties in fact become aggregated or continue to be bilateral in form, they should incorporate several vital reforms to take better account of human rights.[392] The scope of expropriation clauses should be limited, clauses providing for the protection of human rights and for transparency in the dispute resolution process should be inserted, and a mechanism should be instituted for obtaining authoritative treaty interpretations by arbitral tribunals regarding the permissibility under BITs of particular types of regulation. Each of these possibilities is briefly examined below.

### A. A Unified Multilateral Investment Agreement

The bilateral approach to international investment law has certain advantages, including flexibility and customizability.[393] However, the bilateral approach also presents less attractive features:

> asymmetries in bargaining power put weaker economies at a disadvantage in the negotiations of bilateral agreements. Although this applies in all negotiating

---

[390] See, eg, Bachand and Rousseau, above n 9, at 33–34; IISD 2004, above n 11, at 29–30. See also UNCTAD 2003, above n 6, at 15–23 ('Enhancing the Development Dimension of International Investment Agreements').

[391] See above n 35. See also IISD 2003, above n 4, at 35–36 (citations omitted):

> as treaties continue to proliferate, they have not been matched by evidence that they contribute to enhanced flows of investment. Indeed, a recent report of the World Bank is the latest to point to the lack of correlation between investment flows and the conclusion of these treaties. Given that the standard rationale for the creation and extension of such investor rights has not stood the test of time, it stands to reason that states might wish to consider new rationales for negotiating investment protection treaties.

[392] Ideally, existing BITs should also be modified, although States seem more willing to change future agreements than existing ones. The United States has made, and Canada is considering, changes to their respective templates for future international investment agreements, in order to curtail the disproportionality of the rights granted to foreign investors. But neither appears to be considering the amendment of prior BITs, with the exception that the United States will amend its BITs with countries acceding to the European Union, to prevent conflict between the BITs and EU policies. See IISD 2004, above n 11, at 28–29. For details on changes in some model BITs and free trade treaties, see above nn 34, 72; below nn 401–2 and associated text.

[393] As UNCTAD has reported:

> [bilateral approaches] have the advantage of allowing countries the freedom of choosing the partners to enter into an agreement and how to tailor the agreement to their specific

situations, it is particularly relevant in agreements between large developed countries and small and poor developing ones—and when bilateral agreements go beyond a narrow coverage. In some recent cases, the principal objective of investor protection has been complemented with liberalization clauses related to the right of establishment and an expanded list of restricted performance requirements. So, the other side of the 'flexibility' of the bilateral approach is that developing countries may be entering IIAs of broader scope. The implications of this are—for example because of the MFN clause—still far from fully understood. In addition, [if many countries choose the bilateral approach,] the extension of bilateral treaty coverage and the freedom of pairs of countries to define their provisions, could lead to uncertainty, potentially inconsistent rules and legal conflicts.[394]

In response to concerns such as these, the International Institute for Sustainable Development (IISD) has proposed that 'a single sustainable-development-oriented multilateral agreement on investment might represent a preferable alternative to the current, almost anarchical, world of BITs and regional agreements.'[395]

There are many legal obstacles to the realization of such a unified agreement, as the IISD details.[396] First, while BITs often provide for unilateral termination after a minimum period, they provide also that the rights enjoyed by investments established under the BIT will continue for a period of time after the agreement's termination.[397] Second, although both States parties to a BIT can agree to terminate the agreement, they would probably face an argument from investors that 'the rights vested in third parties survive independently of [the BIT], given the nature of investor reliance on such rights.'[398] Third, if reform is attempted on a piecemeal basis, most-favored-nation clauses 'might be used by investors to thwart States that act to narrow the scope of provisions in some BITs, but leave standing more extensive versions of the same rights in other existing treaties.'[399] Potential approaches States

---

situations. They offer countries flexibility in designing their networks of [international investment agreements], concluding them with countries that are key investors, avoiding countries that are less interesting or that may insist on unwanted provisions. Allowing each treaty to be negotiated separately gives developing countries more flexibility than under a multilateral approach. In addition, BITs can be negotiated quickly. Important is also that the overwhelming number of BITs cover only the post-establishment stage of investment, leaving admission and establishment—which have the greatest development implications—to be determined autonomously by host countries.

UNCTAD 2004, above n 7, at 93.

[394] *Ibid.*
[395] IISD 2004, above n 11, at 27. For some pros and cons of the bilateral framework, see UNCTAD 2003, above n 6, at 93.
[396] See IISD 2004, above n 11, at 27–28.
[397] *Ibid* at 27.
[398] *Ibid.*
[399] *Ibid* at 28.

might take to overcome these obstacles include circumscribing the reach of most-favored-nation clauses, 'negotiating all changes to BIT provisions simultaneously with [a State's] various treaty partners, so as to not allow some treaties to remain as anachronisms,' 'renouncing all [the State's] BITs in favour of a single multilateral agreement,' or having 'a broader multilateral negotiation that revises equally the rules in most, if not all, BITs simultaneously.'[400]

## B. Limiting the Scope of the Expropriation Clause

The scope of the expropriation clause in investment agreements should be restricted to eliminate the compensation requirement for 'regulatory takings'. Governments should not be forced to compensate investors if regulation in the public interest decreases the value of foreign investment without depriving the investors of title. Some countries, including the United States and Canada, have attempted to restrict the scope of indirect expropriations as defined in BITs.[401] In addition to limiting the scope of the expropriation clause in its BITs, the United States has recently attempted to limit the scope of expropriation clauses in the investment chapters of its free trade treaties.[402] The United States probably is taking these steps due in part to the civil society backlash against the investment protection provisions in NAFTA.[403] Perhaps it is the power imbalance between developed and developing countries that has sustained the strong investor protections in BITs until now; as developed countries act more and more often as hosts (and not just exporters) of FDI, they may re-evaluate the desirability of having such

---

[400] *Ibid.*

[401] See above nn 72, 392; Luke Eric Peterson, 'India Reportedly Looking to Narrow Reach of Investment Treaty Provisions', *INVEST-SD: Investment Law and Policy Weekly News Bulletin* (International Institute for Sustainable Develepoment, Winnipeg, Canada), 11 May 2004, available at http://www.iisd.org/pdf/2004/investment_investsd_may11_2004.pdf. For changes in US and Canadian approaches to BITs, see IISD 2004, above n 11, at 28–29; Luke Eric Peterson, 'Canada Releases its Revised Model Investment Treaty; Disputes to be Open', *Investment Law and Policy Weekly News Bulletin* (International Institute for Sustainable Develepoment, Winnipeg, Canada), 24 May 2004, available at http://www.iisd.org/pdf/2004/investment_investsd_may24_2004.pdf; Luke Eric Peterson, 'US Releases draft-text of revised bilateral investment treaty', *Investment Law and Policy Weekly News Bulletin* (International Institute for Sustainable Develepoment, Winnipeg, Canada), 23 February 2004, available at http://www.iisd.org/pdf/2004/investment_investsd_feb23_2004.pdf.

[402] See Matthew C Porterfield, International Expropriation Rules and Federalism, 23 *Stanford Environmental Law Journal* 3, at 41–43 (2004) (discussing the Trade Act of 2002, which instructed the US Trade Representative to 'ensure that expropriation provisions in future agreements do not provide foreign investors with greater rights than those afforded to property owners under the [US] Takings Clause'); IISD 2004, above n 11, at 28, n 85 and associated text; Peterson, above n 64, at 25; Trade Act of 2002, 19 USC §§ 2101–401, at § 2102(b)(3) (2002).

[403] See Porterfield, above n 402, at 41.

broad expropriation provisions.[404] The reining-in of expropriation clauses is welcome and necessary, considering the arguable potential of BITs to shape the customary international law doctrine of expropriation.[405]

## C. A Human Rights Clause

Investment agreements should impose express obligations to protect and fulfill human rights on the States parties and on investors who invoke the agreements. As has been noted, '[a]s currently drafted, BITs are extremely narrow in their formulation: according substantive rights to investors, without any need for corresponding duties or obligations on the part of those investors.'[406] To remedy this, investment agreements should include 'a broader set of actors, rights and responsibilities' than is represented by the current focus on investor rights.[407] Such a structure might enumerate rights and obligations for foreign investors, host States, and home States in both the pre-establishment and post-establishment phases of investment.[408] Post-establishment obligations of investors might include an obligation to respect basic human rights, as well as requirements to undertake:

> human rights impact assessments [and] adhere to transparency requirements with respect to royalties and taxes paid to host states; or [agreements might include] an explicit conditioning of rights upon respect for domestic and international human rights rules.[409]

Host State rights might include rights to maintain development priorities, establish performance requirements and establish high environmental and human health standards in the pre-establishment phase, and rights to maintain development priorities as agreed and to regulate in the public interest in the post-establishment phase.[410] Imposing human rights obligations on investors and States would ensure the legal relevance of human rights to the adjudication of investment claims.[411] Ideally, however, the invocation of investor rights under investment treaties should be explicitly conditioned on investor compliance with human rights norms.[412]

---

[404] See Hallward-Driemeier, above n 4, at 8–9 ('[i]t is precisely those cases where FDI flows in substantial amounts in both directions that countries have balked at ratifying BITs').

[405] See above n 41 and associated text.

[406] IISD 2003, above n 4, at 33.

[407] IISD 2004, above n 11, at 30.

[408] See *ibid* at 30 and tbl 1.

[409] IISD 2003, above n 4, at 36. Todd Weiler likewise suggests that BITs include an enforcement mechanism 'for the prosecution of human rights violations committed by private parties whose [investment] activities will be protected under such agreements': Weiler, above n 342, at 437.

[410] See IISD 2004, above n 11, at 32 and tbl 3.

[411] IISD 2003, above n 4, at 33.

[412] *Ibid* (jurisdiction of arbitral tribunals could be conditioned on compliance 'with minimum human rights responsibilities as set out in the treaty, or [as] incorporated by reference').

## D. Reform of the Dispute Resolution Mechanism

In order to alleviate the regulatory chill produced by the lack of transparency, legitimacy and accountability in the dispute settlement process under BITs,[413] it is crucial that the process be reformed. A multilateral court, dedicated to investor–State investment disputes and featuring independent jurists and public proceedings, would go furthest towards rationalizing the development of the body of international investment law.[414] This rationalization is essential due to the increasing impact of investment disputes on matters of public interest.[415]

If the current mechanism is not replaced, it should at least integrate a requirement of exhaustion of local remedies as well as mechanisms to provide for transparency, legitimacy, and accountability, such as a standing body of panelists, public proceedings, third-party *amicus curiae* status, public access to documents, and the availability of an appeal process.[416]

---

[413] See above, section II.3.C.

[414] The IISD has proposed 'the establishment of a multilateral tribunal and/or an appellate process geared specifically to issues of foreign investment agreements and customary international law standards': IISD 2004, above n 11, at 35. Michael D Goldhaber notes that '[i]nvestment has overtaken trade in global economic importance, but, so far, investment has failed to inspire the creation of mature legal institutions': Goldhaber, above n 207. Goldhaber goes on to assert that '[t]he ideal solution would be to establish a World Investment Court, corresponding to the Appellate Body of the World Trade Organization. Such a forum could be called into being by signing a new world treaty, or adding a protocol to existing world treaties. However, prospects for any such agreement are dim': *ibid*.

[415] See, eg, Cosbey, above n 202, at 4 ('more often than not, [arbitration systems in the investor–State context] engage key issues of public policy and the balancing of private and public welfare issues'); Goldhaber, above n 207 (noting that uniformity in investor–State arbitration awards is more important than in arbitrations between private parties because 'the stakes tend to be higher, both in terms of money and public interest').
The IISD emphasizes that the arbitration mechanism for investor–State disputes must reflect its importance to public welfare:

> we believe it is time for the investor–state process to mature and be based on democratic principles that must be reflected in the emerging role of international law in this area ... [c]hanges to the dispute settlement process must, we believe, be seen in the context of a developing international law regime rather than simply as a tinkering with the arbitration procedures.

Cosbey, above n 202, at 3. The IISD acknowledges that its approach would more closely approximate the investor–State dispute settlement mechanism to a judicial apparatus:

> we are fully aware that [our proposed guiding principles of legitimacy, independence, impartiality, accountability and transparency] will tend to diminish the differences between arbitration and judicial proceedings. This is deliberate. The arbitration system in the investor–state context has, quite simply, outlived its original rationale. The primary reason for this is clear: the cases coming before it too often bear no resemblance to traditional commercial or private disputes that arbitration systems are essentially designed to address.

*Ibid* at 4.

[416] IISD 2004, above n 11, at 35. If ICSID were to host the appellate mechanism, it would need to be divested from the World Bank to avoid conflicts of interest:

> a prerequisite for ICSID operating an appellate facility is its divestiture by the World Bank and re-establishment as a single, independent body with individualized governmental

The IISD notes that 'even existing agreements could ... be relatively easily fixed' through a revision of the ICSID and UNCITRAL arbitration rules, which would effectively amend almost all existing BITs.[417]

## E. A Mechanism for Requesting Authoritative Treaty Interpretations

Regulatory chill is pernicious in part because it forces States into a binary choice between regulating, and thereby risking suit by investors, or not regulating at all. States could avoid this straitjacket if there were a mechanism by means of which they could obtain authoritative interpretations of clauses in BITs in advance of promulgating regulations. Such a mechanism would increase both the transparency and predictability of the investment law regime, sparing States from having to withdraw entirely, due to the threat of large arbitral awards against them, from the business of regulating.[418]

control entirely outside the existing World Bank voting system. While the linkage to the Bank may have been necessary at the beginning of the process, it is not demonstrably necessary now ...

[The existence of a conflict of interest] is equally true for the current role of ICSID in terms of arbitration panels, and most pronouncedly in relation to the annulment panels. An independent organization could house both the leading arbitration panel process and the single appellate process. This would create some additional governance and financing needs, beyond those that could be recovered by arbitration and appeal fees. However, given the vital role of foreign investment in the global economy today, and its critical role in the pursuit of development and sustainable development, this cost is one worth bearing.

Cosbey, above n 202, at 13. See also above n 209 (discussing the potential for conflicts of interest arising from ICSID's connection to the World Bank).

[417] IISD 2004, above n 11, at 35. ICSID, noting that 'there is "clearly scope for inconsistencies to develop in the case law,"' recently proposed a reform to its rules that would provide for a single avenue of appeals for review of arbitral awards: Luke Peterson, 'ICSID Secretariat floats proposals for reforms to investor-state arbitration', *Investment Law and Policy Weekly News Bulletin* (International Institute for Sustainable Development, Winnipeg, Canada), 27 October 2004, available at http://www.iisd.org/pdf/2004/investment_investsd_oct24_2004.pdf. The IISD responded with comments that 'urged more radical reform including fuller transparency of proceedings and devolution of ICSID from the World Bank Group': Luke Peterson, 'IISD submits proposals on ICSID reform', *Investment Law and Policy Weekly News Bulletin* (International Institute for Sustainable Development, Winnipeg, Canada), 17 December 2004, available at http://www.iisd.org/pdf/2004/investment_investsd_dec17_2004.pdf. The ICSID proposal is available at http://www.worldbank.org/icsid/improve-arb.pdf and the IISD response is available at http://www.iisd.org/pdf/2004/investment_icsid_response.pdf. For more on the ICSID proposal and the IISD response, see above n 202.

The IISD has also posited that further analysis is needed on the potential for human rights courts to be used to adjudicate investment disputes, with an eye to achieving better coherence in international law. See IISD 2003, above n 4, at 36–38.

[418] One precedent for such a mechanism is NAFTA, which provides in its Art 1131(2) for the issuance of binding interpretive statements. See Aaron Cosbey, International Institute for Sustainable Development, *NAFTA's Chapter 11 and the Environment* (2003), at 10, available at http://www.cec.org/files/PDF/JPAC/JPAC-Ch11-paper_en.pdf. It has been noted in the NAFTA context that 'an interpretive statement can address the "damage control"

The mechanism might consist of a standing panel of independent arbitrators who would receive and answer questions from governments regarding the applicability of particular BIT clauses to proposed regulation.[419] The opinion of the panel would be binding in any subsequent dispute. The mechanism would not be effective if it did not address all of the BITs to which the relevant State is a party, but given the substantial repetition of language in respective clauses across BITs, evaluating all of a State's BITs at once with regard to any particular question should be a manageable task for the panel. The establishment of a such a panel would face legal obstacles similar to those detailed in section V.1.A above; it is likely States would need to negotiate the establishment of the panel with each of their existing BIT partners.

## 2. Summary

In summary, by virtue of their pervasiveness, the strength of their investment protection provisions, and the lack of transparency, legitimacy, and accountability of their dispute settlement procedures, BITs have the potential to have a significant negative impact on human rights enforcement and progressive realization. Until there is wider reform of the international regime governing foreign direct investment, States should consider injecting human rights considerations into investment treaty disputes in an effort to make the investment regime more sensitive to its implications for the public interest and for States' other international obligations which may conflict with the obligations imposed by BITs. Although defenses that are based on human rights are unlikely to be successful in the majority of investment treaty disputes, because such disputes usually implicate human rights obligations subject to progressive realization and thus not amenable to easy proof of

required to mitigate the uncertainties and regulatory chill created by the existing provisions of Chapter 11': Howard Mann and Konrad von Moltke, International Institute for Sustainable Development, *Protecting Investor Rights and the Public Good: Assessing NAFTA's Chapter 11* (2003), at 24, available at http://www.iisd.org/pdf/2003/investment_ ilsd_background_en.pdf (noting, however, that the mechanism is inherently limited in that 'it cannot expand the content of Chapter 11 to include the promotion of sustainable investments').

[419] Under NAFTA, the interpretive statement is to be rendered by the Free Trade Commission, which is comprised of the Trade Ministers of each of the three parties. The parties to NAFTA thus retain some control over the development of doctrine under the treaty, although the limitations of the mechanism have been noted: see Cosbey, above n 418, at 10–11. In the investment context, in the absence of a single multilateral agreement on investment it would not be possible to replicate the NAFTA mechanism due to the multiplicity of BITs participated in by each State, where each treaty establishes a relationship with a different State partner.

breach,[420] attempts at such defenses may raise awareness of the need for reform in the investment treaty regime by prompting an acknowledgement of the value of the kind of regulation that is undercut by investment treaties.[421] Ultimately, however, the legal regime governing international investment requires substantial reforms if it is to avoid impinging on human rights realization and enforcement.

[420] See above n 361 and associated text.
[421] The conflict between human rights and investment goals may not be as severe as it appears, because strong human rights enforcement and other forms of public interest regulation may in fact enhance rather than decrease business profitability, inasmuch as they provide a stable workforce, shield businesses from human rights complaints if they are complying with regulations, and contribute to an environment that will sustain commercial operations into the future. Until the substantive BIT provisions take account of these potential synergies between human rights and investment by incorporating human rights protections, however, States may be subject to conflicting obligations arising under investment treaties and human rights commitments.

# 4

# Competing for Foreign Direct Investment through the Creation of Export Processing Zones: The Impact on Human Rights

CHU YUN JULIANA NAM*

## I. INTRODUCTION

EXPORT-PROCESSING ZONES (EPZs) are traditionally defined as industrial zones with special incentives set up to attract foreign investors, in which imported materials undergo some degree of processing before being (re-)exported again.[1] This chapter first attempts to understand the rationale behind the attention paid to EPZs, which some States consider part of 'legitimate trade policy tools',[2] but which some labor rights activists see as a manifestation of 'the brutal face of globalization'.[3] The small number of empirical studies conducted on the impact of EPZs does not provide sufficient information to make a judgment on whether EPZs are detrimental to social conditions. This debate on whether EPZs are a detrimental source of globalization is still raging, and this chapter does not judge whether EPZs deserve the reputation as a brutal face of globalization. Instead, it will present the complexities of the issues in relation to the use of EPZs as a trade policy. Following that analysis, this chapter suggests that there is an existing set of norms that could be the starting point

---

* This paper was written by the author in her personal capacity as part of the Master of Laws in International Legal Studies program at New York University School of Law in 2004–05.

[1] International Labour Office, Employment and Social Policy in Respect of Export Processing Zones, Third Item on the Agenda, 286th Session (Geneva, March 2003) [hereinafter 'ILO 286th Session, Third Item'], at 1.

[2] See World Bank, *PremNotes Economic Policy Export Processing Zones*, Number 11 (December 1998).

[3] Jagdish Bhagwati, *In Defense of Globalization* (New York, Oxford University Press, 2004), at p 83.

for formulating a rules-based system that regulates how States use EPZs. Given the connection between the consequence of the use of EPZs and the identification of EPZs as an 'investment-related trade measure',[4] the chapter steps into the arena of the multilateral trade regime by considering the available means of conceiving such a regulation by existing international institutions, the World Trade Organization (WTO) and the International Labour Organization (ILO).

## II. THE CREATION OF EXPORT PROCESSING ZONES AND THE PRESUMED IMPACT ON FOREIGN DIRECT INVESTMENT

Although EPZs have a bad reputation among labor rights activists, various reports by international organizations such as the ILO, the Organization for Economic Cooperation and Development (OECD), the World Bank, and the International Confederation of Free Trade Unions (ICFTU) indicate that any presumption that the existence of such zones by definition means that human rights violation occur in such zones is not supported. Of course this chapter does not dispute reports that many individuals have had their rights violated whilst working for enterprises that operate in EPZs. Rather, it questions the rationale behind the particular attention paid to EPZs. Unfortunately, this question remains unresolved. As it stands, there are insufficient empirical studies conducted to provide reliable answers to this question.

### 1. The Phenomenon of Export Processing Zones

A table titled 'Types of Zones: An Evolution' on the ILO's website[5] shows that there are many different types of what could be considered an EPZ. Zones are not a new phenomenon and have existed since the 1920s in Spain. Zones have evolved from sites of initial assembly and simple processing activities to include high-tech and science zones, finance zones, and even tourist resorts. From 25 countries with EPZs in 1975, there are now over 116, which are said to employ 43 million people, according to the ILO's last survey, taken in 2002.[6]

---

[4] United Nations Conference on Trade and Development (UNCTAD), *Investment-Related Trade Measures*, UNCTAD/ITE/IIT/10 (vol IV) (1999), at 23, available at http://www.unctad.org/en/docs//psiteiitd10v4.en.pdf (last visited 21 November 2004).

[5] ILO, *Types of Zones: An Evolutionary Typology* (2003), available at http://www.ilo.org/public/english/dialogue/sector/themes/epz/typology.htm (last visited 21 November 2004).

[6] UNCTAD, above n 4, at 2 (noting that 30 million of the 43 million are from China).

As exemplified by the ILO's table, *special incentives* designed to attract foreign investment—which is part of the definition of EPZs—could include any or all of the following:

— tax holidays, reductions, and exemptions;
— exemption from foreign exchange controls;
— duty-free imports of capital goods, machinery, and raw materials;
— no quotas, nor levies, on imports;
— free repatriation of profits;
— lower administrative and establishment costs, eg, less government red tape; and
— provision of start-up facilities, eg above-average (compared to the rest of the country) communications services and infrastructure. It is also common for governments to subsidize utilities and rental rates for firms operating in EPZs.[7]

However, it becomes evident that in certain countries, special incentives could mean lax labor laws, leading to violation of certain workers' rights, which are also universal human rights. For instance, there are waivers with regard to termination of employment and overtime in the 'Free Ports' of Hong Kong, Singapore, Bahamas, Batam, Labuan and Macao.[8] In the 'Special Economic Zones' of Hainan and Shenzhen provinces of China, restraints are placed on the formation of trade unions.[9] Likewise, despite obligations to respect national employment regulations, there are restrictions on the freedom of trade unions in the 'Industrial Free Zones/EPZs' of Ireland, Taiwan, Malaysia, the Dominican Republic, Mauritius, Kenya, Hungary and the 'Information Processing Zones' in India-Bangalore and the Caribbean.[10] At the more extreme end of the scale, the 'Enterprise Zones' in Indonesia and Senegal prohibit the formation of trade unions, and government mandate on liberal hiring and firing of workers.[11]

It follows that, despite the diverse range of types of EPZs, in many of these States, there is no formal waiver of the enforcement of labor laws. In fact, on the face of the legislative instruments creating EPZs, one would find that labor laws in EPZs are the same as those that are applied elsewhere in the State.[12] Even an ICFTU study concedes that EPZs are by no means the only places were labor rights are violated.[13]

---

[7] Dorsati Madani, *The World Bank, A Review of the Role and Impact of Export Processing Zones* (1998), 97–101, available at http://econ.worldbank.org/docs/965.pdf.
[8] ILO, above n 5.
[9] *Ibid.*
[10] *Ibid.*
[11] *Ibid.*
[12] ILO 286th Session, Third Item, at 8.
[13] International Confederation of Free Trade Unions, *Export Processing Zones—Symbols of Exploitation and a Development Dead-End* (2000) [hereinafter 'ICTFU Study'], at 7.

However, surveys conducted by the ILO suggest that often host States do not enforce their labor laws in EPZs.[14] According to that ILO survey, for instance, in Togo, workers' views are that the special incentives offered in EPZs to foreign investors seriously limit fundamental labor rights, such as basic trade union rights and equality of treatment.[15] Further, although the following example is rare, the Kenyan Government has gone to the extreme and granted temporary exemptions on the application of occupational safety and health laws in its EPZs.[16]

Thus it is not surprising that the results of a limited number of empirical studies on the correlation between EPZs and labor standards are not definitive. A more extensive study of EPZs shows that on aggregate:

— the average wage for workers in EPZs tends to be higher than the average wage outside EPZs in the country concerned;
— as working conditions are positively correlated to the size of firms, it follows that working conditions are better in firms that operate in EPZs as they tend to be larger than firms outside EPZs; and
— most firms that operate in EPZs are foreign-owned companies that are more likely to be better managed than locally owned companies, and frequently offer higher wages and better working conditions than in the surrounding economy.[17]

Nevertheless, we should consider how in certain instances the use of EPZs as a trade policy by some States has in fact led those States to disregard human rights norms in favor of economic development. Essentially, this chapter requires readers to consider EPZs as a phenomenon of developing countries that are seeking foreign investment, exemplifying how certain governments may value or prioritize economic goals over fundamental rights.

## 2. The Purpose and Function Fulfilled by EPZs

To understand the phenomenon of the proliferation of EPZs, one needs to gain at least a superficial understanding of the economic rationale behind its use. As with all explanations behind international economic theories of

---

[14] International Labour Organization, *Seventh survey on the effect given to the tripartite declaration of principles concerning multinational enterprises and the social policy. Part II: summary of reports submitted by governments and by employers' and workers' organizations* (2001), at p 352 referred to in ILO 286th Session, Third Item, at 10.

[15] *Ibid.*

[16] *Ibid.*

[17] Ana Teresa Romero, 'Labor Standards and Export Processing Zones: Situation and Pressures for Change' (1995) *Development Policy Review* 13, 247–76, referred to in David Kucera, *The Effects of Core Workers' Rights on Labour Costs and Foreign Direct Investment: Evaluating the 'Conventional Wisdom'* (Geneva, International Labour Organization), at p 50.

today, it is necessary to refer to the comparative advantage principle, which survived into the modern legal framework that regulates trade between States.[18] The basic premise behind the comparative advantage principle is that 'freer trade leads to each country filling an economic niche that it is most suited to occupy'.[19] As it stands in the global trading system, the reality is that for many developing countries, their comparative advantage is cheap labor.

This is not to say that regulatory competition between States will necessarily lead to optimal results. As explained by prominent economist and development theorist, Hirschman, under the current world trading regime, free trade principles have not translated into free movement of human capital. Restrictions on human capital mobility have lead to fundamental distortions in world labor markets. As Hirschman elaborates:

> [i]f labor were as mobile a factor of production as capital or technology, regulatory competition between jurisdictions might well ensure a close to optimal domestic policy equilibrium with respect to labor rights given that transboundary externalities are not nearly as pervasive in this area as, for example, with environment. However, when workers cannot move and are disempowered domestically, labor rights policy outcomes may well not accurately reflect their preferences.[20]

That is, although labor is a factor of production that is traded in the world market, it is not treated in the same manner as other factors of production. Instead, trade policy tools such as EPZs are applied so as to overcome the obstacles posed by the apparent barriers to trade in human capital. Subsequently, EPZs are 'designed specifically to attract (domestic and) foreign investment'.[21] A World Bank study on the impact and role of EPZs concluded that EPZs are often created by governments in countries with economies that are not open liberally to trade. That is, their establishment is an attempt by these governments to create 'open market oases within an economy that is dominated by restrictions to trade, macro and exchange rate regulations and other regulatory governmental controls'.[22]

---

[18] John J Jackson, William J Davey and Alan O Sykes, *Legal Problems of International Economic Relations Cases, Materials and Text*, 4th edn (St Paul, MN, West Group, 2002), at p 6.

[19] Daniel A Zaheer, 'Breaking the Deadlock: Why and How Developing Countries Should Accept Labor Standards in the WTO' (2003) 9 *Stanford Journal of Law, Business and Finance* 69, at 74.

[20] Albert Otto Hirschman, *Exit, Voice, and Loyalty, Responses to Decline in Firms, Organizations, and States* (1970), referred to in Robert Howse, 'The World Trade Organization and the Protection of Workers' Rights' (1999) 3 *Journal of Small and Emerging Business Law* 131, at 154.

[21] UNCTAD, above n 4, at 23.

[22] Madani, above n 7, at 16–17.

In countries such as Taiwan and South Korea, EPZs were created with specific timeframes to allow these developing countries to make the transition to an open market economy.[23] It is also said that China is using EPZs to experiment with the concept of a market economy.[24]

It is increasingly evident from the reaction of developing nations to the 2003 report by the ILO titled *Employment and Social Policy in Respect of Export Processing Zones* that the developing countries believe that EPZs are designed to promote employment, training, enterprise development, technologies, and skills.[25] Most importantly, as stressed before, EPZs are used to attract foreign direct investment and earn foreign currency in order to achieve those economic goals. Governments of these developing countries express strongly that it is within their sovereign right, as well as a duty to their citizens, to use legitimate policies to create employment opportunities for their subjects so they may earn an income.[26] By their assessment, the establishment and operation of EPZs is a legitimate policy that allows them to meet their economic goals. As discussed above, empirical studies are inconclusive on whether EPZs do achieve these aims. Nevertheless, there are tentative conclusions that EPZs have created substantial employment in these developing countries.[27]

But why would these governments at times implement lax labor laws in their EPZs or not enforce labor laws in EPZs? There appears to be a belief[28] held by many of these States that: (a) lower labor standards lead to lower labor costs, and (b) foreign investors prefer to locate where labor costs are lower, other things being equal, most importantly accounting for differences in labor productivity. As emphasised by the ICFTU study, there is therefore a fear that the proliferation of EPZs is leading to a 'race to the bottom'. This allegation refers to: 'the scenario of countries or regions competing against each other by offering investors ever greater tax breaks and ever weaker regulations'. So, the argument goes that poor

---

[23] *Ibid.*

[24] *Ibid.*

[25] Comments from representatives of the Government of the Republic of Korea speaking on behalf of the Asia Pacific Group, cited in International Labour Office, Governing Body, Fifth Item on the Agenda, Report of the Committee on Employment and Social Policy, GB 286/15, 286th Session (2003) [hereinafter 'ILO 286th Session, Fifth Item'], at 22.

[26] *Ibid.*

[27] International Labour Organization, *Labour and Social Issues Relating to Export Processing Zones* (1998), available at http://www.ilo.org/public/english/dialogue/govlab/legrel/tc/epz/reports/epzrepor_w61/3_1.htm (last visited 21 November 2004).

[28] Interestingly, this is contrary to the results of a survey of managers of transnational corporations (TNCs) and international experts on FDI, which showed that TNCs rate factors such as growth of the market, political and social stability, and quality of labor higher than the cost of labor in deciding location for investment (Kucera, above n 17, at 3). On the other hand, one would question the reliability of such surveys, as it is unlikely, in this public relations-wary society, that corporations would be willing to divulge the actual intentions behind their choice.

countries with only cheap labor to offer to the world market have been engaged in serious competition with each other to attract investment from multinational corporations to set up in their countries and utilize the human capital offered by them as a factor of production. That is, their aim is to create employment and inject much-needed foreign capital into their countries and, as stressed before, ultimately simply to allow their countries to become richer. In this desperate competition for foreign direct investment, many fear that there is a race to the bottom amongst the poor countries, in offering such generous terms to the investors that they wind up net losers.[29]

However, a recent OECD study on competition among countries to attract FDI questions whether there is indeed evidence of a 'race to the bottom'.[30] The study concludes that there is no decisive evidence of 'any inexorable tendency towards global 'bidding wars among governments in their competition to attract FDI'. As one scholar put it, '... competition on the basis of low labour standards can only be explained as political rather than an economic phenomenon, reflecting little more than misguided attempts to secure short term political payoffs—attempts which may be imitated by others'.[31]

But while it may not be inevitable, such a 'race to the bottom' at least appears characteristic in fact of the attitude of a number of countries. Indeed, it is precisely for this reason that the 2000 OECD study makes the point that the 'prisoner's dilemma' nature of the competition creates a permanent danger of such 'wars'.[32] A 'race to the bottom' does not depend on investors being truly attracted to countries with lower labor standards. As Kucera, in reflecting on that 2000 OECD study, pointed out, '[p]erception, true or false, will suffice.'[33]

Yet, a significant weakness in proposals that advocate the prohibition of EPZs is that a ban will not solve the inherent problem of certain States' disregard for human rights. Proscribing the use of EPZs is clearly not the preferable approach, as not all EPZs lead to violation of fundamental rights, particularly since, as made apparent in the developing countries' reaction to the ILO's 2003 study on EPZs, there is a 'concern on the part of

---

[29] ICTFU Study, above n 12, at 5; Herbert Jaunch, 'Export Processing Zones and the Quest for Sustainable Development: A Southern African Perspective' (2002) 14 *Environment & Urbanization* 101, available at http://www.globalpolicynetwork.org/research/namibia/jaunch.pdf (last visited 21 November 2004).

[30] See Charles Oman, Policy Competition for Foreign Direct Investment: A Study of Competition among Governments to Attract FDI (Organization for Economic Co-operation and Development, 2000).

[31] Kevin Banks, 'Globalization and Labour Standards—A Second Look at the Evidence' (2004) 29 *Queen's Law Journal* 533, at 549–50.

[32] Oman, above n 30, at p 10.

[33] Kucera, above n 17, at p 1.

developing countries that the imposition of core labor standards will erode their comparative advantage.' It is commonly argued that developing countries' comparative advantage lies in low wages, as discussed above. Any external pressure that raises labor costs will deny developing countries their right to exercise their comparative advantage in international trade.

### III. THE REGULATION OF THE ESTABLISHMENT AND OPERATION OF EXPORT PROCESSING ZONES

Nevertheless, it is because we are dealing with certain fundamental rights that we need to consider the question: should host States be restricted in, as opposed to prohibited from, using EPZs as a trade policy? As endorsed by a 2000 OECD study on policy competition for FDI, '[f]rom a policy perspective, ... governments [should be encouraged] to move away from incentives-based means of competing to attract FDI in favour of greater concentration on rules-based means of competing that do not weaken environmental and labour standards.'[34] According to that OECD study, 'the most damaging effects appear to stem less from direct financial cost to governments of investment subsidies paid out, or from any lowering of environmental or labor standards, than from the lack of policy transparency and government accountability that the process of competition for FDI tends to engender.'[35] For that reason, the OECD study concludes that:

> [stable, predictable and transparent rules] should help governments collectively to overcome the 'prisoner's dilemma' nature of policy competition, and the 'free rider' problem associated with it, and should favour policies that work to enhance productivity growth in developing and emerging economies in ways that promote sustainable development and improved working conditions in those countries.[36]

That is, in exploring this core issue, it is necessary to consider how a rules-based system could be conceived under which States would be restricted from pursuing economic goals in a way that is incompatible with observance of human rights norms. At the same time, we need to bear in mind the likely negative reception the developing countries will give to any pressure to enact and enforce certain rights in EPZs. One could just imagine such pressures being characterized in the words of another well known trade law expert, Raj Bhala, as 'an unwarranted intrusion into the internal affairs of these countries and an affront to their

---

[34] Preface by Ulrich Hiemenz, in Oman, above n 30, at p 7.
[35] *Ibid.*
[36] *Ibid.*

sovereignty.'[37] As argued by Singer, 'problems of regulatory gaps or regulatory competition are often seen to be outside of the international trade regime because they involve "real conflicts" and "political disagreements" about regulatory standards among sovereign States.'[38]

Further, what some may consider 'business friendly labor laws',[39] as used to describe the characteristics of EPZs in a recent World Bank Report, may mean violation of fundamental human rights to others. More particularly, what would be the point of pressuring desperate countries to agree to a complex rights regime if they simply cannot afford to meet those standards and will therefore always be in violation of such an agreement? The reality is that 'it is economically infeasible and even counter-productive for most companies and governments of developing countries to adopt such a laundry list.'[40]

So we are left with the question: is there a set of universal rights that under no circumstances should be violated? An easy answer is that many believe that there is, under customary international law, a set of core fundamental workers' rights that are part of human rights norms.[41] Howse, a leading international trade law academic, claims that 'certain labor rights or standards have come to be widely regarded as basic human rights with a universal character.'[42]

As one would guess, the place to start is the 1998 ILO Declaration on Fundamental Principles and Rights at Work ('ILO Declaration'), which places good faith obligations[43] on members of the ILO to respect, promote, and realize:

(1) freedom of association and the effective recognition of the right to collective bargaining;
(2) the elimination of all forms of forced or compulsory labor;
(3) the effective abolition of child labor; and
(4) the elimination of discrimination in respect of employment and occupation.

---

[37] Raj Bhala, 'Clarifying the Trade-Labor Link' (1998) 37 *Columbia Journal of Transnational Law* 11, at 26.

[38] Joseph William Singer, 'Real Conflicts' (1989) 69 *Boston University Law Review* 1.

[39] Madani, above n 7, at 9.

[40] Bhala, above n 37, at 33.

[41] *Ibid* at 35, and Howse, above n 20, at 149.

[42] Howse, above n 20, at 149.

[43] However, a major weakness of the ILO Declaration is that the ILO Declaration in itself is not a binding treaty. Despite its universal nature and arguably international customary law status, even the ILO admits that '[t]he Declaration is a promotional instrument—and a reaffirmation by the ILO's government, employer and worker constituents of central beliefs set out in the organization's Constitution': International Labour Organization, 'About the Declaration', available at http://www.ilo.org/dyn/declaris/DECLARATION WEB.ABOUTDECLARATIONHOME?var_language=EN (last visited 20 November 2004).

Even Bhagwati agrees that nations must assert the broad aspirational objectives agreed in the ILO Declaration.[44] This is because, as Howse points out, '[r]espect for the universal normative content of international labor rights does not usually entail identical labor policies or standards. Precisely because universal human rights have important contextual dimensions, even these labor rights elicit quite different views as to their exact scope and meaning.'[45] That is, these standards are universal, but not absolute.

According to this view, to address the 'race to the bottom' predicament whilst ensuring that States retain their regulatory autonomy, States ought to agree on a rules-based system under which States ensure that their use of EPZs as a trade policy does not infringe the workers' rights set out in the ILO Declaration as a minimum. Going back to the prisoner's dilemma, if all countries formally form a consensus to abide by, to protect, and to enforce these core fundamental rights at work, and agree to operate EPZs accordingly, then at least there will be a de jure harmonization of a minimum standard that would halt the reality or the perception of the 'race to the bottom.'[46] That is, the main purpose of such an agreement would be to create a level playing-field for basic labor standards so as to address the main perceived problems behind the image of EPZs as the 'brutal force of globalization'. Under this agreement, States would be obliged to ensure that their laws achieve certain outcomes, that is, non-violation of the core fundamental labor rights in EPZs, but would retain their regulatory autonomy as they would be free to formulate their own domestic laws so as to achieve those end-results.

## IV. SHOULD THE INITIATIVE BE TAKEN BY THE WORLD TRADE ORGANIZATION OR BY THE INTERNATIONAL LABOUR ORGANIZATION?

The question now is: who could enforce this agreement to operate EPZs without infringing core labor rights so that in fact, host States would be held accountable for any violation of those norms? It is widely recognized that: '[t]he difficulty of regulating a global economy has been nowhere more evident than in the attempt to enforce international labor rights.'[47] As noted by Bhala, '[i]n the absence of harmonized enforcement mechanism—such as the WTO or ILO, developed countries are likely to force compliance on developing countries through conditionality of preferential trade benefits, or even unilateral trade action.'[48]

---

[44] Bhagwati, above n 3, at p 177.
[45] *Ibid.*
[46] Bhala, above n 37, at 39.
[47] John C Knapp, 'The Boundaries of the ILO: A Labor Rights Argument for Institutional Cooperation' (2003) 29 *Brooklyn Journal of International Law* 369, at 371.
[48] Bhala, above n 37, at 39.

If unilateral trade actions were to become the preferred approach, the international community would not have an opportunity to decide by consensus that the measure in question was a violation of the core labor standards, nor, as a result, would it have the opportunity to determine, against an objective set of rules as agreed, the appropriate remedy for that particular violation of human rights norms. That is, it should be for the international community to decide whether it ought to withdraw preferential treatment, impose trade sanctions, or apply another appropriate solution against the defaulting State in order to correct that violation. However, as controversial as it may sound, it may be worthwhile to consider alternatives so as to minimize the potential for what could be considered paternalistic or worse, imperialistic interventions.

Consequently, is there a potential for existing multilateral regimes to undertake the task of ensuring that States abide by the obligations to respect these universal rights in their use of EPZs as a trade policy? Both the ILO and the WTO have, in varying degrees, existing mechanisms to hold States accountable for the violation of the relevant treaty provisions, and many would argue that the WTO and the ILO possess 'foundations upon which the apparatus for bringing human right responsibility to bear directly on States might be built.'[49] Any rules-based system administered by either institution would need to cover issues such as who would:

— monitor observance of the obligations;
— decide whether a member State has violated the obligations; and
— decide on the sanctions and remedies for non-compliance,

and how this system could be implemented.

## 1. What is the International Labour Organization's Role in the Context of EPZs?

Historically, the responsibility for characterizing and monitoring labor standards has been allocated to and assumed by the ILO.[50] It carries out its functions through its tripartite structure whereby States, employers,

---

[49] David Kinley and Junko Tadaki, 'From Talk to Walk: The Emergence of Human Rights Responsibilities for Corporations at International Law' (2004) 44 *Virginia Journal of International Law* 931, at 995.

[50] Drusilla K Brown, International Labor Standards in the World Trade Organization and the International Labour Organization 7 (1999), prepared for presentation at the Multilateral Trade Negotiations: Issues for the Millennium Round, Twenty-Fourth Annual Economic Policy Conference, Federal Reserve Bank of St. Louis, 21–22 October 1999, available at http://ase.tufts.edu/econ/papers/200003.pdf (last visited 21 November 2004).

and employee representatives are involved in the creation of labor rights norms.[51] As Professor Charnovitz asserts:

> [t]he probability of ILO approval of new trade controls is very small, but the ILO is a better forum than the WTO for three reasons. First, the ILO is a specialized organization on labor, where labor and foreign ministry officials serve as representatives. Second, the ILO is a champion of workers' rights. Third, the vote required for new labor standards is two-thirds compared to the consensus needed for new rules in the WTO.[52]

Although the ILO was established as the principal agency that sets standards for international labor law, it does not have convincing enforcement powers. As pointed out by various trade law experts, '[t]he International Labor Organization ... has proven largely ineffective in enforcing compliance with even the core universal standards it has delineated.'[53] Arguably, although the Declaration is not a legally binding treaty, each of the Declaration rights is enshrined in separate binding agreements of ILO. Nevertheless, '[t]he tools that the ILO currently has available to attain member compliance are limited to moral persuasion, publicity, shame, diplomacy, dialogue and technical assistance.'[54] That is, as noted by Russell-Brown, the ILO 'cannot legally compel a member state to act nor can it impose sanctions on violators of labor standards.'[55]

More specifically, the way in which the ILO has attempted to deal with extreme situations of violation of the core labor standards in EPZs is said 'to be instructive as to why the ILO has been ineffective (on its own) in bringing such violating countries into compliance with its standards.'[56] For instance, Pakistan enacted and maintained laws that explicitly exempted EPZs from certain labor protections extended to workers outside the EPZs, such as the right to form an association. For over 17 years, the ILO requested many times that the Pakistan government amend its

---

[51] S Cooney, 'Testing times for the ILO: Institutional Reform for the New International Economy' 20 *Comparative Labor Law & Policy Journal* 365, at 367, referred to in Kamil Ahmed, 'International Labor Rights A Categorical Imperative' (2004) 35 *Revue de droit de l'Université de Sherbrooke* 145, at 161.

[52] Steve Charnovitz, Trade Law and Global Governance (London, Cameron May, 2002), at p 267.

[53] Knapp, above n 47, at 371.

[54] Daniel S Ehrenberg, 'From Intention to Action: An ILO–GATT/WTO Enforcement Regime for International Labor Rights', in Lance A Compa and Stephen F Diamond (eds), Human Rights, Labor Rights and International Trade (Philadelphia, University of Pennsylvania Press, 1996), p 164.

[55] Sherrie L Russell-Brown, 'Labor Rights as Human Rights: The Situation of Women Workers in Jamaica's Export Free Zones', (2003) 24 *Berkeley Journal of Employment and Labour Law* 179, at 195.

[56] Michael Gordon, 'Export Processing Zones', in Michael Gordon and Lowell Turner (eds), *Transnational Cooperation Among Labor Unions* (Ithaca, Cornell International Industrial and Labor Relations Reports, 2000), at p 66, referred to in Knapp, above n 47, at 391.

laws to include EPZ workers in its labor protections and refrain from such activities as would be inconsistent with its obligations under ILO Conventions Nos 87[57] and 98[58], respectively.[59]

Pakistan finally stopped ignoring the ILO's demands only after the ILO threatened to request the World Bank and the IMF to suspend assistance to Pakistan if it continued to maintain laws that denied freedom of association to workers in its EPZs.[60] While there are no direct accounts of the effect this warning had on the government's policy position, it is probably no coincidence that shortly thereafter Pakistan announced to the ILO that it would redraft its laws concerning EPZs so as to conform with the relevant ILO resolutions.[61]

## 2. Could the World Trade Organization be the Enforcer of Core Labor Standards?

It might be thought that the WTO is an obvious choice for enforcing obligations to observe fundamental labor rights that concern Export Processing Zones as a trade measure. It is, after all, the leading international organization dealing with the rules of trade between nations. Consequently, it is one of the few international institutions that could legitimately approve or condemn the decision of a member State to provide favorable treatment to, or impose sanctions on, imports from another member State.

Further, this is because the WTO is unique from any other multilateral institution in that it has a relatively solid foundation for enforcing obligations under its dispute settlement mechanism. The Understanding on

---

[57] International Labour Organization, Convention No 87 on Freedom of Association and Protection of the Right to Organize, San Francisco, 14 June 1948.

[58] International Labour Organization, Convention No 98 on Right to Organize and Collective Bargaining, Geneva, 1 July 1949.

[59] Committee on Freedom of Association [hereinafter CFA] Case No 1353, Complaint against the Government of Pakistan, presented by the Trade Unions Action Committee, ILO Report No 253 (Vol LXX, 1987, Series B, No 3); CFA Case No 1726, Complaint against the Government of Pakistan, presented by the International Federation of Building and Wood Workers, the International Confederation of Free Trade Unions and the All Pakistan Federation of Labour, ILO Report No 294, (Vol LXXVII, 1994, Series B, No 2), at para 419(b), and CFA Case No 2006, Complaint against the Government of Pakistan, presented by the All Pakistan Federation of Trade Unions and the Federation of Oil, Gas, Steel and Electricity Workers, ILO Report No 318 (Vol LXXXII, 1999, Series B, No 3), at para 353(a), referred to in Knapp, above n 47, at 400–1.

[60] Dagens Arbete, ILO Warning to Government, 25 January 2000, available at http://www.dagensarbete.se/home/da/home.nsf/pages/9C5E7C3AF112D3134125687400 3ED1A9?OpenDocument, referred to in Knapp, above n 47, at 401.

[61] International Labour Organization, Committee of Experts on the Application of Conventions and Recommendations, Individual Observation Concerning Convention No 87, Freedom of Association and Protections of the Right to Organize 1948, Pakistan (Ratification: 1951) (2002).

Rules and Procedures Governing the Settlement of Disputes ('the DSU'), which forms part of the Agreement Establishing the World Trade Organization 1994 ('the WTO Agreement'), provides a forum for member States to complain of and defend alleged violations of treaty obligations before an independent panel, and even has an appeals procedure. Unlike, for example, the United Nation's International Court of Justice (ICJ), all WTO members must submit to the WTO's Dispute Settlement Body's jurisdiction, and this mechanism is subject to strict deadlines and procedural rules.[62]

So far, however, there is a great reluctance within the WTO to recognize the link between trade and human rights or labor standards. As explained by Howse and Trebilcock, 'the [General Agreement on Tariff and Trade] contains no explicit provision either permitting or requiring trade action against labour rights violations.'[63] Indeed, the WTO is a specialized organization on trade, where trade ministers serve as representatives: human rights are not part of its mandate, and unilateral trade action taken on the basis of human rights violations by one member State towards another member State should be regarded with suspicion.[64] As explained by Howse:

> [t]he system is based, first, on the notion that both domestic and global welfare normally are enhanced by the removal of trade protection and, second, on the fundamental necessity of being able to distinguish protectionist cheating on trade rules from various trade-impacting policies purported to have aims unrelated to commercial interests themselves, whether environment, human rights, or health and safety.[65]

As Daniel Enhrenberg, an international trade lawyer notes, '[w]henever the idea of establishing and enforcing labor standards has been introduced in the [General Agreement on Tariff and Trade] it has always been rejected.'[66] For instance, during the preparatory meetings for the WTO ministerial conference in Singapore, a few trade ministers pressed for the inclusion of labor rights on the agenda.[67] This call was led by the Clinton

---

[62] Art 1 of the Understanding on Rules and Procedures Governing the Settlement of Disputes, Annex 2 of the Agreement Establishing the World Trade Organization, Geneva, 1994: see Hilary K Joseph, 'Symposium: Global Trade Issues in the New Millennium: Upstairs, Trade Law; Downstairs, Labor Law' (2001) 33 *George Washington International Law Review* 849, at 864.

[63] Robert Howse and Michael J. Trebilcock, The Regulation of International Trade, 2nd edn (London and New York, NY, Routledge, 1999), at p 456.

[64] Charnovitz, above n 52, at p 263.

[65] Robert Howse, 'The World Trade Organization and the Protection of Workers' Rights' (1999) 3 *Journal of Small and Emerging Business Law* 131, at 148.

[66] Ehrenberg, above n 54, at p 164.

[67] 'Inside US Trade', in (1996) Norwegian Paper on Trade and Labor,  9 August, at 5–6, referred to in Charnovitz, above n 63, at p 258.

administration, which proposed the establishment of a WTO working party on trade and core labor standards.[68] However, this proposal was fiercely resisted by developing countries, who accused the developed countries of attempting to endorse protectionist measures in this system of free trade.[69]

But because of this discussion, the member States were able to agree on a paragraph on core labor standards in the final WTO Ministerial Declaration. Although it is a pale reflection of what the United States proposed and it certainly does not form part of the WTO Agreements, we could consider this Ministerial Declaration as a consensus acknowledging that member States must observe internationally recognized core labor standards. Nevertheless, the developing countries were able to include an express statement that the comparative advantage of low-wage developing countries should not be called into question and that labor standards should not be used for trade protectionist purposes.

Interestingly, that was not the first time that the subject of labor standards or workers rights was discussed amongst the member States of the General Agreement on Tariff and Trade 1994 (GATT). The historical background to the GATT is that it was initially negotiated as part of a broader international organization to be called the International Trade Organization.[70] However, this idea fell through.[71] But under Article 7.1 of the draft ITO Charter, member States explicitly recognized that measures relating to employment must take into account the rights of workers under inter-governmental declarations, conventions and agreements. In particular, this provision provided that:

> Members recognize that unfair labor conditions, particularly in production for export, create difficulties in international trade, and accordingly, each Member shall take whatever action may be appropriate and feasible to eliminate such conditions within its territory.

### 3. Are Export Processing Zones Illegal under Current World Trade Organization Law?

It follows that, as it currently stands, a member State is not in violation of its obligations under the WTO system if it violates core labor rights without any infringement of international trade rules such as national

---

[68] Ibid.

[69] Gary G Yerkey, 'Developing Countries Block US Plan to Include Labor Issue in Work Agenda' (1966) 13 *International Trade Report (BNA)* 1925, at 259, referred to in Charnovitz, above n 52, at p 259.

[70] See Chapter 6 of Jackson et al, above n 18.

[71] Ibid.

treatment and most-favored-nation principles.[72] As noted by Wai, 'the dominant international trade institutions, the GATT and now the WTO, operate outside the UN system, and have a different set of parties from the human rights conventions and institutions.'[73] As discussed above, the general consensus is to treat the regulation for trade protectionism on the one hand and violation of human rights on the other as involving fundamentally different policy concerns.[74]

However, setting aside the issue of enforcement of labor rights under the WTO system, there has been some speculation on whether the creation of an EPZ could be considered an export subsidy, and whether EPZs therefore are prohibited under the WTO Agreements. Under the Agreement on Subsidies and Countervailing Measures ('the Subsidies Agreement'), many WTO developing member countries have, since 1 January 2003 been prohibited from providing certain export subsidies, calling in some cases for adaptation of their current incentive schemes, including those provided in the context of EPZs producing goods. This depends on whether the incentives offered by host countries to firms operating in EPZs fit within the definition of 'export subsidies' under that Agreement.

In short, Article I:1 of the Subsidies Agreement provides that a subsidy is deemed to exist if:

(a) there is a financial contribution by a government; and
(b) a benefit is conferred.

Article 3 prohibits subsidies contingent on export performance, including those illustrated in Annex I (Article 3.1(a)) of the Subsidies Agreement. On the face of these provisions, it is not likely that lax labor laws or the non-enforcement of labor laws in EPZs would constitute an export subsidy and thereby be prohibited under the Subsidies Agreement. However, as explained earlier, other common characteristics of EPZs, such as duty-free status, tax exemptions, and rental subsidies, are the types of incentives that may be caught under the Subsidies Agreement.

On the other hand, the prohibitions under the Subsidies Agreement do not apply to the least developed countries, or those listed in Annex VII

---

[72] See Howse and Trebilcock, above n 63.

[73] Robert Wai, 'Countering, Branding, Dealing: Using Economic and Social Rights in and around the International Trade Regime' (2002) 14 *European Journal of International Law* 35, at 43.

[74] See ibid; Philip Alston, 'Resisting the Merger and Acquisition of Human Rights by Trade Law: A Reply to Petersmann' (2002) 13(4) *European Journal of International Law*, available at http://www.ejil.org/journal/Vol13/No4/art2.pdf (last visited 3 January 2005).

to the Agreement,[75] all of which have EPZs.[76] In addition, countries which have made timely applications for exemption and which do not have an annual per capital income exceeding US$1,000 for three years in a row may benefit from exemptions until 2007.[77]

As a result, it is not known yet how the application of the Subsidies Agreement could impact on the competitive context in which EPZs will operate in the future. One thing that is clear, however, is that the Subsidies Agreement does not directly change the way host States consider core labor standards. More alarmingly, it is arguable that by not being able to provide other common special incentives, such as tax breaks and tariff waivers, there may be greater inducement to lower labor standards in EPZs as the competitive factor between developing countries that use EPZs as a major trading policy.

## 4. Weaknesses of the World Trade Organization as the Champion of Labor Rights

There are some serious weaknesses in arguments that promote the WTO as a champion of labor rights. First, it is somewhat perverse that the harmful behavior that the WTO system is attempting to prevent is the very enforcement mechanism used within this system.[78] Article 19.1 of the DSU provides that if a member State is found to be in violation of its obligations under any WTO Agreement, that State is obliged to 'bring the measure into conformity with that agreement.' If the member concerned does not withdraw or modify the infringing measure so as to comply with the WTO Agreement within a reasonable time, compensation and the suspension of concessions are temporary remedies available under Article 22 of the DSU.[79] However, Article 22 of the DSU also provides that compensation is 'voluntary', and the complaining member must 'agree not only to be compensated [but also] the specific amount thereof.'[80]

---

[75] Countries listed under Annex VII to the Subsidies Agreement are: Bolivia, Cameroon, Congo, Côte d'Ivoire, the Dominican Republic, Egypt, Ghana, Guatemala, Guyana, India, Indonesia, Kenya, Morocco, Nicaragua, Nigeria, Pakistan, Philippines, Senegal, Sri Lanka, and Zimbabwe.

[76] Jean-Pierre Singa Boyenge, ILO Database on Export Processing Zones (2003), available at http://www.ilo.org/public/english/dialogue/sector/themes/epz/epz-db.pdf (last visited 20 November 2004).

[77] Article 27.2 of the Subsidies Agreement.

[78] Drusilla K Brown et al, Pros and Cons of Linking Trade and Labor Standards, Research Seminar in International Economics, Discussion Paper No 477 (2002), at 7, available at http://www.fordschool.umich.edu/rsie/workingpapers/Papers476-500/r477.pdf (last visited 21 November 2004).

[79] Joost Paulwelyn, 'Enforcement and Countermeasures in the WTO: Rules, Rules and Rules—Toward a More Collective Approach' (2000) 94 *American Journal of International Law* 335, at 337.

[80] Ibid.

As a result, the WTO dispute settlement mechanism does not provide for payment of damages or require compensation. Instead, a finding of inconsistency of the provisions under the WTO Agreements could lead to trade sanctions if the parties to the complaint cannot agree on another resolution to their dispute. As explained by Sykes, the focus of the WTO dispute settlement system is on voluntary compliance, backed up by a staged process to increase pressure from harm to reputation and, ultimately, the threat of suspension of trade concessions by complaining States.[81] This is a paradox as free trade principles essentially aim to liberalize trade by requiring member States to lower their trade barriers. That is, imposing trade restrictions which are economically harmful may be more detrimental to the host State found in violation of core labor standards in its operation of EPZ rather than solving the problem.

Consequently, trade sanctions, if applied, are likely to hurt most the workers who were intended to benefit from the labor standards. If a host State faces a ban on its exports because it has failed to allow the workers in EPZs from forming a trade union, then those workers, who are presumably already suffering from their lack of union representation, would now lose their jobs as well.[82] The essential purpose of using EPZs as a trade policy tool is to attract FDI, to promote export industry, and to create employment. This dilemma has led some economists to advise developing countries to reject proposals to include labor issues in the WTO system.[83] According to them, a monetary fine for breaking the rules may be more desirable in such circumstances.[84]

Another weakness of the WTO system in the context of enforcement of core labor standards is that individuals who have suffered from such a violation do not have standing to sue the host State before the WTO dispute settlement body and seek compensation. As clarified by the WTO Appellate Body in the 2002 case, *European Communities—Trade Description of Sardines*,[85] Article 3.7 of the DSU provides that only member States have the right to bring a case under the WTO dispute settlement regime. That is, although the host State may be condemned by concerned member States under a formal complaints procedure, under the WTO system, the true victims—the workers in the EPZs, complaining about the host State's noncompliance of observance of core labor standards—would have no direct recourse to redress the behavior of the host State. The question is: when

---

[81] Alan O Sykes, 'The Remedy for Breach of Obligations under the WTO Dispute Settlement Understanding', in Marco Bronckers and Reinhard Quick (eds), New Directions in International Economic Law: Essays in Honour of John H. Jackson (The Hague and Boston, MA, Kluwer Law International, 2000).

[82] Brown et al, above n 78, at 22.

[83] *Ibid* at 25.

[84] *Ibid* at 7.

[85] European Communities—Trade Description of Sardines, WT/DS231/AB/R (26 September 2002), at para 158.

member States decide to complain under the WTO system, who are they really seeking to protect—the workers in EPZs or their own industries which cannot compete with their lower-paid counterparts in EPZs?

## 5. Why the International Labour Organization remains the Principal Agency for Monitoring Labor Rights Violations in Export Processing Zones

As explained above, the ILO's lack of power *legally* to compel its members to comply with core labor rights is said to be its key weakness in achieving expedient results. However, the ILO's use of 'social and psychological pressures such as publicly embarrassing, privately cajoling, or otherwise to sway a country to change labor practices that fail to comply with ILO standards' has thus far been the principal multilateral means of influencing member States to change their behavior. Like the WTO system, individuals do not have standing to file a complaint to initiate an ILO investigation of alleged infringement of labor rights. However, unlike the WTO system, trade unions, as the main non-State actors advocating workers' rights in EPZs, have the right to file a representation under Article 24 of the Constitution of the International Labour Organization ('ILO Constitution')[86] against an EPZ host State, if that State is a member of an ILO convention.

Article 24 of the ILO Constitution has at least the potential for the ILO to initiate investigation of alleged abuse of workers' rights in EPZs and address those issues directly. The commencement of these proceedings may lead to the initiation of an Article 26 complaint by the Governing Body of the ILO, which would then proceed to the appointment of a Commission of Inquiry ('Commission') to prepare a report of findings and make recommendations. Following the issuance of the Commission's report, Article 29 of the ILO Constitution provides that the concerned governments may either accept the recommendations of the Commission or submit the complaint to the ICJ. If the ICJ is asked to review the complaint, Articles 31 and 32 of the ILO Constitution provide that the ICJ's decision, to affirm, vary, or reverse the Commission's findings, will be final. If the governments involved fail to comply with the recommendations of the Commission or the decision of the ICJ, Article 33 of the ILO Constitution allows the Governing Body to 'recommend to the Conference such actions it may deem wise and expedient to secure compliance therewith.'

[86] Constitution of the International Labour Organization, Versailles, 28 June 1919.

On the other hand, one view of the ILO is that 'labour standards have been allocated to the ILO precisely because it has no power to punish.'[87] According to Drusilla K Brown of Tufts University, '[t]he low power of the incentives used by the ILO is entirely appropriate given the general inability to identify a set of uniform labor standards that can be applied in all settings.'[88] As discussed above, there is the argument that 'even if developing countries were to agree that a set of standards is desirable; achieving them may be difficult or impossible.'[89] As noted by Brown, this is the type of difficulty which makes the establishment and enforcement of a widely acceptable set of labor standards within the WTO system problematic.[90]

## V. CONCLUSION

The limited empirical studies in this area show that 'the experiences with EPZs have been mixed,'[91] and moreover, that EPZs are not the only places where human rights violations occur. Nevertheless, the focus of this chapter is on the phenomenon of the escalating use of EPZs as a trade policy tool. In considering the apparent dilemmas associated with the negative symbols represented by EPZs, the author is persuaded by arguments that the ILO Declaration should be the basis for a rules-based system that regulates the use of EPZs as a trade policy. That is, States' use of EPZs as a trade policy should be regulated, as opposes to prohibited.

On the question of whether the ILO or the WTO should initiate this regulation, it seems that each institution has strengths and weaknesses in its potential ability to enforce core labor rights. But the fact remains that neither of the existing institutions is capable of policing and penalizing violations of fundamental rights occurring from a host State's use of EPZs as a trading policy. At this stage, the ILO remains the champion of workers' rights, which are the main human rights violated in certain EPZs. Consequently, the most viable option is for a stronger structure of coordination between the two institutions to condemn use of EPZs that undermines fundamental rights. As pointed out by Wai, 'it is more likely, and perhaps normatively less problematic, that emerging system of transnational governance will involve a mix of strategies, including international treaties and institutions, transnational cooperation among governmental actors, national state regulation, transnational NGO activism, transnational litigation, consumer boycotts, and voluntary codes.'[92] Accordingly,

---

[87] Brown, above n 50, at 9.
[88] *Ibid.*
[89] *Ibid.*
[90] *Ibid.*
[91] ILO, above n 27.
[92] Wai, above n 73, at 37–38.

although neither of the institutions is capable of enforcing its members to comply with core labor standards in EPZs, perhaps if the two cooperated and coordinated under a formal agreement and structure, there is a potential for them to establish institutional jurisdiction and competency over all the conditions necessary to ensure the effective protection of the universal labor standards. The mammoth task of regulating EPZs is clearly not for one organization alone.

# 5

# The North American Agreement on Labor Cooperation: An Effective Compromise between Harmonization of Labor Rights and Regulatory Competition?

ANA A PIQUER

## I. INTRODUCTION

THE LINK BETWEEN trade and labor has been widely debated both as a general matter, and as an important part of the debate surrounding the subscription of the North American Free Trade Agreement (NAFTA). Should labor issues be included in the agreement? What could happen to labor in the three States parties (Canada, Mexico, and the United States) if not? Should there be an attempt to harmonize the labor legislation of the three States parties? In the debate, some considered these issues to be necessarily separated. Others looked at the European model, which uses both pre-emptive legislation and harmonization of labor laws.

The result of this debate was the signing of the North American Agreement on Labor Cooperation (NAALC),[1] which acknowledges the link between trade and labor, but sets forth an entirely new model in achieving such a link. This model stands on three main pillars. First, an agreement on 11 labor principles that serve as guidance for the States parties.[2] Second, each State party retains the right to enact its own labor laws, ensuring they provide for high labor standards.[3] And third, each State party acquires the obligation to promote compliance and effectively

---

[1] North American Agreement on Labor Cooperation, 14 September 1993, Can–Mex–US (1993) 32 ILM 289 [hereinafter, NAALC].
[2] *Ibid*, Art 49, Annex 1.
[3] *Ibid*, Art 2.

enforce these labor laws.[4] This is accompanied by procedures for cross-border monitoring of such obligation.[5]

This solution can be seen as a 'second-best compromise',[6] or an in-between solution. On one side, was the criticized possibility of adopting NAFTA without any labor provision at all. On the other side, was the equally criticized possibility of undertaking a harmonization of the labor laws of the three countries, based on commonly agreed standards. Five lines of arguments have been made around these two possibilities, which will be briefly analyzed in the first part of this chapter.

NAALC's 'enforce-your-own-laws' model, as an in-between solution, attempts to get the best of both worlds. It does not undermine sovereignty, but it does have a cross-border monitoring system to control enforcement of labor laws in the States parties. It creates an institutionalized environment for cooperation that can hardly be accused of protectionism. Even though it does not give labor groups any specific influence, its consultation process does give new tools for labor/political activism. Since all countries retain the right to enact their own labor laws, there is leeway for preserving each country's comparative advantages. But, at least in theory, a race to the bottom could be stopped, whether it is legislative or de facto (by lack of enforcement). A legislative race to the bottom could be attacked if it strays too far from the 11 labor principles established in the agreement. A de facto race to the bottom via lack of enforcement could be even more directly attacked by the provisions of the agreement, even leading to trade sanctions in certain limited cases.

In this sense, the NAALC is a compromise. This chapter attempts to test the effectiveness of this compromise. To do so, after analyzing the arguments on both sides of the compromise, it will examine the NAALC model and how it has been re-established in bilateral free trade agreements signed by the United States with several countries from 2000 onwards. With this information, it is possible to study the model from the point of view of what NAALC has really achieved, considering both critical literature and some empirical studies. Finally, we will review some human rights issues which have been largely overlooked in the debates, and evaluate the NAALC from that point of view.

The main conclusion is that the effectiveness of NAALC will depend on what question we are asking. Many policy concerns were actually addressed and probably solved, and led to the repetition of the model in the FTAs

---

[4] *Ibid*, Art 3.

[5] *Ibid*, Arts 20–41.

[6] See eg Stephen F Diamond, 'Labor rights in the Global Economy—A case study of the North American Free Trade Agreement', in Lance A Compa and Stephen F Diamond (eds), *Human Rights, Labor Rights and International Trade* (Philadelphia, University of Pennsylvania Press, 1996), p 199.

which followed. But the ultimate question is: are workers better off? And the answer to this is still unclear, more than a decade since NAALC was signed.

## II. ARGUMENTS SURROUNDING THE SUBSCRIPTION OF THE NAALC

For the purpose of summarizing the large number of opinions raised regarding the NAALC, they will be grouped into five types of arguments: first, arguments that defend sovereignty, opposing arguments that favor the need for NAALC to have some degree of normative influence; second, arguments that favor cooperation between States parties, opposed by those who consider these measures to be disguised protectionism; third, arguments that revolve around the political role that labor should or should not have; fourth, arguments warning of the risk of social dumping, followed by arguments that favor non-interference with the efficiency of world economy; and finally, arguments considering the risk (or not) of a so-called 'race to the bottom'. These will be briefly analyzed below.

### 1. First Argument: Normative Influence and Sovereignty

The arguments in favor of harmonization consider that a strong commitment is necessary for the labor agreement to be effective.[7] The agreement should have normative influence over the labor law of the States parties, and it should be internationally enforceable.[8] Some argue that real protection of labor will not be achieved unless the agreement incorporates its own labor standard-setting mechanism or it incorporates two critical institutional elements: 'a monitoring and enforcement agency, and a permanent, impartial tribunal.'[9] This would be necessary, among other reasons, because 'globalization has undermined the ability of national law to effectively regulate the workplace.'[10]

---

[7] This is linked to propositions to create a 'European-style Social Charter, Structural Fund and Court of Justice': Michael J McGuinness, 'The protection of labor rights in North America: a commentary on the North American Agreement on Labor Cooperation' (1994) 30 *Stanford Journal of International Law* 579.

[8] See Marley S Weiss, 'Two steps forward, one step back—or vice versa: labor rights under Free Trade Agreements from NAFTA, through Jordan, via Chile to Latin America and beyond' (2003) 37 *University of San Francisco Law Review* 689.

[9] *Ibid* at 704.

[10] Sarah H Cleveland, 'Why international labor standards?', in Robert J Flanagan and William H Gould, eds, *International Labor Standards* (Stanford, CA, Stanford Law and Politics, 2003), 129, at p 141. Cleveland further argues that: 'Flexible corporate structures, corporate mobility, and the increasing political and economic power of multinational corporations have combined with employment flexibility and new conceptions of the employment relationship to exacerbate the inherent limitations of states in maintaining and enforcing labor standards': *ibid*.

The mirror argument against such harmonization is sovereignty. Harmonization of labor law has been seen as undermining the sovereignty of the three countries, which is politically not desirable.[11] This 'unifying concern is evident in both the structural arrangement and the substantive commitments of both NAFTA and the NAALC.'[12]

## 2. Second Argument: Cooperation and Protectionism

Harmonization can be promoted because it potentially creates enhanced opportunities for cooperation. Common labor standards allow for truly effective cooperation in their implementation, control, enforcement, and improvement, leading to greater social peace,[13] since it 'sets in motion a process by which countries bring their regulatory frameworks into consistence with one another.'[14] Cooperation is truly possible, because the set standards 'create a common baseline of acceptable employment behavior'[15] against which enforcement and compliance efforts can be measured.

The flip-side of this argument comes mostly from less developed countries (Mexico, in the case of NAFTA). Even when 'it would be surely unfair to label all those who favor international labor standards ... as protectionist'[16], in the case 'of those labor unions and labor ministers in the rich countries that aim to protect their interests against those of developing country workers, the claim of protectionism is a believable one.'[17] Harmonization can be seen as a protectionist measure coming from developed countries, and cooperation is looked at with suspicion under this light.[18]

## 3. Third Argument: Political Role of Labor

Harmonization could give an exceptional opportunity to recover labor's political role. Collectively, 'labor unions articulate the interests and public

---

[11] See Weiss, above n 8, at 703–4.

[12] *Ibid* at 704. Weiss notes that '[o]n the Mexican side in particular, retaining unaltered its corporatist system of industrial relations was deeply intertwined with the preservation of political hegemony for the dominant political party, the Revolutionary Institutional Party ("PRI"). Potential outside intervention in this area was a deal-breaker': *ibid.*

[13] See Katherine Van Wezel Stone, 'Labor and the global economy: four approaches to transnational labor regulation' (1995) 16 *Michigan Journal of International Law* 987, at 1023–24 (comparing harmonization with other three possible models: preemptive legislation, cross-border regulation, and extraterritorial jurisdiction).

[14] *Ibid* at 1024.

[15] Cleveland, above n 10, at 145.

[16] Gary S Fields, 'International Labor Standards and Decent Work: Perspectives from the Developing World', in Robert J Flanagan and William H Gould (eds), *International Labor Standards* (Stanford, CA, Stanford Law and Politics, 2003), 61 at p 68.

[17] *Ibid.*

[18] See Van Wezel Stone, above n 13, at 1025.

policy concerns of a large segment of the population.'[19] Harmonization gives a chance to avoid reducing the labor movement to bargaining for wages and labor conditions, and to return it to the role it traditionally had, as a measure of social justice.[20]

On the other hand, some have argued that 'if labor regulation is not determined at the level of the nation-state, national labor movements lose much of their political clout.'[21] It has also been argued that there are divisions within the trade union movements of the three States parties, and between the movements of each country,[22] which in itself reduces the actual strength of labor as an effective political force.

An optimistic point of view sees harmonization of labor standards as an added opportunity for the labor movement to regroup with renewed strength, based on the new common ground it can work with. A pessimistic viewpoint, however, would consider that harmonization would not make any difference or may even make these weaknesses and divisions worse, since the overall labor environment becomes more complex.

## 4. Fourth Argument: Social Dumping and Efficiency in the World Economy

This is maybe the most repeated argument in the NAALC debate: the risk of 'social dumping' or 'industrial flight'.[23] This is seen as negative, since it 'transforms these developing countries into "dumping grounds" for the dirty industries of developed nations' and 'hurts companies which incur the additional costs of complying with environmental protection and worker health regulations in the developed world.'[24]

In other words, NAFTA raised the concern that many United States companies will choose to relocate in Mexico, taking advantage of lower wages and a persistent lack of enforcement of labor law.[25] This would

---

[19] *Ibid* at 997.

[20] 'Labor is no longer viewed as representing a broad view of social justice in American life,' being reduced to 'one among many "special interest" groups,' which implies 'the loss of a major constituent element in modern political and legal culture': Diamond, above n 6, at 204.

[21] *Ibid* at 996.

[22] *Ibid* at 220.

[23] A definition of 'social dumping' is that it 'takes place when industrialists, in an attempt to avoid stringent labor and environmental regulations in the developed world, transfer their operations to the developing world': Michael Joseph McGuinness, 'The politics of labor regulation in a North America: a reconsideration of labor law enforcement in Mexico' (2000) 21 *University of Pennsylvania Journal of International Economic Law* 1.

[24] *Ibid.*

[25] In this sense, NAALC was negotiated mostly in an effort 'to address concerns raised by organized labor that NAFTA would cause massive job loss': Van Wezel Stone, above n 13, at 1007.

cause a double negative consequence: the loss of jobs in the United States, and the worsening (or at least non-improvement) of the conditions of workers in Mexico.[26] These consequences could be avoided if labor legislation of the States parties is harmonized over the same standards.[27]

However, advocates for free trade have said that so-called 'social dumping' is not necessarily bad. It could have concrete and immediate negative effects, but in the long run, it is merely a redistribution of the world's resources in a more efficient way, which is ultimately beneficial.[28]

On the other hand, this argument has been rebutted from the point of view that the risk of industrial flight is not based on reality. OECD reports in 1996 and 2000 conclude that there is no 'robust evidence' that firms were directing investment to 'no standards' countries.[29] The only 'significant exception' to this conclusion is China,[30] although it is 'a sufficiently giant exception to be of concern'.[31]

Low labor costs is only one out of many factors that companies consider for relocation, and it is not the most important one.[32] Even though there are studies that find that foreign direct investment is attracted to regions with low labor costs, they can be criticized because they do not control for labor productivity.[33] Studies conclude that 'there is no solid

---

[26] McGuinness characterizes what he calls the 'North American Social Dumping Theory' as having three assumptions: (a) Mexico suffers from a disorganized and ineffective labor regulatory structure; (b) due to this weakness, Mexico will be victim of wide-scale social dumping by US and Canadian industries; and (c) this will degrade workplace safety and health conditions in Mexico: McGuinness, above n 23, at 3–4. The author further argues that these assumptions can be in the most part openly questioned with available empirical data: *ibid* at 39.

[27] It is interesting that this was used as an argument against harmonization too: 'An ironic aspect of the adoption of NAALC to improve labor rights was the observation that Mexico has ratified far more ILO labor conventions that the United States. Enforcement of its laws, however, has been uneven': Virginia A Leary, '"Form Follows Function": Formulations of International Labor Standards—Treaties, Codes, Soft Law, Trade Agreements', in Robert J Flanagan and William H Gould (eds), *International Labor Standards* (Stanford, CA, Stanford Law and Politics, 2003), 179, at p 192. If the problem is enforcement, and not existing laws, harmonization via international labor standards would not solve anything at all.

[28] It has been argued that 'permitting firms to relocate in the lowest labor standards environment is desirable because it increases trade and creates more efficient utilization of global resources, which in turn fosters greater social wealth': Van Wezel Stone, above n 13, at 1025.

[29] William B Gould, 'Labor Law for a Global Economy: the Uneasy Case for International Labor Standards', in Robert J Flanagan and William H Gould (eds), *International Labor Standards* (Stanford, CA, Stanford Law and Politics, 2003), 81, at p 93.

[30] China 'has been the object of significant foreign investment and trade in recent years, despite its refusal to allow independent unions and other systematic violations of core labor rights': Cleveland, above n 10, at p 141.

[31] *Ibid*.

[32] Jagdish Bhagwati, *In Defense of Globalization* (New York, Oxford University Press, 2004), p 130.

[33] Drussilla K Brown *et al*, *The Effects of Multinational Enterprises on Wages and Working Conditions in Developing Countries* (NBER–CEPR International Seminar on International Trade, 2002), 24, available at http://www.econ.kuleuven.ac.be/ew/academic/intecon/Home/WorkingGroupSeminars/Files/Deardorff.pdf

evidence that countries with poorly protected worker rights attract FDI. If anything, investors prefer locations in which workers and the public more generally function in a stable environment where civil liberties are well established and enforced'.[34] If this is so, harmonization through international labor standards might be neither necessary nor desirable, at least not for this reason.

## 5. Fifth Argument: The Risk of a Race to the bottom

This last argument is actually the second step of the same process that begins with 'social dumping' or 'industrial flight'. If companies relocate towards countries with lower labor costs, and these countries want to stay attractive for those investments, they will want to maintain or even lower their labor standards in order to attract more investors. This would produce what has been called a 'race to the bottom', in which each country lowers its standards more and more in order to stay competitive.[35] This would further 'weaken labor in the political arena insofar as they create disincentives for labor to lobby for protective legislation.'[36] The fact that empirical data does not support the existence of a true 'industrial flight' effect is not necessarily relevant, since a 'race to the bottom' can happen based only on the belief that an 'industrial flight' will occur.[37] Again, harmonization through common standards could avoid this. It can 'counterbalance these pressures … by removing certain intolerable labor conditions from the labor rights/production costs calculus,' creating 'a floor below which states and managers cannot legitimately go to compete.'[38]

[34] *Ibid* at 27; see also David Kucera, *The effects of core workers rights on labour costs and foreign direct investment: evaluating the 'conventional wisdom'* (International Institute for Labour Studies, 2001), available at http://www.ilo.org/public/english/bureau/inst/download /dp13001.pdf. In the same direction, another study concludes that there is 'no evidence that countries with low labor standards gain competitive advantage in international markets. Poor labor conditions often signal low productivity or are one element of a package of nation characteristics that discourage FDI inflows or inhibit export performance': Robert J Flanagan, 'Labor Standards and International Competitive Advantage', in Robert J Flanagan and William H Gould (eds), *International Labor Standards* (Stanford, CA, Stanford Law and Politics, 2003), 15, at p 48.

[35] Van Wezel Stone, above n 13, at 992–93. This has also been called 'regulatory competition'.

[36] *Ibid* at 993.

[37] Kucera, above n 34, at 1 ('[a] "race to the bottom" does not depend on investors being truly attracted to countries with lower labour standards. Perception, true or false, will suffice'). As some studies conclude, the 'prisoner's dilemma' nature of the competition creates a permanent danger of 'bidding wars' among governments to attract investments: *ibid* (citing Oman, Charles, *Policy Competition for Foreign Direct Investment: A Study of Competition among Governments to Attract FDI* (Paris, OECD, 2000)).

[38] Cleveland, above n 10, at 141.

Arguments against this are also based on empirical data, that show that a race to the bottom does not appear to happen as a general matter, 'at least if you look at recent American experience,'[39] since it is not sustainable in the long run.[40] In fact, some argue that politics might actually shift to a race to the top, 'where you virtually force the exporters into accepting measures that raise their cost of production and hence cut down on their competitiveness,'[41] thus giving rise to arguments related to protectionism, mentioned previously.

### III. THE NORTH AMERICAN AGREEMENT ON LABOR COOPERATION (NAALC) MODEL

In our second step towards evaluating the effectiveness of the compromise behind the NAALC, we will analyze the central elements of the model set forth in the agreement. This same model has been repeated, with some variations, in bilateral Free Trade Agreements that the United States has signed between 2000 and the present. We will also examine what these variations are.

### 1. The NAALC Provisions

The provisions in the NAALC address four basic topics. First, the NAALC establishes its purpose and the substantive principles that the States parties must follow. Second, it defines the precise obligations that the States parties acquire. Third, it establishes an administrative structure. Finally, it creates a procedure for consultation and dispute resolution.

---

[39] Bhagwati, above n 32, at p 127.

[40] The 1996 OECD study concluded that this lacks empirical support, because '[c]ountries can only succeed in repressing real wages and working conditions for a limited period of time. Thereafter, market forces will be such that wages will catch-up, thus wiping out previous competitive gains': Gould, above n 29, at 92.

[41] Bhagwati, above n 32, at p 131. Bhagwati notes the irony in this argument: 'They argue that we should not have to compete with, and lose to, others with lower standards. In short, we want to be virtuous but not have to pay for it!': *ibid* at p 132. Moreover, the 'race-to-the-top' argument is paradoxical, since if it is to be used as an argument for an unregulated global labor market, it must assume either that labor is organized in order to seek a share of gain from improved productivity, or that developed (high standard) countries will place pressure for improvement of standards on developing (lower standard) countries. This makes this argument alone rather weak as support for the improvement of labor standards through an unregulated labor market. However, the argument is buttressed by the apparent lack of empirical data showing the existence of an actual 'industrial flight' and subsequent 'race to the bottom'.

*A. Purpose and Substantive Principles*

The first Article of the Agreement establishes seven objectives, which include to 'improve working conditions and living standards in each Party's territory'[42], 'promote compliance with, and effective enforcement by each party of its labor law'[43] and 'promote, to the maximum extent possible, the labor principles set out in Annex 1.'[44]

These labor principles are set forth in the body of the NAALC in Article 49. This Article defines several concepts used within the Agreement, and defines 'labor law' as 'laws and regulations, or provisions thereof, that are directly related to:

1. freedom of association and protection of the right to organize;
2. the right to bargain collectively;
3. the right to strike;
4. prohibition of forced labor;
5. labor protections for children and young persons;
6. minimum employment standards, such as minimum wages and overtime pay, covering wage earners, including those not covered by collective agreements;
7. elimination of employment discrimination on the basis of grounds such as race, religion, age, sex, or other grounds as determined by each Party's domestic laws;
8. equal pay for men and women;
9. prevention of occupational injuries and illnesses;
10. compensation in cases of occupational injuries and illnesses;
11. protection of migrant workers.'

Annex 1 of the Agreement gives further detail for each of these principles, and clarifies the role that they are intended to have, stating that the principles:

> are guiding principles that the Parties are committed to promote, subject to each Party's domestic law, but do not establish common minimum standards for their domestic law. They indicate areas of concern where the Parties have developed, each in its own way, laws regulations, procedures and practices that protect the rights and interests of their respective workforces.[45]

Thus, as previously said, there is no attempt of harmonization. It is also noticeable that the Agreement makes no reference to international labor standards.

[42] NAALC, above n 1, Art 1(1).
[43] *Ibid*, Art 1(6).
[44] *Ibid*, Art 1(2).
[45] *Ibid*, Annex 1: Labor Principles.

## B. Obligations

Part Two of the Agreement, which deals with 'Obligations', actually starts recognizing a right: 'the right of each Party to establish its own domestic labor standards, and to adopt or modify accordingly its labor laws and regulations.'[46] Then, it establishes that 'each party shall ensure that its labor laws and regulations provide for high labor standards, consistent with high quality productivity workplaces, and shall continue to strive to improve those standards in that light.'[47]

The following five Articles, lay out this general obligation in a more detailed way, dealing with:

(i)   government enforcement action, and the duty to 'promote compliance and effectively enforce its labor law';[48]

(ii)  private action, ensuring that persons have access to administrative, quasi-judicial, judicial, or labor tribunals for the enforcement of the party's labor law;[49]

(iii) procedural guarantees, ensuring a fair, equitable, and transparent procedure and with public and sound final decisions;[50]

(iv)  publication of any ruling of general application on matters covered by the Agreement'[51]

(v)   promotion of public awareness of labor laws.[52]

---

[46] *Ibid*, Art 2.

[47] *Ibid*.

[48] *Ibid*, Art 3. The Article establishes, by way of example, a list of enforcement actions, that go from preventive measures—such as appointing and training inspectors and investigating suspected violations—to direct measures in case of violations of labor law—such as providing or encouraging mediation, conciliation, and arbitration services, and initiating, in a timely manner, proceedings to seek appropriate sanctions or remedies. This list also includes cooperative measures, such as encouraging the establishment of worker–management committees to address labor regulation of the workplace. Finally, this Article states that '? Each Party shall ensure that its competent authorities give due consideration in accordance with its law to any request by an employer, employee or their representatives, or other interested person, for an investigation of an alleged violation of the Party's labor law.'
Art 3 also expressly refers to Art 42 of the Agreement, which establishes that 'Nothing in this Agreement shall be construed to empower a Party's authorities to undertake labor law enforcement activities in the territory of another Party.'

[49] *Ibid*, Art 4. It also states that each Party's law must ensure that persons with a legally recognized interest under its law may have recourse to procedures by which rights arising both under its labor law and collective agreements, can be enforced.

[50] *Ibid*, Art 5. The Article gives further detail, such as the requirement that proceedings comply with due process of law, requirements of the final decisions, that these can be reviewed by an impartial and independent tribunal, that they allow to seek remedies to ensure enforcement of labor rights. However, in its particular care for the preservation of sovereignty, it expressly states that '[f]or greater certainty, decisions by each Party's administrative, quasi-judicial, judicial or labor tribunals, or pending decisions, as well as related proceedings shall not be subject to revision or reopened under the provisions of the Agreement': *ibid*, Art 5(8).

[51] *Ibid*, Art 6.

[52] *Ibid*, Art 7.

## C. Administrative Structure

The Agreement establishes a Commission for Labor Cooperation, which is comprised of a Ministerial Council and a Secretariat.[53] The Commission's activities are financed in equal shares from the three States parties.[54] The Council is the governing body of the Commission[55], and is composed of the Labor Ministers of the three States parties or their designees.[56] It also shall promote cooperative activities, regarding 16 areas specifically established in the Agreement.[57] The Secretariat, headed by an Executive Director,[58] is the executive arm of the Council, assisting it in exercising its functions,[59] and preparing reports and studies.[60]

Additionally, each Party must establish a National Administrative Office (NAO) at the federal government level, designating a Secretary responsible for its administration and management.[61] The main role of the NAO is to serve as point of contact for governmental agencies of that party, for NAOs of the other parties, and for the Secretariat.[62] Each NAO must also 'provide for the submission and receipt, and periodically publish a list, of public communications on labor law matters arising in the territory of another Party.'[63] This last function of the NAOs has possibly become the most relevant, as a first point of access for unions and labor groups wishing to request consultations with regard to violations of the Agreement.

## D. Cooperative Consultations, Evaluations and Dispute Resolution

The Agreement establishes a four-step process for the resolution of disputes: first, consultations between NAOs, 'in relation to the other Party's labor law, its administration, or labor market conditions in its territory'[64]; second, ministerial consultations 'regarding any matter within the scope of this Agreement'[65]; third, if 'a matter has not been resolved after ministerial

---

[53] *Ibid*, Art 8.
[54] *Ibid*, Art 47.
[55] *Ibid*, Art 10. It gives a list of eight specific functions.
[56] *Ibid*, Art 9. It establishes its own rules of procedure, and must convene at least once a year in regular session.
[57] *Ibid*, Art 11.
[58] *Ibid*, Art 12.
[59] *Ibid*, Art 13.
[60] *Ibid*, Art 14.
[61] *Ibid*, Art 15.
[62] *Ibid*, Art 16.
[63] *Ibid*.
[64] *Ibid*, Art 21.
[65] *Ibid*, Art 22.

consultations,' the establishment of an Evaluation Committee of Experts (ECE) can be requested.[66]

The fourth and last step is the dispute resolution mechanism. This is the only step that can eventually lead to sanctions against the country involved, and requires to go through all the previous steps. However, it has a double limitation in comparison with the previous three steps.

The first limitation is substantive. The first two steps can basically refer to any matter within the scope of the Agreement.[67] This would include any issue related to 'labor law', as defined in the 11 guiding principles of the Agreement. However, the dispute resolution mechanism can only refer to the ECE final report, addressing 'enforcement of a Party's occupational safety and health, child labor or minimum wage labor standards.'[68] This implies that all other labor rights (including freedom of association) are not subject to the dispute resolution mechanism, and its lack of enforcement in the States parties cannot lead to trade sanctions under the NAALC.

The second limitation comes from the standard of review established for this process. This mechanism requires the existence of 'a persistent pattern of failure by that other Party to effectively enforce such standards in respect of the general subject matter addressed in the report.'[69] This must be read together with another provision in the Agreement that establishes that a Party has not failed to 'effectively enforce its occupational safety and health, child labor or minimum wage technical labor standards' or to comply with its general obligation to promote compliance and effectively enforce its labor laws

where the action or inaction by agencies or officials of that Party:

1.  reflects a reasonable exercise of the agency's or the official's discretion with respect to investigatory, prosecutorial, regulatory or compliance matters, or
2.  results from *bona fide* decisions to allocate resources to enforcement in respect of other labor matters determined to have higher priorities.[70]

---

[66] *Ibid*, Art 23. The ECE shall analyze patterns of practice by each party, as long as the matter is trade related and covered by mutually recognized labor laws. Arts 24–25 establish rules of procedure and requirements of the drafts and final reports.

[67] NAO consultations can refer to 'the other Party's labor law, its administration, or labor market conditions in its territory': *ibid*, Art 21. Ministerial consultations can refer to 'any matter within the scope of this Agreement': *ibid*, Art 22. An ECE is already limited, since it analyzes 'patterns of practice by each Party in the enforcement of its occupational safety and health or other technical labor standards as they apply to the particular matter considered by the Parties under Article 22': *ibid*, Art 23(2).

[68] *Ibid*, Art 27.

[69] *Ibid*.

[70] *Ibid*, Art 49(1).

The high requirement of a 'persistent pattern of failure', added to the large exception for compliance, could make the standard of review almost impossible to fulfill.

## 2. Variations of the NAALC Model: Jordan, the Bipartisan Trade Promotion Authority Act, and its Progeny

On 2000, the United States entered a bilateral Free Trade Agreement with Jordan.[71] The Agreement included within its main body, labor provisions similar to those of NAALC,[72] addressing the same four basic topics. However, some differences–that might prove important–began to appear.

With regard to the substantive issues, it establishes a list of five principles, instead of the 11 principles of NAALC. These are:

(a)   the right of association;
(b)   the right to organize and bargain collectively;
(c)   a prohibition on the use of any form of forced or compulsory labor;
(d)   a minimum age for the employment of children; and
(e)   acceptable conditions of work with respect to minimum wages, hours of work, and occupational safety and health.[73]

Additionally, the FTA reaffirms the parties' obligations 'as members of the International Labor Organization ("ILO") and their commitments under the ILO Declaration on Fundamental Principles and Rights at Work and its Follow-up,'[74] thus including an international dimension that the NAALC did not have.

The obligations are basically the same, declaring the right of each party to establish its own domestic labor standards, the obligation to 'strive to ensure that its laws provide for labor standards consistent with the internationally recognized labor rights,'[75] which are the five established principles, and the obligation not to 'fail to effectively enforce its labor laws.'[76] An additional provision was included, stating that the parties 'recognize that it is inappropriate to encourage trade by relaxing domestic labor laws,' so each party shall 'strive to ensure that it does not waive or otherwise derogate from, or offer to waive or otherwise derogate from, such laws as an encouragement for trade with the other Party.'[77]

---

[71] Agreement between the United States of America and the Hashemite Kingdom of Jordan on the Establishment of a Free Trade Area, 24 October 2000, US–Jordan, State Dept No 02-11, available at http://www.ustr.gov/assets/Trade_Agreements/Bilateral/Jordan/asset_upload_file250_5112.pdf

[72] *Ibid*, Art 6.
[73] *Ibid*, Art 6.6.
[74] *Ibid*, Art 6.1.
[75] *Ibid*, Art 6.3.
[76] *Ibid*, Art 6.4(a).
[77] *Ibid*, Art 6.2.

There are no specific provisions regarding an administrative structure and dispute resolution mechanisms, and since labor provisions are included in the body of the FTA, it is implied that they are subject to the same proceedings as any other dispute arising from the FTA. However, the large exception regarding compliance of labor laws established in the NAALC is repeated in this FTA with a slightly different wording.[78]

After the subscription of the Jordan FTA, it became necessary to renew fast-track authority for the President to directly negotiate Free Trade Agreements. This renewal came in the Bipartisan Trade Promotion Authority Act of 2002 (BTPAA), which expressly includes labor issues within the trade negotiation objectives,[79] and defines these labor issues as the same five principles established in the United States–Jordan FTA.[80]

Pursuant to the authority of the BTPAA, the United States has entered so far into six Free Trade Agreements (FTAs) with the following countries: Singapore,[81] Chile,[82] Australia,[83] Central American Free Trade Agreement (CAFTA),[84] Morocco,[85] and Bahrain.[86] All these FTAs include a chapter on labor issues, similar to the United States–Jordan FTA in many ways. Again, there are some variations.

[78] *Ibid*, Art 6.4(b). It recognizes the discretion of each party in compliance matters, and that 'the Parties understand that a Party is in compliance with subparagraph (a) where a course of action or inaction reflects a reasonable exercise of such discretion, or results from a *bona fide* decision regarding the allocation of resources.'

[79] The BTPAA establishes among its 'Overall trading objectives', 'to promote respect for worker rights and the rights of children consistent with core labor standards of the ILO … and an understanding of the relationship between trade and worker rights': 19 USC §3802(a)(6). It further establishes within its 'principal trade negotiating objectives' some more detail on labor and environment matters, including the need to ensure a party does not fail to effectively enforce its labor laws in a manner affecting trade, and the right of the parties to exercise discretion in compliance matters and make decisions on the allocation of resources. 19 USC §3802(b)(11).

[80] 19 USC §3813(6).

[81] United States–Singapore Free Trade Agreement, 15 January 2003, US–Sing, State Dept No 04-36, available at http://www.ustr.gov/Trade_Agreements/Bilateral/Singapore_FTA/Final_Texts/Section_Index.html [hereinafter United States–Singapore FTA].

[82] United States–Chile Free Trade Agreement, 6 June 2003, US–Chile, State Dept No 04-35, available at http://www.ustr.gov/Trade_Agreements/Bilateral/Chile_FTA/Final_Texts/Section_Index.html [hereinafter United States–Chile FTA].

[83] United States–Australia Free Trade Agreement, 18 May 2004, US–Austl, available at http://www.ustr.gov/Trade_Agreements/Bilateral/Australia_FTA/Final_Text/Section_Index.html [hereinafter United States–Australia FTA].

[84] Dominican Republic–Central America–United States Free Trade Agreement, 28 May 2004, available at http://www.ustr.gov/Trade_Agreements/Bilateral/CAFTA-DR/CAFTA-DR_Final_Texts/Section_Index.html [hereinafter CAFTA]. The Agreement has been signed by the United States, Costa Rica, Dominican Republic, El Salvador, Guatemala, Honduras and Nicaragua.

[85] United States–Morocco Free Trade Agreement, 15 June 2004, US–Morocco, available at http://www.ustr.gov/Trade_Agreements/Bilateral/Morocco_FTA/FInal_Text/Section_Index.html [hereinafter United States–Morocco FTA].

[86] Agreement between the United States of America and the Government of the Kingdom of Bahrain on the Establishment of a Free Trade Area, 14 September 2004, US–Bahr., available at http://www.ustr.gov/Trade_Agreements/Bilateral/Bahrain_FTA/final_texts/Section_Index.html [hereinafter United States–Bahrain FTA].

The five substantive principles[87] and the inclusion of commitment to ILO declarations[88] is exactly the same as in the United States–Jordan FTA. Some of these treaties include, immediately after the principles, an exception regarding minimum wage.[89] The obligations also have basically the same wording as in the United States–Jordan FTA, including the so-called 'no-relaxation clause'.[90]

The main differences arise from the administrative and dispute resolution regulation. While some of the FTAs refer to the same administrative organs of the rest of the Agreement,[91] some of them establish special labor institutions.[92] All of them establish a Labor Cooperation Mechanism,[93] and a process of consultations, previous to a dispute resolution mechanism.[94] However, if the dispute resolution stage is reached, the mechanism is referred to the general mechanisms for the FTA, with some limitations.[95]

---

[87] See United States–Singapore FTA, above n 81, Art 17.7; United States–Chile FTA, above n 82, Art 18.8; United States–Australia FTA, above n 83, Art 18.7; CAFTA, above n 84, Art 16.8; United States–Morocco FTA, above n 85, Art 16.7; United States–Bahrain FTA, above n 86, Art 15.7.

[88] See United States–Singapore FTA, above n 81, Art 17.1; United States–Chile FTA, above n 82, Art 18.1; United States–Australia FTA, above n 83, Art 18.1; CAFTA, above n 84, Art 16.1 (recalling in a footnote to the Article that 'the ILO Declaration states that labor standards should not be used for protectionist trade purposes'); United States–Morocco FTA, above n 85, Art 16.1; United States–Bahrain FTA, above n 86, Art 15.1.

[89] United States–Chile FTA, above n 82, Art 18.8; CAFTA, above n 84, Art 16.8 (stating, with the exact same wording, that '[f]or greater certainty, the setting of standards and levels in respect of minimum wages by each Party shall not be subject to obligations under this Chapter. Each Party's obligation under this Chapter pertain to enforcing the level of the general minimum wage established by that Party'); US–Morocco FTA, above n 85, Art 16.7 ('[f]or greater certainty, nothing in this Agreement shall be construed to impose obligations on either Party with regard to establishing the minimum wages').

[90] See United States–Singapore FTA, above n 81, Art 17.2; United States–Chile FTA, above n 82, Art 18.2; United States–Australia FTA, above n 83, Art 18.2; CAFTA, above n 84, Art 16.2; United States–Morocco FTA, above n 85, Art 16.2; United States–Bahrain FTA, above n 86, Art 15.2.

[91] United States–Singapore FTA, above n 81, Art 17.4; United States–Australia FTA, above n 83, Art 18.4; United States–Morocco FTA, above n 85, Art 16.4; United States–Bahrain FTA, above n 86, Art 15.4. This includes the creation of a Subcommittee on Labor Affairs, and the designation of an office by each party to serve as point of contact.

[92] United States–Chile FTA, above n 82, Art 18.4 (establishing a Labor Affairs Council); CAFTA, above n 84, Art 16.4 (establishing a Labor Affairs Council).

[93] United States–Singapore FTA, above n 81, Art 17.5 (referring to Annex 17A); United States–Chile FTA, above n 82, Art 18.5 (referring to Annex 18.5); United States–Australia FTA, above n 83, Art 18.5; CAFTA, above n 84, Art 16.5; United States–Morocco FTA, above n 85, Art 16.5 (referring to Annex 16-A); United States–Bahrain FTA, above n 86, Art 15.5 (referring to Annex 15-A).

[94] United States–Singapore FTA, above n 81, Art 17.6; United States–Chile FTA, above n 82, Art 18.6, United States–Australia FTA, above n 83, Art 18.6; CAFTA, above n 84, Art 16.6; United States–Morocco FTA, above n 85, Art 16.6; United States–Bahrain FTA, above n 86, Art 15.6.

[95] It is generally limited to the case of a sustained or recurring course of action or inaction, in a manner affecting trade between the parties, after the entry into force of the Agreement: United States–Singapore FTA, above n 81, Arts 17.6.4–17.6.5; United States–Chile FTA, above n 82, Arts 18.6.6–18.6.8; United States–Australia FTA, above n 83, Arts 18.6.4–18.6.5; CAFTA, above n 84, Arts 16.6.6–16.6.8; United States–Morocco FTA, above n 85, Arts 16.4.4–16.4.5; United States–Bahrain FTA, above n 86, Arts 15.6.4–15.6.5.

## 3. The Free Trade Area of the Americas

The advancements towards a Free Trade Area of the Americas (FTAA) were scheduled to be concluded by January 2005. (The co-chairs of the Trade Negotiations Committee issued a 'joint communiqué'" on 25 February 2005, declaring that they had continued to make progress and were optimistic about the results of this meeting.) The Ministerial Declaration from the Quito meeting in November 2002 was the first directly to acknowledge as an objective to 'secure, in accordance with our respective laws and regulations, the observance and promotion of inter-nationally-recognized labor standards',[96] and renew commitment to the 1998 ILO Declaration on Fundamental Principles and Rights at Work and its Follow-up. It also expressly rejects 'the use of labor or environmental standards for protectionist purposes,'[97] and states that 'Most Ministers recognized that environmental and labor issues should not be utilized as conditionalities or subject to disciplines, the non-compliance of which can be subject to trade restrictions or sanctions.'[98]

The following Ministerial Declarations have not made further reference to the subject, and there is no special working group dealing with labor issues. These have been delegated to a working group of the 'Inter-American Conference of Ministers of Labor (IACML)'. Its work is merely 'acknowledged' in the Ministerial Declaration of the Miami 2003 meeting.[99]

The Third Draft of the FTAA, dated 21 November 2003 included for the first time a Chapter VII on 'Labor Provisions and Non-Implementation Procedures for Environment and Labor Provisions'. However, the draft contains two alternate texts.

The first text is a statement that 'Labor issues are not contemplated in the TCI mandate or in the FTAA negotiation mandate. Therefore, no pro-visions on this issue should exist in the FTAA Agreement'[100] and that 'they shall not be utilized as conditionalities or subject to disciplines, the non-compliance of which can be subject to trade restrictions or sanctions.'[101]

The second possible text is basically the same as the labor chapters included in the bilateral FTAs previously examined: definition of 'labor'; five basic principles; an 'enforce-your-own-laws' model; a 'no-relaxation'

---

[96] Ministerial Declaration, at the Free Trade Area of the Americas Seventh Meeting of Ministers Responsible for Trade in the Hemisphere (Quito, Ecuador, 1 November 2002), para 9, available at http://www.ftaa-alca.org/Ministerials/Quito/Quito_e.asp.

[97] *Ibid* at para 11.

[98] *Ibid*.

[99] Ministerial Declaration, at the Free Trade Area of the Americas Eighth Meeting of Ministers Responsible for Trade in the Hemisphere (Miami, United States, 20 November 2003), para 37, available at http://www.ftaa-alca.org/Ministerials/Miami/Miami_e.asp.

[100] Free Trade Area of the Americas—Draft Agreement, derestricted document FTAA.TNC/w/133/Rev3, 21 November 2003, Chapter VII, available at http://www.ftaa-alca.org/FTAADraft03/ChapterVII_e.asp

[101] *Ibid*.

clause; the wide exception for compliance; procedural guarantees; a procedure for labor consultations and public participation; and a labor cooperation mechanism. It also replaces trade sanctions for monetary assessments.[102]

## IV. WHAT DID THE NAALC REALLY DO (AND WHAT HAS HAPPENED SO FAR)?

As previously stated, the NAALC was intended to be an in-between solution dealing with five lines of arguments both in favor and against harmonization of labor standards. In this section, we will match the NAALC's provisions with these arguments, in an attempt to evaluate if the solution was as effective as expected. In doing so, we will look at academic opinions, as well as some empirical data. The main question, 'are workers better off?' will be considered as a way to arrive at conclusions in this evaluation.[103]

Finally, these basic results will be also matched with the labor model in the bilateral FTAs, considering some of its differences, with reference to the proposed clauses in the FTAA.

## 1. First Argument: Normative Influence and Sovereignty

It is fair to say that in the balance of these two factors, the NAALC tilted towards sovereignty. This is why it does not create uniform supranational standards nor tri-national institutions to implement, enforce, and develop the Agreement, as an agency and/or a tribunal.[104] In this sense, it is essentially different from the European Union model.[105]

However, 'it is the first trade agreement to provide for labor rights,'[106] establishing an important principle that serves as a model for future FTAs, 'notwithstanding the ineffectiveness of remedies.'[107]

---

[102] *Ibid.*

[103] Of course, this is a very indefinite question and may be impossible to measure. However, it is used in its most intuitive meaning as a way of returning the focus towards the protection of workers' rights rather than trade considerations.

[104] It is interesting to view to what extent sovereignty was really preserved. As one author notes, 'empowering the authorities of a Party to review "labor law matters arising in the territory of another Party" putatively breaches sovereignty in the strictest sense,' since it 'subjects domestic law and administration to judgment, including critical judgments, by a foreign entity': Lance A Compa, 'The first NAFTA labor cases: a new international labor rights regime takes shape' (1995) 3 *United States–Mexico Law Journal* 159, at 163.

[105] See, eg Van Wezel Stone, above n 13 (comparing what she calls the 'European approaches' to transnational labor regulation—preemptive legislation and harmonization—with the 'North American approaches' of cross-border monitoring and extraterritorial jurisdiction).

[106] Gould, above n 29, at p 105.

[107] *Ibid.*

This mere inclusion can be seen as an opportunity. Additionally, the mandate given to the Labor Council in NAALC is 'broad and open-ended'[108], which could allow an 'active Council and an aggressive Secretariat' to use it 'to shape critical aspects of the social impact of the NAFTA' and 'it could conceivably serve as a check against the impact of national legislation.'[109] However, from the point of view of its normative influence, the NAALC has been severely criticized in at least five aspects.

The first line of criticism refers to the fact that 'the level of obligation is extremely weak.'[110] Even though 'the strength of the labor law commitment is relatively high,'[111] the NAALC 'neither incorporates international labor law standards nor sets any of its own to apply to domestic labor law.'[112] Rather, 'they opted to transform the domestic labor law regimes of each Party into the basis for their international commitments.'[113]

This links to the second line of criticism: the lack of substantive international labor standards. The agreement encourages member nations to enforce their own labor laws, but 'it has no normative influence over those laws.'[114] The agencies established by the NAALC 'have no authority over the actual labor standards of the member countries.'[115] On the contrary, it states expressly that 'no country is required to alter its labor standards in any way.'[116]

The third criticism comes from the exception in Article 49, in the sense that a failure of enforcement will not be considered as such if it reflects a reasonable exercise of discretion or results from bona fide decisions on allocating enforcement resources.[117] This exception is considered potentially to 'provide a legal excuse for almost all nonenforcement,'[118] since there is almost no instance 'in which government failure to enforce a labor law cannot be characterized so as to fall within one of these exceptions.'[119]

---

[108] Diamond, above n 6, at p 216.

[109] *Ibid.* In this sense, authors consider that 'Mexico has become more democratic since NAFTA has been in existence': Gould, above n 29, at p 105 (referring to the Mexican Supreme Court's decision declaring unconstitutional the law that reserves representation in a firm to one union, and stating that '[n]New and more democratic unions seem to have been set in place as the result of this process').

[110] Diamond, above n 6, at p 215.

[111] Weiss, above n 8, at 711.

[112] *Ibid.*

[113] *Ibid.*

[114] Karen Vossler Champion, 'Who pays for free trade? The dilemma of free trade and international labor standards' (1996) 22 *North Carolina Journal of International Law and Commercial Regulation* 181, at 234.

[115] Van Wezel Stone, above n 13, at 1007. In other words, the Agreement does not 'attempt to harmonize collective bargaining regulation so as to bring labor conditions between countries into parity' *ibid* at 1008.

[116] *Ibid.*

[117] NAALC, above n 1, Art 49.

[118] Van Wezel Stone, above n 13, at 1010.

[119] *Ibid.*

The fourth criticism relates to the established procedures: its steps have been characterized as 'lengthy, complicated and opaque'.[120] Effective trade sanctions for failing to enforce labor laws can only be imposed 'after an arduous and lengthy process of consultations, meetings, panel decisions, failures to agree to action plans, arbitrations, and failures to either pay fines or comply with previously agreed upon action plans.'[121] This procedure 'contrasts sharply with other forms of dispute resolution within the main NAFTA itself.'[122] The main problem is that during all this process, 'any abuses occurring are allowed to continue unchecked, without any effect on free access to the markets of other parties.'[123] Additionally, higher stages of the enforcement process expressly apply to only some of the 11 labor principles and 'are of questionable applicability to the procedural commitments.'[124]

The fifth and last line of criticism is that, even after overcoming the wide exception, and facing the long procedure, a very high standard still has to be met: a 'persistent pattern of failure' in enforcement of the party's technical standards. Thus, 'access to the process requires far more than a single incident,'[125] and 'it seems apparent that the burden of establishing a persistent pattern may be difficult to overcome in many, if not most, instances.'[126]

All this shows that NAALC did not go as far as international labor standards advocates would have hoped for. But, are workers better off? Actually, we cannot know. These arguments address policy reasons that have more to do with economic and political concerns—for which it might create an effective solution—rather than with the improvement of labor conditions. Other elements must be taken into account to evaluate the NAALC from the workers' point of view.

## 2. Second Argument: Cooperation and Protectionism

As with most attempts to limit an eventual race to the bottom, it is possible to accuse the NAALC of being a form of disguised protectionism towards Mexico. As an interference to market forces, it can reduce global

---

[120] Diamond, above n 6, at p 217. According to Diamond, 'to get to the final step in the NAALC over a dispute regarding a technical labor standard can take as many as 1,320 days — nearly four years.' This could be longer if the position prevails that domestic administrative and judicial remedies need to be exhausted prior to going to a NAO: *Ibid.*

[121] Vossler Champion, above n 114, at 235.

[122] Diamond, above n 6, at p 217. For example, investors or defenders of intellectual property rights 'are granted direct access to the courts of any of the parties' and have private rights of action: *Ibid* at p 218.

[123] Vossler Champion, above n 114, at 235.

[124] Weiss, above n 8, at 711.

[125] Diamond, above n 6, at p 217.

[126] Vossler Champion, above n 114, at 234.

wealth in the long run.[127] It has also been said that Mexico, 'which is likely to become the initial significant target of labor rights efforts, may come to resent the apparent intrusion into its previously sovereign territory.'[128]

However, the fact that the only supranational obligation is the enforcement of domestic laws, according to certain agreed principles, allows it to be argued both that there is no protectionism involved, and that cooperation can be truly achieved in the advancement of the principles. In this sense, NAALC is 'has certain hybrid characteristics,'[129] since 'cooperation and contention co-exist.'[130] There are express provisions for cooperative activities, and at the same time, a contentious procedure for solving disputes.[131]

The NAALC system of tying trade agreements 'to the commitment by developing countries to enforce *their own* labor laws,'[132] can be seen as 'a more practical approach' to address the concern of developing countries 'that linking labor standards to trade may be a slippery slope, leading only to further demands from developed countries in the future,'[133] but at the same time acknowledging labor issues as relevant. In this way, 'abridgement of rights including labor rights is acceptable if satisfying the right is too expensive.'[134]

So, the NAALC does address labor concerns and establish certain agreed principles that allow a basis for cooperation between parties. At the same time, it does not impose excessive burdens on Mexico nor does it impose foreign views of how any party should handle its own labor regulations. Are workers better off? Maybe. If actively pursued, cooperation in labor matters can lead to a real improvement of labor conditions in the three countries. But if it does not, there will be no violation of the agreement. The text, once again, on this point is addressing policy concerns other than the workers' conditions.

## 3. Third Argument: Political Role of Labor

An important criticism of the NAALC has been the 'lack of direct influence labor groups have over the functioning of the agreement.'[135] It has

---

[127] This is linked to the idea that 'permitting firms to relocate in the lowest labor standards environment is desirable because it increases trade and creates a more efficient utilization of global resources': Van Wezel Stone, above n 13, at 1025.

[128] Diamond, above n 6, at p 220.

[129] Compa, above n 104, at 163.

[130] *Ibid*.

[131] *Ibid*. Only practice will definitely tell 'how this inherent tension will play itself out in practice': *Ibid*.

[132] Fields, above n 16, at p 72.

[133] *Ibid*.

[134] *Ibid*.

[135] Vossler Champion, above n 114, at 234.

been said that 'if the goal of organized labor is to give voice and power to a previously silenced and disempowered group, then paradoxically the NAALC subverts the goals of the very group it seeks to protect.'[136] This is because the NAALC 'removes the power of real action from the workers and places it in the hands of government bureaucracies, which arguably have very limited powers themselves.'[137]

On the other hand, some have argued that 'the very existence of the NAALC, especially the Secretariat, provides an opportunity to strengthen the participatory components of democratic politics and promote stable and equitable economic growth.'"[138] The NAALC, in this sense, 'provides an *immediate* opportunity for labor activism on a trinational basis,'[139] and 'trade union movements in all three countries have an obligation, not just to society as a whole, but to their own organizational future, to take a full and active role in every possible way in the proceedings of NAALC.'[140]

To some extent, this has actually happened. As of March 2004, 28 public communications had been filed in the three NAOs, 18 of which led to further Ministerial Consultations concluding in either an Agreement on Implementation or a Joint Declaration, and several follow-up measures.[141]

All of the public communications were submitted by unions, labor or public interest organizations. Since complaints relating to one party have to be submitted in another party's NAO, this has required some coordination between labor movements in different countries. In this sense, the NAALC created 'a political debate that became a school for workers and unions in each country, forcing each to learn more about the other.'[142] Some Mexican labor leaders agree that they had to learn 'how to get along with workers and unions in the US and Canada, how to plan together,'[143] and that 'the struggle is very fast, and our response has to be just as fast,' an understanding that 'didn't exist five or six years ago.'[144] So, 'the main impact of the cross-border movement has been in the change of consciousness of

---

[136] *Ibid* at 235.

[137] *Ibid*.

[138] Diamond, above n 6, at p 219.

[139] *Ibid*.

[140] *Ibid*.

[141] See Summary of Public Communications (as of March 2004), available at http://www.naalc.org/english/pdf/pcommtable_en.pdf. Of these 28 public communications, 17 referred to Mexico, nine to the United States, and two to Canada. Most (21) of the submissions have been accepted for review by the NAO, and in only three of those cases, the NAO did not recommend Ministerial Consultations. So far, no submission has gone any further than the Ministerial Consultations stage.

[142] David Bacon, *The Children of NAFTA: Labor wars on the US/Mexico border* (Berkeley, CA, University of California Press, 2004), p 289.

[143] *Ibid* (citing Benedicto Martínez, General Secretary of the 'Frente Auténtico del Trabajo' (FAT) (Authentic Labor Front)).

[144] *Ibid*.

workers, based on their own experience.'[145] However, 'part of the problem has been how to maintain that level of consciousness.'[146]

The cross-border labor movement has achieved concrete success on some issues, the main example being the mere fact that the first submissions made in a NAO—those of the International Brotherhood of Teamsters (IBT) and the United Electrical, Radio and Machine Workers of America (UE)[147]—were actually admitted for review.[148]

Procedural objections were raised, regarding the timeliness of the complaints, the need to allege a 'pattern or practice of violations', that domestic remedies had not been exhausted in Mexico, and that they focused on the wrongdoings of individual companies rather than an enforcement failure by Mexico. The NAO decided to admit the submission for review.[149]

This decision, although grounded in the language of the NAALC, also has a political background, trying to avoid new harsh union reactions against the NAALC system after a strict procedural interpretation.[150] Union activity and pressure is likely to have modeled the NAO's decision, thus broadening the possibilities of submissions.

However, the final NAO report stressed that 'the issue at hand in the review of the two submissions is whether the Government of Mexico is enforcing its labor laws,'[151] and not the conduct of individual companies. Additionally, the NAO did not use the report to give a broad interpretation to Annex I of the NAALC. Instead, 'the NAO said it had found no evidence that Mexico had failed to enforce its labor laws and dismissed the complaints.'[152]

---

[145] *Ibid* at pp 289–90 (citing Teófilo Reyes, an organizer with the Transnational Information Exchange).

[146] *Ibid* at p 290. As an example, Mr Reyes 'points to the relationship between the United Auto Workers local in Minneapolis and the Ford workers at the Mexico City assembly plant in Cuatuhtitlán.' They maintained contact for some time, the union supported labor activity in Ford and even contributed money and material support. However, 'the leadership of the union changed, and the relationship became dormant': *Ibid*.

[147] Both labor submissions were presented in the US NAO, alleging dismissals of groups of employees in late 1993 because of their attempts to form a union affiliated with the FAT in Mexico. See Compa, above n 104, at 165.

[148] Similarly, '[w]hile the NAFTA Labor Side Agreement's enforcement procedures appear to be limited to complaints involving nonenforcement of laws regarding occupational health and safety, child labor, and minimum wages, some union groups have argued that they have a broader applicability': Van Wezel Stone, above n 13, at 1010.

[149] Compa, above n 104, at 168. The NAO agreed with the unions that 'the broad scope of NAO review, "labor law matters", does not restrict review to enforcement issues,' and for further Ministerial Consultations as well. Thus, 'enforcement as such does not appear as to limit the scope of a NAO or subsequent consultations': *Ibid*.

[150] See *Ibid* at 169.

[151] *Ibid* at 175.

[152] Van Wezel Stone, above n 13, at 1011. Even though the NAO noted several issues supporting the claims, it finally declared itself to be 'not in a position to make a finding that the Government of Mexico failed to enforce the relevant labor laws,' because 'the dismissed workers' acceptance of severance pay and the cases of two workers still pending in legal proceedings, were all keeping with Mexican labor law': Compa, above n 104, at 176.

Finally, it is especially noteworthy that of the 28 submissions presented in the NAOs, 23 referred to freedom of association and the right to organize and/or the right to bargain collectively and strike. Of these, 19 were accepted, and only in two cases the NAO did not recommend Ministerial Consultations. This is of relevance because these are rights excluded from the following conflict-solving stages (ECE and dispute resolution stages), and cannot lead to trade sanctions. This, together with the fact that all submissions were presented by unions and/or labor and public interest organizations, might show that the NAALC is being used more as an activist tool, rather than as a road to imposing actual trade sanctions.

Are workers better off? Maybe. A new tool appeared that can be used for labor activism in serious cases. However, the real effects of this activism in the long run are yet to be seen.

## 4. Fourth Argument: Social Dumping and Efficiency in the World Economy

The NAFTA was negotiated in the midst of the presidential election campaign in 1992. Third party presidential candidate Ross Perot 'inveighed about the "great big sucking sound" that would be caused by United States workers' jobs heading south to Mexico if NAFTA were ratified.'[153] This exemplifies the concerns 'as to the effect of lifting all barriers to trade,'[154] focusing particularly on Mexico 'and the effects on American labor of free trade with a nation with substantially lower wages,'[155] with a government 'tendency toward lax enforcement of their laws,'[156] a large informal sector, and unions with a 'suspiciously close relationship with the Mexican government.'[157]

All this creates the inference that the 'opportunity to move production into virgin territory, where new relationships can be established on a much lower wage scale and in a less regulated environment is understandably tempting.'[158] Mexico 'appears as a natural target for US manufacturers.'[159]

The NAALC was then promoted and negotiated by President Clinton 'in an effort to address concerns raised by organized labor that NAFTA would cause massive job loss'[160] to the United States. If the Commission's

---

[153] Weiss, above n 8, at 702.
[154] Vossler Champion, above n 114, at 225.
[155] *Ibid*.
[156] *Ibid*.
[157] *Ibid*.
[158] Diamond, above n 6, at p 211.
[159] *Ibid* (citing a *Harvard Business Review* article, 'Where to find tens of millions of consumers, low-cost workers and a free-market revolution? Right across the Rio Grande').
[160] Van Wezel Stone, above n 13, at 1007.

activities succeed in improving labor conditions in Mexico, it will 'reduce the incentive for industry to migrate South for the wrong reason.'[161]

However, the mere text of the NAALC[162] can raise legitimate doubts as to whether it could effectively achieve this objective.[163] Moreover, the lack of harmonization of labor standards and the 'Commission's complicated, multi-tiered dispute resolution structure will hamper timely settlements'[164] and might 'deter potential complainants from seeking redress through formal Commission proceedings.'[165]

Nevertheless, the real test for this argument is empirical. Did the industrial flight actually take place? A study assembled in 2000 by the Economic Policy Institute shows some evidence that it did, at least to some extent. According to these studies, the United States 'has experienced steadily growing trade deficits for nearly three decades, and these deficits have accelerated rapidly since NAFTA took effect.'[166] Additionally, 'NAFTA and the devaluation of currencies in Mexico and Canada resulted in a surge of foreign direct investment (FDI) in these countries'[167] and '[i]nflows of FDI, along with bank loans an other types of foreign financing, have funded the construction of thousands of Mexican and Canadian factories that produce goods for export to the United States.'[168] However, '[t]he growth of imports to the US from these factories has contributed substantially to the growing US trade deficit and the related job losses.'[169]

This had the effect that 'NAFTA eliminated 766,030 actual and potential US jobs between 1994 and 2000,'[170] which has affected all 50 States and the District of Columbia, affecting the most all States 'with high concentrations of industries (such as motor vehicles, textiles and apparel, computers and

---

[161] McGuinness, above n 7, at 586.

[162] The 'guiding principles … do not establish common minimum standards for their domestic law': NAALC, above n 1, Annex 1.

[163] Additionally, 'the level of resources committed to the NAALC's implementation, the scope of the agreement itself, and the mechanisms of its dispute resolution procedures will all limit the effectiveness of the Commission': McGuinness, above n 7, at 587.

[164] *Ibid.*

[165] *Ibid.*

[166] Robert E Scott, 'NAFTA's Hidden Costs—Trade agreement results in job losses, growing inequality, and wage suppression for the United States', in *Nafta at Seven—Its Impact on Workers in all Three Nations* (Economic Policy Institute, 2000), at 3, available at http://www.epinet.org/briefingpapers/nafta01/nafta-at-7.pdf. The study clarifies that although gross US exports to its NAFTA partners have increased (by 147% to Mexico and 66% to Canada), 'these increases have been overshadowed by the larger growth in imports, which have gone up by 248% from Mexico and 79% from Canada.' This results in a 378% increase in the net export deficit in the United States, from \$16.6 billion in 1992, to \$62.8 billion by 2000: *Ibid.*

[167] *Ibid* at 5.

[168] *Ibid.*

[169] *Ibid.*

[170] *Ibid* at 3.

electrical appliances) where a large number of plants moved to Mexico.'[171] On this point, the study concludes that '[w]hile job losses in most states are modest relative to the size of the economy, it is important to remember that the promise of new jobs was the principal justification for NAFTA.'[172]

In Mexico, employment grew in only very small terms and at a lower rate than what is needed in order to fulfill the yearly demand for new jobs.[173] Additionally, 'the loss of salaried occupations was almost completely offset by the growth in self-employed and unpaid workers,' which 'means that people moved to deteriorating labor occupations.'[174] However, '[t]he maquiladora sector's employment performance contrasts significantly with that of Mexico's other large manufacturing plants'[175] and has 'helped offset weak job creation in other domestic manufacturing industries,'[176] although there has been also a regional relocation of the maquiladoras.[177]

Finally, in Canada '[u]nemployment in the 1990s averaged a 9.6% compared to the US rate of 5.8%—a doubling compared to the 1980s' and 'higher than in any other decade since the 1930s.'[178] A study conducted by the Canadian government concluded that even though employment 'in export industries rose from 19.6% of total business sector employment in 1989 to 28.3% in 1997,'[179] 'the rapid rise in imports displaced (or destroyed) even more employment,'[180] since the 'job-displacing effect of

---

[171] *Ibid* at 6. Net job loss figures range from 395 in Alaska to a high of 82,354 in California. Other highly affected States are Michigan, New York, Texas, Ohio, Illinois, Pennsylvania, North Carolina, Indiana, Florida, Tennessee, and Georgia, each with more than 20,000 jobs lost.

[172] *Ibid*.

[173] Carlos Salas, 'The Impact of NAFTA on Wages and Incomes in Mexico', in *Nafta at Seven —Its Impact on Workers in all Three Nations* (Economic Policy Institute, 2000), at 12, 14, available at http://www.epinet.org/briefingpapers/nafta01/nafta-at-7.pdf.

[174] *Ibid* at 16.

[175] *Ibid* at 17.

[176] *Ibid* at 18. A maquiladora is an assembly plant in Mexico, especially one along the border between the United States and Mexico, to which foreign materials and parts are shipped and from which the finished product is returned to the original market. Maquiladoras accounted for 'about 13% of total manufacturing employment in 1995 and almost 16% in 1999.' 'Maquiladora plants contributed 35% of all new manufacturing employment between 1995 and 1999. Most of the remaining jobs created during this period were in small non-maquiladora plants': *Ibid*.

[177] There were some 'important regional changes as maquiladora plants were established in cities far from the Mexico–US border' and especially, apparel-producing maquiladora plants 'moved to areas where compliance with labor laws is low, such as the states of Puebla and Morelos': *Ibid*.

[178] Bruce Campbell, 'False Promise—Canada in the Free Trade Era', in *Nafta at Seven—Its Impact on Workers in all Three Nations* (Economic Policy Institute, 2000), at 21, 22, available at http://www.epinet.org/briefingpapers/nafta01/nafta-at-7.pdf

[179] *Ibid* at 23.

[180] *Ibid*

imports rose steadily from an equivalent of 21.1% of total business employment in 1989 to 32.7% in 1997.'[181] In other words, 'imports are displacing "relatively" more jobs than exports are adding.'[182] Additionally, 'the labor productivity of the jobs displaced by imports was moderately lower than that of exports.'[183]

Are workers better off? Apparently not. Available data can support the conclusion that the NAFTA did increase previous economic liberalizing trends that actually did provoke the relocation of manufacturing companies in Mexico. Since apparently labor regulation is not the most important reason for that relocation, the existence of the NAALC could have been of little or no effect, and the feared loss of jobs in the United States has taken place, even if in relatively small numbers.

## 5. Fifth Argument: The Risk of a Race to the Bottom

Assuming then that manufacturing companies did relocate from the United States to Mexico, did this translate in a worsening of the labor conditions in the three countries?

On its face, 'the NAFTA model of cross-border monitoring and enforcement has little to contribute to the goal of establishing uniform labor standards or a floor of labor rights,'[184] since it works on a one-time situation-specific basis. Furthermore, NAFTA could 'provide disincentives for member states to legislate labor protections, because each state can be sanctioned for not enforcing its own labor regulations'[185] and because 'each country stands to lose business if it imposes a higher level of regulation than do other countries.'[186] Thus, it is possible that the NAALC's cross-border monitoring system actually 'encourages races-to-the-bottom and regulatory competition, resulting in the lowering of labor standards.'[187]

Once again, this is an empirical kind of question. Has this lowering of standards really taken place? There are studies that give some hints. Some negative effects can be seen in at least four areas: (1) downward pressure on wages; (2) increase in inequalities; (3) negative effects on union activity; and (4) reduction of some labor protections and/or benefits. These effects can be generally seen in all three States parties.

---

[181] *Ibid.*
[182] *Ibid.*
[183] *Ibid.*
[184] Van Wezel Stone, above n 13, at 1024.
[185] *Ibid* at 1025.
[186] *Ibid.*
[187] *Ibid.*

First, with regard to wages, the 'growth in US trade and trade deficits has put downward pressure on the wages of "unskilled" (ie, non-college-educated) workers in the US, especially those with no more than a high school degree.'[188] Research shows that 'expanding trade has reduced the price of import-competing products and thus reduced the real wages of workers engaged in producing those goods.'[189] Because of the elimination of manufacturing jobs, displaced workers tend to find jobs in the service industry, 'with earnings declining by an average of over 13%.'[190] This new supply of workers 'depresses the wages of those already holding service jobs.'[191] Additionally, a 1992 *Wall Street Journal* survey reported that 'one-fourth of almost 500 American corporate executives polled admitted that they were "very likely" or "somewhat likely" to use NAFTA as a bargaining chip to hold down wages,'[192] which has apparently been effectively used.

In Mexico there has been a 'steady erosion' of wages for directly employed workers in the 1990s, and 'the minimum wage in Mexico lost almost 50% of its purchasing power.'[193] In this sense '[f]reer trade has not produced a positive correlation between the growth of real wages and productivity in the manufacturing industry. Negative real wage evolution cannot be attributed to low productivity in the manufacturing firms in Mexico.'[194] Even though there have been 'positive correlation coefficients between real wages and exports to the United States and Canada in export-oriented industry,'[195] the global effect of this in the economy as a whole has been relatively small and 'the differences in wage levels is not significant.'[196] Thus, 'NAFTA has not been an effective mechanism to increase manufacturing wages in a sustainable way.'[197]

Second, the NAFTA might be one of the reasons causing an increase in inequality in all three countries.[198] In the United States, the wage reduction

---

[188] Scott, above n 166, at 7.

[189] *Ibid*. (Even though trade 'is expected to increase the wages of the workers producing exports,' in the end 'the number of workers hurt by imports has exceeded the number who have benefited through increased exports').

[190] *Ibid* at 8.

[191] *Ibid*.

[192] *Ibid*.

[193] Salas, above n 173, at 18. According to this study, labor income in industries whose wage-bargaining process are under federal supervision lost more than 21% of its purchasing power, while manufacturing wages declined by almost 21%, and the purchasing power of the minimum wage fell 17.9% during 1999: *Ibid* at 19.

[194] Enrique de la Garza Toledo, 'Free Trade and Labor Relations in Mexico', in Lance A Compa and Stephen F Diamond (eds), *Human Rights, Labor Rights and International Trade* (Philadelphia, University of Pennsylvania Press, 1996), 227, at p 232.

[195] *Ibid* at p 235.

[196] *Ibid*.

[197] *Ibid*.

[198] This is coherent with other studies regarding FDI and its effect on wages. Although the general findings are that 'foreign-owned firms pay higher wages even after controlling for scale, worker quality, industry, age of facility, inputs and industry and regional characteristics,' 'the largest bonus for working with foreign capital apparently accrues to skilled/white

affected mostly unskilled workers,[199] which might increase the gap with higher-paying jobs. In Mexico, while NAFTA 'has benefited a few sectors of the economy, mostly maquiladora industries and the very wealthy, it has also increased inequality and reduced incomes and job quality for the vast majority of workers in Mexico.'[200] Similarly in Canada, 'market income collapsed for low-income earners and inequality widened, most strikingly during the first half of the decade.'[201] This was initially offset by public transfers, but measures against fiscal deficits 'provided the rationale for social cuts that resulted in a widening of overall income inequality in the latter half of the decade.'[202]

Third, union activity has also been significantly affected in the three States parties. In the United States, a 2000 study showed that 'most employers continue to threaten to close all or part of their operations during organizing drives, despite the fact that, in the last five years, unions have shifted their organizing activity away from industries most affected by trade deficits and capital flight.'[203] These threats are 'simply one more extremely effective tactic in employers' diverse arsenal for thwarting worker efforts to unionize,'[204] and might account for a real reduction in wages. In Canada the effect has been similar: the 'waves of layoffs and plant closures and the threat of closures in heavily unionized manufacturing sectors'[205] have affected unionization rates. However, 'total union membership (not just in manufacturing) has remained remarkably stable.'[206] This shows how, even if the relocation is not as high as it seems, the mere believable threat of relocation is enough to place downward pressure on unionization and labor conditions.

---

collar workers.' So, 'while foreign capital may raise wages on average, it may also tend to worsen the distribution of income': Brown, above n 33, at 23.

[199] Scott, above n 166, at 7.

[200] Salas, above n 173, at 19. These inequalities are increased by the appearance of a 'new, young and unqualified working class with a high female presence and low employment stability,' which is 'clearly the majority in the manufacturing industry, especially if you consider its presence in the maquila': De la Garza Toledo, above n 194, at p 233.

[201] Campbell, above n 178, at 24. Market incomes of the bottom 10% of families with children fell 84% during 1990–96, and those of the next 10% fell 31%. Additionally, '[t]he top 20% of families increased their share of market income from 41.9% to 45.2% during 1989–1998, while the bottom 20% saw their share drop from 3.8% to 3.1%': *Ibid* at 25.

[202] *Ibid* at 24. However, inequality in Canada still remains much lower than in the nited States: *Ibid*.

[203] Scott, above n 166, at 8.

[204] *Ibid*. 'Under the cover of NAFTA and other trade agreements, employers use the threat of plant closure and capital flight at the bargaining table, in organizing drives and in wage negotiations with individual workers. What they say to workers, either directly or indirectly, is if you ask for too much or don't give concessions or try to organize, strike or fight for good jobs with good benefits, we'll close, we'll move across the border just like other plants have done before': *Ibid* at 9 (citing Kate Bronfenbrenner, *Uneasy terrain: The impact of mobility on worker's wages and union organizing*, Commissioned research paper for the US Trade Deficit Review Commission (2000)).

[205] Campbell, above n 178, at 25.

[206] *Ibid*.

In Mexico, the case for unions is different. Traditionally unions are part of a State corporatism scheme, where unionization and collective agreements were government-promoted. In the period surrounding the subscription of NAFTA, 'there was a talk of a crisis in state corporatism, of the need for a new unionism allied with both the state and firms in the battle for competitiveness.'[207] However, 'neither the employers nor the state, and far less the unions, seem to be setting out to democratize labor relations in Mexico,'[208] since 'labor union corporatism seems more interested in reaching a new agreement at the top than in becoming an authentic representative of the workers.'[209] With the proliferation of the maquiladoras, 'official government-affiliated unions also spread, through the process of signing protection contracts,'[210] signed by companies planning to locate in Mexico 'in order to ensure labor peace.'[211] So, 'Mexican labor organizations and groups of workers who are interested in forming real unions to fight the companies have been forced to break the pattern,'[212] sometimes facing strong repression.

Finally, the NAFTA might have caused the reduction of several other labor-related benefits in all three countries. In the United States, the use of the threat of relocation at the bargaining table could have an impact on the agreed benefits that is impossible to measure. In Canada, as 'a cornerstone of this well-known neoliberal family of policies—privatization, deregulation, investment and trade liberalization, public sector cutbacks, tax cuts and monetary austerity—NAFTA has made it easier for Canadian policy makers to bring about a "structural adjustment" of the economy in line with the dominant US model.'[213] In this sense, 'NAFTA and its siblings have put downward pressure on employment and income conditions,'[214] but its impact is highly variable. An important example in Canada is the massive cut of unemployment insurance programs and welfare transfers. The federal government decided this as a measure to '(in its view) strengthen the incentive to work and enhance labor market flexibility.'[215] The measure led to a reduction in the proportion of unemployed people collecting benefits from 75 per cent in 1990 to 36 per cent in 2000, 'essentially the same as the US level.'[216] This was considered a part of the necessary restructuring to 'strengthen the long-term competitiveness of

---

[207] De la Garza Toledo, above n 194, at 236.
[208] *Ibid* at 254.
[209] *Ibid*.
[210] Bacon, above n 142, at 290.
[211] *Ibid*.
[212] *Ibid*.
[213] Campbell, above n 178, at 25. The author warns that 'assessing causality is a complex task' in these matters: *Ibid*.
[214] *Ibid*.
[215] *Ibid* at 28.
[216] *Ibid*.

Canadian business in the new North America.'[217] Although the Canadian employment situation has improved, 'workers have yet to reap any benefits in terms of improved earnings.'[218]

In the case of Mexico, 'NAFTA should be understood as one of the final building blocks of a decade-long process of reintegrating the Mexican economy into the ... US-dominated regional economy.'[219] This included a 'far-reaching program of deregulation,' where more than 'twenty-five sectors of the economy have been deregulated or are under review for future deregulation'[220] and has broadened the 'range of economic sectors open to wholly foreign ownership.'[221] In the specific case of labor relations, the 'most important change in labor relations in Mexico in the 1990s can be summarized by the trend toward work flexibility in large firms.'[222] Although this trend has not yet affected the labor law, it has taken form through unilateral flexibilization and productivity agreements between unions and major firms, and it has been intensified by NAFTA. Also, collective contracts 'are changing in the direction of greater flexibility,'[223] which arguably reduces the protections that workers have within the legal system, against low working conditions and layoff.

The most important question on these four lines of analysis is: how much is NAFTA really to blame? Most of the effects detailed can also be explained as normal effects of a market economy, which will be beneficial in the long run. NAFTA is merely one step in the midst of liberalizing decisions already taken in the economies of Canada and Mexico. If it is used as an excuse to avoid labor regulations, it is a misuse, not its desired effect. However, the NAALC was intended precisely to avoid this. Are workers in the three countries actually better off thanks to the NAALC's existence? Would things be even worse should it did not exist?

This can be answered only through inferences. There is at least one thing that can be said in favor of the NAALC: it is an available tool to complain about labor abuses. An aggressive use of the NAALC's principles, and the broad mandate of its Secretariat, could be useful to place pressure on companies and governments, exercising a certain control on their labor performance. The public communications submitted so far in the NAOs show ways in which this could be possible, and several cooperative activities, such as seminars, forums, educational materials, government-to-government

---

[217] *Ibid.*

[218] *Ibid.*

[219] Diamond, above n 6, at p 208.

[220] *Ibid* at p 209. Some of the deregulated sectors include trucking, telecommunications, petrochemicals, the financial system, insurance, commodities such as sugar, cacao, and coffee, technology transfer, trade secrets, and agriculture.

[221] *Ibid.*

[222] De la Garza Toledo, above n 194, at 238.

[223] *Ibid.*

meetings, and so on, have been held as a consequence. Arguably, this could avoid the worsening of labor conditions in the long run. An optimistic point of view could say that the necessary adjustments—that produced the negative effects previously referred to—have already taken place, and that now the advancement of cooperative efforts can begin to make things better. But a pessimistic view could insist that, with no attempt at harmonization, the NAALC can make no difference whatsoever on the negative effects of NAFTA for the workers in the three countries, and the figures can actually support that view.

### 6. The Case of the Other Free Trade Agreements—and the Free Trade Area of the Americas

The doubts in the conclusions about the effectiveness of the NAALC can be especially important if we consider that the model has been basically repeated in the bilateral FTAs signed by the United States under BTPAA authority which followed. Could its repetition bring similar effects—or non-effects—for the workers in the countries involved? It may be that some of the differences in the texts might also make some improvement on its effects.

The first thing is that the labor provisions are part of the main FTAs, not side agreements. This, in many cases, makes the general dispute resolution procedures for the whole treaty available for labor issues, as long as tradeis affected. Most are preceded by a much shorter consultation procedure.

Additionally, even though the list of principles is reduced to five, all of them are treated equally with regard to the available dispute-resolution procedures, and include rights that were excluded at the later stages from the NAALC, especially freedom of association.

Furthermore, there is an explicit recognition of ILO principles, acknowledging international labor obligations which were not considered in the NAALC, where the only supranational obligation was the enforcement of domestic labor laws. Finally, the existence of the so-called 'no-relaxation clause' could possibly limit at least overt attempts to reduce benefits based on the threat of relocation or competitiveness-related reasons.

The effects of the bilateral treaties, being very recent, are not yet clear. The risks for all parties are probably lowered by the fact that they are all fairly distant countries, instead of bordering countries as in NAFTA, which makes relocation more difficult, and the threat of relocation less credible.

On the other hand, the level of protection given by the labor law of the countries that have entered FTAs with the United States. is extremely variable, and that factor would also—of course—determine the effects.

Some countries could also use the fact they have entered into an FTA with the United States as a reason to improve their labor law enforcement.[224]

Why is the model being repeated if its effects are not clear? Probably because it does solve other policy concerns, such as preserving sovereignty and not imposing additional barriers to trade by way of labor regulations. But maybe workers are not really better off with the inclusion of such clauses in the FTAs, and ultimately in the FTAA.

## V. THE HUMAN RIGHTS ISSUES—A FEW COMMENTS

Several of the labor rights involved in the dispute surrounding the NAALC are actually recognized internationally as human rights. However, this dimension has not really entered the debate. Some comments are worth making on this.

First, at least in the United States and probably in most of the American continent, 'the human rights movement and the labor movement run on tracks that are sometimes parallel and rarely meet.'[225] This is so, even though 'the catalogue of human rights includes numerous rights relating to work',[226] and that the 'status of workers' rights in a country is a bellwether for the status of human rights in general.'[227] Probably this led to the fact that NAALC does not mention in any way the international obligations with regard to labor rights, such as the ILO standards, and 'the only sources of law formally made subject to NAALC commitments are domestic law.'[228]

As a second point, the analysis of the NAALC from the point of view of human rights refers us to the debates regarding what labor standards have 'human rights status'. Even though a full analysis of this point here is impossible, it is fair to say that the most generally accepted baseline is

---

[224] This has been the case, for example, in Chile. Under the concern that the United States–Chile FTA would require enforcement of domestic labor laws, Chile took several legislative measures to give wider powers to the Labor Inspectorate, reforming some aspects of labor laws (both already approved) and reforming the special labor judicial processes and courts (currently debated in Congress).

[225] Virginia A Leary, 'The Paradox of Workers' Rights as Human Rights', in Lance A Compa and Stephen F Diamond (eds), *Human Rights, Labor Rights and International Trade* (Philadelphia, University of Pennsylvania Press, 1996), at p 22. Leary clarifies that it might be a 'largely US phenomenon', that seems 'less accentuated in Canada and in many European countries,' while 'in developing countries, movements for workers' rights are considered human rights issues and the dichotomy is scarcely evident': *Ibid* at p 27. In this last point, my experience in human rights in Latin America is that the issue is mostly associated with gross human rights violations committed during past dictatorships, and not with workers' rights issues, which are usually the concern of unions and union confederations, and not of human rights organizations.

[226] *Ibid.*

[227] *Ibid.*

[228] Weiss, above n 8, at 711.

the four core standards adopted by the ILO: freedom of association, non-discrimination, and prohibition of forced and child labor. These standards 'have been embraced in a variety of fora as well, including the 1995 World Summit for Social Development in Copenhagen and the OECD.'[229] However, some 'have urged that the list of core labor rights should include occupational health and safety, limits on hours of work, right to periods of rest, and protection against abusive treatment.'[230] If we consider the ILO's four core standards, immediately the NAALC shows a limitation in its protection, since freedom of association is not subject to the dispute resolution procedure. This failure is corrected in the bilateral FTAs.

A third point to consider is that most of the labor rights/human rights violations are committed directly by multinational companies operating in developing countries. In this sense, 'globalization has undermined the ability of national law to effectively regulate the workplace.'[231] Currently, 'corporate mobility and layering, MNE economic power, and employment flexibility may create an employer–employee relationship that eludes national regulation.'[232] This is a problem that the NAALC does not address. Since the only supranational obligation is to enforce domestic law, if that domestic law is not effective in controlling the behavior of multinationals, they will remain uncontrolled. Paradoxically, multinationals are basic actors in the opening of trade, and have the greatest chances to relocate and/or believably threaten relocation. Moreover, the first NAO reports on public communications explicitly stated that the review:

> has not been aimed primarily at determining whether or not the two companies named in the submissions may have acted in violation of Mexican law, but rather to gather as much information as possible to allow the NAO to better understand and publicly report on the Government of Mexico's promotion of compliance with, and effective enforcement of its labor law.[233]

The conduct of multinationals, making use of the benefits of NAFTA, remains unchecked via the NAALC.

Finally, as pointed out previously, frequently labor rights can act as a measure for the general human rights situation in the country. The case of the maquiladoras has not only referred to labor conditions, but sometimes also to fierce repression against the labor movement. Some consider that

---

[229] Cleveland, above n 10, at p 152.
[230] *Ibid* at p 153. The limitation is often justified because these four standards 'do not negatively impact a country's comparative advantage': *Ibid*. However, these definitions fall short of the protections guaranteed by the Universal Declaration of Human Rights and International Covenant on Economic, Social and Cultural Rights.
[231] Cleveland, above n 10, at p 141.
[232] *Ibid* at p 143.
[233] Compa, above n 104, at 175.

workers involved in cross-border organizations 'risked their liberty, and even their lives.'[234] Thus, the 'achievements were limited by the repression they've faced. Their jobs are threatened, the legal process they have to follow is very long, and it's hard for workers to last it out. Once worker-activists are marked, it's hard for them to find other jobs where they can use their experience, so often that experience is lost.'[235]

All this shows that acknowledging the human rights dimensions of these debates could add an important perspective towards furthering the same objectives the agreements claim to pursue, since many of these objectives refer to issues regarded internationally as human rights issues.

## VI. CONCLUSIONS

This chapter started by asking if the compromise in the NAALC is actually effective. However, there are multiple answers to that question. If by effectiveness we mean to see if workers in the States parties are better off thanks to the NAALC, the answer is far from clear.

The first two arguments in support of the NAALC—sovereignty and cooperation—do not really address the issue of labor conditions, and the compromise reached ends up solving (maybe effectively) other kinds of policy concerns. If we look at the third argument, probably workers are better off, since the NAALC's procedures, although flawed in many ways, provide a new tool for workers and organizations to use in labor activism. Arguably, this avenue of pressure, in addition to cooperation activities, can lead to a real improvement in working conditions in the States parties.

However, with regard to the last two arguments—industrial flight and race to the bottom—studies show a loss of jobs, reduction of wages and other benefits, and negative effects on unionization. Even though it is not clear that these effects are actually caused by NAFTA, it is also unclear if the NAALC has had any role at all in preventing or reducing them. The effects might respond to a period of adjustment that will be beneficial in the long run.

These unclear results will probably repeat themselves in the development of the FTAs and should be taken into close account if the model is to be repeated in the FTAA, questioning whether the model is actually protecting the rights and principles it acknowledges. The introduction of a human rights perspective in this analysis—which has so far been absent from the debates—might help to guide the debate in this direction.

---

[234] Bacon, above n 142, at 290.

[235] *Ibid* (citing Maria Estela Rios Gonzalez, then chief legal advisor to the mayor of Mexico City and part of the board of the Coalition for Justice in the Maquiladoras, as President of Mexico's National Association of Democratic Lawyers).

# Part II

# Self-regulation by Transnational Corporations

# 6

# Corporate Codes of Conduct and the Human Rights Accountability of Transnational Corporations: A Small Piece of A Larger Puzzle

FIONA McLEAY

## I. INTRODUCTION

### 1. The Context for the Development of Corporate Codes of Conduct

CORPORATIONS ARE INCREASINGLY operating beyond the borders of the home State (the country in which they are registered). A range of mechanisms makes this possible, from wholly owned subsidiaries, joint ventures or other partnerships with foreign companies, to supply-chain relationships with contractors and suppliers of goods and services. This has raised the question of the extent to which transnational corporations (TNCs) have responsibility for the protection, promotion and realization of human rights, and the ways in which they can be held accountable for human rights violations connected with their activities.

The issue is particularly problematic in relation to the activities of TNCs in the developing world. The economic, political and social conditions of many of these countries have often not encouraged the development of domestic mechanisms to protect and promote human rights. Developing country governments in which a TNC operates ('the host State') may not enforce human rights norms because these are seen as conflicting with a regulatory regime which will attract foreign direct investment (FDI). Even a host State which has the desire to implement human rights standards (having signed or ratified international human rights instruments and enacted domestic legislation) may not have the mechanisms and resources necessary to enforce them.

As a result, TNCs are often able to operate in the developing world in an environment where human rights standards (particularly with regard to labor and the environment) are far less stringent than those in place in their home State or the developed world. The problem is accentuated by the benefits TNCs receive from the establishment of export-processing zones and the guarantees afforded under bilateral investment treaties. These often explicitly preclude domestic legislation imposing human rights norms such as limitations on overtime, rights to collective bargaining, and occupational health and safety requirements. TNCs are willing and able to shift their operations to countries where they can produce at the lowest costs, and they may therefore operate in locations where human rights are violated or where the local authorities fail to enforce, for example, laws relating to health and safety in the workplace or the environment. As human rights abuses have increased under these arrangements, human rights NGOs, governments and some business organizations have turned their attention to ways to prevent these abuses and hold TNCs accountable for violations. A range of options have been proposed, from developing the national laws of the host and home States to establishing international and regional treaties or guidelines. In addition, various forms of voluntary non-binding codes have been proposed, such as framework agreements between business and trade unions and individual company codes of conduct.[1]

## 2. A Short History of Corporate Codes of Conduct

The idea of a code of conduct to guide companies when considering the social impact of their activities is not new. In 1981 the World Health Organization developed the International Code of Marketing of Breast-milk Substitutes (although it was not actually adopted at that time).[2] Other codes focused on country-specific issues. The 1977 Sullivan Principles offered guidelines for companies wishing to do business in South Africa during the apartheid regime, and the 1984 MacBride Principles outlined voluntary standards for businesses operating in Northern Ireland during 'the Troubles'.[3] Still others were developed by multilateral institutions. Notable among these are the Organization for

---

[1] B Hepple, 'The importance of law, guidelines and codes of conduct in monitoring corporate behaviour', in R Blanpain (ed) *Bulletin of Comparative Labor Relations: Multinational Enterprises and the Social Challenges of the XXIst Century* (Kluwer Law International, 2000), at p 37.

[2] For a discussion of this, see J Richter, *Holding Corporations Accountable: Corporate Conduct, International Codes and Citizen Action* (Zed Books, 2001), ch 1, 'Regulation of Transnational Corporations'.

[3] www.globalsullivanprinciples.org; http://www1.umn.edu/humanrts/links/macbride.html

Economic Cooperation and Development (OECD) Guidelines for Multinational Enterprises (promulgated in 1976 and revised in 2000) and the 1977 International Labor Organization (ILO) Tripartite Declaration of Principles concerning Multinational Enterprises and Social Policy.[4] More recently, in 2003, the UN Sub-Commission on the Promotion and Protection of Human Rights issued for comment its draft Norms on the Responsibilities of Transnational Corporations and Other Business Enterprises with Regard to Human Rights.[5] This extracts principles with application to the activities of TNCs from the vast body of human rights treaties and instruments. Finally, the United Nations Global Compact sets out 10 human rights norms which apply to corporations. It aims to encourage companies to comply with these norms in all operations and profiles best case examples of 'good corporate citizenship' on its website as a way of promoting this.[6]

The last 15 years have seen the rise of individual company codes of conduct. Levi-Strauss is usually credited as the first TNC to establish a code with comprehensive principles regarding its global sourcing and operations, in 1991.[7] Nike followed later the same year.[8] Since then, company codes of conduct have become more common. In May 2001 the OECD published a review of 246 codes of conduct, noting that this did not cover all codes in existence.[9] A more recent World Bank estimate put the number of company codes at around 1,000.[10] Codes have become an increasingly visible part of the activity of TNCs. They often feature on websites and in annual reports which include assessments of social and environmental performance alongside financial measures.

There are a number of reasons for the rise of codes. The implementation of a code can confer a competitive benefit on a TNC.[11] The 2001 OECD survey noted that 'the protection or enhancement of an organization's reputation and stronger customer loyalty' was often cited as

---

[4] http://www.ilo.org/public/english/standards/norm/sources/mne.htm

[5] UN Economic and Social Council E/CN.4/Sub.2/2003/38/Rev.2, 26 August 2003.

[6] www.globalcompact.org

[7] DM Schilling, 'Making codes of conduct credible: The role of independent monitoring' in O Williams (ed), *Global Codes of Conduct: An idea whose time has come* (Notre Dame, Indiana, University of Notre Dame Press, 2000), at p 221.

[8] SJ Frenkel and D Scott, 'Compliance, collaboration, and codes of labor practice: the *adidas* connection' (2004) 45 No 1 *California Management Review* 29.

[9] OECD Directorate for Financial, Fiscal and Enterprise Affairs, *Codes of Corporate Conduct: Expanded Review of their Contents* (May 2001), Working Papers on International Investment, November 2001/6.

[10] RJ Rosoff, 'Beyond codes of conduct: addressing labor rights problems in China' *The China Business Review*, March–April 2004, 2 at 3.

[11] While some may see this as evidence that codes are inherently illegitimate (springing not from altruism but the profit motive), the adoption of a code motivated in part or whole by a desire for boosting reputation need not in itself be an objection to codes. Of greater importance is the extent to which the human rights principles espoused are implemented, rather than untangling the mix of motivations behind their implementation.

contributing to a decision to implement a code.[12] Although a direct link between 'good corporate citizenship' and the 'business case' is difficult, there is some evidence to support the view that the implementation of a code which includes provision for higher labor standards can in turn produce a more stable and productive workforce and assist a company to increase production, quality and reliability and ultimately profits.[13]

Similarly, some TNCs find their conduct is becoming increasingly visible to a wide range of actors, including consumers, investors, employees, competitors, and NGOs. For such TNCs, implementation of a code can help establish 'social legitimacy'[14]and convey a positive global corporate citizenship image.[15] In addition, a code is flexible and readily adaptable to the operating and industry conditions of a particular company and to new business and operations environments. A TNC which wishes to take human rights norms into account may therefore turn first to a code in order to address the specific employee rights situation of a company in a given location.

## 3. What is a Code of Conduct?

The ILO defines a code of conduct as 'a written policy, or statement of principles, intended to serve as the basis for a commitment to particular enterprise conduct.'[16] The OECD definition is similar, referring to 'commitments voluntarily made by companies, associations or other entities, which put forth standards and principles for the conduct of business activities in the marketplace.'[17] Both definitions highlight the two key distinguishing characteristics of a code; it is entered into *voluntarily*, and it sets out a range of *non-binding commitments*. A code is usually produced by the TNC using a mix of local or national laws and industry and international standards (such as ILO Conventions or UN human rights instruments).[18] Generally, there is no formal role for external agencies in monitoring and reporting on code compliance.

---

[12] OECD *Codes of Corporate Conduct*, above n 9, at 2.

[13] See, eg, Michael E Porter and Mark R Kramer, 'The competitive advantage of corporate philanthropy' (2002) 80(12) *Harvard Business Review* at 56. The example of *adidas*-Salomon in China is discussed below.

[14] Richter, above n 2, at p 298

[15] International Council on Human Rights Policy *Beyond Voluntarism: Human rights and the developing international legal obligations of companies* (ICHRP, Versoix, Switzerland, February 2002), Summary, at 70, available at www.cleanclothes.org/ftp/beyond_voluntarism.pdf

[16] International Labor Organization Governing Body, Working Party on the Social Dimensions of the Liberalization of International Trade, *Overview of global developments and Office activities concerning codes of conduct, social labeling and other private sector initiatives addressing labor issues*, Executive Summary, GB 273/WP/SDL/1, 273rd session Geneva, November 1998.

[17] OECD *Codes of Corporate Conduct*, above n 9, at 8.

[18] The OECD inventory referenced below found that international standards were explicitly cited in only 18% of the 233 codes it reviewed.

Codes can be directed at domestic company issues (such as personnel policies) or international business operations, such as relationships with suppliers, contractors, and even the host State.[19] Their content is as varied as the companies and industry sectors in which they are found, and is influenced by factors such as the size of the TNC and the importance of the area of conduct to its business operations. The OECD survey noted that 'codes from the apparel and extractive industries show that industry factors can be very important in shaping codes' and identified differences between codes in the extractive industry versus the apparel sector which reflected this.[20]

The OECD survey identified the following eight broad areas of conduct covered by codes:

| labor standards | environmental stewardship | consumer protection | bribery |
|---|---|---|---|
| competition | information disclosure | science and technology | taxation |

Of these, labor rights and environmental standards were the most common, with 148 of 246 codes containing some coverage of the former, and 145 codes dealing with the latter. The OECD survey also found that codes were particularly common in the extractive, textile, chemical, and trade sectors.[21]

## II. CODES OF CONDUCT AND THE HUMAN RIGHTS ACCOUNTABILITY OF TRANSNATIONAL CORPORATIONS

### 1. An Overview of the Debate

Many commentators who evaluate the utility of individual company codes of conduct as levers to promote the human rights accountability of TNCs conclude that codes are ineffective. In particular, the lack of enforceable standards, lacunae in the human rights which are included, and the way these are articulated are seen as major deficiencies. In addition, codes are generally judged to be ineffective according to wider criteria, including whether they produce respect for a broad range of human rights in the host State. Westfield's conclusion is typical:

> The continuous reports of labor rights violations in the ubiquitous global marketplace ... raise the question of whether the private, voluntary, self-regulated

---

[19] See G van Liemt, 'Codes of conduct and international subcontracting: a "private" road towards ensuring minimum labor standards in expert industries' in Blanpain, above n 1, at p 167. This chapter focuses on the operation and effect of codes which are non-domestically applicable.

[20] OECD *Codes of Corporate Conduct*, above n 9, at 2.

[21] *Ibid* at 7.

codes of conduct can remain the approach for contending with labor rights violations.[22]

At the other end of the spectrum, many business and industry commentators see voluntary codes of conduct as the most effective means of ensuring that corporations take human rights into account.

However, the evaluation of the effectiveness of codes sometimes lacks methodological consistency and rigor. The various types of codes are often conflated (for example, assimilating individual company codes, framework agreements, and industry codes) and their different aims and areas of application are not distinguished (such as applicability to suppliers and/or contractors or to company activity only). There is also a lack of empirical studies about the overall impact of codes. Attention is often given to whether or not a particular code is being complied with in a particular location, but studies analyzing the overall impact of codes on the promotion, protection, and realization of human rights are rare. Debates tend to rely on a few examples of the operations of companies which have codes of conduct (such as Nike) to draw often broad generalizations about the utility of codes. As one commentator notes:

> to date very little rigorous analysis has been conducted on the impacts and implications of [non-governmental systems of labor standards and monitoring]. And the analysis that has been conducted has been highly contentious, either advocating programmes or dismissing them out of hand.[23]

This chapter attempts to avoid some of these pitfalls. In order to analyze the impact of codes on human rights with some clarity, references to 'human rights' are limited to what might be termed 'employee rights'.[24] These include the right to work and freedom to choose employment, to form and join unions, to be free of discrimination in the workplace (including in hiring, pay and conditions, and promotions), not to be subject to any form of slavery including forced labor, no exploitation of children, and just and favorable conditions of work (including equal pay, a living wage, safe

---

[22] E Westfield, 'Globalization, governance and multinational enterprise responsibility: Corporate codes of conduct in the 21st Century' (2002) 42 *Virginia Journal of International Law* 1075 at 1098. For similar conclusions see also M Shaughnessy, 'The United Nations Global Compact and the continuing debate about the effectiveness of corporate voluntary codes of conduct' (2000) *Colorado Journal of International Environmental Law and Policy* 159.

[23] D O'Rouke, 'Analysing non-governmental systems of labor standards and monitoring' in *Summaries of Presentations Made at the United Nations Research Institute for Social Development Conference on Corporate Social Responsibility: Towards a New Agenda?*, held in Geneva, Switzerland, 17–18 November 2003, at 29, available at http://www.unrisd.org/unrisd/website/document.nsf/(httpPublications)/5FE3FFAE56E19A50C1256F1100518FC5?OpenDocument

[24] See International Council on Human Rights Policy, *Beyond Voluntarism* report, above n 15, at 36.

and healthy work conditions, and reasonable work hours and paid overtime). In particular, the studies examined below illustrate the impact of codes on the right to collective bargaining and to appropriate working conditions.

These rights have been chosen for two reasons. First, they have been the focus of the empirical studies which are reviewed in the next section of this chapter. Second, there is a clear connection between these rights and the capacity of TNCs to influence their promotion, protection, and realization. It is difficult to argue that the 'sphere of influence' of TNCs does not extend to these areas. It is important to state that focusing on the impact of codes on the promotion of these rights does not imply that other human rights are not equally important. It is simply a practical attempt to bring some focus to the discussion about the impact of codes on human rights.

As well as limiting the human rights which are considered, the focus of this chapter is narrowed to consider existing empirical studies on the impact of codes on human rights. It examines a detailed study of the application of a code in operation in China and briefly reviews a recently published report by the University of Iowa's Center for Human Rights ('the Schrage report') which analyzes four case studies of the operation of codes, including in the toy manufacturing sector in China.[25] The final section of the chapter makes conclusions on the role of codes in the human rights accountability of TNCs in the light of these studies.

## 2. A China Case Study

China is a key battle-ground in the fight for the promotion, protection, and realization of human rights. Over the last 20 years its economy has seen astounding growth and it was recently rewarded with membership of the WTO. It is the recipient of a large amount of foreign direct investment, amounting to US$115.07 billion in 2003, and a large number of TNCs have operations there.[26] It now has an estimated 750 million workers, making up a quarter of the world's workforce.[27] The People's Republic of China government has signed most UN human rights conventions and treaties, and China has a comprehensive labor law regime which guarantees its workers a range of labor rights.[28] Despite this, the

---

[25] E Schrage, *Promoting International Worker Rights Through Private Voluntary Initiatives: Public Relations or Public Policy?*, Report to US Department of State on behalf of The University of Iowa Center for Human Rights, January 2004.

[26] From US–China Business Council website: http://www.uschina.org/statistics/fdi1979-03.html

[27] J Sweeney, 'China's workers and the world', in (2004) *China Rights Forum*, No 3, at 15

[28] For a list of human rights treaties that China has signed and/or ratified, see http://www1.umn.edu/humanrts/research/ratification-china.html

rights of China's workers are routinely violated and there is almost total failure to enforce either domestic or international law regarding labor rights in China. In the light of this, and because of the existence of empirical studies, it is a useful case study of the effect of codes on human rights, in particular, employee rights.

At the December 2003 United Nations Research Institute for Social Development (UNRISD) Conference on Corporate Social Responsibility and Development, several presenters outlined the early results of empirical research into the impact of corporate social responsibility (CSR) on development issues in the global south. Monina Wong, from the Hong Kong Christian Industrial Committee (HKCIC), presented her organization's conclusions about the effect of CSR initiatives (including codes of conduct) on labor standards in China.[29] To the question 'have CSR initiatives led to improved labor standards in China?', she answered 'Yes', but qualified this by noting that it depended on the industry and economic sector concerned.

Research by the HKCIC over the last 10 years presented at the conference indicated that there had been some improvements in labor standards in the subcontracting chain in the international toy industry as a result of 'pressure on, and by, the TNC buyers', although Wong notes that there are still a lot of violations. In contrast, she cites the computer manufacturing industry as one which has been largely unaffected by CSR and not 'baptized by international labor or consumer campaigns.' In the case of Hewlett Packard, her organization found evidence that labor conditions in its suppliers' factories in China are in direct contrast to the company's stated policies of CSR, in particular, of choosing 'suppliers and vendors that maintain appropriate standards ...'.[30]

One area where the HKCIC observed a positive impact from TNC codes was in the rise of organized labor in China. Wong states:

> In regard to implementing freedom of association in China, it should be noted that TNC initiatives especially in the area of worker representation and forming unions have created pressure on the labor bureau and the official union in China. The official union, the ACFTU, is under pressure to form new unions in the private sector and the FIEs [foreign invested enterprises] and introduce open elections for the union members and the union chair. ... at least the initiatives help to create legal space and incentives for worker empowerment in China.'[31]

[29] M Wong, 'What difference does CSR make to development?' in *Summaries of Presentations Made at the United Nations Research Institute for Social Development Conference on Corporate Social Responsibility: Towards a New Agenda?*, held in Geneva, Switzerland, 17–18 November 2003, at 18.

[30] *Ibid* at 19.

[31] *Ibid* at 21.

The Schrage report reached a similar conclusion in relation to the toy industry. Schrage reviewed labor conditions in toy production in China, and the response of six major US-based toy manufacturers to human rights issues in the sector. He evaluated the impact of these individual responses as well as the industry-wide code of business practices recently developed by the International Council of Toy Industries (ICTI), a representative body for international toy trades associations comprising representatives from 19 countries.[32] In 1995 the ICTI adopted a 'Code of Business Practices'. Revised in 2001, this aims to ensure that toy factories of ICTI members are operated in a 'lawful, safe and healthful manner ...' and sets out details regarding labor and workplace standards and a compliance regime.[33] Schrage concludes that through this toy industry initiative 'the efforts of some individual toy brands to implement minimum labor standards for their Chinese suppliers have led to concrete improvements in some factories ...' in particular in those wholly owned, or where production was controlled, by Mattel.[34] He notes that 'the Toy Industry Initiative has the potential to promote higher minimum labor standards in Chinese toy factories.'[35] However, he concludes that '... it is too early to evaluate the impact of the PVIs [private voluntary initiatives] of the ICTI on labor standards in the global toy industry.'[36]

## A. The Implementation of the adidas-Salomon Code of Conduct in China

Another study which analyzed the impact of the application of a code in China was undertaken by Stephen Frankel and Duncan Scott, who compared the implementation of the *adidas*-Salomon code of conduct at two factories in China.[37] As a global sporting goods brand, *adidas* ranks second behind Nike, accounting for 15 per cent of world sales, and employing 13,300 people.[38] The *adidas*-Salomon group has approximately 900 factories around the world in its supply chain (only eight of which it owns itself), with 60 per cent of its suppliers based in Asia. Most of these are in the *adidas* side of the business, manufacturing sporting goods.[39]

The *adidas*-Salomon code of conduct, referred to as its Standards of Engagement (SOE) is described as playing a 'critical role in driving the

---

[32] www.toy-icti.org
[33] www.toy-icti.org/resources/code.htm
[34] Schrage report, above n 25, at 125.
[35] *Ibid* at 125.
[36] *Ibid* at 126.
[37] SJ Frenkel and D Scott, above n 8.
[38] *Ibid* at 35.
[39] *adidas*-Salomon *Staying Focused Social and Environmental Report* (2003), at 19.

Group's values and business principles through to the supply chain.'[40] It is used to 'choose supply chain partners, monitor their performance and identify problems.'[41] The company states that it expects its business partners to operate workplaces where the SOE standards and practices are followed. The SOE covers five key areas:

— compliance with legal requirements both in the home and host state (the so-called 'general principle');
— employment standards (prohibiting forced labor, employment of children under 15, discrimination and setting standards for wages and benefits, hours of work, freedom of association, collective bargaining, and disciplinary practices);
— health and safety;
— environmental requirements;
— community involvement.

The SOE seeks to encompass the activities of the *adidas* supply chain; contractors and companies who contract with *adidas*-Salomon sign terms of engagement which require them to uphold the SOE. Handbooks and posters are provided for distribution to workers in factories to educate them about the terms of the code and mechanisms for bringing complaints if it is violated. Responsibility for overseeing the implementation of the SOE is the primary focus of the *adidas*-Salomon Social and Environmental Affairs department.[42] This group has three regional teams (Asia, the Americas, and Europe) and includes people with law, engineering, finance, and human resource management skills. Five members of this team focus on footwear manufacture and three on clothing. These labor practices staff members are responsible for undertaking regular (ideally monthly) visits to suppliers to check code adherence and assist in resolving compliance problems. In addition, an annual formal evaluation of performance against environmental and labor standards forms part of the broader evaluation of the performance of the supplier. The SOE performance score is combined with measures such as price, quality, and delivery times. Where standards are below the SOE requirements, the labor practices team works with the supplier to develop and implement measures to remedy the problem.[43]

---

[40] The code is available at http://www.adidas-salomon.com/en/sustainability/coc/standards_of_engagement/standards_of_engagement.asp. The quote is taken from p 6. This chapter does not analyze the substantive terms of the code, being concerned instead with its implementation, rather than its language.

[41] From 'Frequently Asked Questions: Social and Environmental Affairs', www.adidas-salomon.com/en/services/faq/sea/sea.asp

[42] SJ Frenkel and D Scott, above n 8, at 37–38.

[43] Neither the study nor the *adidas*-Salomon website mentions whether the contract of any supplier has been terminated as a result of persistent violations of the code.

In their study, Frenkel and Scott reviewed the operations of two *adidas* contractors (whom they termed Alpha and Beta), both private companies operating footwear factories in the Chinese province of Guangdong. Beta is part of a Taiwanese-owned company which owns and operates four other factories; Alpha is jointly owned by Taiwanese owners, a community-owned enterprise and a State-owned leather company. The two factories were chosen to be as similar in workplace characteristics as possible in order to minimize the possibility that factors other than the level of code compliance might account for differences in performance between the two companies.

Information regarding the performance of the companies against the SOE was obtained in 'semi-structured' interviews with managers, supervisors, and production workers. In all, over the course of two days, a total of 20 Alpha employees and 17 Beta employees were interviewed.[44] Interviews were carried out in English or with translation either by a workplace manager (when interviewing managers) or a labor practices staff member (when interviewing workers). Workers were interviewed in groups of three in meetings away from the shop floor.

Frenkel and Scott found that Alpha, which showed far better application of the SOE, also performed better than Beta, including demonstrating better levels of pay and health and safety, and lower labor turnover rates. They conclude:

> The differences in workplace outcomes can be explained by Alpha's management having successfully interpreted and implemented the *adidas* code of labor practice as a collaborative relationship. This has been reciprocated by *adidas* labor practices staff and has contributed to a more dedicated and stable contractor management, a more effective labor practices team, and a more committed workforce. By contrast, Beta's management has merely progressed from skepticism towards the code to a position of ambivalent acceptance. [45]

The authors compared the 'collaborative' approach to code implementation at Alpha with the 'compliance' approach taken by Beta's management. In the collaborative approach, characterized by a partnership between *adidas* and the supplier, the SOE was used as a base for continual improvement of workplace conditions and performance. Implementation was jointly monitored, and evolved and developed over time, as both *adidas* and the supplier took a long-term approach to the relationship. By contrast, the compliance approach was characterized by the imposition of

---

[44] Comprising one *adidas* engineer, four senior managers, four middle managers/technical staff, three labor practices staff members, two supervisors, and six workers at Alpha; and one *adidas* engineer, two senior managers, two middle managers, four labor practices staff members, two supervisors, and six workers at Beta.

[45] SJ Frenkel and D Scott, above n 8, at 43.

the code by *adidas*, who remained responsible for its development and enforcement. Beta tended to see the code as one of the conditions it needed to satisfy in order to continue to do business with *adidas*, but the code did not become an integral part of its business operations. This latter, somewhat ambivalent view is captured by the following quote from the manager at Beta:

> We develop these labor practices because this is the *adidas* way. The workers get educated in what their rights are, which is a positive thing. On the other hand, it's Western companies determining what their rights are, which I don't feel is right ... But over the long term, the code of practice is good for the company ... But this is a big cost for us—improving the dormitories, the canteen, and facilities more generally—even though we are compensated for some of the cost by *adidas* ...[46]

Frenkel and Scott conclude that 'codes of labor practice can be a valuable tool for implementing core labor standards among multinationals' contractors in developing countries.'[47] Even in the comparatively poorer performing Beta, Frenkel and Scott found that the 'compliance-type relationship ... also yields distinct benefits that are unlikely to have occurred in the absence of the code.'[48]

There are some difficulties with the methodology adopted in the *adidas*-Salomon study. First, the authors are an employee of *adidas* and an academic from a respected business school in Australia. This background may make it less likely for their analysis of *adidas* to be highly critical. Second, as the authors acknowledge, there were difficulties obtaining comparable information and interpreting its meaning because of the methodology employed. In particular, visits were pre-arranged by *adidas* management, and interviewees selected by a factory manager. The authors attempted to control for the possibility of resulting bias in a number of ways. They set criteria for the selection of interviewees in advance, sought 'facts rather than opinions'[49] about the working conditions in the factories and tried to cross-check the veracity of information by using a variety of sources, including *adidas* engineers working in the factory and documentary records. Despite these efforts, it is difficult to know the extent to which responses received were tainted by a reluctance of workers to reveal the true labor conditions in the two factories or by interviewees being selected on the basis that they were likely to be positive about employment conditions in the factories. There is a real risk that the data was biased towards showing SOE compliance.

---

[46] *Ibid* at 42
[47] *Ibid* at 34.
[48] *Ibid*.
[49] *Ibid* at 37.

These problems are compounded by limitations of the *adidas* inspection report process itself. Resource constraints inevitably affect the ability of the labor practices team both to conduct their regular factory visits, and in the actions they can recommend and enforce when problems are identified. If time and money are limited, the outcome of the inspection reports is likely to be limited to the identification of obvious problems, rather than the encouragement of 'proactive systems to anticipate and prevent problems' as envisaged by the code.[50] In this situation, a company such as Beta which takes the simpler compliance approach can still comply with the SOE without risk of sanction.

## 3. The Beneficial Effects of a Code on Human Rights Accountability

As the above discussion suggests, determining the impact of a company code of conduct on the human rights situation of the employees of a TNC is complex. Codes can produce a range of beneficial effects, but also have a number of inherent limitations. Frenkel and Scott's study also reveals that the same code can be implemented very differently in different contexts. This should come as no surprise. It does show that it is very difficult to draw general conclusions on the effectiveness of codes as a human rights mechanism across industry sectors and countries, when comparisons even within comparable factories in the same country are difficult. In particular, published data of 'code compliance' can mask the real situation—Alpha and Beta both complied with code, but the realisation of employee rights in one workplace was much better than in the other.

In addition as Schrage points out, focusing only on the direct impact of an individual code 'fails to capture the full range of its impact on the global economy.' He proposes additional sets of measures to evaluate the effectiveness of what he terms 'private voluntary initiatives' (PVIs) on global workplace conditions, including:

— their impact on emerging markets, including the extent to which PVIs 'promote civil society and respect for the rule of law'; and
— the changes PVIs bring to TNCs via 'ripple effects' on the way companies source materials and suppliers before production and 'at the very least, sensitizing global corporations to emerging responsibilities under international law.'[51]

---

[50] *Ibid* at 38.
[51] Schrage report, above n 25, at 166.

The following section evaluates the benefits of codes as illustrated by the China case study, and considers both their direct and indirect effects on the human rights accountability of TNCs.

## A. Direct Benefits

The China case study gives some evidence that codes can have a positive impact on the promotion, protection, and realization of core labor and employee rights such as the right to collective bargaining and the prohibitions on child and forced labor and discrimination. Workers in the *adidas*-Salomon factories and the toy industry in China more broadly appear to have benefited in these areas. A well-drafted and well-implemented code can be used to bring about real improvements in employee rights, particularly where the host State has little commitment to such rights and where independent civil society and unions are weak or non-existent. The code may operate as a 'stop-gap' measure until more traditional forms of employee rights enforcement develop.

In addition, Frenkel and Scott note the 'widening of perspectives' of management that occurred through participation in the implementation of higher standards of employee rights.[52] The enculturation of labor standards into overall operations can be a direct benefit of a well implemented code, by educating both management and workers about employee rights. A self-generated code can be more useful in this regard, since it may be more likely to be seen as credible and workable by managers responsible for implementing it, leading to better compliance 'on the ground' than may be possible with externally generated and applied mechanisms for promoting human rights.

## B. Indirect Impacts

Codes may also have an impact beyond company operations. TNCs that use codes in a developing country may help generate acceptance for human rights norms by a host State unable or unwilling to sign up to or enforce international standards. By importing practically applied human rights norms and by showing that FDI and economic development can be consistent with these, the TNC may influence a host State's domestic policy. As noted above, the HKCIC has observed that TNCs have provided a platform for the development of worker representation in China. More recently, Wal-Mart bowed to pressure in China and agreed to allow collective bargaining in its Chinese factories, despite this being against Wal-Mart's usual method of operation.[53]

---

[52] SJ Frenkel and D Scott, above n 8, at 34.
[53] Reported by BBC News on 24 November 2004—see http://news.bbc.co.uk/1/hi/business/4037423.stm

## 4. The Limitations of Codes of Conduct as a Human Rights Accountability Mechanism

The China case study also highlights a number of limitations of codes in promoting the human rights accountability of TNCs. Codes are at best an opaque mechanism for promoting and enforcing human rights standards. As private instruments, there is very little transparency in their development and implementation. While some companies post codes and associated social and environmental reports on their websites, or include references to code compliance in annual reports, many do not. In addition, such information is controlled by the TNC and is difficult to verify. As noted above, even a detailed study on code effects can be subject to criticism because of potential for bias in favor of demonstrating human rights compliance by the company.

Third party monitoring by groups such as human rights and labor organizations can help resolve this, although for such efforts to be effective, these organizations need to be appropriately resourced. Ideally, such monitoring should be done with the support of the TNC to facilitate access to sites and suppliers and by providing financial and other resources to independent groups. The human rights NGO Fédération Internationale des Ligues des Droits de l'Homme (FIDH) has such an arrangement with French retailer Carrefour, allowing for inspections of its suppliers' production sites outside France.[54]

Codes also suffer from inherent inconsistencies which manifest in a number of ways. As noted above, the issues addressed by a code vary from company to company and across industry sectors. Diller notes 'a high degree of selectivity in the choice of labor issues ... [and] ... a wide variation in the way in which the targeted practice was defined.'[55] Decisions to include particular human rights norms in a code may arise from a desire to address issues directly affecting the company, rather than a commitment to a comprehensive scheme for promoting human rights, producing a patchwork approach to human rights in codes. In addition, the ILO report found that international norms were only used in one third or less of codes, suggesting that codes are not necessarily encouraging adherence to generally acknowledged standards of international human rights but to some other, usually simpler, standard.[56] The ILO report also found a focus on procedural rather than substantive requirements in many codes.[57] This produced inconsistencies within codes, and a tendency towards a 'simplistic' approach to human rights norms.

---

[54] For an example of the monitoring carried out by FIDH of Carrefour operations, see http://www.fidh.org/article.php3?id_article=2448

[55] JM Diller, 'Social conduct in transnational enterprise operations: the role of the International Labor Organization' in R Blanpain (ed), above n 1, 17 at p 24.

[56] ILO report, above n 16, at para 52.

[57] *Ibid* at para 119.

As discussed above, the flexibility of codes can make them better adapted and more effective in particular circumstances. However, the diversity in the structure, focus and content of codes also risks diluting human rights standards to the lowest common denominator. It can result in the piecemeal implementation of quasi-human rights principles, with the potential to 'dumb down' human rights to the lowest, most easily achievable norms. The good intentions which underpinned the move to a code may be undone.[58] It also makes it difficult for NGOs, consumers, and the company itself to apply and evaluate codes easily and consistently, particularly in different locations and can produce 'confusion and skepticism ... lead[ing] to the weakening of the phenomenon [of development of codes].'[59] Similarly, this diversity can also mean that less serious codes, which contain little or no monitoring or reporting mechanisms, will crowd out those which are better drafted.

An oft-cited flaw of codes is that most contain no sanctions for non-compliance.[60] The OECD survey found few examples of codes where non-compliance would lead to a serious penalty, such as a financial sanction or even termination of a contract. Instead, as in the *adidas* case study, the response to code violations is more likely to be the maintenance of the relationship and attempts to remedy the breach, rather than the imposition of a penalty on the offending supplier. Code compliance may become no more than an 'optional extra', rather than an important and binding requirement of operation.

This is not to suggest that a serious financial penalty or contract termination should always and inevitably flow from a code breach. For many workers, employment in a TNC operation is the only work available. The imposition of a severe financial penalty for a code violation may simply cause the supplier to, for example, impose more stringent production quotas on employees, by increasing unpaid overtime and decreasing breaks. The termination of a contract may lead to the laying off of workers, leaving them without income. Both outcomes can in fact result in further human rights abuses, rather than remedying them. The question of sanctions for breach of a code thus involves finding a balance between imposing a meaningful penalty, such that the code is taken seriously, without negatively affecting the human rights of the workers whom it aims to protect.

---

[58] See, eg, *ibid* at para 59, where a code in the clothing sector with lesser standards was adopted because of difficulty getting agreement to include stricter standards.

[59] *Ibid* at para 118.

[60] For example, see J Hong, 'Enforcement of corporate codes of conduct: Finding a private right of action for international laborers against MNCs for labor rights violations' (2000) 19 *Wisconsin International Law Journal* 41 at 48.

Van Liemt gives an example of this in the context of the manufacture of soccer balls in Pakistan for Nike and Reebok.[61] Traditionally these were produced in cottage industries in Pakistan and hand-stitched by women and children. In response to criticism of the use of child labor, Reebok and Nike both agreed with local contractors to establish factory sites for the production of soccer balls, where they could set labor standards and monitor compliance. As a result, the use of child labor in the manufacture of soccer balls has been all but eradicated in this industry. However, the shift to factory-based manufacturing resulted in men taking over the jobs previously held by women and children. In the absence of transitional programs and still needing income, women and children were forced to shift to other, less desirable forms of employment, including prostitution. Enforcement of human rights without consultation and programs to compensate workers or assist in their transition to alternative employment simply shifted human rights abuses to another domain.

Some human rights organizations have responded to the lack of internal sanctions for code breach by pursuing external accountability in the courts. In the United States the Alien Tort Claims Act and consumer protection legislation has been used. Recently, litigation was brought against Nike Corporation in California alleging breaches of that State's unfair competition and false advertising laws.[62] In that case, Kasky, on behalf of the citizens of California, alleged that Nike had made false or misleading statements regarding work practices at its factories in Indonesia and Vietnam. The allegation was based on comments made in letters and other statements by Nike in response to media reporting of these labor practices, which were allegedly in conflict with the terms of Nike's code of conduct. After several years at the pre-trial stage, the case settled in September 2003.[63]

While such litigation is successful at raising media and public awareness of human rights violations in the developing world, it is a long, expensive, and difficult road, and the overall impacts are unclear. No case against a TNC for breach of a code has reached trial on the substantive issues. Some, such as the Nike case, have settled, and other claims under the Alien Torts Claims Act have been dismissed for lack of a cause of action, or are still in interlocutory stages. Such litigation may also have unintended consequences. Sutton has detailed the way in which one impact of the Nike litigation has been a decrease in the transparency of

---

[61] G van Liemt, 'Codes of conduct and international subcontracting: a "private" road towards ensuring minimum labor standards in expert industries' in R Blanpain (ed), above n 1, at p 167.

[62] *Kasky v Nike* 27 Cal 4th 939, 45 P.3d 243 (2002); *Nike Inc v Kasky* 123 S.Ct 2554, US 2003, 26 June 2004.

[63] For details of the settlement, see http://www.nike.com/nikebiz/news/pressrelease.jhtml?year=2003&month=09&letter=f

Nike's approach to corporate social responsibility and the operation of its code. Following settlement of the case, Nike announced that it 'would limit its work in corporate accountability, not release its 2002 corporate responsibility report and restrict public platform activities.'[64]

According to Nike's website, its 'commitment to transparency' was 'tempered' by the *Kasky* litigation. Despite this, a number of factors influenced Nike's decision to report again, including a desire for transparency and credibility, increased reporting by its industry sector and improvements in its ability to collect data on its corporate responsibility activities. [65]

Nike released its next corporate responsibility report in 2005, covering the period 1 June 2003 to 31 May 2004. It remains to be seen whether the longer-term impact of such litigation for alleged violation of the code may in fact be less transparency and accountability, instead of more. In addition, as John Sweeney, from the Patagonia sportswear company points out, where there is a strong link between compliance, monitoring, and publicity, the risk is that when the negative publicity fades away, so too will compliance.[66]

## III. CONCLUSIONS

The 1999 World Investment Report estimated that there were over 60,000 TNCs, with over half a million affiliates, employing an estimated 54 million workers.[67] Only a small fraction of these have codes of conduct.[68] The impact of codes on the human rights of the majority of the world's estimated 2.8 billion workers can therefore only ever be minimal.[69] In particular, codes are likely to have little effect on the activities

[64] M Sutton, 'Between a rock and a hard place: Corporate social responsibility reporting and potential legal liability under *Kasky v Nike*' (2004) 72 *University of Missouri KC Law Review* 1159 at 1175.

[65] http://www.nike.com/nikebiz/nikebiz.jhtml?page=29&item=nikereporting

[66] KJ Sweeney, 'Voting with their pocketbooks: The strength and limits of consumer-driven codes of conduct' in O Williams (ed), above n 7, at pp 253–64.

[67] United Nations Conference on Trade and Development, World Investment Report 1999, *Foreign Direct Investment and the Challenge of Development*, at p 16. See also http://www.bigpicturesmallworld.com/Global%20Inc%202/pgs/intro.html, which provides a graph illustrating the rise of TNCs from the English and Dutch East India Companies in the seventeenth century to US telecommunications company Verizon in 2000.

[68] See Peter Utting's introductory remarks at the UNRISD Conference on Corporate Social Responsibility and Development: Towards a New Agenda?, November 2003, available at http://www.unrisd.org/80256B3C005BCCF9/httpNetITFramePDF?ReadForm&parentunid=5F E3FFAE56E19A50C1256F1100518FC5&parentdoctype=paper&netitpath=80256B3C005BCC F9/(httpAuxPages)/5FE3FFAE56E19A50C1256F1100518FC5/$file/confsum.pdf

[69] ILO World Employment Report 2004–05, cited in press release at http://www.ilo.org/ public/english/bureau/inf/pr/2004/54.htm

of TNCs which produce 'intermediate-use' goods, such as metals and rubber, which are purchased by other companies to manufacture end-use goods. These companies are not so image conscious and are unlikely to be motivated by a need to ensure a positive reputation.[70] Indeed, many small TNCs have a limited or non-existent public profile, operating on relatively short-term contracts for governments or other larger companies. They are not visible to activists or consumers, and it is almost impossible to find out whether they seek to meet human rights standards, and if so, how. Codes are likely to play a marginal role in their activities. This difficulty is compounded by the fact that TNCs increasingly use complex and highly devolved supply chains. This makes it harder and harder for even the most responsible of them to control each of potentially hundreds of global contractors, subcontractors, and suppliers.

Even in the apparel industry, traditionally a key focus of monitoring of human rights and labor standards by NGOs, most attention has been concentrated on Reebok, Nike and *adidas*. The behavior of smaller so-called 'B brands' manufacturers such as Puma, Fila and Kappa, many of whom rely on the same suppliers as Nike and *adidas*, has only recently been subject to scrutiny. The Clean Clothes campaign has now turned its spotlight on the labor practices of these TNCs in the lead up to the 2008 Olympic Games in Beijing.[71] However, many others continue to avoid public scrutiny.

It is clear therefore that the question of whether codes of conduct can promote the human rights accountability of TNCs cannot be answered with a simple yes or no. The answer seems to be that the right kind of code may be a useful mechanism to help ensure the realization of some human rights (notably core labor rights). Such a code must clearly articulate the human rights standards it promotes, with reference to international norms and focus on those which it is best placed to address. It needs to be developed and implemented by a company committed not to just the concept of a code, but to its ongoing implementation and open and independent monitoring. Finally, a code will be most effective in industries whose operations are of interest to the public and open to scrutiny by civil society groups. Codes which meet these criteria may also produce indirect benefits to business culture, help educate workers and management about human rights, and improve the host State's attitude to human rights by showing that these are not incompatible with investment.

---

[70] E Westfield, above n 22, at fn 137.
[71] http://www.cleanclothes.org/publications/olympic-profiles.htm

It seems, then, that codes of conduct can be useful:

— to promote and protect human rights which are directly in the sphere of influence of the TNC, in particular, as we have seen, employee or labor rights such as collective bargaining and working conditions like overtime;
— to bring about cultural change within companies and promote an environment where human rights begin to form part of the business plan and everyday operations of TNCs; and
— as role models or examples for host States and workers in the developing world of the way in which human rights can be incorporated into business enterprises.

Within these parameters, the development of codes should be encouraged to maximize their beneficial impacts and address, as far as possible, their limitations. First, TNCs should be encouraged to draft codes of conduct which explicitly source their content from international human rights instruments, to avoid what has been termed 'the tyranny of the minimum'.[72] Governments could assist in this by establishing criteria for codes, publicly acknowledging and rewarding companies who develop and implement such codes and requiring companies tendering for government contracts to implement codes both domestically and overseas. This could extend to the development and promotion of 'model' codes which include recommended content and monitoring mechanisms.

Business organizations should also continue to distill human rights principles for use by companies. For example, the Business Leaders Initiative on Human Rights has sought to address what is sees as the 'conceptual and practical difficulties' TNCs face when seeking to incorporate human rights into corporate operations. It has produced a 'matrix' which seeks to contextualize the UN draft Norms. This lists each of the key areas covered, ranks them as 'minimal, expected or desirable' standards to be met, and then gives examples of ways in which corporations may meet these draft Norms.[73]

Second, there should be continued moves towards benchmarking good companies and their codes, and making this information publicly available and easily accessible. The UN Global Compact is one example of this approach.[74] This will help consumers make informed choices when

---

[72] DM Schilling, 'Making codes of conduct credible: the role of independent monitoring' in O Williams (ed), above n 7, 221 at p 225.

[73] See 'Business Leaders Initiative on Human Rights Report 1', *Building Understanding*, December 2003, Appendix 1, at 11.

[74] The Global Reporting Initiative is another such organization that helps companies to benchmark and report on the economic, environmental, and social dimensions of their activities. See www.globalreporting.org

purchasing products made or sourced from the developing world, which in turn provides an incentive for TNCs to implement 'best practice' codes. Multilateral bodies such as the UN or OECD could also establish a code of conduct standards body, not to enforce but to certify that a code meets acceptable standards of human rights.[75]

NGOs, labor unions and civil society should also continue to work with TNCs to help contextualize the human rights standards expected of TNCs, taking account of the particular industry and country, and the local conditions involved. This is particularly important in the light of the ILO finding that 'reference to international standards occurred proportionately more often in joint enterprise/worker codes and in hybrid codes, in contrast to codes developed by industry associations, employers' organizations or enterprises alone.'[76] Partnerships between TNCs and civil society, particularly in the developing world, thus appear crucial to ensuring that the codes address the real human rights issues 'on the ground'. Both TNCs and civil society must work together to identify where their agendas intersect and be realistic about each other's strengths and limitations. This approach has been adopted in relation to industry-wide framework agreements, negotiated between TNCs and unions, where a problem-solving approach to the implementation of codes is adopted. Here codes are not seen as documents requiring strict observance, but as a learning process with constant modification of targets and expectations over time.

In addition, human rights organizations should consider the desirability of seeking to enforce codes in the courts, both because of the limited success of such attempts to date and also because of the prospect of discouraging companies from making even this small attempt at taking human rights into account. Attempts should continue to encourage both host and home States to take on their full responsibility for the protection, promotion and realization of human rights, according to international norms. This is not to say that human rights abuses committed by, or under the watch of TNCs should be ignored. Human rights NGOs, in partnership with developing world unions, the media and grassroots activists, have a vital role to play in monitoring the behavior of TNCs in developing countries and calling them to account. However, the focus of such efforts should be broader than simply 'naming and shaming'. It should also highlight examples of proper or improving practice and provide consumers and companies with tools to help compare performance, thus providing TNCs with a positive incentive to continue to improve human rights standards in their operations.

---

[75] In much the same way as the International Standards Organization does with business and manufacturing processes.

[76] J Diller, above n 55, at p 25.

A code of conduct is far from the 'silver bullet' solution to address all the complex issues involved in holding TNCs accountable for the human rights impacts of their operations in the developing world. Hong expects far too much when she condemns codes as ineffective because they have 'failed to eliminate the problem of thousands of labor rights violations that occur without punishment.'[77] Indeed, it is not desirable for codes to supplant the role of the home and host State, and the international community, including human rights institutions and NGOs in the establishment and monitoring of human rights norms. However, as Schrage argues, 'the best should not be the enemy of the good and the inability of PVIs to correct all labor violations should not discourage them from correcting some.'[78]

Ultimately, codes are only a very small part of the response to intractable problems of globalization. Finding ways to hold TNCs accountable for the human rights impacts of their operations is a large puzzle, of which codes are only one piece. By far the largest piece of this puzzle is the central incongruity of globalization—consumers, governments and business express anxiety over globalization's impacts on the world's poor, while simultaneously seeking cheaper consumer goods, the most advantageous trade systems, and ever-increasing profits. This double-standard produces a situation where TNCs (and States) can both promote human rights while pursuing economic and trade policies which undermine them. This concern was behind the focus of the UNRISD conference referred to above, which consciously put CSR and development together on the agenda. As Peter Utting notes:

> If CSR is to mean anything, and if large corporations are to contribute in a meaningful way to social and sustainable development, the CSR agenda needs to address the central questions of the structural and policy determinants of underdevelopment, inequality and poverty, and the relationship of TNCs to these determinants.[79]

The developed world, including its TNCs, must face the reality of the world's poor and allow them a place at the global table. To the extent that codes can assist in this, they should be encouraged, as one part of what must be a multi-layered and diverse global response to the needs of the poor and the promotion of human rights universally.

---

[77] J Hong, above n 60, at 48.
[78] Schrage report, above n 25, at 170.
[79] Utting, above n 68, at 7.

# 7

# International Framework Agreements: A Collaborative Paradigm for Labor Relations

LISA R PRICE

## I. INTRODUCTION

O VER THE PAST few decades, globalization has had a great impact on the ability of workers to organize and bargain collectively. International trade and capital flows have increased, together with foreign direct investment and cross-border mergers and acquisitions. Transnational corporations, which employ increasing numbers of the world's workers, have become the dominant economic actors, 'a focal force in integrating national and international economies in global and regional production networks and in coordinating and controlling these production chains and networks.'[1] As a result of these changes, the paradigms and patterns of labor relations have also changed. Transnational corporations can move their operations in order to exploit differences in labor costs. Consequently, workers now compete not only within their home States, but with workers in distant parts of the globe.[2] In addition, workers fear that corporate relocation will leave them without a source of income. As a result, they are reluctant to unionize or to seek better health and safety standards, equal opportunities, or higher wages. The outsourcing of production by many transnational corporations exacerbates this fear.[3]

In the high-risk climate created by globalization, it is extremely difficult for labor unions at the local and national level to accomplish their

---

[1] Lone Riisgaard, International Labor Office, 'The IUF/COLSIBA–CHIQUITA Framework Agreement: A Case Study', Working Paper No 94, at 5, available at http://www.ilo.org/public/english/ employment/multi/download/wp94.pdf (last visited 11 December 2004).

[2] Ibid.

[3] Jesper Nilsson, 'A Tool for Achieving Workers' Rights' (2002) 4 Metal World 4 at 22, available at http://www.imfmetal.org/main/files/4-2002.pdf (last visited 11 December 2004).

objectives.[4] Simultaneously, the protections afforded to workers by national legislation—labor and environmental laws, for example— weaken because States feel that the enforcement of such laws will deter transnational companies from investing further in their economies.[5] The result is a worrisome combination: the under-enforcement of labor rights, and conditions that, by making union organization increasingly difficult, render workers unable to pursue the means to address these problems.

In response to the 'race to the bottom', activists in the labor relations movement have been forced to consider different approaches, strategies, and methods of organizing.[6] Increased global communication, made possible by new technologies, has led to international labor cooperation among and between local and national unions, and also with non-governmental organizations (NGOs).[7] Consumers have also become increasingly aware of corporate behavior, in part as a result of the popularity of investing in pension funds and investment trusts. Transnational corporations have discovered that they must incorporate certain 'values' into their products if they are to compete in the global marketplace. In other words, they must demonstrate a commitment to corporate social responsibility.[8] Labor union activists, in response, have begun to incorporate consumer leverage into a new, 'globalized' labor relations paradigm.

The central point of the preceding discussion is that labor relations, in the wake of globalization, have become increasingly pluralistic and dependent on a multiplicity of international actors for success: transnational corporations, consumers, labor union activists at the local, national, and international levels, NGOs, and of course, workers themselves. The new philosophy of the labor movement is that these groups must work in conjunction with one another, developing partnerships rather than antagonisms, if the world's workers are to be protected. This process, of course, faces its shares of obstacles from heightened global competition, the movement of foreign direct investment, and decreased enforcement of national labor legislation. However, this kind of 'collaborative paradigm' has developed as the most successful means of benefiting workers employed by transnational corporations. Notably, it is not one that draws

---

[4] Riisgaard, above n 1, at 5.

[5] *Ibid.*

[6] Nikolaus Hammer, *International Framework Agreements: Overview and Key Issues*, Industrial Relations in Europe Conference (2004), at 1, available at http://exchange.usg.uu.nl/irec/papers/1_Hammer.pdf (last visited 11 December 2004). Hammer describes dialogue in international bodies including the International Labor Organization (ILO), World Trade Organization, World Bank, International Monetary Fund, and others regarding ways for labor relations to deal with the rising power of transnational corporations, as a result of the failure of national unions to bargain effectively.

[7] Riisgaard, above n 1, at 6.

[8] *Ibid.*

its strength from the efforts of the State. It takes the form of voluntary initiatives and commitments from the relevant players discussed above.

The labor relations paradigm I have described has given birth to a mechanism that is the subject of this chapter: international framework agreements (IFAs). This chapter will discuss the promise that IFAs, negotiated by global unions and transnational corporations, have for preventing the risk of abusive practices in the workplace. Section II will define IFAs and discuss their brief history. Section III will explore the theoretical underpinnings behind the agreements, placing them further within the context of the collaborative paradigm, as I have described it. Section IV will consider several IFAs that have been tested in practice, evaluating the degree to which they have operated successfully. Finally, Section V will identify the problems that continue to plague these agreements, suggesting that the value of the agreements should not be overstated, but that they must be understood in their proper context: not as a cure-all, but as a way of building partnerships, developing corporate social awareness and, eventually, increasing accountability for labor rights in the long term.

## II. THE HISTORY OF INTERNATIONAL FRAMEWORK AGREEMENTS

An IFA is an agreement negotiated between a transnational corporation and a global union federation (GUF)[9] concerning the international activities of that company in all of its workplaces. It commits the corporation to respecting minimum labor standards in its operations around the world, typically addressing such subjects as trade union rights, collective bargaining rights, information and consultation, equal opportunities, safety and health, minimum wage standards, and the abolition of child labor and forced labor.[10] The main purpose of an IFA is to establish a formal ongoing relationship between the corporation and the global union which can solve problems and work in the interests of both parties. IFAs typically incorporate most of the 'core' ILO conventions in their language, including conventions on freedom of association, collective bargaining,

---

[9] GUFs are the international representatives of unions organizing in specific industry sectors or occupational groups. See, eg, *Global Unions*, available at http://www.global-unions.org (last visited 11 December 2004). GUFs that have negotiated IFAs include: the International Union of Food (IUF); the International Federation of Building and Wood Workers (IFBWW); the International Textile, Garment and Leather Workers' Federation (ITGLWF); the International Federation of Chemical, Energy, Mine and General Workers' Union (ICEM); and Union Network International (UNI). These entities will be referenced by their acronyms throughout this chapter.

[10] (2003) 12 *Transport International: The Journal of the International Transport Workers' Federation* (July), available at http://www.itf.org.uk/TI/12/english.index.htm (last visited 11 December 2004).

forced labor, discrimination, child labor, and workers' representatives.[11] Many of the IFAs require transnational corporations to influence the behavior of their suppliers, co-contractors, sub-contractors, and other entities involved in the production process—which, as will be discussed further, can be difficult for the corporation. Because (unlike corporate codes of conduct) the agreements are not unilateral, but are negotiated by two parties, they contain obligations that the signatory corporation should uphold, and often call for regular monitoring meetings to assess the compliance record of the corporation. However, transnational corporate compliance with IFAs is not legally enforceable under any national or international regimes.

IFAs were first concluded in the mid-1980s, the result of social dialogue between IUF and Danone, the dairy products corporation with headquarters in France. Danone and IUF concluded five agreements between 1989 and 1997 on areas affecting the relationship between the company and its employees: (1) information exchange; (2) equal opportunities for men and women; (3) skills training; (4) trade union rights; and (5) changing business activities affecting working conditions.[12] Subsequent framework agreements were signed in the 1990s between GUFs and Accor, IKEA, Faber-Castell, Statoil, and many other transnational corporations. As of August 2004, 32 IFAs have been concluded, covering transnational corporations with total 2003 sales of $741,688.7 million and a workforce of just under 2.9 million.[13] Nearly all of them have been concluded in 2000 or later, reflecting the novelty of this mechanism.[14] Together, they cover industries as diverse as oil production, utilities provision, construction, manufacturing, retailing, cleaning, hotels, and telecommunications.

Interestingly, all except three of the IFAs concluded thus far have been with transnational corporations with headquarters in Europe.[15] This may be a result of the fact that many IFAs were established on the back and at the initiative of headquarters union activities in European Works Councils (EWCs).[16] In 1994, the European Union (EU) adopted the European Works Council Directive, in furtherance of the Agreement on Social Policy. The Directive required the member States of the EU, with the exception of the

---

[11] Hammer, above n 6, at 7–8.

[12] *Ibid* at 3.

[13] *Ibid*.

[14] *Ibid*.

[15] The exceptions are the IUF agreement with Chiquita (with headquarters in the United States); the IUF agreement with Fonterra (with headquarters in New Zealand); and the ICEM agreement with AngloGold (with headquarters in South Africa): *ibid* at 4–5.

[16] Jane Wills, 'Bargaining for the space to organize in the global economy: a review of the Accor–IUF trade union rights agreement' (2000) 9 *Review of International Political Economy* (November) 682, available at http://www.global-labour.org/Accor%20IUF%20agreement. pdf (last visited 11 December 2004).

United Kingdom, to enact legislation requiring the establishment of EWCs by September 1996. EWCs are councils established by the central management or employees of a company that transmit information from management to employees, to ensure that decisions made in a company's operations in one State affecting workers in another State are communicated to those workers.[17] The council requirement applies to companies with at least 1,000 employees within the participating EU States, and with at least 150 employees in each of two States. Importantly, companies in non-adopting countries, such as the United States or the United Kingdom, can still be bound by the legislation if they have divisions located in participating States. The councils are composed of between 3 and 30 members, one from each participating State in which the company has divisions. Employee representation on the council must be proportional to the number of employees in the company as a whole.[18] The relevance of these councils to IFAs is that, arguably, they established in Europe a background of collaborative partnership building and information sharing that provided the foundation upon which IFAs were first concluded.[19] The fact that, in Europe, the formation of these councils is legally required rather than merely voluntary suggests that strong theoretical underpinnings for the development of IFAs in Europe pre-existed the agreements themselves.

## III. THE THEORETICAL UNDERPINNINGS BEHIND IFAS

As discussed briefly in the Introduction, labor union activists have come to realize that, in the face of globalization, it is necessary to conduct industrial relations not only at the local and national level, but at an international level as well. One scholar has called this a 'multi-scalar approach' in the form of 'specific activities and interventions at a variety of scales.'[20] The idea of labor negotiation at multiple levels, and between many different parties, is the central premise behind the development of IFAs. IFAs are regarded not as a substitute for national bargaining systems, but a complement to them. They represent a way to secure recognition from the top of a transnational corporation for the rights of a multinational workforce. The IFA approach seeks to overcome problems associated with the outsourcing of production by corporations, which necessarily means that

---

[17] Council Directive 94/45/EC, 1994 OJ (L 254).

[18] Philip M Berkowitz, *The European Works Councils*, available at http://www.iln.com/articles/euroworks.html (last visited 11 December 2004).

[19] See Liv Torres and Gunnes Stein, *Global Framework Agreements: A New Tool for International Labor*, Fafo Institute for Applied Social Science (April 2003), at 38, available at http://www.fafo.no/lit/global%20framework.pdf (last visited 11 December 2004).

[20] Wills, above n 16, at 696.

workers will be located in many different divisions and factories, without the ability to connect with one another about their shared concerns and desires. By supplementing local and national efforts with international ones, IFAs will make it possible to bridge the geographic divides among workers employed by the same corporation, and to secure the same bargaining rights for all of them.

The notion of IFA complementarity—not substitutability—for national bargaining is an important one because many workers lack the means to connect with a large global union with representatives in far-away locales. Workers must continue to have access to representatives on the ground in the places where they are employed, in order to convey their concerns and goals to those in a position to negotiate. As one scholar aptly put it: 'It would be senseless to take bargaining responsibility away from those with greatest local knowledge, and the most direct accountability to the membership.'[21] As a result, IFAs are considered a way to bargain for more space within which local and national unions *themselves* can unionize. In practice, 'bargaining for space' might take the form of negotiating for the adoption of a 'neutrality policy' within an IFA, under which the transnational corporation affirms that it will not discourage or prevent employees in any part of its operations from unionizing. However, some scholars have criticized the 'bargaining for space' approach as overly reliant on the assumption that bargaining space, and trade union representatives, already exist in the workplace.[22] The substance of this argument is that there hardly seems to be a reason to push for adoption of neutrality policies where conditions for unionization are absent on the ground. The assumption of open space may indeed be unwarranted, given the quality of organization of local and national unions in many workplaces, as will be discussed in Section V. Nevertheless, this is not true in every workplace. Moreover— and more importantly—IFAs may precisely serve to stimulate the unionization at local level, by ensuring that the local union will be recognized a right to function without obstacles or reprisals on workers, and that the local management will agree to a collective bargaining process.

One practical consequence of the 'internationalization' of the labor movement is that workers and union representatives must learn to understand globalization processes, and must consult with colleagues in other countries, in order to be effective in bargaining with transnational corporations. One scholar has noted that 'international work has become the bread

---

[21] Dave Spooner, *International Framework Agreements: Implementing Workers' Rights in Global Corporations*, Global Labor Institute, at 2, available at http://www.global-labour.org/ifas.htm (last visited 11 December 2004).

[22] Terry Collingsworth, *Beyond Reports and Promises: Enforcing Universally Accepted Human Rights Standards in the Global Economy*, Analytical Summary of Achieving Global Justice Seminar (February 2003), Carnegie Council on Ethics and International Affairs, available at http://www.carnegiecouncil.org (last visited 11 December 2004).

and butter of increasing numbers of trade union representatives—down to and including those working in local offices and factories.'[23] These representatives must be skilled at communicating both with workers and with representatives in the global unions who will be negotiating the IFA. The importance to this process of collaborative interaction, and cross-border, cross-cultural, and even cross-class understanding, cannot be overemphasized.

In order to facilitate the new understanding demanded of trade union-ists, many GUFs have begun to provide trade union education programs to their affiliates. For example, the Transport and General Workers' Union in the United Kingdom has been investing in residential shop-steward courses on globalization and development, focusing on the development of IFAs as an instrument of workers' rights protection. Each course invites participants from abroad to discuss their first-hand experiences of union organization and workers' rights.[24] Programs such as these fit with the notion that IFAs are part of a collaborative, pluralistic paradigm that brings different parties together to exchange information and increase global dialogue. In such settings, the exchange of views is not just a means to the goal of improving workers' rights: it is, in itself, also a goal.

Many believe that IFAs can be of particular help to workers in the developing world, where labor legislation or existing collective agreements are either under-enforced, or non-existent.[25] One scholar has described the potential of IFAs to be a 'bridge across geographical difference' uniting labor campaigners in the developed world with workers producing goods in the developing world.[26] Focusing on dialogue among the various parties, she notes, is a way of ensuring that the IFAs actually benefit the appropriate persons—workers—rather than the campaigners who are directly involved in negotiating with transnational corporations. The agreements will mean that negotiators will no longer have to make assumptions about what is in the best interests of workers, because increased dialogue and interaction will mean that those workers can better speak for themselves.[27] At the same time, the hope is that IFAs will also bridge differences between workers in the developing world and workers in the developed world, dispelling notions that the jobs of the latter group must be sacrificed in order to promote labor rights for the former, or that these groups compete against one another for scarce jobs and that such competition necessarily shall entail sacrificing either labor rights, or employment. In the long term, workers located in different parts of the

---

[23] Spooner, above n 21, at 1.
[24] *Ibid* at 6.
[25] Nilsson, above n 3, at 24.
[26] Wills, above n 16, at 678.
[27] *Ibid*.

globe will develop permanent alliances that, together, can exert greater leverage than if each locale were negotiating with a transnational employer by itself. In this way, the IFA becomes not only a labor rights enforcement mechanism, but rather, what one report has called 'a form of international social dialogue.'[28]

Similarly, IFAs are also regarded as a way to enhance trade union cooperation with external parties such as NGOs. Scholars have acknowledged that both NGOs and trade unions have an interest in promoting labor rights, but that sometimes their efforts conflict. For example, NGO attempts to press transnational corporations into adopting codes of conduct have, in the past, provided those companies with an excuse not to negotiate IFAs with trade unions.[29] However, there is no theoretical reason why NGOs should necessarily be an opponent, rather than a partner, of unions in the labor rights movement. Rather, NGOs can work in tandem with labor unions to create conditions favorable to the negotiation of IFAs.

For example, the IFA between IUF and Chiquita was negotiated in conjunction with a public campaign waged by several NGOs in the United States and Europe who sought to draw consumer attention to the banana industry crisis. The crisis began as a result of the EU's 1993 decision to favor bananas produced in Africa, the Caribbean, and the Pacific, rather than in Latin America which accounted for more than 72% of banana exports.[30] This resulted in an oversupply of bananas in the world market, and falling banana prices. The leading transnational corporations in the banana industry, including Chiquita, began to increasingly outsource production to low-pay supplier plantations in Ecuador and along the coast of Guatemala in order to solve their economic difficulties. This, in turn, undermined the bargaining position of the local Latin American union, COLSIBA.

In 1998, several NGOs launched an international campaign to expose publicly working conditions in Chiquita's supplier plantations.[31] They targeted supermarket chains and 'big box' stores, insisting that these retailers hold Chiquita responsible for squashing union activity, using pesticides harmful to workers, and other harmful labor practices.

---

[28] *Organizing For Social Justice: Global Report under the Follow-Up to the ILO Declaration on Fundamental Principles and Rights at Work*, Report of the Director-General, International Labor Conference, 92nd Session (2004), available at http://www.ilo.org/dyn/declaris/DECLARATIONWEB.DOWNLOAD_BLOB?Var_DocumentID=2502 (last visited 11 December 2004).

[29] Riisgaard, above n 1, at 1. See also David Gallin, *Trade Unions and NGOs: A Necessary Partnership for Social Development*, United Nations Research Institute for Social Development (June 2000), at 26, available at http://www.globalpolicy.org/ngos/role/globalact/business/2001/0101tu.htm (last visited 11 December 2004).

[30] Riisgaard, above n 1, at 9.

[31] *Ibid*.

Information regarding Chiquita's conduct also appeared in the *Cincinnati Enquirer*, the home town newspaper of the corporation.[32] COLSIBA participated in this campaign alongside solidarity groups in the United States and Europe such as Banana Link and Euroban, holding press conferences, launching a website to publicize the campaign, and demonstrating in front of supermarkets selling Chiquita bananas.[33] These coordinated efforts are representative of the ways in which trade unions and NGOs can act as partners, cross-fertilizing one another's efforts to protect the rights of workers employed by transnational corporations. In the Chiquita example, mutual organization between the union and the NGOs proved effective. In response to the campaign, Chiquita sought to make corporate social responsibility a part of its image, adopting a range of initiatives including the signing of an IFA with COLSIBA in 2001. The agreement, the first of its kind in the agricultural sector, affirmed the right of workers to bargain collectively and to be represented by an independent and democratic trade union. It commits Chiquita to the ILO 'core' conventions, plus Convention No 135 on protection and facilities for workers' representatives.[34] The 'socially responsible' image that became a part of Chiquita's product as a result of the campaign was not only a way to change public perception of the company, but part of a business strategy to increase its market share and differentiate the corporation from its competitors.[35] Public pressure exerted on the corporation by the joint union—NGO campaign proved to be the kindling behind the negotiation of the IFA.[36]

## IV. INTERNATIONAL FRAMEWORK AGREEMENTS IN PRACTICE

Given that the majority of IFAs have been negotiated only within the past four years, there is little from which to draw conclusions about the success of their implementation—that is, whether the collaborative paradigm has proven workable in practice. However, the evidence that exists is still worth evaluating. Thus far scholars have analyzed, in varying depth, four of the IFAs negotiated between global unions and transnational corporations: (1) Accor; (2) Chiquita; (3) Statoil; and (4) DaimlerChrysler. I will consider each of these agreements in turn, examining the way in which the IFA negotiated with the corporation has been tested, and how well it has withstood labor conflicts and other challenges.

---

[32] *Ibid* at 11.

[33] *Ibid*.

[34] *Ibid* at 12. See also 'IUF, Chiquita and Trade Union Rights' (2001) *International Union of Foodworkers Bulletin* (September), available at http://www.usleap.org/banana/chiquita/iufarticleonglobalagreement9-01.html (last visited 11 December 2004).

[35] Riisgaard, above n 1, at 11.

[36] I will return to the question of the successful implementation of the IFA with Chiquita in Section IV.

## 1. Accor

Accor is a French-owned hotel and associated services company.[37] It is one of the largest groups in the hotel, catering, and tourism industry, best known for its Sofitel, Novotel, Motel 6, and Red Roof Inn chains of hotels.[38] Accor employs more than 120,000 people in 142 countries.[39] Traditionally the hotel sector has been difficult for unions to organize in the developed world due to transitory labor and high turnover; however, in the developing world, hotel workers are relatively well unionized.[40] The trade union rights agreement signed between Accor and IUF in 1995 — the result of relationships formed between the union and a willing Human Resources Director—endorses workers' right to unionize and pledges that Accor will not interfere with this right.[41] The agreement is reviewed annually at a meeting of Accor's EWC, which has delegates from Belgium, Germany, the Netherlands, Amsterdam, Spain, Portugal, France, Switzerland, and Italy.[42]

Accor's IFA has met with mixed success in its various locations. In the United Kingdom, hotel managers in Accor properties in London recognized that every worker had the right to unionize, but refused to allow recruitment facilities and grievance representation. Leafleting by the local union proved useless, because many workers were on short-term placements from Continental Europe, and therefore they were not interested in unionization. Similar problems have occurred in New Zealand, where union organizers have not been able to back up violations of the IFA with organizing activity.[43] In Philadelphia, a local union sought to unionize the Sofitel's 270 workers. When management resisted by hiring attorneys and publishing anti-union literature, the IUF intervened on behalf of the local union, pointing out that such company practice violated the IFA. However, workers were frightened off by the company's behavior, and decided not to pursue unionization after all. In all three of these situations —London, New Zealand, and Philadelphia—the problem was that without local union activity, the IUF was unable to force management to recognize the right to unionize.[44]

---

[37] Wills, above n 16, at 684.

[38] *Ibid*.

[39] *Ibid*.

[40] *Ibid*.

[41] *Ibid* at 685.

[42] *Ibid* at 686–87. Wills notes that the IUF 'is successfully using the EWC as part of its weaponry for promoting union organization across the group'—an idea that supports the hypothesis that Europe, unlike the United States, possesses legislative conditions particularly favorable to the implementation of IFAs.

[43] *Ibid* at 688.

[44] *Ibid* at 689.

However, Accor's IFA has been more successfully implemented in other locales where union activity is more robust, and inter-union alliances are relied upon. For example, Australia had adopted legislation in 1996 allowing employer to negotiate 'non-union' collective agreements which need not obey national labor standards with existing employees. These agreements, which Accor began to negotiate in 1997, provided an escape hatch for Accor not to comply with the IFA. In response, two national unions—the hotel industry union and the construction industry union, which was being denied access to construction sites for the purpose of unionization—together held demonstrations at new Accor building sites, accusing Accor of violating the IFA. In the end, a memorandum was signed between all of the parties to ensure compliance with the IFA. In the memo, Accor agreed not to pursue the allowed non-union collective agreements for 18 months.[45]

Similarly, in New York, IUF successfully intervened to replace union-hostile management at Novotel. Labor relations in the New York hotel industry had been hostile following a city-wide strike in 1985. Novotel management forced the local labor union to undertake a National Labor Relations Board (NLRB) election in order to be recognized as the collective bargaining representative of the hotel's employees. Prior to the vote, management held anti-union meetings, seeking to intimidate the workers as much as possible. They succeeded in preventing the union from organizing at Novotel. Only seven years later, in 1994, did the local union seek to negotiate with Novotel again. This time, the union won the NLRB election, but management refused to acknowledge the result. The union filed a class action lawsuit against Accor, and won at the district court level, but Accor appealed. Simultaneously, IUF contacted the local union to alert them to the provisions of the IFA with Accor. As a result of this intervention by the global union—and a visit by local union representatives to the Accor EWC meeting in Geneva—Accor's European managers decided to appoint new management in North America, and to negotiate with the local union in New York. It was the approach to top Accor management in Europe—through the global union, IUF—that made resolution of the conflict possible.

### 2. Chiquita

The IFA concluded between IUF and Chiquita reveals many of the same implementation problems as the Accor agreement: it has operated to the advantage of workers in workplaces that are already well organized, but has worked less well in locales where workers lack the opportunity, or

---

[45] *Ibid* at 690–91.

lack the structures, that make unionization possible. In a recent study examining the implementation of the Chiquita IFA in Costa Rica, Guatemala, Honduras, and Nicaragua, researchers found that Chiquita management had not widely informed workers of the negotiated agreement. Dissemination of information regarding the IFA was better in Honduras through radio programs, leaflets, and workshops, but in the other countries, distribution was sporadic and limited in scope.[46] In all countries surveyed, the information that did reach workers came from unions and not management. However, union members were the ones to learn of the IFA, not workers who were not unionized.[47] This problem is certainly an obstacle to the idea that the IFA will be useful in increasing unionization.

In Honduras, implementation of the IFA did contribute to the formation of a new local union at a Chiquita supplier, the Buenos Amigos plantation.[48] Importantly, organizing efforts at this plantation began nearly a year before the IFA was signed, with union organizers using the IFA as further leverage to gain access to workers and educate them about their rights.[49] This was not the case in Chiquita's other locales, which may suggest that the positive Honduras experience is an isolated phenomenon.

The Chiquita study also revealed an apparent disconnection between the way management and workers viewed the implementation of the IFA, with management believing it to be successful at protecting core labor rights, but workers and union representatives identifying repeated violations of the agreement.[50] Violations included discrimination against union affiliates, discrimination against women, and denial of plantation access to union representatives. These problems were even more acute at supplier plantations not owned by Chiquita.[51] In fact, on only two out of three supplier plantations surveyed were managers aware of the existence of the IFA.[52] The problem of supplier compliance with IFAs is a particularly serious one in light of increased outsourcing of the production process, as will be discussed in Section V.

The union involved in the negotiation of the Chiquita IFA, COLSIBA, also faced internal problems that made successful implementation of the IFA difficult. The IFA provides for a Review Committee, composed of four IUF/COLSIBA representatives and four Chiquita representatives, to convene periodically to discuss the implementation of the agreement. However, the Committee did not successfully respond to complaints

---

[46] Riisgaard, above n 1, at 13.
[47] *Ibid.*
[48] *Ibid.*
[49] *Ibid.*
[50] *Ibid.*
[51] *Ibid.*
[52] *Ibid.*

received from local unions, even where it discussed in its meetings the issues that those unions had raised. Neither did the Committee distribute reports of its meetings to the local unions, several of which were unsure of the Committee's function in enforcing the IFA.[53] These basic communication problems seem to undermine the collaborative theory from which IFAs are derived. They suggest that, in practice, it has proven more difficult to unite the different 'teams' involved in IFA compliance, or even the varying 'players' within a particular team, such as local and global unions or local unions from different parts of a company's operations.

One particular manifestation of this 'lack of experience in inter-union cooperation'[54] in the Chiquita context was hostility and distrust felt by the local Guatemalan union, UNSITRAGUA, towards the IUF and other local union signatories to the IFA such as SITRABI. During the civil war in Guatemala, UNSITRAGUA and SITRABI were at opposing ends of the political spectrum, and both continue to harbor doubts about considering the other a partner.[55] In addition, some unions regard others as too progressive, intent on revolutionizing industrial relations rather than forming partnerships with both employers and more moderate union elements.[56] This may be the attitude taken by UNSITRAGUA towards IUF, its global partner. Finally, enduring union skepticism at the willingness of Chiquita to improve its labor record after decades of exploitation and ill treatment has also plagued the successful implementation of the IFA.[57] Riisgaard has aptly described these problems as resulting from 'a lack of experience in functioning as a professional partner in an international agreement,'[58] a characterization that points back to the goal of IFAs — collaborative relationships built over time between global allies.

### 3. Statoil

Statoil is an oil and gas company based in Norway, with 24,000 employees, and operations in 28 countries.[59] It is one of the world's biggest suppliers of crude oil, and one of the major suppliers of natural gas to the European market.[60] In 1998, Statoil entered into an IFA with ICEM and the Norwegian Oil and Petrochemical Workers' Union (NOPEF). The IFA enabled ICEM to intervene in an ongoing dispute at one of Statoil's long-term contractors,

---

[53] *Ibid* at 15.
[54] *Ibid* at 16.
[55] *Ibid*.
[56] *Ibid*.
[57] *Ibid*.
[58] *Ibid*.
[59] *Statoil in Brief*, available at http://www.statoil.com (last visited 11 December 2004).
[60] *Ibid*.

the American Crown Central Petroleum Refinery in Pasadena, Texas. In 1996, American Crown had locked out 256 workers after wage negotiations broke down. For five years, the company employed temporary labor to refine the oil. But thereafter, NOPEF and ICEM were able to use the IFA negotiated in the interim period to make contact with local trade unionists in Texas. The dispute was resolved in January 2001 when Statoil made American Crown's refining contract conditional on the re-establishment of normal relations with the local union.[61] While the available research does not document the conditions that made successful resolution of this dispute possible, it is not a stretch to hypothesize severable favorable factors: (1) an active local union engaged in wage negotiations long before the existence of the IFA; (2) harmonious relations between that union and its Norwegian counterpart; and (3) a global union, ICEM, that was willing to bridge the geographic and psychological distance between the two, and to leverage its position as an international signatory with access to the top management of Statoil. In addition, the willingness of Statoil to put pressure on its contractor to comply with the IFA proved key to the resolution of the labor conflict.

### 4. DaimlerChrysler

DaimlerChrysler, a German automotive company with 362,100 employees in 17 countries, and 2003 revenues of $171.9 billion, signed an IFA with the IMF in 2002.[62] The agreement facilitated the resolution of a conflict between one of DaimlerChrysler's suppliers in Turkey that was planning to terminate 200 workers. The conclusion of the IFA encouraged the supplier to sign its first collective agreement with the local union, which guaranteed full-time work and pay to the majority of the workers while providing a 'social plan' for those who could not be retained by the company.[63] As with Statoil, the resolution of this labor conflict depended on collaborative relationships between DaimlerChrysler, the Turkish supplier, the local Turkish union, and the IMF, and upon the effective exchange of information in order to avert worker lay-offs and build a stronger network for the resolution of future conflicts.

### V. PROBLEMS AND POTENTIAL

The four examples raised in the previous section –Accor, Chiquita, Statoil, and DaimlerChrysler—illustrated that IFAs, when implemented, have had a mixed record in terms of their impact on the rights of workers employed

---

[61] *Organizing For Social Justice*, above n 28, at 75.
[62] *Company at a Glance*, available at http://www.daimlerchrysler.com (last visited 11 December 2004); Organizing For Social Justice, above n 28, at 75.
[63] *Organizing For Social Justice*, above n 28, at 75–76.

by transnational corporations. The first problem is that IFAs are less success-ful where labor relations between the local union and the transnational cor-poration are not already well established. If unions are not accustomed to working with management and engaging in a process of negotiation over fundamental needs, it is difficult for them to push for significant change under an IFA. A second problem, closely related to the first, is that the suc-cess of an IFA is largely dependent on the quality of organization of the local unions impacted by the agreement. Many local unions lack both experience and financial and human resources; they may fail to consult with other affiliated unions that are more 'progressive' in mindset, or they may suffer from other internal problems. On the corporate side, the diffi-culties of securing supplier compliance and unfavorable corporate atti-tudes are two other obstacles that often distinguish the reality from the theory of IFA implementation.

Regrettably, the problems described above are not limited to the imple-mentation stage. These same obstacles have manifested themselves when global unions seek to negotiate an IFA in the first place. For example, few IFAs have been negotiated in the garment and textile industries, sectors with characteristically poor labor-management relations and union organ-ization. Textiles, clothing, and footwear (TCF) are characterized by com-plex supply relationships among various transnational corporations: between (1) merchandisers or retailers, such as Nike and Target; (2) supply chain management companies that source and ship bulk orders on the merchandisers' behalf; (3) subcontracted supplier companies that special-ize in the manufacture of raw materials and other component parts; (4) sub-subcontractors; and (5) in some cases, home workers. [64] In the garment industry alone, there are approximately 300,000 supplier firms operating in developing countries.[65] Often, only the direct contracting firm knows of the locations of suppliers and the extent of sub-subcontracting and home working. The transnational corporation most likely to be the candidate for negotiating an IFA—Nike, for example—would not be aware of, much less have control over, these related entities and their activities.

Codes of conduct have been signed in the TCF industries that attempt to express a set of 'corporate responsibility' principles by which the transnational corporation intends to conduct its business, and to which it intends to hold its suppliers as well. Doug Miller, a scholar who has studied

---

[64] Doug Miller, 'Preparing for the Long Haul: Negotiating International Framework Agreements in the Global Textile, Garment and Footwear Sector' (2004) 4 *Global Social Policy* 215, at 217–18. See also *Global Companies, Global Unions*, available at http://www.itglwf.org (last visited 11 December 2004).

[65] Miller, above n 64, at 218. Levi Strauss, for example, subcontracts to approximately 540 companies worldwide, and has supply contracts with Cone Mills and Burlington (denim), Coats plc (thread), and Tibbet & Britten (transport and distribution): *ibid*.

the application of IFAs to these industries, estimates that there are 10,000 different ethical codes currently in place.[66] However, these codes of conduct can often create their own set of problems for the negotiation of IFAs. They often provide an excuse for transnational corporations not to negotiate IFAs with global unions, on the rationale that the corporation is already engaged in the business of corporate social responsibility. These kinds of company initiatives, Miller notes, are 'inappropriate policy tools for addressing the problems of sweated labor along supply chains.'[67] Consequently, the proliferation of such initiatives in the TCF industries can mean the negotiation of fewer IFAs.

In June 2000, ITGLWF, a global union affiliated with the TCF industries, conducted a study to ascertain which transnational corporations in the textile, garment, and footwear industries would respond most favorably to the possibility of negotiating an IFA. The union conducted Internet-based research, attended EWC meetings, and corresponded with human resources personnel in certain 'target' corporations. Miller has documented the results of the study for six of these targets. Some of the results are indicative of the problems that continue to plague the negotiation of IFAs, not just in the TCF sector, but throughout the economy.[68] They suggest that IFAs are not a 'quick fix' to the problem of labor abuses.

Company A, a garment subcontractor, had a history of union dialogue (including an existing EWC) and was open to negotiation with ITGLWF. However, a setback occurred when Company A's parent, a 100% owner of the shares of Company A, decided to sell off some of its constituent parts. The trade union and employee representatives of the EWC became preoccupied with job losses, and did not want to pressure management on the desirability of entering into negotiations with ITGLWF. Eventually, a memorandum of understanding was signed that recognized ITGLWF as a legitimate union representing company A's workers throughout the company, but in 2003 the company became the target of a takeover attempt, throwing the IFA negotiations into limbo.[69] This example highlights the problem of unforeseen business or financial setbacks, coupled with the consequent threats to job stability, which can derail the negotiation of IFAs. During such volatile periods, the desirability of collective bargaining rights and health and safety standards is regarded as secondary to the need for continued employment itself.

Company B, a footwear manufacturer with an uneven labor relations history, had 70 per cent of its production in Chinese factories. Current international trade union policy prevents official approaches being made

---

[66] *Ibid* at 220.
[67] *Ibid* at 223.
[68] *Ibid* at 224.
[69] *Ibid* at 226.

to the All China Federation of Trade Unions, and the International Confederation of Free Trade Unions, ICFTU, does not regard the All China Federation of Trade Unions as a free independent trade union.[70] Therefore, ITGLWF was unable to claim legitimacy on behalf of the company's workers, dooming direct negotiation of an IFA with the company. However, ITGLWF sought to circumvent this problem by proposing an IFA indirectly, through an umbrella organization, the World Federation of Sporting Goods Industries, to which company B's merchandiser clients belong.[71] This innovative approach looked promising in part because many of those merchandisers possessed codes of conduct whose requirements extended to company B itself, suggesting that they might be open to the possibility of an IFA. However, as discussed above, the existence of codes of conduct do not always suggest that IFAs will be regarded favorably by transnational corporations.

Company C was a German textiles company with operations in Europe, Southern Africa, China, and North America. At a workshop designed to organize the company's main centers of production, the owner of the company announced that no overarching guidelines would govern the various operations of the company. However, a coordinating committee with trade representatives from several different countries was soon set up, and the representatives decided to embark on an international workplace petition campaign in favor of an IFA. An information leaflet was distributed to German workers on the need for the IFA. Simultaneously, the German affiliate of the ITGWLF filed a complaint with Germany's labor court to force company C to comply with a statute requiring the establishment of a supervisory board with union representation on it. As a result, the owner of company C was pressured 'on both the international and domestic industrial relations fronts.'[72] He met with a senior member of the German union's executive, who managed to get a commitment from the owner to negotiate an IFA, in exchange for a cessation of the leafleting campaign. The initial IFA draft submitted by the owner lacked bite, and the ITGWLF submitted a counterproposal. However, talks were delayed when the labor court forced the owner of company C to settle the claim and convene a new supervisory board with union representation on it. The IFA is planned as an agenda item at the first meeting of the new board.[73] This example illustrates that the negotiations process for IFAs may be lengthy and fraught with setbacks; there are no quick results.

---

[70] *Ibid.*
[71] *Ibid* at 227.
[72] *Ibid* at 228.
[73] *Ibid* at 229.

Company D was a global apparel corporation with headquarters in the United States. It had only limited trade union presence in many of its overseas operations, and increasingly outsourced production to Central America and Eastern Europe. Forced under the terms of the European Works Councils Directive to establish an EWC, that body was rendered useless by restructuring in company D's European operations. Finally, company D identified its participation in the World Responsible Apparel Production factory certification scheme—a 'code of conduct' of sorts—as a reason why it did not need to negotiate with ITGWLF. The company received low priority as a potential target for negotiations.[74]

Company E, a European company specializing in engineered and exotic textiles, had a 'clear commitment to social dialogue' in the form of involvement in several EU initiatives, including the European Employers Association for Clothing and Textiles. However, company E decided not to pursue IFA talks with ITGWLF, claiming that the company's 'Charta' on employment standards dealt sufficiently with workers' rights in all of its locations. This is just another example of a corporation's making use of an existing human rights mechanism to justify its unwillingness to negotiate an IFA.

Finally, company F, a European merchandiser, was having some problems with employees in its supply chains. It indicated a willingness to discuss training on freedom of association and collective bargaining with ITGWLF. When the global union suggested an IFA, management resisted, claiming that it already had its own set of standards and that it did not want to impose further on its suppliers. The company also wanted ITG-WLF to guarantee good governance of its affiliates, a promise that the union could not deliver since union democracy is the sovereign concern of each affiliate.

Miller's study paints a gloomy picture about the odds of negotiating an IFA in circumstances where union organization is poor, labor–management relations strained, and corporate supply relationships complex. He notes an 'ill-preparedness on the part of the ITGWLF's affiliates in a number of cases' and identifies several resource problems that hinder local unions in the negotiations process: 'no dedicated research capacity of their own,' 'the absence of on-line computers with a constant supply of electricity in some countries,' and 'a lack of commitment on the part of coordinators to report in news or pass on information.'[75]

However, Miller also acknowledges that these kinds of problems were not found across all of the target corporations. Negotiations with companies A and C reached a substantial level of dialogue, and showed the potential of continuing past the duration of the study. Company F recognized the

[74] *Ibid.*
[75] *Ibid* at 231.

value of communication with the labor movement; its objection to negotiation was based upon a different question of union governance. Importantly, none of the target companies in Miller's study—not even company B, with the majority of its production in China—closed the door entirely to the possibility of negotiating an IFA in the future.

Miller also identified features of the IFA negotiation process discovered through the study that offer the most opportunity for success: a 'multi-level research effort,' 'profiling, awareness raising and union network building,' 'a flexible approach on the part of the [global union],' 'coordinated campaigns' between unions and other groups with like goals, and an 'internationalist process'.[76] These qualities proved useful to each and every negotiation pursued by ITGWLF. The fact that these factors created the most favorable conditions for the negotiation of IFAs suggest that the collaborative paradigm envisioned in Section II is beginning to manifest itself, if slowly. At minimum, it is apparent that scholars are beginning to recognize the intrinsic value of inter-union and union–management dialogue, across multiple workplaces and geographic locales. One scholar notes: 'The development of IFAs—albeit still in its infancy, and fraught with difficult problems—offers a practical strategy for building an international trade union movement.'[77] Others have argued that IFAs 'constitute not the least an important framework for further dialogue between management and trade unions at the local level, and not the least at the international level.'[78] This kind of regard for the value of pluralistic, multi-scalar interaction will, over time, trickle down to those individuals who are themselves participants in the formation of the agreements.

## VI. CONCLUSION

On balance, IFAs, although beset by shortcomings in the short term, still remain a strong mechanism for the protection of global labor rights in the long term. Their negotiation—even if not always fruitful—brings together multiple constituencies, fosters partnerships between parties that would perhaps otherwise be opponents, and contributes to a global exchange of dialogue on multiple levels: local, national, and international. IFAs should and can be understood as an initial step in fostering international dialogue and collaboration between transnational corporations, global unions, and local union representatives regarding the problems that workers face in a globalized economy. Once these relationships and conversations begin to form, the parties can work towards more concrete

---

[76] *Ibid* at 231–32.
[77] Spooner, above n 21, at 7.
[78] Torres and Gunnes, above n 19, at 16.

results in terms of creating collective bargaining opportunities, raising health and safety standards, and implementing other labor protection mechanisms.

Most significantly, the examples discussed in this chapter indicate that the 'collaborative paradigm' upon which IFAs are based takes time to develop. It is unrealistic—particularly at this early stage in the development of IFAs—to expect uniformly favorable results across workplaces with varying socioeconomics, trade union cohesion, and corporate culture. Although the International Organization of Employers identifies a dichotomy between the negotiation of IFAs as an 'industrial relations exercise,' and the agreements as 'a vehicle for deepening dialogue,' arguably the agreements can be both at once.[79] As articulated by one scholar, 'leading global enterprises and trade unions can weave together new negotiating patterns that have considerable potential' to change the relationship between transnational corporations and human rights.[80] Despite the initial setbacks that IFAs have faced, the goal of international social dialogue as a means to better labor rights for the world's workers remains both a laudable and a realistic one, even if best suited for the long term. At this early stage, there is no reason to believe that the promise of IFAs—to deliver improved labor and health standards through a voluntary mechanism in which multiple constituencies can participate—will not be borne out.

---

[79] 2003 Annual Report of the International Organization of Employers at 7, available at http://www.ioe-emp.org/ioe_emp/pdf/IOE%20Annual%20Report%202003.pdf (last visited 11 December 2004).

[80] *Organizing for Social Justice*, above n 28, at 76.

# Part III

# Imposing Direct Obligations on Transnational Corporations under International Law

# 8

# The Illegal Exploitation of Natural Resources in the Democratic Republic of Congo: A Case Study on Corporate Complicity in Human Rights Abuses

ASIMINA-MANTO PAPAIOANNOU

## I. INTRODUCTION

INTERNAL ARMED CONFLICTS in countries rich in natural resources constitute a major source of human rights violations worldwide.[1] Convincing arguments have been put forth that countries with abundant natural resources are more susceptible to violent conflicts than those without, and that the key factor behind many of today's wars is not ideological and political differences, but mainly greed and the struggle for control over 'lootable' natural wealth.[2] Without underestimating the importance of other features present in resource-rich countries of the developing world, such as weak rule of law, widespread corruption, an ethos of impunity, and repressive governance,[3] it appears that the availability of valuable commodities plays an important role in the outbreak of conflicts, and most certainly in the financing of them, often leading to a vicious circle. Legal or illegal exploitation of resources accords the means for financing the war efforts, which in turn creates the conditions that permit continuous plunder of those resources.[4] In this unending cycle of exploitation, conflicts, and human rights violations, a substantial number of transnational corporations (hereinafter TNCs) have contributed to the maintenance of resource-based conflicts in various ways, thus posing

---

[1] Arvind Ganesan and Alex Vines, *Engine of War: Resources, Greed, and the Predatory State* (Human Rights Watch, 2004), available at http://www.hrw.org/wr2k4/14.htm

[2] Michael Renner, Natural Resources and Conflict: A Deadly Relationship, *USA Today*, July 2003, at 20, 21.

[3] See Ganesan and Vines, above n 1.

[4] See Renner, above n 2.

questions about enhancing the mechanisms of holding them accountable and promoting corporate social responsibility in conflict areas.

The Democratic Republic of Congo (hereinafter 'the DRC'), a central African country blessed – or cursed – with a distinctive biodiversity and immense mineral and forest reserves,[5] has not been exempted from this fate of illegal resource extraction, brutal conflict, and severe devastation of the civilian population. The war in the DRC, which started in August 1998, has cost more than three million lives – the highest death toll in any war since World War II – and has rendered the country one of the poorest in the world.[6]

As a response to prevalent apprehension about the link between the exploitation of the country's natural resources and the continuation of the conflict, the United Nations Security Council employed a Panel of Experts (hereinafter 'the Panel') as a fact-finding body.[7] It is the aim of this chapter to review the conclusions of the Panel with respect to the role of States and, more significantly, TNCs, in fuelling the war and its subsequent human rights violations. Focus will be placed on the working methods of the Panel and on its overall performance, in order to assess the advantages of establishing such a body and to detect the relevant drawbacks.

After completing this appraisal of the Panel's work, next there will be an examination of the Organization for Economic Co-operation and Development (hereinafter OECD) Guidelines for Multinational Enterprises.[8] The Panel used these guidelines as a yardstick in evaluating companies' involvement in the DRC, and the reaction of countries that have subscribed to the OECD Guidelines will also be assessed. A short reference will also be made to the International Criminal Court (hereinafter 'the ICC') and its launch of investigations into crimes that occurred in the DRC after the establishment of the Court.

## II. HISTORICAL BACKGROUND

The situation in the DRC first began to deteriorate in 1994, when hundreds of thousands of refugees fled into the country due to the war in neighboring Rwanda.[9] The situation further degenerated in 1996, when

---

[5] See Report of the Panel of Experts on the Illegal Exploitation of Natural Resources and Other Forms of Wealth of the Democratic Republic of the Congo, UN doc S/2001/357, 12 April 2001 [hereinafter '2001 Report'], at 6.

[6] Rights & Accountability In Development, *Unanswered Questions: Companies, Conflict and The Democratic Republic of Congo* 1 (2004), available at http://www.unites.uqam.ca/grama/pdf/RAID-DRC_Ex-Summary.pdf

[7] See Statement by the President of the Security Council, UN doc S/PRST/2000/20, 2 June 2000.

[8] *OECD Guidelines for Multinational Enterprises* (revision 2000), available at http://www.oecd.org/dataoecd/56/36/1922428.pdf [hereinafter 'OECD Guidelines'].

[9] 2001 Report, above n 5.

war broke out between Zairian government forces and the Alliance of Democratic Forces for the Liberation of Congo-Zaire (AFDL), commanded by Laurent-Désiré Kabila and backed by Angolan, Rwandan, and Ugandan troops.[10] In May 1997 the war came to an end with the toppling of President Mobutu Sese Seko's 30-year rule, and Laurent Kabila's ascension to the Presidency.[11]

'Ultimately though, international corporations were the ones whose influence was critical in reshaping the political landscape of the country.'[12] Even at the early stages of the rebellion, Laurent Kabila, in order rapidly to generate revenue for the AFDL, negotiated deals with foreign investors, and gave these priority over previous agreements signed by President Mobutu.[13] He also granted concessions arbitrarily, thus demonstrating the same patterns of 'unaccountability, corruption and patronage' as his predecessors.[14] This close relationship between the AFDL and corporations meant that the formation of a new government was affected from the beginning by the eagerness of the AFDL to guarantee beneficial agreements over the country's natural resources.[15]

President Laurent Kabila did not prove to meet investors' expectations, however. They were alarmed by his decision to nationalize a key railway, his expression to United States diplomats that he favored extensive Stateowned projects, and generally with his leftist background.[16] At the same time his efforts to control the influence of Rwanda, Uganda, and their corporate backers adversely affected his relationship with these former allies.[17] President Kabila commanded all foreign troops to leave the country in July 1998, and one month later, in August 1998, Rwanda and Uganda invaded the DRC, this time as Kabila's enemies.[18]

The second Congolese war involved Zimbabwe, Angola, and Namibia on the side of the DRC government, and Uganda, Rwanda, and Burundi on the side of various rebel groups.[19] Again, investors began to construct

---

[10] *Ibid.*

[11] Rights & Accountability In Development, above n 6, at 10.

[12] Dena Montague, 'Stolen Goods: Coltan and Conflict in the Democratic Republic of Congo' (2002) 22 *SAIS Review* 103, at 109.

[13] *Ibid.*

[14] Addendum to the Report of the Panel of Experts on the Illegal Exploitation of Natural Resources and Other Forms of Wealth of the Democratic Republic of the Congo, UN doc S/2001/1072, 13 November 2001 [hereinafter '2001 Addendum'], at 5; see also Montague, above n 12, at 109.

[15] Montague, above n 12, at 110–11.

[16] *Ibid* at 111.

[17] See Colette Braeckman, 'The Looting of the Congo', (2004) *New Internationalist,* 1 May, at 13.

[18] Rights & Accountability In Development, above n 6, at 10.

[19] The Rwandan Patriotic Army (RPA) has supported the Congolese Rally for Democracy, while Uganda has supported a number of rebel groups in the east and the north part of the country: Congolese Rally for Democracy–Liberation Movement (RCD–ML), Congo Liberation Movement (MLC), Congo Liberation Front (FLC), and RCD-National. All these armies have been fighting not only against the DRC government, but also against each

a close relationship with the new rebel leaders and continued the model of treating rebel-occupied territory as de facto sovereign States open for investment.[20]

In July 1999 the Lusaka Ceasefire Agreement was signed by the main participants in the war, and a United Nations body was appointed to monitor the ceasefire lines. However, the peace did not hold and the country was split between four alliances backed by foreign armies.[21] In January 2001 President Laurent Kabila was assassinated and his son, Joseph Kabila, acceded to power.[22] In spring 2002 in Sun City, South Africa, two of the main rebel groups agreed to a peace deal with the DRC government, while Rwanda and Uganda each signed bilateral agreements that resulted in the withdrawal of their troops from the country in October 2002 and May 2003, respectively.[23] In April 2003 an 'All Inclusive Agreement on the Transitional Government' was signed, and President Joseph Kabila designated a transitional government in June 2003 to rule until the first elections in 2005.[24]

In the meantime, the long-suffering Congolese continue to subsist on an average wage of 10 dollars a month, often walking several hours a day to seek work and never knowing in the morning if they will eat that night.[25] And in the eastern regions of Ituri and Kivu, there are still many thousands of armed fighters who make their living primarily by holding local inhabitants to ransom.[26]

### III. UNITED NATIONS PANEL OF EXPERTS

In the context of the devastating war in the DRC and the immense humanitarian crisis that it generated for the Congolese people, the United Nations Security Council in June 2000 authorized the Secretary-General to establish a five-member Panel of Experts, for a six-month period, with the mandate to 'follow up on reports and collect information on all activities of illegal exploitation of natural resources and other forms of wealth' in

---

other: Jeroen Cuvelier and Tim Raeymaekers, International Peace Information Service, *European Companies and the Coltan Trade: An Update, part 2*, (2002), at 5, available at www.ipisresearch.be/download.php?id=61. See also Amnesty International, *Democratic Republic of the Congo—'Our Brothers who Help Kill us'—Economic Exploitation and Human Rights Abuses in the East* (2003), available at http://web.amnesty.org/library/Index/ENGAFR620102003?open&of=ENG-UGA

[20] Montague, above n 12, at 106.
[21] Rights & Accountability In Development, above n 6, at 10.
[22] *Ibid*.
[23] *Ibid* at 2.
[24] *Ibid*.
[25] Braeckman, above n 17.
[26] *Ibid*.

the DRC and, most importantly, to 'research and analyze' the relationship between this exploitation and the prolongation of the war.[27]

The Panel was established in Nairobi in September 2000, and due to the particular complexity of the issues that it was commissioned to deal with, its mandate was extended four times, with the final extension lasting until October 2003.[28] During this period of time, the Panel submitted three reports, together with two interim reports.[29]

What should be stressed from the outset is that the Panel was not a judicial but a fact-finding body, without any 'recourse to judicial authority to subpoena testimony or documents.'[30] Therefore, all the information that the Panel gathered was given to them on a completely voluntary basis, while, according to its statement, the Panel attempted to cross-check every piece of information it obtained and to engage in a comparative analysis of the received data in order to come to a better and more thorough understanding of the issues.[31] During the three-year period of its work, the Panel visited countries directly involved in the conflict as well as countries involved in the transit and end-use of DRC resources. It also met with governmental and military representatives, interviewed members of the various rebel groups as well as civilians and non-governmental organizations (NGOs), collected information from United Nations agencies and numerous international organizations, gathered documentation from several official and secondary sources, talked to companies and private individuals, and, in general, accessed a broad variety of sources in order to fulfill its mandate.[32]

---

[27] Statement by the President of the Security Council, above n 7.

[28] See Statement by the President of the Security Council, UN doc S/PRST/2001/13, 3 May 2001 (extending the mandate for three months); Statement by the President of the Security Council, UN doc S/PRST/2001/39, 19 December 2001 (extending the mandate for six months); Security Council Resolution 1457 (2003), 24 January 2003 (extending the mandate for six months); Security Council Resolution 1499 (2003), 13 August 2003 (extending the mandate until 31 October 2003).

[29] See Interim Report of the United Nations Expert Panel on the Illegal Exploitation of Natural Resources and Other Forms of Wealth of the Democratic Republic of the Congo, UN doc S/2001/49, 16 January 2001 [hereinafter '2001 Interim Report']; 2001 Report, above n 5; Interim Report of the Panel of Experts on the Illegal Exploitation of Natural Resources and Other Forms of Wealth of the Democratic Republic of the Congo, UN doc S/2002/565, 22 May 2002 [hereinafter '2002 Interim Report']; Final Report of the Panel of Experts on the Illegal Exploitation of Natural Resources and Other Forms of Wealth of the Democratic Republic of the Congo, UN doc S/2002/1146, 16 October 2002 [hereinafter '2002 Final Report']; Final Report of the Panel of Experts on the Illegal Exploitation of Natural Resources and Other Forms of Wealth of the Democratic Republic of the Congo, UN doc S/2003/1027, 23 October 2003 [hereinafter '2003 Final Report'].

[30] 2002 Final Report, above n 29, at 4.

[31] See 2001 Report, above n 5, at 4.

[32] See 2001 Interim Report, above n 29, at 3; 2001 Report, above n 5, at 4.; 2001 Addendum, above n 14, at 4; 2002 Interim Report, above n 29, at 3; 2002 Final Report, above n 29, at 4.

## 1. Responsibility of States Present in the Democratic Republic of the Congo

The Panel, drawing from the wide spectrum of evidence that it collected, established even from the beginning the huge magnitude of the exploitation of the DRC's natural resources that the Ugandan and Rwandan armies along with their rebel counterparts engaged in. In the 2001 Report, the Panel demonstrated how the occupying forces embarked on a 'mass-scale looting' that drained the country of available resources with devastating results for the local population.[33] Furthermore, after the resource stores emptied, the warring parties instituted a 'systematic and systemic exploitation' of Congolese minerals (including coltan, diamonds, gold, and cassiterite) and agricultural resources.[34] They also took advantage of financial transactions, taxes, and the use of forced or cheap labor, which also qualify as 'other forms of wealth.'[35]

Despite the denial by Ugandan and Rwandan authorities of any involvement in the utilization of the DRC's wealth, the Panel presented revealing evidence that during the years of its occupation of the eastern DRC, Uganda, while having no known diamond production, started engaging in diamond exports, and its exports of natural resources, such as gold and other minerals, accelerated.[36] In the same vein, while Rwandan officials underscored that their country does not produce diamonds, the Panel referred to substantiated evidence that Rwanda has been exporting the stones and that its 'production' of gold and coltan has increased since the country's involvement in the conflict.[37] Ironically enough, the World Bank has applauded Uganda and Rwanda for their economic achievements and has even recommended them for the new debt assistance program, the Highly Indebted Poor Countries debt relief project, thus posing questions about the institution's policy of disregarding wide governance concerns when 'dealing with its clients.'[38]

Following the 2001 Report of the Panel, Rwanda accused the Panel of insensitivity towards the continuing security threats the country faces from those who committed the genocide, and of failing to understand the customary commercial links in the region.[39] On the other hand, Uganda did establish a Commission of Inquiry, the Porter Commission, to review the allegations of the Panel. Although this Commission did not exhibit the

---

[33] See 2001 Report, above n 5, at 8–9.
[34] See *ibid* at 9–14.
[35] *Ibid* at 13–14.
[36] See *ibid* at 19.
[37] See *ibid* at 25.
[38] *Ibid* at 38–39.
[39] 2001 Addendum, above n 14, at 19.

best cooperation with the Panel, and many times tried to discredit the latter's credibility, it did concede that one of the accused commanders, Major General James Kazini, lied to it under oath with regard to his illegal exploitation activities.[40] Although it is not the purpose of this chapter to examine in detail the various countries' reactions to the findings of the Panel, the Porter Commission should be complimented to the extent that it was the sole State commission in the region assembled to examine the exploitation of resources in the DRC.[41]

Subsequently, in its Final Report of 2002, the Panel extensively demonstrated how three distinct 'elite networks' of political, military, and business leaders have gained control over a variety of commercial activities, including the plunder of natural resources, in the three disparate areas controlled by the DRC government, Rwanda, and Uganda, respectively.[42] According to the Panel's contentions, the withdrawal of the foreign troops from the territory of the DRC should not be regarded as a sign of willingness on behalf of the warring parties to lessen their involvement in the exploitation of precious resources or to diminish the magnitude of the armed conflict in the region.[43] Alternative strategies have been employed to continue the plundering, while less conspicuous armed forces will continue to guarantee the commercial activities of the involved parties.[44]

One of the biggest contributions made by the Panel was the establishment of a clear and indisputable link between the plunder of the resources in the DRC and the ongoing conflict. In spite of assertions to the contrary, the conflict in the DRC continued not due to political or security reasons, but mainly on grounds of access, trade, and control of the country's valuable mineral resources.[45] This contention proves to be true for both government collaborators and rebel backers. At the same time, the resource exploitation funds the war, which in turn provides the conditions which permit access to those resources.[46] The Panel, referring to the continuation of the conflict and the exploitation of the country's resources, clearly stated that 'one drives the other', and that all engaged sides have resorted to 'self-financing activities', without having to bear any actual budgetary onus.[47]

---

[40] 2002 Final Report, above n 29, at 24–26.

[41] See Paul Asiimwe, 'Report of the UN Panel of Experts on the Illegal Exploitation of Natural Resources of the Democratic Republic of the Congo' (2004) 22 *Journal of Energy and Natural Resources Law* 194, at 198.

[42] See 2002 Final Report, above n 29, at 6.

[43] See *ibid* at 5–7, 14–17, 19–23.

[44] *Ibid* at 14. For a more recent account of the continuing conflict over the DRC's natural resources, see Finbarr O'Reilly, 'Rush for Natural Resources Still Fuels War in Congo', *Reuters*, 9 August 2004.

[45] See 2001 Report, above n 5, at 6–7; 2001 Addendum, above n14, at 26–27.

[46] See 2001 Report, above n 5, at 29–30; 2003 Final Report, above n 29, at 19.

[47] 2001 Addendum, above n 14, at 26–27.

In addition, although the Panel's mandate was not specifically to report on human rights violations occurring in the DRC, the Panel demonstrated in an unambiguous way the overwhelming impact of the vicious cycle of conflict and resource exploitation on the humanitarian and social situation in the country. Population displacement was not merely a result of the armed conflict, but also a calculated strategy of the armed forces in gaining control of resource-rich areas or roads leading to those areas.[48] Organized attacks against villages, killings, torture, and rape were inextricably linked to the armies' control of resource exploitation sites,[49] and have also resulted in the creation of an 'abusive social environment'.[50] The destruction of the infrastructure for agricultural production by the warring parties in order to guarantee mining zones and coerce locals into participating in the extraction of resources has led to unprecedented levels of malnutrition, disease, and mortality.[51] Women have been exposed to continual sexual abuse,[52] while locals, including children, have regularly been used as forced labor in the resource extraction sites.[53] Public infrastructure has become almost non-existent, while few to none of the revenues generated from the country's resources have been allocated to public services.[54] Furthermore, the DRC's natural environment, well known for its distinctive diversity of fauna and flora, has sustained severe damage.[55] In short, the resource-driven conflict has condemned the country to an enormous humanitarian crisis and placed it among the poorest in the world, with no real prospect of substantive progress in the near future.

## 2. Responsibility of Companies Involved

Having established the strong connection between the extensive violation of human rights and the exploitation of natural resources in the DRC, the Panel's most notable, and at the same time debatable, contribution to the actual understanding of the situation in the country was the implication of the companies involved in the area. The Panel, by illustrating the interconnections between Congolese participants in the conflict, foreign authorities, and corporations, maintained that business entities, directly or indirectly, have been instrumental in the plunder of the DRC's

---

[48] 2002 Interim Report, above n 29, at 9.
[49] *Ibid.*
[50] 2002 Final Report, above n 29, at 19.
[51] See 2002 Interim Report, above n 29, at 9.
[52] 2002 Final Report, above n 29, at 19.
[53] See 2001 Report, above n 5, at 14; 2002 Interim Report, above n 29, at 9; 2002 Final Report, above n 29, at 18–19.
[54] 2002 Interim Report, above n 29, at 9.
[55] See 2001 Report, above n 5, at 12–13; 2002 Interim Report, above n 29, at 10.

resources, the prolongation of the war, and the commission of human rights abuses.[56]

In its April 2001 Report, which stressed the vital role of the private sector in the situation in the DRC, the Panel published an Annex containing a sample of companies importing minerals from the country, which the Panel accused of being 'ready to do business regardless of elements of unlawfulness and irregularities' and of facilitating the rise in revenues of the warring parties.[57] However, in its 2002 Final Report the Panel went one step further. In an unparalleled move, it named 29 companies and 54 individuals, whose association with the commercial activities of the elite networks in the DRC was well substantiated and against whom it advocated the imposition of travel bans and financial restrictions[58]. At the same time, the Panel listed, in Annex III, 85 companies that were in apparent breach of the OECD Guidelines.[59]

Although the Panel refrained from giving details about all the companies named in its Report, and simultaneously did not connect its concerns with specific provisos of the OECD Guidelines, its examination of the role of the companies in the country revealed several forms of alleged misconduct.[60] The Panel referred to companies that availed themselves of the immediate assistance of the warring parties, such as mining companies that received 'privileged access to coltan sites and captive labour,' and protection by armed forces.[61] Furthermore, some corporations were named as suppliers of arms and military equipment,[62] while others engaged in 'counterfeiting, money-laundering and diamond smuggling.'[63] A number of corporations acquired highly profitable concessions on disproportionably favorable terms by taking advantage of the lawless situation in the country,[64] while the Panel also mentioned companies that made profit from lucrative joint ventures, mostly in the government-controlled area, 'with no compensation or benefit for the State treasury' of the DRC.[65] Furthermore, a number of companies engaged in the trade of minerals (which the Panel regarded as 'the engine of the conflict' in the DRC), thus 'prepar[ing] the field for illegal mining activities in the country.'[66]

---

[56] See 2001 Report, above n 5, at 37–38, 41–42; Rights & Accountability In Development, above n 6, at 3.

[57] See 2001 Report, above n 5, at 38, Annex.

[58] See 2002 Final Report, above n 29, at 32, Annex I, Annex II.

[59] See *ibid* at Annex III.

[60] See Rights & Accountability In Development, above n 6, at 3.

[61] 2002 Final Report, above n 29, at 16.

[62] See, eg, *ibid* at 10–12.

[63] *Ibid* at 9 (naming three 'clans' who operate licensed diamond businesses in Antwerp and engage in criminal activities, while being associated with Sierra Gem Diamonds, Asa Diam, Triple A Diamonds, and Echogen).

[64] See, eg, *ibid* at 9–10.

[65] *Ibid* at 7.

[66] 2001 Report, above n 5, at 42.

Following the publication of the 2002 Final Report, the United Nations Security Council issued Resolution 1457, in which it condemned the illegal exploitation of the natural resources of the DRC, called upon individuals, companies, and States which had been identified in the Panel's last report to submit their reactions, and directed the Panel to carry out:

> [f]urther review of relevant data and analysis of information previously gathered by the Panel, as well as any new information … in order to verify, reinforce and, where necessary, update the Panel's finding, and/or clear parties named in the Panel's previous reports, with a view to adjusting accordingly the lists attached to these reports.[67]

Consequently, the Panel, starting in early April 2003, held personal meetings in Nairobi and in Paris with parties named in its previous report that were interested in contacting the Panel and presenting their reaction for publication.[68] The reactions received were compiled and listed as an attachment to the Panel's 2002 Final Report.[69]

The last Report issued by the Panel in October 2003 was noticeably different from its earlier ones.[70] The Panel, although recognizing that '[i]llegal exploitation remains one of the main sources of funding for groups involved in perpetuating conflict,'[71] focused its attention mostly on the reactions to its contentious 2002 Report.[72] The Panel, obviously anxious to meet the various responses that its previous Report had generated, tried to clarify that its mandate precluded it 'from determining the guilt or innocence of parties that have business dealings linked to the Democratic Republic of the Congo,'[73] and that its purpose was to advance the standard of corporate behavior in conflict areas and to stress the necessity for a more just and transparent exploitation of the lucrative resources of the country.[74]

Furthermore, the Panel provided a re-categorization of the companies listed in its 2002 Final Report. It divided the companies into five groups: 'resolved', 'resolved cases subject to NCP [National Contact Point] moni toring compliance', 'unresolved cases referred to NCP for updating or investigation', 'pending cases with governments', and 'parties that did not react to the Panel's Report'. Forty-two companies previously listed in

---

[67] Security Council Resolution 1457, above n 28, para 9.

[68] Addendum to the Panel of Experts on the Illegal Exploitation of Natural Resources and Other Forms of Wealth of the Democratic Republic of the Congo addressed to the Secretary-General, UN doc S/2002/1146/Add.1, 20 June 2003 [hereinafter '2003 Addendum'], at 2.

[69] *Ibid.*

[70] Global Witness, *Same Old Story: A Background Study on Natural Resources in the Democratic Republic of Congo* (2004), at 11, available at http://www.globalwitness.org/reports/show.php/en.00054.html

[71] 2003 Final Report, above n 29, at 14.

[72] Global Witness, above n 70.

[73] 2003 Final Report, above n 29, at 7.

[74] *Ibid* at 8.

Annex III were now contained in the 'resolved' category, which, however, incorporates a wide variety of cases.[75]

After more than three years since its initial mandate, the Panel completed its work and was dissolved, definitely this time. Through the progress of its mission, it attracted various comments and reactions both by the actors directly involved and by NGOs and civil society. Proceeding to an assessment of its overall performance is necessary in order to draw lessons regarding its positive impact, as well as the inherent restraints and limitations of such a body.

## IV. ASSESSMENT

When assessed as a whole, the Panel's work has conferred an 'invaluable insight' into exploring the self-perpetuating cycle of conflict and resource plunder in the DRC.[76] Drawing from various sources of evidence, the Panel substantiated that the exploitation of natural resources was the main source of revenue for the brutal war, which, in turn, was sustained in order to secure access to those resources. Furthermore, although the mandate of the Panel was not specifically related to examining human rights violations, the Panel documented the widespread human right abuses that the conflict and the extraction of lucrative resources in the country have caused.

In addition, the Panel raised awareness of the situation in the DRC, which had until then attracted very little media attention, and through the progress of its work, it negated any possible future claims by TNCs that they were ignorant of the implications that their business activities in the area might have. The Panel, mainly through its two first Reports, recorded the various ways in which TNCs contributed to the revenues of the warring parties, the continuation of the war, and the ensuing human rights abuses. The Panel enhanced the calls for socially responsible corporate behavior in conflict zones not only by TNCs that directly perpetuate the conflict, but also by TNCs that, by obtaining, trading, or purchasing the illegally extracted resources, fund the groups immediately responsible for extensive human rights violations.[77]

---

[75] A company might be listed in the first category: because it had either conceded the issue mentioned by the Panel and had taken or promised to take remedial action; or because it had only tangential or indirect links to the DRC; or because it had stopped operating in the country or doing business with Congolese parties that could not meet international standards of business ethics; or because the company proved that conduct previously suspect due to a dearth of transparency was actually permissible; or because it had been operating in the country for many years and its business practices could be viewed as acceptable. See *ibid* at 9–11.

[76] Global Witness, above n 70. See also Rights & Accountability In Development, above n 6, at 6.

[77] See Rights & Accountability In Development, above n 6, at 18.

As a result of its findings, many corporations, even before the publication of the Panel's penultimate Report, not only gained a better understanding of their role in the situation in the country, but also ceased
purchasing minerals originating from the DRC. A characteristic example
is the decrease in demand for coltan observed after 2001, which, according to the Panel, could also be attributed to the 'manufacturers' desire to
disassociate themselves with what became known, following release of
the [2001] report, as "blood tantalum".'[78]

The Panel's findings, which have also been confirmed by a rising number of 'independent reports',[79] went one step further. By naming specific
companies contributing to the financing of the parties and the continuation of the conflict, they were not confined to broad allegations with no
expressed addressee. This unprecedented step has been welcomed with
enthusiasm by NGOs and civil society, and as a Congolese businessman
in the United States commented, 'for the first time names are being
named, companies identified and sanctions being recommended.'[80]

At this point, it could be argued that the Panel's naming of companies
that are in breach of their obligations in the DRC, without being a judicial
body with due process restraints, jeopardizes these companies' rights.
However, it should be stressed that the Panel, throughout the course of its
mandate, tried to establish communication with all the implicated companies.[81] Moreover, according to its statement, it employed a standard of
proof based on 'reasonableness' or 'sufficient cause', and for any individual party mentioned it has received information indicating that, prima
facie, that company has violated the OECD Guidelines[82] in existence since
1976. All the companies named in the Annexes have been given the
opportunity not only to communicate their opinions to the Panel, but
also, as already mentioned, to have them published in an Addendum.
Consequently, taking into consideration that the companies have not been
deprived of the right to express their own points of view, overt accusations
of violation of these companies' rights can be soundly refuted.

Another positive contribution made by the Panel was that by using
the OECD Guidelines as a benchmark for assessing corporate behavior in
the DRC, it 'breathed life' into them[83] and gave them new impetus.
Furthermore, the Panel, by employing the OECD Guidelines as the decisive
criterion, and finding in breach even corporations whose home governments

---

[78] 2001 Addendum, above n 14, at 6.

[79] Human Rights Watch, *DR Congo: UN Must Address Corporate Role In War* (2003), available at http://hrw.org/press/2003/10/drc102703.htm

[80] Milan Vesely, 'UN Congo Report Damns Individuals, Companies, Countries' (2002) 282
*African Business*, December, at 16.

[81] See, eg, 2001 Interim Report, above n 29, at 3; 2001 Report, above n 5, at 4.

[82] 2003 Final Report, above n 29, at 7.

[83] *Ibid* at 21.

do not adhere to them,[84] demonstrated that it perceives the OECD Guidelines as a 'global standard'[85] and a tool available to governments to hold individuals and companies accountable for their undertakings.[86] However, as a negative feature of the Panel's findings, it must be added that the Panel did not mention which specific provisions of the OECD Guidelines had been breached, while in some instances it just listed a company in the Annexes without elaborating in the main body of the Report how it had specifically violated ethical business standards in the DRC.[87]

Furthermore, it must be acknowledged that the Panel had to work with restraints and limitations that had to do not only with its restricted powers to gather evidence and testimonies but foremost with the historic and current political environment. Specifically, during the period of its mandate efforts were being made to lead the DRC to peace and democratic governance, and it is obvious that considerations of the Panel's detrimental effect to the whole process were being taken into account. The Panel explicitly recognized this when it stated that, although it had intended to meet with the various participants in the inter-Congolese dialogue in Sun City, according to its mandate and course of action, it decided not to do so in order not to jeopardize the peace efforts.[88] Furthermore, the Panel declared many times in its Reports that it was being mindful of the peace process, apparently in an effort to soothe concerns about its possible implications for the country's efforts toward transition.[89] The decision by United Nations officials not to make public excerpts of the Panel's Final Report that implicate members of the new Transitional Government[90] could be explained on the same basis. Although controversy has followed this decision,[91] the work of a fact-finding body such as this Panel cannot be viewed in isolation from the surrounding political setting, which more often than not will place limitations on its freedom of action and initiative. And voices urging that accountability should take priority over any other considerations should also think of the price that is to be paid by the people most immediately affected.

---

[84] Home governments of corporations listed in the Annexes which have not subscribed to the OECD Guidelines include: South Africa, Ghana, Zimbabwe, Thailand, the DRC, Saint Kitts, Bermuda, Malaysia, Kazakhstan, China, Hong Kong, United Arab Emirates, British Virgin Islands, Uganda, and Rwanda.

[85] Rights & Accountability In Development, above n 6, at 91.

[86] Global Witness, above n 70.

[87] See 2002 Final Report, above n 29, at 32.

[88] 2002 Interim Report, above n 29, at 3.

[89] See, eg, 2001 Addendum, above n 14, at 4; 2002 Final Report, above n 29, at 4–5; 2003 Final Report, above n 29, at 4–5.

[90] Friends of the Earth, *United Nations Expert Panel Investigation of Illegal Exploitation of Natural Resources and Other Forms of Wealth in the Democratic Republic of the Congo—Overview*, available at http://www.foe.org/oecdguidelines/2PageBackground.pdf

[91] David Usborne, 'Congo: UN Says War Fueled by Foreign Firms', (2003) *The Independent* (London), October 31.

When trying to assess the Panel's general efficiency, mention has to be made of the negative criticism against the Panel that it has yielded under pressure from the United Nations Security Council and the home governments of businesses to 'clear' corporations' names in its 2003 Final Report. Allegations have been made by NGOs that many of the listed companies lobbied their governments, together with the Security Council, to secure their deletion from the Annexes.[92] Unfortunately, the formulation of the 2003 Final Report does not help to challenge these assertions, but, on the contrary, raises many questions.

First, the 'resolved' category, which encompasses the majority of the cases, is not adequately defined. While the Panel clearly states, in conformity with Security Council Resolution 1457,[93] that '[t]he overarching goal of the dialogue was to achieve a resolution of the issues that led to parties being listed so that they can be removed from the annexes,' at the same time it declares that 'resolution should not be seen as invalidating the Panel's earlier findings with regard to the activities of those actors.'[94] As a result, it is not possible to differentiate between companies that violated the OECD Guidelines and those that acted in compliance with them. The responsible and the guiltless are placed side by side, which is objectionable 'both from the point of view of accountability and the public interest and also from the point of view of the parties concerned.'[95]

In the same vein, the 'resolved' category incorporates a wide spectrum of TNCs, ranging from companies that have taken or have promised to take remedial action to companies that stopped operating in the country or doing business with Congolese parties that could not meet international standards of business ethics.[96] The Panel does not clarify which companies fit in which subcategory, thus posing the same problem about distinguishing culpable companies from those that did not violate the OECD Guidelines in the first place. Furthermore, although some companies have been included in this category because they acknowledged improper conduct and promised to adopt remedies, no information is given about what these remedies involve, thus making it impossible for civil society and interested parties to test the efficiency of the remedies or whether they are being actually realized.[97]

Furthermore, appreciable omissions seem to characterize the available public record. It should be stressed that out of the 85 companies listed in Annex III, only 10 have been included in the category of parties that did

---

[92] See Rights & Accountability In Development, above n 6, at 4.
[93] See text accompanying n 67 above.
[94] 2003 Final Report, above n 29, at 9.
[95] Rights & Accountability In Development, above n 6, at 15.
[96] See 2003 Final Report, above n 29, at 9–11. For the five subcategories that the 'resolved' category incorporates, see above n 75.
[97] Rights & Accountability In Development, above n 6, at 15.

not react to the Panel's Report. Nevertheless, according to the 2003 Addendum, only 49 companies replied to the Panel, thus raising questions about why 26 companies that did not submit their reactions have been listed as if they had done so. Taking into account that the Panel decided to form a special category for the parties that decided not to reply, the fact that companies for whom no public record of response exists have been allocated to the remaining categories greatly weakens 'the principles of transparency and accountability.'[98]

Moreover, no convincing explanation has been given by the Panel as to why companies that require further investigation have not all been treated in the same way: some are referred to National Contact Points (hereinafter NCPs) for further investigation, while others are to be examined by governments.[99] It cannot be argued that this is so because the former category consists of companies registered in countries which are signatories to the OECD Guidelines, while those in the latter are in countries which are not.[100] On the contrary, four companies in the latter category operate in countries subscribing to the Guidelines[101]. This inconsistency raises serious concerns, because it does not explain why companies operating out of the same jurisdictions, such as De Beers and Euromet,[102] are being treated differently, and why some of them are excluded from the prospective inquiry by NCPs.[103]

However, the noted deficits about the Panel's Final Report cannot negate the fact that when seen as a whole, the Panel made a strong contribution to a deeper understanding of the situation in the DRC, raised awareness with regard to the companies' role in the continuing war, and successfully completed its mandate, which was to substantiate the link between the conflict in the country and the exploitation of its resources. It is possible that the disappointment that its ultimate report generated had also to do with some lack of understanding that the Panel was solely a fact-finding body with limited powers, whose role was to record the various implications of the conflict in the DRC and not to do justice. The onus to investigate further and sanction corporations that totally disregarded their obligations under the OECD Guidelines rests on governments, whose ultimate response will determine whether the findings of the Panel will just

---

[98] *Ibid.*

[99] See 2003 Final Report, above n 29, Annex I: Categories III (Unresolved Cases Referred to NCP for Updating or Investigation) and IV (Pending Cases with Governments for Individuals and Companies).

[100] Rights & Accountability In Development, above n 6, at 15.

[101] These companies are: International Panama Resources Corp (Canada), SLC Germany Gmbh (Germany), Euromet (UK), and Mineraal Afrika Limited (UK): 2003 Final Report, above n 29, Annex I: Category IV.

[102] Both De Beers and Euromet operate out of the UK: *ibid* at Annex I: Categories III and IV.

[103] Rights & Accountability In Development, above n 6, at 15.

stay on paper. No matter how successful such a fact-finding body may be at documenting the corporate irresponsibility in countries devastated by resource-driven conflicts, its work should be complemented by mechanisms that can take remedial measures in order to make corporations truly face the consequences of their opportunistic and sometimes criminal behavior.

## V. OECD GUIDELINES AND FOLLOW-UP ON THE PANEL'S WORK BY ADHERING GOVERNMENTS

The OECD Guidelines, which the Panel used as a benchmark to assess TNCs' conduct with regard to the DRC, are recommendations made by the 38 adhering governments to TNCs operating in or from their territory.[104] The countries subscribing to the OECD Guidelines are the source of most foreign direct investment worldwide, and home to the majority of TNCs.[105] Consequently, taking further into account that the OECD Guidelines reach to all the countries in which TNCs operate, including the DRC, and that they are addressed to both the parent company and the local entities within a TNC,[106], the OECD Guidelines comprise 'one of the most geographically extensive of the corporate codes.'[107]

The OECD Guidelines contain 'voluntary principles and standards' that concern a wide range of TNCs' activities: disclosure of information, employment and labor relations, environmental protection, combating bribery, protecting consumers, science and technology, competition, and taxation.[108] Furthermore, with their revision in 2000, an important improvement was achieved. A specific recommendation on human rights was incorporated into the text, which now reads, 'enterprises should [r]espect the human rights of those affected by their activities consistent with the host government's international obligations and commitments.'[109] The term 'affected by their activities' seems to be broad enough to encompass business stakeholders.[110]

---

[104] There are 30 OECD Members: Australia, Austria, Belgium, Canada, the Czech Republic, Denmark, Finland, France, Germany, Greece, Hungary, Iceland, Ireland, Italy, Japan, Korea, Luxembourg, Mexico, the Netherlands, New Zealand, Norway, Poland, Portugal, the Slovak Republic, Spain, Sweden, Switzerland, Turkey, the United Kingdom, and the United States. Eight non-member countries (Argentina, Brazil, Chile, Estonia, Israel, Latvia, Lithuania, and Slovenia) have also adhered to the OECD Guidelines. See OECD Policy Brief, 'The OECD Guidelines for Multinational Enterprises' (2003) at 1, available at http://www.oecd.org/dataoecd/52/38/2958609.pdf

[105] *Ibid.*

[106] OECD Guidelines, above n 8, I. Concepts and Principles, para 18.

[107] Rights & Accountability In Development, above n 6, at 12.

[108] See OECD Guidelines, above n 8.

[109] *Ibid*, II. General Policies, para 19.

[110] Surya Deva, 'Human Rights Violations by Multinational Corporations and International Law: Where from Here?' (2003) 19 *Connecticut Journal of International Law* 1, at 11.

One of the most important elements of the OECD Guidelines is that they are the first international code on corporate social responsibility that provides for implementation procedures through a government-backed mechanism for supervising and guiding corporate conduct.[111] The adhering countries are committed to establish NCPs, which are vested with the role of furthering the effectiveness of the OECD Guidelines.[112] Among the responsibilities of NCPs are promoting awareness and knowledge of the OECD Guidelines and responding to the enquiries of interested parties.[113] Furthermore, NCPs should submit annual reports to the OECD Committee on International Investment and Multinational Enterprises (hereinafter CIME), which is responsible for overseeing 'the effective functioning of the Guidelines'[114] and for clarifying their meaning.[115] A significant provision of the OECD Guidelines procedures refers to something called 'specific instances', a facility that requires NCPs to examine a particular company's non-compliance with the Guidelines when this is raised by interested parties.[116]

The Panel of Experts in its 2002 Final Report specifically referred to the OECD Guidelines mechanism 'for bringing violations of them by business enterprises to the attention of home Governments,' and went one step further by stating that '[g]overnments with jurisdiction over these enterprises are complicit themselves when they do not take remedial action.'[117] In addition, calls for further inquiries about the corporations' illegitimate conduct in the DRC came from the Security Council, which repeatedly urged governments to follow up on the Panel's findings. In a resolution issued after the Panel's 2002 Final Report, the Security Council requested that the Panel 'establish a procedure to provide to Member States, upon request, information previously collected by the Panel to

[111] Rights & Accountability In Development, above n 6, at 12.

[112] OECD Guidelines, above n 8, Implementation Procedures, Procedural Guidance, I. National Contact Points.

[113] NCPs should handle enquiries about the OECD Guidelines made by other NCPs, the business community, employee organizations, other NGOs, the public, and the governments of non-adhering countries: OECD Guidelines, above n 8, Implementation Procedures, Procedural Guidance, I. National Contact Points, B. Information and Promotion, para 3.

[114] OECD Guidelines, above n 8, Implementation Procedures, II. The Committee on International Investment and Multinational Enterprises, para 6. In April 2004 the Investment Committee was formed by the merger of the CIME and the Committee on Capital Movements and Invisible Transactions (CMIT).

[115] *Ibid* at para 4.

[116] OECD Guidelines, above n 8, Implementation Procedures, Procedural Guidance, I. National Contact Point, C. Implementation in Specific Instances. Mentioned as parties to a specific instance are the business community, employee organizations, and 'other parties concerned'. Therefore, unions, NGOs, and even individuals may bring a company's alleged misconduct to the attention of an NCP. See Rights & Accountability In Development, above n 6, at 13, n 25.

[117] 2002 Final Report, above n 29, at 31.

help them *take the necessary investigative action,*' and encouraged all States to proceed with their own investigations.[118] Calls for further action by governments on the basis of information provided by the Panel was repeated in a following resolution,[119] while in the Security Council's final statement all States were again urged to take appropriate measures to halt these illegal activities and to continue with their own investigations.[120]

Nevertheless, the action that the governments participating in the OECD have taken up to now is far from effective and satisfying. Although the situation is not as disappointing as one year ago, when Human Rights Watch stated that none of the governments adhering to the OECD Guidelines had taken any steps to investigate the behavior of any of the companies listed in the Panel's reports,[121] it appears that countries have been very slow in their reactions to the Panel's findings. One notable exception is Belgium, which initiated criminal investigations against Belgian corporations on tax and money-laundering related charges.[122]

Some home governments tried to excuse their inaction by stating that the Panel had been dissolved and consequently nothing more could be done, or by mentioning the difficulties they faced in obtaining specific information from the Panel.[123] With regard to the first argument, it is no exaggeration to state that it flies in the face of the Security Council's calls and of governments' commitments to promoting the OECD Guidelines. However, it does seem that cooperation between the NCPs and the Panel has not always achieved a satisfactory level, and that some NCPs did, indeed, not receive substantive information from the Panel, or at least not to the desired extent.[124] As a result, the Chair of the CIME wrote a letter to be transmitted to the United Nations Secretary-General and for the attention of the Security Council, outlining deficits in the relationship between the two institutions and containing suggestions for improved cooperation in the future.[125]

---

[118] Security Council Resolution 1457, above n 28, paras 12 and 15 (emphasis added).

[119] See Security Council Resolution 1499, above n 28, para 3.

[120] Statement by the President of the Security Council, UN doc S/PRST/2003/21, 19 November 2003.

[121] See Human Rights Watch, above n 79.

[122] The companies are: Ahmad Diamond Corporation, Banque Belgolaise, and Cogecom. See Friends of the Earth, *Status of Non-US Complaints,* available at http://www.foe.org/new/releases/84drccomplaint.html (last visited 25 October 2004).

[123] See Paul Redfern, 'DRC Plunder: UK Accused of Failing to Act on Firms Named in UN Report' (2004) East African, January 5.

[124] See Public Statement by CIME, 'Illegal Exploitation of Natural Resources in the Democratic Republic of Congo' (2004), available at http://www.oecd.org/document/6/0,2340,en_2649_34889_27217798_1_1_1_1,00.html

[125] The letter by the Chair of the CIME was transmitted to the OECD Secretary-General on 18 December 2003, and subsequently to the United Nations Secretary-General on 9 January 2004. It is available on the OECD website, at http://www.oecd.org/dataoecd/38/57/27225423.pdf

Nevertheless, notwithstanding the difficulties that some NCPs faced in obtaining information from the Panel, it should be noted that the calls for investigation by the Security Council were not confined solely to the evidence gathered by the Panel. Furthermore, the Commentaries to the OECD Guidelines specifically state that when a Guidelines-related issue surfaces in a non-adhering country, the NCP 'may still be in position to pursue enquiries and engage in other fact finding activities.'[126] More importantly, the argument that not enough information exists to pursue an investigation is negated by the counter-argument that the aim of such investigations is to reveal such information in the first place.[127]

The same goal of avoiding scrutiny of their own corporations may help explain the assertion put forth by some adhering governments, including the Bush administration, that TNCs cannot be held in violation of the OECD Guidelines for purchasing illegally exploited resources from their suppliers.[128] This contention does not seem to be supported by the text of the OECD Guidelines, which states that enterprises should '[e]ncourage, where practicable, business partners, including suppliers and sub-contractors, to apply principles of corporate conduct compatible with the *Guidelines*.'[129] It also undermines the Panel's efforts to bring to the attention of the TNCs their responsibilities with respect to the origin of their raw materials.[130] In a statement issued at the June 2003 NCP meetings, the CIME clarified that an investment nexus is necessary for the applicability of the OECD Guidelines, and that the issue of scope is linked to the practical feasibility of TNCs influencing the behavior of their business partners with whom they enjoy an investment like cooperation.[131].This seems to set a worrying precedent that TNCs registered in OECD countries are not responsible for certifying that the raw materials they are purchasing are not indirectly financing conflicts and human rights violations.[132]

As a result of the unwillingness of home governments to adopt a more vigorous approach to following up on the Panel's findings, NGOs have filed complaints to NCPs in order to trigger the specific instance

---

[126] OECD Guidelines, above n 8, Commentary on the Implementation Procedures of the OECD Guidelines for Multinational Enterprises, I. Procedural Guidance for NCPs, para 20. Note that although the Commentaries explain the text of the OECD Guidelines, they are not part of it.

[127] Rights & Accountability In Development, above n 6, at 6.

[128] See Friends of the Earth, *Congo at a Crossroads* (2003), available at http://www.foe.org/oecdguidelines/Oped.pdf

[129] OECD Guidelines, above n 8, II. General Policies, para 10.

[130] See 2003 Final Report, above n 29, at 5–6.

[131] See Statement by Dutch National Contact Point on Chemie Pharmacie Holland BV Complaint (June 2004), and annexed OECD CIME statement on investment, available at http://www.oesorichtlijnen.nl/documenten/NCP_verklaring_NIZA_CPH.pdf.

[132] Friends of the Earth, above n 128.

mechanism[133]. Furthermore, they have not confined themselves to the companies that were listed in the Panel's 2003 Final Report as requiring further investigation, but have also cited companies that were mentioned in the 'resolved' category, resting on the premise that the NCPs should address the inadequacies of the Panel's categorizations.[134]

Although there are signs that NCPs have started taking their role more seriously, and NGOs certainly exert pressure in this direction, it seems that the reaction by the adhering countries to the Panel's work cannot sustain the belief that the OECD Guidelines comprise an effective tool for holding TNCs accountable for human rights violations. The follow-up by adhering countries so far seems to confirm assertions that governments are hesitant to compel their corporations' compliance with international law, out of fear that this will place them at a competitive disadvantage.[135] It also underlines the non-binding character of the OECD Guidelines, which, although one of the most 'authoritative internationally agreed standards for corporate conduct,'[136] cannot escape the criticism and dispute that generally surround soft law.[137]

## VI. CONCLUDING REMARKS

The Panel of Experts, after three years of intense investigative work, produced a documentary account of the vicious circle of illegal exploitation of natural resources and perpetuation of the conflict in the DRC. Furthermore, it proceeded to examine the role of TNCs in the continuation of the war and, by utilizing the OECD Guidelines to evaluate the TNCs' involvement, it emphasized their character as the single most important multilateral instrument for holding corporations accountable.

Without underestimating the positive results that the Panel produced as a fact-finding body, its constraints and deficits should also be acknowledged in order to enhance the efficiency of analogous bodies that may be employed in the future. Political considerations emerging from the ongoing transitional process to peace and democratic governance in the DRC have undoubtedly informed the Panel's work and

---

[133] See Friends of the Earth—United States and Rights & Accountability in Development's Complaint to State Department (2004), available at http://www.foe.org/oecdguidelines/StateDp1.pdf

[134] *Ibid.*

[135] See Sarah Joseph, 'An Overview of the Human Rights Accountability of Multinational Enterprises', in Menno T Kamminga *et al* (eds), *Liability of Multinational Corporations Under International Law* (The Hague, Kluwer, 2000), 75, at 80.

[136] *Ibid* at 84.

[137] See, eg, Deva, above n 110; Stephen Kabel, 'Our Business is People (Even if it Kills Them): The Contribution of Multinational Enterprises to the Conflict in the Democratic Republic of Congo' (2004) 12 *Tulane Journal of International and Comparative Law* 461.

should be acknowledged as an inevitable limitation to any similar efforts taking place in countries which find themselves in periods of evolution.

At the same time, the pragmatic realization should be made that the Panel did not manage to counter political pressure by business lobbies and governments generated by its unprecedented step of naming specific TNCs. This is reflected in the Panel's 2003 Final Report, which raises many questions with respect to the Panel's ultimate categorization of companies and its listing of cases as resolved without including further information.

Additional queries are raised by the Panel's inaction in response to requests by NCPs for more details about its findings, although the Panel emphatically stated that it is the responsibility of each government to verify and update the list of business enterprises in breach of the OECD Guidelines.[138] As for the countries adhering to the OECD Guidelines, although they were also urged by the Security Council to follow up on the Panel's pronouncements, they have not adopted a vigorous approach to the Panel's conclusions. This has caused damage to the 'public confidence in the effectiveness' of the OECD Guidelines,[139] and confirmed voices that call for stronger enforcement mechanisms at the international level and regard the ICC as the appropriate forum for holding TNCs accountable for human rights violations.

The Prosecutor of the ICC, Luis Moreno Ocampo, who after a referral by the DRC commenced official investigations into crimes committed in the country since 1 July 2002, has stated that his office will also look into the way businesses have contributed to the occurrence of war crimes and crimes against humanity.[140] Nevertheless, although the conduct of some corporations in the DRC, particularly with regard to forced labor and forcible transfer of populations, lies within the spectrum of crimes over which the ICC has jurisdiction,[141] the Court may assume jurisdiction only over private persons and not over corporations.[142]

Consequently, only employees or corporate directors might be prosecuted in the ICC, and not their corporate entities as such.[143] Without undermining the argument that holding individuals, and especially

---

[138] See 2002 Final Report, above n 29, at 32.

[139] See Rights & Accountability In Development, above n 6, at 7.

[140] Human Rights Watch, above n 79.

[141] See Art 7 of the Rome Statute of the International Criminal Court, 17 July 1998, 37 ILM 999 (entered into force 1 July 2002) [hereinafter 'Rome Statute'].

[142] See *ibid*, Art 25.

[143] For an account of the possibility of holding business persons responsible in the ICC for crimes committed in the DRC, see Kabel, above n 137; Julia Graff, 'Corporate War Criminals and the International Criminal Court: Blood and Profits in the Democratic Republic of Congo' (2004) 11 *Human Rights Brief* 23.

directors, responsible may have a 'far reaching effect on corporate human rights policies,'[144] the focus solely on individual liability neglects the corporate nature of the abuse, and thus fails to encompass corporate operations and to deter improper corporate conduct.[145]

However, it should be stressed that the proposal by the French delegation at the 1998 Rome Diplomatic Conference on the Establishment of an International Criminal Court to incorporate legal persons in the personal jurisdiction of the Court was abandoned not because the delegates disputed the conceptual premise that legal persons are bound by international criminal law, but mainly due to practical considerations and the delegations' concerns that such an initiation could ultimately lead to the prosecution of State entities.[146] Amendments may be made only after seven years have passed since the Statute's entry into force,[147] and one scholar has asserted that political support for an amendment introducing legal persons in the jurisdiction of the ICC will only be achieved 'should cases arise at the ICC level where there is seen to be a manifest injustice due to the exclusion of corporations from the jurisdiction of the international court.'[148] Conceivably, this first investigation of the Court over international crimes committed in the DRC[149] may comprise the opportunity to demonstrate such 'manifest injustice', thus rending the Panel's contribution and implications far more influential than initially perceived.

## BIBLIOGRAPHY

Amnesty International, *Democratic Republic of the Congo – 'Our Brothers who Help Kill us' –Economic Exploitation and Human Rights Abuses in the East* (2003), available at http://web.amnesty.org/library/Index/ENGAFR620102003?open&of=ENG-UGA

Paul Asiimwe, 'Report of the UN Panel of Experts on the Illegal Exploitation of Natural Resources of the Democratic Republic of the Congo' (2004) 22 *Journal of Energy and Natural Resources Law* 194.

Colette Braeckman, 'The Looting of the Congo' (2004) *New Internationalist*, May 1, at 13.

---

[144] Viljam Engström, *Who Is Responsible for Corporate Human Rights Violations?* (2002), at 44, available at http://www.abo.fi/instut/imr/norfa/ville.pdf

[145] *Ibid* at 43–44. See also Anita Ramasastry, 'Corporate Complicity: From Nuremberg to Rangoon. An Examination of Forced Labor Cases and Their Impact on the Liability of Multinational Corporations' (2002) 20 Berkeley Journal of International Law 91, at 96–97.

[146] Andrew Clapham, 'The Question of Jurisdiction Under International Criminal Law Over Legal Persons', in *Liability of Multinational Corporations Under International Law*, above n 135, 139, at 191.

[147] See Art 121 of the Rome Statute, above n 141.

[148] Clapham, above n 146, at 160.

[149] See ICC website, at http://www.icc-cpi.int/pressrelease_details&id=26&l=en.html

Andrew Clapham, 'The Question of Jurisdiction Under International Criminal Law Over Legal Persons', in Menno T Kamminga *et al* (eds), *Liability of Multinational Corporations Under International Law* (The Hague, Kluwer, 2000), p 139.

Jeroen Cuvelier and Tim Raeymaekers, International Peace Information Service, *European Companies and the Coltan Trade: An Update, Part 2* (2002), available at www.ipisresearch.be/download.php?id=61

Surya Deva, 'Human Rights Violations by Multinational Corporations and International Law: Where from Here?' (2003) 19 *Connecticut Journal of International Law* 1.

Viljam Engström, *Who Is Responsible for Corporate Human Rights Violations?* (2002), available at http://www.abo.fi/instut/imr/norfa/ville.pdf

Friends of the Earth, *Congo at a Crossroads* (2003), available at http://www.foe.org/oecdguidelines/Oped.pdf

Friends of the Earth, *United Nations Expert Panel Investigation of Illegal Exploitation of Natural Resources and Other Forms of Wealth in the Democratic Republic of the Congo—Overview*, available at http://www.foe.org/oecdguidelines/2 PageBackground.pdf

Arvind Ganesan and Alex Vines, *Engine of War: Resources, Greed, and the Predatory State* (Human Rights Watch, 2004), available at http://www.hrw.org/wr2k4/14.htm

Global Witness, *Same Old Story: A Background Study on Natural Resources in the Democratic Republic of Congo* (2004), available at http://www.globalwitness.org/reports/show.php/en.00054.html

Julia Graff, 'Corporate War Criminals and the International Criminal Court: Blood and Profits in the Democratic Republic of Congo' (2004) 11 *Human Rights Brief* 23.

Human Rights Watch, *DR Congo: UN Must Address Corporate Role In War* (2003), available at http://hrw.org/press/2003/10/drc102703.htm

Sarah Joseph, 'An Overview of the Human Rights Accountability of Multinational Enterprises', in Menno T Kamminga *et al* (The Hague, Kluwer, 2000), *Liability of Multinational Corporations Under International Law*, p 75.

Stephen Kabel, 'Our Business is People (Even if it Kills Them): The Contribution of Multinational Enterprises to the Conflict in the Democratic Republic of Congo' (2004) 12 *Tulane Journal of International and Comparative Law* 461.

Dena Montague, 'Stolen Goods: Coltan and Conflict in the Democratic Republic of Congo' (2002) 22 *SAIS Review* 103.

Finbarr O'Reilly, 'Rush for Natural Resources Still Fuels War in Congo', *Reuters*, 9 August 2004.

OECD Policy Brief, *The OECD Guidelines for Multinational Enterprises* (2003), available at http://www.oecd.org/dataoecd/52/38/2958609.pdf

Anita Ramasastry, 'Corporate Complicity: From Nuremberg to Rangoon. An Examination of Forced Labor Cases and their Impact on the Liability of Multinational Corporations' (2002) 20 *Berkeley Journal of International Law* 91.

Paul Redfern, 'DRC Plunder: UK Accused of Failing to Act on Firms Named in UN Report' (2004) *East African*, January 5.

Michael Renner, 'Natural Resources and Conflict: A Deadly Relationship' (2003) *USA Today*, July, at 20.

Rights & Accountability In Development, *Unanswered Questions: Companies, Conflict and The Democratic Republic of Congo* (2004), available at http://www.unites.uqam.ca/grama/pdf/RAID-DRC_Ex-Summary.pdf

David Usborne, 'Congo: UN Says War Fueled by Foreign Firms' (2003) *The Independent* (London), October 31.

Milan Vesely, 'UN Congo Report Damns Individuals, Companies, Countries' (2002) 282 *African Business*, December, at 16.

# 9

# Corporations and the International Criminal Court

## CRISTINA CHIOMENTI

### I. INTRODUCTION

THIS CHAPTER EXAMINES the issue of the possible extension to corporations of the jurisdiction of the International Criminal Court (ICC), now limited to natural persons, in 2009 when the Statute of the ICC may be reviewed and amended.

It is, however, at the same time an occasion to touch upon the principal problems which have been and are being discussed in relation to the general issue of criminal liability of corporations.

There are, of course, numerous delicate problems to be faced when considering the criminal liability of a corporation, and in particular liability for the very special and serious crimes under the jurisdiction of the ICC. In this connection I formed the opinion that it is not possible to deal equally with two entirely different realities: the ordinary corporation, in particular a transnational corporation, which has a lawful purpose and normally conducts its operations in a lawful way; and the 'criminal corporation', which has an unlawful purpose and was formed as a cover-up for the unlawful activities of certain individuals. This chapter is essentially devoted to the ordinary corporation.

### II. THE STATUTE OF ICC, ITS PREPARATORY WORKS, AND ITS FUTURE AMENDMENTS

#### 1. The Present Statute of the ICC

The Statute of the ICC provides in Article 25, which is titled 'Individual criminal responsibility', that 'the Court shall have jurisdiction over natural persons pursuant to this Statute.'[1]

---

[1] 'Rome Statute for the International Criminal Court' in *The Statute of the International Criminal Court: A Documentary History*, compiled by MC Bassiouni (Transnational Publishers, Inc 1998), at 39.

The choice has therefore been made to exclude jurisdiction over legal persons and in particular over corporations.

## 2. The Preparatory Works

If we look at the preparatory works of the Statute on this subject we see the following development.

The UN Draft Statutes for an International Criminal Court of 1951 and 1953 contemplated that 'the Court shall be competent to judge natural persons [only].'[2]

The Draft Statute for an International Criminal Tribunal prepared in 1993 by M.C. Bassiouni, who would subsequently be at all times one of the leading minds in the realisation of the Statute, stated in Article XII that the purposes of the International Criminal Tribunal would be 'to adjudicate the criminal liability of individuals charged by the State Parties with the violation of international criminal law....' In that document, the expression 'individuals' was clearly of a general nature and was meant to include both natural persons (physical persons) and legal persons (juridical persons).[3]

The International Law Commission (ILC) Draft Statute for an International Criminal Court of 1994 provided that the Court could exercise jurisdiction over 'persons'. Although the word 'person' might technically include both natural and legal persons, the remainder of the Draft suggests that the ILC intended to refer to natural persons only.[4]

The Report of the Preparatory Committee on the Establishment of an International Criminal Court of 1996 contained the following two Proposals under Part 3 bis, General Principles of Criminal Law, Article B, Individual Criminal Responsibility, para a, Personal Jurisdiction:

*Proposal 1*
1. The International Tribunal shall have jurisdiction over [natural] persons pursuant to the provisions of the present statute.
2. A person who commits a crime under this statute is individually responsible and liable for punishment.
   [2. bis Criminal responsibility is individual and cannot go beyond the person and his/her possessions.]

---

[2] Revised Draft Statute for an International Criminal Court (Annex to Report of the 1953 Committee on International Criminal Jurisdiction on its Session held from 27 July to 20 August 1953) (GA, 9th Sess, Supp No 12, A/2645, 1954).

[3] MC Bassiouni, Draft Statute: International Criminal Tribunal, in *The Statute*, above n 1, at 760

[4] Report of the International Law Commission on its Forty-Sixth Session, Draft Statute for an International Criminal Court, 2 May–22 July 1994 (GA, 49th Sess, Supp No 10, A/49/10, 1994).

3. The fact that the present Statute provides criminal responsibility for individuals does not [prejudice] [affect] the responsibility of States under international law.

*Proposal 2*
*Physical persons and juridical persons*

1. The Court shall be competent to take cognisance of the criminal responsibility of:
   (a) Physical persons;
   (b) Juridical persons, with the exception of States, when the crimes committed were committed on behalf of such juridical persons or by their agencies or representatives.
2. The criminal responsibility of juridical persons shall not exclude a criminal responsibility of physical persons who are perpetrators or accomplices in the same crime.
3. This provision shall be without prejudice to the responsibility of States with respect to international law.

*Note:* Some delegations indicated that the expression 'juridical persons' should extend to organisations lacking a legal status. Some delegations expressed doubts about including the criminal responsibility of juridical persons into the Statute. As an alternative the possibility of referring to the 'responsibility' of the juridical persons without including the word 'criminal' was proposed.[5]

The Proceedings of the 1996 Preparatory Committee contain the following comments on the subject of 'Criminal liability of corporations': 'Some delegations held the view that it would be more useful to focus attention on individual responsibility, noting at the same time that corporations were in fact controlled by individuals. Several delegations stated that such liability ran counter their domestic law. The point was made, however, that the liability of the corporations could be important in the context of restitution. It was recalled that the principle had been applied in the Nurnberg Judgement.'[6]

The Working Group recommended to the Preparatory Committee of 1997 the following draft: '1. [t]he Court shall have jurisdiction over natural persons pursuant to the present Statute … [5. the Court shall also have jurisdiction over juridical persons with the exception of States, when the

---

[5] Report of the Preparatory Committee on the Establishment of an International Criminal Court, Vol II (Compilation of Proposals) (GA 51st Sess, Supp No 22, A/51/22, 1996).

[6] Report of the Preparatory Committee on the Establishment of an International Criminal Court, Vol I (Proceedings of the Preparatory Committee During March–April and August 1996) (GA 51st Sess, Supp No 22, A/51/22, 1996).

crimes committed were committed on behalf of such juridical persons or by their agencies or representatives],' and added the following note:

> There is deep divergence views as to the advisability of including criminal responsibility of juridical persons in the Statute. Many delegations are strongly opposed, whereas some strongly favour its inclusion. Others have an open mind. Some delegations hold the view that providing for only the civil or administrative responsibility/liability of juridical persons could provide a middle ground. This avenue, however, has not been thoroughly discussed. Some delegations, who favour the inclusion of juridical persons, hold the view that this expression should be extended to organisations lacking legal statues. Some prefer the term 'legal entities'.[7]

The same texts (draft Article and note) were contained in the full Draft Statute transmitted in April 1998 by the Preparatory Committee to the UN Diplomatic Conference on the Establishment of an International Criminal Court to be held in Rome in June of that year.[8]

In the course of the Conference in Rome the issue of jurisdiction over legal persons was addressed, although I understand that it could not be treated at great length in presence of other pending issues of a more central nature and of the overwhelming objective finally to achieve the creation of an international Court of Justice.

The discussion that took place at the Rome Conference over the inclusion of legal persons in the jurisdiction of ICC is illustrated in great detail in an article by A. Clapham, who was present in the capacity of legal advisor for one of the governments.[9] The most remarkable development was the circulation by the French delegation of a working paper containing an articulated proposal for ICC jurisdiction over 'juridical persons', reading as follows:

> Without prejudice to any individual criminal responsibility of natural persons under this Statute, the Court may also have jurisdiction over a juridical person for a crime under this Statute.
>
> Charges may be filed by the Prosecutor against a juridical person, and the Court may render a judgement over a juridical person for the crime charged, if:
>
> (a) The charges filed by the Prosecutor against the natural person and the juridical person allege the matters referred to in sub paragraphs (b) and (c); and

---

[7] Decision Taken by the Preparatory Committee at its Session held in New York 11–21 February 1997 (A./AC.249/1997/L.5, 1997).

[8] Report of the Inter-Sessional Meeting from 19–30 January 1998 held in Zutphen, The Netherlands (A/AC.249/1997/L.9/Rev.1, 1997).

[9] A Clapham, 'The Question of Jurisdiction Under International Criminal Law Over Legal Persons: Lessons from the Rome Conference on an International Criminal Court' in M Kamminga and S Zia-Siarifi (eds), *Liability of Multinational Corporations Under International Law* (The Hague, Kluwer Law International, 2000), at p 139.

(b)   The natural person charged was in opposition of control within the juridical person under the national law of the State where the juridical person
was registered at the time the crime was committed; and

(c)   The crime was committed by the natural person acting on behalf of and
with the explicit consent of that juridical person and in the course of its
activities; and

(d)   The natural person has been convicted of the crime charged.

For the purpose of this Statute, 'juridical person' means a corporation whose
concrete, real, or dominant objective is seeking private profit or benefit, and not
a State or other public body in the exercise of State authority, a public international body or an organisation registered and acting under the national law of
a State as a non-profit organisation.[10]

The Working Paper contains several interesting solutions for the legal
problems connected with the criminal liability of corporations and we
shall refer to it later when dealing with such problems.

### 3. Amendments and Review of the Statute.

The requirements for changing the Statute are very demanding.

During the first seven years after entry into force of the Statute (1 July
2002 to 1 July 2009) only amendments of an exclusively institutional
nature as listed in Article 122 may be proposed. Article 25 is not in the list.

Seven years after the entry into force of the Statute, the Secretary-
General of the United Nations shall convene a Review Conference to consider amendments; further, after the expiry of the seven-year period any
State party may propose single amendments. Any amendments shall
enter into force only if accepted by seven-eighths of the States parties.

Therefore an extension of the jurisdiction of the ICC to corporations
could only be proposed after July 2009 and would have to be accepted by
seven-eighths of the States parties.

### III. CORPORATIONS AND CRIMINAL LIABILITY IN GENERAL

### 1. The General Debate on Criminal Liability of Corporations

In order to better understand the problems associated with a possible
extension of ICC jurisdiction to corporations it is important to consider
first the general debate surrounding the issue of criminal liability of
corporations.

---

[10] A/Conf./183/WGGP/L.5/Rev. 2, 3 July 1998.

Of course, I will consider the current state of the debate only very briefly and essentially in view of the possible ICC extension.

We have seen that during the preparatory works for the ICC, several delegations opposed the inclusion of liability of legal persons stating that such liability ran counter to their domestic law.

As a matter of fact, common law countries, and specifically the United States and England, have abandoned much earlier than civil law countries the traditional position excluding the criminal liability of corporations, which was expressed since the Middle Ages in the mottos *societas delinquere non potest* (companies cannot commit criminal acts) and *societas puniri non potest* (companies cannot be subjected to criminal punishment).[11]

At the basis of the traditional negative position there were certainly some important conceptual reasons deserving consideration: first, the 'abstraction' doctrine of legal persons, according to which legal persons are only 'artificial subjects' created 'by fiction'[12], whilst criminal liability implies a 'naturalistic' evaluation and judgement only suitable to human beings; second, the related consideration that legal entities are incapable by their very nature of the mental attitudes, whether intent, recklessness, or negligence, entailing the blameworthiness which should normally be at the basis of criminal punishment; third, the principle of individual criminal liability which excludes a criminal liability for the acts of other persons and which would therefore forbid criminal sanctions on the

---

[11] On the medieval origin of the principle, aimed at protecting the newly born communal corporations, see L Arroyo Zapatero, 'Persone giuridiche e responsabilità in Spagna' in *Societas Puniri Potest* (Padova, CEDAM, 2003), at p 179.

On the gradual recognition of the criminal responsibility of corporations in England, see C Wells, 'Corporate Criminal Liability in England and Wales' in *Societas Puniri Potest* (Padova, CEDAM, 2003), at p 109, and C De Maglie, *L'Etica e il Mercato, La responsabilità penale delle società* (Milano, Giuffre, 2002), at p 145 ff. In England the first judicial decisions establishing the criminal liability of corporations go back to 1840 and 1844, and are based on the concept of vicarious liability. The identification theory, establishing a direct liability of corporations, was developed one century later, in the 1940s, and found a clear recognition in 1972 in *Tesco v Nattrass* [1972] AC 153, HL.

On the evolution of criminal liability of corporations in the United States, see RL Dixon, 'Corporate criminal liability' in M Spencer and R Sims (eds), *Corporate Misconduct* (Westport, CN, Quorum Books, 1995), at p 41; K Brickey, *Corporate Criminal Liability, A Treaties on the Criminal Liability of Corporations, Their Officers and Agents*, vol 1 (West Publishers Co, 1992), at pp 2–11; De Maglie, above, at p 12 ff. The 'old and exploded doctrine' of corporate immunity from civil prosecution was abandoned by the Supreme Court decision in *Eugene F Moran v New York Central and Hudson River R Co* 212 US 466 (1909). Since then, in the United States the criminal liability of corporations has been generally based on the theory of vicarious liability (*respondeat superior*).

A comparison between the principles of criminal corporate liability in the United States and England can be found in J Coffee, *Emerging Issues in Corporate Criminal Policy*, Foreword, in R Gruner, *Corporate Crime and Sentencing* (London, Lexis Law Publishers, 1994).

[12] The 'theory of fiction' of legal persons was elaborated at the beginning of the 19th century by the great German jurist Savigny. In contrast, another great German jurist, O von Gierke, elaborated a 'theory of reality' at the end of the 19th century.

corporations bearing effects on directors and managers of the corporation as well as on third parties such as minority shareholders, creditors or employees, for acts committed by other individuals working within the corporation.[13] It should be noted that all these conceptual reasons have something to do with the problem of *mens rea* of corporations to which we will revert later on.

However, it is probably correct to say that the main reasons for excluding the criminal liability of corporations have been practical policy considerations. An eminent Italian scholar of criminal law who devoted a research to the subject over 30 years ago concluded that 'the principle *societas delinquere non potest* has no ontological value,' that is no value relating to the essence of corporations and of criminal law.[14]

The practical reasons have probably been on one side the desire of corporations to operate without the burdens of criminal law, but on the other side, and above all, the fact that in different countries society and legislators have perceived at different times the necessity or expediency to impose on corporations as such the legal remedy of criminal liability as opposed to civil liability.

To understand the latter point it is useful to focus for a moment on the distinction between civil and criminal liability. The object of civil liability is to *redress* a situation of fact through the imposition of a conduct (whether the recovery of money or other property or the enforcement of a right or advantage on behalf of the plaintiff), whilst the object of criminal liability is to *deter* (and to *rehabilitate*) through the punishment, and through the pain and blame associated with punishment.

The need to deter (or rehabilitate) a corporation as such had not been widely felt until corporations started to impose themselves as a decisive presence (perhaps *the* decisive presence) in society, pushing aside to a large extent the role of individuals. In a way, it could be said that in contemporary society corporations have abandoned their 'fictional' features, which justified the abstraction doctrine mentioned previously, and have adopted 'real' features which make them equal, from the point of view of the criminal law and its objectives, to natural persons.

This factual transformation of corporations and the consequent expediency or necessity to impose a criminal liability on them, in particular for the purpose of deterrence, has been perceived earlier in the United States

---

[13] These conceptual reasons are amply examined by F Bricola, 'Il costo del principio societas delinquere non potest nell'attuale dimensione del fenomeno societario', in (1970) *Riv It Dir Proc Pen* 991–1031. For a more recent analysis of the same conceptual issues, see C Wells, *Corporations and Criminal Responsibility* (Oxford, Oxford University Press, 2001), at pp 74–83.

[14] Bricola, above n 13, at 1031.

and in England due to the faster pace of industrial development and to the social context of those countries.[15]

At the same time, under the criminal law system of civil law countries the only way in which criminal conduct by groups or associations could be caught was under the offence of 'criminal association' (in Italy *associazione a delinquere*; in France *association de malfaiteurs*),[16] which is close to the criminal conspiracy concept of common law countries. This approach is obviously insufficient in facing the problem of criminal liability of corporations, technically because the crime of 'criminal association' leads to punishment of the individual members and not of the association; factually, because the 'criminal associations' are organisations whose principal object is a criminal activity, while the corporations that we are primarily considering in this chapter are organisations with a perfectly lawful purpose and with perfectly lawful activities in general, but which may in particular circumstances behave contrary to criminal law.

The case of a criminal association or conspiracy is considered by the ICC Statute in Article 25(2)(d), which establishes the criminal liability of a person who 'contributes to the commission … of a crime by a group of persons acting with a common purpose. Such contribution … shall be made with the aim of furthering the criminal activity or criminal purpose of the group …. For the reasons mentioned above, this provision cannot meet the problems of criminal liability of corporations treated in this chapter. The two types of liability, although both broadly relating to a 'group conduct', must be kept distinguished.

At the end of the Second World War, the Nuremberg Military Tribunal took into consideration the criminal conduct of organizations, such as the Gestapo, the SS, and others, for the purpose of a 'declaration of criminality', and of corporations, such as Krupp, accused of violation of the laws of war in connection with labour camps programs. However, after the findings of criminality (for the organizations) and of guilt (for the Krupp firm), the liability was imposed on the individual members of the organizations, and on the owner and other officials of the firm.

In recent years the emergence of dramatic problems in particularly sensitive areas such as corruption and terrorism have convinced legislators all over the world that the solutions cannot be found solely in the criminal prosecution of individuals and must necessarily involve the criminal liability of the corporations as such. The two main objectives in involving the corporations are *deterrence* and *reparations*. Deterrence is now regarded as an essential tool of criminal justice policy, and the ability to focus on

---

[15] See Brickey, above n 11, at pp 7–8, on the early perception by American Congress that criminal liability should be imposed on corporations as a mechanism to control their institutional behaviour, specifically when introducing criminal penalties applicable to corporations in the antitrust legislation of 1890 (the Sherman Act) and 1914 (the Clayton Act).

[16] Italian Codice di Diritto Penale, Art 416; French Code de Droit Penal, Art 450.

and to affect corporate behaviour and image as such can be especially effective for the purpose of deterrence. Further, since the corporate façade is increasingly used as a cover for criminal activities, the current criminal justice policy for such cases is to strike at the corporations in order to deter the individuals hiding behind it. As to reparations, nowadays they can be effectively provided only by the financial resources of corporations rather than by the limited means of individuals.

Accordingly, most civil law countries have gradually introduced in recent years national legislation providing for the criminal liability of corporations, whether in general or with respect to certain categories of crimes, in particular corruption, public fraud, white-collar crimes, money laundering, drug trafficking, and terrorism. For example, legislation establishing a criminal liability of corporations was introduced in France in 1994, in Belgium in 1999, in Italy in 2001, and in Switzerland in 2003.[17]

Further, in recent years an increasing number of international Conventions and instruments, especially in the field of corruption and terrorism, explicitly contemplate a criminal liability of corporations.[18]

In conclusion, the concept of a criminal responsibility of corporations is now generally accepted at the level of both national and international law. The issues now relate to the prerequisites, the contents, and the consequences of such liability. Which crimes? Which rules of attribution of *actus reus* and *mens rea*? Which sanctions? What relation with the liability of the individuals? These issues have no single answer and can only be answered reasonably in relation to the different types of subjects and situations.

## 2. Current Solutions to the Problem of Mens Rea of Corporations

We have seen that the principal conceptual objections to the criminal liability of corporations all centered around the problem of *mens rea*.

---

[17] For a description of the most important national legislations throughout the world establishing the criminal liability of corporations, see De Maglie, above n 11. The liability introduced by the Italian legislation is formally defined 'administrative' but is commonly held, both by scholars and in public opinion, to have a 'criminal' nature. In Europe, the Netherlands (which does not have a pure civil law system) preceded the other countries in introducing into its legislation the principle of criminal liability of corporations as early as 1974.

[18] See, eg, OECD Convention on Combating Bribery of Foreign Public Officials in International Business Transactions, 17 December 1997; Council of Europe Convention on the Protection of the Environment through Criminal Law, 4 November 1998; Council of Europe Criminal Law Convention on Corruption, 27 January 1999; UN Convention for the Suppression of the Financing of Terrorism, 25 February 2000; UN Convention against Corruption, 31 October 2003.

Modern legal doctrine, both in the elaborations of scholars and in judicial decisions, has faced the problem with great attention and offers several possible criteria for attributing *mens rea* to a corporation.[19]

Recognizing that the traditional model of vicarious liability (*respondeat superior*), whereby the corporation is automatically liable for the acts of its employees in the course of their duties, is difficult to support beyond strict liability offences[20], the following alternative 'rules of attribution' have been amongst others suggested:

— the identification doctrine (alter ego): the corporation (as well as the individual) is liable if the criminal action has been committed with the necessary mens rea by an individual who is sufficiently important in the corporate structure for his acts to be identified with the corporation itself, or who is specifically in charge of compliance with the relevant laws or regulations;

— the aggregation doctrine: the corporation is liable if, on aggregating the acts and mental elements of all individuals within the corporation, they would amount to a crime;

— the interest doctrine (often combined with the two above): the corporation is liable if the crime was committed in the interest of the corporation;

— Corporate Compliance Programs (or Codes of Conduct): this is a model which takes into account the modern organizational structure of corporations, where responsibilities for compliance with regulatory matters, such as health, safety, labour, environment, etc, are spread throughout the corporation. At the same time this model emphasizes the objective of prevention in establishing a criminal liability of corporations.[21] Corporate Compliance Programs are formal and detailed rules, often prepared in accordance with the directives of public authority, designed to ensure that employees will know the relevant laws and corporate policies regarding the operations of the corporation, and providing for control over compliance with the laws and for internal sanctions in cases of non-compliance. In basic terms, the corporation can avoid criminal liability if it proves effective adoption of such programs, and surveillance over the compliance with the same.

---

[19] A comprehensive analysis of the responses of the current law to the problems of *mens rea* in corporate criminal liability can be found in CVH Clarkson and HM Keating, *Criminal Law* (London, Sweet and Maxwell, 1998), at pp 229–43.

[20] See, however, Coffee, above n 11, for strong support of a general application of vicarious liability.

[21] B Fisse, 'Reconstructing Corporate Criminal Law Deterrence, Retribution, Fault and Sanctions' (1983) *South California Law Review* 1141, and Gruner, above n 11, at 6.

In conclusion, it can be said that these suggestions and elaborations offer useful instruments for well-balanced legislative solutions of the problem of *mens rea* of corporations, appropriate for the different types of crimes and for the different circumstances.

## IV. CORPORATIONS AND INTERNATIONAL LAW

Most of the international law instruments that contemplate a criminal liability of corporations have adopted until now the so-called 'indirect enforcement method', whereby the international instrument imposes on States the obligation to introduce the liability in their domestic legal systems.[22] For example, the 1999 Council of Europe Criminal Law Convention on Corruption provides, in Article 18, Corporate Liability, that 'each Party shall adopt such legislative and other measures as may be necessary to ensure that legal persons can be held liable for the criminal offences of active bribery, trading influence and money laundering established in accordance with this Convention ....'[23]

But international law no longer deals only with States. Individuals and organisations are increasingly becoming the new subjects of the international law system, having under it both duties and responsibilities, and rights and privileges that single States cannot infringe. This is the widely

---

[22] On the 'indirect' and 'direct' enforcement regimes in international criminal law, see MC Bassiouni, *Introduction to International Criminal Law* (Ardsley, NY, Transnational Publishers Inc, 2003), at pp 18, 333, 387.

The indirect enforcement method means that enforcement over international criminal law takes place through national legal systems. One aspect of the indirect enforcement method relevant for our present discussion is the incorporation in national laws of obligations arising under international criminal law; the method of incorporation is also intended to permit adaptation of treaty obligations to the requirements of national law.

The direct enforcement method contemplates international judicial institutions which have the power of rendering and enforcing their judgments without going through national States. This assumes, of course, the existence of substantive international criminal legislation to be adjudicated by the international institutions. The only fully comprehensive examples of a direct enforcement regime have been the International Military Tribunals set up in Nuremberg and Tokyo after the Second World War. The ICC (following the International Criminal Tribunals for Yugoslavia and Rwanda) is a major example of the direct enforcement method, but is not fully comprehensive since it has to rely on the co-operation of States for the apprehension of accused persons and for the enforcement of its judgments.

[23] Other international instruments, also adopting the 'indirect enforcement method', are less stringent on 'criminal' liability, since they contemplate the imposition of 'criminal or administrative sanctions or measures on legal persons' (Art 9 of the 1998 Council of Europe Convention on the Protection of Environment through Criminal Law). A similarly flexible solution is found in Art 26 of the 2003 UN Convention against Corruption, in Art 3.4 of the 2002 Optional Protocol to the Convention on the Rights of the Child on the Sale of Children, children prostitution and children pornography, and in Art 5 of the 2000 UN Convention for the Suppression of the Financing of Terrorism.

noted process of 'privatisation' of international law,[24] which, as far as criminal law is concerned, started after the Second World War Nuremberg International Military Tribunals, 'direct enforcement' institutions establishing criminal liabilities of individuals irrespective of national laws.[25] The process has expanded with international legislation on human rights granting protection and rights directly to individuals but also imposing criminal responsibilities directly on individuals. The ICC (presided by the International Criminal Tribunals for Yugoslavia and for Rwanda) is a recent major example of a 'direct enforcement' institution directly establishing criminal liabilities on individuals which single States cannot modify.

In this framework some recent international instruments directly contemplate a criminal liability of corporations irrespective of any national State legislation. This may be the final outcome of the UN Norms on the Responsibilities of Transnational Corporations and other Business Enterprises with regard to Human Rights currently under discussion at the United Nations Human Rights Commission after being adopted in August 2003 by the Sub-Commission for the Promotion and Protection of Human Rights.[26] The Norms, although a set of 'soft law' rules (rules that are not strictly binding but may in time become customary international law), directly impose obligations on corporations for the respect of human rights.

---

[24] International law scholars started focusing after the Second World War on the emergence of the international personality of individuals, which departed from the strict positivistic theory that States are the only actors of international law. See M Korowicz, 'The problem of the international personality of individuals' (1956) *American Journal of International Law* 50; H Lauterpacht, *International law and human rights* (New York, NY, Garland, 1973). For a more recent analysis of this process see M Janis, *An introduction to international law*, (New York, NY, Aspen Publishers, 2003), at pp 239–85, and Bassiouni, above n 22, at pp 64–71.

From a conceptual point of view, although it cannot be denied that nowadays individuals sometimes acquire rights and obligations directly by treaty independently of national legislation, several scholars still doubt that these circumstances promote the individuals to true subjects of the international community, which is still regarded as a community among States (the governing entities) excluding the individuals (the governed entities). For this conceptual discussion, eg among Italian scholars, see L Ferrari Bravo, *Lezioni di diritto internazionale* (place of publication, publisher, 1998), at pp 127–49; B Conforti, *Diritto internazionale* (place of publication, publisher, 1997), at pp 20–22.

[25] Art 6 of the Charter of the International Military Tribunal annexed to the Agreement for the Prosecution and Punishment of the Major War Criminals of the European Axis, signed on 8 August 1945, provided: 'The following acts … are crimes coming within the jurisdiction of the Tribunal for which there shall be individual responsibility....' In its judgment the Tribunal stated: 'It was submitted that international law is concerned with the actions of sovereign States, and provides no punishment for individuals …. In the opinion of the Tribunal … this submissions must be rejected. That international law imposes duties and liabilities upon individual as upon States has long been recognized … the very essence of the Charter is that individuals have international duties which transcend the national obligations of obedience imposed by the individual State.'

[26] UN doc E/CN.4/Sub.2/2002/13 at 15–21 (2002)

## V. THE CRIMES WITHIN THE JURISDICTION OF THE INTERNATIONAL CRIMINAL COURT AND THE POSSIBLE INVOLVEMENT OF CORPORATIONS

Under Article 1 of its Statute, the ICC is established to exercise jurisdiction over persons 'for the most serious crimes of international concern, as referred to in its Statute.'

Article 5 specifies that 'the jurisdiction of the Court shall be limited to the most serious crimes of concern to the international community as a whole' and that 'the Court has jurisdiction in accordance with this Statute with respect to the following crimes: (a) the crime of genocide; (b) crimes against humanity; (c) war crimes; (d) the crime of aggression' (however, with respect to the crime of aggression, jurisdiction will be exercised only at a future time and after it is defined and approved by the Assembly of States parties). Articles 6, 7, and 8 contain detailed definitions of 'genocide', 'crimes against humanity', and 'war crimes', respectively.

What type of involvement by corporations can be reasonably imagined with respect to the above crimes?

This question would obviously not make sense for corporations set up to pursue a criminal purpose, which may be instruments for any of the above crimes. In any case it should be noted that with respect to such 'criminal corporations' the primary concern is the prosecution of the individuals who are behind the corporation: this objective can already be pursued under the present text of the ICC Statute making use of Article 25(3)(d), which provides for the criminal responsibility of a person who in any way contributes to the commission of a crime by a group of persons acting with a common purpose.

The interesting issue for purposes of this chapter is what involvement in the ICC Statute crimes can be imagined on the part of corporations (in particular, transnational corporations) which have a perfectly lawful purpose and normally operate in a perfectly lawful way.

It is difficult to imagine that, except in extreme circumstances (such as those considered at the Nuremberg Trials with respect to German industries involved with the Holocaust), a corporation ordinarily operating in the industrial, commercial, or services sector, will act as a principal author to commit any of the crimes falling under the jurisdiction of the ICC, considering their peculiar nature. Some authors have mentioned in this connection the issue of security corporations organising hired troops which may in certain circumstances be involved in war crimes. Also, instances have been mentioned of manufacturing corporations which may make use of 'slave labour'.[27]

---

[27] See Clapham, above n 9, at pp 149–50.

It should be borne in mind that, under whatever rules of attribution, for the crime to be attributed to the corporation the crime must be done on behalf of the corporation and for the benefit of the corporation, not merely by employees of the corporation in a personal capacity or for a personal purpose. Bearing this in mind, the most realistic cases of involvement of corporations in ICC Statute crimes are forms of complicity.

I understand that during the ICC preparatory works the instances which were mentioned by some delegates included forms of complicity such as the commerce of products deriving from violations of human rights, the storage of arms and equipment, the covering up of mass graves by construction companies, and radio broadcasts by communication companies.

In the Reports of the Panel of Experts on the Illegal Exploitation of the Natural Resources of the Democratic Republic of Congo transmitted to the United Nations in 2002 and 2003 certain specified companies are accused 'by contributing to the revenues of the elite networks [of that country], directly or indirectly, to [have contributed] to ongoing conflict and to human rights abuses.'[28]

Of special interest is the case currently pending before the Belgian Courts against the oil company TotalFinaElf, as well as against two of its managers. This action was brought under a Belgian law of 1993 (expanded further in 1999 in order to include not only war crimes but also crimes against humanity and genocide, and then seriously restricted by a further revision in 2003) which—at the time the action was filed—recognized the Belgian Courts as having a universal jurisdiction for the repression of serious violations of international human rights, and under a Belgian law of 1999 which establishes the criminal liability of legal persons. In this action Total is accused, in connection with the building of the Yadana pipeline in Burma, of complicity in crimes against humanity, namely murder and arbitrary execution; enslavement, imprisonment and other severe deprivations of physical liberty; deportation and forcible transfer of population; and torture. The accusation is based on the allegation of a global moral and financial support given by Total to the military regime of Burma with Total's full knowledge of the consequences of this support on the commission by that regime of massive violation of human rights; as well as of a local moral, financial, logistical, and military support given by Total to the military battalions charged with assuring the

---

[28] Final Report of the Panel of Experts on the Illegal Exploitation of Natural Resources and Other Forms of Wealth of the Democratic Republic of Congo, transmitted on 15 October 2003 by the Chairman of the Panel, Mahmoud Kassem to the Secretary-General of the United Nations, Kofi Annan, in accordance with the mandate received by the Panel of Experts from the Security Council of the United Nations and extended to 31 October 2003 (Security Council Resolution 1457 (2003), 24 January 2003, and Security Council Resolution 1499 (2003), 13 August 2003 (UN doc S/2003/1027).

security of the Yadana pipeline, with Total's full knowledge of systematic and widespread violations of human rights by such battalions.[29]

In light of the above it is clear that, in the case of an extension of ICC jurisdiction to corporations, the issue of complicity would deserve the highest attention.

## VI. THE CONCERNS ABOUT THE EXTENSION OF INTERNATIONAL CRIMINAL COURT JURISDICTION TO CORPORATIONS

It is well known that serious concerns have been raised about several aspects of the ICC institution, to the point that the United States has decided not to become a party for the time being. Some of these concerns, although raised in general, give rise to special considerations in relation to transnational corporations and are therefore worth examining in the framework of this chapter.

It is understandable that concerns may exist, considering the very innovative nature of the ICC institution, which combines the two features of being *international* and *permanent*.

Although technically defined as a 'hybrid' system (since it has to rely on the cooperation of the States for the apprehension and surrender of accused persons, legal assistance, and enforcement of its judgments),[30] the ICC is a very strong international institution of direct enforcement at the fundamental levels of investigation, trial, and sentencing.

Further, it is a permanent institution and in this respect it is profoundly different from previous international tribunals such as the International Military Tribunal at Nuremberg, the International Criminal Tribunal for the Former Yugoslavia or the International Criminal Tribunal for Rwanda, which were ad hoc institutions created to judge prior events specifically identified in time and scope.

### 1. Political Use of the Court

The first concern that has been expressed is that the Court, due to its structure, may be used as a political instrument against particular countries; for example, in relation to a country's soldiers operating abroad on missions of any nature, including peacekeeping or humanitarian missions, in order to create obstacles to the mission through the instrument of court proceedings. A similar concern of instrumentality could subsist with respect to the foreign activities of important transnational corporations,

---

[29] *Case brought against X, TotalFinaElf SA*, T Desmarest, H Madeo before the Instructing Judge of the Tribunal de Première Instance de Bruxelles on 25 April 2002.
[30] Bassiouni, above n 22, at p 495.

which also represent a country abroad in a significant way both practically and symbolically.

In order to fully evaluate this concern it is necessary to consider the conditions of jurisdiction and the trigger mechanism of prosecutions under the Statute.

Under Article 12 of the Statute, the Court may exercise its jurisdiction if the crime was committed on the territory of a State party to the Statute or by a person who is a national of a State party to the Statute. In addition, the Court may exercise its jurisdiction on the basis of an express ad hoc acceptance by a State which is not party to the Statute if the crime was committed on the territory or by a national of such State.

It may be noted in passing that, in the light the above jurisdictional principles, the ICC is not a court of 'universal jurisdiction'. However, under the territorial principle, the ICC may also judge nationals of a State which is not a party to the Statute, without such State's consent. Further, where an investigation is promoted by the UN Security Council, the two jurisdictional principles do not apply, so that in such a case the ICC may happen to exercise its jurisdiction over a national of a State not party to the Statute for crimes allegedly committed in the territory of a State equally not party to the Statute. These possibilities increase the concern of the countries which fear a political use of the Court.

As to the trigger mechanism, according to Article 13 an investigation and subsequent prosecution may be started in three ways: (a) a State party may refer to the Prosecutor a situation in which crimes appear to have been committed; (b) the UN Security Council may refer to the Prosecutor a situation in which crimes appear to have been committed; (c) the Prosecutor may initiate an investigation *proprio motu* on the basis of information of crimes within the jurisdiction of the court.

Under Articles 15 and 53 of the Statute it is up to the Prosecutor to evaluate the information received and to determine, based on various considerations, whether there is reasonable basis to proceed with an investigation and then, upon investigation, whether there is sufficient basis for a prosecution.

It is in particular the role of the Prosecutor and his discretion to pursue or not to pursue cases, which raises concerns in the political respect. Article 42 of the Statute states that 'the office of the Prosecutor shall act independently as a separate organ of the Court.' But some see in the Prosecutor a dangerous and potentially enormous source of power. As one critic puts it, 'the risk here is that this independent counsel, not subject to any legitimate political accountability, in fact will be politicized and that it will go after, and it will be presented with, cases based principally on political grounds.'[31]

---

[31] Emory University School of Law Atlanta, Georgia, 'Toward an International Criminal Court? A Debate' (2000) 14 *Emory International Review* 159 (the remarks reported are by John Bolton).

To answer such concerns several considerations should be taken into account. In the first place the Prosecutor is not as unaccountable as suggested above. Under Article 46 of the Statute the Prosecutor may be removed from office by an absolute majority of the States parties 'if he is found to have committed serious misconduct or a serious breach of his duties.'

Further, the decisions of the Prosecutor relating to investigations are not beyond control. On the one hand, Article 15(4) requires the authorisation of the Pre-Trial Chamber before the Prosecutor commences an investigation *proprio motu* as opposed to when a situation is referred by a State party or by the UN Security Council. On the other hand, under Article 53, the Pre-Trial Chamber has the power to review the Prosecutor's decisions not to proceed.

But above all, two important features of the Statute should be considered for their effects on the whole issue of political use of the ICC: the power of the UN Security Council to defer an investigation or prosecution, and the principle of complementarity of the ICC with respect to national legal systems.

Under Article 16 of the Statute, Deferral of Investigation or Prosecution, 'no investigation or prosecution may be commenced or proceeded with under the Statute for a period of 12 months after the Security Council, in a resolution adopted under Chapter VII of the Charter of the United Nations, has requested the Court to that effect; that request may be renewed by the Council under the same conditions.' It will be noted that under this mechanism the veto power of any country in the Security Council may only serve to force the continuation of an investigation or prosecution, never to stop it. The provision reflects the choice of the State parties to the Statute to counter the risks of a political use of the ICC with a remedy which is itself of a political nature. Precisely for this reason the provision may be regarded as an unsatisfactory answer to the concern.

In my opinion, the most convincing answer to the concern over political use of the ICC (although not a perfect answer, which would be impossible) lies in the complementary nature of ICC jurisdiction.

The Preamble and Article 1 of the Statute state that the ICC shall be complementary to national criminal jurisdictions. The principle is developed in Article 17 which provides that 'the Court shall determine that a case is inadmissible where (a) the case is being investigated or prosecuted by a State which has jurisdiction over it, unless the State is unwilling or unable to carry out the investigation or prosecution; (b) the case has been investigated by a State which has jurisdiction over it and the State has decided not to prosecute the person concerned, unless the decision resulted from the unwillingness or inability of the State genuinely to prosecute ....' The concepts of 'unwillingness' and 'inability' are defined in the subsequent part of the Article.

In other words, national criminal jurisdictions have priority over the ICC. Without ignoring the discretional margins of a judgment on the unwillingness or inability, for a State fearing the political nature of an ICC procedure there is the opportunity to have the matter dealt with by its own national courts.

## 2. State-related Corporations or Organisations

It is obvious that States are careful not to incur liability under the ICC just as they have always avoided involvement in any form of criminal liability. Paragraph 4 of Article 25 of the Statute specifies that 'no provision in this Statute relating to individual criminal responsibility shall affect the responsibility of States under international law.'

In the event of an extension of ICC jurisdiction to legal persons, States would want not only to make it clear that the definition of legal or juridical person does not include States, but would also want to specify that public organizations would be excluded from liability. It is obvious that in this area the risk of a political use of the ICC would be especially high. At the same time, it would not be reasonable to exclude from liability profit-making corporations simply because they are owned by the State.

The Working Draft presented during the preparatory works of ICC (and mentioned under Section II.2 above) contains a definition of 'juridical person' which is an interesting effort in this direction: 'For the purpose of this Statute, "juridical person" means a corporation whose concrete, real or dominant objective is seeking private profit or benefit, and not a State or other public body in the exercise of State authority, a public international body or an organization registered, and acting under the national law of a State as a non profit organization.'

## 3. Extended Interpretation of the Crimes

One complaint about the ICC Statute is the allegation that crime definitions are 'vague and elastic' so that there would be a risk of an extended interpretation. An answer to this complaint has been that the ICC Statute contains remarkably detailed definitions of many of the crimes, and that the crimes as defined in the Statute are largely codified in international treaties.[32] Furthermore, the risk of undue expansion should be reduced by the solemn statement in Article 5 that 'the jurisdiction of the Court shall be limited to the most serious crimes of concern to the international community as a whole.'

[32] See 'Toward an International Criminal Court? A Debate', above n 31 (these answers were provided by Kenneth Roth).

However, it must be recognised that if corporations were covered by the Statute the temptation would be great to extend the Statute to new areas, in particular those bordering on crimes against humanity. An example is given by an article which deals with environmental liability in connection with the ICC.[33] Another indication of this trend towards expansion is given by the discussion over the subject-matter jurisdiction of the US Alien Tort Claims Act.[34]

Therefore, if in the future the ICC Statute were to be extended to corporations it would be advisable to give specific indications on the ICC's subject-matter jurisdiction in those areas where doubts might subsist considering the developments of international law at that time.

## VII. ISSUES TO BE ESPECIALLY CONSIDERED IN THE CASE OF AN EXTENSION OF INTERNATIONAL CRIMINAL COURT JURISDICTION TO CORPORATIONS

### 1. Mens Rea: The Rules of Attribution

We have seen that the question of how to attribute to a corporation *actus reus* and *mens rea* of the individuals acting within the corporation is one of the major problems in establishing the criminal liability of a corporation. We have also seen that various different 'rules of attribution' have been elaborated by the scholars who have analyzed the organic relation between the corporation and the individuals acting within it, as well as the modern organizational structure of corporations.

The Draft Statute submitted to the Rome Conference contemplated that legal persons would be liable 'when the crimes committed were committed on behalf of such legal persons or by their agencies or representatives.'[35]

The working paper of the French delegation contemplated that a juridical person would be liable if (a) the natural person convicted of a crime 'was in a position of control within the juridical person under the national law of the State where the juridical person was registered at the time the crime was committed,' and (b) 'the crime was committed by the natural person acting on behalf of and with the explicit consent of that juridical person and in the course of its activities.'

It is interesting to compare the above projects with the rules of attribution adopted in the 1999 Council of Europe Criminal Law Convention

---

[33] P Sharp, 'Prospects for Environmental Liability in the International Criminal Court' (1999) 18 *Victoria Environmental Law Journal* 217.

[34] 'Corporate Liability for Violations of International Human Rights Law' (2001) 114 *Harvard Law Review* 2025.

[35] Report of the Inter-Sessional Meeting from 19 to 30 January 1998 held in Zutphen, The Netherlands (A/AC.249/1997/L.9/Rev.1, 1997).

on Corruption. This Convention provides that 'legal persons can be held liable for the criminal offences [of active bribery, trading in influence and money laundering] committed for their benefit by any natural person, acting either individually or as part of an organ of the legal person, who has a leading position within the legal person, based on: a power of representation of the legal person; or an authority to take decisions on behalf of the legal person; or an authority to exercise control within the legal person.' Further, the Convention provides that 'apart from the cases already provided for [above], each Party shall take the necessary measures to ensure that a legal person can be held liable where the lack of supervision or control by a natural person referred to [above] has made possible the commission of the criminal offences mentioned [above] for the benefit of that legal person by a natural person under its authority.'

It will be noted that the Council of Europe Convention adopts a combination of the identification and interest doctrines as far as the conduct of the leading individuals of the corporations is concerned, while for the conduct of individual at the lower levels of the corporation the Convention refers to lack of supervision or control, thereby opening the way to the model of Corporate Compliance Programs.

As a consequence, national legislation enacted pursuant to the Council of Europe Convention has extensively adopted the Corporate Compliance Program method, providing that corporations will not be held liable when they have adopted, have effectively applied, and have supervised the functioning of and compliance with, organizational and management models apt to prevent the relevant crimes.

It is arguable which rules of attribution would be most appropriate for the very special type of crimes contemplated by the ICC Statute. There is no doubt that a corporation could only be liable for crimes under the ICC Statute if the criminal conduct was adopted on its behalf and in its interest.

It is more arguable whether liability should only be linked to the conduct of individuals in a senior position within the corporation or should also cover staff at lower levels.

I believe that if the liability were to extend to staff at lower levels, in consideration of the size and complexity of transnational corporations a Corporate Compliance Program solution should be adopted in order to exclude liability in some extreme cases. Although it is very unlikely that this type of crime could be committed in blameless ignorance, there might be circumstances where, for example, a crime against humanity or a war crime is committed (whether as a principal or as an accomplice) at the initiative of a local manager of the corporation notwithstanding the existence of a contrary corporate policy and of reasonable surveillance.

## 2. Mens rea: The Substantive Rules

The Statute of the ICC contains an express and detailed definition of the mental element required for liability. Such a definition was not present in the charter of the prior ad hoc Tribunals and constitutes therefore a very important indicator for international law in general. Article 30 of the Statute reads as follows:

*Mental Element*

1. Unless otherwise provided, a person shall be criminally responsible and liable for punishment for a crime within the jurisdiction of the Court only if the material elements are committed with intent and knowledge.
2. For the purposes of this article, the person has intent where:
    (a) in relation to conduct, that person means to engage in the conduct;
    (b) in relation to a consequence, that person means to cause that consequence or is aware that it will occur in the ordinary course of events.
3. For the purposes of this article 'knowledge' means awareness that a circumstance exists or a consequence will occur in the ordinary course of events. 'Know' and 'knowingly' shall be construed accordingly.

This provision sets a particularly high standard, requiring a particularly high level of mens rea before liability will ensue. This is understandable in light of the very serious nature of the crimes and of the very serious potential punishment, both in terms of pain and blame, that may derive. It should be noted, however, that, exceptionally for some particular crimes, the Statute specifically sets different rules on mens rea (for example, negligence or recklessness are sufficient to impose responsibility on military commanders and other superiors, respectively; a specific intent is required for the crime of genocide).

First, the provision requires both intent *and* knowledge with respect to the material elements of the crimes, that is as regards the conduct, the consequences, and the circumstances. This implies that the criminal conducts described in general terms under Article 25(3) ('commits a crime …', 'solicits, orders …', 'aids, abets or assists …', 'contributes …', 'incites …', 'attempts …') are not criminally relevant and punishable, lacking the intent or the knowledge in the terms set out in Article 30.

Further, the provision does not contemplate recklessness as a possible mental state. Recklessness or negligence is relevant only where expressly and exceptionally contemplated for some particular crimes. In this respect, the general rule of the Statute sets a higher standard than has been adopted by some decisions of the ad hoc international tribunals.

Finally, the definition specifies that a person has intent (or, respectively, knowledge) with respect to consequences only if he is aware that such consequences 'will occur in the ordinary course of events.' This definition appears to correspond to the concept of 'direct intent', as opposed to 'possible intent', and excludes liability if consequences are merely possible.

## 3. Complicity

Complicity is a particularly complex area in criminal law. It becomes even more complex when examined with regard to the conduct of transnational corporations and violations of human rights in countries where they operate.

In this respect, the issue has been the subject of passionate discussions from both a political and a legal point of view, and present expectations are set at a very high level.

This is clearly apparent if we look at the types of possible complicity which are now currently listed when the issue is dealt with:

— *direct* complicity, when a corporation actively assists violations of human rights committed by other persons;
— *indirect* complicity, when a corporation through its lawful activities in a country gives financial support (for example through investments and the payment of taxes) or moral support to a country whose regime commits violations of human rights;
— *beneficial* complicity, when a corporation benefits from the violation of human rights even though it does not give any specific support;
— *silent* complicity, when a corporation remains silent and inactive in the face of human rights violations.

The *Total* case before the Belgian courts provides a very clear example of alleged complicity of the first two types: direct complicity, where Total is accused of local financial and logistical support given to the military battalions charged with assuring the security of the pipeline; and indirect complicity where Total is accused of a global moral and financial support to the military regime.

Careful observers of the issue understand that in order to achieve progress it is necessary to draw clear and reasonable lines both politically and legally: 'what is needed is a model of complicity that is not so restrictive as to be ineffective except against the most egregiously bad multinational corporations but neither so inclusive that it will be politically unacceptable except to the most ethically compliant states. This is the threshold question—what is the minimum level of involvement and of knowledge before liability is triggered.'[36] In this chapter I will obviously examine the issue only from the legal aspect.

From the point of view of criminal law, complicity has two necessary requirements: (1) the causation element, that is the necessary connection between the act of the accomplice and the act of the principal author; and (2) the mental element, that is the necessary mens rea of the accomplice.

The legal issue of complicity in the violation of human rights under international criminal law has been dealt with recently and specifically by the ad hoc International Criminal Tribunals addressing the crimes committed in Yugoslavia and Rwanda. Of course, these tribunals, which had no jurisdiction over corporations, have dealt with cases of complicity by individuals.

The tribunals have affirmed the following main principles relevant for our purposes:

— as to the causation element, that mere presence at the scene of the crime may constitute complicity in the form of moral support even without practical assistance, when combined with authority and encouragement. Absent these circumstances, a failure to act cannot constitute complicity;[37]
— (2) as to the mental element, that it is not necessary for the accomplice to share the mens rea of the perpetrator, in the sense of positive intention to commit the crime. Instead, the clear requirement is for the accomplice to have knowledge that his actions will assist the perpetrator in the commission of the crime.[38]

Under the ICC Statute, the relevant provisions are Article 25(3)(c) and Article 30. Article 25(3)(c) describes the conduct of complicity, providing that a person shall be criminally liable if 'for the purpose of facilitating the commission of such a crime [any crime within the jurisdiction of the Court] [it] aids, abets or otherwise assists in its commission or its attempted commissions, including providing the means for its commissions.' Article 30 deals with the mental element in the way examined above.

Article 25, in describing the material conduct of complicity, essentially mirrors the classical forms contemplated in both civil law and common law.

[36] C Wells and J Elias, 'Holding Multinational Corporations Accountable for Breaches of Human Rights', discussion paper based on 'Catching the conscience of the king: Global players on the international stage', in Alston (ed), *Non-State Actors in International Law* (Oxford, Oxford University Press, forthcoming).

[37] *Furundzija*, Case No IT-95-17/1-T 10, ICTY, Judgment 10 December 1998.

[38] *Akayesu*, Case No ICTR-96-4-T, Judgment 2 September 1998; *Furundzija*, Case No IT-95-17, above n 37.

With respect to the mental element it is arguable whether the ICC rules set a more demanding standard than the judicial precedents mentioned above. The mens rea required in the decisions of the ad hoc tribunals is only the accomplice's *knowledge* that his conduct assists in the commission of the crime. Article 30 of the ICC Statute requires as a general rule both *intent* and *knowledge*; further, attention should be paid to the words '*for the purpose of* facilitating the commission' in Article 25 (my emphasis). In any case, even if higher standards as to intent are set by the ICC Statute, this would never mean that the accomplice must share the mens rea of the perpetrator, and even less that the accomplice must share the 'specific intent' of the perpetrator in those cases where this *dolus specialis* is required (for example, in the crime of genocide the 'intent to destroy in whole or in part a national, ethnical, racial or religious group, as such').

If we now try to assess the four types of complicity described above (direct, indirect, beneficial, and silent) from a legal point of view, and in particular under the rules of the ICC Statute, we can make the following points.

The direct complicity conducts fall within the conducts described in Article 25(3)(c) and are governed as to the mens rea requirement by the rules in Article 30 on intent and knowledge.

Beneficial complicity and silent complicity, on the contrary, do not appear capable of giving rise to criminal liability under the present law, due to lack of the causation element. If on the part of the corporation there has been no material support to the perpetrators of the crimes and no moral support through authority *and* encouragement, the mere failure to act cannot amount to complicity under the present law.

The most difficult situation to assess is so-called indirect complicity, which should obviously be examined case by case in the light of the specific circumstances. In general, it would appear that if the allegation is of material support to the country, such as investments and the payment of taxes, the crucial issue seems to be the existence of a causation link between such general provision of means and the commission of the crimes. The causation link should not only be examined from the material point of view, that is, whether such means contributed to the country's government's perpetration of the crimes, but also from the point of view of mens rea of the corporation, that is, whether the corporation had the knowledge (and the intent?) to assist in (or to facilitate) the commission of the crimes. In this connection the concept of 'awareness that a consequence will occur in the ordinary course of events' might be relevant.

If, on the other hand, the allegation is of moral support, then in the light of the judicial precedents the crucial issue is whether the corporation accused of complicity had the *authority* and gave the *encouragement*, as these have been indicated as the two necessary elements of the *actus reus*. Both concepts, authority and encouragement, are easier to establish for physical persons than in the more complex situation of a corporation.

In conclusion, should the jurisdiction of ICC be extended to corporations, more specific rules and criteria would be required with respect to complicity.

## VIII. SANCTIONS

The ICC Statute provides that (in addition to imprisonment) the court may order a fine under the criteria provided for in the Rules of Procedure and Evidence, and a forfeiture of proceeds, property, and assets derived directly or indirectly from the crime.

The Statute therefore already contemplates sanctions generally suitable for corporations. Probably, in the case of an extension of jurisdiction to corporations it would be useful to take into account the complex debate which has taken place on the issue of appropriate corporate sanctions, particularly in the United States, where specific Federal Sentencing Guidelines have been elaborated.

## CONCLUSIONS

The preamble of the UN Norms on the Responsibilities of Transnational Corporations and other Business Enterprises with Regard to Human Rights[39] states that 'transnational corporations ... are also obligated to respect generally recognized responsibilities and norms contained in .... international instruments such as ... the Rome Statute of the International Criminal Court.'

It would be consistent with this statement to create a mechanism under which the liability of corporations for international crimes could be imposed. This objective may be pursued either through national laws and jurisdiction or directly through the rules and jurisdiction of an international institution such as the ICC.[40]

The national solution would be easier for States to accept, for numerous reasons, including easier adaptation to domestic legal systems, and would also probably permit speedier judicial proceedings; overall, this solution would therefore be faster in operation.

On the other hand, the extension of the ICC jurisdiction to corporations would undoubtedly have the advantages of (a) the authority attached to the ICC Statute and (b) the mechanism of direct enforcement (although

---

[39] Above n 26.
[40] See Part IV above as to the distinction between an 'indirect' and a 'direct' enforcement method.

with its current limitations);[41] it would therefore constitute a significantly stronger deterrent against criminal conduct by corporations.

An amendment of the ICC Statute in 2009 to extend its jurisdiction to corporations is unlikely to be achieved easily. It took over 50 years of efforts to create the permanent international court. The concept of including legal persons was contained in the draft submitted by the Preparatory Committee to the Conference, was examined at the Conference and was not accepted. The majorities required for the amendment (seven-eighths of the States parties) are very high.

Furthermore, the extension of the ICC's jurisdiction to corporations would inevitably require an extensive and delicate review of the Statute. We have seen, for example, the problems encountered with respect to complicity, which would require a review of the general principles of criminal law contained in Part 3 of the Statute.

The objective of submitting corporations to the deterrence of criminal law in the field of human rights, and in particular with respect to the especially serious matters covered by the ICC, will be probably pursued more easily through other avenues.

The concept of a criminal liability of corporations has been making its way both in national and international legislation, beginning with 'soft laws' and 'indirect enforcement' instruments. Although the current attention is more focused on the issues of terrorism and financial criminality, the issue of human rights will obviously continue to be pursued.

The ICC Statute, although not yet extended to corporations, will inevitably be a fundamental reference point also for the conduct of corporations. As concerns the 'criminal corporation', Article 25(3)(d) on group criminality will be an available tool. As concerns normal corporations, any serious departure from lawful conduct in the areas covered by the Statute may be examined and faced under the point of view of the individual liability of the persons (directors and managers) having a leading position in the corporation.

---

[41] See Part VI above as to the strength and limitations of the ICC's direct enforcement mechanism.

# 10

# The Lack of Enforcement in the United Nations Draft Norms: Benefit or Disadvantage?

JACOB GELFAND

## I. INTRODUCTION

IN THE PAST few decades, the rise of globalization and transnational markets has not only altered global patterns of production and consumption, but created incredibly powerful corporate actors with major impacts on human rights, often negative ones.[1] At the same time, national governments, non-governmental organizations (NGOs), and international agencies, particularly the United Nations (UN), have been increasingly dedicated to codifying and protecting an ever-expanding range of human rights. The tension between globalization and protection of human rights raises a great number of philosophical and practical issues, such as which actors should be responsible for rights violations, which enforcement mechanisms are effective, and how they can be implemented.

In August 2003, the UN Sub-Commission for the Promotion and Protection of Human Rights formally adopted the draft Norms on the Responsibilities of Transnational Corporations and Other Business Enterprises with Regard to Human Rights ('the Norms'), which was a new, comprehensive list of norms geared at improving the compliance of

---

[1] See Abbas J Ali, 'Globalization: Part III' (1998) 8(2) *International Journal of Commerce & Management*, at 3 (tracing the human suffering caused by powerful corporations); Robert McCorquodale and Richard Fairbrother, 'Globalization and Human Rights' (1999) 21 *Human Rights Quarterly* 735 (arguing that globalization creates new threats to human rights as well as new avenues of rights protection). As of 2004, the hundred largest economies in the world included over 50 TNCs: Claudia T Salazar, 'Note: Applying International Human Rights Norms in the United States: Holding Multinational Corporations Accountable in the United States for International Human Rights Violations Under the Alien Tort Claims Act' (2004) 19 *St John's Journal of Legal Commentary* 111, at 113–14.

transnational corporations (TNCs) with human rights.[2] The Norms are the product of a drafting process led by the Working Group on Transnational Corporations ('the Working Group') and especially Professor David Weissbrodt of the University of Minnesota.[3] The Working Group, after compiling an initial draft version of the Norms, met with various actors to garner commentary and suggestions.[4] The current version of the Norms reflects five years of revisions and input from governments, corporations, and international institutions.[5] The Norms consist of a long preamble referencing numerous UN documents, standards, and empirical trends related to globalization and human rights protection; they then outline which rights corporations have an obligation to protect.[6] The Norms also contain a commentary on each set of human rights, as well as the obligations it intended to create.[7] They include an impressive array of rights, ranging from environmental and consumer protection to non-discrimination, workers' rights, and national sovereignty.[8]

The Norms were developed partially as a response to unsuccessful earlier attempts to produce standardized corporate human rights obligations, such as the UN Code of Conduct for Transnational Corporations,[9] and in order to address the shortcomings[10] of a voluntary approach to corporate responsibility.[11] In an article explaining the Norms, Weissbrodt argues that it is the 'first nonvoluntary initiative accepted at the

---

[2] Jim Lobe, 'Rights: Groups Praise New UN Guidelines For Business', *Global Information Network*, 16 August 2003.

[3] Penelope Simons, 'Corporate Voluntarism and Human Rights: The Adequacy and Effectiveness of Voluntary Self-Regulation Regimes' (2004) 59 *Relations Industrielles* 101.

[4] David Weissbrodt and Muria Kruger, 'Norms on the Responsibilities of Transnational Corporations and Other Business Enterprises with Regard to Human Rights' (2003) 97 *American Journal of International Law* 901, at 904. This article provides great detail about the process by which the Norms were created.

[5] *Ibid* at 906–7.

[6] UN Sub-Commission on the Promotion and Protection of Human Rights, Norms on the Responsibilities of Transnational Corporations and Other Business Enterprises with Regard to Human Rights, UN doc. E/CN.4/Sub.2/2003/L.II (2003).

[7] *Ibid*.

[8] *Ibid*.

[9] Carolin F Hillemanns, 'European & International Law: UN Norms on the Responsibilities of Transnational Corporations and Other Business Enterprises with regard to Human Rights' (2003) 4(10) *German Law Journal* 1065.

[10] Andrew Pendleton, 'The Real Face of Corporate Social Responsibility' (2004) 14(3) *Consumer Policy Review*, at 77 (using numerous studies to show that despite corporate claims, voluntary regimes have failed to stop major human rights violations in several countries).

[11] See Weissbrodt and Kruger, above n 4. Although Weissbrodt and Kruger argue that the norms are not voluntary, other commentators disagree, claiming that '[t]he document is not directly binding against corporations and has been described by some of its drafters as a mere restatement of existing international human rights laws': Troy Rule, 'Developments: Using "Norms" to Change International Law: UN Human Rights Laws Sneaking in through the Back Door?' (2004) 5 *Chicago Journal of International Law* 325, at 325.

international level.'[12] Although this language could imply that the full content of the Norms is already binding, and creates enforceable obligations on a variety of possible entities, in reality they are far from completely binding. Although the Norms may contain provisions that are beyond hortatory, their main binding power may come from their restatement of already existing international law, in which case their value as a new and comprehensive human rights instrument is questionable.[13] Even so, adoption by the UN Human Rights Council would at least denote an acceptance of the goals behind the Norms, which could in turn support arguments that the Norms reflect customary international law, thus allowing their use as the basis for treaties.[14] Over time, incorporating provisions from the Norms into multilateral treaties, and ultimately the hardening of their content into customary law, would be definitive proof that the Norms can move from non-binding to binding.

The Norms also supplement existing international agencies and instruments, including those proposed by NGOs such as Amnesty International;[15] relevant documents including the Universal Declaration of Human Rights; and bodies such as the UN Commission on Human Rights, which 'has authority to investigate potential violations of international human rights laws by states.'[16] However, although various groups share the goal of increasing human rights protection, none of these efforts has provided a comprehensive or binding basis for implementing this goal. Instead, the current attitude is still focused on corporate volunteerism.[17]

In light of the failures of volunteerism, the potential for the Norms to be adopted by the UN Human Rights Council, and the various obligations they could create or be used to supplement, one central question arises: Is the lack of an obligatory enforcement mechanism in the Norms, at least for rights not already codified in international law, beneficial or harmful? The answer depends upon the response of TNCs and governments alike, as well as the UN and NGOs. Similarly, the value of the Norms depends upon their value as an internationally accepted instrument, which requires simultaneously convincing TNCs and host governments that they are not

---

[12] David Weissbrodt and Muria Kruger, 'Human Rights Responsibilities of Businesses as Non-State Actors', in Philip Alston (ed), *Non-State Actors and Human Rights*, Oxford, Oxford University Press, 2005, 315–50, at p 318.

[13] Geoffrey Chandler, *Commentary on the United States Council for International Business 'Talking Points' on the United Nations Norms on the Responsibilities of Transnational Corporations and Other Business Enterprises with Regard to Human Rights*, available at http://209.238.219.111/Chandler-commentary-on-USCIB-Talking-Points.htm (last visited 26 February 2005).

[14] Lobe, above n 2.

[15] Rule, above n 11, at 327.

[16] *Ibid* at 326.

[17] *Ibid* at 327.

too rigid or unrealistic, while facilitating flexible enforcement mechanisms. However, given the reality of a potentially long window of time before the Norms can possibly become binding, their voluntary nature leaves time and space for clarification and negotiation, which has the beneficial potential to facilitate cooperation from the multiple groups that can and should work together to enforce human rights.

After analyzing general critiques of the Norms from corporate actors and commentators, this chapter will analyze enforcement mechanisms at various levels, continually asking whether the non-binding nature of the Norms is beneficial or not.

## II. GENERAL CRITIQUES OF THE NORMS AND THEIR VIABILITY

### 1. Are the Norms Overly Vague or Properly Holistic?

The publication of the Norms was hailed by human rights groups as a major victory.[18] They embraced a renewed hope that a comprehensive document would ensure that important human rights were not forgotten; in fact, the Norms outline a veritable laundry list of human rights, including many that are far from recognized by all States.[19] Without explicit or binding enforcement mechanisms in place, the breadth of the human rights included in the Norms has the potential to make corporations and governments either overwhelmed or reluctant to accept so many obligations. Academic and corporate critics have addressed these issues in a series of related arguments.

First, academics have criticized the universalization of norms for being unrealistic and potentially counterproductive.[20] Surya Deva argues that 'the right to a safe and healthy working environment or the right to fair and reasonable subsistence wages is universal only in abstract terms and in each case the quantification of what is safe and healthy or fair and reasonable is bound to vary from place to place.'[21] Therefore, considering the imperfect conditions in many countries where TNCs operate, particularly developing nations, the attempt to localize universal norms will be impossible. This is problematic because many of the enforcement mechanisms suggested in the Norms are potentially undercut by an empirical lack of resources and incentives. On the other hand, the aspirational nature

---

[18] Lobe, above n 2. See also below pp 332–333.
[19] Norms, above n 6.
[20] See Surya Deva, 'UN's Human Rights Norms for Transnational Corporations and Other Business Enterprises: An Imperfect Step in the Right Direction?' (2004) 10 *ILSA J International and Comparative Law* 493, at 512.
[21] *Ibid*.

of the Norms may be consistent with long-term goals to incorporate the Norms into binding documents such as treaties. As efforts and information to protect human rights increase, situations on the ground can evolve to support local realization of an expanding group of rights. This gradual implementation is supported by Weissbrodt himself, when he argues that enforcement and complaint mechanisms are just two of the local changes that will be required to create an infrastructure, which itself is a prerequisite to real enforcement of the Norms.[22]

Second, corporate actors have criticized the Norms for including a range of human rights that are not currently accepted by all State actors.[23] Because many of these rights are 'appropriately decided by national governments ... [i]t would be highly inappropriate to, in effect, privatize the policing of those rights by making companies the enforcing agent,'[24] the United States Council for International Business (USCIB) argues. In its Talking Points on the Norms, the USCIB claims that the Norms would privatize human rights obligations, removing the ability of governments to define which human rights they accept, and making enforcement difficult.[25] In a direct response, Sir Geoffrey Chandler[26] argues that the Norms do not shift any responsibility away from States, quoting the first paragraph of the Norms, which reads: 'States have the primary responsibility to respect, ensure respect for, prevent abuses of, and promote human rights recognised in international as well as national law, including ensuring that transnational corporations and other business enterprises respect human rights.'[27] However, this argument undercuts the practical viability of the Norms, not only because it allows individual States to define the scope of enforceable rights, but also because it relies upon corporations to adopt the Norms as good citizens in the absence of any binding requirements.[28] Therefore, in future developments regarding the Norms, its advocates should focus on strictly defining which rights are included, and how much leeway States have in defining exceptions. More importantly, to avoid letting States and corporations alike skirt their responsibilities to protect and enforce human rights, the UN should provide stronger incentives for compliance than 'good citizenship'.

---

[22] Weissbrodt and Kruger, above n 4, at 916.

[23] United States Council for International Business, *Talking Points on the Draft 'Norms on the Responsibilities of Transnational Corporations and Other Business Enterprises with regard to Human Rights'*, available at http://209.238.219.111/USCIB-text-Talking-Points.htm (last visited 1 March 2005) [hereinafter 'Talking Points'].

[24] *Ibid.*

[25] *Ibid.*

[26] Geoffrey Chandler, above n 13.

[27] Norms, above n 6.

[28] See Chandler, above n 13 ('Adherence to the Norms would visibly demonstrate a belief in principle as well as profit, analogous in principle to the good citizen following the moral code embedded in society, and help to restore trust').

Third, one of the most common criticisms of the Norms has been that their 'one size fits all' approach is inconsistent with global ideological and political diversity.[29] This is not only a problem with regard to defining which rights the Norms can codify realistically, but also a problem in legal interpretation of what the provisions of the Norms actually mean. In their commentary on the Norms, the International Organization of Employers (IOE) and International Chamber of Commerce (ICC) argue that individual balancing is required in all situations, and that balancing must be contextual and not based upon '"jargon" like "norms" and "standards".'[30] Their argument, that incanting the names of rights and other UN buzzwords is a mistake that ignores the complex situations in various countries, is important to address, because if the Norms cannot make the lead from aspiration to reality, any clear approach to enforcement will be difficult to implement. One initial response is that all words are abstractions that require contextualization to give them meaning, and using vagueness as a justification for inaction is simply irresponsible.[31] In his response to the IOE and ICC, Chip Pitts also argues that the terms in the Norms have already been used in various global documents, and are part of standards that the UN, member States, and corporations already are familiar with.[32] Ironically, Pitt and others responding to the IOE/ICC neglect to point out that 'one-size-fits-all' is itself meaningless jargon, and hardly a substantive objection to a document that is necessarily broad and flexible. Moreover, to the extent that the Norms restate already existing and binding international agreements, these are at least theoretically accepted by all nations, but that does not mean they cannot adapt to diverse circumstances.

Linguistic quibbling aside, the broad language and aspirational rights in the Norms can be both beneficial and problematic when considering the lack of an enforcement provision. As Weissbrodt and Kruger point out, for the Norms to become the basis for treaties, the obligations they define must become widely agreed upon by multiple States.[33] With this in mind, it makes sense that the Norms would

---

[29] International Organisation of Employers and International Chamber of Commerce, *Joint Views of the IOE and ICC on the Draft 'Norms on the Responsibilities of Transnational Corporations and Other Business Enterprises with Regard to Human Rights'*, available at http://www.businesshumanrights.org/ Links/Repository/179848/jump (last visited 29 January 2005).

[30] *Ibid.*

[31] See Chip Pitts, *Response to IOE/ICC Concerns Regarding the UN Norms for Business*, available at http://www.business-humanrights.org/Links/Repository/260001/jump (last visited 11 February 2005).

[32] *Ibid.*

[33] Weissbrodt and Kruger, above n 4, at 914.

include certain rights that are not yet widely agreed upon. In the mean-time, this could provide an incentive for NGOs and other agencies to encourage working toward acceptance and realization of the as yet aspirational standards. Moreover, those adopting or encouraging the use of the Norms in domestic law or corporate codes of conduct can stress that they are indeed aspirational.[34] Deva argues that this facili-tates gradual adoption of the Norms in two ways: internalization; and compliance between business partners.[35] Internalization focuses on 'developing a corporate culture of respect for human rights,' including training individuals within the corporation and increasing internal pro-tective measures.[36] At the same time, interactions between corporations and subcontractors, suppliers, and other businesses could require a greater mutual respect for human rights.[37] This approach requires time and flexibility, both of which are facilitated by the broad language and lack of enforcement mechanism in the Norms. Additionally, if the Norms were already binding, this could in effect freeze human rights protection at current standards, setting the status quo as a definitive floor that might be difficult to raise in the future. This goal would be well served by clearer directives than those which the Commentary to the Norms or Weissbrodt's later contributions provide; simply assert-ing that governments and corporations will be expected to enforce all the provisions in the norms is clearly unrealistic.[38] Instead, future inter-pretations should focus on reasonable and gradual adoption of the admittedly now aspirational content, encouraging companies to protect as many rights as possible and encouraging their business partners to do the same.

Finally, there are unique benefits to a general and flexible approach with regard to the Norms' lack of enforcement. An Amnesty International booklet on the Norms argues that 'the value of the UN Norms lies in their universality, and, because they comprise an international standard, of necessity they adopt a general approach.'[39] Therefore, the advisory status of the Norms is valuable because it outlines considerations for businesses without internal limitations on the scope of Norms and variety of approaches.[40]

---

[34] Deva, above n 20, at 514.

[35] *Ibid* at 514–15.

[36] *Ibid* at 515.

[37] *Ibid.*

[38] Weissbrodt and Kruger, above n 4, at 912–13 (arguing that the Norms cannot justify lack of government enforcement and should be incorporated by TNCs).

[39] Amnesty International, *The UN Human Rights Norms for Business: Towards Legal Accountability,* available at http://web.amnesty.org/aidoc/aidoc_pdf.nsf/Index/IOR420022004ENGLISH/$File/IOR4200204.pdf (last visited 24 February 2005).

[40] *Ibid.*

## 2. The Privatization Controversy: Do the Norms Shift Responsibility Away from States?

One of the most common, and most controversial, criticisms of the Norms is that it moves responsibility for monitoring and enforcement away from States and toward corporate actors.[41] Individual businesses and economic institutional actors have generally made this the focus of their critique of the Norms; the USCIB has even threatened 'developing countries that the Norms would lead to disinvestments.'[42] Although it is unclear whether its 'aggressive'[43] campaign will actually damage the success of the Norms, what is clear is that critics are basing their argument on a specific reading of the Norms that is not supported by members of the Working Group and other advocates.[44] However, even if the Norms do not intentionally or directly advocate removing responsibility from States, critics claim that implementing them would inevitably begin such a process. In the face of these arguments, reminding critics that the Norms are not indeed binding yet may mitigate their concerns, although it will create the need to clarify enforcement for future cooperation.

Critics claim the Norms privatize responsibility for human rights protection, first, because they present a change from the historical focus of human rights protection exclusively on State actors. Unlike domestic law, international law has no generalized basis for holding corporations responsible for harmful actions.[45] Although the 1998 Rome Conference attempted to give the International Criminal Court (ICC) power to try corporations as legal persons for offenses it states in its statute, 'the proposal failed to gather sufficient support.'[46] However, there is counter-evidence that TNCs have some international obligations based upon their 'existing rights or duties under international law.'[47] Therefore, there is

---

[41] See Corporate Europe Observatory, *Shell Leads International Business Campaign Against UN Human Rights Norms*, available at http://www.corporateeurope.org/norms.html (last visited 15 December 2004) [hereinafter 'Shell Leads Campaign']; John Elkington, *In the Hot Seat: Shell VIP Robin Aram*, available at http://www.greenbiz.com/news/reviews_third.cfm ?NewsID = 26884 (last visited 26 February 2005); Menno T Kamminga, *Corporate Obligations Under International Law*, available at http://www.business-humanrights.org/Links/ Repository/928980/jump (last visited 3 January 2005); Talking Points, above n 23.

[42] 'Shell Leads Campaign', above n 41.

[43] *Ibid*.

[44] See, eg, Kamminga, above n 41 ('[o]n the contrary, the drafters of these treaties apparently considered companies to be such important players that in order to achieve the treaty's objectives they had to be addressed directly, in addition to states').

[45] *Ibid*.

[46] *Ibid*. See, on this issue, Cristina Chiomenti, ch nine in this volume.

[47] David Kinley and Junko Tadaki, 'From Talk to Walk: The Emergence of Human Rights Responsibilities for Corporations at International Law' (2004) 44 *Virginia Journal of International Law* 931, at 946 ('[f]or example, both the International Convention on Civil Liability for Oil Pollution Damage and the Convention on Civil Liability for Damage Resulting from Activities Dangerous to the Environment directly impose liability on legal persons including corporations').

precedent to undercut arguments that the Norms' implications of corporate responsibility are a drastically new development. The lack of binding enforcement provisions in the Norms strengthens this argument. The Norms do not clarify how corporations 'could be held directly liable under international law for any breaches of these obligations, beyond implying that such a possibility exists.'[48] In the short term, at least, this implies that corporate obligations would always be mediated by State actors, without precluding long-term changes toward direct corporate responsibility. In this respect, the lack of an enforcement provision enables flexibility, although it does not guarantee any specific short-term action.

Second, critics argue that the Norms imply unrealistic and unfair positive obligations on TNCs to provide goods and services to their employees in order to fulfill human rights obligations.[49] However, because the Norms recognize that TNCs should be held to varying degrees of responsibility based upon their spheres of influence, scope, and power, it is unlikely that such obligations would put too much strain on specific corporate actors.[50] Additionally, because of the massive resources many TNCs have, it is perhaps not only realistic, but equitable, to expect the gradual creation of a positive obligation to use some of those resources to improve conditions for workers and take other measures toward human rights protection. Regardless of the proactive implications the Norms will have on TNCs, however, the lack of enforcement provisions ensures that this argument is not actually immediate, and moreover, the Norms 'clearly distinguish between the primarily responsibilities of governments and the secondary responsibilities of business within their respective sphere of influence.'[51] However, because business paranoia will undoubtedly continue as the Norms are debated and perhaps adopted, addressing such concerns will remain vital.

Finally, regardless of the need to address such concerns, I would suggest that they represent a fundamentally wrong framing of the issue of corporate responsibility. Instead of panicking over whether corporations will take over responsibilities that host governments should and historically do hold, it might be more productive to determine *when* and *which* obligations should be transferred to corporations. The USCIB is counterproductive when it focuses on the possibility of corporations being held responsible for rights they have no control over.[52] The reality that the

---

[48] *Ibid* at 947.

[49] Amnesty International, above n 39 (summarizing arguments that the Norms might obligate TNCs 'to provide essential goods or services (such as housing, food, health care or education) that are government responsibilities').

[50] Weissbrodt and Kruger, above n 4, at 912 (arguing that the flexible approach of the Norms is rooted in its definitions of corporations and their spheres of influence).

[51] Amnesty International, above n 39.

[52] Talking Points, above n 23.

drafters correctly addressed is that many TNCs are 'such important players that in order to achieve the treaty's objectives they had to be addressed
directly, in addition to states.'[53] TNCs are often more powerful, and frequently much more so, than their host States; therefore, there is political
pressure for States to avoid enforcing corporate responsibility.[54] The
Norms have the opportunity to prevent corporations and weak States from
cooperatively shirking human rights obligations. This may be undercut by
the lack of enforcement provisions. In the future, the Working Group and
its allies should work to balance obligations, especially in developing
countries, keeping in mind that the power and influence of TNCs, combined with their rights and corresponding duties under international law,
expose fears of transferring obligations to them as unfair and problematic.

### III. SPECIFIC POSSIBILITIES FOR IMPLEMENTATION OF THE NORMS

## 1. Implementation at the Corporate Level

*A. Defining Corporations and the Scope of Their Responsibilities*

The account by Weissbrodt and Kruger of the drafting history of the
Norms illustrates that much thought and effort was put into the issue of
defining TNCs.[55] There were concerns that unclear definitions would
allow corporations to evade responsibility by claiming they were not technically TNCs under the law.[56] Therefore, the Norms' definition is fairly
broad, basically encompassing any enterprise operating in more than one
State.[57] Although this definition is beneficial in that it minimizes restrictions on the application of the Norms to TNCs, it also raises concerns that
applying the Norms uniformly will be impossible, since they could be
applied equally to businesses of widely varying size and scope. However,
this problem can be mitigated with constant guidance from the Working
Committee as the status of the Norms changes in the future. Although the
Norms do not place stringent limits on the definition of TNCs, they do
limit the accountability of TNCs to their 'spheres of activity and influence.'[58]

---

[53] Kamminga, above n 41 ('[t]he proper question to ask therefore is not whether direct
international legal regulation of companies is possible but whether or not it is appropriate
in specific instances').

[54] *Ibid.*

[55] Weissbrodt and Kruger, above n 4, at 908–9.

[56] *Ibid* at 909.

[57] Norms, above n 6. The full definition reads: "The term 'transnational corporation' refers
to an economic entity operating in more than one country or a cluster of economic entities
operating in two or more countries—whatever their legal form, whether in their home country or country of activity, and whether taken individually or collectively." *Id.*

[58] *Ibid.* See also Kamminga, above n 41.

This limitation is important because it builds more flexibility into the Norms; that is, TNCs with more influence, and probably more resources, will have greater obligations than smaller businesses.[59] These provisions deal with concerns that the Norms will impose unfair or unrealistic obligations; however, given the lack of an enforcement mechanism, the question of what obligations TNCs have, directly or indirectly, remains.

## B. Enforcement by Internal Adaptation, Monitoring, and Applications to Business Transactions

The first suggestion Weissbrodt makes for corporate use of the Norms is through internal adoption of certain provisions.[60] He argues that businesses should incorporate the Norms into their codes of conduct, and ensure their officers are aware of these human rights provisions.[61] Additionally, TNCs could make their internal rules 'available to anybody with an interest in the company' and 'adequately train managers and workers to comply with the guidelines outlined in the Norms.'[62] These steps would promote transparency, allowing those looking for businesses to interact with to be informed on whether they are likely to act in accordance with the Norms. This provides an economic incentive for TNCs to provide proof of compliance, or at least proof of incorporating as many provisions from the Norms as possible into their codes of conduct, at the risk of exposure to businesses and economic actors who have the ability to affect the TNC's economic viability. Additionally, there is a strong incentive for corporations to take positive steps in order to maintain a good public image.[63] In fact, Cynthia Williams argues that 'companies are often more concerned with damage to their reputation than they are concerned with the possibility of legal liability.'[64] The importance of corporate reputation should provide an incentive for the UN to make the Norms publicly accessible and promote awareness by the media, businesses, and consumers alike. Creating publicity and the ensuing pressure on corporations to comply with the Norms, then, may be more powerful than a technically binding obligation without these related conditions. In this respect, making the Norms immediately binding could dissuade TNCs from adapting the Norms because of implementation and resource limitations. Because the Norms are so comprehensive and aspirational,

---

[59] *Ibid.*

[60] Weissbrodt and Kruger, above n 4, at 915–16.

[61] *Ibid* at 916.

[62] 'United Nations Update' (2003) 11 *Human Rights Brief* 34, at 35.

[63] Cynthia A Williams, 'Symposium: Oil and the International Law: The Geopolitical Significance of Petroleum Corporations: Civil Society Initiatives and "Soft Law" in the Oil and Gas Industry' (2004) 36 *New York University Journal of International Law and Politics* 457, at 496.

[64] *Ibid.*

corporate incentives may be created more effectively by keeping them non-binding for the time being.

Internal adaptation of the Norms by TNCs can be effective only if accompanied by monitoring to ensure they are enforced and utilized.[65] The Commentary to the Norms specifies several avenues, including collaboration with stakeholders and unions, and developing avenues for worker complaints to be filed and handled effectively.[66] Even without a binding obligation to ensure monitoring occurs, in the very least the Norms will 'increase pressure on TNCs to provide greater compensation, better working conditions, and more extensive human rights protections for workers in developing countries than would result in market equilibrium.'[67] However, the same pressures could impose a 'market floor' for rights in international markets, reducing 'the incentive for TNCs to expand their operations in some third-world countries, potentially leaving such countries worse off than before.'[68] Balancing these concerns raises the need for emphasizing consistency in enforcement, and preventing a situation where only the richest TNCs would be able to implement enforcement effectively. The Commentary to the Norms gives TNCs advice on how to develop internal enforcement mechanisms; it advises businesses to disclose information constantly, maintain transparency, and offer periodic reports to inform interested parties on their successful implementation of rights protections.[69] Increasing transparency through these mechanisms will be a gradual process, and one that might be deterred by forcing immediate and strict compliance with the entire Norms.

Along with internal implementation and monitoring, TNCs have a third direct option: 'incorporat[ing] the Norms into all their business dealings or cease doing business with that business partner.'[70] Although this is a potentially powerful avenue to increase incentives for enforcement, it has also led to worries by business organizations. Specifically, the USCIB claims this would create a legal obligation for companies to break contracts with suppliers who did not implement the Norms.[71] However, Chandler responds that the Norms only aim to 'deal with the first levels of a company's contractual relations.'[72] Additionally, the Commentary specifies that TNCs should initially work with non-complying subcontractors and then, 'if they will not change, the enterprise shall cease doing business with them.'[73] The flexibility built into the Norms is beneficial

---

[65] See Weissbrodt and Kruger, above n 4, at 915–17.
[66] Norms, above n 6; Weissbrodt & Kruger, above n 4, at 916.
[67] Rule, above n 11, at 331.
[68] *Ibid.*
[69] Weissbrodt and Kruger, above n 4, at 916–17.
[70] Hillemanns, above n 9.
[71] Talking Points, above n 23.
[72] Chandler, above n 13.
[73] Norms, above n 6.

here; however, the language is almost so flexible that it seems difficult to ensure any remotely consistent standard of enforcement. Therefore, future clarifications should specify the types of interactions TNCs should engage in to ensure compliance by business partners, and how long they should attempt to improve non-complying suppliers before they cross a threshold where business transactions become impermissible. An additional complaint could be that the expense of monitoring all suppliers, no matter how remote, would require huge amounts of resources. Although the same answers mitigate this concern as the concern about contracts, it is also addressed in the Norms' definition limiting the responsibility of TNCs to their spheres of activity and influence.[74] Ultimately, these arguments do not easily resolve each other; instead, in the future, more clarification will be necessary to define the scope of obligations between TNCs and business partners. Such clarification should be provided by the UN or other legal bodies before the Norms are adapted as binding. This goal can be facilitated by a window of flexibility, during which time the Norms gradually move from being hortatory to binding.

In light of public controversy about the implications of globalization on human rights, increased scrutiny from the media and the public, and the potential implications these forces could have on profitability, TNCs are under strong incentives to protect human rights. Such an incentive-based mechanism would be threatened by making the Norms binding in the near future.

## 2. Implementation Mechanisms at the State Level

The first paragraph of the Norms posits that 'States have the primary responsibility to promote, secure the fulfillment of, respect, ensure respect of, and protect human rights[.]'[75] However, the same paragraph goes on to say that corporations have similar duties '[w]ithin their respective spheres of activity and influence[.]'[76] Underlying these dual premises is a potential tension between government and corporations, exacerbated by power disparities, particularly in developing nations.[77] This potential tension necessarily frameworks a realistic discussion of what obligations the Norms should give to States. Although the Norms are part of a shift toward imposing international human rights obligations on corporations,[78] these are

---

[74] *Ibid.* See also Kamminga, above n 41.
[75] Norms, above n 6.
[76] *Ibid.*
[77] See, eg, Mahmood Monshipouri *et al*, 'Multinational Corporations and the Ethics of Global Responsibility: Problems and Possibilities' (2003) 4 *Human Rights Quarterly* 965. The authors write that 'MNCs' power to control international investment, especially portfolio investments, has had enormous bearing on the economies of developing countries': *ibid* at 966.
[78] *Ibid* at 970.

fairly major changes from the historical focus on States.[79] Critics disagree on whether the Norms actually focus on States instead of corporations.[80] Emeka Duruigbo claims that '[t]he essential aims of the Norms were to help governments identify what types of legislation they should enact and what enforcement mechanisms they should implement.'[81] Aside from assuaging fears of transferring responsibility to corporations, focusing on State implementation has the additional benefit of allowing courts to develop laws internally that reflect their contextual ability to protect human rights. Additionally, because there is no binding obligation in the Norms, gradual adoption of their content by domestic law avoids a rush to implementation that could have a chilling effect on certain governments, turning them against the Norms by fears that adopting them would require huge amounts of resources for monitoring potential violations and providing redress.

The Norms envision a variety of specific mechanisms for State enforcement. Weissbrodt and Kruger suggest that States 'use the Norms to establish and reinforce the necessary legal or administrative framework' for corporate activities, as well as 'encourage their application by national courts in connection with the determination of damages and criminal sanctions,' and other legal responses.[82] Additionally, domestic courts could use the Norms to determine 'whether a company has provided consumers or investors with adequate information about its products and sendees.'[83] United States domestic courts could also use the Norms 'as a yardstick … for determining whether a company has acted with the due diligence or due care that may be expected from it.'[84]

Incorporating standards from the Norms into domestic law may be a positive long-term goal, but in the short term, many governments might worry that imposing new restrictions could result in a huge amount of litigation. Therefore, the non-binding status of the Norms may ease fears States have of being forced to deal with so many claims. In addition to establishing long-term goals for States, the Norms also restate, or potentially encourage the broadening of, already existing national enforcement mechanisms.[85] However, this begs the question of how effective these mechanisms already are. Developing States may lack the resources to monitor TNCs, and any States may simply lack the incentive. Therefore, until the Norms harden or are adopted into binding domestic law, the

---

[79] Kamminga, above n 41 (providing examples, including multilateral treaties such as the ILO Convention on Forced Labor, and the 1997 OECD Convention against Bribery).

[80] See Section II.B, above; Emeka Duruigbo, 'The Economic Cost of Alien Tort Litigation: A Response to Awakening Monster: The Alien Tort Statute of 1789' (2004) 14 *Minnesota Journal of Global Trade* 1, at 33.

[81] *Ibid.*

[82] Weissbrodt and Kruger, above n 4, at 921.

[83] *Ibid.*

[84] Kamminga, above n 41.

[85] Hillemanns, above n 9.

efficacy of domestic monitoring will probably remain fairly constant. Although this lack of immediate change is not heartening, the opposite result could be counterproductive: binding domestic governments to increased monitoring requirements 'risks undermining the resources and attention necessary to improve the capacity of national governments to implement and enforce their existing human rights laws.'[86] Additionally, forcing local governments to dedicate resources specifically to human rights violations by TNCs could 'shift the focus away from some of the worst cases of human rights and labor abuses that take place in local economies.'[87] These concerns raise important issues that should be kept in mind as the Norms are further developed: obligations should be incorporated gradually and contextually, keeping in mind the resources and abilities of governments to enforce human rights obligations. Additionally, obligations under the Norms should be balanced with other human rights obligations, tailoring them to the context of various States. For example, States dealing with ethnic cleansing or other extremely serious human rights situations should not be bound by rigid obligations related to TNCs that would compromise their ability to protect other fundamental rights. As the Norms continue to develop, and are implemented by local governments, these issues should continue to guide efforts at encouraging action by domestic governments.

One final problematic aspect of domestic State enforcement is the possibility that governments will simply choose not to enforce the Norms.[88] Given the lesson learned from the Guidelines, that a focus on domestic enforcement is likely to be sunk by lazy or incapable States, it may be important to focus on making the Norms binding.[89] However, because this will elicit the concerns detailed above about unrealistic strain on resources, transfer of obligations from corporations to businesses, and other complaints from TNCs and States alike, it will be important to make the Norms binding gradually, perhaps focusing on one issue or one State at a time.

Aside from supplementing TNC obligations through enforcement, States are also important actors because they can ratify treaties that impose binding obligations on a variety of actors, most importantly TNCs themselves. One of the ultimate goals of the Norms' drafters is for their content to harden from soft law to hard law through multilateral treaties.[90] Before this is realistic, a sizeable number of States would have to support the

---

[86] Talking Points, above n 23. Talking Points voices this fear as irrelevant to whether the Norms impose binding obligations immediately or in the future; however, the former scenario is contradicted by the text of the Norms, and Weissbrodt's interpretation of it. See Norms, above n 6; Weissbrodt and Kruger, above n 4.

[87] Talking Points, above n 23.

[88] See 'United Nations Update', above n 62, at 35 (adding that Human Rights Watch alleges that this is the main problem with current Guidelines).

[89] See *ibid*.

[90] Weissbrodt and Kruger, above n 4, at 907.

obligations, which is not currently the case.[91] However, State support for the Norms and involvement in their drafting, as well as maintaining a realistic role for States in enforcement, would create incentives for treaties to eventually be adopted. Therefore, it may be beneficial in the short term that the Norms are not hard law, since the process of hardening cannot be instant in the case of TNC obligations. If States do eventually ratify treaties that impose direct obligations on corporations, they will not be doing so without precedent. For example, the 1969 Convention on Civil Liability for Oil Pollution Damage 'provides that the owner of a ship (which may be a company) shall be liable for any pollution damage caused by it.'[92] Of course, the same businesses and organizations that criticize the transfer of any rights obligations to TNCs would doubtlessly criticize treaties with similar effects; however, at the opposite extreme, such treaties could actually encourage States and corporations to work together. Although this is currently very optimistic, it is an important long-term goal that should guide steps to incorporate the Norms into binding obligations.

## 3. Implementation by the United Nations

There are a variety of bodies within the UN that can play a role in implementing the Norms, beginning with the Sub-Commission for the Promotion and Protection of Human Rights. The Sub-Commission is composed of independent human rights experts with the 'mandate to examine human rights issues through the lens of the Universal Declaration of Human Rights (UDHR) and to make recommendations to prevent human rights abuses and violations of fundamental freedoms, and to protect racial, national, religious, and linguistic minorities.'[93] Although their powers are hortatory, the Sub-Commission also has the ability to work with other UN organs toward methods of implementation. If the Norms are adopted by the UN Human Rights Council, the Council can utilize various mechanisms to take action toward the realization of its goals. For example, it can request assistance from the Office of the High Commissioner for Human Rights to help State governments.[94] Adoption of the Norms by the Human Rights Council would greatly increase the likelihood of positive action, since it would be an official endorsement of the Norms and would

---

[91] *Ibid.*
[92] Kamminga, above n 41.
[93] 'United Nations Update', above n 62, at 34.
[94] Commission on Human Rights, at http://www.unhchr.ch/html/menu2/2/chrintro.htm (last visited 2 February 2005) ('[t]his assistance takes the form of expert advice, human rights seminars, national and regional training courses and workshops, fellowships and scholarships, and other activities aimed at strengthening national capacities for the protection and promotion of human rights').

add it to the agenda of the Council. Perhaps more importantly, special procedure, are available to implement human rights protection.[95] To this end, the Human Rights Council has access to a network of 'experts, representatives and rapporteurs' whose annual reports assist it.[96] On a general level, the UN has the ability to galvanize consumers, spreading information about TNCs to ensure that those who do not follow the Norms lose business.[97] By mobilizing public opinion in a current atmosphere where both TNC human rights abuses and protests are prominent in the media,[98] the UN could utilize external media outlets without over-using its limited resources.[99] Although public pressure would not have the same effect as making the Norms binding, it could create stronger incentives based upon economic viability rather than technicalities that corporations could perhaps more easily evade.

The Commentary to the Norms specifies several other specific enforcement mechanisms at the UN level. First, human rights treaty bodies could use the Norms to create 'additional reporting requirements for states.'[100] The Commentary suggests that treaty bodies could use the Norms to create these requirements, which would force States to report information about TNC compliance with the Norms.[101] The vagueness of this suggestion allows for flexibility, as treaty bodies could determine which areas to focus on and how to implement the requirements. However, additional recommendations could help guide implementation efforts, and could be specified as the Norms develop. Weissbrodt also suggests, in addition to the specifics in the Commentary, using treaty bodies with 'individual reporting procedures' to obtain information about countries where the Norms are not being effectively enforced.[102] Monitoring could be both indirect and direct. Indirectly, the UN can work with 'international or national mechanisms already in existence or yet to be created,' such as NGOs.[103] Directly, the UN could ask special rapporteurs to 'use the Norms to raise concerns' about TNC actions.[104] The UN could also create a new special rapporteur whose role would be specifically to monitor TNCs for compliance with the Norms. This would cover gaps in content not covered by already existing special rapporteurs, although it would also require

---

[95] *Ibid.*

[96] *Ibid.*

[97] See Hillemanns, above n 9.

[98] See, eg, Williams, above n 63, at 467–68 (chronicling social responsibility campaigns, anti-globalization protests, and other signs of public dissatisfaction).

[99] *Ibid.*

[100] Weissbrodt and Kruger, above n 4, at 917; Norms, above n 6.

[101] *Ibid.*

[102] Weissbrodt and Kruger, above n 4, at 917.

[103] Hillemanns, above n 9.

[104] Weissbrodt and Kruger, above n 4, at 918 (mentioning the special rapporteur on housing as an example of this monitoring).

more time and resources, and require holistic monitoring that might be difficult to implement comprehensively. If the Norms were to become binding, the value of these reporting mechanisms could be increased, and the incentives for compliance by both States and TNCs would be greater.

Another option at the UN level would be to establish a specific thematic procedure under the UN Human Rights Council[105] or even to rely on a procedure similar to the current '1235 procedure'.[106] For instance, a working group could be established to examine violations of human rights by corporate actors and the insufficiences of States' protection of those rights, thus creating incentives for protection at the State level regardless of the Norms' status as binding or not.[107]

## 4. Implementation by Other Actors

### A. Non-governmental Organizations

NGOs have been strong supporters of the Norms.[108] Although public statements by NGOs regarding the Norms sometimes can seem overly optimistic, the enthusiastic response is a good predictor that NGOs will assist in implementing the Norms, making them useful even if not binding. Amnesty International, in its pamphlet supporting the Norms, suggests that NGOs and 'other industry groups would be encouraged to use the UN Norms as the basis for monitoring, dialogue, lobbying and campaigning activities with businesses.'[109] Not only can NGOs use the Norms to monitor businesses, but they can also encourage governments, unions, and other bodies to do the same.[110] Moreover, with the use of prominent websites,[111] NGOs can disseminate valuable information about compliance to the public, increasing scrutiny and economic and political

---

[105] Kinley and Tadaki, above n 47, at 997.

[106] A 1235 Procedure 'is a procedure on the basis of which the Commission holds an annual *public* debate on gross human rights violations committed by a given state': Ewa Skoczkowa and Maria Bal-Nowak, *How to Protect Human Rights?*, available at http://www.hrea.org/erc/Library/monitoring/HFHR/2-UN-text.html (last visited 12 February 2005) ('[i]f the situation still does not improve, one possible outcome can be the adoption of an ECOSOC resolution condemning the authorities of a given state for the violations. Such a resolution severely effects [sic] the prestige of the ruling authorities': *ibid*.

[107] Kinley and Tadaki, above n 47, at 997.

[108] See, eg, Amnesty International, above n 39; Lobe, above n 2 (citing NGOs including Human Rights Watch, Amnesty International, and Christian Aid).

[109] Amnesty International, above n 39.

[110] See *ibid*.

[111] Examples include the sites of Amnesty International (http://web.amnesty.org) and Human Rights Watch (http://www.hrw.org). In April 2003 alone, the latter received '29,252 average daily user sessions and 81,477 average daily page views.' Additionally, '[o]ver 28,700 users receive the monthly email update': Human Rights Watch, *Some Frequently Asked Questions About Human Rights Watch*, at http://www.hrw.org/about/faq/ (last visited 5 January 2005).

incentives for States and TNCs to comply with the Norms. Along similar lines, Amnesty International suggests that NGOs can '[s]upport the further dissemination and development of the [Norms].'[112] Together, these processes can ensure that NGOs are involved in the future development of the Norms. Far from fixing as static the Norms' current content and status, their non-binding nature, combined with input from various NGOs, ensures that they can evolve and be adapted to different contexts and States. This facilitates flexibility and experimentation before the Norms become binding, and ensures their acceptance will be, as is appropriate to their aspirational content, gradual.[113]

### B. Other Actors

Weissbrodt and Kruger suggest a number of enforcement options for economic and intergovernmental organizations, including unions, trade associations, and investment groups.[114] Most of these suggestions supplement the core mechanisms existing at the State and TNC level. For example, Weissbrodt and Kruger recommend that investors and business groups use the Norms to monitor TNCs, adapt their own guidelines to be consistent with the Norms, and use information about TNC compliance 'in making their investment decisions.'[115] By encouraging powerful economic actors to refuse to give loans to non-complying TNCs, and limiting investment as well, this could provide another strong economic incentive. Because these organizations may not have the ability to monitor TNCs internally as well as institutions such as the UN and NGOs, cooperation between various actors would be a beneficial method of monitoring. Overall, because almost all groups which engage with TNCs, whether as watchdogs, trade partners, or consumers, have different abilities and incentives, an intersectional approach can encourage cooperative monitoring. The power of these groups, if combined, can do more to create incentives for transparency and human rights protection than one isolated group. Ultimately, encouraging cooperation between multiple and diverse actors should be one goal, in tandem with the goal of hardening the Norms into binding international law. Because different actors obviously have disparate and sometimes conflicting interests, bargaining and working to increase incentives to cooperate is vital while the Norms are still non-binding and adaptable to change. Negotiation and communication must stress the realities of TNC human rights abuses, and what different groups are able and willing to do in order to increase international compliance.

---

[112] Amnesty International, above n 39.
[113] See 'United Nations Update', above n 62, at 36 (encouraging 'periodic monitoring and input by NGOs').
[114] Weissbrodt and Kruger, above n 4, at 918–20.
[115] *Ibid* at 920.

## IV. CONCLUSION

The Norms are the latest in a series of documents attempting to limit human rights abuse by TNCs. Considering the lack of success of preceding efforts, it could be asked whether another holistic, aspirational document is even necessary. However, the Norms can and must be distinguished as an effort that has a real possibility of creating positive change toward increased human rights protection by TNCs.

Since the Norms are not yet binding, at least to the extent they diverge from existing obligations, it is important to clarify their content and what obligations they impose. Importantly, the Norms certainly 'synthesize a wide range of international human rights standards into one document that targets business entities as powerful non-state actors.'[116] This synthesis clarifies the full range of norms, from environmental to labor standards, non-discrimination, and beyond, that TNCs are intended to respect. Setting a goal for States and TNCs is important, and while the goal the Norms sets may be unrealistic, it is at least clear and comprehensive. As such, the Norms have 'an important expressive function (one that can coordinate action towards a focal point, even without sanctions).'[117] The coordination of various actors is an important step, one that should be accomplished while the Norms are non-binding. Steering diverse groups toward a common goal, and a common path, ensures that monitoring and enforcement are effective and come from various sources.

While clarification and coordination are important in the meantime, other actions are necessary before the Norms are adopted. Deva suggests that 'an enforcement mechanism should be put in place before the Norms being adopted' and that mechanism must 'not only preempt human rights violations but also offer speedily an adequate remedy to the victims in cases of violation.'[118] I suggest that enforcement should not come from one mechanism alone. Although the UN could create a special rapporteur or even a distinct organ specifically for enforcement of the Norms, and one or more NGOs could be devoted to the Norms as well, there are simply too many interested parties to focus the huge task of enforcement on one actor. However, enforcement mechanisms should be made clear to States and TNCs before the Norms are adapted, specifying which obligations each should expect to have.

As Weissbrodt and Kruger comment, 'more educational work for businesses, unions, and governments remains to be done before the Commission is likely to begin considering or adopting the Norms and Commentary.'[119]

---

[116]  *United Nations Update*, above n 62, at 36.
[117]  Williams, above n 63, at 496.
[118]  Deva, above n 20, at 520.
[119]  Weissbrodt and Kruger, above n 4, at 907. The author refer to the UN Commision on Human Rights, as they write before the creation of the Human Rights Council.

This work includes facilitating a constant and critical discourse on the Norms at the UN level, while encouraging States, TNCs, and other organizations to gradually incorporate provisions into their daily activities and guiding documents.

Until the Norms are widely enough accepted to be used in multilateral treaties, or a majority of them are hardened into customary international law, they will remain non-binding. While attaining binding status is a legitimate goal, it is not realistic in the short term. Instead, the Norms should be used as an explicitly non-binding, and therefore flexible, document that restates human rights obligations, suggests new means of enforcement and monitoring, and ultimately encourages corporate, political, and social actors to work together to ensure human rights protection by TNCs becomes less aspirational and more of a reality.

*Editor's Note*: The author was unable to review the final version of this chapter, initiallly prepared prior to the establishment of the Human Rights Council by the UN General Assembly Resolution, 60/251 of 15 march 2006. All the adaptations to the text resulting from this change are the sole reponsibility of the editor.

# 11

# *Overt and Hidden Accomplices: Transnational Corporations' Range of Complicity for Human Rights Violations*

INÉS TÓFALO

## I. INTRODUCTION

T HERE HAS BEEN a general move in international law towards findings of corporate responsibility for human rights violations, particularly when perpetrated by State actors in close relation with transnational corporations (TNCs). But how far does this notion of TNCs' complicity for human rights violations extend? Must TNCs and State actors violating human rights act in concert? Must TNCs assist governments in the design or implementation of their repressive policies? Are TNCs' operations in an area where human rights abuses are pandemic enough to attribute responsibility?

Attributing corporate complicity for human rights violations is a complex theoretical pursuit, given its multiple dimensions and types. It is also a complex area of the law, which is currently in disarray. Multiple international and domestic fora have addressed issues of corporate complicity. They have developed inconsistent vocabularies, relied on disparate doctrines, and followed different types of precedent, and hence, the relevance of studying this issue and attempting to provide structure and ordered distinctions across the spectrum of accomplice responsibility.

A majority of international legal bodies, from the Nuremberg Tribunals to the International Criminal Court, did not or do not have jurisdiction over legal persons. However, useful precedent has evolved directly or indirectly from these institutions; as well as from non-adjudicatory bodies such as relevant United Nations Committees. National litigation or reconciliation processes that look towards international law for a doctrine and standard to attribute corporate complicity have found significant inspiration. However, given the multitude and variability of sources and theories, a doctrine and standard have proved hard to discern. Litigation in the United States under the Alien Torts Claim Act (ATCA), which incorporates international law, exemplifies this lack of legal structure and consistency. ATCA cases have been particularly puzzled by the question of corporate complicity, since the Acts of State Doctrine impedes United States courts from prosecuting sovereign States for human rights violations, but does not impede them from attributing accomplice liability to corporations involved in those abuses. The notion of corporate complicity is consequently the cornerstone to these disputes. ATCA courts cite an array of sources in their decisions, ranging from ad hoc international criminal tribunals to domestic legislation. They have not yet resolved what constitutes controlling precedent, nor have they articulated a consistent vocabulary and standard.

In a different, non-litigious, scenario South Africa's Truth and Reconciliation Commission has commented on TNCs' complicity with the apartheid regime. This study reached more extensively, incurring into the outer circles of the spectrum of complicity. However, it still confronted methodological difficulties in the drawing of significant moral and legal distinctions for varying types of accomplice responsibility. Part of these difficulties lay in the continuous and amorphous features of the spectrum of complicity, which render it hard to establish universal distinctions without drawing arbitrary lines.

Yet another complexity subsists in the multiple dimensions through which accomplice responsibility can be examined: criminal, civil, and moral. The extent to which complicity will be established is highly dependent on the purpose and consequences of such finding. Criminal complicity and moral complicity are not the same notion, and are certainly conformed by different elements and call for different standards and sanctions. While criminal accomplice liability would ordinarily attach only where there is a closer and more substantial relation between the TNC and the human rights abuses, moral accomplice responsibility is appropriate even in the outer circles of the spectrum of complicity.

In this chapter I outline the spectrum of responsibility for human rights violations in which TNCs may participate. I introduce a structure and a more consistent vocabulary as tools to argue distinctions across different types of complicity. In order to more systematically describe this spectrum, I elaborate a working typology of complicity that ranges from direct violations by TNCs' agents or under color of state law, to indirect complicity, to mere presence in an area where human rights abuses are pandemic. I comment on the intricacies of these three types of complicity and subtypes within each of these categories.

This chapter identifies three subtypes of direct complicity and responsibility: (1) joint execution of abuses, where the TNC and the State act conjointly and they both directly violate human rights; (2) State commission of abuses in furtherance of a joint venture, where the State and the TNC have a close relationship, and the State commits the abuses in the execution of their common endeavor; and (3) TNC participation in shaping an abusive regime by design and implementation, where a TNC shares a repressive policy agenda with a government and assists the formulation and enforcement of these policies.

Next, I delve into two types of indirect complicity: (1) financing a repressive regime, where a bank provide a government with a bad human rights record with funding that serves its abusive policies; and (2) supplying tools for human rights abuses to a repressive regime, where a TNC procures an overtly repressive regime with tools that knowingly will be directly used to violate human rights.

Finally, I explore four criteria relevant to incidental complicity: (1) silent complicity, where a TNC operates under an abusive regime and fails to protest violations; (2) intent and benefit, where a TNC derives an advantage from a State's abusive policies and shares the State's intention to violates human rights; (3) existence of a sanctioning regime, where a TNC's operation in a country violates national or international embargoes; and (4) proximate causation.

This typology should not be seen as a finite and comprehensive tool. Quite on the contrary, the number of subtypes is potentially infinite, since each event of TNC complicity in human rights violations is unique. Moreover, the spectrum is continuous and non-linear. Changes can be so subtle and gradual that not all distinctions are systematically relevant. Therefore, this chapter simply attempt to provide a working structure and vocabulary. For this reason, I elaborate on prototypical forms of TNC complicity for human rights abuses. The elements of these prototypical forms supply criteria relevant to distinguish varying forms of complicity in different settings. These criteria include, among other things, existence of a legal relationship, de facto dominance, intent, and/or benefit from the perpetration of abuses and knowledge and power to prevent them. In order to avoid a purely theoretical and elusive discussion, examples are provided under each prototype. I also describe arguments that have been advanced for and against findings of complicity for each case.

Throughout this chapter, I follow Peter Muchlinski's working definition of a TNC as any firm which 'owns (in whole or in part), controls and manages income generating assets in more than one country.'[1] As Beth Stephens explains, 'control is central to this definition—multilateral corporations do not merely have a financial stake in foreign ventures but also

---

[1] Peter Muchlinski, *Multinational Enterprises and the Law* (Oxford, Blackwell Publishers, 1995), p 12 (cited in Surya Deva, 'Human Rights Violations by Multinational Corporations and International Law: Where from Here?' (2003) 19 *Connecticut Journal of International Law* 1, at 1, fn 2).

exercise managerial control. This level of control enables a level of coordination among the various subparts that transforms the multinational corporation from a mere network of independent entities into an entirely new business structure.'[2] However, I have established my own definitions and types for degrees of complicity, which I elaborate in the body of this chapter.

Although there is a growing agreement amongst scholars that TNCs should be held responsible for human rights violations in certain circumstances, the identification of the situations where such a responsibility should be found to exist is more complex than it is for sovereign States. This complexity has halted attempts to enlarge the scope of TNCs' responsibilities towards human rights. States generally have human rights obligations towards all persons on their territory, although some duties do not run to non-nationals.[3] This stems from an assumption that governmental control and jurisdiction is determined on a territorial basis. For TNCs, however, a territorial scope for determining the universe of relevant right holders will not work insofar as businesses do not exercise such a geographically fixed form of jurisdiction. Therefore, the determination of corporate duties must address the company's links with individuals possessing human rights.[4] A few contemporary scholars, Marilyn Friedman, Barbara Herman, and Bernard Williams among them, structured the debate on scope of responsibility in terms of partiality and impartiality. Impartiality supporters require endorsing equal treatment of all persons under all circumstances, regardless of family or group connections.[5] Under such a structure TNCs would owe equal duties to a more diffuse population. Partiality advocates favor overt identification with close relatives and limited moral duties towards others,[6] and would impose on TNCs duties to protect the human rights of those who are associated with it, employees, contractors, their families, and so on. The United Nations Global Compact Program has phrased TNCs' obligations to respect human rights 'within their sphere of influence.'[7] This latter terminology encourages responsibility over those people on whom they have an effect and where the TNC can have an impact.

---

[2] Beth Stephens, 'The Amorality of Profit: Transnational Corporations and Human Rights' (2002) 20 *Berkeley Journal of International Law* 45, at 47–48.

[3] *Ibid* at 506.

[4] *Ibid* at 507.

[5] See *ibid*, at 507, n 266 (referring, for helpful reviews of the modern debate, to Marilyn Friedman, 'The Practice of Partiality' (1991) 101 *Ethics* 818; Barbara Herman, 'Agency, Attachment, and Difference' (1991) 101 *Ethics* 775; and Hugh LaFollette, 'Personal Relationships', in Peter Singer (ed), (Oxford, Blackwell Publishers, 1993) *A Companion to Ethics* 327. The principal modern advocate of the partialist stance is Bernard Williams: see Bernard Williams, *Moral Luck* (Cambridge, Cambridge University Press, 1981).

[6] *Ibid*.

[7] UN Global Compact Program.

## II. THE SPECTRUM OF COMPLICITY

The notion of complicity, as it has evolved in international law across adjudicatory and advisory bodies, is an amorphous concept of unclear breadth. It has been used in a range of situations: from joint action where TNCs and perpetrators of human rights violations are acting in concert, to mere presence situations where TNCs are merely participating in an economic system, and indirectly enhancing the viability of an abusive regime. However, such distant forms of involvement do not carry the same weight, and nor should the same legal and moral responsibility be attached to these acts.

Through a working typology, I lay out the spectrum of TNCs' complicity in human rights violations. A panoply of authors have used varying nomenclature, as well as disparate definitions for recurrent terms for distinguishing levels of complicity. I find the standard categorization which focuses on two notions, direct and indirect complicity, highly unsatisfactory. Therefore, I supply a more nuanced terminology and working structure, which covers direct, indirect and incidental complicity, and various sub-types within each of these three forms. I intend this typology to be a simplified working framework that covers archetypal forms of complicity, rather than a comprehensive description that captures and crystallizes what is, indeed, an amorphous and evolving spectrum.

Besides elaborating on the elements that compose each typology, I provide examples of TNCs that have acted under each form of alleged complicity, and explore the rulings or conclusions of fora (judicial or not) that have addressed the notion of complicity in these cases. I do not intend to cover all fora having dealt with similar questions of complicity, but focus on a few examples that are most relevant to determinations or recommendations in each instance. My analysis covers not only notions of legal complicity, which judicial fora have adjudicated, but also matters pertaining to moral responsibility, which have been elaborated to a greater extent in non-judicial or academic writings.

## 1. Direct Complicity and Responsibility

### A. Joint Execution of Abuses

The most commonly accepted forms of TNCs' direct complicity in human rights violations are symbiotic joint actions, where the State and the TNC act in concert. In cases where there is joint execution of human rights violations by both the State and the TNC, findings of complicity are unavoidable. Examples of such joint abuses are epitomized in German Nazi-era industrialists who used forced labor during the Holocaust. The US Military Tribunal at Nuremberg tried officials from three German firms: I.G. Farben; Flick; and Krupp. These defendants were indicted for plunder and spoliation of civilian property and factories, deportation of and use of prisoners of war and concentration camp inmates as forced laborers, and complicity in aggression and mass murder. Five Farben directors and 11 Krupp defendants were held criminally liable for the use of slave labor.[8]

It is impossible to not attribute responsibility for human rights abuses to these corporations,[9] particularly when 'Auschwitz was financed and owned by Farben … The Auschwitz construction workers furnished by the concentration camp lived and labored under the shadow of extermination'[10]. Krupp appropriated factories stolen by the Nazi regime from their Jewish owners, submitted requests for free labor of concentration camp inmates offered to the armaments industry by the SS in 1944, and engaged in massive human rights abuses.

## B. State Commission of Abuses in Furtherance of a Joint Venture

The differences between joint execution of human rights abuses and State execution of such abuses in furtherance of a joint venture are subtle and, for legal purposes, this distinction is almost meaningless. Nevertheless, joint execution might be an aggravated form that is lessened as the degree of closeness and interaction between the TNC and the State diminishes, as occurs in this latter type of State violations of human rights in furtherance of a joint State—TNC venture.

Anita Ramasastry has elaborated a test for direct complicity, arguing that it is present where there is: '(1) a strong and interdependent business

---

[8] Anita Ramasastry, 'Corporate Complicity: From Nuremberg to Rangoon—An Examination of Forced Labor Cases and Their Impact on the Liability of Multinational Corporations' (2002) 20 *Berkeley Journal of International Law* 91, at 1081, 1205–9.

[9] In the cases cited, individual directors, rather than the corporations themselves, were convicted, as the jurisdiction of the military tribunals did not extend to legal persons. Indeed, the argument most frequently raised against findings of complicity in cases of joint execution of human rights violations comes from several jurisdictions' domestic criminal laws. Many criminal regimes, particularly in civil law countries, follow the principle of *societas delinquere non potest* and deny that criminal responsibility can be attributed to corporations. The main premise behind this doctrine is the problematic notion of corporate intent. Establishing *mens rea* is a difficult issue in individual criminal liability, and becomes exponentially more complex for corporate criminal liability. Therefore, several jurisdictions have rejected corporate criminal responsibility and would not recognize corporate complicity. Regardless, such jurisdictions structure their proceedings by identifying individual criminal responsibility for acts that are perpetrated through the corporate form. Consequently, this counter-argument does not create an obstacle, in principle, to findings of TNC complicity and liability. Indeed, the US Military Tribunals did not have the power to attribute corporate responsibility. They found, eg, that I.G. Farben was an instrumentality through which individual actors were able collectively to engage in criminal acts (Ramasastry, above n 8, at 106), and the responsible individuals were condemned for those actions.

[10] 'The I.G. Farben Case', in *VIII Trials of War Criminals Before the Nuremberg Military Tribunals*, iii–iv (1952) at 1183–84 (cited in Ramasastry, above n 8, at 106, fn 53).

relationship between the [TNC] and the host government; (2) the [T]NC is aware of the human rights violations; and (3) the [T]NC continues to provide financial support to the host state and continues to perform under contractual arrangements, particularly in furtherance of a collaborative project or endeavor.'[11] I build on these three elements to construct a type I have labeled State execution in furtherance of a joint venture. However, for human rights violations to fall within this type, I require a determinative degree of corporate dominance over State actors. Where control is not present, I would consider complicity to be indirect, rather than direct. Control is, therefore, a key element to this type of complicity. Other factors, such as intent to effect the abuses or deriving a benefit from them, can be interesting features to aggravate responsibility but are not elements of the complicity type.

Steven R Ratner considers the issue of benefiting from and intending human rights abuses to be irrelevant in any determination of direct complicity. He believes that it is enough if the TNC or its agents knew or should have known of the likely effects of their assistance, and they need not intend these effects for direct complicity to attach to their actions.[12] However, factual determination of benefit and intent can help establish the degree of closeness and joint operation between the State and the corporation. Considerations of intent or benefit may not affect findings of civil legal responsibility based on damages. However, in my view, they should affect moral and criminal responsibility, in turn lessening or aggravating the seriousness of the crime and the consequent sentence.

The actions of Unocal Corporation in Burma are a clear example of this type of complicity. In this case, Unocal and the Burmese government engaged in a form of joint venture to construct a pipeline. The Burmese government supplied several services such as the clearing of helipads and building of roads through the use of forced labor and other human rights abuses, which in turn benefited Unocal. The US Ninth Circuit empowered by the Aliens Tort Claims Act, found Unocal liable for its complicity in the perpetration of these human rights abuses.[13]

A number of legal doctrines may favor or reject complicity findings in cases where a host State violates human rights in the furtherance of a joint doctrine. The legal doctrine of *respondeat superior*, adopted in several jurisdictions' civil laws, provides strong grounds for findings of TNC

---

[11] Ramasastry, above n 8, at 103.

[12] Steven R Ratner, 'Corporations and Human Rights: A Theory of Legal Responsibility' (2001) 111 *Yale Law Journal* 443, at 446 .

[13] *John Doe I v Unocal Corp*, Nos. 00-56603, 00-57197, Nos. 00-56628, 00-57195, United States Court of Appeals for the Ninth Circuit, 395 F.3d 932; 2002 US App LEXIS 19263; 2002 Cal Daily Op Service 9585; 2002 Daily Journal DAR 10794, 3 December 2001, Argued and Submitted, Pasadena, California, 18 September 2002, Filed, Vacated by, Rehearing, en banc, granted by *Doe v Unocal Corp*, 395 F.3d 978, 2003 US App. LEXIS 2716 (9th Cir., 2003).

complicity. This theory on agency holds a principal responsible for the acts of its agent if those acts were committed during the course of the agent's employment and were within the scope of the agent's duties. This doctrine conventionally does not permit limiting a principal's responsibility for the acts of his or her agent by claiming that the agent's scope of employment was limited to lawful and non-tortious performance of his or her duties. Through the lenses of *respondeat superior*, TNCs which act as principals in a business relationship and request or invite government human rights abuses could be held directly responsible for State perpetrations of such abuses. In many situations it will be hard to establish that a TNC and a host State's links constitute even a joint venture. However, when a TNC requests or hires State security forces which commit human rights abuses, the applicability of *respondeat superior* would establish TNC liability in a fairly straightforward manner.

A similar variation of such legal theory, commonly used in both domestic and international criminal law, is the command responsibility doctrine. Command responsibility attributes culpability to superiors, when a superior knew, or should have known, that the subordinate had committed, or was about to commit, the acts in question, and he did not take any reasonable measures to prevent the acts or punish the subordinate. Moreover, according to the International Criminal Court Statute, 'the crimes [must] concern activities that were within the effective responsibility and control of the superior.'[14] The key factor in determining responsibility is control. Where there is State control over other actors, there is a possibility of establishing State action. Consequently, if it can be established that a TNC exercises control (which could be in the form of overwhelming influence) over a State at least in one regard, it could be possible to establishing corporate responsibility for State acts.

Despite the fact that it will be even more difficult to define a TNC/host State relationship as a commander/subordinate than a principal/agent relationship, the command responsibility doctrine is of significant applicability. This doctrine is particularly relevant in those cases where TNCs' powers dwarf the State's powers. Where it can be established that TNCs have enormous leverage over a host State, in at least one or more respects, direct command and, consequently, direct responsibility is appropriate.

One major counter-argument to complicity findings comes from international criminal law. For example, the International Tribunal for the Former Yugoslavia has held that '*actus reus* of aiding and abetting in international criminal law requires practical assistance, encouragement, or moral support which has a substantial effect on the perpetration of the

---

[14] Rome Statute of the International Criminal Court, UN doc A.CONF/189/9, 17 July 1998, Art 28(b).

crime.'[15] Corporations such as Unocal have raised this defense. They claimed that practical assistance is required to establish complicity in an attempt to limit Unocal's complicity for Burma's human rights abuses committed in furtherance of their joint venture to construct a pipeline. Unocal has claimed that doing business with the government in the course of a project that has increased human rights abuses in its area of operations does not constitute that *actus reus*, and therefore findings of complicity are inappropriate. However, this counter-argument has been dismissed by the Court of Appeals for the Ninth Circuit, since it is also established in international criminal law that 'assistance need not constitute an indispensable element, that is, a condition *sine qua non* for the acts of the principal.'[16] Consequently, the 'act of assistance need not have caused the act of the principal,'[17] and participation in such a joint venture with a repressive State can be enough to establish corporate complicity under international criminal law.

### C. TNC Participation Shaping an Abusive Regime by Design and Implementation

The State and the TNC act in tandem in the design of human rights abuses when corporations play a significant role at influencing the governmental design of abusive policies that benefit these same corporations, and governments shape their policies accordingly. Although the TNCs are not physically executing the human rights abuses, nor do they have a joint venture relationship with the government, they have enough leverage and use their influence on the government to advance and sustain policies that infringe human rights.

One archetypal example of this type of complicity is embodied in South Africa's mining firms under the apartheid regime. South Africa's Truth and Reconciliation Commission has extensively documented this government—corporation relationship, particularly in the development of labor policies, where mining firms' strategies included 'influencing legislation that forced black workers into the wage system (and managed their allocation within it); state-endorsed monopolistic recruiting practices; the capping of African wages; divisive labor practices in managing compounds.'[18] The Truth and Reconciliation Commission accordingly held that corporations that played a central role in helping to design and implement the abusive policies engaged in first-order involvement with

---

[15] *Prosecutor v Furundzija*, IT-95-17/1-T (10 December 1998), reprinted in (1999) 38 ILM 317, para 235.

[16] *Ibid* at 209.

[17] *Prosecutor v Kunarac*, IT-96-23-T & IT-96-23/1-T, para 391.

[18] *Final Report of the Truth and Reconciliation Commission (South Africa)*, vol 4, ch 2, 'Business and Labour', p 7.

the abusive regime and 'must be held responsible and accountable for the suffering that resulted'.[19] Other corporations responsible for similar activities are contractors building prisons or providing armoured vehicles. It is true, however, that it might be difficult to draw a stopping-point in what constitutes design and implementation of an abusive regime, and this might be a de facto question related to actual influence in the shaping and carrying out of policies. Major Craig Williamson (a former security police spy) exemplifies this matter explaining:

> 'Our weapons, ammunitions, uniforms, vehicles, radios and other equipment were all developed and provided by industry. Our finances and banking were done by bankers who even gave us covert credit cards for covert operations. Our chaplains prayed for our victory and our universities educated us in war. Our propaganda was carried by the media and our political masters were voted back into power time after time with ever increasing majorities.'[20]

This perception of omnipresent responsibility for the design and implementation of an oppressive regime reflects the complexity and subjectivity involved in distinguishing between various types of complicity, and even finding a stopping-point to it. One plausible argument to defend against such accusations of complicity is contending that rent-seeking through licit means does not render an interest group complicit of norms and violations perpetrated by a State. Lobbying and influencing the legislature or supporting an administration does not mean full endorsement of all of its acts. Neither does the influencing group have final responsibility for the end product that might have been in some way affected by its communications with or support for the government. However, these provisos do not absolve interest groups that advanced a repressive agenda from responsibility for violations of human rights. Consequently, the legality of the modes of exercising influence resorted to by corporate actors is not a good standard to assign direct complicity. Level of involvement and extent to which such corporations influenced the abusive regime to pursue repressive policies are more relevant criteria. Significant involvement with significant influence in the design and implementation of abuses determine direct complicity.

## 2. Indirect Complicity

I define indirect complicity as otherwise lawful conduct that closely serves to aid a State in violating human rights, where there is knowledge of State human rights abuses, but no intertwined connection between the

---

[19] *Ibid*, at p 3.
[20] *Ibid*.

State and the TNC that would be sufficient to establish an agency relation. In cases of indirect complicity, the TNC does business with the abusive system, but it does not shape the workings of the abusive regime to extract an advantage by engaging with the government in the system of human rights violations. In indirect complicity cases, although there is a close relationship between the abusive regime and the TNC, the host government is a customer rather than a business partner of the TNC. No joint venture, goal or profits in furtherance of which human rights abuses are perpetrated exist. No relation of joint ownership and decision-making is established. Moreover, the TNC's transaction with the host State must directly assist the government in its implementation of abusive policies. That assistance cannot be phrased in a remote or hypothetical fashion, but ought to remain concrete. It is not enough to establish that the government profits from the broader or market relationship to establish indirect complicity.

### A. Financing a Repressive Regime

I would distinguish financing a repressive State from other forms of indirect complicity. Arguments for finding indirect complicity in the banking activities of financiers is straightforward as they provide substantial assistance that constitutes a key empowering link to the perpetration of human rights abuses. Nevertheless, most domestic and international fora that have addressed complicity for providing financial assistance to regimes which abuse human rights have declined to extend both criminal liability and civil liability. The main reasons behind this reluctance to extend complicity are fears that the links are too attenuated and might open the floodgates to finding complicity in too vast of a range of cases. Absence of *mens rea* in the financiers also plays a role in criminal proceedings.

For example, Karl Rasche, the Chairman of Dresdner Bank, a private commercial bank in Germany that has been characterized as 'the Third Reich bank', was tried under the Nuremberg Charter for facilitating slave labor on the grounds that he made loans to entities using slave labor.[21] The US Military Tribunal ruled 'We cannot go so far as to enunciate the proposition that the official of a loaning bank is charged with the illegal operations alleged to have resulted from loans or which may have been contemplated by borrowers.'[22] Other Holocaust litigation against Swiss banks is currently also confronting legal arguments that, even where banks had knowledge of the purpose of such financing, passive investment has

---

[21] See *United States v Von Weizsaecker (Ministries Case)*, in *XIV Trials of War Criminals Before the Nuremberg Military Tribunals* (1952) 852 (cited in Ramasastry, above n 8, at 113, fn 94).
[22] *Ibid* at 854.

not been considered to trigger liability.[23] However, new developments, for example in anti-terrorist funding laws, as well as UN Security Council resolutions on asset freezes for such funding, indicate that both international law and the domestic laws of several jurisdictions are evolving towards the recognition of liability for institutions who finance criminal activity.[24]

## B. Supplying Tools for Human Rights Abuses to a Repressive Regime

TNCs supplying overtly repressive or discriminatory States with materials used to abuse human rights, such as those building prisons or selling armored vehicles, police batons, arms, and so on, also constitute good examples of indirect complicity. Findings of responsibility are relevant in these contexts, since these corporations empower these governments to perpetrate abuses. Although in most jurisdictions criminal complicity would be inappropriate, given the absence of *mens rea*, there is a strong case for finding civil and moral responsibility in such instances. These corporations, after all, provide significant assistance that empowers States to commit such abuses.

It has been used as a defense to such allegations that State action would not have been prevented had the corporation refused to contract with it. This argument claims that market forces would regardless fulfill these States' requests for the supplied materials. Counter-factual claims hypothesizing that the aggregate would have the same effect as the singular act are futile theoretical attempts to disclaim responsibility. Responsibility attaches to those who participate, empower, or facilitate the commission of abuses, and does not attach to those who do not. Speculations about other TNCs' behavior if a particular TNC chooses not to be an accomplice neither add to nor subtract anything from that complicity.

## 3. Incidental Complicity

Incidental complicity is the least developed and least accepted theory of TNCs' responsibility for host States' human rights violations. Precisely for this reason, this chapter will provide a more elaborate analysis of this type of complicity. The doctrine of incidental complicity was most vocal during the campaigns to end South Africa's apartheid regime. However, it is also representative of theories of corporate responsibility in a disparate range of States including Cuba, North Korea, Burma, Libya,

---

[23] See Anita Ramasastry, 'Secrets and Lies? Swiss Banks and International Human Rights' (1998) 31 *Vanderbilt Transnational Law Journal* 325, at 416.
[24] See Ramasastry, above n 8, at 113.

Angola, and China, to name just a few. Trade embargoes, restrictions on TNCs' operations, and limits on individuals' visits to some of these countries are clear examples of how mere presence in a country with a bad human rights record, can be problematic. Even when there is no active participation or cooperation between the host government and TNCs, mere presence in such areas has been blamed for enhancing the viability of oppressive system, bolstering their economy and legitimizing their political system, and consequently perpetuating their subsistence. Incidental complicity proponents believe, for example, that the speed at which South Africa's apartheid regime crumbled after the establishment of a comprehensive ban 'is the final proof of the way in which international business sustained apartheid.'[25]

On top of this principle of sustaining the economic and financial viability of a State that ought to be ostracized until the incumbent's regime becomes untenable given its repugnant human rights practices, there is a second reason behind the notion of incidental complicity. Some State omissions favoring corporate commissions of human rights violations have been considered sufficiently linked to government actors to be categorized as abuses under color of State where such abuses benefited from what might be called official tolerance. Widespread non-enforcement of the minimum wage or health and safety laws is one example of this phenomenon. Conversely, some TNC omissions favoring State commissions of human rights abuses ought to give rise to corporate responsibility. Inaction in the midst of a repressive structure can amount to complicity if the capabilities to protect from such violations exist and the duty to ensure compliance with basic rights is not fulfilled. Where a corporation has the capability to prevent human rights abuses, it might have imposed on it a responsibility to do so.

Nevertheless, some groups are absolutely opposed to the notions of incidental complicity. Quite on the contrary, rather than criticizing mere presence in countries with governments abusive of human rights, optimists of TNCs' influences on these regimes view TNCs' presence as constructive engagement, rather than complicity. Constructive engagement advocates believe the presence of TNCs serves to improve the local economy, consequently creating a less precarious and more enlightened class that will push for democratization and respect for human rights. Furthermore, TNCs' presence can be influential on the government and build some leverage that could directly serve to reduce human rights abuses.

Under constructive engagement theories, ostracizing an oppressive regime is more problematic and leads to more human rights abuses than working in such countries, and thus improving their economy and their

---

[25] *Final Report of the Truth and Reconciliation Commission (South Africa)*, vol 4, ch 2, 'Business and Labour', p 14.

ties with better regimes could create a leverage on those rogue States to improve their human rights policies. William H Meyer actively supported constructive engagement after finding a positive correlation between TNC investment and human rights in a cross-study of several countries.[26] In fact, however, Meyer retreated from his initial position that presence of TNCs is positively correlated to good human rights records of host countries after confronting and embracing numerous critiques to his prior work.[27]

Despite the spurious causality relation established in Meyer's quantitative work, the argument that TNCs can positively influence governments' human rights records in multiple contexts finds some grounding in empirical and anecdotal evidence. But whether there may be such an impact will be highly context-specific, and it seems implausible to derive any general rules from the evidence at our disposal. Reasonable minds differ on whether operating in regions with endemic human rights abuses empowers or weakens a regime, improves or worsens the human rights situation, has a positive or a negative effect in the long run. These disparate views render applying the notions of incidental complicity more complex. Regardless of which paradigm is preferred—constructive engagement or incidental complicity, a number of variables may be considered relevant to the analysis of TNCs' effects on the local regime and their responsibility towards human rights. These variables are reviewed below.

A second cornerstone of incidental complicity on which reasonable minds could differ is the definition and assessment of regimes with a sufficiently repugnant human rights record to warrant TNC disengagement. It is difficult to articulate a standard that is comprehensive enough to cover the panoply of human rights abuses that a State can inflict on its population, and flexible enough to exhibit proportional incidence across varying situations. This is a problem national procurement policies often confront. Political stands, protectionist agendas, historical rivalries, and idiosyncratic clashes pushed on to the national legislature's policy making agenda by interest groups can distort a nation's assessment of another regime's human rights record. Neither international bodies' resolutions nor public opinion are good tools to measure a regime's respect for human rights, since public awareness campaigns and resolutions are

---

[26] See William H Meyer, 'Human Rights and MNCs: Theory v Quantitative Analysis' (1996) 18 *Human Rights Quarterly* 368–97; and William H Meyer, *Human Rights and Political Economy in Third World Nations. Multinational Corporations, Foreign Aid and Repression* (Westport, CN, Praeger, 1998).

[27] William H Meyer, 'Activism and Research on TNCs and Human Rights: Building a New International Normative Regime', in Jedrzej G Frynas and Scott Pegg (eds), *Transnational Corporations and Human Rights* (Victoria, Australia, Palgrave Macmillan, 2003), ch 2, pp 33–52.

highly influenced by political and economic concerns. For example, China's repression of Falung Gong practitioners appears more brutal and abusive than Cuba's treatment of dissidents. Nonetheless, the level of political condemnation these abuses have received is inversely correlated.

## A. Silent Complicity

A first relevant distinction in findings of incidental complicity is whether TNCs remain silent about human rights violations and fail to protest or attempt to prevent them, or whether they engage in some type of resistance and opposition. There is growing acceptance within TNCs and the general public that there is something culpable about failing to exercise influence when the leverage exists and abuses are endemic. Sir Geoffrey Chandler, Chair of the Amnesty International UK Business Group has affirmed that 'silence or inaction will be seen to provide comfort to oppression and may be adjudged complicity … Silence is not neutrality. To do nothing is not an option.'[28]

Consequently, the notion of silent incidental complicity reflects the expectation that TNCs raise systematic or continuous human rights abuses with the appropriate authorities,[29] the press, their home governments, or the international community. The complicity is lacking where a TNC denounces abuses, engages in civil disobedience, or adopts social practices that subversively act to challenge the abusive system in place.

In such cases indeed, TNCs can be perceived as an outside pressure for change rather than as an incidental accomplice. They can distinguish themselves from endemic rights abuses by engaging in conduct that is progressive in the face of the local human rights situation. Examples of such forms of resistance or disobedience are recognizing unions even where the local government does not recognize them, or maintaining codes of conduct that follow international standards such as the Sullivan Code (or arguably more progressive ones) even if they set standards higher than local practices or even conflict with local requirements.

It is unlikely that TNCs will undertake such activities, given that repressive regimes might not allow TNCs to criticize government policies and still continue to operate in the region. Moreover, TNCs in many respects are more concerned about fiduciary duties to shareholders than with human rights abuses throughout the world. Nevertheless, the home State's consumer pressure on TNCs not to get involved in human rights abuses might be sufficient incentive to bring about these improved standards or civil disobedience by TNCs. Indeed, the Sullivan Code of

---

[28] Cited in Christopher L Avery, *Business and Human Rights in a Time of Change* (London, Amnesty International, 2000), at p 22.

[29] Andrew Clapham and Scott Jerbi, 'Categories of Corporate Complicity in Human Rights Abuses' (2001) 24 *Hastings International and Comparative Law Review* 347–48.

Conduct required not only non-discrimination in the workplace, but also training and investment to improve the opportunities of oppressed racial groups. Despite the challenge this represented in the context of the South African apartheid regime, it was adopted by more than '125 companies … including giants such as Exxon, Mobil, IBM, Citicorp and Merck.'[30] Its relative effectiveness as a political tool for change, nonetheless, remained questionable.

## B. Intent and Benefit

Another distinction within incidental complicity is the notion of benefit. On one hand, in incidental beneficiary complicity cases, TNCs with few or no links to the host State might benefit from an abusive regime, even if they do not participate in, encourage, or shape its policies. The benefit in such instances is present, for example, in downward pressure on wages, or the non-unionization of workers, which are results of discriminatory practices that regimes such as South Africa's apartheid-era governments, or repressive States such as China, practiced or practice. TNCs might, in many cases, factor the existence of these abusive conditions as a positive aspect when they do a cost—benefit analysis of establishing TNC presence in such countries. Indeed, in some cases, TNCs might not have a presence in such areas if it were not for those practices and how they impact on their cost and revenue structures.

One critical question that might be asked is whether it is financially and administratively viable for TNCs to operate in such localities under non-abusive conditions. Although a positive answer does not convey much valuable information, a negative response implies that the TNC has an interest in the perpetration of human rights violations and that it would not be present if it were not for them. Consequently, some moral responsibility ought to be attributed to the TNC for the subsistence of such violations.

Therefore, incidental complicity is also framed as a plain duty to abstain from even remotely or incidentally benefiting from or otherwise dealing with regimes responsible for an atrocious system of human rights violations. Consequently, advocates of the notion of benefit from incidental complicity call for corporate duties not to invest at all in a repressive society, or to ensure that the TNC does not in any way benefit from a government's lax human rights policy.

On the other hand, in instances of non-beneficiary incidental complicity, TNCs neither participate in nor benefit from host State human rights abuses. They merely do business in a country where such abuses are

---

[30] Barbara A Frey, 'The Legal and Ethical Responsibilities of Transnational Corporations in the Protection of International Human Rights' (1997) 6 *Minnesota Journal of Global Trade* 153, at 175.

endemic. TNC presence is, regardless, criticized since it strengthens the very same State that perpetrates such violations by paying taxes to such governments, tolerating their behavior and bolstering their economy.

The distinction between beneficiary complicity and non-beneficiary complicity is unsatisfactory for several reasons. Neutral businesses with no engagement in human rights violations can incidentally benefit from them even if they are on the other side of the world and have never been confronted with such abuses. Consumers around the world may also incidentally benefit, regardless of the degree of knowledge or awareness. TNCs or other corporations which do not operate in countries with pervasive human rights abuses might benefit from deflated prices for some of their materials even if they purchase them in the market from corporations that have no contact whatsoever with countries which violate human rights. Downward pressure on global market prices is hard to isolate or respond to. The issue, therefore, is not geographical area of operation.

As argued in earlier sections of this chapter, notions of intent and benefit could be factored into analyses of moral responsibility aggravating the offense of complicity. However, benefit (just as intent) per se is not a distinction that affects finding of legal responsibility in any meaningful way.

## C. Existence of a Sanctions Regime

The existence of a sanctions regime that massively encourages TNCs to avoid operations or investment in a country with a record of human rights abuses is a factor that can be taken into account when evaluating TNC complicity. Whether such regime is in place, or not, does not shed much light on the complicity question, given that the establishment of sanctions regimes might be influenced by multiple factors. Nevertheless, reviewing the arguments for and against the establishment of such sanctions regimes enriches the dialogue on how TNC presence may be complicit or not with the abusive State.

Proponents of sanctions and embargoes believe that the nature of global business has changed, and that international law must evolve together with such changes. Although the imposition of a duty on TNCs to abstain from operating in countries with atrocious human rights violations was not always desirable, the changing nature of TNCs calls for an evolution towards such a system. TNCs are currently denationalized entities that can move and restructure themselves around the world. TNCs' fiduciary duties to their shareholders makes them more detached from their duties to the community in which they operate, and more responsive to shareholders that do not suffer the consequences of the way in which TNCs do businesses. This accountability deficit calls for a different kind of regulation. There is an undisputable need to build greater incentives for TNCs to be accountable and positively engaged in the communities in which they operate. An example of how this can be done successfully is the international campaign to end apartheid in South Africa, where a coordinated embargo brought about regime change.

One caveat is that, in order for advocacy on sanctions not to lose its credibility, it is important to avoid having such propositions hijacked by interest groups. Not all claims for the establishment of sanctions regimes are genuine. Frequently, supporters of trade bans or bans on investments and operations by TNCs in countries with bad human rights records have hidden agendas. Other groups not particularly concerned about human rights might mask their true motives in favoring the introduction of a blockade behind human rights claims. The most common hidden agenda is a protectionist, anti-free trade position. For activists wishing to have a positive impact on the human rights agenda, an effective strategy requires that they distinguish themselves from such interest groups and their covert intentions.

The most fervent opponents of the notion of incidental complicity have advanced equally strong counter-arguments. They believe restricting TNCs' operations in areas with pandemic human rights abuses is, at best, counter-productive. Investment is a source of economic and social growth. TNCs' mere presence, rather than contributing to human rights abuses, seeds a source of resistance and change. TNCs improve the living conditions of their workers and bolster the economy, creating jobs and providing revenues. This allows for greater education and training, for their workforce and also for their families. Through taxes, the multiplier effect, subcontracting, and other social and economic engagements, TNCs improve the socio-economic conditions and favor the establishment of a middle class which is better suited to engage in intellectual activities and political resistance. Consequently, restricting TNCs from operating in countries with repressive regimes results in hindering economic and social development where it is most needed. This only delays democratization and improvements in the human rights situation. Skeptics of such theories doubt, of course, that TNCs have such a spill-over effect in the local population. They point at the barely subsistence wages they pay in such countries and the poor working conditions they provide, denying that TNCs create a middle class, let alone an educated elite of inchoate resistance.

A second interesting argument opposing findings of incidental complicity for TNCs' mere presence in countries with bad human rights records is that it is now commonly accepted that international sanctions on trade and investment risk punishing mainly the innocent. Consequently, establishing a regime that encourages or obliges TNCs to restrain from operating in such countries is detrimental for the very people whom advocates of incidental complicity claim to aid. International economic sanctions are conceived by some to be a human rights violation per se.

The application of comprehensive economic sanctions has often caused enormous unintended humanitarian consequences for the civilian population in target States. Drastic declines in the quality of life in Iraq following the first Gulf War, or in Fidel's Cuba and Kadafi's Libya, are blatant examples.

As asserted in the Bossuyt Report to the United Nations Economic and Social Council '[t]he sanctions regime against Iraq [was] unequivocally illegal under existing international and humanitarian law and human rights law.'[31] In 2000:

> [i]n marked contrast to the prevailing situation prior to the events of 1991—1992, the infant mortality rates in Iraq [were] among the highest in the world, low infant birth weight affect[ed] at least 23 per cent of all births, chronic malnutrition affect[ed] every fourth child under five years of age, only 41 per cent of the population ha[d] regular access to clean water, 83 per cent of all schools need[ed] substantial repairs.[32]

Human rights are not only negative rights (the right to be free from oppression, torture, etc.) but also include positive rights, primarily economic and social rights that are necessarily tied to resources to ensure that health care, nutrition, and so on, are guaranteed to all people. Therefore, banning TNCs' economic activities or prohibiting international investment and trade in order to make an economic and political system unsustainable is extremely problematic. Active efforts to make a country's economy non-viable, rather than improving human rights, could result in increased violations, if not of negative rights, at least of positive ones. Doubtless, indefinite unemployment is worse than lack of recognition for workers' unions, endemic malnutrition is worse than racial discrimination, and so on.

Over the last century, transnational corporations have attained unprecedented economic power, as well as geographic scope

> which have given them enormous influence over the enjoyment of a broad range of human rights. These rights fall into three general categories: economic, social and cultural rights; civil and political rights; and rights protected under international humanitarian law.[33]

---

[31] *The Bossuyt Report: The Adverse Consequences of Economic Sanctions on the Enjoyment of Human Rights*, E/CN.4/Sub.2/2000/33 (21 June 2000), para 70.

[32] Report of the second panel established pursuant to the note by the President of the Security Council of 30 January 1999 (S/19999/100), concerning the current humanitarian situation in Iraq, S/1999/356 (30 March 1999) annex II (cited in *The Bossuyt Report,* above n 31, at para 65).

[33] Symposium contributor, 'Corporate Liability for Violations of International Human Rights Law' (2001) 114 *Harvard Law Review* 2025, at 2027.

In my opinion, advocacy of sanctions that restrain TNCs from operating in countries with systematic human rights abuses, in most cases, utilizes an extremely narrow conception of human rights which focuses solely on the last two categories of rights, but neglects economic, social, and cultural rights. These rights are just as crucial and extremely difficult to protect in countries affected by poverty and weak economies. Human rights are not a monolithic block of entitlements that are either respected or not. Quite on the contrary, they are a bundle of rights that interact, overlap, and might even compete against each other. Human rights are a matter of degree, and the amount of funds and freedoms available to ensure their respect determines the extent to which some or all of them will be protected.

Attempting to address this dilemma, Bossuyt proposes a six-stage test to evaluate the legitimacy and limitations of sanctions. This test poses the following questions: (1) Are the sanctions imposed for valid reasons (for example, a breach of peace and security) and not for political reasons?; (2) Do the sanctions target the proper parties?; (3) Do the sanctions target the proper goods or objects? (4) Are the sanctions reasonably time-limited?; (5) Are the sanctions effective (reasonably capable of achieving a desired result)?; and (6) Are the sanctions free from protest arising from violations of the 'principles of humanity and the dictates of the public conscience'?[34] The limitations of such a test are nonetheless obvious, since answers to such questions are inherently subjective and could hardly be detached from the political climate resulting in the pressures that led to the imposition of economic sanctions in the first place.

Further contributing to this debate, the UN Committee on Economic, Social and Cultural Rights issued a General Comment on 'The Relationship between Economic Sanctions and Respect for Economic, Social and Cultural Rights'. In this Comment, the Committee affirms that international human rights instruments

> cannot be considered to be inoperative, or in any way inapplicable, solely because a decision has been taken that considerations of international peace and security warrant the imposition of sanctions. Just as the international community insists that any targeted State must respect the civil and political rights of its citizens, so too must the State and the international community itself do everything possible to protect at least the core content of the economic, social and cultural rights of the affected peoples of that State.[35]

It is precisely for this reason that the international community, particular through the United Nations, has been shifting its strategy away from

---

[34] *The Bossuyt Report*, above n 31, at paras 41–47.
[35] Committee on Economic, Social and Cultural Rights, General Comment No 8, The Relationship between Economic Sanctions and Respect for Economic, Social and Cultural Rights, C/C.12/1997/8 (12 December 1997).

economic sanctions and towards 'smart' sanctions. Such sanctions have been developed to eliminate or minimize the unintended atrocious consequences of economic sanctions on civilian populations. Smart sanctions set no restraints on trade, investment, or corporate activities. They focus on the individuals or entities responsible for human rights violations (or other policies condemned by the international community) and leave international trade relations and their impact on the local economy unaffected. These targeted sanctions include travel bans and financial sanctions against designated individuals or entities (asset freezes), as well as arms embargoes. In the face of such developments, it is hard to argue that imposing duties on TNCs across the board to abstain from operating in countries with oppressive regimes is sound policy.

Contexts in which sanctions will be an appropriate tool for the international community and will not have devastating effects on the civilian populations are rare, but nonetheless exist. I believe two principles are paramount for economic sanctions to realize their objectives. First, sanctions must be universal or at least include all nations with more than de minimis trade relations with the abusive regime, and target limiting resources if they are not comprehensive. Second, a viable civil society, and a political alternative, must exist in the country on which sanctions are imposed. Non-strategically targetted partial sanctions, just like sanctions in a country with little civic life and no other political route, are not likely to achieve their intended result. In the former cases, the sanctions strategy would not be coercive enough. In the latter, sanctions would only foster further repression, but would not advance any alternative that would have otherwise remained inchoate for organizing resistance and bringing about social change.

For this reason, despite the overall unpopularity of economic sanctions, support for sanctions in present-day Burma subsists. TNCs' presence in Burma, which is primarily restricted to energy companies, has effects almost exclusively on the government's budget and very little impact on the local economy.[36] In this rare situation, arguments about the weakening of the local economy become irrelevant, since only the government's finances and not household budgets would shrink if all TNCs were to divest from the region. In the case of Burma, political alternatives also exist in the pro-democracy movement embodied in Aung San Suu Kyi. The viability of sanctions regimes under this type of factual pattern makes them a lot more appealing.

*D. Proximate Causation*

It is very difficult to draw a line between what does or does not constitute complicity. But it is important to find a stopping-point. Otherwise, findings

---

[36] See, eg, the report of the International Confederation of Free Trade Unions, *Doing Business with Burma*, 25 January 2005, available at www.icftu.org

of complicity where practically no relation exists might undermine the rationale and case for apportioning responsibility in difficult cases of indirect and incidental complicity with significant TNC participation. I would draw the line at active or immediate assistance, rather than allowing for complicity where actors only have broad or economic relations with human rights abusers. Proximate cause is an important component of attributions of responsibility. A 'but for' causality link, a standard which exists in all legal systems and requires a close connection between the act under review and the damage should be present in our analysis of complicity. Alternative criteria may be equally suitable. The Yugoslav War Crimes Tribunal has stated, for example, as a requirement for the predicate act for accomplice liability that such act must have a 'direct and substantial effect' on the commission of the offense.[37] This is a lesser standard than 'but for' causation, but remains an articulated, contained and manageable scheme.

It is hard to sustain a legal system where mere causation that amounts to little more than theoretical or loose relations would be enough to identify responsibility. Otherwise, establishing incidental complicity could open the floodgates to finding complicity everywhere, and consequently eviscerating this notion of any power. If any act which could have the effect of benefiting a human rights perpetrator is considered to extend responsibility to its agent, regardless of the degree of proximity between the act and the abuser's benefit and also regardless of the agent's intent, we could all be accomplices of all human rights violations. How far can the accomplice's net be cast without rendering complicity a meaningless notion?

If incidental complicity is attributed to TNCs for merely keeping an abusive regime's economy afloat, are individuals who buy the products of TNCs that directly violate human rights any less responsible for keeping those corporations in business and therefore any less complicit for those human rights abuses? Are shareholders who own stock in TNCs that directly violate human rights accomplices? If TNCs are condemned for incidental complicity, why not tourists who visit such countries and contribute to their economies? Why not non-governmental organizations (NGOs) which also prevent the humanitarian situation in the host State from being so unbearable that it causes the abusive regime's downfall? Why not news broadcasters, health workers, diplomats? Why not all agents who act in the region, regardless of their intentions and effects?

If proximate cause is not an essential element of complicity, responsibility would be attributed to the very same actors that are key to redressing human rights violations: the international press, social activists, humanitarian workers, and so on. Although some authors like

---

[37] *Prosecutor v Tadic*, Case No IT 94-1, Trial Judgment, 7 May 1997, p 692.

James Petras, Henry Veltmeyer, and Steve Vieux[38] are particularly critical of the NGO 'band-aid' approach of acting to prevent crises, and consequently assisting the abusive regimes to remain in power, it is generally accepted that such humanitarian work, far from being guilty of complicity, is highly desirable. Ironically, notions of incidental complicity not incorporating proximate cause as a necessary element could hold those who do not benefit and are most antagonistic to human rights abuses more responsible than those who do benefit but do not operate in the area, or are indifferent to such abuses.

It is valid to question the real extent of TNCs' influence on the behavior and sustainability of host governments. Often, international financial and economic sanctions do not work. South Africa's apartheid regime boycott is considered to have been fairly effective at assisting the demise of apartheid. Nevertheless, several authors argue that this success will rarely be replicated elsewhere, since South Africa had a 'particular vulnerability [due to its] reliance on international investment networks.'[39] Clearly, similar approaches have not worked in Iraq, Libya, or Iran. If there is little claim for influence, the notion of complicity becomes devoid.

Richard Dicker, Associate Counsel at Human Rights Watch, 'would recommend no new private investment, a suspension of business operations, a boycott, or even a withdrawal of all foreign private investment'[40] in extreme cases. 'Such situation[s are] characterized by several of the following factors: grave and systematic rights abuses, abuses of such a nature that no business enterprise can avoid taint by operating in the country; no form of pressure from the international community has had, or has, any reasonable prospect of having a significant effect on those abuses.'[41] Dicker's recommendation points out a factor I consider most significant: the likelihood of having an effect.

### III. CONCLUDING REMARKS

The spectrum of TNCs' complicity for human rights violations committed by the State in which they operate leads to the distinction of three types of complicity—direct, indirect, and incidental—and their subtypes. A special emphasis has been placed on incidental complicity, given that this is the most complex and unexplored form of TNC complicity for human rights violations. However, even those who are favorable to findings of

---

[38] See Petras, Veltmeyer and Vieux, *Neoliberalism and Class Conflict in Latin America: A Comparative Perspective on the Political Economy of Structural Adjustment* (Victoria, Australia, Palgrave Macmillan, 1997), p 176.

[39] Robert Stumberg, 'Preemption and Human Rights: Local Options After *Crosby v NFTC*' (2000) 32 *Law and Policy in International Business* 109, at 190.

[40] Richard Dicker, Symposium Article (Spring 1999) 11 *Pace International Law Review* 231.

[41] *Ibid.*

complicity in most cases should recognize the importance of establishing elements that must be present to attribute responsibility. Such elements have therefore been outlined for each category, focusing on legal issues such as agency control, aiding and abetting, and proximate cause.

This chapter has argued in favor, in all but the most extreme cases, of integrationist policies of constructive engagement that embrace abusive regimes and try to work with them towards social and political change. I prefer such approaches to exclusionary policies that attempt to favor human rights by ostracizing abusive regimes. Segregation, discrimination, and punishment tend to generate antagonism and, in turn, a tightening of hostilities. Mutual dependency and mutual influence are more likely to foster improvements in respects for human rights. It is, nonetheless, undeniable that not all regimes are willing to cooperate or even to be co-opted and that international pressure and influence are not omnipotent. Where human rights abuses cannot be influenced and connections between the State and the TNC are minimal and indirect, I do not attribute complicity.

Moreover, humans rights cannot be conceived as falling into two categories: one where they are respected and the other where they are abused. On the contrary, human rights can be respected to varying extents throughout an entire spectrum. Consequently, when attributing responsibility to TNCs for human rights abuses committed by State actors or under color of State law, it is important to take a holistic approach. I believe policies for the improvement of human rights ought to be comprehensive and consider not solely a few civil and political rights, but the panoply of human rights and how they interact.

# Part IV

# Incentivizing Socially Responsible Corporate Conduct

# 12

# *The Promotion Of Human Rights by Selective Public Procurement Under International Trade Law*

KATHERINE ZEISEL

## I. INTRODUCTION

SELECTIVE PUBLIC PROCUREMENT is a unique type of governmental measure tailored to ensure fulfillment of international human rights obligations in that it requires companies that wish to bid on public contracts to make a specific level of commitment to protecting human rights. It is one of the few tools of a government by which it can hold a company producing goods outside its borders directly accountable for its practices that has some enforcement power behind it, namely that the government can deny a contract based on failure to meet specific human rights-based criteria. Such policies create incentives for companies and their host States to improve human rights conditions. It is, however, important to remember that such policies are usually just one of the components of a multi-tiered trade policy intended to combat a specific practice or to target a specific country, and are unlikely to be effective without other forms of pressure.

Once the decision to implement selective public procurement policies has been made, the question of the legality of selective public procurement clauses under international trade law then becomes important. Fundamentally, selective public procurement policies are trade policies and, as such, are subject to the discipline of international trade law, which is largely defined in the context of the World Trade Organization (WTO).

This chapter argues that selective public procurement policies by States are permissible under international law, including under international trade law generally and under the GATT (General Agreement on Tariffs and Trade)/WTO agreements specifically. This discussion revolves around the fundamental question of whether States may have selective public procurement policies, not whether international human rights law requires them to do so.

The first section will provide background on selective public procurement, including a typology of the kinds of selective public procurement.

The second section will examine examples of selective public procurement in practice in the United States and the European Union, as well as the perspective of developing States and international institutions. The third section will examine the legitimacy of selective public procurement through discussion of theoretical and pragmatic justifications for and against. The fourth section will analyze the legality of selective public procurement in the context of the law of the WTO.

## II. SELECTIVE PUBLIC PROCUREMENT BACKGROUND

Selective public procurement can be defined as the use of non-economic, human rights standards to evaluate the awarding of public contracts for goods or services by governments. The broad goal of these policies is either a change in domestic policy, such as impacting on the criteria used by a specific government agency in procuring supplies, or a change in the policy of foreign States. Additionally, States are increasingly using these policies as a means of ensuring corporate accountability for production of the good or service provided rather than just hiring the company that meets only economic criteria.[1]

Public procurement is an important part of the economies of many States, and government procurement is believed to compose 10 per cent to 30 per cent of the gross national product (GNP) in all States.[2] In the United States, government procurement is valued at between $1.4 billion and $1.6 billion annually.[3] In the European Union, public procurement represents 10 per cent to 15 per cent of the GNP, or 25 per cent to 30 per cent of public expenditure.[4] Thus, public procurement represents a significant part of these economies, and implementation of selective procurement policies could have a major effect on the practices of suppliers.

This section will provide a typology for the various methods of selective public procurement policies and will then discuss the implementation of these policies in the United States and the European Union.

## 1. Typology of Selective Public Procurement

Before exploring selective public procurement in more detail, it is useful to lay out the various types of selective procurement policies. The first is

---

[1] Naomi Roht-Arriaza, 'From Country-Based to Corporate-Based Campaigns' (2003) 21 *Berkeley Journal of International Law* 185, at 186.

[2] G Callendar and D Mathews, 'Government Purchasing: An Evolving Profession?' (2000) 2(2) *Journal of Public Budgeting, Accounting & Financial Management* 272.

[3] Khi V Thai, 'Public Procurement Re-Examined' (2001) 1 *Journal of Public Procurement* 9, at 24.

[4] *Public Procurement*, SIGMA Policy Brief No 3, available at: http://www.oecd.org/dataoecd/60/7/1820856.htm (last visited 3 January 2005).

domestically oriented and is designed with the goal of aiding the remedying of current or past discrimination. For instance, this type of policy is
commonly used in the United States to require the hiring of minority contractors in public works projects, and South Africa openly uses public
contracts to try to decrease post-Apartheid disparities.[5]

The other types of selective procurement, and the ones which this
chapter will largely focus on, are practices outside of the contracting
State's borders. These policies either target businesses interacting with a
specific country, such as prohibiting public contracts with businesses that
buy, sell or make products in Burma, or target a specific manufacturing
product or process, such as child labor or the use of a chemical pollutant.
Regulation of process, although controversial in international trade law, is
not without precedent in selective public procurement policy. For example, in 1999, President Clinton barred federal agencies from purchasing
goods made with exploitative child labor.[6]

In addition, selective public procurement requirements may be a condition of execution of the contract or may be a condition of selection of the
vendor. Generally, a regulation that is a condition of the contract will be
more specific to the nature of the contract, such as a particular environmental requirement. On the other hand, a condition for the selection of
the vendor will tend to be broader, and may require the vendor not to
engage in a particular practice more generally.

The compliance component policy itself may also take several forms. It
may require adherence to a specific code of conduct, such as the
Organization for Economic Cooperation and Development's (OECD's)
Principle of Corporate Governance.[7] Other policies require that companies agree not to do business with a specific country or that they pledge
not to use child labor or harmful environmental pollutants, but not that
they adhere to a specific code of conduct. Companies are frequently
required to shoulder the cost of compliance, although those costs may be
minimal depending on the current practices of the company and the
strength of the compliance mechanism.

Finally, the actual rationale behind the creation of the selective public
procurement policy can vary, and is instrumental in choosing the type of
policy. The most common goal is to try to eliminate a specific practice that
a State finds contradictory to its public values. However, the justifications
behind even this basic goal differ. States may justify such policies on the
basis of their international obligations: as will be discussed in more detail

---

[5] Christopher McCrudden, *Buying Social Justice* (forthcoming), at p 1.

[6] Exec Order No 13,126, 64 Fed Reg 32,383 (1999) (the order does not apply to products
from countries that are parties to NAFTA or the WTO Agreement on Government
Procurement).

[7] OECD Principles of Corporate Governance, available at: http://www.oecd.org/
dataoecd/32/18/31557724.pdf (last visited 12 January 2005).

below, States may wish to avoid complicity in human rights violations or they may wish to create an international environment that is beneficial for the realization of rights. Alternatively, policy-makers may feel some obligation to citizens to ensure that they are ethical consumers through the purchase of goods that are not abhorrent to public morality. The theory is that in situations where consumers purchase their own products in the marketplace, they want information about the process by which the product is made so they can act as ethical consumers.[8] While labeling schemes may be sufficient in a case in which the consumer is directly purchasing the product, in the case of public procurement, the government is acting as an agent of the people. Thus, since consumers have no ability directly to purchase these goods, the government should reflect the desires of its citizens to purchase products made in a way that is consistent with human rights norms. This theory can be criticized as being overly paternalistic in that the government can be seen to be protecting the citizens. In reality, however, this theory is an embodiment of representative democracy, and is about fulfilling consumers' market preferences as expressed to and through their elected representatives. Since they have no direct access to the purchasing other than through the election of representatives, those representatives ought to act in accordance with the desires of the public. Although there are few examples of selective public procurement in practice, these policies could exist in many varieties and for many rationales.

## 2. Implementation of Selective Public Procurement Policies

Integrated approaches are ones which form part of a larger policy scheme and which systematically implement the procurement policies through official procedures.[9] These policies can be implemented in several ways. Some States that have rewritten their constitutions in recent years chose to incorporate requirements that public procurement favor certain historically disadvantaged populations or to incorporate specific non-economic criteria directly into the constitution.[10] Other States have incorporated

---

[8] There are concerns that, on an individual level, consumers do not act to preserve their true best interests through their process preferences, but that critique is irrelevant to the specific discussion of government exercise of economic power to reflect the will of its citizens on a social rather than individual level. See Douglas A Kysa, 'Preferences for Processes: The Process/Product Distinction and the Regulation of Consumer Choice' (2004) 118 *Harvard Law Review* 525, at 531.

[9] McCrudden, above n 5, at pp 37–39.

[10] The South African Constitution provides that procurement must be fair and transparent and that it: '... does not prevent the organs of state or institutions referred to in that subsection from implementing a procurement policy providing for a. categories of preference in the allocation of contracts; and b. the protection or advancement of persons, or categories of persons, disadvantaged by unfair discrimination': South African Constitution (1996), Art 217.

policies through statutes or administrative declarations.[11] The most effective selective public procurement policies are implemented in an integrated approach as part of a comprehensive policy with respect to a specific practice, because selective public procurement is unlikely to be effective if not used in concert with other mechanisms.[12]

The most significant model code for governmental procurement was drafted by the United Nations Commission on International Trade Law.[13] The goal of this model code, as with most international procurement reform efforts, was to increase transparency in the procurement process. Therefore it does not address the issue of selective public procurement explicitly. However, if such measures are implemented in a way that fulfills the requirements of transparency, they would be permissible under the model code.

The specific method employed by selective public procurement programs to ensure accountability of contractors varies. In recent years, the trend has been to link procurement programs to adherence to a specific voluntary corporate code of conduct, such as the Sullivan Principles or the MacBride Principles.[14] The MacBride Principles are designed to ensure that companies are not discriminating against religious minorities in Northern Ireland, and they provide an external tool for States to utilize in evaluating the actions of a particular corporation.[15] Currently, New York, Rhode Island, and Massachusetts require companies that conduct business with Northern Ireland and that want to bid on State contracts to adhere to the MacBride Principles.[16] Other States may require specific environmental, labor, or other human rights norms to be applied within constraints they specify by the company bidding on a contract. For instance, a company may be required to demonstrate that it meets specific environmental criteria determined by the government in accordance with appropriate scientific evidence.

## III. SELECTIVE PUBLIC PROCUREMENT IN PRACTICE

This section will provide a brief discussion of the examples of the United States and the European Union with respect to their utilization of selective

---

[11] McCrudden, above n 5, at 64.

[12] *Ibid*.

[13] United Nations Commission on International Trade Law, UNCITRAL Model Law on Procurement of Goods, Construction and Services, available at: http://www.uncitral.org/english/texts/procurem/ml-procure.htm (last visited 12 January 2005).

[14] Craig Forcese, 'Globalizing Decency: Responsible Engagement in an Era of Economic Integration' (2002) 5 *Yale Human Rights and Development Law Journal* 1, at 41.

[15] The MacBride Principles are modeled on the Sullivan Principles. The relationship between the Sullivan Principles and the MacBride Principles will be discussed further below.

[16] Carol E Head, 'The Dormant Foreign Affairs Power: Constitutional Implications for State and Local Investment Restrictions Impacting Foreign Countries' (2000) 42 *Boston College Law Review* 123, at 130; Jorge Perez-Lopez, 'Promoting International Respect for Workers' Rights Through Business Codes of Conduct', 17 *Fordham Int'l Law Journal*, 7 (1993).

public procurement. Analysis of the United States and the European Union is important, because they have more defined public procurement policies and have utilized selective public procurement in a way that other States have not. This section will then look at the current position that developing States are generally taking towards selective public procurement, and towards international procurement policy more broadly. Finally, it will address the policies of several international institutions with respect to procurement.

## 1. The United States and Selective Public Procurement Policies

In the United States, federal, state and local governments can have independent public procurement policies. Currently, the only limitation is the preemption doctrine which prevents state governments from having laws that conflict with federal law. This limit was clarified with respect to procurement policies when Massachusetts implemented a public procurement policy prohibiting state agencies from contracting with companies that do business with Burma. President Clinton subsequently instituted his own policy in reaction to the massive human rights abuses in Burma and sued Massachusetts to prevent the state from continuing its procurement policy.[17]

The European Commission submitted an amicus brief in the case. It argued that allowing Massachusetts to set policy towards Burma would undermine relations between the United States and the European Union.[18] The European Commission was primarily concerned with the sanctions aspect of selective public procurement rather than the fact it was selective public procurement per se.[19]

The Supreme Court ultimately held that states could not have trade policies that conflicted with federal trade policy under the doctrine of preemption.[20] The decision did not, however, forbid states from implementing their own policies in the absence of federal action. Therefore, the question of whether outwardly directed public procurement policies by individual states are permitted under the foreign affairs doctrine, which delegates all foreign policy decisions to the federal government, is still open.

New York, Rhode Island, and Massachusetts have a selective public procurement policy that requires all contractors that do business with Northern Ireland to adhere to the MacBride Principles.[21] During the era of South African apartheid, public procurement policies that required

---

[17] *Crosby v National Foreign Trade Council* (2000) 530 US 363.
[18] Brief for European Commission, *Crosby v National Foreign Trade Council*, 2000 WL 177175 (US, 2000) (No 99-474), at 4.
[19] *Ibid*, at 6.
[20] *Crosby*, above n 17, at 374.
[21] Head, above n 16, at 3.

adherence to the Sullivan Principles was common.[22] The Sullivan Principles were publicly proposed in 1971 by Reverend Leo Sullivan, a member of the board of directors for General Motors.[23] At the time, 12 major United States corporations were already voluntarily adhering to the Principles.[24] These Principles created a framework for ethical business under the apartheid regime by requiring companies to subvert the separation policies.[25] They became the first important voluntary code of behavior within corporate America.[26] In 1984, they were amended to include the explicit objective of encouraging changes in the practices of other businesses.[27] The Sullivan Principles were the basis for codes of conduct in various other parts of the world, and particularly in Northern Ireland and the former Soviet republics.[28]

In 1986, Congress passed the Anti-Apartheid Program, which codified much of the Sullivan Principles.[29] It specifically prohibited procurement by the United States Government from the South African Government, as well as importation of South African steel, and agricultural and oil products.[30] It also required the United States government to make affirmative efforts to procure goods and services from South African businesses that were majority-owned by South Africans harmed by apartheid.[31]

At this time, there is no widespread movement to utilize selective public procurement as a tool of the national government to influence the human rights behavior of other governments. It seems likely that if states or federal governments decide to pursue selective public procurement they will follow the voluntary code model that has existed thus far since it requires the least oversight and the least interference with business practices.

## 2. The European Union and Selective Public Procurement Policies

The European Union has taken two contradictory positions on the issue of selective public procurement. In October 1998, the European Union

---

[22] David D Caron, 'Cities, States, and Foreign Affairs: The Massachusetts Burma Case and Beyond: The Structure and Pathologies of Local Selective Procurement Ordinances: A Study of the Apartheid-Era South Africa Ordinances' (2003) 21 *Berkeley Journal of International Law* 159, at 160.

[23] Head, above n 16, at 5.

[24] *Ibid*, at 6.

[25] Caron, above n 22, at 160.

[26] Perez Lopez, above n 16 [to be added?], at 7.

[27] *Ibid*.

[28] Stephen G Wood and Brett G Scharffs, 'American Law in a Time of Global Interdependence: US National reports to the XVIth International Congress of Comparative Law: Section IV Applicability of Human Rights Standards to Private Corporations: An American Perspective' (2002) 50 *American Journal of Comparative Law* 531, at 558.

[29] 22 USS §5001–5117 [Repealed].

[30] 22 USC §5057 [Repealed].

[31] 22 USC §5001(e)(2) [Repealed].

asked for a consultation in the WTO with respect the Massachusetts policy towards Burma.[32] The European Community claimed that such policies were a violation of the Government Procurement Agreement (GPA) and should not be permitted.[33] While the complaint was withdrawn once the United States Supreme Court struck down the Massachusetts measures,[34] the fact remains the European Communities took a decisive position that selective public procurement policies are a violation of the GPA.

This stance is in sharp contract to several directives issued by the European Parliament, and the case-law of the European Court of Justice (ECJ), all of which clearly permit the use of non-economic criteria in public procurement. In *Concordia Bus Finland*, the ECJ held that the city of Helsinki could consider non-economic criteria, in this case environmental considerations, in awarding its public transportation contracts.[35] Prior to *Concordia Bus Finland*, the Court had made similar pronouncements in *Commission of the European Communities v France*[36] and *Beentjes v Netherlands*.[37] The Court in *Beentjes* held that member States may take environmental considerations into account when assessing the economically most advantageous tender.[38] In *Commission of the European Communities v France*, the Court held that Article 30(1) of Directive 93/37, which lays out the criteria public authorities must consider in awarding public contracts, does not preclude the use of non-economic criteria.

In its most recent directive on public procurement issued in March 2004, the European Parliament and Council expanded upon and clarified this jurisprudence by declaring that the awarding of contracts by member States is subject to principles of free movement of goods, equal treatment, non-discrimination, proportionality and transparency.[39] Article 6 clarifies that:

---

[32] See United States—Measure Affecting Government Procurement: Request for Consultations by the European Communities, WTO Doc WT/DS88/1 (26 June 1997) [hereinafter 'European Request'].

[33] Specifically, the European Communities argued that the United States violated provisions that Article VIII(b), which requires that only conditions related to the firm's capability to perform the contract, be included; Article A, which requires that economic criteria and not political criteria be the basis for qualification of potential contractors; and Article XIII, which requires that the awarding of contracts be based on economic rather than political criterion: European Request, above n 32.

[34] *Crosby*, above n 17.

[35] Case C-513/99, *Concordia Bus Finland v Helsingin kaupunki* [2002] ECR I-07213, Recital 55, 63 (judgment of 17 September 2002).

[36] Case C-225/98, *Commission of the European Communities v France* [2000] ECR I-7445 (judgment of 26 September 2000).

[37] Case 31/87, *Beentjes v Netherlands State* [1988] ECR 4635.

[38] *Ibid*, para 37.

[39] Directive 2004/18/EC of the European Parliament and of the Council of 31 March 2004 on the coordination of procedures for the award of public works contracts, public supply contracts and public service contracts, Art 2.

Nothing in this Directive should prevent the imposition or enforcement of measures necessary to protect public policy, public morality, public security, health, human and animal life or the preservation of plant life, in particular with a view to sustainable development, provided that these measures are in conformity with the Treaty.[40]

Thus, while States are not required to utilize selective public procurement policies, they are clearly permitted to do so under European Union law. Functionally, this means that States that wish to utilize non-economic criteria in order to evaluate the economically most advantageous tender are free to do so.[41] The Directive does not explicitly authorize the creation of requirements to respect human rights or to accede to a monitoring mechanism, although it may still be technically possible to do so within the constraints of the Directive and the Court jurisprudence.[42] It is not unthinkable, therefore, that international trade requirements such as non-discrimination, proportionality, and equal treatment could be compatible with non-economic criteria.

The internal position of the European Union clearly is at odds with the position that it took as a member of the WTO. While the conflict has never been explicitly resolved, the recent directive and the case-law indicate there is space for selective public procurement policies in European law.

## 3. Developing States and Public Procurement

International public procurement reform has largely been targeted at developing States, and has been developed with the goal of increasing transparency and decreasing corruption. In recent years, there has been a trend among developing States to resist further development of international procurement standards because of concern about the perceived negative effects of the reforms particularly as they curb government authority to award contracts.[43] This is consistent with the increasing resistance of developing countries to the development of international labor standards and other norms that they perceive as interfering with international investment.[44] While not all developing States take this position, those that do have argued at recent WTO meetings that increased transparency requirements would limit their ability to conduct procurement in a way that benefits local

---

[40] *Ibid*, Art 6.

[41] Olivier De Schutter, 'The Accountability of Multinationals for Human Rights Violations in European Law', Working Paper No 1 (Center for Human Rights and Global Justice, 2004), at 71.

[42] *Ibid*, at 70–71.

[43] McCrudden, above n 5, at p 60.

[44] David Kinley and Junko Tadaki, 'From Talk to Walk: The Emergence of Human Rights Responsibilities for Corporations at International Law' (2004) 44 *Virginia Journal of International Law* 931, at 973.

economies or disadvantaged people.[45] Developing States are resisting further interference with their public procurement systems, and would be likely to resist any additional reforms that would limit their discretion.

The implication of this resistance is felt not only in terms of international model procurement codes, but also with respect to assessing the legality of selective public procurement policies under international trade law. Developing countries are unlikely to support a position that such policies are consistent with international law. This reluctance is also guided by an additional concern about the qualification of goods produced in their countries, and the economic ramifications of the inability to meet standards set by selective public procurement policies.

From a development perspective, developing States may also disagree with the underlying assumption of selective public procurement: that such policies are the best means to increase protection of human rights. Many States argue that the best way to achieve protections in the long run is trade liberalization because increased trade leads to increased resources.[46] From this perspective, attempting to change internal human rights policies of developing States may impede increased protections for human rights to the extent that such policies limit free trade. However, it is not clear that selective procurement policies would result in less free trade of goods, and so these concerns are unwarranted at this time.

Thus, the main objections to selective public procurement policies by developing States are not necessarily directed at the policies per se, but rather are part of a general resistance to increased international procurement reform.

## 4. International Institutions and Procurement

While the procurement policies of international institutions are beyond the scope of this chapter, it is interesting to note that several utilize non-economic criteria. UNICEF will not contract with suppliers that use child labor or suppliers that manufacture land mines or any of the components for land mines.[47] As detailed in the accompanying Draft Commentary, the Norms on the Responsibilities of Transnational Corporations and Other Business Enterprises with Regard to Human Rights propose that all United Nations agencies should consider human rights treaty obligations as a basis for procurement decisions.[48]

---

[45] McCrudden, above n 5, at 60.

[46] John O McGinnis and Mark L Movsesian, 'Against Global Governance in the WTO' (2004) 45 *Harvard International Law Journal* 353, at 365.

[47] UNICEF, *Procuring Supplies for Children: Becoming a Supplier*, available at http://www.unicef.org/supply/index_suppliers.html (last visited 13 November 2004).

[48] Norms on the Responsibilities of Transnational Corporations and Other Business Enterprises with Regard to Human Rights, ESC Res 2003/16, UN ESCOR Commission on Human Rights, 55th Sess, Agenda Item 4, UN doc. E/CN.4/Sub.2/2003/12/Rev.2 (2003).

These examples are instructive in that they indicate that the concept of selective public procurement is penetrating the international consciousness at least on one level. In assessing the merits of such policies, the United Nations has, at least tentatively, taken the position that the benefits outweigh the harms. However, these decisions do not necessarily provide a sound basis for States to proceed with similar policies, because the United Nations is not subject to the discipline of international trade law, which is the most significant legal obstacle for selective public procurement policies.

## IV. THE LEGITIMACY OF SELECTIVE PUBLIC PROCUREMENT

The legitimacy of selective public procurement is an important question because it draws on both the theoretical legal and economic basis for these policies as well as practical concerns. If these policies are to be utilized in a significant way, challenges to their legitimacy must be addressed. This section will first look at the justifications for selective public procurement. It will then address the concerns about selective public procurement policies on the part of human rights activists. Finally, it will discuss additional concerns of proponents of trade liberalization.

### 1. The Use of Selective Public Procurement Policies is a means by which States comply with their human rights obligations under international law

*A. States have an Obligation not to be Directly Complicit in the Violation of Human Rights*

As Robert Howse observes, 'The very existence of international human rights ... and the institutions developed to deal with these areas suggest that the international community accepts that a state's legitimate concern about the morality of the treatment of individuals is not limited to its own nationals.'[49] States voluntarily sign and ratify treaties, thereby accepting the obligations embodied in those treaties; to respect, protect and fulfill the rights protected in the specific treaty.[50] These treaties do not limit

---

[49] Robert Howse, 'Back to Court After Shrimp/Turtle? Almost but Not Quite Yet: India's Short Lived Challenge to Labor and Environmental Exceptions in the European Union's Generalized System of Preferences' (2003) 18 *Am U Int'l L. Rev* 1333, at 1369.

[50] For instance, the Preambles of both the International Covenant on Civil and Political Rights and the International Covenant on Economic and Social Rights, as well as Art 2 of the Convention on the Rights of the Child and Art 3 of the Convention on the Elimination of Forms of Discrimination Against Women all call for to States to respect, protect and fulfill human rights in some form. See International Covenant on Civil and Political Rights, GA res 2200A (XXI), 21 UN GAOR Supp (No 16) at 52, UN doc A/6316 (1966), preamble, 999 UNTS 171; International Covenant on Economic, Social and Cultural Rights, GA res 2200A (XXI), preamble, 21 UN GAOR Supp (No 16) at 49, UN doc A/6316 (1966), 993 UNTS 3; Convention on the Rights of the Child, GA res 44/25, annex, Art 2, 44 UN GAOR Supp (No 49) at 167, UN doc A/44/49 (1989).

these obligations to only the citizens of one particular country, and signatories are obligated to uphold the rights contained in the treaty to the best of their abilities within the constraints of international law generally. For example, the International Covenant on Economic and Social Rights, which currently has 160 parties,[51] recognizes the rights within the convention as basic to human dignity[52] and states that everyone has the basic worker protections.[53] The treaty could logically be read to say, at the very least, that parties are required to not to be complicit in violating rights that all people deserve and which are fundamental to human dignity. Under the general principles of treaty interpretation, as embodied in the Vienna Convention on Treaty Interpretation, it can be said that States are required, at the very least, not to act in a contrary manner to a treaty to which they are a signatory.[54] These obligations ought to have the same status in domestic and international law as other treaty-based responsibilities unless specific reservations are made at the time of the ratification of the treaty. There is some responsibility on the part of States for non-State actors, particularly when there is a direct interaction as occurs in a public contract.[55]

The natural corollary, although one which is often resisted, is that although States owe no affirmative obligation to protect the rights of persons outside their territory, they do have an obligation not to undermine the core of a treaty by actively violating the basic rights codified in the treaty. Thus, in the context of selective public procurement, States ought not contract with companies or other States if, in order to fulfill the contract, the State knows or ought to know that relevant rights will be violated.

Even this idea of complicity can be understood in various ways. It could mean that States should not utilize vendors who will violate human rights in the actual fulfillment of the contract. Alternatively, complicity could mean that States should not allow vendors who violate human rights in any way to be eligible to bid on public contracts, regardless of

---

[51] Status of Ratifications as of 3 November 2004, available at http://www.ohchr.org/english/law/cescr-ratify.htm (last visited 11/20).

[52] ICESCR, above n 50, preamble.

[53] *Ibid*, Art 7.

[54] Under Art 18 of the Vienna Convention, States are obligated not to defeat the object and purpose of a treaty when it is signed and prior to ratification. This provision, read in conjunction with Art 26, which obliges States to perform their treaty obligations in faith, and Art 27, which obliges States not to undermine the treaty through internal law, can be read to indicate that States should not undermine the purpose of a treaty. Contracting with corporations that the State knows will violate treaty obligations, particularly human rights obligations, undermines the object of upholding these basic rights for all people: Vienna Convention on the Law of Treaties, 1155 UNTS 331, reprinted in (1969) 8 ILM 679, Arts 18, 26–27.

[55] McCrudden, above n 5, at p 37.

whether or not they will do so to fulfill the particular contract. Just as a person is complicit in murder whether he commits the murder himself or whether he contracts with an assassin under domestic criminal law, a State that knowingly contracts for such abuses should be liable for breaches of its international obligations. There is something inherently wrong, in both the moral and legal sense, if States are allowed to escape human rights obligations merely by contracting with actors who will abuse rights to fulfill contracts cheaply rather than the government abusing rights and providing the services or goods itself.

## 2. States that Fulfill Contracts with Companies that Violate Labor Standards Benefit from Unfair Competition

Companies that violate basic human rights in order to make a product more cheaply do so either because the States they operate in do not fulfill their obligations to legislate against the violations or because they fail to enforce such prohibitions where they exist. Companies look to invest where labor standards are lowest so they can maximize profit, and in doing so encourage these practices.[56] If companies stay in States with higher labor standards, they are frequently at a disadvantage in the marketplace when forced to compete with companies in States with low or no labor rights protections. Thus, companies are unfairly benefiting from the fact that some States are ignoring their obligations under international law.

There is some dispute about the accuracy of claims that States will decrease labor and environmental standards in order to attract business investment. However, the point here is not that States will lower protections, but rather that companies will seek out States with lower standards, and thereby provide a disincentive to raise standards. The movement of factories owned by multinational corporations along the border of Mexico and the United States to South Asian countries with lower human rights and environmental standards is just one example of this phenomenon.[57] It should be noted that there is a distinction between seeking the lowest production costs and seeking low labor standards.

[56] Frank Emmert, 'Labor, Environmental Standards and World Trade Law' (2003)10 *UC Davis Journal of International Law and Policy* 75, at 96.

[57] While it has many parallels, this critique must be distinguished from the 'race-to-the-bottom' critique. There is little empirical evidence that States lower their labor or environmental standards to attract foreign investment as is hypothesized in one formulation of the race-to-the-bottom theory: José E Alvarez and Jagdish Bhagwati, 'Afterword: The Question of Linkage' (2002) 96 *American Journal of International Law* 126, at 131. However, there is still a strong disincentive to increase labor and environmental standards because of the fear of losing or discouraging additional foreign investment: see Daniel A Zaheer, 'Breaking the Deadlock: Why and How Developing Countries Should Accept Labor Standards in the WTO' (2003) 9 *Stanford Journal of Law Business & Finance* 69, at 86.

Lower production costs, such as cheap labor, do not necessarily imply low labor standards, since the price of labor can vary according to local economies. Lower labor standards, although they often accompany cheap production costs in practice, are distinct because these standards often fall below international norms and usually permit violations of international labor norms.

## 2. Critiques by Trade Liberalization Proponents

### A. There is No Logical Endpoint for this Type of Regulation

One critique by the advocates of trade liberalization is that the potential to create trade policies based on non-trade values could potentially be without end, and could therefore interfere with the primary purpose of trade liberalization, to get the lowest price for products.[58] This critique arises from the fear that the protection of human rights is a vague objective, and therefore run the risk of being instrumentalized for protectionist purposes. While there are real concerns over States being permitted to invent policies that they link to some nebulous conception of human rights, this critique is ultimately unconvincing. Human rights generally may be a broad concept, but, as with any developing area of law, certain concrete minimum standards have evolved, particularly in the context of labor rights, which are most relevant in this discussion. It is possible, by looking to both treaty law and jurisprudence, to interpret human rights in a concrete way. Thus, in the event a State began to instrumentalize human rights, its policy could be challenged in the same way that policies based on other developing standards of international law may be questioned.

States logically can have both the goal of promoting trade liberalization and that of promoting human rights. It is up to the State to balance those goals and decide upon the best policy. It is not the purpose of trade law to determine social policy for States, but rather to encourage transparency. So long as a State is clear about the policy and does not implement it as a protectionist measure, there ought to be space in international trade law for that decision.

### B. Selective Public Procurement Policies Violate Sovereignty of Other States

In a broad human rights context, this critique says that by attempting to influence the policies of other States in which companies reside, the State implementing the policy is violating the autonomy of the other State to make its own policy decisions.[59] This is a relevant critique for selective procurement policies that are explicitly designed to affect the human rights policies of another State, particularly ones directed at companies

---

[58] McCrudden, above n 5, at p 48.
[59] Emmert, above n 57, at 87.

that conduct business with the target country. Under general public international law, however (without prejudice to specific requirements of international trade law), this argument is unpersuasive because interference to protect human rights is generally accepted, particularly in this context where one State is interfering through economic policy rather than physical interference with the country. It is not clear that selective public procurement policies even constitute direct interference because they are only indirectly targeted at States through regulation of bidding by companies, and it is companies that must meet a certain level of rights protection. Companies and States can make economic decisions about whether a particular practice or trade with a particular State is more valuable, and thereby decide if they wish to comply with the requirements of a selective public procurement program.

However, even if it is interference, the very concept of *erga omnes* obligations and *jus cogens* norms illustrate this obligation of States to ensure the protection of human rights in at least some contexts.[60] The International Court of Justice has held that all States have an interest in *erga omnes* obligations.[61] In its recent Advisory Opinion on the construction of the Wall in the occupied Palestine Territory, the International Court of Justice also held that all States have an obligation not to render aid or to assist in maintaining a violation of *erga omnes* obligations.[62] Human rights violations by a government against its citizenry, including the failure to protect citizens, constitutes a violation of the State's obligation not just to its citizens but also to the international community.[63] This breach allows other States to intervene to protect human rights, including through policies such as selective public procurement, as appropriate to the situation.[64] Article 28 of the Universal Declaration on Human Rights reinforces this idea with the obligation to consider human rights norms at all levels of societal interaction.[65]

## C. Cost–Benefit Analysis Suggests that Selective Public Procurement Policies are not the Most Efficient Mechanism to Protect Human Rights

Some critics argue that it is more complex and expensive to meet the requirements of selective public procurement contracts, particularly in the

---

[60] *Barcelona Traction, Light and Power Company, Limited (Belgium v Spain)*, Second Phase, 1970 ICJ 3, at 32 (5 February).

[61] *Ibid.*

[62] Legal Consequences of the Construction of a Wall in the Occupied Palestinian Territory, Advisory Opinion (ICJ, 9 July 2004) (2004) 43 ILM 1009, para 159 [hereinafter 'Advisory Opinion on the Wall'].

[63] *Barcelona Traction*, above n 60, at 32.

[64] Margo Kaplan, 'Using Collective Interests to Ensure Human Rights: An Analysis of the Articles on State Responsibility'(2004) 79 *New York University Law Review* 1902, at 1910.

[65] Dinah Shelton, 'Protecting Human Rights in a Globalized World' (2002) 25 *British Columbia International & Comparative Law Review* 273, at 284.

context of domestic policies designed to remedy past discrimination by the affirmative recruitment of a diversified workforce, and so only large companies will be able to bid on such contracts.[66] The argument continues that there may be better ways to resolve social problems without driving small and medium-sized business out of the market.[67] This criticism is not necessarily relevant to broader subcategories of public procurement. In most cases, small businesses can easily comply with guidelines because there is less institutional change to be made and they possibly can move production locations more easily than large companies. They may, however, be hampered by an inability to absorb additional costs associated with meeting higher labor standards, whereas a larger company could spread the costs between various customers more easily. Thus, this critique can also apply if compliance assessment mechanisms are burdensome and their cost must be absorbed by the company, or if compliance itself requires significant changes in business practices.

If States determine that it is an important policy goal to encourage small and medium companies to bid on the contracts, they could either be prepared to assume the additional costs, though this may be incompatible with the obligation to choose the most economical offer, or they could find ways to ensure compliance that minimize costs to the company. For instance, requiring adherence to the OECD Guidelines, which have a monitoring mechanism already included, would minimize the costs to companies themselves. Ultimately, this concern is an insufficient reason to prevent States from utilizing selective procurement as a tool to fulfill their human rights obligations, because there are sufficient mechanisms to ensure that both small and large businesses can meet the requirements set by selective public procurement policies. States have sufficient information to decide how to spread costs if they value this policy enough to implement it, and small businesses have capacity to change location or production in a way that larger companies may not.

## V. THE LEGALITY OF SELECTIVE PUBLIC PROCUREMENT: THE WORLD TRADE ORGANIZATION

International trade law as regulated by the WTO is the major obstacle to the realization of selective public procurement programs. Although many proponents of trade liberalization argue that human rights and trade law should be maintained as two separate disciplines, the coexistence of these international regimes nevertheless should be considered in order to fully understand either.

---

[66] McCrudden, above n 5, at p 46.
[67] *Ibid.*

The question of the consistency of human rights obligations and GATT/ WTO obligations is one which goes to the very purpose of the WTO. The GATT/WTO system was originally intended not just to protect States, but to allow States to protect the rights of individual merchants.[68] Human rights law is also fundamentally designed to protect individuals, and so a conflict between the two laws challenges the way in which the systems value individuals or which individuals are valued. Turning a blind eye to such conflicts is not a viable solution and simply exacerbates those that already exist.[69]

This section will first examine the relevant instruments within the WTO, and will then discuss the types of human rights that could be considered in selective public procurement policies. The third section will discuss the challenge of extraterritorial regulation of the process by which contracts are fulfilled. The fourth will examine the debate about inclusion of human rights norms in WTO proceedings. Finally, the fifth section will analyze possible routes for including human rights standards in public procurement programs within the context of the WTO.

## 1. Relevant Instruments

### A. The 1947 General Agreement on Tariffs and Trade

The 1947 GATT agreement forms the basis of modern international trade law. Among the most relevant provisions for a discussion on the incorporation of human rights principles are: Article I: Most Favored Nation Treatment;[70] Article III: Non-discrimination;[71] and Article XX: Exceptions to the GATT. The provisions for non-discrimination and 'most favored nation' mean that non-origin neutral or otherwise arbitrary or discriminatory measures must be justified under the exceptions outlined in Article XX to be consistent with the GATT.

### B. Government Procurement Agreement

In 1994, as part of the Uruguay Round of negotiations that created the WTO, a new Government Procurement Agreement (GPA) was drafted.[72]

---

[68] Stephen Charnovitz, 'Globalization of Economic Human Rights' (1999) 25 *Brook Journal of International Law* 113.

[69] Andrew T Guzman, 'Global Governance and the WTO' (2004) 45 *Harvard International Law Journal* 303, at 349.

[70] Article I requires that all Member States must grant any privileges, advantages, favors, or immunities given to one member State to all member States: General Agreement on Tariffs and Trade, 30 October 1947, Art XX(e), 61 Stat A-11, TIAS 17000, 55 UNTS 194.

[71] The principle of non-discrimination in Article III requires that States treat imported products in the same way they treat like and/or directly competitive domestic products.

[72] Agreement on Government Procurement, opened for signature 15 April 1994 (entered into force 1 January 1996), 1915 UNTS 103.

This agreement is critical to a discussion of selective public procurement because the area of government procurement is exempted from the scope of the GATT. The main goals of the agreement were to increase transparency and to promote trade liberalization.[73] The agreement is a plurilateral treaty, which means it is enforceable only between States parties, as distinguished from the member States of the WTO, of which there are 14, including the United States and the European Communities, as well as 21 observer governments and four observer international organizations. Nine States are currently negotiating accession.[74] Very few of the current members are developing countries, but the GPA is still extremely relevant to a discussion of selective public procurement because these policies are most frequently used by developed countries.

The GPA is currently undergoing formal review, with the first phase focusing on improving and simplifying the text.[75] Ultimately, this new round of review is centered on creating better mechanisms to improve transparency.[76] The review is also attempting to achieve consensus on the extent of the enforceability of the GPA and the strength of the enforcement mechanism.[77]

In its current form, the majority of the GPA covers the rules of tendering offers, including the specific criteria that may be considered in accepting offers. The GPA is problematic because it requires that 'any conditions for participation in tendering procedures shall be limited to those which are essential to ensure the firm's capability to fulfill the contract in question.'[78] Furthermore, the GPA requires that, unless it is in the public interest not to issue the contract, a State must accept the lowest tender offer that meets economic criteria.[79] In its challenge against the United States over Massachusetts' policy regarding Burma, the European Communities cited both of these provisions.[80]

Article XXIII of the GPA contains exceptions similar to those in Article XX of the GATT. These exceptions could provide a possible ground for integration of human rights criteria in public procurement. It is not clear if this is the case, since there has been no decision by any panel on the scope of the most relevant exceptions in either the GATT or the GPA, particularly the public morals exception. The relevant GATT exceptions will be discussed with relation to the GPA, since there is no GATT jurisdiction

---

[73] *Ibid*, preamble.
[74] Committee on Government Procurement, Members and Observers, available at http://www.wto.org/english/tratop_e/gproc_e/gp_gpa_e.htm (last visited 14 November 2004).
[75] Sue Arrowsmith, 'Reviewing the GPA: The Role and Development of the Plurilateral Agreement After Doha' (2002) 5 *Journal of International Economic Law* 761.
[76] *Ibid*, at 763.
[77] *Ibid*.
[78] GPA, Art VIII:2
[79] *Ibid*, Art XIII:4(b)
[80] European Request, above n 32.

over public procurement. The potential for incorporation of human rights through the exceptions will be discussed in detail below.

While the dispute settlement body has not defined the scope of these exceptions, there is significantly more jurisprudence and scholarly work on the exceptions in the GATT. It is useful to consider Article XX, therefore, in analyzing the limits of the exceptions to the GPA. Under the canons of treaty interpretation, particularly Articles 32 and 33 of the Vienna Convention on the Law of Treaties,[81] it is reasonable to use the GATT to interpret the GPA, since there is the same or similar language, and both are meant to be read as part of a larger system.

## 2. Types of Human Rights that could Potentially be Considered

### A. Jus Cogens Rights

*Jus cogens* rights are ones which are universally recognized under international law and which all States have an obligation to protect. The only rights consistently recognized as *jus cogens* rights are the rights to be free from genocide, from crimes against humanity, from piracy, and from slavery, including slavery-like practices such as forced or compulsory labor.[82] By definition, such obligations should be universal and extend beyond the territory of a specific nation, but many trade liberalization advocates do not recognize the right of a State to prohibit products made by slave or forced labor. While these rights are critical, they are limited in scope. In addition, there is controversy over whether *jus cogens* obligations extend beyond borders.

The underlying question with respect to selective public procurement is not whether States must have such policies, but whether it is permissible to utilize public procurement to protect *jus cogens* norms under the relevant WTO agreements. Arguments that such rights cannot be protected under WTO law are inconsistent with international law. The ICJ *Advisory Opinion on the Wall* makes it clear that *erga omnes* obligations must be protected by all.[83] This principle can be transferred to *jus cogens* norms since both create binding, inviolable obligations on the part of the State to protect the norm in question. It is not necessary to argue that States are obligated to use selective public procurement in this context, but at the very

---

[81] Vienna Convention on the Law of Treaties, above n 53, Arts 32–33.

[82] The International Labor Organization Commission of Inquiry on Burma concluded that there was sufficient international practice to consider a right to be free from forced or involuntary labor as a peremptory norm under international law: Report of the Commission of Inquiry appointed under Article 26 of the Constitution of the International Labour Organization to examine the observance by Myanmar of the Forced Labour Convention, 1930 (No 29), para 203 (July 1998), available at: http://www.ilo.org/public/english/standards/relm/gb/docs/gb273/myanmar.htm (last visited 3 January 2004).

[83] *Advisory Opinion on the Wall*, above n 62, at para 169.

least States ought to be allowed to utilize selective public procurement to ensure the protection of *jus cogens* norms.

The obligations recognized in the *Advisory Opinion on the Wall* are even stronger under the draft Norms on the Responsibilities of Transnational Corporations and Other Business Enterprises with Regard to Human Rights.[84] There is a general obligation for both States and corporations under this agreement to promote and secure the fulfillment of and respect for human rights, including ensuring that transnational corporations respect the rights codified within the document.[85] Selective public procurement is a mechanism for fulfilling the clear obligation to ensure that transnational corporations respect human rights by exerting leverage over the State's buying power.

The GATT and WTO agreements form part of a larger body of international law, and as such, must be subordinate to *jus cogens* norms.[86] Simply, the WTO must either find a way to make its policy consistent with *jus cogens* norms, or such norms must trump conflicting international norms. With respect to *jus cogens* norms, there is a strong argument, which will be examined in detail below, that the exceptions listed in Article XX of the GATT or Article XXIII of the GPA allow for protection of *jus cogens* norms by member States.

States are obliged to abide by peremptory norms of international law, including the prohibition on the utilization of forced or involuntary labor. The prohibition against slave-like labor practices is a clear peremptory norm, and as such, it is clear that at least in this realm States should both protect against such practices and ensure that they are not perpetuating these practices. While States may not be obliged to protect *jus cogens* norms through selective public procurement policies, they do have authority to invoke these peremptory norms in creating these policies. Selective public procurement is a mechanism to ensure the fulfillment of these obligations, and as such is a legitimate tool that can be used by States when they invoke these preemptory norms. If they could not use such tools, then the ability to invoke preemptory norms would have little value in practice, since they still could not take actions that differ from treaty obligations, particularly under the GPA.

## B. Broader Human Rights Protections

Protection of rights that are not *jus cogens* norms pose greater theoretical and practical challenges within the doctrine of the WTO. These include labor rights, basic civil and political rights, and economic and social rights. Most member States of the WTO have also ratified the major

---

[84] Above n 48.
[85] *Ibid*, at para.1.
[86] Gabrielle Marceau, 'Dispute Settlement and Human Rights' (2002) 13 *European Journal of International Law* 753, at 794–98.

human rights treaties, yet the WTO system as it currently exists leaves little space for States to create measures that take into account their obligations under these treaties.

This chapter argues that there is space in the WTO for protection of rights that are beyond *jus cogens* norms within the theoretical and legal confines of the GATT/WTO agreements. However, without a shift in institutional culture, it seems unlikely that the legitimacy of protecting these rights will be recognized since it is trade lawyers and States' trade representatives who argue and decide the cases and who negotiate the agreements. In 1996, the Singapore Ministerial Declaration gave tepid support for labor rights, but it did not provide any specific mechanisms for protection.[87] None of the subsequent declarations make specific mention of any form of human rights. Without the support of the Ministers, it is unlikely systematic change will occur.

As with the exception model generally under the GATT, selective public procurement is a unilateral policy decision by a member State to fulfill its international obligations under other treaties through a specific mechanism. The Appellate Body in *Shrimp-Turtle II* states:

> [C]onditioning access to a Member's domestic market on whether exporting Members comply with, or adopt, a policy or policies unilaterally prescribed by the importing Member may, to some degree, be a common aspect of measures falling within the scope of one or another of the exceptions (a) to (j) of Article XX. ... It is not necessary to assume that requiring from exporting countries compliance with, or adoption of, certain policies ... prescribed by the importing country, renders a measure *a priori* incapable of justification under Article XX. Such an interpretation renders most, if not all, of the specific exceptions of Article XX inutile, a result abhorrent to the principles of interpretation we are bound to apply.[88]

Member States have the autonomy under the GATT structure to create unilateral exceptions to protect public morality or health, and this autonomy ought to extend to their fulfillment of their international obligations so long as measures are implemented in a fair and just way.

## 3. Extraterritorial Regulation of Process

### A. Regulation of Final Product vs Regulation of Process

One of the most contentious areas in the discussion about incorporating human rights into the WTO generally and with respect to selective public

---

[87] WTO, Singapore Ministerial Declaration, Doc WT/MIN(96)/DEC (18 December 1996).

[88] United States – Import Prohibition of Certain Shrimp and Shrimp Products, WTO Doc WT/DS58/AB/R (adopted 6 November 1998), reprinted in (1999) 38 ILM 118 [hereinafter *Shrimp-Turtle*] at para 121 .

procurement specifically is whether regulation of the process by which a product is made, including the labor standards for workers, rather than of the final product is acceptable. It is clear from the text of both the GATT and WTO jurisprudence that regulation of products within the Article XX and GPA exceptions may be acceptable.[89] However, there is no consensus on whether the regulation of process is permissible, and few States have tried to do this in practice. It is a central issue in this context because by their nature selective public procurement policies frequently include the regulation of the process by which the contract is fulfilled in either the creation of the required products or in the fulfillment of the service.

At the time of the drafting, human rights law was also new and was probably not considered in drafting this agreement, since the drafters had no way to anticipate the widespread influence it would eventually have. However, Article XX(e) of the GATT creates an exception to the requirements of the GATT by permitting regulations designed to prohibit products made by prison labor. The inclusion of this exception by the drafters of the GATT in 1947 shows that they were concerned with process in at least this one instance.

In addition, a failure to accept process-based policy generally would have perverse results. For instance, it would mean that all measures designed to prevent entry into the market of products made by organized crime or racketeering schemes would be inconsistent with the GATT.[90] Clearly, neither the drafters of the GATT nor the current member States would want this absurd result, so there must be some consideration of process allowed.

The question of the permissibility of regulation of process has not been directly answered by the WTO adjudicatory bodies. In *Shrimp-Turtle II*, however, the Appellate Body upheld regulations prohibiting imports of shrimp caught in a manner that is not turtle-safe.[91] The Appellate Body stated that an importing member State may not impose a specific method to ensure its public policy goals under Article XX so long as exporting member States have measures that have comparable effectiveness.[92] In a human rights context, this means that if a particular human right can fit into the Article XX exceptions, then an importing member State could institute a measure that required, for instance, that products made to fulfill a public

---

[89] GATT Dispute Settlement Panel Report on Thailand – Restriction on Importation and Internal Taxes on Cigarettes, DS10/R, GATT BISD (37th Supp) (7 November 1990) [hereinafter *Thai Cigarettes*] at 200 .

[90] Robert Howse, 'The World Trade Organization and the Protection of Workers' Rights' (1999) 3 *Journal of Small and Emerging Business Law* 131, at 143–44.

[91] United States – Import Prohibition of Certain Shrimp and Shrimp Products, Recourse to Article 21.5 of the DSU by Malaysia, WT/DS58/AB/RW (22 October 2001).

[92] *Ibid*, at Recital 144.

contract should not be made with child labor, but that it could not dictate specific laws that should be passed in another State.[93]

Therefore, while there is no consensus on the regulation of process by an importing member State of the WTO, there is textual support for the regulation of at least one specific process, and there has been some Appellate Body support for regulation to meet certain goals that are achieved only through some regulation of process. It will probably remain difficult to prevail against challenges to process-based regulations in the current WTO climate, however.[94]

## 4. Dialogue on the Inclusion of Human Rights in World Trade Organization Proceedings

In addition to the general critiques about the integration of human rights law and international trade law discussed above, there are several WTO-specific objections. Some of these objections relate more generally to the incorporation of human rights norms into the WTO. These arguments do not strictly apply in the public procurement context because selective public procurement policies do not ask the WTO to apply human rights standards directly, but rather only ask that States be permitted to do so within the scope of interpretation of those standards by competent bodies. However, it is important to understand these arguments because selective public procurement is often conflated with the broader goal of incorporating human rights norms, and the same critiques are made. The real conflict therefore is whether or not human rights exceptions are understood to fall within the general exceptions of the GPA, and whether those exceptions include policies that regulate process requirements.

### 1. Overextension and Capacity of the World Trade Organization

According to some critics, interpretation and application of the body of international human rights law will overextend the WTO dispute settlement system. Closely related to this critique is one that argues that the WTO does not have the institutional capacity to hear cases involving

---

[93] In its unadopted opinion in *Tuna Dolphin*, the WTO Panel held that member States may not regulate beyond their boundaries. The decision in *Shrimp-Turtle II* indicates, however, that there may be some room for regulations which may indirectly affect the process by which a product is made outside the boundaries of the member State creating the regulation. Selective public procurement would fall into this second category since it only indirectly affects process. An unadopted opinion is one that does not have jurisprudential value in the WTO system: *United States – Restrictions on Imports of Tuna*, Report of the GATT Panel (16 August 1991), reprinted in (1991) 30 ILM 1594 [hereinafter *Tuna Dolphin*].

[94] Kysa, above n 8, at 548.

human rights since the WTO panels and the Appellate Body are comprised of trade experts.

There are two responses to these critiques on a broader level. First, on a theoretical level, the international trade and human rights systems cannot remain on parallel tracks. States have obligations to both, and deliberative bodies must consider the full scope of States' obligations. While the panel is not bound by these obligations, it is important to consider them if human rights and trade law obligations are going to be integrated in any meaningful way.[95] Thus, a WTO dispute panel or the Appellate Body ought to consider certain regulations within the context of a State's obligations to protect, respect, and fulfill human rights.

On a practical level, there is no need for the WTO deliberative bodies to interpret human rights law. Under the current structure of the dispute settlement bodies, panels and the Appellate Body are not permitted to interpret and enforce non-WTO law.[96] In fact, most human rights advocates would be loath to ask the WTO to interpret human rights norms, since it is a body comprised almost exclusively of trade experts who are not expert in human rights law and may actually be hostile towards it.

Instead of asking the WTO to conduct analysis of human rights norms, dispute settlement bodies should consider human rights norms in the same way they consider the standard of 'sufficient scientific evidence' under the Agreement on Sanitary and Phytosanitary Measures (SPS Agreement). SPS panels are asked to consider whether sanitary and phytosanitary measures are based on either international standards or a legitimate risk assessment based on scientific fact.[97] Panels are not asked to make any assessment of the standards or scientific evidence, but rather are required to examine only whether the measure promulgated by the member State was based on sufficient scientific evidence or international standards.[98]

Although the SPS Agreement establishes different rules for justifying trade-restrictive measures than the GATT, this type of methodology could be applied in the analysis of measures based on human rights that fall under the Article XX and GPA exceptions. Panelists would not be required

---

[95] The corollary of this argument is human rights bodies ought to acknowledge and consider trade obligations in their deliberations. This is not to say that human rights bodies ought to begin interpreting trade treaties, but perhaps acknowledgement of trade obligations would advance integration of the two types of law in a way that would allow States effectively to utilize both.

[96] Marceau, above n 88, at 765.

[97] 86 Agreement on the Application of Sanitary and Phytosanitary Measures, 15 December 1993, Art 5, WTO Agreement, Annex 1A, in Results of the Uruguay Round of Multilateral Trade Negotiations, vol 27 (1994), (1994) 33 ILM 1144.

[98] European Communities – Measures Concerning Meat and Meat Products (Hormones), WTO Docs. WT/DS26/R, WT/DS26/AB/R (1998), at 8.56.

to interpret other agreements, but rather they would have to analyze whether the measure is justified based on a State's obligations under those agreements according to the authoritative body for those agreements.[99] Additionally, the Appellate Body has created mechanisms for the receipt of amicus curiae briefs, and such input can be used to clarify human rights obligations.[100] Consequently, adequate mechanisms could exist for the evaluation of human rights measures that fall under the Article XX and GPA exemptions that would not overextend or be beyond the capacity of the WTO dispute settlement bodies.

Another form of this critique is that not only does interpretation of human rights overextend the WTO and ask it to act beyond its capacity, other international bodies are better equipped to make judgments about trade and human rights. The International Labor Organization (ILO) in particular has been highlighted as a more feasible outlet for human rights and trade concerns because it can make decisions without consensus, as is required in the WTO.[101] While the ILO is best equipped to set standards, it does not have an effective enforcement mechanism, and if the WTO prevents such standards from being implemented through trade mechanisms, then the ILO standards have little value because States will not choose to enforce them over WTO obligations. This leads back to the same conclusion as with the other critiques: namely, that the ILO and other human rights bodies are the appropriate organs to set the standards, but do not have the enforcement capacity of the WTO.[102] The WTO should only be inquiring into whether a country is using these standards in its application of a restrictive trade measure.

In fact, one dispute settlement panel actively requested participation by other international organizations. In a case challenging Thailand's ban of cigarette imports, the panel called on the World Health Organization to submit formal reports about the dangers of cigarettes and the specific practices of United States cigarette manufacturers.[103] The mechanisms currently exist in the WTO to allow States autonomously to decide the level of protection they wish to accord to human rights under internationally recognized standards. The possibility exists either explicitly to add mechanisms similar to those in the GPA or to read such mechanisms into the agreement's exceptions.

---

[99] Marceau, above n 88, at 765.

[100] Emmert, above n 57, at 132.

[101] Steve Charnovitz, 'Trade, Employment and Labour Standards: The OECD Study and Recent Developments in the Trade and Labor Standards Debate' (1997) 11 *Temple International and Comparative Law Journal* 131, at 160 (reviewing OECD, Trade, Employment, and Labour Standards: A Study of Core Workers' Rights and International Trade (1996)).

[102] Guzman, above n 74, at 315.

[103] Alvarez, above n 59, at 22.

## B. Access to Justice

Critics also argue that developing countries are less able to obtain favorable judgments in the WTO due to the expense and complexity of the litigation. Therefore, protectionist measures designed to protect human rights are used against them and they will be less able to challenge them.[104] While the WTO system may favor large developed States, this is an institutional problem and should not in and of itself be reason to prevent the legitimacy of measures designed to protect human rights. This argument could be applied to international law generally, but at the same time developing countries are getting more of a voice in the creation of international law and are increasingly winning cases in front of the WTO dispute settlement bodies.

## 5. Possible Routes for Inclusion of Human Rights Standards in Public Procurement Programs within the Context of World Trade Organzation Law

### A. Amendment or Creation of Additional Agreements

The only option that would remove all doubt as to the acceptability of human rights norms is specifically to include a social clause in the form of an amendment or additional agreement that delineates the types of rights protected. The addition of a social clause is the most common suggestion to include human rights formally and is increasingly being called for by non-governmental groups.[105] Governments, however, have not responded favorably to proposals for a social clause. In the negotiation of the Marrakesh Declaration, which ended the Uruguay Round of negotiations, the Ministers declined to establish a permanent committee within the WTO to study the link between trade and labor standards.[106] During the Singapore Ministerial Conference, the most the Ministers could agree on was a lukewarm recognition of labor rights.[107]

---

[104] Emmert, above n 57, at 91.

[105] Adelle Blackett, 'Whither Social Clause: Human Rights, Trade Theory and Treaty Interpretation' (1999) 31 *Columbia Human Rights Law Review* 1, at 3.

[106] *Ibid*, at 43.

[107] The Ministers declared:

'We renew our commitment to the observance of internationally recognized core labour standards. The International Labour Organization (ILO) is the competent body to set and deal with these standards, and we affirm our support for its work in promoting them. We believe that economic growth and development fostered by increased trade and further trade liberalization contribute to the promotion of these standards. We reject the use of labour standards for protectionist purposes, and agree that the comparative advantage of countries, particularly low-wage developing countries, must in no way be put into question. In this regard, we note that the WTO and ILO Secretariats will continue their existing collaboration.'

Singapore Ministerial Declaration, above n 89.

Yet, even if the WTO Member States were prepared to consider a social clause, it is not clear what that clause would include. This perhaps explains some of the resistance of member States to the concept generally.[108] Proposals range from inclusion of broad human rights standards to limiting the clause to only basic labor rights. Focusing on labor rights is appealing because they are narrowly defined and widely accepted, and therefore a clause based on these rights might have more likelihood of success. However, focusing only on labor rights could foreclose the possibility of protection of other rights through trade mechanisms. For example, States restricted trade with South African during the apartheid regime as a way to try to stimulate regime change, but such action could be foreclosed with a narrowly written social clause.[109]

## B. Integration through Exceptions: GPA Article XXXII and GATT Article XX

a. Opening the door to Integration Through Jurisprudence

Article XXXIII of the GPA creates the exception that, subject to the limitation that measures are not arbitrary or unjustifiable discrimination between countries or disguised restrictions on trade, the GPA shall not prevent members from instituting measures that are 'necessary to protect public morals, order or safety, human, animal or plant life or health or intellectual property; or relating to the products or services of handicapped persons, of philanthropic institutions or of prison labour.'[110] The limits of these exceptions have not been tested in any case.

While the GATT does not apply to government procurement, the exemptions in Article XX of the GATT were the basis for the exceptions in Article XXIII of the GPA as is clearly evident by the parallel language of the two agreements. Instead of creating one general exception, Article XX is divided into sub-articles that create separate exceptions: Article XX(a) for the protection of public morals; Article XX(b) for the protection of life or health; and Article XX(e): for the prohibition of products produced by prison labor. Article XX also contains other exceptions that were not included in the GPA and so will not be discussed further.

There are two key cases that shed some light on the interpretation of Article XX generally. In *Shrimp-Turtle*, the Appellate Body suggests that policy objectives must be read in light of contemporary concerns and not solely through the lens of 1947, when it says '[t]hey must be read by a

---

[108] Blackett, above n 106, at 1.
[109] *Ibid*, at 30–32.
[110] GPA, Art XXIII:2. There is some suggestion that because the GPA includes other forms of labor, it is limited in a way that the GATT may not be. However, it seems unlikely that the drafters intended completely to foreclose the possibility of prohibiting of forms of labor that are considered abhorrent under international agreements, such as hazardous child labor.

treaty interpreter in the light of contemporary concerns of the community of nations about the protection and conservation of the environment.'[111] The significance of this statement is clear: it opens the door to broader reading of the exceptions.

Critics argue that the Appellate Body in *Shrimp-Turtle* was referring only to environmental concerns and that the Appellate Body is unlikely to interpret other provisions as broadly.[112] In the decision, the Appellate Body cites the preamble of the GATT 1994 agreement that created the WTO, which refers to the goal of sustainable development, and to the proliferation of multilateral and bilateral treaties designed to protect the environment.[113] Similar analysis could be performed in the context of other rights protections. The preamble to the 1994 GATT also refers to improving standards of living, which could be explicitly linked to public morality as demonstrated through widely recognized multilateral human rights treaties designed to improve living standards by establishing basic respect for human dignity.

Essentially, *Shrimp-Turtle* opened the door to a balancing of broad policy considerations and WTO obligations in a more decisive way.[114] Thus, under the criteria laid out by the Appellate Body in *Shrimp-Turtle*, it is possible that human rights protections could legitimately be the basis for a non-discriminatory measure by a member State.

*Tuna-Dolphin I* and *II* seem to imply that Article XX exceptions should be interpreted narrowly.[115] Yet, there is no reason under the canons of interpretation that these exceptions must be interpreted narrowly.[116] While this interpretation is consistent with the institutional culture of the WTO, it is not necessarily the proper interpretation. A narrow reading of the exceptions would undermine the policy autonomy of a State by limiting the types of policy that are legitimate, even if the State implements GATT-consistent measures.[117]

b. Protection of Public Morals

Both Article XX(a) of the GATT and Article XXIII of the GPA create exceptions for measures based in public morals, although there has been no definitive interpretation of either. The nexus between the exception and human rights seems to most clearly fall within the public morals exception.

---

[111] Shrimp-Turtle, above n 88, at para 129.
[112] Robert Howse, Human Rights in the WTO: Whose Rights, What Humanity? Comment on Petersmannn (Jean Monnet Working Paper No 12, 2002), at 9.
[113] Shrimp-Turtle, above n 88, at paras 129–31.
[114] Robert Wai, 'Countering, Branding, Dealing: Using Economic and Social Rights in and Around the International Trade Regime' (2003)14 European Journal of International Law 35, at 62.
[115] Blackett, above n 106, at 73.
[116] Ibid.
[117] Ibid, at 73.

Originally, the exception was intended to allow States to protect against pornography and other products that were against the standards of morality of society.[118] However, at the time of the drafting of the original GATT, the modern conception of human rights was just evolving and there was no broad international agreement on norms. This is no longer true today, and most States have ratified several international human rights treaties. As such, agreement can be inferred both from those ratifications and from other domestic policies and laws. It is clear that *jus cogens* norms could fall within the sphere of public morality since they are universally accepted norms, but since they are also peremptory norms in international law it may not be necessary to use the Article XX exceptions to justify creating measures to uphold these obligations.

The purpose of this exception is to allow a member State to create a measure designed to prevent the importation of products that would violate these standards of public morality. Where an understanding of public morality exists, consumers should not be forced to pay taxes for policies that violate those conceptions.[119]

It is at this point that the product/process question becomes pressing. The drafters of the GATT did not clearly consider the possibility of restricting market access for products that themselves are innocuous but that are made in ways that breach public morality. These could include, for example, products made with child, slave, or forced labor, or manufacturing products that harm the rainforest. It is here that examination of Article XX(e), the exception for prohibition of products made with prison labor, may be useful. It illustrates that, in at least this particular case, the drafters were concerned about process. It is important to consider that in 1947 concerns about child labor and forced labor were simply not part of the broader social discussion on the international level.[120] It could be said that in a modern context the drafters were concerned with processes that clearly violated international agreements and a concept of basic fairness

---

[118] Salman Bal, 'International Free Trade Agreements and Human Rights: Reinterpreting Article XX of the GATT' (2001) 10 Minnesota Journal of Global Trade 62, at 85.

[119] Michelle Leighton and Elena Castaneda, 'Civil Society Concerns in the Context of Economic Globalization' (2002) 15 Transnational Law 105, at 114.

[120] It was not until the 1980s that there was any serious international effort to limit the employment of children in hazardous industries. The ILO Minimum Age Recommendation (Convention 138) was drafted in 1973 and was the first international effort to end child labor in specific industries: Minimum Age Recommendations (ILO No 138) (1973) 56 ILO Official Bulletin No 1, at 34–37. The United Nations Convention on the Rights of the Child, which contains a specific prohibition on hazardous employment for young persons, was not signed until 1989: Convention on the Rights of the Child, GA res 44/25, annex, 44 UN GAOR Supp (No 49) at 167, UN doc A/44/49 (1989). The ILO Convention on the Worst Forms of Child Labor, which calls for end to particularly hazardous child labor, was drafted in 1999: Convention concerning the Prohibition and Immediate Action for the Elimination of the Worst Forms of Child Labor (ILO No 182), (1999) 38 ILM 1207.

which, if translated into modern parlance, would include a much broader range of processes.

Limited acceptance of modern standards as a basis for policy is indicated in *Tuna-Dolphin*, which suggests that the use of an animal cruelty standard is legitimate under this exception.[121] If it is possible to create norms that are within the exceptions to protect animals, it is logical that measures designed to protect humans should also be within the exception.

Article XX(a) and the identical language of Article XXXIII of the GPA should be understood in this modern context. It is consistent with the recognition of the regulatory autonomy of States to allow them to act unilaterally by enacting public procurement policies that prevent the government from being complicit in contracting for products that are made in ways that breach the basic public morality of the society which the government is serving.

## C. Protection of Life Or Health

The parameters of this exception have been slightly better defined by the WTO. Thus far, it has only been held to apply to domestic populations, but there has also been no explicit prohibition on extraterritorial measures of the Appellate Body. In *Tuna-Dolphin*, the panel held that the extraterritoriality of the measure was problematic, but the measure was ultimately interpreted so as not to be extraterritorial by the Appellate Body. In *Thai Cigarettes*, the panel held that Article XX(b) 'clearly allowed contracting parties to give priority to human health over trade liberalization.'[122] This is an indication that panels may be receptive to a non-economic basis for policies that limit trade, at least in cases where the measure is the least restrictive possible to address the goal.

If Article XX(b) can be read broadly to include working conditions that violate human rights, then it could encompass certain human rights norms related to the process by which products are made. Again, the pragmatic reality that the dispute settlement body may hesitate to read the exception broadly does not exclude the possibility that the exception can properly be interpreted to include protection of these rights.


## VI. CONCLUSION

Ultimately, the question is not whether selective public procurement policies are the most efficient or desirable way to protect human rights. There is insufficient evidence about their efficacy to make that judgment. Rather, the essential issue is whether States should be free to implement such

---

[121] Bal, above n 119, at 76–77.
[122] *Thai Cigarettes*, above n 89, at 1137.

policies or whether they are prohibited under the current international trade law regime as is defined largely by the WTO.

It is clear that States should be allowed to protect rights in the category of *jus cogens* norms since these are peremptory international legal norms. While the exact scope of rights to be protected in the GATT/WTO framework is not clear, there is room for integration of broader human rights protections in the exceptions framework. The legal framework exists for States to enact selective public procurement policies in spite of pragmatic challenges, the most difficult of which is the institutional culture of the WTO. Although such policies raise many of the same issues that the debate over the integration of human rights and international trade law generally raises, selective public procurement is a narrowly tailored policy designed to affect the behavior of companies that choose to bid on public contracts. States should be and can be consistent with their obligation not to be complicit in human rights violations under international human rights law and with their international trade obligations, because the exceptions in the GPA create adequate space in the trade law regime for policies that regulate the standards under which products that fulfill public contracts are created. Thus, although selective public procurement is a legitimate and legal mechanism for States to utilize in order to give meaning to their obligations under international human rights law, they are not obligated to do so.

# 13

# A Role for The International Finance Corporation in Integrating Environmental and Human Rights Standards into Core Project Covenants: Case Study of the Baku–Tbilisi–Ceyhan Oil Pipeline Project

TERRA EVE LAWSON-REMER

## I. INTRODUCTION

THE PURPOSE OF this chapter is to explore the relationship (or lack thereof) between the legal framework underlying the Baku–Tbilisi–Ceyhan (BTC) oil pipeline project and the International Finance Corporation (the member of the World Bank Group responsible for financing private-sector projects), and to argue that the International Finance Corporation (IFC) would more effectively further its mission of promoting environmentally and socially sustainable development by requiring this legal framework to be compatible with the effective enforcement of evolving international environmental and human rights norms. The BTC pipeline project illustrates both the risk of States being pressured by foreign investors wishing to obtain government guarantees that insulate their investment from risk, and the potential role multilateral lending institutions might play in limiting the detrimental effects of such imbalance in bargaining power.

My purpose is not to look at the myriad critiques regarding implementation in the pipeline project of the IFC's existing social and environmental safeguard policies,[1] nor to explore the ongoing general

---

[1] See, eg *Baku Ceyhan Campaign*, available at http://www.bakuceyhan.org.uk; IFC/MIGA, Office of the Compliance Advisor/Ombudsman, *Assessment Report: Seven Complaints regarding the Baku-Tbilisi-Ceyhan (BTC) Pipeline Project: Borjomi Region, Georgia* (issued September 2004); IFC/MIGA, Office of the Compliance Advisor/Ombudsman, *Assessment Report: Complaint*

controversy regarding the adequacy of the IFC's safeguard policies,[2] although both these issues will be touched upon. This chapter instead seeks narrowly to examine the controversial legal framework governing the BTC project.

Oil is often called black gold[3] because its discovery and sale can generate such immense wealth. The revenue from oil is particularly seductive for cash-strapped developing countries, which is all the more ironic since those are the countries least well-positioned to invest the substantial resources necessary for oil extraction and export. With the dissolution of the Soviet Union and the disappearance of the Second World into the Third, Azerbaijan, Turkey, and Georgia find themselves lacking cash to fund everything from basic government services to investment in public projects necessary for development, including roads and schools.[4] The object of this case study, the BTC oil pipeline, is predicted to generate between $500 million and $1 billion in government revenue for each of the host States over the life of the project[5]—providing the three governments with enough revenue to make substantial investments in all these areas, if the governments so choose.

In theory, the development of oil for export brings other benefits in addition to the generation of government revenue. The IFC and the BTC

---

*regarding the Baku-Tbilisi-Ceyhan (BTC) Pipeline Project: Tba, Tsemi and Sadgeri, Georgia*, available at http://www.cao-ombudsman.org/html-english/ombudsman.htm (issued October 2004).

[2] I refer readers to Compliance Advisor/Ombudsman (CAO), *A Review of IFC's Safeguard Policies* (January 2003) for an exploration of the efficacy of IFC's existing safeguard policies (available at: www.cao-ombudsman.org/pdfs/Review%20of%20IFC%20SPs%20final %20report%20english%2004-03-03.pdf). The CAO's mandate is to provide policy and process advice on environmental and social performance, to conduct environmental and social compliance audits and reviews as an aid to institutional learning, and to receive complaints and—through an Ombudsman mechanism—seek to resolve issues for people who are directly, or are likely to be directly, affected by IFC and/or MIGA projects.

[3] See, eg Bryan Rostron, 'Is "black gold" blessing or curse?', *Business Day (South Africa)*, 2 December 2004, Opinion & Editorial, at 15; Sonia Shah, 'The end of oil? Guess again', 15 September 2004, available at http://dir.salon.com/story/tech/feature/2004/09/ 15/no_end_to_oil/index1.html.

[4] Azerbaijan is a low-income country with Gross National Income (GNI) per capita of US$710; in 2001, some 50% of the population lived in poverty and 17% in extreme poverty: International Finance Corporation, *Azerbaijan Country Brief*, available at http://www.ifc.org/eca (last visited 1 December 2004). After an economic crisis in 2000/01, Turkey faces high public debt ratios; World Bank assistance is targeted to reduce those ratios: International Finance Corporation, *Turkey Country Brief*, available at http://www.ifc.org/eca (last visited 1 December 2004). Georgia's economy collapsed following independence in 1991, and incomes are currently 40% of 1991 levels at a GNI per capita of US$730. Unemployment and poverty remain high. The health of the poor and the quality of education is also deteriorating, with a rise in the prevalence of chronic diseases: International Finance Corporation, *Georgia Country Brief*, available at http://www.ifc.org/ eca (last visited 1 December 2004).

[5] International Finance Corporation, *Baku-Tiblisi-Ceyhan Pipeline: Summary of Project Information*, Attachment 2: Principal Economic Benefits, available at http://www.ifc.org (disclosed 31 July 2003) [hereinafter 'Principal Economic Benefits'].

Consortium predict that the BTC pipeline project will produce economic spillover effects by providing employment in the region,[6] supporting the emergence of backward-linked businesses that supply inputs to the pipeline,[7] creating a 'multiplier effect' as initial expenditures circulate and are re-spent in the local economy,[8] and establishing the host governments as 'safe bets' in the eyes of the global investment community, thereby generating further foreign direct investment (FDI) in a virtuous cycle.

This is not to say that the road paved with black gold always—or even usually—leads to development. In fact, many oil-rich developing countries remain corrupt dictatorships renowned for simultaneously perpetrating human rights abuses and blatantly pilfering the public coffers.[9] Others have been torn apart by civil wars fueled, in part, by the desire of competing factions to control oil revenues.[10] My point here is not to argue that the development of oil resources is 'good' or 'bad' for development,[11] but merely to illustrate the promise oil development theoretically holds, in order to illuminate why the governments of Turkey, Azerbaijan, and Georgia so desperately want the pipeline project to happen.

Unfortunately for developing countries, the construction of a mammoth oil pipeline such as the one that will soon stretch from the Caspian to the Mediterranean requires enormous capital investment[12] and technical expertise.[13] It would be extremely difficult for a developing country to

---

[6] *Ibid*; see also BTC Co, *A Lasting Benefit*, available at http://www.caspiandevelopmentandexport.com/ASP/BTC_LastingBenefit.asp (last visited 3 December 2004).

[7] Principal Economic Benefits, above n 3; BTC Co, above n 6.

[8] Principal Economic Benefits, above n 5.

[9] See Nathan Jensen and Leonard Wantchekon, 'Resource Wealth and Political Regimes in Africa', *Comparative Political Studies* (forthcoming), available at http://www.nyu.edu/gsas/dept/politics/faculty/wantchekon/research/regimes.pdf (presenting empirical evidence suggesting a robust and negative correlation between the presence of a sizeable natural resource sector and the level of democracy in Africa).

[10] See, eg, Amnesty International, *Oil in Sudan: Deteriorating Human Rights*, 3 May 2000, available at http://web.amnesty.org/library/index/ENGAFR540012000 (arguing that oil was the final spark for uprisings and the formation of armed opposition groups in Sudan); Nick Shaxson, 'Fuelling the War: Diamonds and Oil', BBC News, 28 January 1999 (documenting the role diamonds and oil have played in financing Angola's long civil war).

[11] This debate has crystallized in the Extractive Industries Review (EIR) and reactions to the EIR by civil society and World Bank Management. The EIR, an independent two-year study commissioned by the World Bank and concluded in 2003, was charged with examining the impact of extractive industries on human rights, poverty alleviation, and the environment in developing countries. The EIR and the Bank Management's Response are available at http://www2.ifc.org/ogmc/; for a broad cross-section of civil society responses, see www.eireview.info.

[12] International Finance Corporation, *Baku-Tiblisi-Ceyhan Pipeline: Summary of Project Information*, Attachment 1: Project Costs and IFC Proposed Investment, BTC Project Indicative Ownership and Financing Plan (as of June 2003), available at http://www.ifc.org

[13] 'The construction of the BTC pipeline poses a vast engineering challenge, spanning 1760 kilometres of widely differing terrain, rising to a height of over 2800 metres in the Caucasus mountains and east Anatolia, and passing beneath hundreds of roads, railway lines and watercourses': BTC Co, *Construction*, available at http://www.caspiandevelopmentandexport.com/ASP/BTC_Construction.asp (last visited 3 December 2004).

sustain such a massive infrastructure project on its own. The only real option, therefore, is for Turkey, Azerbaijan, and Georgia to induce foreign oil companies to raise the capital, supply the technical expertise, and develop the project.

This enables foreign investors such as BP Co, the lead investor in the BTC pipeline,[14] to bargain with potential host governments with the aim of obtaining terms guaranteeing a more favorable investment climate. The bargaining strength of host governments in such a negotiation depends on a wide array of factors, including the existence of alternative economic growth opportunities, the dynamics of internal political pressures, the interest of competing oil investors, and international legal/political constraints. In the case of the BTC project, bargaining positions between BP and the host governments were not so unequal as to allow the BTC Consortium unilaterally to dictate the investment terms—after all, the 11 members of the consortium stood to profit from the pipeline or else they would not have engaged in the project, and therefore they also had much to lose if the project had not gone forward.[15] But the simple fact remains that oil fields exist in other parts of the world.[16] If those had appeared to offer more profitable opportunities than the one presented by the BTC project, the companies that compose the BTC Consortium would certainly have invested elsewhere.

In order to identify how, against such a background, human rights may be better integrated in the policies of the IFC, I begin with a short description of the BTC pipeline project, including a chronology of events leading to development of the project that highlights the potential influence the IFC could exert on the content of project legal frameworks. I then move into an overview of the IFC and its core mission of promoting the progressive realization of human rights in the context of sustainable development. Section IV summarizes the IFC's safeguard policies and the existing relationship between the BTC project and the IFC, in order to contextualize the potential role of the IFC vis-à-vis the legal frameworks of the projects it sponsors. Section V of the chapter examines the legal underpinnings of the BTC pipeline project as embodied in an Inter-Governmental Agreement (IGA), the Host Government Agreements (HGAs), and a series of subsequent project agreements, concentrating on both the specific mechanisms by which provisions in the agreements could impede the realization of human rights and the efficacy of side-undertakings in addressing those concerns. I conclude by illustrating how

---

[14] BTC Co, *Project Participants*, available at http://www.caspiandevelopmentandex port.com/ASP/BTC_ProjectParticipants.asp (last visited 1 December 2004).

[15] Natalia Antelava, 'Oil Is Still the Game', Forbes.com, at 'Companies & Strategies', 9 June 2003, available at http://forbes.com/global/2003/0609/020sidebar.html.

[16] US Geological Survey, Central Energy Team, *Country Break-down of World Oil Reserves*, available at http://energy.cr.usgs.gov/energy/stats_ctry/Stat2.html

the IFC could better operationalize its commitment to human rights and sustainable development by requiring core project covenants to be compatible with State measures to support the effective enforcement of evolving international legal norms.

## II. PROJECT BACKGROUND

The 1,760 km BTC oil pipeline originates in Azerbaijan on the shores of the Caspian Sea. Crude oil is received from oil fields under the Caspian at Sangachal, a medium-sized town south of Baku. From here the pipeline is routed west, closely following the existing Western Route Export Pipeline, which is currently used to transport limited amounts of crude oil production. The BTC pipeline then crosses into Georgia, heading north-west towards Tblisi, Georgia's capital. It continues west and south, jumping the border into Turkey and traversing the breadth of the country, ending at the Ceyhan terminal on the shores of the Mediterranean. The mammoth BTC pipeline has the capacity to transport up to one million barrels of crude oil per day from the Azerbaijan sector of the Caspian Sea to the Mediterranean coast in Turkey.[17]

The BTC pipeline is being developed by an international consortium of 11 partners, known as the Baku-Tbilisi-Ceyhan Pipeline Company (BTC Co). BP (UK) is the largest stakeholder in the project, and is leading the design and construction phases. The other oil companies who are partners in this endeavor are: SOCAR (the State oil company of Azerbaijan); TPAO (Turkey); Statoil (Norway); Unocal (USA); Itochu (Japan); Amerada Hess (USA); Eni (Italy); TotalFinaElf, now renamed Total (France); INPEX (Japan), and ConocoPhillips (USA).[18]

The estimated aggregate cost of the BTC project is US$3.7 billion, the financing of which will include total debt of approximately US$2.6 billion.[19] The export credit agencies financing the project are: USExim and OPIC (US), JBIC and NEXI (Japan), ECGD (UK), Hermes (Germany), COFACE (France), and SACE (Italy).[20] The International Finance Corporation has provided loans of US$250 million—and its imprimatur of approval—to finance the project.[21]

---

[17] BTC Co, *Overview*, available at http://www.bp.com/genericarticle.do?categoryId = 9006669&contentId = 7014358 (last visited 28 March 2006).

[18] BTC Co, above n 14.

[19] International Finance Corporation, above n 12.

[20] BTC Co, *BTC Signs Project Finance Agreements* (Press Release), 3 February 2004, available at http://www.caspiandevelopmentandexport.com/Downloads/MediaLibrary/Download/78/BTC%20Financing%20Press%20release_Eng.pdf

[21] International Finance Corporation, *IFC Board Approves Investments in Caspian Oil and Pipeline Projects: Expected high development impact with environmental, social, and transparency safeguards* (Press Release), 4 November 2004, available at http://www.ifc.org/btc (last visited 3 December 2004).

As the central thrust of this chapter is to argue that the IFC can and should enact safeguard requirements regarding the terms of project agreements for the projects it supports, we must examine to what degree such IFC constraints could influence the content of project agreements. The chronology of events leading to the development of the BTC pipeline is very relevant to understanding the 'micro'- bargaining process which produced the terms of the legal framework governing the project.

In 1997 BP formed a working group composed of its partners in the development of the offshore oil fields under the Caspian Sea (hereinafter 'the Azeri–Chirag–Gunashli project') and the governments of Azerbaijan, Georgia, and Turkey to examine the development of additional export routes for Caspian crude oil;[22] the working group concluded that a pipeline would be the most economically viable way of transporting oil from the Azeri–Chirag–Gunashli (ACG) fields to export markets in Europe and the United States. The IGA laying the legal groundwork for the project was signed by Turkey, Georgia, and Azerbaijan in Istanbul on 18 November 1999.[23] BTC Company and the three host governments executed the HGAs between November 1999 and October 2000.[24] After the legal framework was substantially established, in November 2000, anthropologists, ecologists, and other specialists began conducting extensive environmental and social impact studies (ESIAs), while engineers worked on pipeline design.[25] Two years later, with the ESIAs well

---

[22] BTC Co, Project History, available at http://www.caspiandevelopmentandexport.com /ASP/BTC_ProjectHistory.asp (last visited 1 December 2004).

[23] Agreement Among The Azerbaijan Republic, Georgia and The Republic of Turkey Relating to the Transportation of Petroleum Via the Territories of The Azerbaijan Republic, Georgia and The Republic of Turkey Through the Baku-Tbilisi-Ceyhan Main Export Pipeline (18 November 1999), available at http://www.caspiandevelopmentandexport.com/ Downloads/BTC/Eng/agmt4/agmt4.PDF [hereinafter IGA].

[24] Host Government Agreement Between and Among the Government of the Azerbaijan Republic and the State Oil Company of the Azerbaijan Republic, BP Exploration (Caspian Sea) Ltd, Statoil BTC Caspian AS, RAMCO Hazar Energy Limited, Turkiye Petrolleri AO, Unocal BTC Pipeline, Ltd, Itochu Oil Exploration (Azerbaijan) Inc, Delta Hess (BTC) Limited, 17 October 2000, available at http://www.caspiandevelopmentand export.com/ASP/PD_BTC.asp [hereinafter 'HGA of Azerbaijan']; Host Government Agreement Between and Among the Government of Turkey and [The MEP Participants], 18 November 2000, available at http://www.caspiandevelopmentandexport.com/ASP/PD _BTC.asp [hereinafter HGA of Turkey]; Host Government Agreement Between and Among the Government of Georgia and [The MEP Participants], 28 April 2000, available at http://www.caspiandevelopmentandexport.com/ASP/PD_BTC.asp [hereinafter 'HGA of Georgia']. '*MEP Participants* means any one or more, or all, of the Parties to this Agreement (including by novation and/or accession as an MEP Participant pursuant to any Project Agreement), other than the State Authorities, and any successors and permitted assignees of any of the foregoing': *ibid*, Appendix 1, 17 October 2000.

[25] BTC Co, above n 22.

under way, the consortium formally approached the IFC for financing.[26] The ESIAs were concluded in May 2003 and made public on 11 June,[27] pursuant to the IFC's requirement of a 120-day formal disclosure period. On 4 November 2003, shortly after the end of the 120-day disclosure period, the IFC approved the project loans.[28]

Civil society opposition to the BTC pipeline project reached a noticeable pitch in the summer of 2002. In August of that year, an international coalition of non-governmental organizations (NGOs) issued a press release slamming the IGA–HGA legal framework for paving the way for human rights abuses and environmental disasters in the pipeline corridor.[29] Given Turkey's long history of human rights abuses in its ongoing battle with Kurdish secessionists,[30] the NGO community focused initially on the potential impact of the agreements on the Turkish government's treatment of its Kurdish minority.[31] In the first shot across the bow, the press release claimed that the agreements 'divided Turkey into three countries ... the area where Turkish law applies; the Kurdish areas under official or de facto military rule; and a strip running the entire length of the country from North to South, where BP is the effective government.'[32] The legal framework was decried as a 'backdoor MAI [multilateral agreement on investment]' that would allow BP 'to waive the rules, destroying the environment and trampling on the rights of local communities with impunity.'[33] At the same time, the coalition of NGOs released a series of fact-finding reports, based on investigative missions sent to Turkey, Azerbaijan, and Georgia, excoriating the project for the threat that pipeline construction and operation posed to human rights

[26] Email correspondence from Oliver Broad <BroadO@bp.com>, Site Administrator and Communications Specialist for the BTC Project, to Terra Lawson-Remer, New York University School of Law (19 November 2004, 7:35 am EST) (on file with author).

[27] BTC Co, above n 22.

[28] *Ibid*.

[29] Cornerhouse, FOEI, CRBM, KHRP, PLATFORM, CEE Bankwatch, Network, Ilisu Dam Campaign, *Oil Companies Colonise Turkey: MAI by the Back Door?* (Press Release), 30 August 2002, available at www.bakuceyhan.org.uk/press_releases/press_release%20_oil_companies_colonise_turkey.doc.

[30] Paul J Magnarella, The Legal, Political, and Cultural Structures of Human Rights Protections and Abuses in Turkey (1994) 3 *DCL J Int'l L & Prac* 439 (citing at fn 1, *Human Rights in Turkey: Briefing of the [US] Commission on Security and Cooperation in Europe* 20 (5 April 1993); at fn 2, Human Rights Foundation of Turkey, *500-Day Report* (21 November 1991–5 April 1993), Ankara (1993); and at fn 2 US Department of State Dispatch, *Turkey Human Rights Practices, 1993* [Washington, DC] (1994).

[31] Cornerhouse *et al*, above n 29.

[32] *Ibid*.

[33] *Ibid*. The MAI was an OECD initiative to establish investor rights similar to those created by Ch 11 of NAFTA. The MAI negotiations were called-off in December 1998 in the face of widespread civil society opposition.

and the environment.[34] Public concern continued to mount over the fall and winter of 2002–03[35], reaching a crescendo when Amnesty International released a comprehensive critique of the HGA–IGA framework in May 2003.[36]

In direct response to the criticisms raised by NGOs and local people affected by the project, Turkey, Azerbaijan, Georgia, and BTC Co issued three new project agreements between May and September 2003, clarifying and modifying the terms of the IGA and the HGAs.[37]

The chronology of events demonstrates that, although excluded from the initial stages of project planning, outside forces such as the IFC and NGOs had significant influence on project design and operation, including the content of the legal framework. Civil society groups did not become active in opposing the project until 2002, after the core project agreements were concluded, but succeeded nonetheless in pressuring project participants to execute three subsequent project agreements addressing social and environmental concerns. The influence of the IFC on project development is even more dramatic—although BTC Co did not

[34] Campagna per la Riforma della Banca Mondiale, Kurdish Human Rights Project, The Corner House, and the Ilisu Dam Campaign, *International Fact-Finding Mission: Preliminary Report: Azerbaijan, Georgia, Turkey: Pipeline Project: Turkey Section* (August 2002), available at http://www.foe.org/camps/intl/worldbank/pipelines-factfinding-turkey.pdf; Green Alternative, National Ecological Centre of Ukraine, CEE Bankwatch Network, Campagna per la riforma della Banca mondiale, Friends of the Earth US, Bank Information Center, Ilisu Dam Campaign, The Corner House, Kurdish Human Rights Project, Platform, *International Fact-Finding Mission: Preliminary Report: Azerbaijan, Georgia, Turkey: Pipeline Project: Georgia Section* (July 2002), available at http://www.foe.org/camps/intl/worldbank/pipelines-factfinding-georgia.pdf; Green Alternative, National Ecological Centre of Ukraine, CEE Bankwatch Network, Campagna per la riforma della Banca mondiale, Friends of the Earth US, Bank Information Center, Ilisu Dam Campaign, The Corner House, Kurdish Human Rights Project, Platform, *International Fact-Finding Mission: Preliminary Report: Azerbaijan, Georgia, Turkey: Pipeline Project: Azerbaijan Section* (September 2002), available at http://www.foe.org/camps/intl/worldbank/pipelines-factfinding-azerbaijan.pdf.

[35] See, eg, Baku Ceyhan Campaign, BP's new oil project a 'disaster waiting to happen', say Campaigners: BP Refuses to Discuss Concerns in Public (Press Release), 28 October 2002. The Baku Ceyhan Campaign is a UK based NGO dedicated to 'raising public awareness of the social problems, human rights abuses and environmental damage that will be caused by the Baku-Tbilisi-Ceyhan oil pipeline': see www.bakuceyhan.org.uk/about.htm. For a list of other press releases from the Baku Ceyhan Campaign and other NGOs, visit: http://www.bakuceyhan.org.uk/news

[36] Amnesty International, *Human Rights on the Line: The Baku-Tiblisi-Ceyhan Pipeline Project*, available at http://www.amnesty.org.uk/images/ul/H/Human_Rights_on_the_Line.pdf (May 2003) [hereinafter 'Human Rights on the Line'], at 12.

[37] Implementation Commission established pursuant to Article VI of the Agreement Among The Azerbaijan Republic, Georgia and The Republic of Turkey Relating to the Transportation of Petroleum Via the Territories of The Azerbaijan Republic, Georgia and The Republic of Turkey Through the Baku-Tbilisi-Ceyhan Main Export Pipeline (the 'IGA'), Joint Statement on the Baku-Tbilisi-Ceyhan Pipeline Project, 16 May 2003 [hereinafter 'Joint Statement']; Baku–Tiblisi–Ceyhan Pipeline Company, *BTC Human Rights Undertaking*, 22 September 2003 [hereinafter 'BTC Human Rights Undertaking']; Republics of Azerbaijan, Turkey, and Georgia, Protocol for the Provision of Security for the East-West Energy Corridor, 23 July 2003 [hereinafter 'Security Protocol'].

formally approach IFC for funding until 2002,[38] and the IFC did not approve financing until 2003,[39] BTC Co commissioned environmental and social impact assessments as early as 2000,[40] in anticipation of IFC safeguard guidelines and requirements regarding impact assessments. The conclusion is inevitable: outside players impacted on the terms of the BTC project agreements. If investors are aware of IFC guidelines ex ante, they are likely to anticipate these constraints and abide by them in developing project agreements.

### III. THE MISSION OF THE INTERNATIONAL FINANCE CORPORATION

The International Finance Corporation (IFC) is a member of the World Bank Group, which also includes the International Bank for Reconstruction and Development (IBRD), the International Development Association (IDA), the Multilateral Investment Guarantee Agency (MIGA), and the International Centre for the Settlement of Investment Disputes (ICSID).[41] The purpose of the IFC is to support private sector projects in developing countries; it operates by providing loans, equity, and technical advice to private sector actors in order to finance sustainable development projects.[42]

Implicit in the purpose of the IFC is the duty to promote the progressive realization of human rights and environmental sustainability. The central mission of the IFC 'is to promote sustainable private sector investment in developing countries, helping to reduce poverty and improve people's lives.'[43] The first 'shared principle' underlying this mission is a commitment to 'promoting sustainable projects … that are economically beneficial, financially and commercially sound, and *environmentally and socially sustainable*.'[44] In 1987 the Brundtland Report solidified the ascendance of 'sustainable development' in the social imaginary,[45] defining sustainable development as 'development which meets the needs of the

---

[38] Oliver Broad, above n 26.

[39] International Finance Corporation, *Baku-Tiblisi-Ceyhan Pipeline: Summary of Project Information*, available at http://www.ifc.org (last visited 8 December 2003).

[40] BTC Co, Project History, available at http://www.caspiandevelopmentandexport.com/ASP/BTC_ProjectHistory.asp (last visited 1 December 2004).

[41] The World Bank Group, *About Us*, http://www.worldbank.org (last visited 23 November 2004).

[42] International Finance Corporation Articles of Agreement, as amended through 28 April 1993, Art I, available at http://www.ifc.org/ifcext/about.nsf (last visited 9 December 2004).

[43] International Finance Corporation, *Mission Statement*, available at http://www.ifc.org/ifcext/about.nsf (last visited 9 December 2004).

[44] *Ibid* (emphasis added).

[45] Simon Dresner, *The Principles of Sustainability* (Earthscan, 2002), at pp 31–37.

present without compromising the ability of future generations to meet their own needs.'[46] The Brundtland Report and subsequent literature clarify that 'sustainable development' is concerned with preserving equity between generations (by not depleting the 'natural capital' of the earth's resources), fostering equity within each generation, and promoting growth in order to better provide for people's material well-being.[47] As Roberto Danino, General Counsel for the World Bank, has noted, 'Social equity is a rich and complex notion ... Nobel Laureate Amartya Sen has argued [that] we must view development in terms of freedom and the removal of obstacles to it, including poverty, tyranny, poor economic opportunities, systemic social deprivation, the neglect of public facilities as well as intolerance.[48] Danino continued, emphasizing that 'Social equity thus includes fighting poverty and inequality, giving the poor and marginalized voices, ie empowerment; freedom from hunger and fear, as well as access to justice. *Social equity has, therefore, an obvious human rights component.*'[49] The IFC's mission of promoting sustainable development through private sector investment entails a commitment to social equity, and therefore to environmental sustainability and human rights.

It is important to mention briefly an argument that has been advanced at one time or another over the World Bank's lifetime—that the Bank's charter prohibits it from considering human rights when selecting projects.[50] Although this ongoing debate has mostly concerned the IBRD and the IDA, and not the IFC, which has its own separate and independent charter, the debate is relevant because the IFC's Articles of Agreements contain language substantively similar to the controversial clause in the

---

[46] *Ibid* at p 67.
[47] See, eg, *ibid*; Nigel Cross, *Evidence for Hope: The Search for Sustainable Development* (Earthscan, 2003); World Commission on Environment and Development (WCED), *Our Common Future* (Oxford, Oxford University Press, 1987), ch 2, 'Towards Sustainable Development'.
[48] Roberto Danino, 'The Legal Aspects of the World Bank's Work on Human Rights', in Mary Robinson and Philip Alston (eds), *Human Rights and Development: Towards Mutual Reinforcement* (Oxford, Oxford University Press, 2006), at p 6. Roberto Danino is Senior Vice-President and General Counsel of the World Bank Group.
[49] *Ibid.*
[50] Halim Moris, 'Article & Essay: The World Bank and Human Rights: Indispensable Partnership or Mismatched Alliance?' (Fall, 1997) 4 *ILSA J Int'l & Comp L* 173, at 182–92 (summarizing the arguments levied against IBRD consideration of human rights; the arguments principally focus upon the intrusion into national sovereignty and alleged ineffectiveness of World Bank human rights practices); John D Ciorciari, 'The Lawful Scope of Human Rights Criteria in World Bank Credit Decisions: An Interpretive Analysis of the IBRD and IDA Articles of Agreement' (2000) 33 *Cornell International Law Journal* 331 (citing, at fn 2, two analyses of human rights considerations under the IBRD and IDA Articles of Agreement that were written approximately two decades ago: Victoria E Marmorstein, 'World Bank Power to Consider Human Rights Factors in Loan Decisions'(1978) 13 *Journal of International Law & Economics* 113; Robert W Kneller, 'Human Rights, Politics, and the Multilateral Development Banks' (1980) 6 *Yale Studies in World Public Order* 361.)

IBRD's charter.[51] I will not explore this argument in detail here; adequate treatment would require a lengthy paper, or possibly a book, and has been addressed quite sufficiently elsewhere.[52] Suffice it to say that the World Bank's former General Counsel, Roberto Danino, recently reiterated that he believes that the purported conflict between promoting human rights norms and the IBRD's charter is illusory, and that the Bank's Articles of Agreement do not constrain the Bank from adopting a human rights-based approach to development.[53] The World Bank's policy on human rights has never been static, and Danino's interpretation represents a significant evolution from the position of the Bank's previous General Counsel, Ibrahim Shihata, who liberalized the interpretation of the IBRD Charter somewhat but nevertheless supported the Bank's traditional distinction between human rights concerns of a preponderantly 'economic' and 'political' nature.[54] Although it would perhaps be flippant to assert that no dispute remains regarding the legality of the Bank's consideration of human rights in assessing the merits of potential development projects, it is to be hoped that further statements by World Bank Counsel can definitely clarify that furthering the progressive realization of human rights is at the core of the World Bank's mission of sustainable development.

Significantly, the leadership of the IFC has reiterated the IFC's commitment to promoting the fulfillment of human rights as part of the development agenda. Peter Woicke, IFC Executive Vice-President and Managing Director, in 2004 affirmed '[w]e believe that ... human rights is part of our mission of sustainable development ... [and] I believe that IFC, as one of a handful of organizations that has become a global standard-bearer for environmental and social issues, has a great opportunity and arguably a special responsibility to address these issues.'[55] The question

---

[51] The International Bank for Reconstruction and Development Articles of Agreement state: 'The Bank and its officers shall not interfere in the political affairs of any member; nor shall they be influenced in their decisions by the political character of the member or members concerned. Only economic considerations shall be relevant to their decisions, and these considerations shall be weighed impartially in order to achieve the purposes stated in Article I' (amended 16 February 1989), Arts 4, 10, available at http://www.worldbank.org. The International Finance Corporation Articles of Agreement state: 'The Corporation and its officers shall not interfere in the political affairs of any member; nor shall they be influenced in their decisions by the political character of the member or members concerned. Only economic considerations shall be relevant to their decisions, and these considerations shall be weighed impartially in order to achieve the purposes stated in this Agreement': above n 42, Arts 3, 9.

[52] See, eg, Moris, above n 50; Ciorciari, above n 50; Ko-Yung Tung, 'Comment on the Grotius Lecture by Mary Robinson at Shaping Globalization: The Role of Human Rights (2 April 2003)' (2003) 19 *American University International Law Review* 27, available at 35–37. Ko-Yung Tung is the former Vice-President and General Counsel of the World Bank.

[53] Danino, above n 48.

[54] Ciorciari, above n 50, at 337.

[55] Peter Woicke, 'Draft Remarks (presented 1 March 2004 at NYU School of Law)', in Mary Robinson and Philip Alston (eds), *Human Rights and Development: Towards Mutual Reinforcement* (Oxford, Oxford University Press, 2006), at p 4.

we examine in this chapter is how the IFC could better ensure the promotion of sustainable development and human rights by implementing safeguards regarding the content of the legal covenants that govern large-scale development projects.

## IV. THE INTERNATIONAL FINANCE CORPORATION'S SAFEGUARD POLICIES

Projects are assessed primarily for economic viability, but in order for a project sponsor to receive funding it must comply with various IFC social and environmental guidelines. At the time the BTC Pipeline Project was being funded, the IFC operationalized its commitment to human rights and sustainable development through the imposition of safeguard policies, environmental guidelines, and environmental and social review procedures.[56] The safeguard policies, adopted in 1998, were based on those then in place at the International Bank for Reconstruction and Development (IBRD).[57] In February 2006 the IFC Board of Directors updated the IFC's environmental and social standards.[58] The new Sustainability Policy,[59] Performance Standards,[60] and Disclosure Policy[61] became operational in April 2006.

The purpose of this section is twofold: (1) to illustrate how IFC social and environmental safeguard policies influenced the development of the BTC Pipeline by imposing constraints with which BTC Co was forced to comply, and (2) to overview the IFC's longstanding social and environmental policy framework in order to illustrate the feasibility of introducing IFC-imposed guidelines regarding Project Agreements into revised safeguard policies. I do not here explore in-depth the benefits and shortcomings of the IFC's environmental and social policies and procedures, except insofar as one significant shortcoming is the current lack of guidelines regarding the project-specific legal covenants that are the topic of this chapter.

---

[56] International Finance Corporation, *Environmental and Social Review Procedure* (December 1998), at 1, available at http://ifcln1.ifc.org/ifcext/enviro.nsf/Content/ESRP

[57] *Ibid.*

[58] International Finance Corporation, *IFC Adopts New Environmental and Social Standards*, Press release, 21 February 2006, available at http://www.ifc.org/ifcext/policyreview.nsf/Content/SafeguardPolicesUpdate

[59] International Finance Corporation's Policy on Social and Environmental Sustainability, 30 April 2006, available at http://www.ifc.org/ifcext/policyreview.nsf/Content/SafeguardPolicesUpdate

[60] International Finance Corporation's Performance Standards on Social and Environmental Sustainability, 30 April 2006, available at http://www.ifc.org/ifcext/policyreview.nsf/Content/SafeguardPolicesUpdate

[61] International Finance Corporation's Policy on Disclosure of Information, 30 April 2006, available at http://www.ifc.org/ifcext/policyreview.nsf/Content/SafeguardPolicesUpdate

At the time the BTC pipeline funding was approved, the IFC had environmental and social polices governing: environmental assessment, natural habitats, pest management, indigenous peoples, safeguarding cultural property, involuntary resettlement, forestry, safety of dams, and projects on international waterway.[62] The IFC also required projects to conform to the World Bank Group's Occupational Health and Safety Guidelines.[63] Subject to a reasonableness test, several types of projects were excluded from IFC financing altogether, including: production or trade in any product or activity illegal under host country laws or international conventions; production or trade in weapons and munitions; production or trade in alcoholic beverages (excluding beer and wine), tobacco, and gambling casinos; production or trade in pesticides/herbicides and phar-maceuticals subject to international phase-outs or bans; and production or trade in radioactive materials, products containing PCBs, and ozone-depleting substances subject to international phase-out.[64]

Although the new Policy and Procedures on Social and Environmental Sustainability have altered the constraints on environmental and social impacts governing IFC projects,[65] it is important to detail the pre-existing system because this is the regime under which the BTC pipeline was conceived and financed. Moreover, the new social and environmental policies have only just been introduced, so it remains uncertain how they will function in practice. A brief sketch of the IFC's long-standing environmental and social safeguards illustrates the constraints placed by the IFC on the BTC project sponsors.

Under the pre-existing safeguard policies, all projects proposed for IFC financing required an environmental assessment (EA) to ensure that they were environmentally and socially sustainable, as mandated by the Environmental Assessment Policy (OP 4.01).[66] The new Procedures on Social and Environmental Sustainability likewise require a comprehensive assessment of the social and environmental impacts of a proposed project.[67] The breadth, depth, and methodology of the assessment varies according to the type and complexity of the project, as determined according to the category in which the IFC places the project. A proposed project is classified as 'Category A' if it is likely to have significant adverse environmental impacts that are sensitive (an impact is considered 'sensitive'

---

[62] *Ibid*.

[63] Above n 1, at 2.

[64] *Ibid*., Annex A, at 19.

[65] International Finance Corporation, *IFC Fact Sheet: Policy and Performance Standards on Social and Environmental Responsibility and disclosure of information*, available at http://www.ifc.org/ifcext/policyreview.nsf/Content/SafeguardPolicesUpdate (last visited 28 March 2006).

[66] Above n 1, Annex A, at 19,

[67] International Finance Corporation's Performance Standards on Social and Environmental Sustainability, above n 5, Performance Standard 1.

if it may be irreversible, affect vulnerable groups of ethnic minorities, involve involuntary displacement and resettlement, or affect significant cultural heritage sites), diverse, or unprecedented. [68] A proposed project is classified as 'Category B' if its potential adverse impacts on human populations or environmentally important areas—including wetlands, forests, grasslands, and other natural habitats—are considered site-specific and not irreversible. The scope of assessment for a Category B project may vary from project to project, but it is narrower than that of an assessment for Category A projects.[69] A proposed project is classified as 'Category C' if it is likely to have minimal or no adverse environmental impacts. Beyond screening, no further EA action is required for a Category C project.[70] A proposed project is classified as 'Category FI' if it involves investment of IFC funds through a financial intermediary in subprojects that may result in adverse environmental impacts. Examples of Category FI projects are corporate loans to banks, credit lines, and private equity funds. [71] Under the current system, the process of categorizing a project A, B, or C is internal to the Bank and not subject to public participation or review.

The BTC pipeline was a Category A project.[72] As a Category A project, the EA examined the project's potential positive and negative impacts, compared them with those of feasible alternatives (including the 'without project' scenario), and recommended any measures needed to prevent, minimize, mitigate, or compensate for adverse impacts and improve performance. [73] A full environmental and social impact assessment (ESIA) was required, which included an environmental audit and a hazard/risk assessment.[74] For Category A projects an Environmental Action Plan (EAP) is an essential part of the EA report and must be included as a part of the draft EA report that is released locally for public consultation.[75] OP 4.01 also set forth requirements for public consultation and public disclosure for projects. [76] In order to comply with OP 4.01, BTC Co engaged in an ESIA and developed a comprehensive EAP, as well as a Public Consultation and Disclosure Plan (PCDP).[77] The process, while laudable, has shortcomings: the NGO community has criticized both the content of

---

[68] *Ibid.*
[69] *Ibid.*
[70] *Ibid.*
[71] *Ibid.*
[72] International Finance Corporation, *Baku Tiblisi-Ceyhan Pipeline: Summary of Project Information,* available at http://www.ifc.org (last visited 9 December 2004).
[73] International Finance Corporation, above n 56.
[74] *Ibid.*
[75] *Ibid.*
[76] *Ibid.*
[77] International Finance Corporation, above n 69.

the BTC Consortium's PCDP, as well as BTC's failure to abide by its terms.[78]

The IFC's initial involvement in a project normally occurs after a feasibility study has been completed (that is, after site selection, preliminary design work, etc).[79] In the case of the BTC project, the IFC was approached for funding in 2002, two years after pipeline design began.[80] After the BTC project sponsor submitted an initial proposal, the IFC conducted an Early Review in order to give the sponsor a quick decision on whether the IFC was interested in engaging in the project. The evaluation process was led by an Investment Officer, who consulted with environmental and social specialists as appropriate. The basis for the early management decision was the Project Data Sheet Early Review (PDS-ER), which contained a project description, highlighted any policy issues and potential deal-breakers, and reviewed development impact.[81] Based on the information in the PDS-ER, IFC senior management assessed the appropriateness of the project as an investment for IFC and authorized project appraisal. Environmental and social impact concerns could have been deal-breakers, but they are not in themselves grounds for approving a project for appraisal.[82] In other words, projects are chosen because they are economically viable, unless they threaten unacceptable social and environmental impacts, as opposed to being selected primarily because they promote human rights, public health and safety, or environmental sustainability.

Once the Environment Division was satisfied that the project could comply with appropriate IFC environmental and social requirements, the Division sent an Environmental and Social Clearance Memorandum (ESCM) to the Investment Department. After completion of the appraisal and receipt of the ESCM, the Investment Department decided to process the project, based on considerations of financial viability. The IFC then negotiated with the project sponsor to establish the terms and conditions of IFC participation in the project, including environmental and social aspects, such as conditions of disbursement and covenants, performance and monitoring requirements, and resolution of any outstanding issues.[83]

IFC projects are finally submitted to the Board for approval after the investment officer considers all outstanding issues to be resolved. After project approval, the investment officer, in consultation with the lawyer

---

[78] See, eg, Office of the Compliance Advisor/Ombudsman, *Assessment Report: Complaint regarding the Baku-Tbilisi-Ceyhan (BTC) Pipeline Project: Rustavi, Georgia* (issued July 2004), available at http://www.cao-ombudsman.org/pdfs/Final%20Revised%20Assessment%20Report%2008-12-04.pdf

[79] International Finance Corporation, above n 56.

[80] Oliver Broad, above n 26.

[81] International Finance Corporation, above n 56.

[82] *Ibid.*

[83] *Ibid.*

and environmental and social development specialists, ensures that environmental and social requirements are reflected in the IFC legal documentation for the project. The investment agreement contains covenants which require the project company to comply with IFC and host country requirements, including applicable IFC policies and guidelines. As a Category A project, the investment agreement for the BTC project required the company to comply with the requirements described in the agreed EAP and the PCDP. [84]

The Office of the Compliance Advisor/Ombudsman (CAO) conducted a comprehensive review of the impact and implementation of environmental and social safeguard policies in 2003. [85] The review concluded that the overall framework of safeguard policies and loan conditionalities was having a positive effect in furthering the Bank's mission of poverty alleviation through sustainable development,[86] but that a number of shortcomings remained.[87] The report recommended that the IFC should: focus on selecting loan recipients with a genuine commitment to implementing environment and social best practices; increase the IFC's staff capacity of environmental and social specialists; clarify expectations regarding social issues included under the EA policy (OP 4.01), measurable outcomes, and disclosure and consultation requirements; better integrate social and environmental standards into overall project assessment; and hold management and staff accountable for specific environmental and social goals derived from performance at the project and portfolio level.[88] It remains to be seen whether the new Policies and Procedures on Social and Environmental Sustainability have effectively incorporated the CAO's recommendations, or whether the new system will be more or less successful in operationalizing the IFC's commitment to social and environmental sustainability.

As mentioned at the outset, I have not here attempted to evaluate the sufficiency or effectiveness of the IFC safeguard polices in the context of the BTC pipeline project. This is a critical topic, which has been explored in depth elsewhere.[89] The purpose of outlining the pre-existing IFC framework for encouraging social and environmental responsibility is instead to illustrate the feasibility of imposing IFC requirements regarding the legal structure of project agreements (HGAs and IGAs). Such requirements could be incorporated into the structure of IFC safeguard policies and guidelines, as that structure continues to be modified and improved.

---

[84] *Ibid.*
[85] Compliance Advisor/Ombudsman, above n 16.
[86] *Ibid* at 21.
[87] *Ibid.*
[88] *Ibid.*
[89] See, e.g., http://www.bakuceyhan.org.uk and related links (http: //www.bakuceyhan.org.uk/links.htm).

## V. LEGAL FRAMEWORK OF THE BTC PROJECT PIPELINE

The building and operation of the pipeline is governed by two major types of agreements. The IGA between Azerbaijan, Georgia, and Turkey aims 'to establish more firmly favourable conditions to justify the commitment of capital and resources to the Baku-Tbilisi-Ceyhan MEP Project'[90] by committing the States to upholding the HGAs, providing security to MEP Project personnel, and protecting the freedom of transit of petroleum in their respective territories.[91] A second set of agreements, known as HGAs, was made between each State separately and BTC Co.[92] The HGA concept is not new, and variations on this model have been used since the beginning of post-Soviet oil exploration in the Caspian region.[93] Together these agreements establish the legal framework that governs the adjudication of any issues relating to the construction and operation of the pipeline for the next 40 years, with the possibility of extension for 20 additional years.[94]

Three additional documents were issued in 2003 seeking to respond to criticisms directed at the HGA–IGA structure by the NGO community. These new project agreements (the Human Rights Undertaking, the Joint Statement, and the Security Protocol) directly address most—but not all—of the primary problems outlined here and in various NGO reports regarding the social and environmental implications of the legal framework. According to the consortium, the three project agreements are an integral part of the prevailing legal regime governing the BTC project, and binding on the parties.[95] Despite these assurances, it is not clear whether a court would interpret the undertakings as integral to the core project covenants, and thus the legal value courts or arbitrators would attach to their terms remains an open question.

Yet the Human Rights Undertaking, along with the Joint Statement and the Security Protocol, are highly significant in another respect—despite their ambiguous legal status. The fact that BTC Co and the three host governments executed the agreements demonstrates that it is indeed politically possible and economically feasible to establish a legal framework that allows States to promote the progressive realization of human rights and environmental sustainability. The clear commitments in the three new

---

[90] IGA, above n 23, preamble.
[91] *Ibid.*
[92] HGA of Georgia, above n 24; HGA of Turkey, above n 24; HGA of Azerbaijan, above n 24.
[93] Christopher PM Waters, 'Who Should Regulate the Baku-Tbilisi-Ceyhan Pipeline?' 16 *Georgetown International Environmental Law Review*, Spring 2004, 403, at 406.
[94] HGA of Georgia, above n 24, Art 3.1; HGA of Turkey, above n 24, Art 3.1; HGA of Azerbaijan, above n 24 24, Art 3.1.
[95] BTC Company, *Citizens Guide to the BTC Project Agreements: Environmental, Social, and Human Rights Standards*, at 9, available at http://www.caspiandevelopmentandexport.com (last visited 4 December 2004).

project agreements provide a possible model for provisions that should be incorporated into the core covenants of future investor-government agreements.

Our analysis begins from the premise that there are no rights without remedies. This is both a fundamental legal notion and a commonsense fact. What value is a promise without a mechanism to ensure that the promisor performs? What rights are guaranteed without a way of holding parties accountable if they violate those rights? Our point of departure, therefore, is the legal remedies available under the HGAs and the IGA to BTC Co, the host States, and the private individuals impacted by the pipeline project. We concentrate on how the terms of the HGAs could be interpreted in a manner that would impede the realization of sustainable development and human rights, and conclude with an overview of the subsequently enacted project agreements that aim to address these concerns.

## 1. Host Governments Obligated to Compensate the BTC Company

The three host governments are bound by the agreements to provide monetary compensation if they fail to satisfy fully all of their obligations under the project agreements.[96] If the States violate any of the terms of the agreements 'whether as a result of action or inaction'[97] they must compensate BTC Co for any loss occasioned. The compensation clauses aim to stabilize the investment climate in Turkey, Azerbaijan, and Georgia by removing financial risks and uncertainties for BTC Co. The requirement of compensation in case of contract breach is not uncommon; what is uncommon—and the source of great concern in the NGO community[98]—is the extent of the obligations placed upon the host States. The reach of these obligations, coupled with the compensation requirement, infringe the regulatory autonomy of host States and make it difficult for them to promote effectively the progressive realization of human rights and sustainable development.

### A. Obligations

**1. Governments Prevented From Taking Any Actions To Protect Public Welfare That Interfere With Project**    The HGA explicitly prevents the host governments from taking actions and applying laws and regulations to protect the public welfare when such actions or regulations would

---

[96] HGA of Georgia, above n 24, Art 9; HGA of Turkey, above n 24, Art 10; HGA of Azerbaijan, above n 24 24, Art 9.

[97] HGA of Turkey, above n 24, Art 10.1(iii).

[98] See, eg, Human Rights on the Line, above n 36.

interfere with the smooth running of the project.[99] This ban unambiguously extends to regulation for security, health, safety, or environmental reasons.[100] The only exception is when there exists a material, imminent threat to public health or safety.[101] Article 5.2 in each of the Turkish, Georgian, and Azerbaijani HGAs guarantees that

> the State Authorities shall not act or fail to act in any manner that could hinder or delay any Project Activity or otherwise negatively affect the Project or impair any rights granted under any Project Agreement (including any such action or inaction predicated on security, health, environmental or safety considerations that, directly or indirectly, could interrupt, impede or limit the flow of Petroleum in or through the Facilities, except under circumstances in which continued operation of the Facilities without immediate corrective action creates an imminent, material threat to public security, health, safety or the environment that renders it reasonable to take or fail to take, as the case may be, such action and, then, only to the extent and for the period of time necessary to remove that threat).[102]

If Turkey, Georgia, or Azerbaijan take actions to protect the health and safety of their citizens in the absence of an 'imminent, material threat', they will be obliged to compensate BTC Co. The requirement that a threat must be 'imminent' and 'material' in order for State corrective action to be allowed is incompatible with broadly accepted international human rights standards.[103]

**2. Governments Must Maintain 'Economic Equilibrium', Thus Precluding Legal Or Regulatory Changes Through Domestic Legislation, International Treaties, Or Court Decisions**   One of the central obligations placed on the States is to maintain the 'economic equilibrium' vis-à-vis the investment.[104] 'Economic equilibrium' is used to mean the expected economic value of the combination of legal rights and obligations in place when the HGA was signed.[105] If Azerbaijan, Turkey, or Georgia fail to maintain the pre-existing 'economic equilibrium', they must compensate the consortium for lower profit expectations.

This obligation therefore precludes any legal or regulatory changes that may impact on the pipeline—including improvements to environmental

---

[99] HGA of Georgia, above n 24, Art 5.2(iii); HGA of Azerbaijan, above n 24, Art 5.2(iii); HGA of Turkey, above n 24, Art 5.2(iii).

[100] *Ibid.*

[101] *Ibid.*

[102] *Ibid.*

[103] Human Rights on the Line, above n 36, at 13.

[104] HGA of Georgia, above n 24, Art 7.2(x).; HGA of Turkey, above n 24, Art 7.2(xi); HGA of Azerbaijan, above n 24, Art 7.2(x).

[105] *Ibid.*

and human rights standards. The Agreements specify that any and all changes in law—whether originating from domestic democratic action, court interpretations of existing law, or through accession to international treaties—constitute a disruption in 'economic equilibrium' if such changes negatively affect the project.[106] Article 7.2(xi) of the Turkish HGA states in relevant part: 'the State Authorities shall take all actions available to them to restore the Economic Equilibrium established under the Project Agreements if and to the extent the Economic Equilibrium is disrupted or negatively affected, directly or indirectly, as a result of any change (whether the change is specific to the Project or of general application) in Turkish Law (including any Turkish Laws regarding Taxes, health, safety and the environment)'. Article 7.2(vi) further specifies that the foregoing commitment likewise precludes the application of newly signed international treaties, stating 'if any domestic or international agreement or treaty … [or] any other form of commitment, policy or pronouncement or permission, has the effect of impairing, conflicting or interfering with the implementation of the Project, or limiting, abridging or adversely affecting the value of the Project or any of the rights, privileges, exemptions, waivers, indemnifications or protections granted or arising under this Agreement or any other Project Agreement it shall be deemed a Change in Law under Article 7.2(xi).'[107] The freeze imposed also covers any interpretation of existing law that could adversely affect the economic equilibrium of the project. Article 7.2(xi) further specifies that 'the interpretation or application of Turkish Law (whether by the courts, the executive or legislative authorities, or administrative or regulatory bodies), the decisions, policies or other similar actions of judicial bodies, tribunals and courts, the State Authorities, jurisdictional alterations' constitutes a change in law and a disruption of economic equilibrium. This prevents the Turkish courts from developing their case-law in a way that has negative implications for the project, thereby compromising an important element in the rule of law.[108] By requiring compensation, the agreements effectively freeze the regulatory regimes of the three host governments for the next 40 years, precluding democratic governance, the evolution of case = law, and the application of evolving international legal norms.

In case the terms of the Agreement left any doubt, the Appendix reiterates that: 'If any regional or intergovernmental authority having jurisdiction enacts or promulgates social regulations or guidelines applicable to areas where Project Activities occur … in no event shall the Project be subject to any such standards to the extent they are different from or

---

[106]   *Ibid.*
[107]   HGA of Turkey, above n 24.
[108]   *Ibid.*

more stringent than the standards and practices generally prevailing in the international Petroleum pipeline industry for comparable projects.'[109]

**3. Land Acquisition and Resettlement**   The three host governments have also committed to take a number of positive actions under the agreements that could pose a threat to human rights and environmental sustainability.

Turkey, Azerbaijan, and Georgia each promised to secure a range of land use rights for BTC Co along the pipeline route.[110] Some 30,000 owners or tenant/sharecroppers will be affected by the land acquisition process in Turkey alone.[111] The process of acquiring land for the pipeline raises a number of human rights concerns. First, because the IGA declared that the pipeline project is not in the public interest[112] in order to ensure the signatory States could not violate the terms of the HGAs unilaterally[113], the States lack the legal right to purchase the land or resettle users compulsorily.[114] Of course, due to the enormity and strategic importance of the project it would not be a workable solution to have the consortium acquire the land it needs through the process that has to be followed by any private developer—negotiating voluntary sales—so land use rights are being acquired through compulsory purchase and resettlement.[115] The human rights violation this contradiction engenders could be offset by the provision of independent legal aid to all the people affected, thus allowing them the opportunity for fair negotiation regarding the price paid by BTC Co for using the land. According to Amnesty International, 'The majority of the people in the pipeline zone are rural and would have practically no experience in a court of law … In these circumstances, the provision of legal aid is fundamental to a fair hearing.'[116] Presently there is nothing in the IGA, HGA, or any other project documentation guaranteeing legal aid to landowners or those displaced (even temporarily) by the project. Was Turkey to provide the legal aid, and ensure fairness in the process of land acquisition, then any resulting delay could well interfere with the economic equilibrium of the project, triggering the compensation clause in the HGA.[117]

---

[109] HGA of Georgia, above n 24, Appendix 5.2; HGA of Turkey, above n 24, Appendix 4.2; HGA of Azerbaijan, above n 24, Appendix 4.2.
[110] *Ibid*, Art 7.
[111] Human Rights on the Line, above n 36, at 17 (citing IFC, *Project Document Chapter 6: Impacts and Mitigation* (November 2002), available at http://www.ifc.org, at 3).
[112] IGA, above n 23, Art II, 8.
[113] Human Rights on the Line, above n 36, at 1.
[114] See, eg European Convention on Human Rights, Protocol 1, Art 1 (20 March 1952); Human Rights on the Line, above n 36, at 17 (citing the Constitution of the Republic of Turkey, Art 35).
[115] Human Rights on the Line, above n 36, at 17–18.
[116] *Ibid.*
[117] *Ibid.*

The land acquisition process also threatens to reinforce discrimination against women. Amnesty International reports:

> According to the Land Acquisition Plan, the vast majority of the land is owned by males, or is in the male's name or under customary rules will be considered to belong to the male head of household … Additionally, the documents note that women rarely participate in consultation meetings and it is expected that they will not be represented equally in negotiations on land compensation. The result is twofold. Firstly, only the person authorized to engage in dispute resolution for compensation of the land acquisition will be the named owner or user of the land, generally the male in the family. Secondly, the money paid out by BTC will be paid into a bank account in the male's name or directly to the male in cash, as is [already] happening in Georgia. This excludes women from the process and from enjoying benefit from land on which they have labored and lived. It leaves the women vulnerable in that they cannot promote their own rights (as unnamed landowners and users), and it gives them no means of controlling the assets gained once land has been acquired.[118]

Historical experience suggests that the threat to women's rights is not merely hypothetical. For example, the final report of an international fact-finding mission to examine how the planned Yusufeli Dam in north-east Turkey violated international standards and people's rights stated that: 'The needs of women and other vulnerable groups have not been taken into account and women have not been involved in the decision-making process even to the limited degree that men have been.'[119] The HGAs create disincentives for the host governments to modify the process in ways that would better protect the rights of women, because if such modifications slow-down the project in any way, the State would be required to compensate BTC Co.

**4. Security**   The HGAs each provide that:

> the Government, at its sole cost and expense, but in regular consultation with the MEP Participants[120], shall use the security forces of theState to provide physical security for the Rights to Land, the Facilities and Persons within the Territory involved in Project Activities … the Government shall be solely liable for the conduct of all operations of the security forces of the State and neither the MEP Participants nor any other Project Participants shall have any liability or obligation to any Person for any acts or activities of the security forces of the State.[121]

---

[118]   *Ibid*, at 19.
[119]   *Ibid* (citing Friends of the Earth, *Damning Indictment: How the Yusufeli Dam Violates International Standards and People's Rights*, September 2002, at 3).
[120]   '[O]ne or more, or all, of the Parties to this Agreement … other than the State Authorities': HGA of Turkey, above n 24, Appendix 1.
[121]   HGA of Georgia, above n 24, Art 11.3; HGA of Turkey, above n 24, Art 12.3; HGA of Azerbaijan, above n 24, Art 11.3.

This obligation to provide security for the project threatens to encourage human rights abuses by host State governments. Demonstrations against the pipeline are a virtual certainty given the large number of people affected and the possibility of conflicts over resettlement, land compensation, environmental pollution, and fishing and grazing rights. If the pipeline engenders local resistance and protests it is possible that the police and military security forces will maintain order with violent crackdowns, particularly given that failure to protect the pipeline will trigger the compensation obligation.

Both the history of analogous projects in other countries and the human rights track records and political climates in Turkey, Azerbaijan, and Georgia strongly support the prediction that the host governments will perpetrate human rights abuses in maintaining pipeline security. All three governments have long records of illegal detentions, torture, and repressing freedom of speech.[122] The recent and ongoing response of the Turkish police forces to demonstrations against the Ilisu Dam Project in south-east Turkey and the Ovacick gold mine in western Anatolia are illustrative.[123] According to Amnesty International, 'The Turkish security forces have a record of violently suppressing all forms of protest, in many cases detaining peaceful demonstrators and further subjecting them to torture or ill-treatment, and charging them with offences not directly related to the demonstration.'[124] Oil pipelines and other extractive industry projects often precipitate human rights abuses by State governments. According the World Bank's Extractive Industries Review (EIR), concluded in the fall of 2003, 'In a number of countries, extractive industries have been linked to human rights abuses and civil conflict. Such abuses have been documented, for example, in cases where the army has been called in to guard extractive industries projects.'[125] In the absence of enforceable, contractual constraints to the contrary, the linkage between pipeline security and human rights abuses will only be exacerbated by the HGAs' compensation requirement.

---

[122] Bureau of Democracy, Human Rights, and Labor, State Department, *Azerbaijan: Country Reports on Human Rights Practices—2003* (25 February 2004), available at http://www.state.gov/g/drl/rls/hrrpt/2003/27826.htm; Bureau of Democracy, Human Rights, and Labor, State Department, *Turkey: Country Reports on Human Rights Practices—2003* (25 February 2004), available at http://www.state.gov/g/drl/rls/hrrpt/2003/27869.htm;Bureau of Democracy, Human Rights, and Labor, State Department, *Georgia: Country Reports on Human Rights Practices—2003* (25 February 2004), available at http://www.state.gov/g/drl/rls/hrrpt/2003/27838.htm

[123] Human Rights on the Line, above n 36, at 24–25.

[124] *Ibid.* at 23.

[125] Extractive Industries Review, above n 11, vol 1, at 6.

## C. Dispute Resolution

The HGAs establish that any dispute regarding the project or arising under the terms of the project agreements shall be subject to international binding arbitration.[126] Amnesty International and other NGOs initially expressed concern that this dispute resolution mechanism prevented local residents affected by the pipeline from seeking remedies if BTC Co violates domestic laws relating to human rights, labor rights, and the environment.[127] Amnesty contended that under the terms of the HGAs, anyone wanting to seek redress against the oil pipeline companies would need to prosecute the case in Geneva, Switzerland, in the English language, pursuant to international laws with which all except sophisticated international investors are utterly unfamiliar.[128] The lack of a reasonably available venue with jurisdiction to adjudicate claims against the BTC Consortium would mean that, de facto, no remedy exists for local populations injured by the construction and operation of the pipeline project.

The legal interpretation advance by Amnesty International is debatable, however: a plain reading of the language of the HGAs indicates that the dispute resolution clauses apply only to the parties to the agreement (the three host governments and the BTC Consortium), and thus do not preclude private parties from seeking remedies in local courts for violations of domestic laws.[129] In other words, local residents would have redress against BTC Co in domestic courts for violations of domestic laws. Yet the issue remains important, as there is no guarantee that future legal frameworks will be similarly worded. Drafters should take precautionary measures to ensure that the rights of private citizens to seek remedies against investors are protected.

A second concern regarding dispute resolution under the HGAs also deserves notice. Let us return to our starting framework—there are no rights with remedies. Private individuals, who are not parties to the agreements, do not have the right to bring suit against the consortium for violating the terms of the agreements. The HGAs do not establish that local people have standing to enforce the project agreements. Therefore the impoverished rural farmers, herders, and workers impacted by the pipeline cannot act on their own to hold the BTC Consortium accountable for human rights commitments made under the agreements, particularly the unilateral commitments discussed below, in section V.3. Instead, enforcement of BTC Co's human rights commitments depends entirely on host governments. If the host government turns a blind eye to BTC Co's violations of its commitments—due to domestic or international political

---

[126] See, eg, HGA of Georgia,above n 24, Arts 17.2–17.4.
[127] Human Rights on the Line, above n 36, at 14, 19.
[128] *Ibid.*
[129] *Ibid.*

pressures—all guarantees made by BTC Co under the HGAs or subsequent project agreements, no matter how exemplary in theory, in practice cannot be enforced by the people who suffer injury stemming from violations of these guarantees.

*D. The Joint Statement, the Security Protocol, and the BTC Human Rights Undertaking*

The consortium and the host governments reject the concerns detailed above as illusory,[130] pointing out that subsequent project agreements issued in 2003 definitely clarify that the IGA–HGA framework cannot be interpreted so as to impede the enforcement of international norms relating to human rights and environmental sustainability.

The Joint Statement, the Security Protocol, and the BTC Human Rights Undertaking were executed in response to intense pressure from local activists and the international NGO community. The first of the three agreements, issued in May 2003, begins: 'We note concerns expressed by various non-governmental organizations about the BTC Project. We take these concerns seriously. We are determined to make the BTC Project a model project in all respects, and the environmental, social, and human rights aspects of the project are of fundamental importance. We are committed to BTC Co's objective of, "No accidents, no harm to people, and no damage to the environment."'[131] The BTC Human Rights Undertaking, executed five months later, aimed to address criticisms regarding the ability of host governments and third parties to advance claims against project participants.[132] To the extent that these three project agreements do effectively address the primary problems with the HGAs, the NGO community and local human, labor, and environmental justice activists must be given credit for demanding accountability. Their demands led directly to the establishment of a prevailing legal regime far friendlier to the progressive realization of human rights, environmental protection, and sustainable development.

The Joint Statement[133] was the first official document to address and attempt to ameliorate the criticisms directed against the IGA–HGA

---

[130] 'As part of our dialogue with the NGO community, we are aware of speculation regarding the intent of the parties with respect to provisions of the Project Agreements, and speculation that those provisions might be interpreted or used in a manner that could permit the Project, or the host States, to act in a manner contrary to international human rights, environmental, or social and labor norms. We have considered each of the provisions identified and have concluded that none of the speculation included in recent correspondence reflects the intent or understanding of the parties with respect to their meaning or operation. We are determined to uphold the highest international standards for BTC and we cannot agree with those speculations': Joint Statement, above n 37, Art 4.

[131] *Ibid.*, Art 1.

[132] BTC Company, above n 94, at 14.

[133] Joint Statement, above n 37.

framework. Issued by the three host governments in consultation with the BTC Co, it addresses the social and environmental concerns outlined above in two ways. First, it asserts and clarifies the intent of the parties that 'the Project be developed and operated as a model for good environmental, labor and social practices.'[134] This clarification would make it difficult for BTC Co to prosecute a claim for compensation springing from the enforcement of evolving international legal norms. Second, and more concretely, the Statement affirms that the project will be bound by international environmental and labor standards. With regard to environmental risk management, 'The IGA commits each State to the application of environmental standards and practices that are "no less stringent" than those generally applied within member states of the European Union from time to time.'[135] The clause continues, clarifying that 'The HGAs and other BTC Project Agreements give effect to this commitment, and provide a dynamic benchmark that will evolve as EU standards evolve, and as international standards and practices within the petroleum pipeline industry also evolve.'[136] With regard to labor rights, the Statement confirms 'that International Labor Organization conventions on Forced Labor, Freedom of Association and Right to Organize, Collective Bargaining, Discrimination, Equal Remuneration and Minimum Age, all as in effect from time to time, will apply to the development and operation of the Project, and that the Project is and will remain subject to the standards set forth in any and all other international labor and human rights treaties to which any host State is a party from time to time.'[137]

The Security Protocol, issued by Georgia, Turkey, and Azerbaijan in July 2003, primarily addresses a number of issues regarding coordination of security operations between the three countries.[138] Chapter Two of the Protocol, however, addresses human rights, affirming that all security measures will be implemented in accordance with the UN Declaration of Human Rights, the UN Convention Against Torture and Other Cruel Inhuman or Degrading Treatment or Punishment, the International Convention on the Elimination of Racial Discrimination, the UN Code of Conduct for Law Enforcement Officials, the UN Basic Principles on the Use of Force and Firearms by Law Enforcement Officials, the European Convention for the Protection of Human Rights and Fundamental Freedoms as amended by Protocol 11, the European Convention for the Prevention of Torture and Inhuman or Degrading Treatment or Punishment, and the Voluntary Principles on Security and Human Rights.[139]

---

[134]   *Ibid*, Art 1.
[135]   *Ibid*, Art 7.
[136]   *Ibid*.
[137]   *Ibid*, Art 8.
[138]   Security Protocol, above n 37, ch 1, Arts 1–11.
[139]   *Ibid*, Arts 12, 13.

In the BTC Human Rights Undertaking, dated 22 September 2003, the BTC Co promises it will: (1) not assert any claims that would prevent Host Governments from applying domestic laws to regulate human rights or health, safety, or environmental issues; (2) not assert or advance any claim that would prevent host governments from applying dynamic and evolving norms of international law as related to human rights or health, safety, and environmental standards; (3) not prevent claims by private parties from proceeding against Project Participants in State Courts; and (4) that 'economic equilibrium' will not be used to seek compensation for actions required under international treaties relating to human and labor rights or health, safety, or environmental protections.[140]

To return to our initial frame of analysis grounded in rights and remedies, the Undertaking is potentially more legally significant than either the Joint Statement or the Security Protocol because it directly addresses the core issue of remedies. The Undertaking promises that BTC Co will not seek compensation for the economic impact of government actions that reasonably protect public health and safety or promote adherence to international human and environmental norms. The Undertaking also promises that people affected by the project can hold BTC Co legally accountable in domestic courts, declaring that the international arbitration clauses of the HGAs are not to be interpreted so as to preclude private parties from seeking remedies against project participants in local courts for violations of domestic law.[141] Significantly, the Undertaking *does not* establish the right of locally affected populations to hold the BTC Co accountable for injuries resulting from breach by BTC Co of project agreement standards relating to human rights, health, safety, or the environment.[142] In other words, the Undertaking by BTC does not establish a 'private attorney general right of action', meaning that it remains solely up to the host governments to demand redress from BTC Co for any breach of its human rights commitments.

Although, as mentioned earlier, the importance of the project agreements should not be overlooked, their legal significance under international law remains somewhat ambiguous. On the one hand, the Undertaking states that it cannot be revoked without the consent of the Governments of Turkey, Azerbaijan, and Georgia,[143] and warrants that the commitments it contains 'constitute a legal, valid, and binding obligation.'[144] The Joint Statement likewise declares that it 'constitutes a Project Agreement as defined under the BTC IGA and HGAs,'[145] while the Security Protocol

---

[140] BTC Human Rights Undertaking, above n 37, at 3–4.
[141] HGA of Georgia, above n 24, Arts 17.2–17.4.
[142] BTC Company, above n 94, at 14.
[143] *Ibid.*
[144] *Ibid.*
[145] Joint Statement, above n 94, Art 9.

establishes that it 'shall remain in force throughout the commercial operation of the projects.'[146] On the other hand, the Undertaking was issued unilaterally by the BTC Co, without consideration from the host governments, and may be unenforceable for that reason.[147] To the extent that the terms of these instruments directly conflict with provisions in the core project covenants, a court might decide that the terms of the HGAs and IGA control. Despite assurances to the contrary, the legal value courts or arbitrators would attach to the three documents remains an open question. It is also worth noting that none of the three project agreements (the Joint Statement, the Security Protocol, and the BTC Human Rights Undertaking) address concerns regarding involuntary resettlement procedures or the way the land acquisition process discriminates against women.

### E. Contrasting the BTC Agreements with Standard Bilateral Investment Treaties

The purpose of the stabilization clauses in the HGAs is to protect BTC Co from financial risks associated with operating in a foreign country with an unfamiliar legal system and an unpredictable political climate. Bilateral investment treaties (BITs) between States also aim to protect foreign investors from the same risks. It is important to recognize the key differences between the terms of the BTC pipeline project HGAs and the BITs that govern foreign investments worldwide, of which there are currently more than 2,265.[148]

The key provisions of BITs are generally: (1) national treatment, guaranteeing that foreign investments will be treated no less favorably than domestic investments; (2) most-favored-nation treatment, guaranteeing that foreign investments will be treated no less favorably than investments of investors of any third country; (3) establishment that expropriations

---

[146] Security Protocol, above n 94, Art 17.

[147] Under the doctrine of consideration—applicable under common law but not civil law—a contract and/or a subsequent modification to an existing contract is unenforceable unless there has been a bargain for exchange. Subject to specific exceptions, if a promise is made by one party, unilaterally, without receipt of consideration from the other party, there is no contract:see Restatement (Second) of Contracts §17, §71 (1981). On the other hand, promissory estoppel might prevent BTC Co from invalidating its unilateral statement, if the host States have relied on the assertions it contains: see Restatement (Second) of Contracts §139 (1981). Since the HGAs are governed by the law of England (see HGA of Azerbaijan, Art 17.12; HGA of Georgia, Art 17.13; HGA of Turkey, Art 18.12), the doctrine of consideration applies.

[148] The number of BITs has grown steadily: they numbered 385 by 1989, and 2,265 in 2003, encompassing 176 countries. The number of double taxation treaties reached 2,256 in 2002: United Nations Conference on Trade and Development, *Quantitative data on bilateral investment treaties and double taxation treaties*, available at http://www.unctad.org/Templates/WebFlyer.asp?intItemID = 3150&lang = 1 (last visited 8 December 2004).

must be done for a public purpose, in accordance with the law, and on payment of compensation; (4) prohibitions on performance requirements, including local purchasing and balance of payments requirements; and (5) the specification of a dispute settlement mechanism, usually under the rules of the International Centre for the Settlement of Investment Disputes (ICSID) and/or the United Nations Commission on International Trade Law (UNCITRAL).[149]

The most important distinction between the BTC Project HGAs and BITs is that the HGAs are contracts between a private investor and the host States, while BITs are treaties between sovereign governments. The national treatment, most-favored-nation, and performance requirement provisions are irrelevant to the BTC project contract because the HGAs concern a specific investment (the pipeline project), not possible future investments. Moreover, BTC Co can act in its own interest to hold host governments accountable for violations of the HGAs, without relying on the home State government to intercede on its behalf, as is necessary under BITs.

Another area in which a distinction must be drawn between the BTC legal framework and BITs is the compensation requirement of the HGAs, and the expropriation/compensation constraint imposed by BITs. At first glance, the compensation requirement of the BTC HGAs appears to mirror the 'no expropriation without compensation' requirement generally established by BITs, but this semblance is illusory—the compensation requirement in HGAs establishes a somewhat more expansive obligation than do corresponding BIT expropriation/compensation clauses. As detailed above in Section V, the HGAs between Turkey, Azerbaijan, Georgia, and BTC Co require the host governments to compensate for regulations that upset the 'economic equilibrium' of the pipeline project, even slightly. In contrast, the value of a property must be substantially diminished in order for an expropriation to have occurred.[150] Determinations regarding regulatory takings involve complex, fact-based analysis of many factors, including the extent of a purported diminution in value, the nature of the 'property right' infringed upon, and whether a regulation represents a legitimate exercise of police powers.[151] The HGAs short-circuit this nuanced analysis, requiring the host governments to compensate BTC Co for legal and regulatory actions that would not be

---

[149] See Foreign Trade Information System (SICE), Organization of American States, *Investment Agreements in the Western Hemisphere: A Compendium and accompanying treaty texts*, available at http://www.sice.oas.org/bitse.asp (last visited 8 December 2004).

[150] For an extended discussion regarding international regulatory takings jurisprudence, see Vicki Been and Joel Beauvais, 'The Global Fifth Amendment? NAFTA's Investor Protections and the Misguided Quest for an International "Regulatory Takings" Doctrine' (2003) 78 *New York University Law Review* 30.

[151] Ibid.

likely to constitute an expropriation under international law—and would therefore not trigger the corresponding compensation requirement established by BITs. The HGAs thus establish a greater financial liability owed by governments to the pipeline project investors than would be imposed under BITs, constraining the regulatory autonomy of Turkey, Azerbaijan, and Georgia to a correspondingly greater extent.

The agreements conflate property and contract law, replacing the rationality that generally governs expropriations jurisprudence with the doctrine underlying contracts. By requiring the host governments to 'restore the Economic Equilibrium established under the Project Agreements' or pay compensation,[152] the HGAs protect BTC Co's right to expected future profits. This idea of expectation damages[153] is common to contract law[154]— courts generally award expectation damages in order to give parties incentives to breach only when breach would be socially efficient[155]—but is not an established principle of international takings jurisprudence.[156] When protecting private property from uncompensated government expropriation, a court must first ascertain the property interests in question (the rights of a claimant in relation to a resource).[157] Only if a property right exists can it have been abrogated by the government. Even in the United States, arguably one of the most pro-private property regimes in the world,[158] the inclusion of expected profits as a protected property right is highly contested.[159] Enshrining an absolute private property right

---

[152]   HGA of Georgia, above n 24, Art 7.2(x).; HGA of Turkey, above n 24, Art 7.2(xi); HGA of Azerbaijan, above n 24, Art 7.2(x).

[153]   The purpose of expectation damages in case of contract breach is to put the promisee in the position he or she would have been in had the promisor performed the contract.

[154]   Default measure of damages is expectancy': Restatement (Second) of Contracts §347 (1981).

[155]   A socially efficient breach occurs when a promisor stands to gain more by breaching than the promisee stands to gain if the promisor fulfills the contract terms—thus the promisor is willing to breach even if he or she must compensate the promisee for the full amount the promisee would have received if the contract had been fulfilled.

[156]   For a history of international jurisprudence regarding regulatory takings and compensation in the context of NAFTA, see Been and Beauvais, above n 149, at 40–59.

[157]   The greater the number of rights recognized as legally protected property interests, the more likely it becomes that a government regulation will infringe on these rights and therefore require compensation: Howard Mann and Julie Soloway, Untangling the Expropriation and Regulation Relationship: Is there a way forward?, Report to the Ad Hoc Expert Group on Investment Rules and the [Canadian] Department of Foreign Affairs and International Trade, 31 March 2002, s 4(D).

[158]   For a comparison between Canadian, Mexican, and US takings jurisprudence, see Gregory Starner, 'Note, Taking a Constitutional Look: NAFTA Chapter 11 as an Extension of Member States' Constitutional Protection of Property' (2002) 33 *Law and Policy in International Business* 405.

[159]   Although the US Supreme Court has ruled that the abridgement of 'distinct investment-backed expectations' may constitute a 'taking' that requires government compensation, in *Lucas v SC Coastal Council*, 505 US 1003, at 1027–1029 (1992), the court has also ruled that many regulations that diminish but do not extinguish property value are not 'takings': see, eg *Penn Central Transport. Co v New York City*, 438 US 104, at 124 (1978).

to expected profits would make the normal functioning of government virtually impossible—most laws and regulations alter the 'economic equilibrium' surrounding businesses to some extent; clearly the vast majority of standard regulations are not considered compensable expropriations. In conflating the contract remedy of expectation damages with a property right in expected profits, the expropriation/regulation/compensation regime established under the HGAs greatly increases the private property protections afforded to the BTC Consortium, and sharply circumscribes the ability of Azerbaijan, Turkey, and Georgia to enact laws and regulations in the public interest.

## VI. THE INTERNATIONAL FINANCE CORPORATION SHOULD REQUIRE CORE PROJECT AGREEMENTS TO SUPPORT THE EFFECTIVE ENFORCEMENT OF EVOLVING HUMAN RIGHTS AND SUSTAINABLE DEVELOPMENT NORMS

What is to be done, and who is to do it? How can the international community better ensure that human rights and principles of sustainable development are not undermined by the legal frameworks governing large-scale private development projects, such as the BTC pipeline project?

This chapter has so far examined the background of the BTC pipeline, the IFC's commitment to sustainable development, current safeguard policies the IFC has implemented to further that mission, the problematic aspects of the BTC Project HGAs and IGA, and the positive steps Turkey, Azerbaijan, Georgia, and BTC Co have taken to address social and environmental critiques leveled against the HGAs and IGA.

The legal framework of the BTC project is a case study of both the risks and opportunities presented by project covenants. As detailed in Section V, the initial IGA–HGA legal framework agreement threatened to thwart the protection of health, safety, human rights, and the environment. Yet the execution of subsequent project agreements addressing many of these concerns demonstrated that it is both legally possible and economically feasible to create a legal framework that instead enables the progressive realization of human rights and environmental sustainability.

In order better to further its mission of promoting environmentally and socially sustainable private sector projects, the IFC should implement standards regarding the legal frameworks that govern the projects the Bank finances. The current review and revision of the safeguard policies presents an opportunity to incorporate such standards into core IFC social and environmental project guidelines. Large-scale investment receiving IFC loans or assistance, particularly in the extractive industries, should be required to ensure than any covenants executed with host governments enable the protection and promotion of environmental sustainability and human rights.

Any HGAs should: (1) require project investors to uphold international environmental and human rights norms; (2) provide host governments the right to seek redress in international courts if such norms are violated; (3) bar investors from asserting any claims for compensation if or when host governments apply evolving international laws to regulate human rights or health, safety, or environmental issues; (4) establish the 'private attorney general right' of private parties to bring suit against project investors in local courts if investors violate either the terms of the project agreement or international or domestic laws; and (5) implement contractual mechanisms to prevent providers of security services from perpetrating human rights abuses against dissidents. Central to all these recommendations is the principle—put forth in recommendation (3)—that host States may protect and promote human rights by imposing obligations on transnational corporations, and that transnational corporations may not seek compensation for economic loss. Allowing host States the latitude to enforce human rights norms is all the more important because international human rights obligations are primarily directed towards States, and substantial legal ambiguity exists as to the content of human rights norms when addressed to private parties. Therefore the host States have a pivotal role to play in transforming idealized human rights into concrete, legal obligations.

The IFC is well positioned to influence the content of legal agreements used to structure future projects such as the BTC pipeline. This influence is both direct and indirect.

First, project sponsors seeking IFC financing can be required to comply with guidelines regarding project agreements in the same way that they are required to abide by existing IFC safeguard policies. IFC safeguard policies and project assessment procedures already impose a web of conditionalities on large-scale projects such as the BTC pipeline. Guidelines regarding stabilization instruments could be incorporated into this already existing web. To the extent that sponsors are aware of the guidelines, they can take them into account ex ante; to the extent that they become aware only through the IFC loan appraisal process, sponsors can work with IFC lawyers to incorporate IFC mandated terms into the legal framework ex post, as occurred in the BTC project case study.

Second, IFC policies exert influence beyond the immediate realm of the project the Bank finances. According to the CAO, case studies show that the safeguard policies have a demonstration effect by introducing government regulators, sponsors, and industry sectors to best practices.[160] In one case, a project sponsor's use of the safeguard policy encouraged suppliers and producers to adopt the best practice throughout the supply

---

[160] Compliance Advisor/Ombudsman, above n 16, at 24.

chain.[161] By establishing a 'best practice' benchmark vis-à-vis stabilization clauses, the IFC will encourage companies to adopt a similar framework in subsequent agreements.

Critics may object to the imposition of additional constraints on private sector investors, arguing that constraints will discourage investors from seeking IFC funding and thus prevent the IFC from having positive impact on the sponsor's project in other ways. This specious assertion has two powerful rejoinders. First, World Bank financing adds not only investment to the project, but a stamp of multilateral respectability as well. As one observer puts it, BP and its partners could have raised the money on their own, what they needed was 'the political blessing of the two agencies to avoid claims that the project fails to meet international standards.'[162] Second, as the recent review of IFC safeguard polices attests, the largest determinant of the effectiveness of safeguard policies is the attitude of project sponsors.[163] If sponsors are not interested in upholding basic standards regarding health, safety, the environment, and human rights, their commitment to *any* of the social and environmental policies is likely to be questionable. In other words, if a project sponsor is deterred from applying for IFC funding because of the IFC's safeguard policies, then all the better—the sponsor would likely make a poor and underperforming IFC partner anyway.

The self-proclaimed mission of the IFC is to promote economic development that is socially responsible and environmentally sustainable.[164] This mission requires that the IFC refuse to finance projects when their legal structure impedes the effective enforcement of international and domestic laws regarding health, safety, human rights, and the environment. The BTC pipeline project illustrates the immediate relevance of this issue, as well as a case study of some possible best practices. The IFC should seize the opportunity presented by the ongoing safeguard policy overhaul to include standards regarding legal framework agreements in the Policy on Social and Environmental Sustainability, thus enabling the effective enforcement of evolving international norms regarding human rights, environmental sustainability, labor, health, and safety.

---

[161] *Ibid*.

[162] Christopher PM Waters, above n 92, at 23 (citing Carl Mortished, 'BP Awaits Pipeline Ruling' (2003) *The Times*, 27 October.

[163] Compliance Advisor/Ombudsman, above n 16, at 40.

[164] International Finance Corporation, above n 43.

# Index

242